Britain's Aircraft Industry

Triumphs and Tragedies since 1909

Dedicated to the engineers, the designers, the draughtsmen – the innovators – who saw a specification and said:

'I don't care, they're wrong, this is what we need.'

For Pam

Britain's Aircraft Industry
Triumphs and Tragedies since 1909

Ken Ellis

Crécy
www.crecy.co.uk

Crécy Publishing Ltd

www.crecy.co.uk

Published in 2021 by Crécy Publishing Limited

A CIP record for this book is available from the British Library

ISBN 9781910809426

Printed and bound in Turkey by Pelikan Print

Crécy Publishing Limited
1a Ringway Trading Estate, Shadowmoss Road,
Manchester M22 5LH

www.crecy.co.uk

Front cover: Bristol's unfortunate Brabazon. *Bristol*

Front flap (top): Eurofighter Typhoon - Britain's last manned fighter? *Richard Hall*

Front flap (bottom): Handley Page W.10 G-EBMR and the prototype Airspeed Courier, G-ABXN, during flight refuelling trials, 1933. *Flight Refuelling*

Back cover inset: Hatfield-built Mosquito IVs of 105 Squadron, Marham, late 1942; Tornado F.3 ZE785, Tornado GR.1, Sea Harrier FRS.1, Harrier GR.5, Hawk 200 Hawk 50, EAP. *Both courtesy and copyright BAe Systems*

Back cover, main: Fairey Gannet line-up at Culdrose, 1955. *RNAS Culdrose*

Table of Contents

Introduction

O N A VISIT to British Aerospace at Woodford in 1993 to cover the restoration of Avro XIX G-AHKX for *FlyPast* – then and still Britain's top-selling aviation monthly – I was taken on a quick tour of the heritage centre. I was fascinated by a well-used wooden workbench and a label declaring it to have been used by Alliott Verdon Roe. The bench's provenance is *possibly* apocryphal, but a story I was told at the time serves my purpose well. (Today, the impressive Avro Heritage Museum charts the legacy of the pioneering company on the former airfield site and needs to be on your 'must-see' list.)

The Avro XIX – the civilian version of the ubiquitous Anson – built in 1946, was sharing floor space with British Aerospace (BAe) 146 four-jet airliners and Woodford was busy launching the rejuvenated RJ – Regional Jet – version. As Chapter 12 reveals, BAe was increasingly unsure about its future in airliners and negotiations had been started with the Taiwan Aerospace Corporation about possible co-operation, or the transfer of the entire programme. Part of the courtship involved a tour of Woodford by a Taiwanese delegation. The management requested that *Kilo-Xray* be moved out of the way, for the duration. As it was perched on trestles, the retiree craftsman working on it declared that to be impossible. A compromise was reached: the venerable Avro would be screened off.

The visit was a great success, but the inscrutable visitors insisted on knowing what was behind the partitions: in the interests of full transparency. A call was made, bringing a couple of the volunteers in to talk through the restoration project.

With the assembly line returned to normality, the volunteers 'clocked on' as usual but were horrified to find something missing – Alliott Verdon Roe's workbench. It was normally in a place of honour alongside the 'Annie': in its stead was a hi-tech, metal

equivalent. A retiree – let's call him 'Bob' – dialled an internal number to talk to a member of the management team – let's call him 'Suit'. The conversation went something like this:

Bob: 'Where's A V Roe's bench?'

Suit: 'The old, wooden thing?'

Bob: 'The very same.'

Suit: 'You were so good coming in and giving the visitors a talk that we thought we'd upgrade you with a new, state-of-the-art one.'

Bob: 'You don't understand, it's a very precious item – it's A V Roe's.'

Suit: 'Sorry, give me his extension number and I'll talk to him.'

Alan Crossthwaite and Harry Wheeler working on Avro XIX Series 2 G-AHKX's port Armstrong Siddeley Cheetah 17 at Woodford in 1992. After a painstaking restoration, lasting nearly two decades, *Kilo-Xray* took to the skies again on 8 March 2001. Today, as part of the BAE Systems Heritage Flight, G-AHKX is based at Old Warden. *British Aerospace*

The wooden artefact had not been thrown into a skip ready for disposal, but it was heading that way: it was retrieved. The Taiwan deal was never consummated. That a member of 1990s senior management had no idea who was the founder of the company came as no surprise to the team breathing life into G-AHKX.

Whatever happened to...

Born and bred in Liverpool, as my fascination with all-things aeronautical grew, whenever I could I would venture to Warton to watch English Electric Lightnings blasting around; or to Hawarden near Chester hoping to glimpse Hawker Siddeley HS.125 corporate jets; or I'd head east to Woodford where HS.748s and Nimrods were the highlights. 'Aviation heritage' became a speciality of mine and it evolved into a thirty-year career in publishing. Having passed on the helm of *FlyPast* to Nigel Price in 2010, my new boss asked if there was a series I'd like to write. Over the years, readers had often asked questions like: 'What happened to Gloster?' 'Or: 'Why don't we build airliners anymore?' I'd never lost my interest in the British aircraft industry so I offered to cover the post-1945 manufacturers. The series was well greeted and that response helped me to take the plunge and embark on this mammoth project. I had no pretentions that 'Suit' would benefit; spreadsheets are his preferred reading.

I'd always read avidly on British-built aircraft, among the titles on my shelves was the entire 'run' of 'Putnams' – a generic label from the original publisher's name – on leading manufacturers. I regarded these as the 'bee's knees' for a long time, although the more words I consumed and compared I realised that *some* of them were not the pinnacle of knowledge I had assumed they were.

As well as the Putnams, there were other titles charting the life and times of a particular firm, endless books on individual types, plus the occasional study of a famous designer. Some authors had tackled the *entire* industry, but these tended to stick to a nuts-and-bolts approach – a relentless procession of each and every machine produced.

The fascination of Britain's industry lies in the way it has been inter-linked, not just in terms of takeovers and mergers, but in its personnel. It dawned on me that the book I've always wanted to see needed writing. This is a narrative history of the major 'players': the triumphs and turkeys, the vital interdependence, shrewd decisions and breakthroughs, and the schemes and concepts that led to fame or disaster. Most importantly, this is a tribute to the designers and engineers – the innovators – that made Britain's aircraft industry a world-class enterprise.

The bibliography lists books and websites referred to in order to help those who wish to take this fascinating subject further. If the 'bug' has really bitten, there are two out-of-print quintets that you should seek out. Ron Smith's *British Built Aircraft*, published between 2002 and 2005, is breathtaking in its coverage: essentially site-based, it chronicles the smallest workshop to the largest production line. The other is part of the exceptional body of writing by Westland test pilot Harald Penrose: the iconic *British Aviation* appeared between 1967 and 1980, ranging from 1903 in *The Pioneer Years* to the *Ominous Skies* of 1939, and has the gravitas of someone who *was there*.

How to use the main data tables

Tables provide at-a-glance details to support the narrative. Some zoom in on more specialised subjects, but the majority give the following:

From/To: Denote the 'life' of the design, including overseas licences. This extends from the year of the first flight of the prototype – not necessarily when production began – to when the last example was completed.

Total: For some types, particularly during World War One,

Alliott Verdon Roe's workbench, treasured Avro heritage artefact. *Ken Ellis*

establishing a production total is a nightmare and the figure given may or may not be qualified in the 'Notes'. The amount includes British manufacture, be it from the original designer, sub-contractors *and* overseas licence construction, where applicable. It does *not* include refurbishing for second use.

Name and/or **Designation**: For the general reader designations are off-putting, for those that are 'into' such things, no further detailing will be needed. To avoid turning the book into a data-fest, type *names* are used wherever possible.

This is a good moment to explain that in 1944 it was decreed that once a type reached Mk.XX, subsequent versions would adopt Arabic numbers: hence the Spitfire XX was followed by the Mk.21. In early 1948 Roman numerals were dropped altogether, eg. Spitfire PR.XIXs became PR.19s.

Type: A *much* abbreviated description of the main role and/or configuration of the aircraft. Arbitrarily, 'fighters' start at 1916, prior to that, they are 'scouts'. 'GP' denotes 'general purpose', in the military sense; ie. essentially patrol and liaison but with a limited offensive role.

A floatplane is a type with a float, or more likely floats, attached to the fuselage; some of these may have an amphibious capability. A flying boat is a type in which the fuselage has boat-like features and comes fully into contact with the water; some of these may have an amphibious capability. A floatplane or a flying boat could *also* be termed a 'seaplane'.

Readers should be well familiar with 'biplane', triplanes', 'pusher', 'tractor', etc, but two terms perhaps less so: A 'two-bay' biplane (or indeed triplane) will have two sets of inter-plane struts at intervals across the wings; more complex structures will have more – see the illustration of the multiple-bay Wight Twin Landplane. A 'sesquiplane' biplane (or triplane) has one wing (or more) much shorter in span – see the image of the Port Victoria PV.2.

Engine(s): That of the prototype, or as used for the *majority* of the production run. Designations are restricted to the *general* type name.

Notes: Numeric keys to additional material given as footnotes at the base of the table.

What makes an 'industry'?

A lot of time was spent in pondering at what point does a workshop become a factory? How many factories constitute an industry? The line had to be drawn somewhere and entry into the 'big league' – of industrial stature – has been determined as: the construction and flying of at least five original, individual, types and a grand total of at least 250 machines built. This does not include sub-contractors, some of which built thousands of aircraft, but did not originate them. If 250 seems a small amount it should be noted that in the 1920s and early '30s a production run breaking into double figures was often considered a very satisfying achievement. The 'five types, 250 machines' rubric is *occasionally* strayed from to include 'names' that deserve a higher profile, or provide further insights into the nature of British industry: for example Beardmore, Comper and Folland.

Before kicking off, time for some 'terms and conditions' … The narrative does not attempt to be a type-by-type chronicle, nor does it dwell on military serials, civil registrations or construction numbers. While the emphasis is on aircraft being manufactured and flown; the occasional mention is made of a type that was built but remained flightless. There is scant reference to projects: there are plenty of books on that fascinating subject, including some brilliant ones in the Crécy Publishing catalogue. Several manufacturers branched out into other specialities, for example Boulton Paul's gun turrets and Bristol's guided missiles: mention

of these is necessarily brief. Aircraft companies that also built engines – eg. Armstrong Siddeley and de Havilland – merit slightly more coverage as they were crucial to their own designs and powered other aircraft detailed throughout the book.

Gliders, gyroplanes, 'homebuilds', 'kitplanes' and microlights are really a world of their own and only a few find their way into these pages. As might be expected, there *are* exceptions … Assault gliders, true warriors, and experimental types that paved the way for powered designs: for example the Airspeed Horsa and the Armstrong Whitworth AW.52G, respectively. The pioneering 'autogiro' work of Juan de la Cierva, mostly carried out via established manufacturers, was both ground-breaking *and* on an industrial scale. While some homebuilt designs have been created in impressive numbers, these are *individual* achievements – even if only to open the box the kit came in – and fall beyond the book's scope. Similar reasoning follows with microlights, be they weight-shift or three-axis.

The liberty has been taken to explain the meaning of the more opaque names given to aircraft. The Air Ministry and its successors adopted several 'systems' littered with inconsistencies and bafflement – the Blackburn *Blackburn* being the crowning glory! The author hopes that readers do not think he is teaching them to suck eggs!

No attempt has been made to chronicle the post-delivery service history of the hundreds of types covered here. Again, there are plenty of tomes dealing with derring-do, plying the airways and similar exploits. Even this cannot be a hard and fast ruling when the

The one-off Wight Twin Landplane under construction at Cowes, 1915. Despite building more than a dozen types, the output of J Samuel White and Company falls below the 'radar' of this book. Count the pairs of struts: this is a seven-bay biplane. *KEC*

operational career had a bearing on the manufacturer: the Comet jetliner disasters being a classic example. That said, for this book the choice of images leans far less towards prototypes and more to in-service images. For a plethora of first-of-breed illustrations the two-volume story of Britain's test pilots, *Testing to the Limits*, is available from Crécy.

Aviation glories in abbreviations but here they have been kept to a minimum. It is hoped that readers will forgive some repetition of background within the company 'biographies' as the book is designed to be 'dipped into'; although they are more than welcome to read it cover to cover!

Vital characteristics

Throughout the text, reference is made to the vital characteristics that make for a great 'industrial' aircraft. Aircraft that hit some, or all, of these parameters enter the history books and are pivotal to the company that made them:

- Reasonable – ideally minimal – research, design and set-up costs.
- The right solution to the requirement.
- Meeting an expanding and enduring market, ideally both civil and military.
- The potential for further development and/or licensed manufacture.
- Keeping the manufacturer in prime position to create the replacement.
- Scope for support and update contracts.
- Capability for refurbishment and resale after initial service and…
- Above all, profitable.

Some of these characteristics may not be apparent from inception but a business that notices them as they arise and exploits them is on to a winner. In the author's humble opinion, the following aircraft 'tick' all of these 'boxes': **Airco**: DH.4 – DH.9 – DH.9A. **Avro**: 504 'family'; Anson; Lancaster–York–Lincoln–Shackleton. **Bristol**: F.2B Fighter 'family'; Blenheim–Beaufort–Beaufighter. **British Aerospace** (Eurofighter) Typhoon. **BAE Systems**: F-35 programme participation. **British Aircraft Corporation**: One-Eleven; (Panavia)

The naval experimental depot at Port Victoria on the Kent coast devised several experimental types. The PV.2 scout floatplane of 1915 was intended to intercept Zeppelins. Note the unconventional sesquiplane format. *KEC*

Tornado: **Britten-Norman**: Islander: **de Havilland**: Moth 'family' leading to the Tiger Moth; Dragon/Dragon Rapide; Mosquito; Vampire and Venom. **English Electric**: Canberra. **Fairey**: Series III 'family' from Campania to Gordon/Seal and the much-developed Swordfish: **Gloster**: the 'wooden' Nighthawk–Grebe–Gamecock 'family'; the 'metal' Gauntlet–Gladiator 'family'; Meteor. **Handley Page**: the O/100 bomber 'family' to the Hinaidi and 'W' series airliners; Halifax and civil evolutions, Hermes and Hastings. **Hawker**: the Hart biplane 'family'; the Hurricane–Typhoon–Tempest–Sea Fury progression; Hunter: **Hawker Siddeley**: HS.125 (born a de Havilland); P.1127–Kestrel–Harrier; Hawk. Remaining as wing builder to Airbus when the government pulled out. **Hunting**: Jet Provost and Strikemaster. **Miles**: M.2 Hawk and the developed 'family' through to the Magister. **Royal Aircraft Factory**: B.E.2/R.E.8 'family'; S.E.5/a. **Shorts**: Naval Tractor biplane floatplane 'family'; Empire flying boats and the Sunderland; Skyvan/330/360 generation. **Sopwith**: the 1½ 'Strutter', Pup, Camel, Dolphin and Snipe design progression. **Supermarine**: the S.4, S.5 and S.6 racers – crucial technology 'generators'; the Spitfire and Seafire in all its versions. **Vickers**: Vimy–Virginia and transport spin-offs; Wellington and its Viking–Valetta–Varsity 'family'; Viscount. **Westland**: Wapiti and Wallace; the Sikorsky licences; Lynx, Merlin.

Leicestershire Aero Club's 1993-built Slingsby T.67 Mk.II Firefly G-BUUB awaiting the author in June 2010. Derived from the French Fournier RF-6, around 250 T.67s were built by Slingsby at Kirkbymoorside. The company produced a long series of original gliders, but few 'indigenous' powered types. *Ken Ellis*

Acknowledgments

As MARCH 2020 was drawing to a close, the 'send' button was about to be pressed to propel this book to the printers. But just around the corner was the COVID-19 global pandemic. The Crécy Publishing team sagely decided to keep their powder dry and await more optimistic times. Now, after a few text revisions to take in developments and sore arms from 'jabs' we're ready for roll-out.

As ever, the crew at Crécy embraced this project and turned it from concept to reality. Jeremy Pratt whole-heartedly made suggestions, all of which enhanced the book. Charlotte Stear patiently guided this mostly errant author with serenity. Paul Middleton edited and smoothed the narrative and kept it on course. Rob Taylor took pixels and turned them into the finished, polished, product.

Alan Curry and Hugh Trevor checked, revised and enriched the manuscript. That said, all errors and omissions are to be laid firmly at my door.

Over the many decades that I have followed the highs and lows of the British aircraft industry, a vast number of people have supplied information, guided me in the right direction, passed on illustrations and thoroughly encouraged me. Listing them all would be impossible – they know who they are. Providing support of all natures during the immediate preparation of this book were the following: Tony Buttler, Chris Clifford, Richard Hall, Ian Haskell, Mike Ingham, Graham Pitchfork, Col Pope, Nigel Price, Dave Scott, Dean Wright. Thanks to one and all.

Every effort has been made to secure permissions for quotes extracted from books that appear in the text. I'm used to getting a 'minority response' from such 'trawls' but this time the result was a complete 'nil' return.

Finally, and especially, Pam and feline Rascal provided their unique brands of encouragement during the creation of this enormous project.

Ken Ellis
People's Republic of Rutland
March 2021
ken@sillenek.com

The incredible Eurofighter Typhoon: is it destined to be the last manned interceptor built in the United Kingdom? *Richard Hall*

CHAPTER ONE

From Boxkite to Brexit

'All modern aircraft have four dimensions: span, length, height and politics.'
Sir Sydney Camm on the cancellation of the TSR.2 in 1965

As the last elements of this book were coming together Britain departed the European Union, without 'Big Ben's' participation. I had hoped to call this book *From Boxkite to Brexit* but the publishers – probably wisely – chose the title on the cover. The quote from Sir Sydney Camm above highlights that politics and the aviation industry are inescapable. No matter what your views on Brexit are, the final paragraph in Chapter 12 holds true. Hence the table charting governments: their decisions and prevarications litter these pages.

Aviation is about long-term thinking and a search for something to show the fragility of the passage of time turned to the superbly readable history of the British Aircraft Corporation by Charles Gardner. He was writing in 1981 when the Panavia Tornado was nearing entry to service. The three-nation swing-wing workhorse took very nearly thirteen years from the formation of Panavia in the spring of 1969, to firm orders in July 1976, to acceptance by the RAF's 9 Squadron in 1982. The successor programme, Eurofighter, was set up in June 1986. Britain, Germany, Italy and Spain committed in December 1997 and the RAF's 17 Squadron took its first Typhoons in 2003. For such a complex weapon system that's a very creditable 16¾ years.

Gardner adopted a ten-year rule-of-thumb from go-ahead to first deliveries of a programme to show just how vulnerable a project was

to political whims. As the table shows, from 1945 to 2020 there have been sixteen governments: it makes no matter be they Conservative, Labour or Coalition. Between the first post-war PM, Clement Richard Attlee, and the advent of Alexander Boris de Pfeffel Johnson the average tenure in power has been just over six years. That timespan provides plenty of opportunity for the next incumbent to tear up any agreement. Chapter 12 shows how short-lived the nationalisation of the British aircraft industry was before Margaret Hilda Thatcher put it back on the commercial market: she exceeded Gardner's decade by nineteen months.

With some adjustment, Gardner's ten-year theory applies throughout the history of the industry. In the 1920s and '30s a five-year measure would be a better yardstick. For the BAE Systems Tempest – should it see the light of day – a *minimum* of two decades seems more likely. The clock is ticking…

A Boxkite replica, built by Miles, at Filton in 1966. Today, this machine flies regularly with the Shuttleworth Collection at Old Warden. *Rolls-Royce*

Prime Ministers and Governments

Tenure	Prime Minister	Political Party
1908 to 1916	Herbert Henry Asquith	Liberal: Coalition from 1915
1916 to 1922	David Lloyd George	Liberal: Coalition to 1918
1922 to 1923	Bonar Law	Conservative
1923 to 1924	Stanley Baldwin	Conservative
1924	Ramsay MacDonald	Labour
1924 to 1929	Stanley Baldwin	Conservative
1929 to 1935	Ramsay MacDonald	Labour: Coalition from 1931
1935 to 1937	Stanley Baldwin	Conservative
1937 to 1940	Neville Chamberlain	Conservative
1940 to 1945	Winston Churchill	Conservative: heading Coalition
1945 to 1951	Clement Attlee	Labour
1951 to 1955	Winston Churchill	Conservative
1955 to 1957	Anthony Eden	Conservative
1957 to 1963	Harold Macmillan	Conservative
1963 to 1964	Alec Douglas-Home	Conservative
1964 to 1970	Harold Wilson	Labour
1970 to 1974	Edward Heath	Conservative
1974 to 1976	Harold Wilson	Labour
1976 to 1979	James Callaghan	Labour
1979 to 1990	Margaret Thatcher	Conservative
1990 to 1997	John Major	Conservative
1997 to 2007	Tony Blair	Labour
2007 to 2010	Gordon Brown	Labour
2010 to 2016	David Cameron	Conservative: Coalition with Liberal Democrats to 2015
2016 to 2019	Theresa May	Conservative
2019 to date	Boris Johnson	Conservative

Fragile time

As the book is based alphabetically on the 'major players' of the British aircraft industry, a chronology may help see the 'bigger picture'.

1 Apr 1897: HM Balloon Factory formed at Aldershot.

1908: S E Saunders Ltd set up at East Cowes.

1908: George Harris Handasyde and Helmut Paul Martin entered a partnership. Martin and Handasyde, also known as Martinsyde, was formed on 24 March 1915: the company was liquidated in late 1920.

16 Oct 1908: Samuel Franklin Cody made the first powered, controlled and sustained flight in Britain, at Farnborough.

Nov 1908: Short Brothers inaugurated: Leysdown became the world's first aeroplane factory.

1909: Blackburn Aeroplane Company set up. It was renamed Blackburn Aeroplane and Motor Company Ltd in May 1914.

17 Jun 1909: Handley Page Ltd formed at Barking Creek.

Jul 1909: On the 13th and 23rd Alliott Verdon Roe made two flights in his Triplane at Lea Marshes, Essex. He became the first British person to pilot an all-British aircraft.

Jan 1910: A V Roe and Company formed.

19 Feb 1910: Sir George White set up four companies: Bristol Aeroplane Co, Bristol Aviation Co, British and Colonial Aeroplane Co and British and Colonial Aviation. Trading started as British and Colonial Aeroplane Co; with the simple generic name 'Bristol' being adopted from the start.

1911: Grahame-White Aviation Company formed.

26 Apr 1911: HM Balloon Factory renamed HM Aircraft Factory at Farnborough; prefix 'Royal' granted from April 1912.

20 Jan 1912: Vickers Ltd's Aviation Department established.

13 May 1912: Royal Flying Corps (RFC), including a military wing and a naval wing, formed.

5 Jun 1912: Aircraft Manufacturing Company (Airco) registered.

Jun 1912: Sopwith Aviation Company inaugurated; later renamed Sopwith Aviation and Engineering Company.

27 Jun 1914: Pemberton Billing Ltd founded at Woolston.

Jun 1914: Blackburn Aeroplane and Motor Company Ltd formed.

1 Jul 1914: Royal Naval Air Service (RNAS) formed out of the naval wing of the RFC.

4 Aug 1914: Great Britain declared war on Imperial Germany.

Jul 1915: Fairey Aviation Company formed; restructured as Fairey Aviation Ltd on 9 March 1921.

Jun 1915: Petters Ltd began sub-contract construction and adopted the name Westland Aircraft Works.

1916: The Burbidge and Bailhache commissions examined the role of the Royal Aircraft Factory and RFC procurement arrangements.

20 Sep 1916: Pemberton Billing Ltd renamed Supermarine Aviation Works Ltd.

5 Jun 1917: Gloucestershire Aircraft Company Ltd set up: soon the name 'Gloster' was being used and it was officially adopted on 11 November 1926.

3 Jan 1918: Lord Rothermere appointed as first Secretary of State for Air – the Air Ministry had been created.

1 Apr 1918: The Royal Air Force was inaugurated as an amalgamation of the RFC and RNAS.

Jun 1918: Royal Aircraft Factory renamed the Royal Aircraft Establishment and aircraft production wound down.

11 Nov 1918: The Armistice brought the Great War to an end.

14 Dec 1918: English Electric Company formed from Coventry Ordnance Works; Dick, Kerr and Company and the associated United Electric Car Company; and Phoenix Dynamo. It stopped aircraft construction in 1926.

1920: George Handasyde set up the Handasyde Aircraft Company.

1920: George Parnall and Company established.

Mar 1920: The Aircraft Manufacturing Company was bought out by the Birmingham Small Arms Company; aircraft construction brought to a close.

4 Mar 1920: Handley Page formed the Aircraft Disposal Company (ADC or 'Airdisco'). It was restructured as ADC Aircraft Ltd in 1925 and closed down in 1930.

Apr 1920: Sir W G Armstrong Whitworth Aircraft Company inaugurated.

11 Sep 1920: Sopwith Aviation and Engineering Company closed down.

25 Sep 1920: de Havilland Aircraft Company established.

15 Nov 1920: H G Hawker Engineering Company emerged out of the liquidation of Sopwith. Renamed Hawker Aircraft Ltd in 1933.

24 Mar 1926: Cierva Autogiro Company founded.

11 Nov 1926: Gloster Aircraft was registered, replacing the name Gloucestershire Aircraft Company Ltd.

Mar 1927: de Havilland Aircraft Proprietary set up – later de Havilland Australia.

1928: Phillips and Powis Aircraft (Reading) Ltd established, from 1932 the company manufactured Miles types. It was renamed Miles Aircraft in 1943.

1928: Simmonds Aircraft, Weston, Southampton, formed.

1928: Vickers (Aviation) Ltd set up as independent from Vickers Ltd.

1928: de Havilland Canada formed. It was sold to the Canadian government in June 1974.

May 1928: Avro acquired by the Armstrong Siddeley Development Company.

Passengers boarding de Havilland DH.86B G-AEAP *Demeter* of Imperial Airways at Croydon, 1938. *KEC*

Oct 1928: Saunders-Roe Ltd, Saro for short, previously S E Saunders Ltd, formed.

Nov 1928: Vickers (Aviation) Ltd acquired Supermarine: it continued to trade under its own name until 1959.

Mar 1929: Comper Aircraft formed.

1930: Simmonds Aircraft renamed as Spartan Aircraft, at East Cowes. It was absorbed into Saro in 1935.

27 Feb 1931: General Aircraft Ltd formed out of the Monospar Wing Company.

13 Mar 1931: Airspeed Ltd inaugurated.

12 Sep 1931: Société Anonyme Belge Avions Fairey established at Gosselies, near Charleroi. Later named Fairey SA, it was acquired by the Belgian government in 1977.

1933: British Klemm Aeroplane Company set up, renamed British Aircraft Manufacturing Company in 1935; ceased trading in 1938.

1933: G and J Weir began development of rotorcraft: operations suspended in 1940.

1933: Percival Aircraft created.

May 1934: Gloster acquired by Hawker.

Aug 1934: Comper Aircraft folded; re-formed as Heston Aircraft on 10 August 1934. Heston was renamed as Hestair in the 1950s, no longer building aircraft.

30 Jun 1934: Boulton and Paul Ltd established Boulton Paul Aircraft Ltd.

1935: Prestwick Airport and Scottish Aviation inaugurated.

May 1935: Parnall Aircraft Ltd formed from George Parnall and Company and Hendy Aircraft Ltd. Aircraft construction stopped in 1939.

25 Jun 1935: Hawker Siddeley Aircraft inaugurated, encompassing Armstrong Whitworth, Avro, Gloster and Hawker.

4 Jul 1935: Westland Aircraft Works renamed Westland Aircraft Ltd.

Feb 1936: British Maritime Aircraft established. It was renamed Folland Aircraft in October 1937.

2 Jun 1936: Short and Harland Ltd inaugurated at Sydenham.

Oct 1938: Supermarine and Vickers (Aviation) Ltd brought under the aegis of Vickers-Armstrongs.

21 Nov 1938: Taylorcraft Aeroplanes (England) Ltd founded.

Apr 1939: English Electric returned to aircraft manufacturing; running the 'shadow factory' at Samlesbury.

3 Sep 1939: Great Britain declared war on Germany.

1940: A W Hawksley Ltd – a play on Armstrong Whitworth Hawker Siddeley – created for administrative purposes to oversee production of the AW Albemarle at Hucclecote.

Jun 1940: Airspeed (1934) Ltd acquired by de Havilland – reverted to the name Airspeed Ltd in January 1944.

8 Dec 1941: Great Britain declared war on Japan.

1943: Rotorcraft interests of G and J Weir and Cierva merged.

23 Mar 1943: Short Brothers nationalised as Short and Harland Ltd.

Sep 1944: Hunting acquired Percival. It was renamed Hunting Percival Aircraft on 25 April 1954 and on 5 December 1957 became Hunting Aircraft Ltd.

8 May 1945: World War Two ended in the European theatre and in Asia on 15 August 1945.

1 Dec 1945: Avro Canada formed: Malton factory acquired by de Havilland Canada in July 1962.

8 Mar 1946: Taylorcraft Aeroplanes (England) Ltd renamed Auster Aircraft.

Nov 1947: Short Brothers and Harland Ltd formed from Short and Harland; absorbing Short Brothers at Rochester.

1948: Miles Aircraft ceased trading.

Jul 1948: Handley Page (Reading) Ltd formed to take over the Miles assets.

1 Jan 1949: Blackburn Aircraft and General Aircraft merged as Blackburn and General Aircraft Ltd.

Intended to break records, the specially configured High Speed Spitfire, N.17, ground-running at Eastleigh, late 1938. Spitfires soon had other things to do! *KEC*

22 Jan 1951: Cierva bought out by Saro.

Jun 1951: F G Miles Ltd set up.

1954: Edgar Percival Aircraft formed. Acquired by Samlesbury Engineering and renamed Lancashire Aircraft Corporation in October 1958. Stopped aircraft manufacture in 1961.

1955: Britten-Norman Ltd established. Restructured as Britten-Norman (Bembridge) Ltd in November 1972.

Jan 1958: The Aircraft Manufacturing Company consortium of de Havilland, Fairey and Hunting inaugurated to build the DH.121 tri-jet: dissolved 1960.

9 Jan 1959: English Electric Aviation Ltd inaugurated, to define elements of the company going on to join the British Aircraft Corporation in 1960.

Aug 1959: Saunders-Roe bought up by Westland.

Oct 1959: Hawker Siddeley acquired Folland Aircraft.

6 Feb 1960: Fairey Aviation purchased by Westland.

Mar 1960: Rotary-wing division of Bristol taken on by Westland.

May 1960: Blackburn acquired by Hawker Siddeley.

1 Jul 1960: British Aircraft Corporation inaugurated: comprising English Electric, Vickers and minority partner Bristol.

Sep 1960: British Aircraft Corporation took a majority holding in Hunting.

7 Oct 1960: British Executive and General Aviation Ltd (Beagle) established.

Nov 1960: Beagle acquired Auster.

1961: Boulton Paul and Dowty joined together as specialists in control systems.

16 Feb 1961: Bulk of the assets of F G Miles Ltd acquired by Beagle.

May 1966: Société Européenne de Production de l'Avion d'Ecole de Combat et d'Appui Tactique (SEPECAT) established to govern the Jaguar project, involving British Aircraft Corporation and Bréguet of France.

1 Oct 1966: Westland Aircraft renamed Westland Helicopters. Also Vickers and Westland combined their air cushion vehicle interests as the British Hovercraft Corporation at East Cowes.

1968: Cierva Rotorcraft formed to develop the Grasshopper helicopter; ceased trading 1973.

26 Mar 1969: Britain (British Aircraft Corporation), Germany (Messerschmitt Bölkow Blohm) and Italy (Aeritalia) formed Panavia Aircraft GmbH to oversee the Multi-Role Combat Aircraft – later Tornado – programme.

Apr 1969: French and German governments formed Airbus Industrie. Hawker Siddeley announced it would remain as a private-venture investor.

8 Aug 1969: Handley Page Ltd liquidated; Handley Page Aircraft Ltd formed nine days later but folded on 27 February 1970.

Dec 1969: Beagle Aircraft went into receivership.

31 Aug 1972: Britten-Norman acquired by the Fairey Group, becoming Fairey Britten-Norman. Receiver called in on 3 August 1977, company restructured as BN (Bembridge) Ltd.

1 Jan 1973: United Kingdom joined the European Economic Community.

1977: NDN Aircraft formed to develop the designs of Desmond Norman. Norman Aircraft Company set up 1985, but wound up in 1988.

17 Mar 1977: Aircraft and Shipbuilding Industries Act, leading to the creation of British Aerospace (BAe) on 1 January 1978. BAe comprised: British Aircraft Corporation, Hawker Siddeley Aviation and Scottish Aviation. BAe completely denationalised in May 1985.

24 Jan 1979: BN (Bembridge) Ltd bought by Pilatus of Switzerland, renamed Pilatus Britten-Norman.

The Armstrong Whitworth AW.52G glider, RG324, in the spring of 1945. It pioneered the way for the jet-powered AW.52 flying wing. *Armstrong Whitworth via Tony Buttler*

Fresh from active service at Kandahar in Afghanistan, Harrier GR.9A ZD433 was retired and presented to the Fleet Air Arm Museum at Yeovilton on 20 December 2011. Although wearing the badge of the RAF's 1 Squadron, as part of Joint Force Harrier, ZD433 was also crewed by 800 Squadron pilots. *Fleet Air Arm Museum*

Jun 1980: European Helicopter Industries, joint venture founded by Westland and Agusta of Italy.

1981: Aircraft Designs (Bembridge) Ltd and later Sheriff Aerospace founded to develop John Britten's Sheriff light twin. Ceased trading 1984.

1984: Short Brothers Ltd (previously Short Brothers and Harland) denationalised.

Jun 1986: Germany, Italy, Spain and the UK formed Eurofighter Jagdflugzeug GmbH to create EFA, later known as Eurofighter 2000 and named Typhoon in September 1998.

7 Jun 1989: Bombardier Group acquired Short Brothers.

Jan 1993: Avro International Aerospace launched by British Aerospace to manage the Avroliner (HS.146 and RJ) family.

Apr 1993: British Aerospace formed Jetstream Aircraft Ltd to oversee twin-turboprop ventures.

1 Nov 1993: The European Union is formed, with the UK as a member.

18 Apr 1994: Westland Helicopters renamed and restructured as GKN Westland.

1 Jan 1996: Aero International Regional established by Aérospatiale of France, Aeritalia of Italy and British Aerospace: mutually dissolved July 1998.

18 Jun 1997: Britain signed up to become the only full collaborative partner in the Lockheed Martin F-35 Joint Strike Fighter programme.

20 Nov 1997: Airbus UK formed.

July 1998: Pilatus Britten-Norman sold; Britten-Norman Group set up, trading as BN Aviation from 2010.

30 Nov 1999: British Aerospace and Marconi Electronic Systems merged to form BAE Systems.

26 Jul 2000: Finmeccanica of Italy and GKN Westland enter a joint venture: AgustaWestland; GKN disposed of its 50% to Finmeccanica on 25 May 2004.

Oct 2006: BAE Systems sold off its 20% share in Airbus.

1 Jan 2018: Finmeccanica rebranded: AgustaWestland became Leonardo SpA.

31 Jan 2020: United Kingdom left the European Union.

Same as it ever was

Two quotes, from very different eras, prove that 'progress' is not linear, or certain. The next chapter is devoted to the genial and far-sighted George Holt Thomas, a victim of the lack of vision of Lloyd George's government as Britain moved from trench warfare to the Armistice. Harald Penrose's *British Aviation – The Adventuring Years 1920–1929* cites Thomas from March 1920: 'Minister after minister had publically stated that we must retain our lead. We are far from doing so. This is a new science, still in its infancy. Ordering aeroplanes in quantity could not be expected, but £1 million a year spent on experimental machines distributed among design firms, would be a national insurance and maintain the technical staffs.'

Stig Abell's *How Britain Really Works* (John Murray 2019) is a thought-provoking tour-de-force of the United Kingdom in the early 21st century. His words concern our manufacturing base in general, but they are precisely on target for the aerospace industry: 'Spending on research and development is well beneath the global average. We do not innovate or develop much anymore; it is as if our creative impetus has dissipated over the last century, like a former athlete whose muscles have softened and sagged, and whose former glory is scarcely visible beneath the surface.'

Artist's impression of the next generation fighter – the BAE Systems Tempest. *Copyright and courtesy BAE Systems*

CHAPTER TWO

Journalistic Foresight

Airco – Aircraft Manufacturing Company
1912 to 1920

'the largest aircraft enterprise in the world' Airco advert 1919

OWADAYS aviation in one form or another is seldom out of the media. It was no different during the 'pioneering' days of powered aeronautics from 1903 to the outbreak of the Great War. Then such coverage was the domain of the newspapers; the 'wireless' – radio – arrived in the 1920s, television's first trials were made in the late 1930s and the 'internet' and its dubious offspring began their revolution in the final decade of the century. Some newspaper proprietors went much further than covering the new-fangled flying machines, recognising their potential and, in turn, a way to boost circulation. Prizes were offered for increasingly demanding exploits and events were sponsored.

Perhaps the most outstanding of these 'air-minded' print magnates was the First Viscount Rothermere, who was briefly the first Secretary of State for Air in 1918. This appointment was very significant but paled against a commission he placed with the Bristol Aeroplane Company in March 1934. That was for a twin-engined executive transport, the Type 142, which first took to the air on 12 April the following year. With this his lordship bequeathed to the nation what became the Blenheim. Viscount Rothermere had been born Harold Sydney Harmsworth, and both he and his elder brother, Alfred Charles William (the first Viscount Northcliffe), used the *Daily Mail* and other titles to further the cause.

Another newspaper publisher encouraged the Harmsworth brothers to foster aviation and went on to become the owner of Britain's largest aeroplane manufacturer. This was George Holt Thomas (Thomas from now on), whose name does not trip off the tongue in the same manner as Blackburn, Handley Page, Roe, the Shorts, Sopwith and Sir George White (founder of Bristol) who spearheaded the birth of Britain's aircraft industry. This is a great pity as not only did he eclipse all of those named above during the Great War, he fostered two other 'names' that came to rank among the giants – de Havilland and Gloster – and helped to turn Westland from a sub-contractor into a specialist design house.

Built by Airco in 1917, DH.9A E8700 was refurbished by de Havilland at Stag Lane in 1925, going back into service in 1925 in the Middle East. It ended its days with 30 Squadron at Mosul, Iraq, in 1929 as a target tug. A spare wheel is attached to the Liberty 12A cowling, an additional radiator is fitted under the observer's position and the rear fuselage is bedecked with guards and wires to prevent target flags from snagging. *KEC*

In 1890 Thomas joined his father's *Daily Graphic* group at the age of 21. He rose through the ranks to launch *Empire Illustrated* and *The Bystander*, becoming a respected and rich entrepreneur. Thomas founded the Aircraft Manufacturing Company in June 1912, which became known in 'the trade' simply as 'The Aircraft Company' and was referred to by its proprietor as 'Airco' – it is the latter that this book will adopt. An advert in the 1919 edition of *Jane's All the World's Aircraft* referred to Airco as: 'the largest aircraft enterprise in the world'. By the end of the Great War, Thomas headed up a complex chain of organisations that would in later years be termed 'vertical integration' – he was king of his 'supply chain'. This incited Charles G 'CG' Grey, the *Jane's* compiler and frequently malicious, occasionally eloquent, editor of the weekly magazine *Aeroplane* to declare Thomas 'a monopolist', although he was fulsome in his obituary after George's death in 1929.

Unsung aviation industrialist, George Holt Thomas at the wheel of one of his motor cars, 1914. *Lambeth Libraries*

Shopping list: licences and companies

In 1906 Thomas was offloading his publishing responsibilities. He met up with French pioneer Henri (or Henry) Farman and was galvanised by the potential of aviation, although he never became a pilot. Thus began an association that lasted into the Great War. Thomas also struck up a friendship with French pilot Louis Paulhan and became his agent for competitions and demonstrations in Britain, flying a Farman, from 1909. Convinced that his country was lagging behind Europe, Thomas became a single-handed pressure group promoting the expansion of military aviation and the fledgling aircraft industry.

Henri Farman had been building pusher biplanes in a limited manner since 1908. With his brother, Maurice, Henri established a factory at Billancourt, to the west of Paris, in 1912. Prior to this Thomas acquired the sole British rights for Farman types and set up The Aeroplane Company, soon changed to the Aeroplane Supply Company, at Merton in south-west London. Thomas's brother, Augustus 'Gus' Thomas was appointed as a director. Ambitions did not just lie with fixed-wing types, Thomas also established Airships Ltd, taking a licence from the Parisian Société Astra for the Astra-Torres non-rigid 'blimp'. The French shopping list was still not complete; Thomas signed agreements for British production of Gnome and, later, Le Rhône rotary engines.

With the collapse of Horatio Barber's Aeronautical Syndicate in April 1912, Thomas acquired its premises at Hendon aerodrome. Factory space was also acquired on the Edgware Road in Hendon and this was added to by the occupation of a former bus and tram garage in 1915. On 5 June 1912 the Aeroplane Supply Company and Airships Ltd amalgamated and the Aircraft Manufacturing Company was born. A French-built Farman was entered into the Larkhill Trials in August 1912, winning a £100 'consolation' prize. This became the basis of the Longhorn general-purpose biplane and Airco began production in November 1912, initially assembling Billancourt-made sub-assemblies before churning out all-British versions. Further development of the Longhorn disposed of the forward elevator and this version was appropriately named the Shorthorn. Among the airships manufactured was the SS-class – Submarine Scout – most fitted with modified Shorthorn 'fuselages' as crew/engine gondolas.

Airco Farman biplane production

Type	Total	From	To	Notes
MF.7 Longhorn	318	1912	1917	[1] [2]
MF.11 Shorthorn	939	1914	1917	[3]
F.20	211	1913	1914	
F.22H floatplane	6	1914	-	

Longhorns and Shorthorns also produced by Grahame-White and by Brush Electrical, Loughborough, South Coast Aviation Works, Shoreham, and Whitehead Aircraft, Richmond. **[1]** MF.7 – popular designation for 'Série 7' biplane. **[2]** Early 'production' assembled from French-made components; followed by all-British airframes. **[3]** MF.11 – popular designation for 'Série 11' biplane.

Manufacturing logjams were endemic during the Great War, generated by sub-contractors being slow to get a 'flow' going, tardy supply of engines and poor quality control. Conscious of all of these potential dilemmas, Thomas began a policy of company acquisition to protect his supply chain. In 1914 he contracted precision engineers Peter Hooker Ltd of Walthamstow in east London to build a batch of Gnome Monosoupape rotaries and ended up purchasing and dramatically expanding the business. Other assets were snapped up, including: the Camden Engineering Company in north-west London, to manufacture fittings; the Hendon-based Integral Propeller Company and high-quality coachbuilder Vanden Plas, with works in Hendon making wings and tail surfaces. A Belgian concern, the British Vanden Plas had been established in London by Warwick Wright.

Not content with airships, landplanes, engines, fittings and propellers, Thomas also embraced marine aviation – flying boats. Airco secured a sub-contract for Felixstowe F.2As, but the pressures of building DH.4s and developing the DH.9 was too much for Hendon. So Thomas turned his attentions to Hythe on the River Solent and set up a 'sub-sub-contract' with May, Harden and May – renowned marine engineers also engaged in flying boat construction. Typically, Thomas invested in the company and it became a part of the 'empire'.

The search for sub-contractors went as far as Cheltenham and in 1915 the woodwork specialist H Martyn and Co Ltd was signed up to make assemblies for Farmans and DH.2s, followed by fuselages for DH.4s and later whole DH.6s. Workmanship was excellent and talks about setting up a new business resulted in Airco and Martyn going into a 50:50 partnership as the Gloucestershire Aircraft Company on 5 June 1917.

de Havilland's mentor

At the heart of Thomas's corporate acumen was a sharp eye for talent. An early appointment was Francis St Barbe, whose fluency in French made him an ideal liaison and translator with all aspects of Airco's French connections, and in 1916 furniture creator Arthur Hagg joined the rapidly expanding design department. But it was the contract drawn up on 23 May 1914 that was the most spectacular of Thomas's appointments. He was looking for someone to: 'design and supervise the construction of such aeroplanes as the company may require', and to 'pilot any such aeroplanes designed by him.' Latterly frustrated at the Aeronautical Inspection Directorate at Farnborough and before that with the Royal Aircraft Factory and the Balloon Factory, the man signing the document was 32-year-old Geoffrey de Havilland. (To differentiate between the man and the company that came to bear his name, Geoffrey is referred to here as GDH.)

Geoffrey's personal 'back story' is dealt with in Chapter 17 and must receive scant coverage here. Suffice it to say that Thomas had snapped up the man who had created the most adaptable of the 'first generation' military types, the B.E.2, among others. Thomas built a relationship of mutual respect and trust with his gifted chief designer. This was underlined in the designation of Airco machines, each prefixed 'DH'. Writing in his autobiography *Sky Fever*, GDH declared his new annual salary as £600: the annual salary of a train driver in 1914 was approximately £192. Airco supplemented GDH's salary by something he never had at 'The Factory' – commission on sales and life insurance. The perceptive Thomas was transforming his enterprise from that of a licence builder of French designs into an innovator.

GDH's early days with Airco suffered from administrative chaos. He had signed up as a special reservist in March 1913 and on the day that Britain declared war on Germany, 4 August 1914, he was mobilised and despatched to Montrose in Scotland to pilot a Blériot XI on coastal patrol. All of this was rescinded on the 26th, but GDH did not return to Hendon, going instead to Farnborough. There he kicked his heels test flying while Thomas campaigned to get his chief designer back; this was achieved in November: fifteen weeks wasted.

Also eventually making the transition from the Royal Aircraft Factory was GDH's former boss, Lt Col Mervyn O'Gorman, who signed up with Airco in November 1917.

The DH.1 prototype: the rudder carries the lettering 'THE AIRCRAFT MFC CO LTD' and, above that, a stylized 'H' with a 'de' below the crossbar – clear indication of the maker and the designer. *Hawker Siddeley*

Demise of the pusher

Despite his championing of the tractor biplane – GDH's B.E.2 had become the backbone of British military aviation – his first design for Airco reverted to the pusher layout. This was not the Airco ethos; it was that of the War Office. So, initial drawings for a tractor type were shelved and the company's first original machine, the DH.1, was a tandem-seat pusher biplane of the same format as GDH's original Royal Aircraft Factory F.E.2 of 1911. As with his days at Farnborough, GDH was at the helm of his prototypes for their maiden flight; in the case of the DH.1 he did the honours in January 1915.

Priorities had already changed; the War Office wanted an agile single-seater – urgently. As aerial combat evolved, armed reconnaissance types – such as the DH.1 – required escort and enemy incursions needed intercepting. Keeping to the recce theme, such machines were called 'scouts'.

So it was that Airco built a solitary DH.1; the rest were sub-contracted to Savages Ltd of King's Lynn to keep factory space available for the new scout. Renowned for making fairground 'rides', the Norfolk company found the transition to warplanes challenging and it was November 1915 before the first example appeared. By then, time had largely passed the DH.1 by and a modest total of ninety-nine was completed; Savages continued as a sub-contractor, including DH.6s.

Why was a novice organisation entrusted with a combat type? Instead of DH.1s, should King's Lynn have taken on Farmans? It needs to be remembered that apart from a few established aircraft manufacturers, *any* placing of a contract was going to be with a firm that was finding its feet. (This was just as true with those making engines, lorries, guns and all the other equipment vital for a massive war of attrition.) Plodding and 'old tech' as they may have been, the Farman trainers coming out of the sheds at Hendon were *as vital* as types such as the DH.1; the Royal Flying Corps (RFC) and the Royal Naval Air Service faced a desperate shortage of pilots.

British developments in gun synchronization (or 'interrupter') gear, allowing machine guns to fire through the propeller arc, were slow to become reliable. This gave GDH no option but to create the DH.2 using the DH.1 format scaled down, with a fixed forward-firing 0.303in Lewis gun in the pilot's nacelle. GDH took the prototype of what was arguably Britain's first true fighter for its maiden sortie on 1 June 1915. On the first day of July a German Fokker monoplane downed a French Morane-Saulnier in what is believed to have been the first use of an 'interrupter' gear in anger. Manufacture of the DH.2 was quickly instigated at Hendon and the type remained the sole domain of Airco, with 202 coming off the line.

During the summer of 1916 GDH flew a twin-pusher bomber, the DH.3, for the first time. Although an order for fifty was placed in September, the prototype DH.3 remained solitary as the contract was cancelled. The fin and rudder of the DH.3 exhibited the 'signature' de Havilland shape that became so well known in the 1920s and '30s. The twin-pusher format was revived in 1917 when the need for long-range bombers had become a prime concern. Refined as the DH.10, the first example flew on 4 March 1918 as a pusher, but production was standardised on a tractor layout. The DH.10 was named Amiens in the spring of 1918, long before the town in northern France astride the River Somme became famous for the offensive of that August. As well as Airco, manufacture of the 273 DH.10s was spread piecemeal across six sub-contractors. Delays brought about by the flawed ABC Dragonfly engine meant that the more advanced DH.11 Oxford long-range day bomber did not fly until the spring of 1919. Having 'missed the boat', it remained a prototype.

The second prototype DH.10, C8659, at a muddy Hendon in the spring of 1918. *Hawker Siddeley*

Innovation and simplification

By the time Airco was again asked to supply a scout that word was out of style. Instead, a single-seat *fighter* was sought. Although British synchronization gear was gaining in maturity, soon after its first flight in the autumn of 1916 the prototype DH.5 was given an elevating nose-mounted gun, which fired above the propeller disc. Production examples had 'interrupters' fitted to the single 0.303in machine gun from March 1917. While the DH.5's firepower was a novelty, this paled against its format. To overcome the poor view tractor biplanes afforded their pilots, GDH gave the DH.5 a *backward* stagger to the upper wing. This gave exceptional views upward and sideways but solicited poor comments regarding the very poor rear view – compromise is never an easy task! More than 500 DH.5s were produced, but it was not destined to be the type that took Airco into the realms of four figures – that lay with the company's two-seat tractors.

Airco-built DH.5 A9197 'New South Wales No. 15 – 'The Upper Hunter' of 68 Squadron, Australian Flying Corps, 1917. *Australian War Memorial*

The lowly DH.6 trainer deserves to be elevated in importance because of its significance to Airco and its legacy to de Havilland. By late 1916 the RFC was engaged in another flat-out expansion scheme and although Farman types remained a staple into 1917, the time had come for a tractor, tandem-seat trainer. The result was the no-frills DH.6 featuring: ease of construction – and hence sub-contracting (the hallmark DH fin and rudder was forsaken for an angular version); the ability to take a variety of 80 to 90hp engines; good low-speed handing, although this took some perfecting; and a roomy cockpit allowing ease of communication – verbal and physical – between pupil and instructor.

A typical training accident, Airco-built DH.6 B2715 and a Royal Aircraft Factory B.E.2 after a collision at Wyton, May 1918. *Peter Green Collection*

Sub-contracts were scattered about and the DH.6 proved its worth; just over 1,000 were completed in the first quarter of 1918. The DH.6 became the standard trainer of the latter war years. It even attracted a licence agreement in Spain and was still being made there in the early 1920s. The little biplane gained a series of nicknames, including the 'Skyhook' from its ability to hang in the air (in the right hands) and the 'Clutching Hand' from a pupil's stress-laden grasp of the stick. The Australians affectionately called it the 'Dung Hunter', apparently because the cockpit area resembled a farmyard cart. Once the DH.6's aerodynamic foibles were ironed out, GDH had gained invaluable knowledge of biplanes that were forgiving to fly and easy to build upon which his own company was to thrive.

Mother lode

'The significant success of the [DH.]4 and its derivatives was, I believe, due to the same reasons that make all "good" aeroplanes, and which applied equally to the later Moth. These are simplicity, right size, cleanness of design, and of course, a very reliable engine. The value of simplicity is to be found in weight saving, ease of production, reliability and lower cost. Size is governed chiefly by power of the chosen engine, and if the size is right, the aeroplane becomes more versatile in use – again exemplified more recently in the Mosquito.'

These words appear in GDH's autobiography, *Sky Fever*, on the triumph of the DH.4 and its successors, the DH.9 and the DH.9A. Confidence in Airco was such that the War Office ordered the DH.4 off the drawing board, two months before GDH took the prototype aloft at Hendon in August 1916. Its layout of pilot in the front, gunner/observer positioned behind – the reverse of the B.E.2 – was much praised. So was its dual-control ability – the 'back seater' having stowable controls to allow him 'options' should the pilot be incapacitated; this feature was also available on the 'Nines'. Its good performance led to a rethink of its role. Intended as a day bomber, it was reclassified as a fighter-reconnaissance type but soon was undertaking ground-attack, photo-recce and deep penetration raids across the lines.

The appeal of the DH.4 was such that it was hoped it could provide a much-needed degree of standardisation within the diverse ranks of RFC types. Despite the arrival of the more powerful and sophisticated DH.9 and DH.9A, the 'Four' remained in production beyond the Armistice, such was its utility. The variety of engines fitted did not reflect the adaptability of the airframe; the aim was to achieve a one aircraft–one engine formula. The never-ending problems of supply and/or quality of powerplants gave rise to many headaches. Not by choice, but by force of circumstance the DH.4 flew operationally with the following: the BHP – later known as the Galloway Adriatic); the Fiat A.12; the Royal Aircraft Factory 3a and the Rolls-Royce Eagle. Power ran from the 200hp of the 3a all the way to 375hp from the superb Eagle VIII. A total of 1,430 DH.4s were built, but this was eclipsed by American licence production of 'Liberty Planes' – beyond the remit of this book – which ran to a staggering 4,841 units. The author has been unable to ascertain if royalties were attached to this transaction.

It was clear the DH.4 could be developed still further and GDH proposed a dedicated day bomber version in July 1917, which was pounced on by the Air Board. It featured the BHP-derived and initially problematic Siddeley Puma. The prototype DH.9 used a converted DH.4 airframe and was ready for testing in August. The fuselage was rearranged so that the pilot and the gunner/observer were located further aft and a bomb bay was fitted within the centre section. Despite the Puma's traumas, the DH.9 was ordered in huge numbers and, like the DH.6, attracted a contract for manufacture in Spain. The final figure for the DH.9 was 1,782 – Airco had found the mother lode in the DH.4 and its offspring.

DH.4 A7995 parked out at its birthplace, Hendon, in 1917. *Hawker Siddeley*

The first DH.4 built by Dayton-Wright is displayed at the National Air and Space Museum at Washington DC, USA. Completed in 1917, it was retired in April 1919. *NASM*

Airco DH.4, DH.9 and DH.9A compared

	DH.4	**DH.9**	**DH.9A**
Engine	RR Eagle III	Siddeley Puma	Liberty 12
	250hp	230hp	400hp
Span	42ft 5in	42ft 5in	45ft 11in
Wing area	434sq ft	434 sq ft	486¾ sq ft
Length	30ft 3in	30ft 6in	30ft 3in
Loaded weight	3,313lb	3,669lb	4,645lb
Max speed at 15,000ft	102.5mph	97.5mph	106mph
Climb to 10,000ft	16 min 25 sec	20 min 5 sec	15 min 48 sec
Endurance	3½ hours	4½ hours	5¾ hours
Bomb load	448lb	460lb	660lb

Ordinarily, the fixing of a letter suffix to a designation implies a modification; not so with the DH.9A, as the table shows it was a *very* different beast from the 'Nine' and is best considered to be a new type. In December 1917 thoughts were turning to giving the DH.9 a power boost, by replacing the 230hp Puma with a 375hp Rolls-Royce Eagle VIII. A DH.9 airframe was converted and fitted with enlarged wings, and it flew for the first time in February 1918. The following month it received the designation DH.9A and became known throughout its long service life as the 'Ninak' from the phonetics of the era – Nine-Ack.

Understandably, the exceptional Eagle VIII was in much demand for other uses and the search for a suitable engine for the DH.9A looked across the Atlantic to the US War Department's Liberty 12 of 400hp. Hendon was hard at work on the promising DH.10 long-range bomber and the decision was taken to entrust Westland with design leadership on the Liberty DH.9A. Westland had proven to be a capable and consistent sub-contractor and it flew the new variant on 19 April – making it a Royal Air Force type by eighteen days. This contract for the Yeovil-based firm was to have far-reaching consequences; it set Westland up as a specialist in general-purpose military types. The Ninak's post-1918 career was principally in aerial policing and the much-modified Walrus of 1921 and even the Wapiti of 1927 owed much to Airco ancestry.

A large number of manufacturers benefitted from the longevity of the DH.9A when a large refurbishing/rebuild programme was undertaken from 1924 to 1927. Some of the resurrected airframes were given metal wings, such was the 'depth' of the project. What had been an Airco venture gave de Havilland much-valued work together with Blackburn, Gloster, Handley Page, Parnall, Saunders, Shorts and Westland, as well as the RAF's 4 (Central) Aircraft Repair Depot at Ascot.

As GDH wrote, the DH.4 was such a 'good aeroplane' that it spawned a family that ran beyond the end of the war. Sadly, circumstances were such that this success did not have a long-lasting effect on its parent company. The British aircraft industry has had similar potent dynasties, the one initiated by the Hawker Hart being a classic example. de Havilland reproduced the versatility and agility of the DH.4, DH.9 and Ninak but without the need for a stream of variant names; all that was needed was one – Mosquito.

Airline pioneer

Building aeroplanes was only part of Thomas's passion and with incredible foresight, on 5 October 1916, he founded an airline, Aircraft Transport and Travel Ltd (ATT), as a subsidiary of Airco. He patiently waited for the day when civil aviation would have the upper hand. He was joined by the dynamic, dapper Sir Sefton Brancker in 1919 as the airline started proving flights. On 25 August 1919 ATT staged the first British scheduled service from Hounslow Heath to Le Bourget, Paris, using modified DH.4As and a more practical 'airliner', the DH.16. By widening the DH.9A's fuselage, four passengers were accommodated in the DH.16's rudimentary cabin. ATT initially acquired all nine DH.16s; this was a case of 'robbing Peter to pay Paul', keeping the design office and the factory going by moving money around Thomas's empire.

The DH.16 was an interim solution and GDH conceived a more ambitious eight-seat airliner, the DH.18. This had its maiden flight during early 1920 and entered service with ATT in March. Only the prototype was flown at Hendon; another two were under assembly when Airco folded. They were removed for completion to Stag Lane, where another three were built. Operating tentative services with no subsidies, ATT was haemorrhaging cash and it did not long outlive its parent, calling it a day on 17 December 1920. Airco was not alone in diversifying into air transport; Handley Page dabbled in airline work, while Avro turned to joy-riding.

Writing on the wall

Switching some of Thomas's factories to building car bodies could put off the meltdown that faced the entire industry after the Armistice. Working tirelessly to diversify and sell off viable assets while suffering from throat cancer, Thomas watched as the house of cards collapsed. To all intents and purposes, it looked as though Britain had opted out of manufacturing aircraft.

As already related, the DH.11 twin-engined bomber did not fly until 1919, by which time it was regarded only as a contractual obligation. The last new Airco military design was the DH.14 Okapi (a short-necked central African member of the giraffe family) intended as a DH.4 replacement. Three had been ordered, but only one was flown at Hendon, in late 1919; the other two were completed by GDH's new enterprise at Stag Lane, Edgware. There was some solace in conversions for the civilian market, or for export, of DH.4s, DH.9s and DH.9As, but these were small beer and Airco found itself in competition with former sub-contractors also keen to supplement their meagre incomes with similar work.

In 1916 David Lloyd George's newly elected Liberal Coalition government introduced Excess Profits Duty, which hit the fledgling

Airco

From	To	Total	Name or Designation	Type	Engine(s)	Notes
1915	1916	100	DH.1/DH.1A	Pusher recce	1 x Renault	[1]
1915	1916	202	DH.2	Pusher scout	1 x Gnome	
1916	-	1	DH.3	Pusher bomber	2 x Beardmore	
1916	1919	1,430	DH.4	Day bomber/recce	1 x BHP/Eagle	[2]
1918	1919	4,841	DH.4 'Liberty Plane'	Day bomber/recce	1 x Liberty 12A	[3]
1916	1917	550	DH.5	Fighter	1 x Le Rhône	[4]
1917	1922	2,362	DH.6	Trainer	1 x RAF 1a	[5]
1917	1931	3,162	DH.9	Day bomber	1 x SD Puma	[6]
1918	1919	1,782	DH.9A	Day bomber/recce	1 x Liberty 12	[7]
1918	1919	273	DH.10/A Amiens	Day bomber	2 x Liberty 12	[8]
1919	-	1	DH.11 Oxford	Day bomber	2 x ABC Dragonfly	
1919	1920	3	DH.14/A Okapi	Day bomber	1 x Napier Lion	[9]
1919	-	1	DH.15 Gazelle	Day bomber	1 x B'more Atlantic	
1919	1920	9	DH.16	Transport	1 x Napier Eagle	
1920	-	1	DH.18	Airliner	1 x Napier Lion	[10]

All tractor, piston biplanes unless noted. **[1]** All but prototype sub-contracted to Savages, King's Lynn. **[2]** DH.4 also sub-contracted to Berwick and Co, London; Glendower Aircraft, London; Palladium Autocars, London; Vulcan Motor, Southport; and Westland. Does not include DH.4s 'reverse-engineered' by Polikarpov at Duks, Moscow, Russia, 1920–21. **[3]** Licensed in USA as DH.4A and DH.4B, plus sub-variants by Dayton-Wright Airplane, Dayton, Ohio; Fisher Body Corp, Cleveland, Ohio, and Detroit, Michigan; Standard Aircraft Corp, Elizabeth, New Jersey. Does not include major rebuilds – with steel tube fuselages – by Atlantic Aircraft and Boeing. **[4]** Also sub-contracted to British Caudron, Cricklewood; Darracq, London; and Marsh Jones and Cribb, Leeds. **[5]** Also sub-contracted to Gloucestershire (Gloster) and Grahame-White, Harland and Wolff, Belfast; Kingsbury Aviation, Kingsbury; Morgan and Co, Leighton Buzzard; Ransomes, Sims and Jefferies, Ipswich; and Savages, King's Lynn. Licences: 1 by Canadian Aeroplanes, Toronto, 1917; 60 by Hispano-Suiza, Guadalajara, Spain, 1921–22. **[6]** Also sub-contracted to Alliance Aeroplane, London; Berwick and Co, London; Mann Egerton, Norwich; National Aircraft Factory 1, Waddon; National Aircraft Factory 2, Heaton Chapel, Vulcan Motor, Southport; Waring and Gillow, London (including a 'sub-let' to Wells Aviation, London); G and J Weir, Glasgow; also Shorts and Westland. Licences: 130 by Hispano-Suiza, Guadalajara, Spain, 1925–27; 30 by Société Anonyme Belge de Constructions Aéronautiques (SABCA), Belgium, 1922–23. A DH.9J was built from stock by DH Technical School, Hatfield, 1931. **[7]** Also sub-contracted to Berwick and Co, London; Mann Egerton, Norwich; Vulcan Motor, Southport; Whitehead Aircraft, Richmond; and Westland. Licensed in USA as USD-9/A by Dayton-Wright Airplane, Dayton, Ohio (6) and Engineering Division US Army Air Service, McCook, Ohio (7) in 1918. Does *not* include: unlicensed production of about 100 R-1s in USSR by Polikarpov, 1922–23. From 1924 Soviet state factories built 2,800 improved R-1s from scratch. See under Armstrong Whitworth and Westland for Tadpole and Walrus. **[8]** All but the prototype were tractors. Also sub-contracted to Birmingham Carriage, Birmingham; Daimler, Coventry; Mann Egerton, Norwich; National Aircraft Factory 2, Heaton Chapel. **[9]** Three built at Hendon but only one flown; other two completed by DH at Stag Lane in 1920. **[10]** Prototype flown at Hendon, production recommenced by DH at Stag Lane.

aircraft industry particularly hard. The superb biography of AHT by David Scott and Ian Simmons explains the burden: 'As mostly new ventures [the companies] were being asked to expand rapidly to fulfil the nation's ever-growing wartime requirements. New plant, new buildings, new labour and ever-increasing material costs were putting an endless pressure on their industrial finances. Yet it was proposed to levy a tax on any profits made in excess of the normal 25% peacetime [figure] applied at a rate of 60% [above that] … without any consideration or allowance for the incurred extra costs.'

Overstretched and exhausted, Thomas began secret negotiations with BSA – Birmingham Small Arms – in December 1919. This consortium made guns for the military and for sportsmen, bicycles, motorcycles and car bodies among many other products. BSA had no interest in aircraft; it wanted Airco for its production capacity, premises and workforce. Excess Profit Duty of £119,652 – more than £13 million in present-day prices – was levied on Airco in early 1920 – with a whopping £207,680 held over for another day. Despite this the company showed a profit in its final accounts, just prior to 'amalgamating' with BSA in March 1920. The tax was a hammer blow, there could be no recovery. By the summer, the last Airco machines had flown.

In 1919 Oxford student Nevil Shute Norway applied to work at Airco out of term-times for no money; what used to be called 'work experience' but these days is dressed up in the grandiose term 'internship'. In his autobiography, *Slide Rule*, Norway gives a taste of the twilight of Airco: 'By modern standards the factory at Hendon would be small, but in those days it was enormous and far too large to be kept going on the peacetime demand for aircraft … Airco at that time was near its end … de Havilland and Walker [Charles Clement Walker had been with GDH at Farnborough and worked

alongside him at Airco; he became a founding director of de Havilland Aircraft, retiring from the board in 1954 as C Walker CBE] were already making plans to start a new company on their own … In the meantime they were allowed to go on working in the empty design offices that had been so busy in the war, with a very small staff, most of whom were working out their notice.' Norway went on to join de Havilland and then co-founded Airspeed.

GDH established his own company on 25 September 1920, initially taking on unfinished work from Airco. One of those backing the new venture – to the tune of £10,000 – was the ailing Thomas. As well as Charles Walker, several Airco personnel went with GDH, including: Frank Halford, creator of the Gipsy engines; Francis St Barbe, who championed the marketing of the Moth 'family', and Arthur Hagg, designer of such breathtaking creations as the Comet racer and Albatross airliner, ending his career with Airspeed and the Ambassador.

Thomas succumbed to illness and died in France on New Year's Day 1929 – he was 59. He had the pleasure of seeing the British aircraft industry revive from the post-war ashes and it must have been very satisfying to see his protégé, GDH, make a 'go' of it. We shall turn to Harald Penrose and his exceptional *British Aviation – The Pioneer Years* to pay tribute to George Holt Thomas: 'Though the greatest and most influential constructor in the British aircraft industry, he was too remote to be well known. By encouragement and selection of the right men in his companies, coupled with visionary understanding of the sky's potential, he forced progress, despite official apathy and even hostility against British aviation.'

The name Airco was reused – for a consortium – during the early days of the Trident jetliner – see Chapters 17 and 26.

CHAPTER THREE

Novel Inspiration

Airspeed
1931 to 1951

'… these orders did nothing to restore the spirit that had once inspired the company' Nevil Shute Norway

Skeletal ruins strewn across the French countryside marked the end of the British rigid airship industry. Flagship of a new era, the R.101 was on its first overseas voyage when it came to grief near Beauvais on 5 October 1930. Among the forty-eight who perished as a result of the crash (six survived) were Lord Thomson, the Secretary of State for Air and the man tasked with overseeing the Imperial Airship Scheme; Sir Sefton Brancker, Director of Civil Aviation; Lt Col Vincent Richmond, Director of Design and others of his staff.

The State-supported R.101 was a product of the Air Ministry's Royal Airship Works at Cardington and one element of a two-pronged programme; the other being the private-venture R.100 built by the Airship Guarantee Company (AGC), a Vickers-Armstrongs subsidiary, at Howden, west of Hull. In December 1930 Lord Thomson's successor, Lord Amulree, closed down the entire venture. At Howden the R.100's chief designer, Barnes Neville Wallis, had already departed to find new challenges with Vickers at Brooklands. But chief engineer Alfred Hessell Tiltman and his deputy, Nevil Shute Norway, were not so fortunate; like many others they were left kicking their heels.

management and Tiltman tackled design and technical matters. Some company names roll off the tongue, rich with inspiration and promise: such was Airspeed, coined by Tiltman's wife, Miriam. In present-day parlance, Airspeed was a 'start-up' and quickly asserted itself, living up to the romantic, high-performance image generated by its title.

Nevil Shute Norway has already been mentioned in Chapter 2. Under the pen name Nevil Shute. he wrote novels and in 1954 his absorbing autobiography, *Slide Rule*, appeared. Before charting the founding years of Airspeed, *Slide Rule* provides an insightful appraisal of both the airships and the angst inherent in a ministry-administered programme.

Inspiration and promise

The pair had ambitions and lost no time; 101 days after AGC was closed down they formed Airspeed Ltd in York on 13 March 1931. They were joint managing directors; Norway looked after sales and

The second prototype Ambassador was converted by Rolls-Royce at Hucknall in 1958 as a test bed for the Tyne turboprop, flying with the 'B Condition' serial G-37-3. It was unveiled at that year's SBAC display at Farnborough. *Rolls-Royce*

In 1919 the 20-year-old Norway was accepted for work experience in Airco's Hendon design office under the tutelage of Geoffrey de Havilland. Norway was studying engineering science at Balliol College, Oxford. In the spring of 1921, after Airco had collapsed, Geoffrey was happy to invite the youngster back to the newly established de Havilland Aircraft (DH) at Stag Lane, near Edgware. The seeds were sown; Norway took up a full-time post there in January 1923. Spending his days at the drawing board, of an evening Norway toiled away writing: his first novel, *Marazan*, was published in 1926.

Norway's time with DH was brief, as a significant step up the career ladder presented itself. He became an early employee of AGC at Howden in 1924, initially as chief calculator to Wallis. Setting up Airspeed with Tiltman was both nerve-racking and satisfying but as the outfit expanded – by 1938 the workforce had reached 1,035 – Norway became disillusioned. There was a rift with Tiltman; for a while both looked set to depart, but it was Norway that resigned during the summer. In *Slide Rule* he describes the Oxford crew trainer's increasing success but was far from euphoric: '... these orders did nothing to restore the spirit that had once inspired the company. Perhaps it had all become too easy.'

During the war Norway served in the Royal Navy Volunteer Reserve and was involved in weapons and systems development. In this work he was reunited with 'Dennis' Burney, who had been AGC's managing director. (Burney is profiled in Chapter 11.) Shute became a very successful novelist, his titles including *Pied Piper* (1942), *No Highway* (1948), *A Town Like Alice* (1950) and *On the Beach* (1957) – the last three being transformed into acclaimed movies. *No Highway* told the story of a Royal Aircraft Establishment 'boffin' who calculates a structural failure in a new airliner – the Rutland Reindeer – and takes positive action to ground the fleet. Norway's writing acquired new meaning in 1954, when the Comet disasters were investigated and solved by scientists just like *No Highway's* Theodore Honey. Nevil Shute Norway died on 12 January 1960: most of his books remain in print to this day.

Alfred Hessell Tiltman's tenure with Airspeed began and ended with gliders – the Tern and the Horsa – but in between were single- and twin-engined types that were more advanced than those of longer-established rivals. With a degree in engineering from London University, at 19 he joined the British Daimler engine company, but in 1911 bridge design became his forte and he worked in Canada for a while. His aviation career began with Airco in 1916, alongside Geoffrey de Havilland, and went with the great man to Stag Lane in 1920. There he struck up a relationship with Norway, and like his friend, decided that AGC offered greater prospects in 1924.

With Norway taking the brunt of the growing pains at Airspeed, Tiltman concentrated on creating a series of innovative types, crowned by the Oxford and the Horsa. His skills were recruited by fellow Airspeed board member Sir Alan Cobham in 1938 when he was taken on as an engineering and design consultant for Flight Refuelling Ltd (FRL). At this time, the kinship between himself and Norway had fractured and Tiltman may have hoped the FRL post would become full time.

DH took a controlling interest in Airspeed in June 1940 and from this point Tiltman found things increasingly frustrating. He particularly begrudged having the Horsa design office relocated to Salisbury Hall, London Colney, near Hatfield, where decisions that had previously been reached quickly became mired in the complexities of a much larger organisation. In his splendid book *Airspeed the Company and its Aeroplanes*, Don Middleton – who knew Tiltman well – described the attitude of DH staff: 'who probably felt a little piqued that two fairly junior de Havilland designers should have started this small firm and have developed the Oxford, which the [Air] Ministry instructed DH to build at Hatfield. Tiltman, to the day he died, was convinced that this caused resentment and led to his resignation in 1942.' Among other positions, Tiltman advised the Ministry of Aircraft Production (MAP) and the Society of British Aircraft Constructors (SBAC), linking up with Marcus Langley of FRL to form a research consultancy, Tiltman Langley Laboratories, in 1944. Alfred Hessell Tiltman retired in 1955 and died on 28 October 1975.

A 1968 view of the former York bus depot that was Airspeed's first factory. *Don Middleton*

Cobham's influence

Setting up in a disused bus garage in York, Airspeed was fortunate to have Sir Alan Cobham as a director and financial backing from Lord Grimthorpe (Ralph W E Beckett). Norway and Tiltman had launched a company aiming to offer high-value products in the teeth of the Great Depression. They had planned a high-wing monoplane two/three-seat tourer but lacked the capital and instead Tiltman embarked on the AS.1 Tern single-seat sailplane – named after a seabird. This is best described as a foot-in-the-door, allowing the small concern to establish the workshop and get its name put about. The first of two Terns had its maiden flight at Sherburn in Elmet in August 1931.

By this time Cobham had signed a contract for two short-range transports for use as 'joy-riders' with his touring National Air Day 'circus'. These needed to be robust, capable of getting in and out of unprepared fields and provide ten 'punters' with the feeling they had sampled a fully-fledged airliner. Although the Ferry trimotor was wrapped around Cobham's specific needs, it might well appeal to other operators. Cobham had pump-primed the nascent company and the much-needed cash flow allowed Tiltman to commence a bigger

version of the original tourer project – the ground-breaking Courier. The prototype Ferry had its maiden flight at Sherburn on 5 April 1932. Eight months later DH flew its Dragon, eclipsing the Ferry's chances with the smaller airlines. While the Ferry could take ten passengers on three engines, the DH biplane could carry six and baggage on two. Only four Ferries were built, the last one being completed at Portsmouth in 1933.

In September 1930 Airspeed was approached by Forward View Aeroplanes Ltd to build a prototype tandem two-seat pusher parasol monoplane. This was the Shackleton-Murray SM.1 created by former Beardmore and ANEC designer William Shackleton and Australian Lee Murray. It first flew at Sherburn early in 1933 and remained a one-off.

The former bus depot had served its purpose; Airspeed needed much more space and an aerodrome alongside the factory. Across Britain, municipal corporations were offering all sorts of businesses favourable terms in order to stimulate recovery from the Depression. Portsmouth came up with a package at the city's airport that was too good to refuse. Ground was broken on a purpose-built assembly line and flight sheds on 2 December 1932.

The prototype Ferry, G-ABSI, serving with Portsmouth, Southsea and Isle of Wight Aviation, at Shoreham in 1939. *KEC*

Right: The third Courier, G-ACLF, under construction at Portsmouth, late 1933. *Airspeed*

Below: A line-up at Portsmouth, probably for the handover of the second Courier G-ACJL in 1933. Third from left is Nevil Shute Norway, then Hessell Tiltman and Lord Grimthorpe. *via Don Middleton*

Growing pains

Among the lorry loads making the trek from York to Portsmouth in the spring of 1933 was the airframe of the final Ferry and a radical prototype that was to be crucial to Airspeed's prospects. This was the five/six-seat Courier, which had its maiden flight on 11 April. Norway and Tiltman were convinced that their original thoughts of a two/three-seat tourer were no longer valid, believing that private owners and aero clubs would take longer to recover from the Depression. Instead, they had created a more substantial single-engined design that could embrace the light transport/air taxi roles and the emerging business travel markets.

Sir Alan Cobham had commissioned the first example, providing vital cash flow of £5,000 at a very challenging time. The large cabin made the Courier the ideal vehicle for Cobham's ambitious non-stop flight to India, topping up the tanks using his pioneering in-flight refuelling system. A forced landing at Malta put paid to the venture on 22 September 1934, but the concept had been proven. The heads of designers and directors of rival companies must have turned when two Couriers were shown at the July 1934 SBAC display at Hendon. A sleek monoplane with a large cabin was advanced enough, but the Courier was the first British aircraft with retractable undercarriage to achieve series production. Bristol's corpulent and troublesome Racer of 1922 was so equipped but the type only made seven flights before being quietly forgotten.

The Airspeed board had already committed to the relocation to Portsmouth and to a batch of Couriers. This was eye-watering enough for the small enterprise, but In November 1933 they backed a twin-engined Courier – the Envoy. Prospects for the single-engined design proved to be limited – only sixteen were built – as the airline, charter and corporate marketplace preferred twins. The costs were racking up; five Envoys, and a special order long-distance racer Viceroy, were laid down before the end of the year. The prototype Envoy was airborne on 26 June 1934 and the response was immediate and encouraging, including a licence production agreement with Japan and a single example for the nascent King's Flight.

South Africa placed an order for seven specially configured Envoy IIIs in late 1935, for delivery in the summer of 1936. It was these that changed the focus at Airspeed and put it on the road to massive expansion. Four of the South African Envoys were for the national airline, the others for the air force. The military examples were fitted with a dorsal gun turret, a fixed machine gun in the nose and centre section bomb racks. The quartet for South African Airways could be quickly converted to military guise, or the South African Air Force examples could equally swiftly take on a more peaceful aspect. These adaptable Envoys provided Airspeed with the experience necessary for its next venture.

Specification T.23/36 was issued on 10 July 1936 for a twin-engined aircrew trainer capable of twin conversion, night flying, bombing and gunnery practice, navigation and radio tuition. Within two months the engine choice had settled on Wolseley Scorpio IIs – of which more anon. For a company formed only five years previously, the Air Ministry paid Airspeed an incredible compliment by making T23/36 uncontested and placing an order for 160 'straight off the drawing board'. Initially referred to as the 'Envoy Trainer', the type was named Oxford. Did Nevil Shute Norway influence the choice of name for the new machine? With his Balliol College education, it must have brought a smile to his face.

Powered by a pair of Armstrong Siddeley Cheetah X radials, the first of 8,581 Oxfords took to the air on 19 June 1937. To achieve this total, DH, Percival and Standard Motors became sub-contractors, making 1,515, 1,356 and 750 respectively. Oxfords were built at Hatfield from February 1939 to January 1942, by which time the Mosquito was absorbing practically all of its capacity. As mentioned earlier, in June 1940 DH acquired the controlling interest in Airspeed and so technically ceased to be a sub-contractor, becoming a co-producer.

Such large orders brought about other demands on Airspeed and necessitated still more personnel and logistics. British and Commonwealth units required service liaison – modification alerts, utilisation monitoring, checking Civilian Repair Organisation workshops and more. At first DH staff took the lead, having greater experience of this task, but by 1940 Portsmouth and Hatfield shared the responsibility. Service liaison was a requirement that all major manufacturers needed to establish; it was an extension of the support peacetime customers would expect, but it occasionally put staff in harm's way.

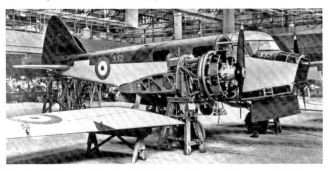

Right: An Oxford II under assembly at Portsmouth early in 1940. Chalked on the airframe is its construction number, 552; this machine was delivered to the Royal New Zealand Air Force. *KEC*

Below: N9107, one of a pair of Envoy IIIs delivered to India in the summer of 1938 for use by the RAF's Delhi Communications Flight. *Peter Green Collection*

Corporate intent

With a new factory and an expanding product line thanks to the Courier and the Envoy it was not surprising that by the summer of 1933 Airspeed was running up large debts. Salvation came from Newcastle-upon-Tyne, where the shipbuilding giant Swan Hunter and Wigham Richardson Ltd was attempting recovery from the Depression by diversifying, perhaps using its existing workforce. Swan Hunter took a controlling interest in Airspeed and to streamline this process the original company entered voluntary liquidation, re-emerging as Airspeed (1934) Ltd. One of the reasons for the relocation to Portsmouth had been its proximity to waterfronts, allowing Airspeed the possibility of entering the flying boat business. This also appealed to Swan Hunter, although its management had a fantasy that 'flying ships' could be fabricated on the empty slipways of Tyneside.

By 1935 the shipwrights turned their thoughts to a tie-up with Fokker for licences on the Dutch manufacturer's airliner and fighter designs. Fokker also held the European rights to the revolutionary Douglas DC-2 twin-engined airliner. The hope was to build the American type in Britain under the Airspeed label, as the AS.23, but this came to nought. (Fokker only ever assembled DC-2s after shipment from Santa Monica, California; no production was undertaken in the Netherlands.)

With the advent of the Envoy, Airspeed developed a close relationship with another start-up, the aero engine division of Wolseley Motors. The Birmingham-based company had made aero engines during the Great War and sub-contracted for the Royal Aircraft Factory but it reverted to vehicles after 1919. Motor car industry mogul Sir William Morris (Lord Nuffield from 1934) acquired Wolseley in 1931 and encouraged the development of the AR series, the Aquarius, Aries and Scorpio radials. Apart from a handful of Hawker Tomtit trainers, Airspeed was the only customer for Wolseley aero engines and intended to power the Oxford with 250hp Scorpio IIs.

By September 1936 Lord Nuffield's infatuation with aviation powerplants had evaporated and the plug was pulled. Left in the lurch, Airspeed approached Nuffield for the manufacturing rights. In *Slide Rule*, Nevil Shute comments: 'Our shipbuilding controllers, perhaps rightly, were averse to any further adventures till we had shown that we were capable of working at a profit.' Shute regretted this, but it was a wise move; much more investment was needed to mature the Wolseley 'family', particularly to take them beyond 300hp. The Oxford accepted the 375hp Armstrong Siddeley Cheetah X with ease and never looked back.

Turning the tables

In June 1940 DH turned the tables on Airspeed. Prior to this, Hatfield had been both a rival and a sub-contractor. Shortly to have its maiden flight, there were great hopes for the Mosquito and DH had a pressing need to expand. Airspeed's factory, workforce and design capacity – not its existing or potential product lines – were ideal. By then Swan Hunter couldn't build ships quickly enough and divesting itself of a small subsidiary was an easy decision. DH took control, although Airspeed continued to trade under its own name. Hatfield called the shots from this point and the writing was on the wall for Tiltman's departure. On 25 January 1944 the company name reverted to Airspeed Ltd but this was no indicator of greater independence: complete share transfer to DH took place in 1948.

This is a good moment to discuss a diverse trio of Airspeed types. First flown on 11 June 1937, the Queen Wasp biplane target drone was summed up by H A Taylor in *Airspeed Aircraft since 1931* as: 'much too good-looking to be shot out of the sky'. Designed to replace the Tiger Moth-based Queen Bee, a handful of production

The one-off Fleet Shadower, N1323. Its 53ft 4in wingspan folded backwards for stowage on a carrier's flight deck. *KEC*

examples appeared in 1940 but by then they were a diversion of vital resources and the programme was axed. The four-engined Fleet Shadower or 'Special Observation Aircraft' of 1940 is related in more detail in Chapter 21 on General Aircraft, who also built and flew a contender for this bizarre requirement. Specification T.4/39 was issued in July 1939 for an advanced trainer and Airspeed was given a contract for two, named Cambridge to maintain the university theme. The prototype took to the air on 19 February 1941, by which time it was realised that it brought nothing new to the party: the RAF was well served by the North American Harvard, which entered service in December 1938, and the Miles Master from May 1939.

The Luftwaffe bombed the Airspeed factory on 11 July 1940. This was the first British aircraft plant to receive such treatment, which was not surprising considering its proximity to a vast naval base. The Luftwaffe was back on 9 April, 1941, this time causing one fatality and many injured. Some sources give this exposure as the reason for the construction of a factory down the coast to the west, at Christchurch, which opened on 22 March 1941. While the attentions of the Luftwaffe had a bearing on the decision, Airspeed needed to expand and find another workforce. Christchurch was a MAP 'shadow factory', with the buildings and plant supplied by the state but staffed and managed by Airspeed. Major Hereward de Havilland DSO, the younger brother of Geoffrey, was put in charge, emphasizing the pecking order in post-1940 Airspeed. Oxfords and Horsas were manufactured there along with Spitfire-into-Seafire conversions and other contracts.

By late 1944 it was clear that Christchurch was under-utilized and a new assembly line for the Mosquito was established. Such things take time and by VJ-Day – marking the capitulation of Japan on 15 August 1945 – only a dozen Mk.VIs had been completed and it is likely the first of those were finished off at Portsmouth. The last Airspeed-built 'Mossie', a B.35, was ready for collection in February 1948.

Airspeed-built Mosquitos

Variant	Total	From	To	Notes
FB.VI	57	1945	1947	[1]
B.35	65	1947	1948	

As a de Havilland-owned company, this was an 'internal' sub-contract. [1] First six, or so, possibly completed at Portsmouth, all others – including the B.35s – built at Christchurch.

While Airspeed did not get its hands on the Wolseley aero engine concern in 1936, three years later the company set up a business that was vital to the war effort and would have a lasting effect on British industry. A Frenchman had invented a simple process to make aircraft fuel tanks fire-resistant. Airspeed took up the British rights in 1939, just in the nick of time. Within two years Fireproof Tanks Ltd had three factories, headquartered at Portsmouth, and manufactured more than 250,000 fuel tanks. Today the venture is known as FPT Industries and is still at Portsmouth, part of GKN Aerospace.

A D-Day-striped Horsa I – note the Y-shaped tow rope – being pulled aloft by a Handley Page Halifax. *KEC*

War chariots

After the Oxford, it is the Horsa assault glider for which Airspeed is most remembered. Horsa was a 5th-century Kentish warrior, the brother of Hengist, the family having come from present-day Denmark/Germany. (The name Hengist was given to a smaller, and unsuccessful, assault glider from Slingsby.) Germany pioneered the use of glider-borne troops in 1940, but Britain was quick to take up the concept. Specification X.26/40 required an easy-to-build and fly, low-value – and therefore expendable – glider capable of taking up to twenty-five troops, depending on what equipment they were carrying.

Shortly after the DH buyout, Tiltman and his team were installed in the former Technical School at Hatfield. Bombing raids in October 1940 made the move a couple of miles south to Salisbury Hall at London Colney expedient. The prototype was built in a hangar alongside the 17th-century manor house. It was towed aloft behind an Armstrong Whitworth Whitley from the Great West Aerodrome – now swallowed within the vastness of Heathrow – with test pilot George Errington at the controls. He praised the all-wood 88ft-span glider: 'of all of the hundreds of production Horsas we made, we never had an accident of any sort though every landing was "forced".' The Mk.I was a pure 'trooper' with tow attachment points on the leading edges of the wing; the Mk.II featured a hinged nose that permitted the loading of Jeeps or small artillery pieces, as well as soldiers. The Mk.II's tow rope was not Y-shaped like the Mk.I, it attached to the nose wheel strut.

The largest number of Horsas came from Harris Lebus of Tottenham. The famed furniture maker assembled them from elements brought in from other carpentry and bodywork companies at a variety of sites as well as the main factory at Tottenham. Completed gliders were taken to Christchurch or RAF maintenance units, including 9 MU Cosford, 15 MU Wroughton and 27 MU Shawbury, for final erection and flight test.

A cuckoo in the nest

Hessell Tiltman parted company with Airspeed in 1942. In that year, a new design office was set up at Fairmile Manor, near Cobham in Surrey. In charge of this branch was a gifted old-hand who had been responsible for two of the most beautiful aircraft of the inter-war period, the DH.88 Comet and the DH.91 Albatross. Arthur Ernest Hagg was appointed to the Airspeed board on New Year's Day 1943 as technical director and director of design.

Hagg's biography could just as easily appear under Chapter 17, but that is already crowded, so it is related here. He joined Airco at Hendon in 1915, working for Geoffrey de Havilland on types including the DH.4, DH.9 and DH.9A. Hagg followed his boss to Stag Lane where he crafted a wide range of aeroplanes, from the Fox Moth to the four-engined Albatross.

In late 1936 he raised eyebrows when he resigned his post at Hatfield and reverted to a lasting passion as a boat designer, forming

Airspeed

From	To	Total	Name	Type	Engine(s)	Notes
1932	1933	4	Ferry	Biplane airliner	3 x DH Gipsy	
1933	1936	16	Courier	Light transport	1 x AS Cheetah	
1934	1939	61	Envoy/Viceroy	Light transport	2 x AS Cheetah	[1]
1937	1945	8,581	Oxford I, II, V	Crew trainer	2 x AS Cheetah	[2]
1937	1940	5	Queen Wasp	Biplane target drone	1 x AS Cheetah	
1940	-	1	Fleet Shadower	Shipborne recce	4 x Pobjoy Niagara	
1941	-	2	Cambridge	Advanced trainer	1 x Bristol Mercury	
1941	1945	3,799	Horsa I/II	Assault glider	nil	[3]
1947	1953	23	Ambassador	Airliner	2 x Centaurus	

Based upon: *Airspeed Aircraft since 1931*, H A Taylor. All piston monoplanes unless noted. **[1]** Licence production of ten by Mitsubishi, Nagoya, Japan as the Hina-Zuru ('Young Crane'). AS.8 Viceroy was a one-off for long-distance racing. **[2]** Also sub-contracted de Havilland and Percival, and to Standard Motors, Ansty. Oxfords refurbished and resold as AS.65 Consuls 1946–48. **[3]** Also built by Austin Motor, Birmingham and Harris Lebus, Tottenham.

The seventh Ambassador, G-ALZR of BKS Air Transport, on approach at Teversham, Cambridge, on one of its last flights, July 1969. *Roy Bonser*

his own company, Walton Yacht Works at Shepperton. There he devised air-sea rescue craft for the RAF among other commissions; post-war his luxury cabin cruisers gained a Bentley-like reputation. Hagg was also a consultant for D Napier and Sons, specialising in engine installations. Along with George Cornwall Hagg designed the ill-fated Napier Sabre-powered Heston Racer of 1940. It was the Napier connection that brought Hagg to Airspeed – effectively a return to DH – to supervise the fitting of the 2,310hp 24-cylinder, H-format Sabre VI to the AS.56 fighter project.

The AS.56 did not get off the drawing board, but Hagg stayed on, DH wanted his airliner expertise. By January 1944, the Brabazon Committee – chaired by aviation pioneer Lord Brabazon of Tara – devised a series of broad concepts for the time when Britain could re-enter the airliner business. (See Chapter 11 for the Brabazon recommendations.) Hagg was tasked with meeting the Brabazon Type IIA requirement for a 40-passenger medium-range machine.

Although the result carried the Airspeed brand it was a DH initiative – a cuckoo in the nest. As was to be expected from Hagg, he came up with a shapely solution, the AS.57 Ambassador. From the start, this could be powered by a pair of Bristol Centaurus pistons or four Napier Naiad turboprops and there was a military fall-back, a tactical transport version, the AS.60 Ayrshire. The turboprop option and the AS.60 did not come to fruition.

With production of the Horsa and Oxford coming to an end in 1945, the Ambassador was intended to take up factory capacity at Portsmouth and Christchurch, but delays on the programme meant that other work was needed to fill the gap. As well as the already mentioned Mosquitos, the ever-dependable Oxford came to the rescue. There was demand for reconditioned examples for export and 121 were refurbished for the RAF. A more refined conversion, the Consul, appeared in March 1946 and close on 150 were delivered. All of this and the manufacture of fuselage 'pods' for the Vampire jet fighter helped to keep the workforce going.

The Ministry of Supply backed two Centaurus-powered Ambassador prototypes and the type had its maiden flight on 10 July 1947. Arthur Hagg retired in mid-1949 with staff from Hatfield taking up the mantle. He returned to a love he had been cultivating; designing luxury motorboats that are today eagerly sought after. It was not long before Hagg was back in de Havilland's corridors; this time as a visitor. In 1950 he had been recruited by Sir Alan Cobham as a consultant technical director for Flight Refuelling Ltd to investigate extending the Comet jetliner's range by topping it up from Avro Lincoln tankers. Arthur Ernest Hagg, creator of beautiful furniture, aircraft and boats, died on 21 January 1985, aged 97.

The nationalised British European Airways (BEA) was the obvious launch customer for the Ambassador and in December 1947 it committed to an order, but it was September of the following year before a contract for twenty was signed. As will be seen under Vickers, BEA was also interested in the Viscount four-turboprop, a response to the Brabazon Type IIB scheme. The Viscount turned out to be in a league of its own and BEA's twenty – known as the Elizabethan class in service – was the only order placed for the Ambassador.

On 1 January 1948 the former Christchurch 'shadow factory' was handed over to Airspeed on lease. The so-called DH 'second unit' at Leavesden had begun to wind down in 1947 and the former MAP plant at Hawarden, near Chester, was taken over in 1948. Thus, DH completed its plan for three production centres: Hatfield, Christchurch–Portsmouth and Hawarden. Airspeed's independent status was becoming administratively more and more cumbersome; for example staff transferred from Hatfield technically needed to be sacked, then re-employed on arrival at Portsmouth. On 21 July 1951 Airspeed was subsumed within de Havilland, becoming a division of the parent. When the last Ambassador was handed over to BEA on 6 March 1953 the name Airspeed passed into history.

CHAPTER FOUR

Pacemakers of Progress

Armstrong Whitworth
1913 to 1959

'Always a discerning man, Siddeley was confident of the future of flying' Armstrong Whitworth brochure

EVEN IN THE 21ST CENTURY a Midlands-built jet that first took to the skies in late 1947 is regarded by many as the most futuristic-looking British aircraft ever. The Armstrong Whitworth AW.52 flying wing certainly stirs the author's blood. It was so advanced, so radical that the manufacturer's publicity department went into overdrive. Test pilot Eric 'Frankie' Franklin took the prototype aloft for its maiden flight from Boscombe Down on 13 November 1947. It was revealed to incredulous press, radio and newsreel representatives at Bitteswell on 16 December. The occasion was captured in a specially commissioned watercolour that was used for a 'splash' advert in the aviation press with the banner headline 'The air occasion of '47'. The advertising agency had been briefed well, prominent in the foreground of the image were cars made by sister company Armstrong Siddeley. To emphasize the new epoch, the Armstrong Whitworth 'wing sphinx' logo was upstaged by a stylized AW.52 coupled with reflective 'AWA' lettering. Alongside this was a catchy jingle: 'Pacemakers of Progress'.

On hand to answer questions were Franklin and John 'Jimmy' Lloyd, the AW.52's designer, who had started out on wooden biplanes with the Siddeley Deasy company in 1917 and thirty years later was a champion of swept-back wings, laminar flow and boundary layer control. Sir Thomas Sopwith, chair of AWA's parent, Hawker Siddeley, and Sir Ben Lockspeiser, chief scientist of the Ministry of Supply, gave speeches. A *Flight* staffer reported hot-foot from frozen Leicestershire in the issue dated 25 December: 'Less than five hours'

flying has been completed to date, chiefly as a result of the bad weather, and since the flight from Boscombe Down to Bitteswell cloud has persisted and prevented all but the simplest of handling trials. After two or three low passes across the airfield, at speeds between 200 and 250mph, Sqn Ldr Franklin made a long, shallow approach, culminating in a faultless nose-up touchdown…'

Despite this spectacular renaissance, AWA's post-1945 production of its own designs amounted to a mere seventy-seven units. For this reason the company tends to be dismissed as a spent force whose glory days ended with the Whitley bomber. But the AWA of the 1940s and '50s had a stature and a stability that its peers

Both AW.52s dominated the 1948 SBAC display at Farnborough: illustrated is the Derwent-engined second example, TS368, arriving on 6 September. *via Tony Buttler*

Stylish advert of February 1948 unveiling the AW.52 and AWA's new logo. *KEC*

With the letters 'AW' proudly embossed on the cowling, FK.8 B3354 at Chingford in 1918. *Peter Green Collection*

craved. In 1958 the Baginton factory and the assembly and flight test centre at Bitteswell employed around 11,500 people. This was not far behind the 1944 high of 12,873 personnel when AWA was also looking after six additional dispersed factory sites.

North-east heavyweight

The origins of AWA lie in Newcastle upon Tyne and Coventry, with two very different industrial concerns. In Newcastle upon Tyne the giant Sir W G Armstrong, Whitworth and Co Ltd (referred to from now on as 'Whitworth') had an enviable reputation in structural engineering, shipbuilding, munitions, artillery and vehicles. From 1912 it began to construct aero engines for ABC Motors, but this soon lapsed. During the Great War the Tyneside Elswick foundry made top-class engine blocks and 'internals' for other aero engine companies. The Admiralty approached Whitworth in the spring of 1913 asking if it could manufacture airships and aeroplanes. In June vacant premises at Scotswood on the north shore of the Tyne became a makeshift factory and production of Royal Aircraft B.E.2s began. During 1914 the move was made a couple of miles north to Gosforth, which boasted a rudimentary airfield. Whitworth began talks with Lt John William Dunne's Blair Atholl Syndicate in 1913 but these petered out the following year.

In 1913 the British Deperdussin Aeroplane Company of Highgate, London, folded leaving Dutch-born Frederick Willem 'Cully' Koolhoven jobless, but not for long. Whitworth snapped him up and the 27-year-old designed and flew the FK.1 single-seater. This remained a one-off but in 1915 Koolhoven devised the FK.2 two-seat

biplane that improved on the B.E.2. This was refined into the FK.3, which went into volume production. Another Dutchman reacquainted himself with Whitworth in 1916. Robert 'Bob' Noorduyn had served an apprenticeship with the company before taking a post in the Sopwith design office. After this he joined the Farnborough-based Aeronautical Inspection Directorate and was assigned to keep an eye on Whitworth. Koolhoven offered Noorduyn a job and the pair began a partnership that outlasted their time at Gosforth.

The experience of the FK.3 was applied to the larger FK.8 for use in the armed reconnaissance role. First flown in May 1916, the FK.8 was a direct rival to the much better-known Royal Aircraft Factory R.E.8. The latter reached a production total of 2,262, while the FK.8 achieved 1,652 units, the majority built by another Newcastle firm, Angus Sanderson. The FK.3 and FK.8 proudly carried the initials 'AW' embossed on the cowling. This gave rise to the nickname 'Ack-W' for the FK.3, from the phonetics of the day. With the advent of the FK.8, it became the 'Big Ack', with the FK.3 adopting 'Little Ack'.

Koolhoven was an advocate of multi-winged formats and in 1916 he created two triplanes, the FK.5 and the FK.6, intended as heavily armed escorts. Both had 'fighting tops' – faired positions for a gunner mounted on each side of the middle wing – giving the two airmen a wide field of fire. The FK.5 was a sesquiplane, with the middle wing of far greater span than the upper and lower components, and is believed not to have flown. The FK.6 followed the same concept but was more conventional looking, but also remained a one-off. Koolhoven turned to a single-seat quadruplane, which initially appeared as the FK.9 before a major transformation into the FK.10. Production plans included sub-contracting to Angus Sanderson and Phoenix Dynamo, Bradford, but only ten were completed.

Koolhoven became disenchanted with Whitworth, which shunned his increasingly radical multi-winged designs, including the FK.11 that would have boasted *fifteen* lifting surfaces. In 1917 he and Noorduyn left for the newly established British Aerial Transport (BAT) at Willesden, London. After BAT folded, Koolhoven returned to the Netherlands in 1920 and was employed by Nationale Vliegtuigindustrie (national aircraft industry) before starting his own Koolhoven Vliegtuigen in 1934. There he created transports and military types until his factory was destroyed in the German blitzkrieg of May 1940. Bob Noorduyn established his own business in Canada in 1933 and two years later his famous Norseman 'bush plane' flew; it remained in production until December 1959.

Fred Murphy took over the Whitworth design office. Two of his creations followed: the FM.4 Armadillo and Ara (a generic name of the macaw parrot family) single-seat fighters; neither went beyond the prototype stage. Murphy had started off with Bristol at Filton, before moving to Hamble in 1914 to devise the HL.1 floatplane for

The flightless FK.5 triplane at Gosforth showing its sesquiplane format and the proximity of the 'fighting tops' to the propeller. *KEC*

Hamble River, Luke and Co. Gosforth built a batch of Bristol F.2B Fighters through to the autumn of 1919, when the aeronautical department was closed down.

Armstrong Whitworth/Siddeley Deasy World War One sub-contracts

Type	Total	From	To	Notes
R A/c Factory B.E.2a, 'b, 'c	83	1913	1915	[1] [2]
R A/c Factory R.E.7	100	1916	-	[3]
R A/c Factory R.E.8	1,027	1916	1918	[3] [4]
Bristol F.2B	250	1918	1919	[1] [2]

[1] Built by Armstrong Whitworth at Scotswood – to 1914 – and Gosforth thereafter. [2] Total estimated. [3] Built by Siddeley Deasy. [4] The three improved RT.1s were extracted from this order – see narrative.

A tale of two Johns

John Davenport Siddeley resuscitated the Deasy Motor Car Manufacturing Company to such an extent that it was renamed the Siddeley Deasy Motor Car Company in 1912. That was not the only time that a business carried his name: his own Siddeley Autocar Company was founded in 1902 and a series of Wolseley-Siddeley motor cars was launched in 1908. In aviation terms Hawker Siddeley was dominant from 1935 to 1977. That conglomerate included a large number of 'tech' firms and today Hawker Siddeley Switchgear continues to commemorate a great industrialist. The dynamic John Davenport Siddeley (to differentiate John from Siddeley companies, he is referred to as JDS from now on) was knighted in 1932; he retired in June 1936 and became Baron Kenilworth in 1937. He died in November 1953, aged 87.

The War Office approached Siddeley Deasy (SD) in 1915 to construct the BHP aero engine at its plant in Parkside, Coventry (see under Beardmore for more on the BHP). Typically, JDS was not content and the BHP was revised and refined as the Puma, beginning a powerplant dynasty that ended with the Sapphire turbojet in the late 1950s. The War Office returned in 1917 wanting SD to manufacture aeroplanes, with contracts for Royal Aircraft Factory R.E.7s and R.E.8s. Just as sub-contracting aero engines led to a successful standalone venture, JDS reasoned that the same could happen with aircraft.

Appointing Jimmy Lloyd as assistant designer in 1917, under Major Frederick Michael Green, proved to be a masterstroke. Green began his career making engines with the British Daimler company, before taking the post of engineer-designer in 1910 at what was then the Balloon Factory – becoming the Army Aircraft Factory from the following year and the Royal Aircraft Factory from 1912. It was Green who 'found' Geoffrey de Havilland, who signed up with the 'Factory' in December 1910.

Apprenticed in the steel industry, Lloyd was also a Farnborough man. From 1916 he was head stress calculator, one of his first tasks being the R.E.8. Green moved over to SD in January 1917 as chief engineer and Lloyd also migrated to Coventry. Lloyd went from strength to strength, being promoted to chief designer in 1924 and technical director in 1948. He retired in March 1955 and died aged 90 in 1978. It remains a great pity that so few people know his name; he was among the 'greats'.

Lloyd's first creation for SD was the RT.1, based on the R.E.9, itself a refined and improved R.E.8. Using airframes from the company's sub-contract, three were manufactured, but with the R.E.8 and the FK.8 in volume production there was no need to reinvent the wheel. The Sinaia twin-engined bomber employed a more practical form of Koolhoven's 'fighting tops'. The engine nacelles of the two Tiger radials extended well beyond the low wing's trailing edge, concluding in a gunner's position. (Sinaia was the name then given to what is today the Sinai peninsula, Egypt.) The Sinaia programme was drawn out: the only prototype was initiated under the SD aegis in 1918, but did not fly until 25 June 1921, by which time the company had changed name.

It was the SR.2 Siskin – named after a bird of the finch family – that was to shape the future for JDS's new enterprise. Flown in 1919, the first of three prototypes suffered from the problematical 320hp ABC Dragonfly engine; when fitted with a 325hp Armstrong Siddeley Jaguar in 1921, its reliability and performance were transformed. The Air Ministry recognised the SR.2 for what it was; the basis of an excellent fighter. Both Green and Lloyd had been involved with the S.E.5 at the Royal Aircraft Factory and the SR.2 doubly benefitted from this experience. Green's responsibility encompassed aircraft and engines and during 1916 Farnborough was developing the Type 8, a 14-cylinder radial of around 300hp. The Burbidge Committee was exceptionally critical of the 'Factory' and it was reborn in 1918 as a pure research facility. In 1919 Siddeley Deasy took on the RAF Type 8 and it evolved into the Jaguar, which remained in production into the late 1920s.

In his excellent *Armstrong Whitworth Aircraft since 1913*, Oliver Tapper wrote of the familial likeness of the S.E.5 and the SR.2: 'It has been suggested that the design which emerged as the [SR.2] Siskin had already been roughed out by Green before he left Farnborough, but both he and Lloyd have denied that this was so: nevertheless, it seems likely that, but for the change in government policy towards [the Royal Aircraft Factory], the aeroplane that became the Siskin might very well have been the SE.7.' Paul Hare, author of *The Royal Aircraft Factory*, also speculates about the relationship, while explaining that the S.E.6 and S.E.7 were follow-ons to the S.E.5, the latter to have been fitted with an RAF 8. Whatever its parentage, the Siskin was AWA's launch pad.

Merged, buying spree, acquired

During the Great War, Whitworth and SD had worked closely on the 6-cylinder Puma and both concerns manufactured aeroplanes of their own design and under sub-contract. With the collapse of orders after the Armistice, JDS approached Whitworth about a closer relationship, which evolved into Newcastle buying out Coventry. Whitworth would continue to concentrate on ships and the 'heavy end' of engineering, and it closed the aviation element. In May 1919 the Armstrong Whitworth Development Company was formed as the holding group for the Coventry businesses. Armstrong Siddeley Motors (ASM) was the new name for SD products – classy cars and an expanding range of aero engines. (See the tables for SD and ASM engines: ASM was absorbed into Bristol Siddeley Engines in 1959.) The Sir W G Armstrong Whitworth Aircraft Company (AWA) came into being in April 1920.

Siddeley-Deasy (SD) and Armstrong Siddeley piston engines

Name, Type/Format	From	Application*	Notes
SD Puma, 6-cy in-line	1915	Airco DH.9	[1]
SD Tiger, V-12	1918	SD Sinaia	[2]
Lynx, 7-cy radial	1920	Avro 504N	
Jaguar, 14-cy radial	1923	AW Atlas	
Genet, 5-cy radial	1926	Blackburn Bluebird	
Mongoose, 5-cy radial	1926	Hawker Tomtit	
Leopard, 14-cy radial	1927	Hawker Horsley	
Genet Major	1929	Cierva C.30A	[3]
Panther, 14-cy radial	1929	Fairey Gordon	
Serval, 10-cy radial	1931	Saro Cloud	
Tiger, 14-cy radial	1932	Blackburn Shark	[4]
Hyena, 15-cy radial	1933	AW XVI	
Deerhound, 21-cy radial	1935	AW Whitley II	
Cheetah, 7-cy radial	1935	Avro Anson	

* Typical, or only, use. [1] See Chapter 8. [2] Entirely separate from the ASM Tiger of 1932. [3] Major I was 5-cylinder, Major IA, III and IV was 7-cylinder. RAF called the Genet Major IA the Civet. [4] Entirely separate from the SD Tiger of 1918.

Prior to 1920, SD aircraft had been test flown from Radford, north-west of Coventry, but in that year AWA bought land at Whitley, to the south, and in 1923 the factory and aerodrome was fully operational. Lloyd's design department remained at Parkside until relocating to Whitley in 1930. Both Radford and Whitley are now covered in the city's urban sprawl.

By the mid-1920s Whitworth was struggling and JDS was frustrated that Coventry's endeavours were keeping the parent going. He bought the enterprise back in December 1926, under the Armstrong *Siddeley* Development Company (ASDC) banner, the full names of ASM and AWA remaining unchanged. This purchase might well have cost JDS £1.5 million but the cash injection did little to help the ailing Newcastle giant. Rival Vickers pounced and on 31 October 1927 acquired Whitworth, the amalgamation trading as Vickers-Armstrongs.

Whitworth was not the only concern willing to sell off subsidiaries. Crossley Motors was looking to unload its interests in Avro. Seeing another manufacturer that could use his aero engines, JDS snapped up the Manchester-based firm in May 1928. His buying spree continued, securing majority ownership of the stumbling High Duty Alloys Ltd

later in 1928. Having gained independence from Whitworth, within two years JDS was at the helm of a large combine, with two design and production centres. Through ASM he commanded a major aero engine manufacturer and High Duty Alloys gave access to the latest thinking in metallurgy and structures.

By the mid-1930s, it was ASDC that was the focus of others with a view to purchase. This time the sale was not through weakness; the Siddeley 'empire' was a very attractive package. 'Tommy' Sopwith and Fred Sigrist at Hawker saw this great opportunity and on 25 June 1935 the organisations came together, along with Gloster (which had been acquired in May 1934), as the massive Hawker Siddeley *Aircraft* Company. The constituent businesses continued to trade under their own names. The enterprise was reorganised in 1948 as the Hawker Siddeley Group and again in January 1959 when it became Hawker Siddeley *Aviation*. To prevent confusion between the 1935 to 1948 HSA and the HSA formed in 1959, throughout the book the earlier HSA is referred to as the Hawker Siddeley (HS) consortium.

Inter-war big numbers

The SR.2 Siskin provided Green and Lloyd with the basis of a military biplane family that sustained the factory into the 1930s and attracted export orders. The ability to adapt a proven airframe to other tasks was the recipe for success during the 1920s and early '30s. The intermediate Siskin II of 1922 represented a very different machine from the SR.2 of 1919 and the projected S.E.7 of two years before that. The Mk.II was bigger, more stable, had a robust undercarriage able to absorb the most alarming rate of sink and gave the pilot an enhanced field of view. The Mk.II – the prototype was a two-seater – retained wooden wings, but boasted a steel tube fuselage. It was an interim stage because the Air Ministry had taken the plunge and announced that types entering service in 1924 would have all-metal structures.

The all-metal Siskin III had its maiden flight on 7 May 1923 and was rewarded with a contract to replace the RAF's Sopwith Snipes, thus ending the Great War fighter era. Siskin IIIs were the first series production all-metal type to join the RAF. From 1928 they took over from Gloster Grebes and Gamecocks and the RAF also ordered dual-control trainers. More advanced developments of the Siskin theme

Blackburn-built Siskin IIIAs of Tangmere-based 43 Squadron in 1930. *KEC*

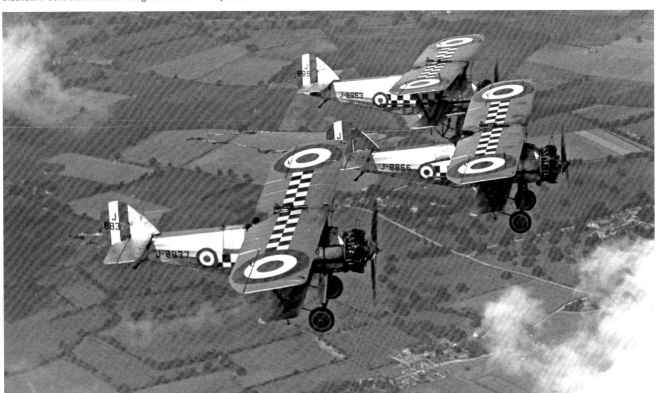

Three of four Scimitars delivered to the Norwegian Army Air Service in 1936. *KEC*

Heavyweights

Prior to his promotion to chief designer in 1924 Jimmy Lloyd worked on his – and AWA's – largest aircraft to date; the Awana troop transport, which took its name from a New Zealand township. The first of two flew on 28 June 1923, but it was defeated by the Vickers Victoria, which had its debut in the previous year. This was not a wasted effort; it was preparation for a trio of airliner commissions from Imperial Airways. In the spring of 1926 the first of seven Argosy twenty-passenger trimotors flew. By modern standards, such a tiny order seems a disastrous state of affairs, but the circumstances of the 1920s were very different. With routes to Africa, the Middle East and beyond, Imperial Airways represented the largest market for airliners outside the USA. The potential number of passengers was limited and these could be met by small numbers of aircraft. The prestige of being a 'flag carrier' meant that each country was protectionist, placing orders with indigenous manufacturers whenever possible. Airliners were a niche market but types such as the Argosy – named after a capacious merchant vessel – were designed conservatively to minimise risk. With a customer such as Imperial, cash flow was assured and small runs were, more or less, viable.

That was the case for the next airliner, the company's first monoplane. Clearly pleased with the Argosy, Imperial ordered eight AW.XVs without going to the accepted 'fly before you buy' procedure. Lloyd produced a very sleek four-engined machine with fuselage-mounted, spatted, main undercarriage. The cabin could take nine passengers, their luggage and a large load of mail. The first example carried the name *Atalanta* – a virginal Greek huntress – on the nose and this was adopted as the name for the type.

The relationship with the airline remained strong and the AW.27, AWA's response to Imperial's requirement for an 'Empire Route Airliner' taking up to forty passengers, was accepted. After the development costs were 'loaded' on the prototype, the remaining thirteen that were eventually ordered cost Imperial Airways around £37,000. The Atalanta had convinced Imperial that the high wing was popular with passengers and allowed easy access from the apron to the cabin. Taking the name Ensign, the AW.27 was very advanced, benefitting from the experience of the Whitley bomber.

With a span of 123ft and an all up weight of 48,500lb, the AW.27 Ensign was the largest British aircraft to date when it had its maiden flight on 23 January 1938. That momentous event took place at Hamble, on the Solent, and not from Whitley. When AWA signed the contract, it was fighting to get the Whitley into mass production at a new factory. Such a large and complex project as the Ensign was an inevitable drain on already stretched resources. In the early 1930s it had become clear that Whitley was too small and a colossal factory and airfield was established in 1936 at Baginton, south of Whitley and now Coventry Airport. The Whitley site was maintained, going on to become the centre of AWA's post-war foray into guided missiles: it closed in 1968, by which time it was an HS Dynamics facility.

Extensive hangars could be made available at sister company AST as the Ensign assembly line. The first of these giants was expected to be handed over to Imperial in mid-1936 but the programme suffered delays from the relocation, the need to concentrate on Whitley manufacture and the airline tinkering with the specification. The last of fourteen Ensigns was delivered to what by then was British Overseas Airways Corporation in December 1941. Had the war been averted, it is worth speculating that the Ensign might well have attracted more orders, perhaps even exports.

Manchester being land-locked, the rapidly expanding Avro decided in 1916 to find an airfield alongside water on which to build a factory and, perhaps, flying boats. The choice fell upon Hamble, the site was bought and A V Roe (Southampton) Ltd was constituted on

followed, the Starling, AW.XVI and Scimitar but in each case orders failed to reach double figures. (See the 1915 to 1936 data table for notes on the occasionally opaque AW designation 'system'.)

In the 1920s rarely did the Air Ministry acquire aircraft in an uncontested manner, and a requirement for an army co-operation type saw AWA's Wolf and the Hawker Duiker under evaluation at Martlesham Heath in 1923. Neither made the grade, but three Wolfs were adapted as trainers by the RAF. From July 1923 AWA established a flying school at Whitley and by 1930 the fleet was substantial and a revenue earner, keeping personnel from the Reserve of Air Force Officers current. Three more Wolfs were built in 1923 for the school. With the setting up of Air Service Training (AST) in 1931 – see below – other AWA types were recruited as civilian-operated trainers. A trio of Wolf-based Apes – purpose-built flying test beds for the Royal Aircraft Establishment – appeared in 1926. To alter the centre of gravity, bays could be added to or subtracted from the fuselage, changing the length pre-flight, while the 'tail feathers' could have their incidence varied in the air.

In 1924 the Air Ministry began the process of replacing the venerable, much-remanufactured, Bristol F.2B Fighter, although rebuilt Mk.IVs continued to be delivered up to 1928. This was potentially a very lucrative contract and AWA found its Atlas up against the Bristol Boarhound, de Havilland Hyena, Short Chamois and Vickers Vespa. Clearly showing Siskin thinking and experience, the private-venture (PV) Atlas was the victor and when production ended in 1933 a total of 478 had been built. A small batch of Ajax day bomber variants also appeared in 1925. Hoping to extend the assembly line, an improved Atlas, the Aries, failed to attract attention in 1930. Another PV type, also unsuccessful, was the AW.19 general-purpose biplane that was flown in 1934. It was one of *seven* PV entrants and three Air Ministry-sponsored contestants striving for Specification G.4/31 to succeed Fairey Gordons and Westland Wapitis.

Siddeley Deasy SR.2 Siskin and AWA Siskin IIIA compared

	SR.2	Siskin IIIA
First flown	1919	1925
Structure	All-wood	All-metal
Engine	ABC Dragonfly 320hp	AS Jaguar IV 385hp
Span	27ft 6in	33ft 2in
Wing area	247sq ft	293sq ft
Length	21ft 3in	25ft 4in
Loaded weight	2,181lb	3,012lb
Max speed at 15,000ft	139mph	153mph
Climb to 10,000ft	7 min 5 sec	6½ min

Pre-delivery image of the first Argosy II, G-AACH. It was named *City of Edinburgh* when accepted by Imperial Airways in mid-1929. *KEC*

The penultimate Atalanta, G-ABTL *Astrea*, delivered to Imperial Airways in April 1933. *Peter Green Collection*

The first Ensign, G-ADSR, probably on show to the AWA workforce at Whitley, in early 1938. *Rolls-Royce*

the last day of the year. With the purchase of Avro by ASDC in May 1928 the Hamble design staff were consolidated with their colleagues in Manchester; a new use was sought for the Solent aerodrome. Expanding on the theme of the Whitley flying school, AST was founded and was up and running by April 1931. As well as the Ensigns, the two prototype Albemarles – see below – were assembled and tested at Hamble. AST was transferred from ASDC management in 1940, coming under the parent HS consortium.

From Whitley to Lincoln

A competition for a bomber-transport resulted in the AW.23, which flew on 4 June 1935. It was AWA's first aircraft with retractable undercarriage and with manually operated gun turrets at the nose and tail – both innovations from the ever-inventive Lloyd. The AW.23 and the Handley Page HP.51 lost out to the Bristol Bombay but both runners up found other success. The HP.51 evolved into the bomber-configured Harrow, while Lloyd used the wings, engine grouping, undercarriage and tail surfaces to create the Whitley heavy bomber. In the same way that the Ensign suffered from the advent of the Whitley, so too did AWA's bid for Specification P.27/32 for a light day bomber. The AW.29 took to the air on 6 December 1936, nine months after the Fairey contender; the latter clinched the order, becoming the ill-fated Battle.

Thanks to the AW.23 bomber-transport, AWA was in a commanding position to respond to the urgent request for a twin-engined heavy bomber. The prototype Whitley first flew on 17 March 1936 from the airfield it was named after as Baginton was being readied for volume production. Two months after that maiden flight the Air Ministry placed an order for eighty Mk.Is. When the RAF's previous heavy bomber, the Fairey Hendon, had its debut in November 1930 it took just over two years to sign a contract and it was for a paltry fourteen. Six years later the world was a very different place and Britain had a lot of catching up to do. Hitler, having gained absolute power in 1933, was rearming Germany at an alarming pace. Ten days before the first Whitley took to the air, the German army occupied the previously demilitarised Rhineland, and four months later the Spanish Civil War erupted.

The Whitley assembly line at Baginton, 1938. *KEC*

Bombing up a Whitley III of 58 Squadron at Linton-on-Ouse, 1940. *KEC*

In 1938 AWA took responsibility for Specification 17/38 for a twin-engined recce-bomber using the minimum of strategic materials. This had been commenced by Frank Barnwell's team at Filton as the Bristol Type 155. Barnwell, the creator of the Bulldog and Blenheim among others, was killed in a light aircraft of his own design on 2 August 1938. This put huge pressures on his deputy, Leslie Frise, and it is likely that the Type 155 was offloaded as the Beaufort was only two months away from its maiden flight when Barnwell died.

Named after George Monck, 17th-century military leader, politician and the first Duke of Albemarle, the resulting AW.41 was a major departure for Lloyd. Having established a reputation as a 'metal master', Lloyd needed to incorporate as much wood as he could and break the airframe down into 'chunks' that could be distributed around as many sub-contractors as possible. With classic Bristol-style nose glazing, the Albemarle had the distinction of being the first mass-produced type with a tricycle undercarriage to enter RAF service. Two prototypes were completed at Hamble, the first taking to the air on 20 March 1940.

Baginton was far too busy building front-line bombers so final assembly and flight test took place at another HS consortium factory,

Newly completed Albemarle I Series II at Hucclecote, 1941.
Peter Green Collection

the Gloster plant at Hucclecote. The programme remained AWA-managed and to distinguish the supply chain A W Hawksley Ltd – a play on Armstrong Whitworth Hawker Siddeley – was created for administrative purposes. It was late 1940 before Albemarles began rolling out of the Hucclecote 'shadow' factory. Soon the machine that had been initiated as a bomber, relegated to bomber-reconnaissance had become a special transport – a parachute platform and glider tug.

At Baginton, the last of 1,814 Whitleys appeared in July 1943. The management was already working on the complex logistics required to take on Lancaster production in place of the Whitley. To smooth this, by that time AWA was *already* building the Avro bomber. A 'shadow factory' had been created at Sywell and the first Lancaster II completed in September 1942. Upwards of thirty-eight examples were assembled and flown from the all-grass aerodrome; after that, the plant's output consisted of sub-assemblies that travelled by road to Baginton. The first Coventry-built Lancasters came off the line in autumn 1943. AWA was the only manufacturer constructing the 'insurance' Mk.II, which was powered by Bristol Hercules VI radials, after Avro had flown the prototype on 26 November 1941. A 'famine' of Rolls-Royce Merlins never occurred and after 300 Mk.IIs, AWA switched to Mk.Is and Mk.IIIs.

In 1943 another assembly line was set up at Bitteswell and it was from there that the last of 1,329 AWA Lancasters took to the air. By the end of World War Two, AWA was gearing up to build Avro Lincolns but that work was due to peter out in 1947 and other products were urgently needed. The design office was busy with two projects, but both would take time to come to fruition. Conversions and overhauls helped but diversification was the name of the day. To quote an AWA brochure, the company turned to: 'such mundane equipment as wheelbarrows, lawn mower parts and even metal huts'. With the advent of the jet age, Baginton's runway length was becoming marginal and from May 1952 Bitteswell undertook final assembly and flight test; AWA acquired the site outright in 1956. The last AWA-built machine to depart Baginton was the prone-pilot modified Gloster Meteor F.8 on 10 February 1954.

Hangars 1, 2, 3 and 4 on the 'Old Site' at Bitteswell circa 1952. The road in the foreground is the A5. *KEC*

Armstrong Siddeley turbine engines

Name, Type/Format	From	Application*	Notes
Mamba turboprop	1946	AW Apollo	
Adder turbojet	1948	GAF Pika	[1]
Sapphire turbojet	1948	Hawker Hunter F.2	
Python turboprop	1949	Westland Wyvern	[2]
Double Mamba coupled turboprop	1949	Fairey Gannet	
Viper turbojet	1951	Hunting Jet Provost	

* Typical, or only, use. [1] Pika 1950 manned version of Australian Government Aircraft Factories Jindivik drone. [2] Originally known as the ASP.

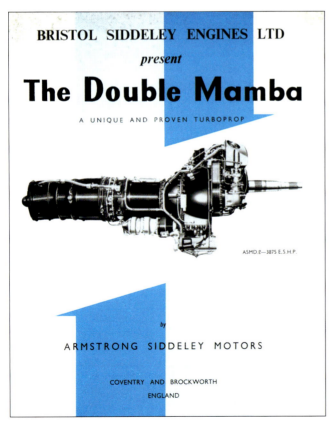

Brochure published under the Bristol Siddeley banner for the ASMD.8 Double Mamba coupled turboprop. *KEC*

Flying wings and Greek heroes

In 1942 Lloyd was looking into laminar flow and a Hawker Hurricane was modified to examine this method of improving the efficiency of wings at Farnborough. By coupling this technique with a tail-less, swept-wing layout and turbojet propulsion there was great potential for high-speed, long-range types, be they bombers or airliners. A private-venture, all-wood glider was created to examine handling, ready for a jet version. The one-off AW.52G went aloft – towed by a Whitley – on 2 March 1945.

Specification E.9/44 was issued in 1944 to cover two prototypes roughly twice the size of the glider. The ability to carry a 4,000lb payload was intended to demonstrate the AW.52's potential as a bomber and it was also proffered as a civil mailplane. Powered by a pair of Rolls-Royce Nenes, the first AW.52 flew from Boscombe Down on 13 November 1947. It was followed ten months later by the second example, fitted with Derwent turbojets. On a sortie in the first AW.52 on 30 May 1949 test pilot J O 'Joe' Lancaster encountered violent flutter and had to abandon it courtesy of his ejection seat. He became the first person to use the Martin-Baker escape system 'in anger'. Results from the AW.52s had not been encouraging and by the end of the decade AWA was preparing for a production surge of jet fighters; the project was abandoned and the second machine had a short career at the Royal Aircraft Establishment.

Lloyd's last design, before taking up the post of technical director in 1948, was an airliner named after the Greek god, Apollo. This was in response to the Brabazon Committee's wartime deliberations over the civilian types Britain would require when peace returned. Powered by four 'in-house' ASM Mamba turbines, the AW.55 was originally to have been called Achilles, after the vulnerable Greek hero, but better counsels prevailed. The first Apollo took to the skies on 10 April 1949, nine months after its competitor, the Vickers Viscount, had flown.

Both rivals were afflicted with the British 'disease' of being too small for the market, but the Viscount could be stretched relatively easily and its Rolls-Royce Dart turboprops were destined to make powerplant history. The Mamba had teething problems and a beefier version for an enlarged Apollo would take a long while to bring about. Eventually the Mamba became very reliable and a coupled version, the Double Mamba, powered the Fairey Gannet. The second Apollo did not fly until 12 December 1952 and by 1954 the programme was moribund.

The AW.52G RG324 in the static at Farnborough in July 1955 to celebrate the airfield's golden jubilee. It is dwarfed by Vickers Valiant B.1 WP209 of the Royal Aircraft Establishment. Returned to Baginton, the AW.52G was scrapped not long after this. *KEC*

The first Apollo, G-AIYN, in 1951. Underneath the cockpit is a Hawker Siddeley Group logo. *AWA*

Super-priority

While the AW.52 and Apollo went nowhere, AWA had manufacturing capacity available just when it was needed. The advent of the 'Cold War' generated a pressing need for rearmament to face the apparent threat of the Communist Bloc. Fellow HS consortium member Gloster could not build Meteors fast enough and AWA started making Mk.4s and Mk.8s from 1949. A night fighter version was an urgent priority and AWA was given design authority to create a two-seat, radar-equipped interceptor based upon the T.7 trainer. The prototype NF.11 first flew at Baginton on 31 May 1950. Production amounted to four versions and at its peak AWA was churning out thirty-two examples per month.

With the Hunter declared a 'super-priority', sister company Hawker handed on all but the initial thirty-five Sea Hawk shipborne fighters to AWA from 1953. This was followed by large contracts for Hunters and the final Gloster product, the delta-winged Javelin.

Armstrong Whitworth contracts for Hawker Siddeley

Type	Total	From	To	Notes
Hawker Hart	456	1933	1937	[1]
Avro Lancaster I, II, III	1,329	1942	1945	[2]
Avro Lincoln I	281	1945	1951	[3]
Gloster Meteor F.IV (F.4)	46	1949	1950	[3]
Gloster Meteor F.8	430	1950	1954	[4]
Gloster Meteor NF.11 to '14	578	1950	1954	[5]
Hawker Sea Hawk	490	1953	1959	[6]
Hawker Hunter F.2, '5, '6	278	1953	1957	[7]
Gloster Javelin FAW.4, '5, '7	133	1956	1958	[8]
Hawker Siddeley Hawk T.1	39	1979	1982	[8]

[1] Built at Whitley. The first Hart handed over in July 1933 and at this point, AWA was a sub-contractor: it became part of the HS consortium two years later and production continued as a sister firm. [2] Assembled at Baginton and later Bitteswell. At least 38 Lancaster IIs assembled at Sywell, 1942 to 1943. [3] Assembled at Baginton. [4] Majority assembled at Baginton. Last F.8, WK935 was completed as a prone-pilot test bed and first flown 10 February 1954 from Baginton. [5] Majority assembled at Bitteswell. [6] F.1, F.2, FB.3, FGA.4, FGA.6, Mk.50 and Mk.100 variants, majority assembled at Bitteswell. [7] AWA sole source for Sapphire-engined F.2s and F.5s; majority of Hunters assembled at Bitteswell. [8] All at Bitteswell.

Whistling Wheelbarrow

As well as transforming the Meteor into a long-nosed nocturnal predator and prone-pilot test bed, the AWA design office, headed by H R Watson from 1948, tackled plenty of projects, but none went any further than brochures. It was beginning to look as though the Apollo would be the final true AWA product. However, E D Keen took over in 1955 and he headed the creation of the last AWA aircraft. The new machine was going to be called Freightliner, although the name 'Coventry' had been flirted with until the marketing department held sway. With a nod to history, the new venture finally took the name Argosy. In RAF service it was given the affectionate nickname of 'Whistling Wheelbarrow' from the signature whine of its Dart turbines and the handle-like twin booms.

While responding to an RAF requirement for an airlifter in 1955, AWA's design team widened the thinking to include a commercial freighter. The military need vaporised and the management took a very brave decision; to develop a PV transport optimised for airline use but with an eye to a future RAF purchase. The board took a mighty gamble, authorising ten aircraft, including the prototype, *ahead* of any orders. A high-wing, rear-loading 'pod-and-boom' layout was adopted with full-width cargo doors in the nose and in the rear, allowing simultaneous loading and unloading. The projected wing structure was very close to that of the Avro Shackleton maritime patroller, production of which was winding down in 1959. Using the existing jigs, HS consortium member Avro became a major sub-contractor. Choice of engine was easy; the incredible Rolls-Royce Dart that had helped to foil the Apollo.

BEA Argosy 222 G-ASXP at Heathrow, June 1966. *Roy Bonser*

The prototype Argosy had its maiden flight from the snow-cleared runway at Bitteswell on 8 January 1959 and four more followed it before year end. With a unit price of £460,000, the Argosy was an expensive piece of kit, but it was aimed at a niche market. Building a batch straight off paid handsome dividends; in early 1960 Riddle Airlines of Miami placed an order – a superb breakthrough into a difficult market – and a year later British European Airways (BEA) also came on board. The RAF was again looking for a replacement for its venerable, Wellington-descended Vickers Valetta transports and placed a conditional, but still off-the-shelf, order for twenty Argosies in January 1959. This was later upped to fifty-six and the first Argosy C.1 took to the air on 4 March 1961. The RAF version did not have a nose door and had a clamshell 'beaver' ramp at the rear for air-dropping men or supplies. On 21 November 1966 Argosy Series 222 G-ATTC departed Bitteswell for Heathrow, the last of a line that could be traced back to 1914.

Reshuffle

By the time *Tango-Charlie* had been delivered, technically it was a Hawker Siddeley Argosy. On 2 October 1961 AWA was merged with Gloster (both already part of the HS consortium) becoming Whitworth Gloster Aircraft Ltd with headquarters at Baginton. HS was reorganised on 1 July 1963 and Whitworth Gloster morphed into the Avro Whitworth Division, based at Chadderton, Manchester. (The irony was not lost that thirty-five years earlier John Siddeley had bought the ailing Avro outfit lock, stock and barrel!) Baginton closed in December 1965. Bitteswell found plenty of work in upgrades of Shackletons, Vulcans and other types, and even became a second production line for the HS Hawk trainer from 1979. On 22 March 1982 British Aerospace – which had absorbed HS in 1977 – announced the closure of Bitteswell and the end of an exceptional era.

Armstrong Whitworth/Siddeley Deasy multi-winged types

From	To	Total	Name or Designation	Type	Engine(s)	Notes
1914	-	1	FK.1	Scout	1 x Gnome	[1]
1915	-	6	FK.2	Recce	1 x RAF 1a	[2]
1915	1917	500	FK.3	Recce/trainer	1 x RAF 1a	[3]
1916	-	1	FK.6	Heavy escort triplane	1 x RR Eagle	[4]
1916	1918	1,652	FK.8	Armed recce	1 x Beardmore	[5]
1917	-	10	FK.9, FK.10	Fighter quadruplane	1 x Clerget	[6]
1917	-	3	RT.1	Armed recce	1 x Hispano-Suiza	
1918	-	1	FM.4 Armadillo	Fighter	1 x Bentley	
1918	-	2	Ara	Fighter	1 x ABC Dragonfly	
1919	-	3	SR.2 Siskin	Fighter	1 x ABC Dragonfly	
1920	-	1	Tadpole	Shipborne recce	1 x Liberty	[7]
1921	-	1	Sinaia	Bomber	2 x SD Tiger	[8]
1922	1929	482	Siskin II. III, IV, V	Fighter	1 x AS Jaguar	[9]
1923	-	6	Wolf	Armed recce/trainer	1 x AS Jaguar	
1923	1924	2	Awana	Troop transport	2 x AS Lion	
1926	-	3	Ape	Aerodynamic test bed	1 x AS Jaguar	
1925	1933	489	Atlas/Ajax/Aries	Army co-op/Bomber	1 x AS Jaguar	[10]
1926	1929	7	Argosy I, II	Airliner	3 x AS Jaguar	
1927	1929	3	AW.XIV Starling	Fighter	1 x AS Jaguar	[11]
1930	1932	6	AW.XVI	Fighter	1 x AS Panther	
1934	-	1	AW.19	General purpose	1 x AS Tiger	
1934	1936	6	AW.35 Scimitar	Fighter	1 x AS Panther	[12]

All tractor piston biplanes unless noted. FK types, the FM.4 and Ara all Newcastle types. RT.1, Sinaia and SR.2 all Deasy types, remainder AW. **[1]** At time referred to as the Sissitt – best 'translation' for this is a Baltic freedom fighter! **[2]** Tapper, in *Armstrong Whitworth Aircraft since 1913*, does not refer to the FK.2, calling them FK.3s; Bruce, in *Aeroplanes of the Royal Flying Corps*, does and in some detail. **[3]** Also sub-contracted to Hewlett and Blondeau, Luton and London. **[4]** Single FK.5 to similar specification built, not flown. **[5]** Bruce – see Note 1 – denotes prototype as FK.7, Tapper does not. Also sub-contracted by Angus Sanderson, Newcastle upon Tyne. **[6]** FK.9 prototype, much redesigned FK.10 was 'production' machine. Also sub-contracted to Angus Sanderson, Newcastle upon Tyne and Phoenix Dynamo, Bradford. **[7]** Major modification of an Airco-built DH.9A. **[8]** Construction commenced in 1918, completed under the AW aegis. **[9]** Also sub-contracted to Blackburn, Bristol, Gloster and Vickers. **[10]** Includes 10 under licence by the Blackburn-managed Greek National Aircraft Factory, Old Phaleron, Athens. **[11]** Siskin derivative, possibly only 2 built. **[12]** AW.XVI derivative; possibly only 5 built.

Armstrong Whitworth monoplanes

From	To	Total	Name or Designation	Type	Engine(s)	Notes
1932	1933	8	AW.XV Atalanta	Airliner	4 x AS Serval	
1935	-	1	AW.23	Bomber-transport	2 x AS Tiger	
1936	-	1	AW.29	Day bomber	1 x AS Tiger	
1936	1943	1,814	Whitley	Heavy bomber	2 x AS Tiger	
1938	1941	14	Ensign	Airliner	4 x AS Tiger	[1]
1940	1944	602	Albemarle	Bomber recce/transport	2 x Bri Hercules	[2]
1945	-	1	AW.52G	Tail-less research glider	nil	
1947	1948	2	AW.52	Tail-less research	2 x RR Nene	
1949	1952	2	Apollo	Airliner	4 x AS Mamba	
1959	1966	73	Argosy	Freighter/transport	4 x RR Dart	

All piston-engined except AW.52 turbojet, Apollo and Argosy turboprop. **[1]** Assembled at Hamble. **[2]** Both prototypes at Hamble. Production by A W Hawksley Ltd at Hucclecote.

CHAPTER FIVE

One-Trick Pony?

Auster
1938 to 1969

'He loved to break a rule, not for the mischievous pleasure of doing so, but to create a new standard.' Tribute to Lance Wykes

Britain had replaced the privations of the Depression years with a boom based on massive rearmament in the face of German expansionism. Prime Minister Neville Chamberlain got out of a British Airways Lockheed Super Electra at Heston on 30 September 1938 and announced an accord with Adolf Hitler that provided: 'Peace for our time'. Despite the apparent euphoria, it hardly seemed like a good time to be launching a light aircraft manufacturer. Yet fifty-two days after Chamberlain waved his bit of paper in the air, Leicester-based entrepreneur Alexander Lancelot Wykes did just that, founding Taylorcraft Aeroplanes (England) Ltd ('Taylorcraft' hereafter) on 21 November. Known as 'Lance' to business associates or 'A-L' – from his initials – to his friends, he was smitten with an American-designed two-seater. He intended to change the face of the British flying club and private owner market. The war that Chamberlain was trying to prevent probably saved Wykes's venture from collapse as the Taylorcrafts joined the conflict in large numbers. With the return of peace, the dream of dominating the British market was realised but tragically the man who started it all was not to see it.

Ironically, the man that had drawn Wykes and his chequebook across the Atlantic in late 1938, Clarence Gilbert Taylor, was also from the East Midlands, born in Nottingham in 1898. Self-taught Taylor, a year older than Wykes, had established Taylor Brothers in the USA in 1928. With backing from William Thomas Piper he embarked on creating the ultimate light aircraft, inexpensive, stable and easy to build. The result was the famous tandem-seat Cub that was destined for an incredible production history. Piper and Taylor went their own ways in 1936 and the latter created his Model A with side-by-side seating – ideal for training and sociable aviating.

Trained by the Royal Air Force in 1918, Wykes saw no action during the Great War. By the early 1930s this enterprising, determined motivator was the managing director of Crowthers Ltd of Thurmaston, to the north of Leicester. The company's Britannia Works specialised in making machine tools for the textile, garment and shoe industries for which the East Midlands was famous. Wanting to return to piloting, Wykes signed up with the County Flying Club at Rearsby. The group had imported a trio of J2 Cubs (one of which was G-AEXZ, which is still extant in Leicestershire) and ordered a Taylorcraft Model A, which arrived in the summer of 1938. Sampling these, Wykes was impressed and moved fast; he wanted to secure an exclusive deal before someone

Cover of the brochure for the Aiglet Trainer. KEC

The first British Taylorcraft, Plus C G-AFNW, at the Britannia Works, Thurmaston, April 1939. *KEC*

Works superintendent Ray Carlson (left) in conversation with Lance Wykes at Thurmaston, May 1939. *KEC*

else realised the potential of the American product. Off he went to Alliance, Ohio, to negotiate with the Taylor-Young Airplane Company. He came away with the British rights, including the ability to vary the build specification, a stock of Lycoming O-145 'flat four' engines, a fuselage jig and a brand new Model B on order. The 'B was registered to Taylorcraft as G-AFKO in December 1938 – more of this machine soon. Wykes had what that he needed to go into production, except for the trivial matters of a factory and a workforce.

Cheap and overstretched

Space was found at the back of the Britannia Works and hasty recruiting resulted in a handful of staff. The fuselage structure tubing and the wing spars were 'beefed up' for the British version, making a more robust airframe. This led to the Anglicised machine becoming the Model C and, to spice up the marketing, it was called the Plus C. Construction of the prototype began in February 1939 and crucial was another 'import' from Ohio, Ray Carlton on 'secondment' from Taylor-Young. Having taken just nine weeks to create, the first Plus C had its debut on 3 May 1939 from Ratcliffe, north of Leicester.

An extensive press and advertising campaign was launched with assertions that 500 machines a year could be churned out. Early examples were offered for a neat £500, which was claimed to be 25% cheaper than rivals. That may seem a bargain but a three-bedroomed house in 1938 cost £350 and the average salary was £200: the Plus C was not for the masses. There were high hopes that it was perfect for the Civil Air Guard, a government-subsidised organisation training up pilots as a flying reserve, but nothing came of this.

By the time Britain declared war on 3 September 1939, more than twenty Plus Cs had been delivered. Rumours had been growing that Britain's latest lightplane was being sold too cheaply and that Taylorcraft was under-funded and overstretched – a state that was to be repeated in the decades to come. Building aircraft for civilians was banned but salvation was at hand. Sub-contract work, making sub-assemblies for other manufacturers, was sought. The firm also overhauled and repaired DH Tiger Moths, later Hawker Hurricanes and Typhoons, as part of the Civilian Repair Organisation (CRO).

Eyes of the Army

Days before Europe fell into conflict, a new version, the Blackburn Cirrus Minor-engined Plus D, had been certificated. This changed the fortunes of the breed as the Air Ministry was wary of aircraft with imported engines, wisely determining that supplies could be intermittent or terminated. The hunt was on for an air observation post (AOP) – eyes for the guns. In the autumn of 1939 Old Sarum was the venue for an eclectic gathering of types hoping for the contract: the Plus D, the General Aircraft GAL.47 and the Arpin A-1. The first two had entered production and General was alone in having a sustained manufacturing capability.

From this motley bunch, the Plus D was deemed the winner, albeit with reservations. The next step was an operational evaluation to prove the concept and devise tactics. Taylorcraft turned to locating Plus Cs and converting them to take Cirrus Minors. With a poor view for pilot and observer, especially above and behind, and no flaps the Plus D was not perfect but it was soon rewarded with an order for 100 examples. Taylorcraft needed to expand, taking on factory premises at Syston, to the north of Thurmaston, and adopting the former County Flying Club aerodrome at Rearsby. The first fully militarised Plus D had its maiden flight on 7 May 1942.

A name was needed for the RAF's new aircraft – a modern-day R.E.8 charting the 'drop' of artillery shells. Wykes came up with Icarus, a character from Greek mythology. However, it was pointed out that while flying courtesy of feathers attached by wax to his arms, Icarus suffered a catastrophic 'structural' failure. Instead of Greek, Latin was chosen and the Taylorcraft became the Auster, after a southerly Italian wind. The Air Ministry could not have known that it had come up with a name that post-war became almost generic for a British light aircraft.

From 1942 until the '60s, Rearsby built military Austers. During the war the type reverted to American Lycoming 'flat-fours' as the U-boat threat diminished and supplies became more assured. On 5 July 1943 a bizarre version began unsuccessful trials. In the USA Taylorcraft had created the TG-6, a two/three-seat training glider, by fitting a glazed cockpit in place of the firewall and engine. Mimicking

An Auster AOP.IV with the name 'Sammie 17' on the cowling, in its element, Italy 1944. *Peter Green Collection*

this, Taylorcraft came up with the Model H, a conversion of Wykes's G-AFKO mentioned above. This was intended as a simple-to-produce trainer for assault glider pilots, but that task remained the domain of the General Aircraft Hotspur.

While displaying the prototype Auster AOP.IV (MT454, a conversion of a Mk.III) over a 'Salute the Soldier Week' event at Leicester's Abbey Park, Wykes was killed when the machine crashed.

Two books on Auster come from the heritage group of the International Auster Club: *Austers – Nearly All You Wanted to Know* by Mike Preston and Mick Ames, and *The History of the Auster Aeroplane* by Ambrose Hitchman and Mike Preston. They are the most engaging on the subject because they dwell on the people behind the aircraft. Hitchman and Preston quote K G Potterton – a member of the '39 Club' founding employees – on Wykes: 'Perhaps one of his greatest qualities was expressed in his ability to make small things big enough and great things no longer [awe-inspiring]. He possessed an unquenchable spirit which made us believe [that] with him no difficulty was insurmountable or no task impossible. … He loved to break a rule, not for the mischievous pleasure of doing so, but to create a new standard. … He would cut across an involved technical discussion and lift the problem clean out of it. Maybe another rule would be broken, but there would be one less problem to contend with.'

Peacetime doldrums

Taylorcraft was quick to prepare for peace. In April 1945 modified AOP.V G-AGOH (still extant with Leicestershire's museum service) was fitted with an in-line Blackburn Cirrus Minor – a new slant on the Plus D. This became the interim prototype for a successful run of civil versions, beginning with the J1 Autocrat. A month after *Oscar-Hotel* flew, the new standard observation post had its debut – the AOP.VI. (During 1948 British designations changed from Roman to Arabic numbers, hence the AOP.VI became the AOP.6.) Although nearly 400 Mk.VIs were ordered, they were made in piecemeal batches through to 1953; nevertheless they were the most important part of the firm's cash flow. Taylorcraft became Auster Aircraft on 8 March 1946, to emphasize its independence from the US organisation and capitalising on what had become a famous brand.

Just as Airco – see above – suffered from war-surplus airframes flooding the market and stifling the sales prospects of new models, Auster found the going tough with brand new machines. The workforce in 1944 had reached 1,600, but it was down to 200 in 1947. In that year, bowing to the inevitable, Auster began to buy 'demobbed' Lycoming-engined versions to refurbish and sell on. It was a hand-to-mouth existence, giving an entirely new meaning to *auster*ity. This was not enough to keep the business going and it was 1948 before rescue came.

When civilian production was banned in September 1939 the firm survived by diversifying into sub-contract and repair programmes. The state of the post-war aircraft industry was such that these options were not available. Auster was too far down the 'food chain' for such business to filter past the major players. While aviation was in the doldrums, the motor vehicle industry was on the up. Rearsby was no distance from the Midlands-based car giants and sub-contracts were there for the taking. What grew into the so-called 'Auster Commercial' division occupied buildings to the north of the Rearsby to Ashby Folville road, emphasizing its separation from the assembly line and aerodrome on the southern side. While automotive contracts predominated, aviation work was also gleaned, for example building parts for the Hunting Jet Provost. The automotive industry suffered its ups and downs, but throughout the existence of Auster it provided the means to finance aviation ventures and often was a source of friction between the 'wings' and 'wheels' protagonists. With the decline of Beagle – see later – 'Auster Commercial'

survived to stand alone in 1966 as Rearsby Automotive Ltd. Vehicle sub-contracting on the site lasted through to the early 2000s.

Ever-decreasing circles

Post-war just over 1,200 civilian Austers with variant names such as Aiglet, Alpha, Alpine, Arrow, were made at Rearsby, all relying on the tried and tested Taylorcraft formula. It was not until the J1U Workmaster, first flown on 22 February 1958, that the wooden wing spar was exchanged for an alloy one. From the early 1950s onwards, Auster was gravitating from volume production to niche market batches. Chief designer 'Dickie' Bird was responsible for tweaking the established product line, but he was also evaluating new civil markets or forthcoming military requirements, in order to break away from the ever-decreasing circles of rehashing a 1930s design.

A life with aeroplanes was all Ronald Edward 'Dickie' Bird would consider and in 1936, at the tender age of 14, he was apprenticed to Percival Aircraft at Luton. He befriended another student, Bernard Sarna, who was a year older. In between their work and studies the pair built a Mignet HM.14 Pou du Ciel, which they fitted with a 2-cylinder ABC Scorpion and painted the name *Mister Hercules* on the fuselage sides. In August 1939 they moved the 'Flying Flea' to a farm next to Luton aerodrome for testing. It was state-of-the-art with the pivoting rear wing safety feature and had been inspected by the Air Ministry ready to issue an Authorisation to Fly. (Many builders avoided, or were oblivious of, the Air Ministry but with careers in the aviation industry looming, the two lads needed to be completely legitimate.) Both 'hopped' the Flea on Saturday, 2 September 1939. That was the only chance they got; the following day Britain declared war on Germany and their creation was grounded.

Having got his 'ticket' from Percival, Bird became the chief draughtsman with CRO contractor Herts and Essex Aviation, which specialised in the repair and overhaul of Proctors at Broxbourne. The company also worked on a variety of former civilian light aircraft that had been impressed into military service, including Taylorcrafts. He moved to Rearsby in 1943 and in 1947 was appointed as chief designer, later technical director. With no major challenges to tackle, Bird parted company with Auster in 1959, joining the Miles brothers and their consultancy at Shoreham. He began to reacquaint himself with Rearsby when Beagle absorbed Miles and Auster in late 1960 and guided the Beagle 206 twin through its evolutions. With Beagle behind him, in 1965 he took the ferry to the Isle of Wight and signed up with Britten-Norman as chief designer. Bird went on to guide the Britten-Norman Islander into production and it was his drawing board that created the radical Trislander. Ronald Edward 'Dickie' Bird died on 10 May 2010, aged 88.

The Rearsby works, looking north, in the late 1990s. What was the Rearsby Automotive factory is the other side of the road. *Roy Bonser*

The second A.2/45, VL523, wearing a 'P-for-prototype' markings, 1950. *Auster*

Breaking the mould

Under Bird's tutelage the Rearsby design office created a large number of schemes, only a handful of which came to fruition. As might be imagined, there were lightplanes of differing formats, including pod-and-boom, but there were also transports and even a tip-jet driven helicopter. In the summer of 1945 the Air Ministry decided to re-examine the AOP role and issued Specification A.2/45 seeking a two-seater with a 240hp DH Gipsy Queen, an endurance of 2½ hours and a 600-mile range – parameters twice that of an AOP.5.

Auster was in competition with Heston Aircraft, which submitted the pod-and-boom pusher configured JC.6: two prototypes of each rival were ordered for a fly-off. Auster had been lent a Fieseler Fi 156 Storch during the summer of 1945 and Rearsby test pilot Geoffrey Edwards tried it out. When the Type N had its debut on 27 April 1948 its similarity to the German machine was remarked on. While they shared the same power, roughly equivalent dimensions including wing area, the Auster had a loaded weight that was nearly 400lb heavier. By March 1950 the Air Ministry had realised there was no need to reinvent the wheel and that the Auster AOP.6 and further developments on the theme would continue to fit the bill. The A.2/45 project had been a costly gamble and conservatism increasingly became the company watchword.

This thinking led to a private venture in 1951 that kept to the Taylorcraft legacy while greatly improving its utility. Nicknamed the 'Pygmy Pantechnicon', the prototype B4 freighter took to the air for the first time on 7 September 1951. In the previous year, the Type S had appeared with a Blackburn Bombardier engine – soon to be chosen for

the AOP.9 – and the B4 capitalised on this installation. A wider cabin with a reinforced floor ended in a hinged fairing allowing easy access for bulky goods; the rear of this stubby fuselage was supported by a *pair* of tailwheels. For long loads or even parachuting, the fairing could be dispensed with. The tail 'feathers' were carried at the end of a boom extending from the top of the fuselage. As well as lacking capital to support more ambitious designs, market research was something that Auster could not afford. The B4 was destined to remain a one-off.

Slippage and overruns

Reliance on the 'classic' Auster continued at Rearsby but there was a desperate need to penetrate new markets. In the early 1950s two expensive ventures were cleared by the board for development. One was to follow the other to keep the investment reasonable, but overruns almost brought the outfit to its knees. After the Specification A.2/45 fiasco the Air Ministry returned to the AOP theme in late 1949, initiating a replacement for the AOP.6. Dickie Bird and his team embarked on the Blackburn Bombardier-powered AOP.9, which owed only its format to previous Austers – it was an entirely new creation. An initial order for fifty-six units was placed in November 1951 and it looked as though the company had turned the corner. Progress was dogged by ministry changes to the requirement, the last revisions arriving on 21 January 1954. The prototype AOP.9 had its maiden flight on 19 March; only weeks after the ink had dried on the last amendment document. Once accepted, the AOP.9 became profitable, also capturing export orders from India and South Africa. The cash flow-boosting assembly line closed in 1962.

With its rear fairing removed, B4 G-AMKL shows its ability to carry outsized loads, 1951. *Auster*

'Classic' Auster types 1939 to 1969

From	To	Total	Designation/Name	Engine	Notes
1939	-	23	Plus C	O-145	
1942	-	107	Plus D/D1, AOP.I	CM	
1942	1944	468	E AOP.III	GM	
1942	-	2	F AOP.II	O-290	
1943	1944	253	G AOP.IV	O-290	
1943	-	1	H	Nil	[1]
1944	1946	805	J AOP.V/Alpha 5	O-290	
1945	1951	564	J1 Autocrat	CM	[2]
1946	1947	42	J2 Arrow	C-75	
1946	-	2	J3 Atom	C-65	
1946	1947	29	J4 Archer	CM	
1946	1953	378	K AOP.6	GM	
1947	1959	389	J5 Autocar	GM	[3]
1947	-	1	P Avis	GM	
1948	1951	86	Q T.7	GM	[4]
1950	-	1	S 'AOP.8'	702	[5]
1954	1962	183	B5 AOP.9	702	
1960	1962	33	D4/108	O-235	[6]
1960	1969	162	D5	O-320	[7]
1960	-	6	D6/180 Husky	O-320	
1961	-	1	E3 'AOP.11'	IO-470	[8]

Based upon: Wenham-Simpson-Fillmore *Auster – The Company and the Aircraft*, which taught the author the correct presentation of Auster designations! All high-wing piston-engined 'tail-dragger' monoplanes. AOP I to V wartime military air observation posts; AOP.6 and AOP.9 post-war military; T.7 post-war military trainer. All others two/three/four-seat trainer/tourers and specialist role for largely civil market. Many in-house conversions post-war, including the AOP.6-based Tugmaster and Terrier. Engine abbreviations: O-145, O-290, O-235, O-320 – Lycoming; CM – Blackburn Cirrus Minor; GM – DH Gipsy Major; C-65, C-75, IO-470 – Continental; 702 – Blackburn Bombardier. **[1]** Training glider prototype, converted from US-built Model BC. **[2]** Sub-variants: J1 and J1A Autocrat; J1B Aiglet; J1N Alpha; J1U Workmaster; J1W. **[3]** Sub-variants: J5 Adventurer; J5B Autocrat; J5D, J5E, J5P, J5V Autocar; J5F, J5K, J5L Aiglet Trainer; J5G Cirrus Autocar; J5Q and J5R Alpine; J5T. **[4]** Includes two T.7s modified to C2 Antarctic configuration. **[5]** AOP.6 with Bombardier engine. **[6]** Includes nine assembled under licence by Oficinas Gerais de Materiel Aeronáutical (OGMA), Alverca, Portugal. **[7]** Sub-variants: D5-160; D5-180 Husky. Includes 139 assembled under licence by OGMA, Alverca, Portugal. **[8]** Technically this is the Beagle A.115, but essentially a 'late-production' Auster.

Slippage on the AOP.9 project diverted Bird's staff from the other plan; Auster was committed to creating a dedicated, flexible agricultural aircraft. This was the low-wing B8 Agricola, a 240hp crop-duster, capable of lifting a very efficient 1,680lb of chemicals.

With its rear fairing removed, B4 G-AMKL shows its ability to carry outsized loads, 1951. *Auster*

Cover of a brochure on the Agricola, showing the prototype wearing its New Zealand identity ZK-BMI. *KEC*

With a span of 42ft, this was the largest type to be built at Rearsby. The jury is out on the origin of its name, the Latin for farmer, or was it after the 1st century AD Roman general who played a major part in the conquest of Britain. This Agricola was intended to take another country by storm – New Zealand.

Aerial application was a major business in New Zealand, with the hard-working, but load-limited, DH Tiger Moth comprising the bulk of the fleet. To encourage modernisation the Auckland government substantially subsidised top-dressing operations and this was the motivator for Auster. Bird visited New Zealand in 1953, paying great attention to what was needed in a new-generation crop duster. The resulting Agricola was very advanced, offering almost everything a 'Kiwi' ag-pilot could want, but it was expensive. When it was conceived, the project was set to dominate a burgeoning market but by the time the first B8 flew, on 8 December 1955, rivals were gathering. To hit the floor running, as well as the prototype the company authorised a batch of fourteen laid down.

As finished Agricolas rolled out at Rearsby in 1956 for shipment to the other side of the world the short-term subsidies were withdrawn. Orders from New Zealand dried up while Bird's team urgently examined light transport or even counter-insurgency versions of the B8. The board waved the white flag in 1957 and brought the project to a halt. *The History of the Auster Aeroplane* lamented: '… production ceased forthwith and the balance of the "bits and pieces" [substantial sub-assemblies from the initial batch] were sold to New Zealand to support the few aircraft which were in operation. This was a severe blow to Auster after having invested a total of £250,000 … This capital had been carefully accumulated in the profitable ventures of previous years …'

Back to basics

British import levies were keeping the flood of US-designed light aircraft from making much headway in the late 1950s, but elsewhere they were dominating the marketplace and squeezing out the increasingly archaic Austers. With the Agricola wiping out revenues from the AOP.9, Auster could be forgiven for keeping its head down, but it had to compete or face severe contraction. On 3 July 1957 the C6 Atlantic four-seater made its debut, offering car door-like access, a tricycle undercarriage, a 180hp Continental 'flat-four' engine and two models, the more basic 'Winchester' and the deluxe 'Windsor'. Getting the machine into production was estimated to cost £100,000 that would need 300 machines to be sold to reach break-even. The money was just not there to properly develop, produce and support the Atlantic and the prototype was soon dismantled.

Wearing the Beagle logo on the fin and 'Beagle Mk Eleven' on the cowling, the Model E3 in racing guise at Coventry, August 1965. *Roy Bonser*

Other Auster types 1948 to 1958

From	To	Total	Designation/Name	Type	Engine(s)	Notes
1948	1949	2	N A.2/45	Air observation post	DH Gipsy Queen	
1951	-	1	B4	Ambulance/freighter	Bombardier 702	
1955	1957	9	B8 Agricola	Agricultural duster	Continental O-470	[1]
1958	-	1	C6 Atlantic	Tricycle u/c tourer	Continental E-185	

See narrative for details. **[1]** Includes an additional B8 built from spares in New Zealand.

In the aftermath of the Atlantic decision, Cessna made an approach in 1958 regarding licence production for the European market of its single-engined types. This was not to be; a lucrative agreement was signed in France two years later with increasingly large numbers of Cessnas fresh out of the Reims factory heading for Britain.

Lessons learned, Auster knuckled down to concentrate on what it knew best. Another prototype went aloft from Rearsby on 22 May 1958, the utilitarian J1U Workmaster. From this stemmed the D4, D5 and D6 family. These won a licence-build contract with Portugal's Oficinas Gerais de Materiel Aeronáutica (OGMA) for the nation's air force. Signed on 4 November 1959, the order amounted to 148 units and was valued at £150,000. A magazine article chronicling the ups and downs of Auster referred to it as 'A One-Trick Pony', be that as it may, twenty-one years after the agreement with Taylor was secured, the little high-wing monoplane was still paying dividends. The OGMA deal was a great shot in the arm, but without significant capital input Auster was on the road to nowhere.

Beagle buyout

The Beagle story appears in Chapter 7, but it is best that we deal with the 'Auster-ish' products here. With the backing of the Cowley-based Pressed Steel Company (PSC), British Executive and General

Aviation Ltd was formed on 7 October 1960. Beagle acquired Auster that November for a reported £525,000 – not a huge amount and reflecting Auster's relatively poor prospects. Not only was Auster the *only* light aviation builder of substance in the UK, as we have seen it was also an important sub-contractor to the automotive industry – PSC had a double interest in the Leicestershire enterprise.

The Rearsby factory was crying out for investment but it would be some time before new designs started to flow off the assembly lines. The plan was to stick with warmed-over Austers in the form of the Tugmaster and Terrier revamps of surplus AOP.6s and a brisk marketing effort on the Husky, a development of the D5. The marriage of Beagle's Shoreham factory and Rearsby was never smooth and often acrimonious but it did give the 'Auster' workforce another nine years of employment.

A lot of time and money was devoted to the E3, the so-called 'AOP.11', a Continental-engined refinement of the AOP.9, which took to the air on 18 August 1961. The Army Air Corps was committed to a wholly helicopter-based fleet, but the Beagle management naively believed they'd settle for fixed-wing. The one-off prototype, G-ASCC, is still airworthy. Let's turn to *Nearly All You Wanted to Know* to sum up Shoreham's input to the last 'Auster': 'the only Beagle contribution being the spats and the undercarriage fairings and even these were later removed.'

CHAPTER SIX

Pioneering Wings

Avro
1907 to 1959

'… pilots who flew the wartime Lancasters speak of their machines with nostalgic admiration,
and regard Roy Chadwick as the greatest aircraft designer of all.' Harald Penrose

VISITORS TO THE FANTASTIC Brooklands Museum, near Weybridge in Surrey, can walk along the famous finishing straight of the world-famous motor racing circuit. Across from the beautifully restored clubhouse – it once served as Barnes Wallis's drawing office – is a wooden shed that looks very out of place among the Edwardian racetrack architecture. With the words 'Avroplane' above the doors, this is a replica of a structure that stood close to that very spot more than a century ago. The original was rented by Edwin Alliott Verdon Roe during 1907 and 1908, and inside he kept the biplane for which he had high hopes. At the end of each session trying to get the fragile craft airborne, it would be manoeuvred sideways into the hut to await the next attempt.

Inside the facsimile shed is an exacting replica of that biplane, along with a full-size cut-out of the aviation pioneer himself. A stroll from the shed towards the racetrack banking takes onlookers to the site where a photo of Roe was taken, sitting within the struts and wires of his creation. If it were not for the unenlightened views of the Clerk of the Course, Ernst de Rodakowski, who had the 30-year-old pioneer removed from the site in July 1908, it may well have been that the venue for the first all-British flight would have been Brooklands and not near Walthamstow in north London.

Lancaster nose sections inside the huge plant at Chadderton, Manchester, in June 1944. *British Aerospace*

Born in Patricroft, to the west of Manchester, preferring Alliott to Edwin, and known to his friends as 'AV', Roe had been building model gliders since 1901. At Alexandra Palace in north London in mid-April 1907 he won the considerable sum of £75 for his rubber-powered, Wright-like biplanes, which outflew the opposition. Samuel Franklin Cody attended the contest: on 16 October the following year the American-born showman became the first person to carry out a sustained powered flight in Britain. If £75 doesn't sound like winning the lottery, Roe's winnings were a 'fiver' more than the average annual salary of 1908.

This cash helped with the construction of a full-size machine that is commemorated in the Brooklands Museum shed. Roe tested the biplane

Above: A V Roe with his 1907 biplane on the finishing straight at Brooklands. *Brooklands Museum*

Left: With his back to the camera and wearing a waistcoat, A V Roe and friends with the 1909 triplane outside the arches of the Clapton railway viaduct at Lea Marshes. *British Aerospace*

along the finishing straight at Brooklands, under tow behind a car, in December 1907. Initially fitted with a 9hp JAP twin-cylinder, the biplane needed more power. With a borrowed French Antoinette rated at up to 24hp installed, Roe managed a few minimal 'hops' on 8 June 1908, but time was not on his side. In just over a month, Rodakowski succeeded in 'evicting' Roe from Brooklands – seeing the experiments as troublesome and distracting from motor racing. All of this was to change in late 1909 when Major Frederick Lindsay Lloyd took over as Clerk of the Course: he saw aviation as an ideal use for the land on the inside of the track, turning it into a flying field. Roe was eventually to return to Brooklands, testing his designs up to the Type 500.

In 1909 Roe turned his thoughts to a triplane format. Retrospectively referred to as the Roe Triplane Type I, this was started at Putney and assembled in a railway arch under the Clapton railway viaduct at Lea Marshes, south-west of Walthamstow, London. The triplane was powered by a vee-format JAP twin-cylinder of a hoped-for 10hp, but gave only 9hp, built by John Alfred Prestwich – hence JAP – at his Tottenham works. Roe's brother, Humphrey Verdon Roe or 'HV', backed his brother and they drew up a partnership on 27 April 1909. Roe had already adopted the name Avroplane – based on his initials – which would appear on the side of the triplane. HV was a successful businessman, he owned the Everard Manufacturing Company and among its products were the very popular 'Bulls Eye' trouser braces. This trade name appeared in larger lettering on the triplane's minimalist fuselage, an early instance of the importance of sponsorship.

Hops from land close to the arches were achieved on 5 June. On 13 July Roe made a more prolonged sortie and ten days later he achieved a distance of 900ft at a giddy height of 10ft. These were the first sustained flights by an Englishman in a British-designed and built machine with a likewise indigenous engine. In the dawn of 25 July Louis Blériot flew the English Channel and any chance of Roe dominating the headlines vanished.

Like many pioneer aircraft, the Triplane I had a brief career, it last appeared at the Blackpool Flying Carnival, held over 18–24 October 1909. This incredibly significant machine survived and was presented to the Science Museum, South Kensington, on short-term loan in 1925. This arrangement was made permanent on 20 June 1950, Roe himself signing the donor document. The Lea Marshes triplane is a gem among gems in the top floor of the Science Museum.

Into business

The brothers were quick to exploit their achievement: the triplane was ripe for development. In January 1910 they established A V Roe and Company. Growth was so rapid that in January 1913 the business took on limited status with a capital of £30,000. The name Avro – a contraction of the previous Avroplane 'brand' – had been rapidly adapted. Elder brother HV was doing much more than monitoring the double-entry book-keeping: he was guaranteeing the fledgling outfit in an uncertain market where most fell by the wayside and backing Roe's potential to the hilt. Space was made available within the Brownsfield Mills in Ancoats, Manchester – part of HV's Everard empire. Construction of the improved Triplane II, named *Mercury*, began. At this point one of many shrewd appointments was made: 23-year-old Reginald 'Reg' John Parrott, who took the role of draughtsman. Parrott transformed Roe's often nebulous sketches into workable plans and quickly established an eye for detail. In March 1910 *Mercury* was taken to the Aero Show at Olympia in London and picked up an order for another example from Walter Windham for £550 – a drop of vital cash flow.

The firm turned its hand to building to commission, but soon gave this up. The Waterbird of 1911 for the Lakes Flying Company was Britain's first successful floatplane. A version of the Type D – see below – was ordered by Australian John Duigan and carried his name. It was flown at Brooklands during 1912 and was later transformed into the Lakes Seabird. The Burga Monoplane was built for the Peruvian naval attaché in 1912 and was Roe's first experience of a single wing. It had a novel control system of Burga's invention, including rudders mounted above and below the centre section in addition to a conventional example at the tail. It was not successful. Another venture was an ad hoc flying school, established at Brooklands in 1910. Part and parcel of any sale to an individual was tuition and other would-be aviators were made welcome. Brooklands was awash with such operations and in October 1911 the move was made to Shoreham and the Avro Flying School (Brighton) Ltd was formally created. The Sussex aerodrome also provided access to the adjacent River Adur, allowing floatplane training.

Brownsfield Mills workshop in Ancoats, early 1912. In the background is the Burga Monoplane with the Type E in the foreground. *Hawker Siddeley*

Formal portrait of A V Roe in 1927 as the head of the company bearing his name; the model is of the projected military version of the Type 607 tri-motor flying boat. *Hawker Siddeley*

The triplanes evolved into more workmanlike aircraft, but the availability of more powerful engines and the need to simplify construction meant that for Roe the day of the biplane was approaching. The Type IV triplane of 1910 proved to be the last of the line until a decade later when the anachronistic Type 547 four-passenger transport appeared. Even then the thinking was the reduction of wingspan to keep the structure simple. The Type D, which in tandem two-seat form became the backbone of the Avro Flying School, was essentially a biplane version of the Type IV triplane. Both initially employed a 35hp Green C.4, devised by British aero engine pioneer Gustavus Green at his Twickenham workshop, yet the wing area of the Type D was only 16sq ft greater than that of the triplane. First flown on 1 April 1911, the Type D was stable and pleasant to fly. The step to the machine that marked the transformation of Avro from a build-to-order workshop into an industry was the Type E and this will be detailed when we turn to Roy Chadwick.

During 1912 two machines appeared that broke away from the rugged, reliable two-seater format. The Type F single-seater monoplane allowed Roe to realise a dream, it was the world's first fully enclosed cabin aircraft – it took to the air on 1 May but was out of use by the autumn. The theme was repeated with the Type G, a two-seater cabin biplane entered into the Larkhill military aeroplane trials of August. The G was awarded £100 for being serviceable for all of the evaluations, but remained a one-off.

Architect of Wings

Between Bolton and Manchester is Farnworth in what was then lush Lancashire countryside; Roy Chadwick was born there in 1893. By the age of 11 he was building and flying intricate model aircraft, just like the man who became his boss – Roe. Three years later Chadwick was employed as a trainee draughtsman at an engineering firm and was known to most as 'Chad'. In July 1910 young Chadwick peeked inside the 'Avroplane' factory at the Brownsfield Mills and later that month he joined the huge crowds attending the second Blackpool Aviation Meeting where Roe and others were performing.

Afterwards Chadwick could think of nothing else. Surely there was employment to be had for an aircraft-mad, trained draughtsman from this inspiring pioneer aviator, fellow modeller and Lancastrian? Approaching his 18th birthday, Roy took the plunge and asked the great man – sixteen years his senior – for a job. Roe said yes, and from that day the prospects for the lad from Farnworth, Avro and British aviation were transformed.

Mention has already been made of the prolific writing of Harald Penrose, the multi-talented test pilot for Westland. Of all the tens of thousands of words devoted to Roy Chadwick, there are none finer those that appear in Penrose's *Architect of Wings*, a studious and loving biography of the great designer. Penrose describes Chadwick's first day at work: 'Alliott Roe introduced him to his keenly intelligent 24-year-old engineering assistant Reginald Parrott, and he was allocated a table in the latter's small office on the ground floor [of Brownsfield Mills] adjacent to the main erecting hall. [Chadwick's] mentor was a man of cool detachment who had given practical reality to the many sketches made by Alliott on the back of envelopes … By now, the elegance of detailed design compared with rival aircraft was becoming a hallmark of Avro construction.'

Under the guidance of Roe and Parrott, Chadwick was tasked with a rethink of the Type E 'Military Biplane', which appeared in March 1912. Practical, and with great potential, it was rebranded as the Type 500 and formed the basis of the famous 504. Chadwick was itching to get airborne, but most of the early machines had just one seat. The Type 500 had two and even offered then revolutionary dual control. Here was Chadwick's chance to experience the end product of his drawings and calculations. In July 1912 the third Type 500 was

Roy Chadwick ready to receive an honorary associateship of the Manchester College of Technology, November 1946. *British Aerospace*

Avro 504J fuselages outside the extension to the Mather and Platt premises at Newton Heath, Manchester, 1914. *British Aerospace*

taken from Brownsfield Mills to the cricket pitch at Eccles for its maiden flight. Enquiries with test pilot Wilfred 'Parky' Parke brought about a 'nod' and Chadwick climbed into the front seat. A swift circuit was followed by a bounce on landing and the biplane ended up on its nose. Pilot and aspirant designer were unhurt.

Expansion and new horizons

The all-important order from the War Office in mid-1912 – see below – meant that Brownsfield Mills was rapidly becoming too small. Additional space was secured at Clifton Street, Miles Platting, north-east of Ancoats, from March 1913. A short distance away, at Newton Heath, the engineering company Mather and Platt had completed a major extension to its foundry in early 1914 but it was still unoccupied by the summer. Little more than a handshake with HV was required for Avro to take it over and begin series production of 504s. This all helped, but the bullet had to be bitten; a purpose-built factory was the solution and work began at a site further along the Oldham Road, still in Newton Heath. By early 1918 the new plant was up and running and in 1934 it encompassed 250,000sq ft with further extensions in 1940 and 1943.

Ever since the Avro Flying School was established at Shoreham, Roe had his sights on the south coast of England as an additional factory, but more importantly a flight test base that the company could call its own. The choice settled upon Hamble, alongside the Solent estuary. Grandiose plans were drawn up to create a Victorian-inspired 'garden village' with bespoke accommodation for workers as well as extensive hangars. Wartime privations prevented this, but the aerodrome was ready by the spring of 1916 and A V Roe (Southampton) Ltd was established on the last day of that year. Perhaps as many as 150 Avro 504Js were assembled at Hamble, but essentially it was where the prototypes were erected and flown, with production remaining the domain of the Manchester sites. It made sense for the design office to relocate to Hamble and an appreciative Chadwick and his team moved into spacious, well-equipped offices. The following had their maiden flights at Hamble: Types 523 Pike, 529, 529A, 530, 531 Spider and 533 Manchester. Several 504 developments, Cierva autogiros, Avians and most post-1919 prototypes also had their debut at Hamble, up to the Avenger fighter and Buffalo torpedo bomber of 1926.

From 1925 until its closure in 2012 Woodford, south of Manchester, was synonymous with Avro and today's heritage museum, sited on the former airfield, flies the flag for the magnificent aeronautical legacy of the region. New Hall Farm was purchased early in 1925 to give Avro its own assembly and flight test site. Several airfields had been used previously, mostly the former Aircraft Acceptance Park at Alexandra Park, south of Manchester city centre. Three hangars from Alexandra Park were moved to the new site. Production got rolling at Woodford in 1926. During World War Two the Manchesters, Lancasters and Lincolns from the Metropolitan-Vickers factory at Trafford Park were also assembled and tested at Woodford. The present-day Manchester Airport, Ringway, was co-opted as a test centre from the spring of 1939 to relieve pressures on Woodford. It was ideal for maiden flights and the Manchester, Lancaster, York and Lincoln prototypes all had their debuts there. By late 1946 Avro had closed its Ringway office.

With the Anson in mass production and the Manchester under development, construction of an enormous government-sponsored factory at Chadderton in north-east Manchester, south of Rochdale, commenced in the autumn of 1938. Manufacturing within the 750,000sq ft building started in April 1939. Located on Greengate, the site took over from Newton Heath as the corporate headquarters, the telephone number was Failsworth 2020 and the telegram address reflected the company's early days: Triplane Manchester. The Chadderton plant had an exceptionally long tenure, only closing on 2 March 2012.

Supporting the Lancaster in Bomber Command and the huge fleets of Ansons required two further facilities, initially under the A V Roe Repair Organisation banner. Just south of Lincoln, Bracebridge Heath had been built during World War One and handled the output of Clayton and Shuttleworth, and Robey. Avro took over the 'Belfast truss' hangars in 1940 and it was used for Manchester and Lancaster repair and overhaul; the aircraft arriving at adjacent Waddington before being towed along the A15 main road to Bracebridge. From 1945 Anson reworks dominated and two of the 707 mini-deltas – see below – were assembled there ready for testing at Waddington. The plant also made sub-assemblies for HS, finally closing in the 1980s. The other airfield was Langar from 1942. Post-war this was a centre for Shackleton upgrades and overhauls: it closed in 1968 with the task transferring to Bitteswell.

In 1938 Roy Dobson – of which more soon – was looking for a site suitable to relocate the Anson production line, lock, stock and barrel. The Doncaster area seemed favourite, but a chance meeting with Australian-born Henry Vernon Worrall DSC* CDG changed all of that. Chief instructor for the Yorkshire Aeroplane Club, Worrall convinced Avro's redoubtable Yorkshireman that Yeadon was the solution. The club's base since it opened in October 1931, Yeadon was run by the Leeds and Bradford Joint Airport Committee and today is Leeds-Bradford Airport.

The factory, on the northern edge of the airfield, was completed in February 1941 and the efficient Dobson 'machine' got into gear. The jigs were moved from Newton Heath to Yeadon in May and seven Mk.Is rolled off the line the following month. Another type was intended to be built in quantity from 1941; the Hawker Tornado under sub-contract from the fellow HS consortium member. The Tornado was a version of the Typhoon, powered by a Rolls-Royce Vulture – the engine that stymied the Avro Manchester. A batch of five Tornados was commenced at Yeadon but only one, R7936, was completed. It was tested at Woodford on 29 August 1941, a month after the programme was scrubbed. More than 4,600 Ansons were made at the Yorkshire outpost up to the end of 1946: Mk.Is, Xs, XIs, XIIs and XIXs. The plant also built 695 Lancasters, six Lincolns and 113 Yorks. Closure of the factory was announced on 18 April 1946, with the last aircraft leaving before the end of the year.

The 504 generations

Some aircraft tick all the right boxes and the Introduction gives eight vital characteristics that make a great 'industrial' aircraft. Some of those attributes may not be apparent from inception but a company that notices them as they arise and exploits them is on to a winner. The Avro 504 was all of this and more. The most-produced British type of the Great War; the 504 set the standard for trainers for decades hence.

The stepping stone to the 504, using the experience of the Type D, was the 'E' aimed at securing an order from the War Office's 1911 requirement for a general duties military machine. It had its maiden flight on 3 March 1912 powered by a 60hp ENV Type F water-cooled 8-cylinder. Based at Willesden in London, the ENV Motor Syndicate was a British offshoot of a French company that took its name from its V-format engines – en vée. Roe was impressed with the performance of the Type E, but the water-cooled ENV was heavy and he turned to the faithful 7-cylinder Gnome Omega rotary. Despite having 10hp less than the ENV, the far lighter Gnome made the second example much sprightlier when it appeared two months later. Roy Chadwick was responsible for redesigning its forward fuselage to accept the rotary. Three were ordered for use by the Central Flying School at Upavon, with the promise of more to follow, and the Portuguese government ordered one. The War Office had recognised Avro as a contractor and the company was an exporter: vital credentials.

This was the watershed, Avro had a viable product. Around this time the decision was taken to create a more expansive designation system – the alphabet was too limited. The Gnome-engined 'E' became the Type 500. Penrose writes that when asked why the start at 500, Roe replied that it was a case of: 'drawing office swank!' When HSA reduced Avro to a division in 1963, that designation system had got as far as the projected four-turboprop maritime reconnaissance Type 784.

Under Chadwick's leadership the stage was set for a revision of the 500 to create the 504, destined in its 'first-generation' form to remain part of the Avro product line well into the 1920s. Parrott ran through the main improvements when it was unveiled at the start of the Aerial Derby at Hendon in September 1913: 'a heavy wing stagger to increase efficiency and improve downward and forward view; increased span and wing chord; a better wing section; improvement in streamlining the fuselage; fitting a unique undercarriage.' Trainers and single-seaters followed and, as the Great War erupted, sub-contractors began to churn out 504s as well as Avro.

During late 1916 manufacture standardised on the Gnome Monosoupape – single-valve – rotary as the 504J. By the autumn of 1917 the 'Mono' was ending its production life but there were huge stocks of British- and French-made 9-cylinder 130hp Clerget 9Bs and Le Rhône 9Cs and 9Jas of 80hp and 110hp. What if the 504 could be adapted to take *any* of these, as the situation permitted? Hamble-built 504J B3157 was adapted to take a Clerget and became the prototype of the incredibly successful 504K. Harry Broadhurst, part of Chadwick's team, came up with universal bearer plates on the firewall and a cowling that could accommodate any of the three rotaries. A legend had been born.

The Armistice of 11 November 1918 precipitated the wholesale cancellation of warplanes and disaster for the industry. Avro did its share of manufacturing baby carriages, billiard tables and motor car bodies but the 504K rode through all of this. The standard trainer for much of the war was to continue in that role with the RAF for the foreseeable future. Overseas air arms needed trainers and, new, reworked or licensed 504Ks were eagerly sought after. The mass 'demobbing' of aircraft, engines and components with the return of peace meant that new 504s were facing competition from surplus stocks. There was concern at Avro that spares from sub-contractors should not be traded under the 'Avro' name in case claims were made against it. These fears led to intervention in the dealings of the Aircraft Disposal Company – see Chapter 24. The 504 also was perfect for peacetime 'joy riding' operators. Keen to diversify, Avro entered this expanding business, creating Avro Transport in 1919, although it was disbanded in April of the following year.

The best replacement for a 504...

... is another one. Replacing 504Ks across the RAF did not require any major increase in performance, what was needed were the hallmark flying characteristics, robustness, reliability and minimal investment. The requirement was not contested but the parlous finances of the 1920s meant that the replacement process was a leisurely one. Specification 32/24 outlined the need for what was designated the 504N, while Specification 3/27 launched it into production and 6/30 defined the final RAF iteration, which boasted a steel tube fuselage frame and Frise ailerons. Prior to the metal fuselage, the main change was the substitution of the rotary with a radial and the choice was narrowed down to the 100hp 3-cylinder Bristol Lucifer or the 184hp Armstrong Siddeley (AS) Lynx II. The distinctive overturn skid was no longer a feature of the much tougher undercarriage and, among other refinements, the upper wing featured cutaways in the centre section's leading and trailing edge to provide better upward vision for instructor and student. Having chosen the Lynx, deliveries to the RAF commenced in early 1928 and the type was referred to as the 'Lynx-Avro' or simply 'Lynx' in service. During that year the Armstrong Siddeley Development Company (ASDC) acquired Avro, meaning that the 504N was powered by an in-house engine, further increasing its profitability. As well as 512 ordered as new-builds, about eighty conversions of 504Ks to Lynx status were also carried out. The 504N was also an export success, including licence manufacture.

The Lynx-Avro was an important stopgap for both Avro and the RAF but its development potential was at an end. When it came to superseding the 504N the result was a wholly new design, the summation of all Chadwick's experience of what a military trainer should be. Initially simply named Trainer, the Type 621 and the family it spawned was another resounding triumph for Avro with 1,220 of all versions built – an incredible figure for the late 1920s/early 1930s. First flown in 1929, the Type 621 was ordered by the RAF in 1932 as the Tutor.

Avro 504 'family'

From	To	Total	Designation/Name	Type	Engine	Notes
1912	1914	18	Type E (500, 502)	Military biplane	1x ENV/Green	
1913	1916	2,059	504, 'A to 'H	Military biplane	1 x Gnome	[1]
1916	1918	1,918	504J	Trainer	1 x Gnome	[2]
1916	-	12+	521	Fighter trainer	1 x Clerget	
1916	-	1	527	Armed recce	1 x Sunbeam	
1917	1927	5,125	504K	Trainer	See narrative	[3]
1919	-	43+	504L	Floatplane	1 x Clerget	[4]
1919	-	1	504M 'Limousine'	3-seater coupé	1 x Gnome	[5]
1919	-	22	536, 546	'Joyrider'	1 x Clerget	
1921	1925	32+	552/A	Trainer/floatplane	1 x Wolseley Viper	[6]
1924	-	1	504K Mk.II	Trainer	1 x Gnome	
1924	-	1	504Q	3-seat floatplane	1 x AS Lynx	
1926	1934	122+	504R Gosport	Trainer	1 AS Genet	[7]
1927	1934	616	504N 'Lynx-Avro'	Trainer	1 x AS Lynx	[8]

Great War production totals, establishing who-built-what and how many, etc, is far from a precise study. Figures are a 'best fit' from several sources. Post-1918 large numbers of airframes were supplied as 'spares' to operators both civil and military and remanufactured: these are *not* included. **[1]** Also sub-contracted to Parnall; S E Saunders; Blériot and Spad, Addlestone; Brush Electrical, Loughborough; Eastbourne Aviation, Eastbourne; Humber, Coventry; Regent Carriage, Fulham; and Sunbeam Motor, Wolverhampton. Some of these runs were ended with 504Js or 'Ks. **[2]** Also sub-contracted to Brush Electrical, Loughborough; Harland and Wolff, Belfast; and Sunbeam Motor, Wolverhampton. Some of these runs ended with 504Ks or 'Ns. **[3]** Also sub-contracted to Grahame-White and Parnall; and to Brush Electrical, Loughborough; Eastbourne Aviation, Eastbourne; Harland and Wolff, Belfast; Henderson Scottish Aviation Factory, Aberdeen; Hewlett and Blondeau, Luton and London; Humber, Coventry; London and Provincial, Edgware; Morgan and Co, Leighton Buzzard; Sage and Co, Peterborough; and Savages, King's Lynn. Some of the Brush run completed as 504Ns. Licence production by Australian Aircraft Engineering (6); Canadian Aeroplanes (2), Nakajima Aircraft, Japan (73+) from 1921 and 33 by Société Anonyme Belge de Constructions Aéronautiques (SABCA), Belgium. **[4]** Completed by Avro and Eastbourne Aviation, Eastbourne, plus conversions of 504K airframes. Licence production by Nakajima, Japan, from 1921 of around 30+. **[5]** Completed at Hamble from unfinished/surplus 504K. **[6]** Three created by contractor C B Field, Kingswood, 1933–34 from 'spares'. Licensed by Canadian Vickers (4). **[7]** Includes 100+ licensed to Fábrica Militar de Aviones, Argentina. **[8]** Several delivered for export as 504O – as in O or orange – floatplanes. Licensed by Canadian Vickers (13), Blackburn-managed Greek National Aircraft Factory, Old Phaleron, Athens (24), Orlogsvaerlet, Denmark, as LB.1 (5), Royal Thai Aeronautical Workshops (20) and SABCA, Belgium (31).

As with the 504, the design and marketing departments at Avro combined to maximise the concept and swell the coffers. Across its products, Avro built private-venture demonstrators and launched sales tours worldwide to help drum up sales – a ploy that paid dividends. The Tutor was adapted as the Prefect navigation trainer for the RAF. For export, the multi-purpose Type 626 had the provision for a third crew member for gunnery training and the armed 637A offered a limited offensive capability. The less complex Cadet appeared in 1931 hopefully to attract orders from schools and clubs. It was regarded as expensive by civilians but attracted air arms, including Australia and Ireland. The final military application was the elegant Type 667 fighter trainer of 1935, powered by a 460hp AS Jaguar VI and ordered for the Irish Air Corps. By this stage the biplane's reign was rapidly drawing to a close. Fully enclosed cabin versions of the Tutor and the Cadet, respectively the Commodore and the Club Cadet, were aimed at well-to-do owner-pilots, but only attracted a handful of orders.

Yorkshire plain speaking

There's another character that is overdue introduction, a Yorkshireman among Lancastrians. Aged 23, Roy Hardy Dobson – 'Dobbie' to almost everyone – asked in July 1914 about employment with Avro. He started on 2 August and two days later Britain was at war. The post was for a

'Lynx Avro' K1244 of the Central Flying School with the student 'under the hood' on instruments, summer 1930. *KEC*

A trio of Wittering-based Tutors of the Central Flying School, 1934. *Hawker Siddeley*

draughtsman, not part of the engineering fitter's training. Dobson was so determined to get into aviation that he was ambiguous when questioned about his skills. He got the job and was set to work under Roy Chadwick, but after six months he was moved to the section involved with materials testing. So the paths of the two Roys separated, but they were destined to be interwoven. Occasionally there were fireworks between them but both shared a passion for all things Avro. Dobson's expertise was motivational and organisational; he had the ability to take a Chadwick prototype and recreate it by the hundreds and later in thousands. When Dobson started at Avro, the workforce was a couple of hundred, but rising swiftly. In the spring of 1945 Sir Roy Dobson CBE, as he had become, was presiding over the production of 150 Lancasters a month in twenty-two factory sites employing 40,000 people.

Dobson's story could just as well be cited under HSA, but it is best told here. Dobson was soon immersed in all aspects of manufacture, from sorting out supply chain problems to flight testing machines off the assembly line, and delivering them. An early exploit gives a vivid insight into his grasp of a situation. The Pike bomber of 1916 was powered by a pair of Sunbeam pushers and it was test pilot Frederick 'Freddy' Phillip Raynham's first experience of a twin. In *Architect of Wings* Raynham is quoted as discounting the safety aspects of two powerplants, declaring that they gave: 'twice the chance of engine failure'. While engaged in acceptance testing at the Isle of Grain in May 1916, Raynham was flying the Pike with Dobson acting as observer in the gunner's position behind the wings. The aircraft proved to be exceptionally tail heavy and Raynham realised that throttling back could precipitate a stall. Dobson soon grasped the predicament and the nature of the pilot's hand signals. He climbed along the top of the fuselage, over Raynham's open cockpit and deposited himself in the nose gunner's 'office', transforming the centre of gravity. Freddy made a safe landing.

Dobson's rise through the ranks was swift; work on the flight line at Hamble was followed by promotion to assistant manager of the Manchester factories and in 1919 he became manager. In 1934 he was the entire company's general manager and gained a place on the board two years later. By then he was gearing up Avro to build Ansons and Bristol Blenheims at the vast Chadderton factory, but problems with the Manchester bomber threatened the company's future. A gifted redesign under Chadwick and ferocious replanning of the manufacturing process from sub-contractor to flight shed spearheaded by Dobson saved Avro from building Handley Page Halifaxes. Co-ordinating the Victory

Sir Roy Dobson shortly after becoming chairman of the Hawker Siddeley Group, 1960. *Hawker Siddeley*

Aircraft Lancaster output led to a directorship of HS in 1944 and he headed up Avro's Canadian division.

Knighted in January 1945, Sir Roy became managing director of the HS Group in January 1959 and chairman of HSA in 1963. He had the difficult task of overseeing the integration of the 'independent' constituent companies into divisions and the assimilation of Blackburn, de Havilland and Folland. No matter if he was in the hangars, or the factory floor or the boardroom, Dobson was plain speaking and forthright, knowing what was required to get a job done. He retired in 1967 and died on 7 July 1968, aged 77. In its obituary *Flight* magazine quoted the citation on Dobson's Air League Founders' Medal: 'his great services to the British aircraft industry sustained with unremitting vigour for over 50 years … there are few men … so universally respected.'

Search for new markets
As well as perfecting the 504 during the Great War, Chadwick's fertile mind turned to bombers, including the twin-engined Pike and Manchester biplanes, and fighters such as the pusher Type 508 and the Spider, but these achieved only meagre orders. In 1917 the 24-year-old was appointed chief designer, presiding over the extensive drawing

Avro types 1907 to 1918*

From	To	Total	Name/Designation	Type	Engine(s)	Notes
1907	-	1	Biplane	1-seat pusher	1 x JAP	
1909	-	2	Triplane I 'Bulls Eye'	1-seat tractor	1 x JAP	[1]
1909	1910	7	Triplane II, III, IV	1-/2-seat tractor	1 x Green	[2] [3]
1911	-	8	Type D	School biplane	1 x Green	[4]
1912	-	1	Type F	Monoplane	1 x Viale	
1912	-	1	Type G	Military, cabin biplane	1 x Green	
1912	1913	5	Type H (501, 503)	Training floatplane	1 x Gnome	
1913	-	1	508	Armed recce, pusher	1 x Gnome	
1914	1915	6	510	Military floatplane	1 x Sunbeam Nubian	
1914	-	1	511	Scout	1 x Gnome	
1916	-	4	519	2-crew bomber	1 x Clerget	
1916	1917	2	523/A Pike	Bomber	2 x Sunbeam	[5]
1916	-	1	528 Silver King	2-crew bomber	1 x Sunbeam	
1916	-	2	529/A	Long-range bomber	2 x RR Falcon	
1917	-	2	530	2-crew fighter	1 x Hispano-Suiza	
1918	1919	2	531 Spider	Fighter	1 x Clerget	[6]
1918	-	3	533 Manchester	Bomber/recce	2 x AS Puma	

* For Type 504 and derivatives, see separate table. All tractor biplanes unless noted. [1] See narrative. [2] First to be built under the aegis of A V Roe and Co. [3] Type III two-seat, others single-seat. [4] Single- and two-seaters, includes the similar Duigan Biplane commissioned by John Duigan. [5] Type 523 and 523A both initially pushers. The 523 converted to tractor format in 1917. [6] Second machine finished as Type 538 sportsplane.

Above: The prototype Aldershot outside the flight shed at Hamble in late 1922 in Mk.II guise with a 16-cylinder X-format 1,000hp Napier Cub. Count the wheels on the undercarriage: four each on independently sprung legs. *Avro*

Right: Roy Chadwick (left) with Avro test pilot Bert Hinkler (centre) and general manager Reginald Parrott (right) in front of Avian G-EBOV at Hamble in 1928. *British Aerospace*

office at Hamble. Reg Parrott went on to become the general manager at Hamble, moving to the London headquarters office from 1928 when ASDC took over and the Avro operation retreated back to Manchester.

Avro needed to diversify into markets other than trainers. As the table covering 1919 to 1935 shows, a wide range of types was built, from sporting ultralights to torpedo bombers, but most remained at the prototype stage, thankfully the majority paid for by the Air Ministry. Two designs broke through to the modest numbers that were typical in the cash-strapped 1920s, the Bison and the Aldershot. The former was a portly shipborne spotter with a crew of three or four. The deep fuselage contained a large cabin with room for a navigator's plotting table and a radio bench. Production ran to fifty-six units. With a 68ft span, the single-engined Aldershot day bomber of 1922 was massive. Beyond two prototypes, fifteen were ordered by the RAF, just sufficient for 99 Squadron at Bircham Newton.

Roe was determined to break into light aviation and Chadwick's initial foray in that direction was the single-seat Baby sports biplane. Occasionally test piloting at Hamble was Harold Hamersley and one of his tasks was to teach Chadwick to fly. On the last day of April 1919 he took the prototype Baby up for its maiden flight. At about 300ft Hamersley accidently knocked off the ignition switches and the little 35hp Green stopped; the Baby entered a spin and splattered into the mud of the River Hamble. Hamersley was not sent packing; he successfully flew the second Baby on 10 May.

Chadwick piloted this machine frequently, but it nearly brought a dazzling career to an abrupt end on 13 January 1920. In a website devoted to her father, Margaret Dove (who died in 2008) described what happened: 'Roy had gone up without his flying jacket. It was a cold day, and he fainted. He came to as he was crashing into trees beside the aerodrome. His right arm, left leg and pelvis were severely fractured and the joystick went through his neck! He later made a full recovery, thanks to the skill of the great World War One surgeon, Sir Arbuthnot Lane.'

For Avro, the real breakthrough came in 1926 with the Avian two-seat tourer/trainer. It was not to rival de Havilland's exceptional Moth

dynasty in terms of numbers, but it did enter volume production. Like the 504, it made the leap from all-wooden airframe to the steel tube fuselage structure. The 'metal' Avian IV succeeded in penetrating the American market, although a licence agreement soon fizzled out.

European links

The company established close relations with two European pioneers. Like several British manufacturers, Avro embraced the rotorcraft ambitions of the Spanish-born Juan de la Cierva. Also, a delegation visited Fokker in 1928 and came away with a licence for the F.VIIb/3m trimotor airliner across the British Empire, other than Canada. This was potentially lucrative and gave Chadwick insights into welded steel tube fuselage structures and the one-piece cantilever ply wing for which the Dutch company was famous. Fokker transformed its single-engined F.VII into a trimotor in 1925 and brokered licensing agreements in Belgium, Italy, Poland and the USA as well as with Avro. The Type 618 appeared in 1929 and was essentially an F.VIIb/3m with Imperial measurements and British fittings. With a crew of two and eight passengers it was marketed as the Avro Ten after the number of seats if offered. As the first examples emerged, Britain entered economic depression and on 31 March 1931 an American-built version suffered a structural failure of the wing and crashed, killing all on board. This tainted the image of the Fokker trimotor – no matter where it was made. Sales of the Avro version amounted to a disappointing fourteen.

Adopting the F.VII's layout, in 1929 Chadwick conceived a completely new type, a five- or six-seater powered by 105hp AS

Genet Majors. Intended for the charter or corporate market, the Avro Five and Six also suffered in the economic climate and only seven were made. Avro returned to the Fokker theme in 1934 by marrying the Avro Ten wing to an entirely new airliner fuselage as the Type 642, offered in either two- or four-engined formats. The Ten's fuselage was 47ft 6in long, while the new design was 54ft 6in and could take a crew of two and sixteen passengers, hence its name: Eighteen. On this occasion only, Avro's designation system reflected that of Fokker, the Type 642 carrying the suffix /2m or /4m depending on the number of engines. The 642 was a costly exercise; only two prototypes were completed.

Type 642/2m G-ACFV was delivered to Midland and Scottish Air Ferries in January 1934 and wrecked five months later. *KEC*

Corporate shuffles

The return to peace in November 1918 saw Avro in a far better condition than some of its rivals but it was still in a parlous state. Its potential was obvious, but steady work and a cash injection was vital.

John Lord, latterly with HV's Everard company and the Roe brothers' partner from the early days of 1913, cast the net wide for new associations and negotiations with Crossley Motors bore fruit. Crossley had had a 'good war' and was capitalising on the post-war boom in motor cars. On 6 May 1920 Crossley acquired the majority shareholding in Avro. This was not an asset stripping exercise like Birmingham Small Arms had inflicted on Airco the previous year. Crossley certainly needed the spare capacity at Newton Heath to churn out car bodies, but was determined to keep its new acquisition in the aviation business. During the war Crossley had successfully managed 2 National Aircraft Factory at Heaton Chapel. Here was a kindred spirit, although its management made it plain from the outset that Avro needed to pay its way.

The wheel of fortune had turned by the mid-1920s: it was Crossley that was not doing well, with revenues from Avro helping to keep it afloat. In May 1928 Sir John Siddeley, through his ASDC holding company, bought up Crossley's holdings in Avro. This spelt the end for Hamble as the experimental station, but otherwise the Manchester business continued as an independent organisation and a prolific consumer of Armstrong Siddeley engines.

This was not the end of the corporate shuffling. By the mid-1930s the Siddeley 'empire' was a very attractive package. 'Tommy' Sopwith and Fred Sigrist at Hawker recognised this great opportunity and on 25 June 1935 the organisations came together, along with Gloster (which had been acquired in May 1934), as the massive Hawker Siddeley *Aircraft* Company. The constituent businesses continued to trade under their own names. The enterprise was reorganised in 1948 as the Hawker Siddeley Group and again in January 1959 when it became Hawker Siddeley *Aviation*. To prevent confusion between the 1935 to 1948 HSA and the HSA of 1959 onwards, throughout the book the earlier HSA is referred to as the Hawker Siddeley (HS) consortium.

Avro types 1919 to 1935

From	To	Total	Name/Designation	Type	Engine(s)	Notes
1919	1921	9	534, 543 Baby	Sportsplane	1 x Green	
1919	-	1	539	Racing floatplane	1 x AS Puma	
1920	-	2	547	Transport, triplane	1 x AS Puma	
1921	1925	56	Bison	Naval recce	1 x Napier Lion	
1922	1924	17	Aldershot	Heavy bomber	1 x RR Condor	
1927	-	2	Ava	Torpedo bomber	2 x RR Condor	
1923	-	2	558	Ultralight	1 x Douglas	
1923	-	1	560	Ultralight monoplane	1 x Tomtit	
1924	1925	4	Andover	Transport/ambulance	1 x RR Condor	
1924	-	1	Avis	Ultralight	1 x Thrush	
1926	-	1	Avenger	Fighter	1 x Napier Lion	
1926	-	1	Buffalo	Torpedo bomber	1 x Napier Lion	
1926	1930	194	Avian	Lightplane	1 x ADC Cirrus	[1]
1927	-	2	Avocet	Shipborne fighter	1 x AS Lynx	
1928	-	1	Antelope	Day bomber	1 x RR Kestrel	
1929	1933	202	Avian IVM	Lightplane	1 x Cirrus Hermes	[2]
1929	1936	14	Ten	Transport	3 x AS Lynx	[3]
1929	1932	7	Five/Six	Transport	3 x AS Genet Major	
1929	1936	855	Tutor	Trainer	1 x AS Lynx	[4]
1930	-	2	Avian	Lightplane, monoplane	1 x Cirrus Hermes	
1930	1940	223	626, Prefect, 637	Crew trainer	1 x AS Lynx	[5]
1931	-	1	Mailplane	Long-range mailplane	1 x AS Panther	
1931	1939	103	Cadet	Trainer	1 x AS Genet	
1933	1935	27	Club Cadet	Club trainer	1 x AS Genet	[6]
1934	-	2	642/2m and 642/4m	Transport	2 x AS Jaguar	[7]
1934	-	6	Commodore	Light transport	1 x AS Lynx	
1935	-	4	667	Fighter trainer	1 x AS Jaguar	[8]

All tractor biplanes unless noted. [1] Prototype 581, Avian I, II, III, IV all Type 594. [2] Licensed by Ottawa Car Manufacturing (18+) and Whittlesey Manufacturing Co, USA (about ten). [3] Licensed-build of Fokker F.VIIb/3m. [4] Licensed by Orlogsvaerlet, Denmark (3) and South African Air Force Aircraft and Artillery Dept (57). [5] Prefect navigation trainer for RAF and RNZAF, 537 armed version for Kwangsi, China. Licensed to Oficinas Gerais de Materiel Aeronáutical (OGMA), Portugal (17). [6] Includes one-off Type 639 Cabin Cadet and 9 Type 640 Three-Seaters. [7] Known as the Eighteen. Type 642/4m powered by 4 AS Lynx. [8] Batch of four for the Irish Air Corps were technically Type 667s, but were always referred to as Type 636s.

Two brothers – different directions

Humphrey Roe was not prepared to build aeroplanes as his part of the war effort; he wanted to take part. He left the company he had founded with his brother on the last day of July 1917. Cashing in his share-holding yielded just over £20,000 – a fortune in Edwardian Britain. He'd backed AV to the hilt, putting his own business at risk, and had been well rewarded for his faith and hard graft.

This was Humphrey's second war. When aged 21 he had fought with the Manchester Regiment in the Second Boer War, including the siege of Ladysmith. In December 1917 Humphrey was accepted into the Royal Flying Corps. Initially he instructed, but he was determined to go into combat. He was posted to a bomber unit, piloting Royal Aircraft Factory F.E.2bs on night raids across the Western Front. He was wounded and brought back to 'Blighty' to recover. His military and aviation exploits were far from over, but they were put on hold in 1918 when he married Dr Marie Stopes. Humphrey had a new venture to support, his wife's trailblazing family planning clinics.

Humphrey re-entered aviation in 1936 when he set up the Aeronautical Corporation of Great Britain as UK licensees for American Aeronca lightplanes. He was back in uniform in 1940 serving with the RAF, retiring two year later. There was one more aeronautical link; divorced in 1936, he married Mary Eyre Wallis – the daughter of Barnes Wallis – in 1948. Sadly this union was a brief one, Humphrey Verdon Roe died on 27 July 1949, aged 71.

The deal with ASDC in 1928 transformed the prospects at Avro, but was also a turning point for Roe. Aged 51, Roe was looking for new diversions and with people like Chadwick and Dobson at the 'coalface', his role was increasingly corporate or as a figurehead. One of the reasons for establishing the 'outstation' at Hamble was Roe's ambition to build flying boats and in the autumn of 1928 he and his friend and colleague John Lord sold up their shares in Avro in search of a marine aviation business. Their focus settled on the other side of the Solent, at Cowes on the Isle of Wight. The pair acquired the majority share of Sam Saunders's company and in the following year it was renamed Saunders-Roe, Saro for short. Harry Broadhurst, another Avro stalwart and the man who had devised the 504K's 'universal' engine mount, pitched in, becoming general manager at Cowes.

Roe was knighted in 1929 and four years later changed his name, subtly adding a hyphen to Verdon-Roe to honour his mother, maiden name Sofia Verdon, equally with that of his father, Dr Edwin Hodson Roe. Roe lost two sons during World War Two, both serving as pilots in Bomber Command. Sqn Ldr Eric Alliott Verdon-Roe, aged 26, was killed along with the rest of his crew when his 102 Squadron Armstrong Whitworth Whitley V was shot down by a Luftwaffe night fighter during a raid on Hanover, Germany, on 26 July 1941. Sqn Ldr Lighton Verdon-Roe DFC, aged 22, was at the helm of an Avro-built Lancaster III of 156 Squadron on 13 May 1943 when it came down in the target area, Duisburg, Germany, killing all seven on board.

The second Type 652, G-ACRN *Avatar*, on early air test; March 1935. *Peter Green Collection*

From the late 1920s Roe lived in Hampshire, handy for Cowes where he remained chairman of Saro until his death. Sir Edwin Alliott Verdon-Roe OBE, Britain's first fully indigenous aviator and co-founder of an aviation dynasty, passed away at the age of 81 on 4 January 1958, two years after the Avro Vulcan entered service with the RAF.

Avro sub-contracts, licences* and Hawker Siddeley work

Type	Total	From	To	Notes
Lakes Waterbird	1	1911	-	[1]
Burga Monoplane	1	1912	-	[2]
Cierva C.6C and 'D*	2	1926	-	[3] [4]
Cierva C.8V and 'L *	5	1927	1928	[3] [5]
Cierva C.9 – Type 576*	1	1927	-	[3]
Cierva C.17*	2	1928	1929	[3] [6]
Cierva C.19 Mk.I to V*	34	1930	1935	[3]
Cierva C.30, 'A and 'P *	78	1934	1936	[3] [7]
Hawker Audax I	244	1936	1938	
Bristol Blenheim I, IV	1,000	1938	1941	
Hawker Tornado	1	1941	-	[8]
EE Canberra B.2	75	1952	1955	

[1] Pusher biplane floatplane of Curtiss format commissioned by E W Wakefield of Lakes Flying Company, Windermere. [2] Monoplane designed by Peruvian Lt R Burga, used a Type 500 fuselage. [3] For all Cierva types see Chapter 15. [4] Types 574 and 587. [5] Types 575, 586, 587, 611 and 617. [6] Types 586, 575, 612, 620 apply. Second of these almost certainly converted to C.12 'Hydrogiro'. [7] Type 671, RAF examples called Rota. [8] HS consortium member, technically an in-house work share.

'Faithful Annie'

Niche markets such as trainers and tourers were all very well, but more complex military types offered the greatest growth potential. The breakthrough came when Avro responded to an Imperial Airways requirement released in May 1933 for a twin-engined luxury charter aircraft. Frank 'Tommy' Tomkins took Type 652 G-ACRM *Avalon* for its maiden flight at Woodford on 7 January 1935. Imperial only wanted a pair of 652s, but Chadwick recognised the type's applicability to Air Ministry coastal patrol Specification 18/35. Sixty-six days after *Avalon* flew, Sidney Albert 'Bill' Thorn, piloted Type 652A K4771 on its first sortie. The 652A was up against an armed de Havilland Dragon Rapide, but the biplane was no match for the sleek, retractable undercarriage monoplane. An order for 174 Anson Is was placed in July and such was the preparedness at Woodford that the first example was ready for handover just five months later. The type was named after the 18th-century admiral of the fleet, Lord George Anson.

The last Anson, T.21 WJ561, over Woodford on 15 May 1952. Behind, looking to the south-east is the massive assembly hall with five Lancasters and a York out on the airfield. *Avro Media Centre*

Anson refurbishing at Bracebridge Heath, Lincoln, 1947. *British Aerospace*

Manchester I L7515 of 207 Squadron having fun with a Handley Page Hampden, which was acting as a photo-ship, in November 1941. *KEC*

Like the 504 before it, the Anson was a world-beater. Avro began and ended World War Two with it *still* in production; it was the springboard that turned the company into an industrial giant. With an enlarged fuselage and metal wings, a 'second generation' Anson and a civilian version, known as the Nineteen, were offered to the post-war marketplace. The last example, RAF T.21 crew trainer WJ561, was flown from Yeadon on 15 May 1951. Manufacture of Chadwick's multi-purpose Anson ran for seventeen years and 11,020 units, through an incredible number of variants, with extensive exports and licences.

Two into four

The Anson gave Avro the credentials to pitch for the bomber contracts that were looming as Britain geared up for another European war. An invitation to tender was sent out on 8 September 1936 – just two months after Bomber Command came into being. The statistics were challenging; the winning design was to carry up to 8,000lb of bombs at no less than 275mph for a maximum range of 2,000 miles. But Air Ministry Specification P.13/36 wanted much more of the RAF's next spearhead. In order to use existing airfields while carrying the greatest weapon load, the bomber had to be stressed to use a catapult launch system to hurl it into the air. It would also be called upon to serve as a torpedo bomber, with a pair of 18in 'tin fish' carried internally. To increase the accuracy of weapon aiming and reduce time over the target, it should be capable of dive attacks at 60 degrees. Use in the general reconnaissance – maritime patrol – role with minimal equipment changes was to be possible. Oh, and the ability to transport sixteen fully equipped troops long distances was desirable.

Avro, Boulton Paul, Bristol, Handley Page, Shorts and Vickers were all asked to see what they could come up with. Large orders awaited, but such a demanding 'shopping list' made the venture extremely high-risk. Avro and Handley Page (HP) were awarded contracts to build prototypes. The end products would be named Manchester – the second use of the name –

and Halifax respectively. In terms of aerodynamics, construction techniques, armament and hundreds of other aspects, P13/36 was an awesome commission.

By far and away the greatest hurdle was the powerplant; the Avro and HP design teams at Woodford and Radlett both opted for the Rolls-Royce (RR) Vulture, a relatively compact 24-cylinder, X-format supercharged brute that could belt out 1,800hp. The Air Ministry later instructed HP to redesign its proposal to take four RR Merlins. Avro, which had been given an off-the-drawing-board production order in July 1937, was told to stick with the Vulture.

Gradually all of the non-bomber requirements for P13/36 were dropped; bizarrely the last to go was the troop-carrying role. As the design had long since been 'frozen', many elements of the original specification had to stay in place, with weight penalties. But some of P13/36's latent demands played a major part in making the Manchester's successor, the Lancaster, a war-winner. The torpedo requirement necessitated a huge bomb bay and to be able to accommodate soldiers, the fuselage had to be broad and deep, giving the Lancaster versatility when it came to internal equipment changes. This also made the post-war airliner version, the Lancastrian, possible. Ease of production and maintenance was stipulated by P13/36. Chadwick created a modular airframe that permitted major sections to be built off-site by sub-contractors and easily dismantled and returned by road for repair.

The prototype Manchester had its maiden flight on 25 July 1939. Chadwick's team faced endless redesigns, changes in systems and fittings in an attempt to prove that the twin was a viable war machine. Throwing the towel in was not an option. While the Anson was a spectacular production success, if the Manchester failed, in the medium term Avro faced a future as a sub-contractor for others. Wisely, Chadwick had been looking at engine options. Staying with a twin format, there was the Bristol Centaurus and the Napier Sabre, but both were in their earliest stages. If four engines were required, the radial Hercules or Taurus from Bristol might suffice, but the RR Merlin dominated.

On 18 April 1940 Avro proposed the bigger-winged Manchester III with four Merlins. Roy Dobson was working furiously to achieve the changes needed in the supply chain and the assembly line to make a possible switch of powerplant as seamless as possible. That month Stuart 'Cock' Davies was appointed as head of the experimental department to oversee the design changes. This crucial task was pivotal to the 34-year-old's career. It was a nail-biting time for Avro. In November 1940 the Ministry of Aircraft Production gave consideration to switching the Avro and Metropolitan-Vickers assembly lines to churning out Halifaxes. Thankfully it was more efficient to introduce the Manchester III than stop everything and re-jig for the HP bomber, so approval was given to go ahead.

Lancaster – giant leap

Chadwick's original design was sound and a weight-reduction scheme coupled with operational experience meant that the Merlin-powered version was a giant leap ahead of its predecessor. The alterations were so comprehensive, and as the Manchester 'brand' was hardly bathed in glory, a name change was needed. On 28 December 1940 the prototype Mk.III, BT308, began engine runs at Ringway. Chadwick signed its clearance to fly on 5 January 1941 and the document referred to BT308 not as a Manchester III, but a Lancaster. It first flew four days later. The Vulture was cancelled in September 1941 and the last Manchester was issued for service in March of the following year.

Once freed from the neutering Vultures, Chadwick's bomber excelled. Like the 504 and the Anson before it, it matched the categories needed for longevity. The British-based Lancaster Production Group and Victory Aircraft in Canada created 7,377 examples up to the spring of 1946. In peacetime the type still had 'legs'; sixty-plus reworked GR.3s for Coastal Command were joined by refurbished exports to Argentina, Egypt and France, with the last departing in February 1954. There was also a healthy demand for Lancastrian transports for military and airline use.

York G-AHEY of Skyways at Luton in August 1963 at the end of a varied service life that began in the summer of 1946. *Roy Bonser*

Australian-built Lincoln Mk.30s of the RAAF's 1 Squadron, over Malaya, 1950. *RAAF*

Built in the summer of 1943 by Armstrong Whitworth, Lancaster II DS771 showing the variant's Bristol Hercules radials. This Lancaster served with two RCAF units and went missing over Stuttgart on 16 March 1944 with the loss of all seven on board. *British Aerospace*

An early post-war view of the Chadderton factory, looking north-east. The power station was demolished in the mid-1980s and much of the factory site has been redeveloped; some of the buildings in the right foreground remain. *British Aerospace*

By grafting Lancaster wings and tail feathers to a new, boxy fuselage, Chadwick's team created the York airlifter, the prototype flying on 5 July 1942. Priorities did not lie with transports at the time, but the York came into its own from 1944 with 258 built for the RAF and airlines; the last rolling off the Yeadon line in mid-1948. Avro was still refurbishing Yorks for customers in 1955.

With a stretched fuselage, greater span wings, more powerful Merlins and improved systems, the Lincoln was the obvious replacement for the 'Lanc'. The prototype had its maiden flight at Ringway on 9 June 1944 and the bomber entered RAF service in August 1945. Avro, Metropolitan-Vickers and Armstrong Whitworth built 536 Lincolns; the last one in mid-1951. Canada completed a solitary example and the Government Aircraft Factory in Australia produced fifty-four for the RAAF. Systems upgrades provided regular contracts for Avro, including its 'special fit' workshops at Langar.

Tudor tragedy

In December 1945, Chadwick was rewarded for his incredible endeavours when he was appointed technical director; he'd been on the Avro board since 1936. Experience with the York and the Lancastrian encouraged Avro to enter the post-war airliner market and the result was the elegant-looking Tudor 1 for British Overseas Airways Corporation (BOAC). The prototype had its debut at Woodford on 14 June 1945 but two years later BOAC abandoned the type. In parallel with the Tudor 1, BOAC requested the high-capacity Tudor 2. With a fuselage length of 105ft 7in, it was the longest British aircraft at the time. This was not 'merely' a stretch; the fuselage

The ill-fated Tudor 2 prototype, G-AGSU, at Woodford, 1946. *Avro*

diameter was increased by 12in, requiring almost entirely new tooling and jigs, a massively expensive exercise. The first Tudor 2, G-AGSU, flew on 10 March 1946.

On 23 August 1947 chief test pilot Bill Thorn, prepared to take *Sugar-Uncle* for a test with a crew of three and a trio of keen passengers: Roy Chadwick; Stuart Davies – Chadwick's nominated successor – and Sir Roy Dobson. An important telephone call pulled Dobson away and the sortie continued without him. As the airliner climbed, it banked violently to starboard and cartwheeled; the fuselage broke in two places and the wreck plummeted into a large pond. Miraculously, flight-test engineer Eddie Talbot and Davies survived. Thorn and Sqn Ldr David Wilson drowned in the cockpit; Chadwick and radio operator John Webster were both thrown clear and died of fractured skulls.

It was discovered that during maintenance, *Sugar-Uncle's* ailerons had been rigged wrongly – starboard down on the control wheel produced 'up' and the opposite to port. Before he could establish this cross-over, Thorn's control inputs put the Tudor into an ever-deepening roll. The long fuselage meant that a visual check from the cockpit to see that the ailerons were functioning as they should be was not physically possible; this could only be done with help from ground crew indicating 'starboard aileron down', etc. It was a salutary lesson in quality control, pre-flight procedure with large aeroplanes and about not letting crucial personalities go flying in aircraft under test. The Tudor never recovered from this tragedy and was a rare dismal failure for Avro.

Everyone at Woodford was stunned; the loss of the flight crew was terrible enough, but Roy Chadwick CBE was synonymous with Avro – a giant of his time. Among his last work had been overseeing mock-ups for the upcoming Shackleton maritime patroller and sketches confirming the delta configuration of what would become the Vulcan. By far and away the best tribute is in *Architect of Wings*: 'His inspiration lived on. The designs of the Athena trainer, Coastal Command Shackleton, Tudor development into the jet-powered Ashton, and the thunderous long-serving Vulcan bomber were

completed in due course by Stuart Davies. To this day the surviving pilots who flew the wartime Lancasters speak of their machines with nostalgic admiration, and regard Roy Chadwick as the greatest aircraft designer of all.'

Trainer swansong

Avro returned to trainers when the RAF issued Specification T.7/45 to replace the ubiquitous North American Harvard. The vagaries of this requirement included two, perhaps three seats; capable of arrested deck-landing, then not; powered by a turboprop before switching to the trusted Merlin 35. The name Athena, the Greek goddess of wisdom, was selected for this inheritor of the legacy of the 504 and the Tutor.

On 12 June 1948 Avro's first turboprop, AS Mamba-powered Athena prototype VM125, flew at Woodford. It was followed by the Merlin version, the T.2, in August. Avro was up against Boulton Paul and that concern's Balliol won a large contract. Bizarrely, fifteen Athena T.2s were *also* ordered for the RAF as armament trainers, delivered at a leisurely pace from late 1949 to 1951. (See Chapter 10 for a comparison of the two types.)

Canadian adventure

Canadian Lancasters were assembled and flown from Malton, Ontario, by a government-owned organisation appropriately named Victory Aircraft. Once the line had been set up, leading Avro personnel, most often Dobson and Davies, made regular transatlantic trips to liaise with their Canadian counterparts. During the summer of 1945 Dobson was being given a tour of the plant, where the workforce was coming to terms with probable closure. The Avro board had discussed the possibility of acquiring Malton to increase Avro's potential, but no decision had been reached. In a classic Dobson moment on return from his inspection, he amazed the rest of the Manchester delegation by announcing: 'Well, I've taken it – the bloody lot!' A V Roe Canada Ltd – most often referred to as Avro Canada – was formed on 1 December 1945 with 'Dobbie' as its chairman.

Avro from Anson to Lincoln

From	To	Total	Name/Designation	Type	Engine(s)	Notes
1935	-	2	652	Light transport	2 x AS Cheetah	
1935	1952	11,020	Anson	Patrol/crew trainer	2 x AS Cheetah	[1]
1939	1942	200	Manchester	Heavy bomber	2 x RR Vulture	[2]
1941	1946	7,377	Lancaster	Heavy Bomber	4 x RR Merlin	[3]
1942	1948	257	York	Long-range transport	4 x RR Merlin	[4]
1945	1946	82	Lancastrian	Long-range transport	4 x RR Merlin	
1944	1951	586	Lincoln	Heavy bomber	4 x RR Merlin	[5]

[1] Includes Canadian production – 2,882 units – involving Canadian Car and Foundry, de Havilland Aircraft of Canada, Federal Aircraft, MacDonald Brothers, National Steel Car Corp, Ottawa Car and Aircraft. **[2]** Also sub-contracted to Metropolitan-Vickers, Trafford Park. **[3]** Also sub-contracted to Armstrong Whitworth; Austin, Birmingham; Metropolitan-Vickers; Vickers Armstrong. Includes licensed (430 Mk.Xs) by Victory Aircraft, Canada. Mk.X. Mk.I, III, III, VI, VII, X all Merlin-powered; Mk.II with Bristol Hercules. **[4]** Licence production by Victory Aircraft, Canada, got no further than a prototype. **[5]** Also sub-contracted to Armstrong Whitworth, Metropolitan-Vickers. Licensed to Government Aircraft Factory, Australia – Mk.30 – 54 examples and Victory Aircraft, Canada – one prototype only.

This book is about *British* industry, but it would be wrong not to give at least passing reference to an incredible fifteen-year enterprise. There were contracts to convert Royal Canadian Air Force (RCAF) Lancasters for maritime patrol and other roles, but Avro's Canadian offshoot had greater ambitions. The C-102 Jetliner designed by James 'Jim' C Floyd was capable of carrying up to fifty passengers and capitalised on the parent company's experience with the Tudor 8 of 1948 and the forthcoming Ashton research test bed – see below for more on these. Woodford test pilot Joseph Harold 'Jimmy' Orrell took the four-engined prototype for its maiden flight on 10 August 1949; this was the first time a jet transport had flown in North America. The occasion was only the second inaugural flight by a dedicated jetliner anywhere in the world; fifteen days previously John Cunningham had lifted the prototype de Havilland Comet into the skies at Hatfield. The Comet was the main reason why the C-102 remained a one-off.

Avro Canada

Type	Total	From	To
C-102 Jetliner 4-jet airliner	1	1949	-
CF-100 Canuck jet fighter	692	1950	1958
CF-105 Arrow jet fighter	5	1951	1967
VZ-9V Avrocar experimental	2	1959	1960

This was far from the case with the second Malton creation, the CF-100 Canuck two-seat, twin-engined all-weather fighter. This had a production run of 692 in five different versions, the bulk for the RCAF and fifty-three for the Belgian Air Force. Another British test pilot, supplied by the HS consortium, Gloster's Canadian-born William 'Bill' Waterton, took the prototype up for the first time on 19 January 1950. The intended replacement for the CF-100 was the twin-engined, supersonic interceptor, the CF-105 Arrow. Another Gloster test pilot, Russian-born Janusz 'Jan' Zurakowski, presided over the maiden flight of the prototype on 25 March 1958. Four more examples followed it into the sky but the entire programme was cancelled on 20 February the following year. This was the death knell for Avro Canada but one more first 'flight' took place on 12 December 1959. This was the saucer-shaped, twin-jet research aircraft, the Avrocar. In

the middle of the disc was a fan that provided lift and propulsion, with a cockpit on either side. Two machines, designated VZ-9V, were built for a joint US Army and Air Force project. Both made 'hops' but no real flying was achieved. The Malton plant was sold to de Havilland Canada in July 1962 and eventually used to build sub-assemblies for the Douglas DC-9 twinjet airliner.

Maritime giant

Avro's most enduring design – the Shackleton – could trace its roots back to the Manchester, Lancaster and Lincoln. Looking to replacing Coastal Command's Lancaster GR.3s, a development of the Lincoln was initially considered, but the fuselage was not capacious enough. Instead a new, broader, version was mated to a Lincoln wing, and fitted with four RR Griffon 57As driving contra-rotating propellers. The inaugural flight of the prototype Shackleton took place on 9 March 1949. This maritime giant paid homage to early 20th-century Antarctic explorer Sir Ernest Henry Shackleton CVO OBE.

The phrase 'weapon system' was not then in vogue, but that was exactly what Coastal Command was taking on – a hugely sophisticated aircraft with a wide variety of weaponry and complex radar and detection equipment. The Shackleton, and the Vulcan that followed it, became 'rolling' programmes of improvement that proved highly profitable for Avro, long after the production line closed.

Between 1950 and 1952 a total of seventy-seven MR.1s and MR.1As was produced. Almost seamlessly, the improved MR.2 came on line in 1952, with fifty-nine built. The final variant, thirty-four examples manufactured from 1955 to 1959 plus eight for South Africa in 1957–58, was the MR.3. This featured wing tip tanks and tricycle undercarriage among many internal enhancements. A major contract in the mid-1960s brought about the MR.3 Phase 3 with an AS Viper 203 turbojet mounted in the rear of each outboard engine nacelle to provide extra boost in overload conditions. This mod almost certainly shortened the fatigue life on MR.3s, which retired in the early 1970s, requiring a life-extension programme for venerable MR.2s.

The prototype CF-105 Arrow being put through its paces, summer 1958. *Avro Canada via Tony Buttler*

Above: Second of eight Shackleton MR.3s for the South African Air Force, 1717 was handed over in May 1957. *Avro*

Left: The Shackleton overhaul and modification line at Langar in the summer of 1957. *British Aerospace*

and operators, and the required endurance. The first AEW.2 conversion flew at Woodford on 30 September 1971 and it was followed by eleven more, all created at Bitteswell. The follow-on Nimrod AEW.3 was axed in 1986 and the Boeing Sentry ordered instead. The AEW.2 fleet soldiered on until 1 July 1991. The first delivery to the RAF had been MR.1 VP260 on 30 March 1951 – Avro's Shackleton had clocked a staggering forty years of service.

Jet generation

There was a shred of redemption from the tainted Tudor programme as Avro entered the jet age. To provide a research test bed for the Royal Aircraft Establishment, the second prototype Tudor was given four 5,100lb RR Nene 5 turbojets in twin, under-wing pods. Tudor 8 VX195 took to the air on 6 September 1948 and was the world's first four-engined jet transport. An order for six improved versions followed, based upon the bigger fuselage section of the Tudor 2 and with tricycle undercarriage. This was the Ashton, a purpose-built test bed capable of engine trials, radar evaluation and more. The type took its name from the town of Ashton-under-Lyne, east of Manchester. The first example flew on 1 September 1950, the last on 18 November 1952.

Through the war and into the early 1950s *other* concerns built Avro designs under sub-contract or by licence. Between April 1953 and March 1955 the compliment was returned when Woodford manufactured a batch of seventy-five English Electric Canberra B.2s.

Just as the Lancaster gave its wing to the York and the Lincoln passed its wing structure to the Shackleton, so Avro's maritime patroller came to the aid of a fellow member of Hawker, Armstrong Whitworth. The wing was adopted for the AW Argosy four-turboprop airlifter, which first flew at Bitteswell in January 1959.

The MR.2's longevity provided an opportunity that neither the manufacturer nor the RAF could have foreseen. The Royal Navy was retiring its carriers and Fairey Gannet AEW.3s and the HS Nimrod airborne early warning 'command post' was still a 'paper' project. Something was needed to bridge the gap. Underneath the upward-slopping nose of the MR.2 the Gannet's heavy and bulbous AN/APS 20 radar would fit nicely, plus it had a roomy fuselage for consoles

Avro post-1945

From	To	Total	Name/Designation	Type	Engine(s)	Notes
1945	1950	25	Tudor	Long-range airliner	4 x RR Merlin	[1]
1946	1949	12	Tudor 2	Long-range airliner	4 x RR Merlin	[2]
1948	1951	22	Athena	Advanced trainer	1 x RR Merlin	[3]
1949	1954	148	Shackleton MR.1/2	Maritime patrol	4 x RR Griffon	[4]
1949	1953	5	707	Delta research	1 x RR Derwent	[5]
1950	1952	6	Ashton	Research test bed	4 x RR Nene	
1952	1958	42	Shackleton MR.3	Maritime patrol	4 x RR Griffon	
1952	1959	47	Vulcan B.1	Heavy bomber	4 x BS Olympus	[6]
1958	1964	89	Vulcan B.2	Heavy bomber	4 x BS Olympus	
1960	1988	382	748/Andover	Airliner/transport	2 x RR Dart	[7]

Vulcan, Ashton and 707 all turbojet powered. **[1]** Tudor 1, 3 and 4: one example converted to 4 x RR Nene turbojets 1948 as Tudor 8. **[2]** Tudor 2 and 5 plus one-off Tudor 7 with Bristol Hercules. **[3]** Three initial aircraft, two powered by AS Mamba and one by RR Dart turboprops. **[4]** Conversions to T.4 crew trainer and AEW.2 airborne early warning picket. **[5]** 707 and 707B dorsal air intake, 707A and 'C inboard leading edge intake. Single-seat, except two-seat 707C. **[6]** Includes two prototypes, first of which was powered by RR Avons. **[7]** Detailed in Chapter 26.

Spare capacity in the factory helped swell the numbers of the jet bomber for the RAF and gave the company valuable experience in readiness for volume production of the Vulcan.

Chadwick's choice of a delta concept for the Type 698 'V-bomber' required as much data as possible before the prototype made its first flight. One answer to this pressing need was for a series of small delta-wing research aircraft to fly prior to the full-size machine, in order to better assess the aerodynamic properties. The first of five Type 707s, all powered by RR Derwents, was short lived. VX784 took to the air at Boscombe Down on 4 September 1949, piloted by Samuel Edward 'Red' Esler DFC, but it crashed twenty-six days later, killing Esler. The second machine was airborne a year later and the third, with engine intakes in the wing roots and therefore a layout very similar to the Vulcan itself, flew in June 1951. A batch of four 707Cs was also ordered, but in the end only WZ744 was completed, in 1953. The 707C was a two-seat, side-by-side, trainer that the RAF envisaged would help transition to the Vulcan, but in the end such a step-up was not needed. The table gives a chronology of the 707s and the prototype Vulcans. The 707s probably appeared too late to provide much feedback for the Vulcan but passed on considerable data for other projects. They also allowed test pilot Roland 'Roly' John Falk and others to try out the new format before strapping in to the full-scale version.

Four 707s taxiying out for a performance at the September 1953 Farnborough display. Clockwise from the front: 707B VX790, 707A WZ736, 707C WZ744 and 707A WD280. *via Tony Buttler*

Avro delta chronology

Date	Type	Serial	Status
4 Sep 1949	707	VX784	prototype; dorsal intake, fatal crash 30 Sep 1949
6 Sep 1950 envelope	707B	VX790	dorsal intake, low-speed
14 Jun 1951	707A	WD280	wing root intakes, high-speed envelope
30 Aug 1952	698	VX770	prototype Vulcan, RR Avons
20 Feb 1953	707A	WZ736	wing root intakes, high speed envelope
3 Sep 1953	698	VX777	2nd proto Vulcan, BS Olympus
1 Jul 1953	707C	WZ744	wing root intakes, two-seater
4 Feb 1955	Vulcan B.1	XA889	first production example
31 Aug 1957	698	VX777	aerodynamic prototype B.2
30 Aug 1958	Vulcan B.2	XH533	first production example

Note: 707s VX784, VX790 and WD280 maiden flights at Boscombe Down; WZ736 and WZ744 built at Bracebridge Heath and first flown at Waddington. All Vulcans flew from Woodford.

God of fire

Once recovered from the Tudor 2 disaster, Davies set to turning Chadwick's sketches into the formidable reality of the Vulcan. Stuart 'Cock' Davies was apprenticed in the automotive industry before taking a post as a draughtsman with Vickers. There he was involved in the transition of the Virginia heavy bomber from wood to the all-metal structure of the Mk.X in 1927. He joined Hawker in 1931, becoming part of Sydney Camm's team on the monoplane fighter that emerged as the Hurricane four years later.

Movement of talent within the HS consortium was made easier by early warning of job opportunities and he was offered the post of assistant chief designer at Avro, under Chadwick, in January 1936. It was an exceptional time at the company and, as mentioned earlier, he had the heavy responsibility of quickly and carefully morphing the twin-engined Manchester into the four-engined Lancaster. This was followed by the York transport and the Lincoln bomber.

With the death of his friend and mentor in 1947, Davies took the role of chief designer with a heavy heart. His first 'clean sheet' design was the Athena, but it was the Type 698 strategic jet bomber that was

The third Ashton, Mk.3 WB492, was delivered to the Royal Radar Establishment in 1951. *Avro*

his greatest creation. Davies left Avro in 1955 and his successor, Roy Ewans, took on the redesign that produced the Vulcan B.2. After Avro, Davies worked for undercarriage and propulsion specialist Dowty Rotol, rising to the managing directorship of its fuel systems division. The pull of HS remained strong and he re-joined the organisation in 1958 to 1964. Stuart Duncan Davies CBE, the man who took the

Vulcan B.1s on the assembly line at Woodford. XA896 on the right first flew on 30 January 1957. *British Aerospace*

Vulcan from paper to metal, died on 22 January 1995, aged 88.

The background of the V-bomber programme and the incredible 'solution' of ordering three different designs into production are debated within Chapter 24. Operational Requirement OR.229 was issued on 17 December 1946 seeking a replacement for the Lancaster and Lincoln. In January 1947 Specification B.35/46 was released as OR.229 was firmed up. Among the stipulations was the ability to carry a 10,000lb 'special' – atomic – weapon 1,724 miles. The Ministry of Supply accepted Avro's tender for the Type 698 delta-winged four-jet on 28 July. Twenty-six days later, Roy Chadwick was killed and Davies stepped into very big shoes.

Falk was at the helm of the prototype on 30 August 1952. Sixteen days before this the first production contract, for twenty-five B.1s, was signed. The bomber was named after the Roman god of fire on 2 October. The testing went well and the first Mk.1 was handed over to the RAF in May 1956. Even as 230 Operational Conversion Unit was coming to grips with the new bomber, Avro was working on a much more refined version to exploit the increases in power promised from the Bristol Siddeley Olympus 201s and 301s. The B.2 was far more than

a 'tweak'; it was a major redesign, with the span increasing from the B.1's 99ft to 111ft, the wing area expanding from 3,544sq ft to 3,964sq ft and the loaded weight spiralling from an estimated 170,00lb to 200,000lb. The leading edge was 'kinked' at the outer wing and the trailing edge boasted four-section elevons in place of a combination of ailerons and elevons.

The other big design challenge for the B.2 was to integrate another Avro product, the 35ft Blue Steel rocket-propelled nuclear cruise missile. From 1960 it was decided that the Vulcan would be equipped with the Douglas AGM-87 Skybolt air-launched ballistic missile, one under each wing. A B.2 flew with dummy missiles at Boscombe Down from March 1961. Although the project was cancelled in 1962, the hardpoints fitted to some of the fleet proved vital two decades later. The Falklands conflict of 1982 brought about an astounding response from what was then British Aerospace, refitting Vulcans with in-flight refuelling probes and adapting the Skybolt points for the carriage of Shrike anti-radar missiles. An urgent post-conflict requirement for tankers gave rise to the Vulcan's final iteration, the K.2, the first of which flew on 18 June 1982.

Glittering inheritance

In 1957 the future of military aviation was thrown into chaos with the Defence White Paper. Conservative minister Duncan Sandys appeared to rule out anything other than missiles to fight the wars of the future – a man far ahead of his time, as this *still* has yet to be achieved! Such wisdom helped Avro to get back into the airliner business. Lessons learned from the Tudor paid dividends as the design department conceived the robust 748 twin-turboprop aimed at a broad commercial and military customer base. The prototype had its maiden flight on 24 June 1960. Part of the HS consortium since July 1935 and a member of HS Aviation since 1959, Avro was absorbed fully on 1 July 1963, becoming a part of the Avro-Whitworth Division. HSA inherited a superb cash cow in Woodford's new product, which morphed from being the Avro 748 to the HS.748 and it is in Chapter 26 that its story is told. In 1963 the design office was already looking into turbojet-powered successors, but the 748 was the last Avro type to take to the air.

The name Avro was reused – initially by a British–Taiwanese consortium called Avro International Aerospace from January 1993 and then with the RJ derivatives of the HS.146 jetliner – see Chapter 12.

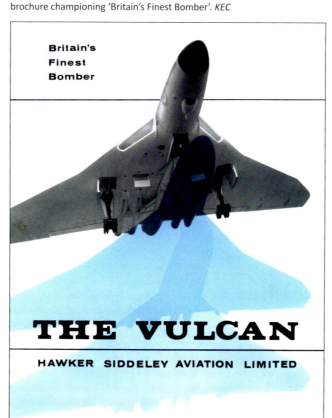

A Blue Steel-equipped Vulcan B.2 on the cover of a Hawker Siddeley brochure championing 'Britain's Finest Bomber'. *KEC*

Britain's Finest Bomber

THE VULCAN

HAWKER SIDDELEY AVIATION LIMITED

CHAPTER SEVEN

Too Much, Too Late

Beagle
1960 to 1970

'…had I known the personality and political problems which would confront the Beagle enterprise,
I would never have ventured to start it!' Sir Peter Masefield

HINDSIGHT IS A WONDERFUL, precise, thing. The author grew up hoping that Beagle was a long overdue renaissance of the British general and light aircraft industry. It was bringing a barrage of wondrous types to the party while freshening up the legacy of Auster and Miles. Like the Beatles, it ended in acrimony with the boys from the band going off to do their own things. Even the great north–south divide reared its head. It seemed that it was the nasty Tony Benn that put paid to the dynamic venture. Later I was to discover that Beagle was a very British institution, a complete and utter, self-destructing shambles even before the ink was dry on the articles of incorporation. No wonder Tom Wenham titled his exhaustive book on the company's life and times *False Dawn*.

Beagle was the brainchild of Peter Gordon Masefield (Sir Peter from 1972), who became passionate about aviation from an early age. He learned to fly while at university and joined Fairey as a draughtsman in 1935, working on the Swordfish and the Fulmar. Five years later, aged 26, he became a war correspondent, taking part in some combat missions in USAAF B-17 Flying Fortresses. Having written in the aviation press since his days at Fairey, he founded the magazine *Aeroplane Spotter*, which ran from 1940 to 1948. Lord Beaverbrook appointed him as an adviser in 1944 as plans were made for British commercial aviation in peacetime. In 1945 Masefield began a stint as civil air attaché with the British embassy in Washington DC. A directorial position with the Ministry of Civil Aviation followed in 1946, leading to employment in the state-run British European Airways (BEA). Masefield rose to be the airline's chief executive and championed the development of the Vickers Viscount. He returned to the aircraft industry in 1955, as managing director of Bristol, of which more anon.

Beyond his time at Beagle Masefield held several boardroom posts, including the British Airports Authority and British Caledonian Airways. Throughout his exceptionally varied career he also championed all sorts of societies and committees, for example the Royal Aero Club and the Brooklands Museum Trust: every day was brim full. Retiring in 1996, he died on 14 February 2006, aged 91. Working alongside Masefield at Beagle, as a production test pilot and in the marketing department, was his son Charles Beech Gordon Masefield (Sir Charles from 1997). After Beagle, Charles test piloted for Hawker Siddeley and was president of BAE Systems from 2003 to 2007.

The quote at the header comes from *Flight Path*, Masefield's autobiography, written with the help of prolific author Bill Gunston.

Key Publishing, producers of *FlyPast* – Britain's top-selling aviation monthly – operated 206 Series 2 G-FLYP from Cranfield from 1998 to 2015. It was originally delivered to the British Aircraft Corporation, as G-AVHO, in November 1967. *Duncan Cubitt – courtesy and copyright Key Publishing www.flypast.com*

Many captains of industry would argue that anyone finding themselves affronted by personal or political adversity should never have entered business. By the time he took control of Beagle, Masefield's exposure to the cut and thrust of commercial enterprises had been limited. From the beginning his undoubted fervour was no match for the ever-changing circumstances that appeared before him. His vision of founding, almost overnight, a new force in general and light aviation with an expanding 'family' of products proved the well-known adage: 'What is the first casualty of war? The plan!'

General aviation renaissance

After his time at BEA, Masefield was appointed as managing director of Bristol Aircraft at Filton on 29 August 1955. By that time the company was in a gentle slide into oblivion, with the Britannia programme mired in technical delays and the helicopter programmes running out of options. Such was the decline that the former giant became the junior partner in the British Aircraft Corporation when it was set up in 1960. In *Flight Path*, it is clear that Masefield faced a torrid time at boardroom level with apathy or opposition to thoughts about new products – the prospect of the Type 198 supersonic transport, the Concorde precursor – dominating all else. A jetliner design to take the place of the Britannia ran out of steam – de Havilland's DH.121 tri-jet was the one that attracted BEA. *Flight Path* describes the state of play: '[the firm] was reduced to drawing things that it knew it had almost no chance of actually building.' Ironically, this could also sum up much of the activity at Beagle.

From 1958 Masefield had turned his attention to general aviation. He managed to inspire William 'Bill' Strang, Bristol's chief fixed-wing designer, and Ron Woodhams to examine possible layouts for five-seat singles and twins that gelled as the Types 219 and 220 respectively. The notion of the British light aircraft industry's rebirth was gaining traction. A huge concern such as Bristol would only be interested in such a venture if there was government money to be had, and the 220 – known as the 'Masefield Twin' at Filton – was conceived with an Air Ministry operational requirement (OR) in mind. In *Flight Path*, Masefield writes about an OR to replace the Avro Anson C.19 to which he attached great significance. It is certain that within the Air Ministry there would have been thoughts about replacing the RAF's do-it-all light transport, but there was nothing formal. Masefield seems to have taken a large order – he writes of an *initial* need for up to eighty – as a 'given'.

Increasingly cheesed off with the torpor at Bristol, Masefield began to look for a backer for his scheme. A chance meeting in 1959 at Oxford's Kidlington airfield with Mike Bellhouse, chief executive of Cowley-based Pressed Steel Company (PSC), brought together a pair of kindred spirits. There was not a moment to lose; in that same year Harold Macmillan's Conservative government lifted a wide series of bans and heavy tariffs on imports. Included in this were light aircraft – a flood of types was heading for the UK, particularly from across the Atlantic.

Purchasing the rights for the Type 219 and 220 from Bristol for £1,000, Masefield resigned his post at Filton. (That would be £25,000 in present-day values, a hefty sum but in theory Beagle had a from-new design that apparently was just what the RAF was looking for.) British Executive and General Aviation Ltd was formed on 7 October 1960 with Peter Masefield at the helm. Immediately BEAGAL was referred to as Beagle and a canine theme was established. PSC was a giant in the automotive supply business, making car bodies and other sub-assemblies, but was also a major domestic refrigerator manufacturer. During World War Two PSC had sub-contracted on aviation programmes and this had continued into peacetime with the Hawker Hunter.

PSC had the leasehold on a substantial amount of land around Kidlington, including the airfield. Looking after its interests, including training and sales was a subsidiary – British Executive Air Services Ltd (BEAS); another nature-based acronym, pronounced 'Bees'. PSC was cash-rich and keen to diversify further into aviation; Bellhouse saw 'synergies' in aircraft manufacture. Kidlington seemed like the ideal location but it never became Beagle's base. Amazingly, PSC never made pressed steel components for Beagle types, although the Pup adopted the car door handles the company churned out.

Three in a bed

Beagle needed to hit the floor running and while Kidlington had many advantages, it made sense to acquire an existing manufacturer. In November 1960 Auster was snapped up. Not only was it the *only* light aviation builder of substance in the UK, since 1948 it had been an important sub-contractor to the automotive industry – PSC had a double interest in the Leicestershire company. The Rearsby factory was crying out for investment, but time was of the essence: the new outfit needed something to offer immediately and opted to stick with warmed-over 'classic' Austers in the form of the Tugmaster, Terrier and Husky.

Airedales nearing completion on the Rearsby assembly line, 1962. *Beagle*

With Cessna gaining a major foothold in the British market, work also started on a four-seat high-winged, tricycle undercarriage tourer. This resulted in the underpowered Airedale, which first flew on 16 April 1961. Production ground to a halt in mid-1963 at forty-three units – 524 fewer than its projected break even! A lot of time and money was devoted to the Beagle E3, the so-called AOP.11, a refinement of the AOP.9, which took to the air in August 1961. The Army Air Corps (AAC) was committed to a wholly rotorcraft-based fleet, but Beagle naively believed they'd settle for fixed wing, ordering both new AOP.11s and retrofit kits for existing AOP.9s. Only the prototype was built.

Throughout Beagle's existence Rearsby's capabilities were doubted or even derided. Yet it was the Leicestershire 'branch' that baled out the business: taking on the relocated 206 assembly line and making mass manufacture of the Pup a possibility. With its automotive and aviation elements, Rearsby could have been all that Beagle needed in terms of industrial real estate and heft. Not so, Beagle's sights were set in a southerly direction, on Shoreham.

The exploits of Frederick George Miles ('FG') and his younger brother George Herbert Miles are told in Chapter 28. F G Miles Ltd was a design consultancy, a plastics technology specialist and a sub-contractor with stressed-skin capabilities and operator of Shoreham aerodrome. The talented brothers were also at work on the M.114 Martlet and M.115 Merlin four-seat single and twin respectively. Both of these used extensive amounts of glass-fibre reinforced plastics (GFRP) on a metal 'base frame'. At first Beagle engaged F G Miles Ltd to create the Bristol 220-based prototype 206 on a sub-contract basis. But the Shoreham company was a logical 'target' for Beagle and on 16 February 1961 the design rights to the M.114 and M.115 and other elements of the Miles business, including the running of the aerodrome, were acquired and the brothers were employed under the Beagle-Miles banner.

The M.115 was redesignated Beagle 218 and it first flew at Shoreham on 19 August 1962. The Air Registration Board (ARB, then overseeing airworthiness certification; it became the Civil Aviation Authority in 1972) quite rightly wanted massive research and development before considering the adoption of GFRP. The Miles brothers argued that 'plastic' would give Beagle an edge on its principally American opposition. Wisely, Masefield was not prepared to commit to this; his company had neither the time nor the capital to devote to this level of pioneering. Why then was the attractive, but very challenging, 218 ever built? Having recognised this cul-de-sac, the 218 was redesigned to incorporate an all-metal airframe and was back in the skies again, as the Beagle 242, on 27 August 1964 – an incredible achievement. While the 218 and the 242 shared a basic layout, Beagle had designed and developed two *separate* airframes in the space of three years. The 242 was mothballed in 1966, but by then the horrified Miles brothers had washed their hands of Beagle and left. (FG departed in 1962, George a year later.) Vast amounts of cash and time had been consumed to no advantage.

The Miles brothers were passionate advocates of light and general aviation and so was Masefield. Clashes became a regular occurrence at Shoreham; they openly questioned Masefield's ability to run Beagle yet their own track record at running an aircraft manufacturing company was no shining example. The 206 was bitterly and overtly criticised but the brothers did successfully push the view that the prototype was too small for the task. Inevitably the 206 project was taken away from the brothers and 58-year-old Marcus Langley was appointed chief designer to see the project through. Langley, via his research consultancy Tiltman Langley Ltd, had already been 'parachuted in' to Rearsby, overseeing the Airedale in early 1961. At the same time Ron Woodhams, who had penned the Type 220 drawings at Bristol, was also engaged.

Langley cut his teeth at Shorts in 1924, after which came a procession of jobs, mostly as a draughtsman: Supermarine (from 1925), Handley Page (from 1928), Desoutter (from 1928) and Saunders-Roe (1930–31). He was at Hatfield 1931 to 1935, tutoring at the de Havilland Technical School. He joined the newly formed British Aircraft Manufacturing Company at Hanworth in 1935, eventually as chief designer his work including the Double Eagle six-seater retractable twin. Langley took the post of technical manager of Flight Refuelling Ltd at Ford in 1938. Joining up with Hessell Tiltman (see Chapter 3) the pair acted as consultants, before forming Tiltman Langley Laboratories Ltd in 1947 – later simplifying the name to Tiltman Langley Ltd.

Top left: Shoreham, looking north-east towards the River Adur. The 1936 art deco terminal is central, with the Beagle offices and 'blister' hangar to the right. *Beagle*

Bottom left: George Miles piloting M.218 G-ASCK alongside the second prototype 206, G-ARXM, wearing 'B Condition' serial G-35-62. Eight days separated their first flights, 12 and 19 August 1962, respectively. *Beagle*

Below: The Beagle 242 G-ASTX performing at Farnborough in September 1964; it had first flown the previous month. *Peter Green*

So a *third* element of the already multi-faceted concern was formed, nicknamed 'Masefield-Beagle', which functioned until the Beagle-Miles debacle was absorbed into the rest of the operation. Langley and Woodhams were 'let go' in October 1962 during the first of several cutbacks. By mid-1961 the design and technical staff had reached around 180 at Shoreham. They all occupied the same building, but each worked for one of the 'empires' with only some cross-over. At Wichita, Kansas, in 1962 giant US rival Cessna was getting by with just seventy design personnel in its non-Department of Defense ventures.

With three 'divisions' there is a temptation to regard Beagle as a large organisation, but it was a comparative minnow with many limitations and obvious flaws. Masefield thought otherwise, as he explained in *Flight Path*: '… we opened [in 1961] a small corporate head office at Sceptre House in London's Regent Street. … The outgoings each month were awesome, but with Pressed Steel behind us and careful management I had no fears. In any case, we intended soon to be selling lots of aircraft.'

Irreplaceable Anson

To return to the Bristol 220 that was the catalyst for Beagle's meandering. Predictably, the 220 – the Beagle 206 – was over-engineered, as might be expected from a concern used to the Britannia and Concorde airliners. Frantic redesign began, all the while aiming for an undefined RAF need. On 15 August 1961 the prototype, G-ARRM, had its maiden flight. *Romeo-Mike* is still extant, having been a denizen of several museums. The much-refined and enlarged second example, 206Y G-ARXM, took to the air on 12 August 1962. Six months earlier, Masefield's relentless lobbying had made headway; the Air Ministry was to order two examples for evaluation.

As the table shows, after the Anson C.19 RAF orders for light transports were sporadic and ever dwindling: indeed, since 2015 when the last of the HS.125 executive jets were withdrawn, the service has done without such machines. Not being a front-line asset, light transports and trainers tend to have long service lives, affording lots of time to consider their replacement. Years in service for the five types in question are as follows: Anson C.19 – twenty-three; de Havilland (DH) Devon C.1/C.2 – thirty-seven years; Percival Pembroke C.1 – thirty-five years; Beagle Basset CC.1 (the military 206) – ten years; Hawker Siddeley HS.125 CC.1/CC.2/CC.3 – thirty-three years. While the radial-engined Anson may have looked antiquated in 1962, by that time the youngest had only been in service

sixteen years, making them mere teenagers! The RAF's last six Ansons were retired on 28 June 1968.

Duties for the Anson during the 1950s and '60s included personnel transport (the 'top brass' preferring the Devons, Pembrokes and later the jets), moving spares, tools and supplies and taking V-bomber crews (Avro Vulcans and Handley Page Victors) to dispersed operating bases should 'the balloon' go up. It was this nuclear deterrent support role that seems to have transfixed Masefield – convinced that this was the route to huge contracts. A modicum of 'homework' would have revealed the true potential. The first Anson Mk.XIX (C.19) was delivered to the RAF in 1945, the final one in 1947. Crew trainer variants – T.20, T.21, T.22 – continued in production until 1952 and some of these were pressed into transport roles. In 1963 there were seventy-six Ansons *on charge* with the RAF, but of these upwards of forty were in store or awaiting disposal.

Bomber Command's tactic of sending off its V-bombers to dispersed bases to improve survivability in the event of a Soviet strike had all but ceased with the introduction of the Avro Blue Steel stand-off weapon in June 1962. The sophisticated cruise missile needed the infrastructure of dedicated V-bomber bases. December that year provided the death knell of the 'scatter' ploy when the Blue Steel's replacement, the Douglas GAM-87 Skybolt air-launched ballistic missile, was cancelled by the Americans. The Royal Navy was going to take on the nuclear retaliation mantle with its Polaris submarines – these became operational on 30 June 1968. The need for 'Annies' to run crews around was fading rapidly; there was no pressing need to order a replacement.

RAF Post-Anson Light Transports

Type	Total	Delivered	Retired	Notes
de Havilland Devon C.1	36	1947 to 1949	1984	[1]
Percival Pembroke C.1	44	1953 to 1958	1988	[2]
Beagle Basset CC.1	22	1965 to 1966	1974	[3]
Hawker Siddeley HS.125 CC.1	6	1971	1994	[4]
Hawker Siddeley HS.125 CC.2	2	1973	1998	
Hawker Siddeley HS.125 CC.3	6	1982 to 1984	2015	

[1] Military version of the Dove; does not include four C.1s delivered in the 1950s for use by test and trials establishments or Royal Navy Sea Devons. [2] Includes six special fit C(PR).1s. Does not include Royal Navy Sea Prince comms and crew trainer versions. [3] Including two pre-series 206Zs used for test, trials and the Empire Test Pilots School. The second 206Z, XS743, soldiered on at Boscombe Down, carrying out its last flight on 7 November 2014. [4] Does not include the Dominie T.1 crew trainer or a former civilian Series 1 used for test and trials 1970 to 1992.

The fourth Basset CC.1, XS768, alongside Anson C.19/2 VM325, circa 1965. The Anson entered service with 4 Ferry Pool at Hawarden in the spring of 1947 and was struck off charge in September 1968: it survives with a museum in Pembrokeshire. The Beagle was taken on charge in July 1965 and was sold off in July 1974: it was wrecked on a transatlantic delivery to a civilian Paraguayan owner the following year. *KEC*

Achieving the impossible

The Ministry of Aviation (MoA) in part functioned as the purchasing agent for the Air Ministry. (In 1964 the Air Ministry fused into the Ministry of Defence and MoA was subsumed into the Ministry of Technology – 'Min Tech'.) MoA also existed to promote Britain's industry. Ordering Beagles for the RAF would provide a real shot in the arm for the new company, but MoA could not impose on the Air Ministry. Beagle's hopes for a large order of 206s fell between two stools. From the RAF's point of view, Beagle was a 'start-up' with no track record; to be sure of longevity of product support a well-established supplier was essential. Sniffing possible orders, Shorts realised that any procurement would be in small numbers and so an off-the-shelf type, built under licence, was the only sensible approach. Shorts had an agreement with the US manufacturer Beech and it examined the Twin Bonanza and the larger Queen Air – an Anglicized version of the latter got as far as preliminary design status, as the PD.58. DH was in pole position, it was still building the Dove – the civil version of the Devon – and the Series 8 would seamlessly settle in alongside the earlier models the RAF had taken. (The last Dove was handed over to a customer in September 1967.)

The Air Ministry was not impressed with Beagle's infrastructure, and with good reason. Shoreham was ramshackle, Rearsby was not much better but did have the potential for a properly laid out assembly line. MoA was keen to hand on the lease of Christchurch in Dorset where DH was busy vacating the former Airspeed factory to centralise on Hatfield. Cash-strapped Beagle declined – it was stuck with Shoreham and Rearsby. Consideration was given by the MoA to treat Beagle as a design house with one of the 'biggies' – the established manufacturers – making Bassets for the RAF. Boulton Paul, Shorts and Westland were all considered, but the idea went no further. Eventually, it was agreed to construct RAF Bassets at a reconfigured Rearsby and the rudimentary 'production line' at Shoreham was moved lock, stock and jig to Leicestershire. Boulton Paul picked up the contract to build the wings for all Rearsby 206s.

On 6 May 1963 MoA announced a contract for twenty Bassets along with mutterings that there might be another thirty or so in due course. The order had not been contested by the rest of the industry: Masefield had gone through hoops to achieve this result, no mean achievement in the circumstances. Yet he was not celebrating, he was mortified. The 'balance sheet' for the already wildly overspent 206 was reliant on at least seventy-plus RAF examples, ordered from the beginning. The deal was fixed price and with performance guarantees. Beagle was about to discover what a harrowing roller coaster meeting RAF requirements would be, and it is to that subject we must turn.

Prevaricate and inflate

Throughout the dealings with the MoA and the RAF, Beagle constantly complained that the goalposts was always being moved, causing considerable delay and cost. A battered copy of the MoA's *Aircraft Specification C.238 D&P (Issue 2),* originally issued to Beagle on 1 October 1963, makes interesting reading both in terms of the travails at Shoreham and what the British industry at large has always faced. Thankfully the fading pink card cover carries the wording 'UNCLASSIFIED' in red ink all over it. Created on a rotary ink duplicator, the document refers to the 206R with a handwritten amendment calling it a 'Bassett [sic] CC Mk.1'. Inside is an appendix charting Air Staff Requirement 379 of 25 April 1963 – the nitty-gritty of what was expected from Beagle. The circulation list notes seventy-two copies to forty-four separate 'addresses', including the ministry at St Giles Court, London, the Admiralty and the ARB.

Spread through the stapled pages are more than fifty amendments to the requirements, the last dated 20 September 1965. Most of these changes take the form of an appendix, others are carefully cut out strips of paper from a duplicator attached by clear sticky tape – long since discoloured and lacking in adhesion – to the appropriate paragraph, some are written in blue or green ballpoint pen. Examples show what any design office responding to the whims of such a high-powered customer had to juggle with. The provision of a Walter Kidde continuous fire detector system in each engine nacelle was estimated to increase the weight by 10lb and reduce the guaranteed range by 14 nautical miles. (The weight increase is flagged as 'provisional', which seems optimistic.) The upholstery did not escape scrutiny: the seats were changed from grey to dark blue leather – with no impact on weight or range. Dated 19 February 1965 and running to four close-typed sheets dropped into the document were details of additional instruments (eg. a Sperry horizon gyro) and radios (eg Plessey UHF, Cossor identification, friend or foe). There are estimations of the increased electric power required, including peak loading. This lot added 450lb to the airframe and was estimated to reduce the guaranteed range by a whopping 601 nautical miles.

While the colour of the seats would involve no more than a look through a book of swatches, any additional change to a system was a case of 'back to the drawing board'. The introduction of fire detectors, for example, would require trial-and-error installation, creation of mountings, rerouting wiring, recalculating weight and balance, new drawings necessitating amendments to both the assembly procedure and the supply chain. Although MoA might absorb some costs through methods such as 'embodiment loans' (sourcing and paying for third-party items – eg. engines, radios) or expanding the budget, the manufacturer was faced with additional design and process costs, programme delays and cash flow nightmares. Such prevarications would be regarded as par for the course by the seasoned design staff at Fairey in the late 1920s, trying to achieve what became the Hendon heavy bomber, and the British Aerospace (BAE Systems from 1999) team grappling with the Nimrod MRA.4 maritime patroller, which was axed in 2010. They would have considered the changes to the Basset programme as chickenfeed; just day-to-day occurrences in British defence procurement.

Costly diversions

By the late 1950s the ever-inventive Wg Cdr Kenneth Horatio Wallis was convinced that light autogyros represented a multi-purpose platform for pleasure, commercial and military use. He acquired a kit of a US-designed Bensen B7, G-APUD, which he flew for the first time from Shoreham on 23 May 1959. (*Uniform-Delta* is preserved by The Aeroplane Collection.) Wallis used Shoreham for his test flying with the blessing of F G Miles and the two entered into an informal relationship regarding potential developments.

Wallis schemed a series of patents, including an offset gimbal rotor head providing exceptional stability and a spin-up drive for the blades. On 2 August 1961 Wallis flew the prototype WA-116 Agile, G-ARRT, from Boscombe Down. *Romeo-Tango* was a completely original design and formed the basis of a family that followed up to the late 1980s. With no knowledge of rotorcraft, Beagle took the WA-116 under its umbrella and pitched it for OR 353 seeking to evaluate autogyros for use as 'local theatre' reconnaissance and liaison for the AAC. Seduced by the prospect of another military contract, from the spring of 1962 parts for six WA-116s were created at Shoreham, using G-ARRT as a pattern. It transpired that only one machine was considered a purchase, two others were for loan only. The first Beagle-built WA-116, XR942, had its debut at Shoreham on 10 May 1962 and was wrecked forty-eight hours later. The next example, also painted as XR942, appeared two months later, followed by three more; the sixth never flew.

The second WA-116 to wear the serial XR942 with a streamlined nacelle at Shoreham in the spring of 1963. *Beagle*

In *The Lives of Ken Wallis – Engineer and Aviator Extraordinaire*, biographer Ian Hancock writes that: 'the WA-116 was fully certificated at some expense to Beagle in expectation of securing orders but when the [AAC] trials were conducted [during the winter of 1962–1963 at Middle Wallop] the aircraft was encumbered with a heavy valve radio taken from a tank plus 'wet' batteries.' The inappropriate radio frustrated Wallis, but this was eclipsed by a string of defects reported as the AAC quickly realised that the autogyro had no place on a battlefield. Beagle's ignorance of military needs doomed the project to be a mere interlude. Although a civil demonstrator, G-ASDY, was built, Hancock notes that: 'Beagle's interest had been solely in a military application and they were not convinced that any likely civil application would justify production, so their support lapsed.' Wallis went his own way in 1964.

Beagle is thought to have spent a cool £50,000 on the venture that was probably always just academic interest to AAC tacticians. In Chapter 5, the company's talented chief designer, Ronald Edward 'Dickie' Bird, was recorded as leaving Rearsby bound for F G Miles Ltd in 1959. He joined the short-lived Beagle-Miles and Beagle 'proper' the following year. His main task was design manager responsible for achieving the 206, but the WA-116 and the Brantly B-2 helicopter (see below) was also dropped on his desk, further watering down the time available for what was the founding product. In 1965 Bird took the ferry to the Isle of Wight and signed up with Britten-Norman. We will continue his 'CV' under that heading.

There was another flirtation with rotorcraft. In 1963 the AAC was involved in another evaluation, seeking a two-seat 'ultralight' helicopter to replace the Saro Skeeter. PSC subsidiary BEAS was the UK agent for the American Brantly B-2 and it and the Hughes 269 were pitched against each other at Boscombe Down and later Idris in Libya. At Shoreham plans were put forward to build the B-2 under licence, should it win. The well-proven and reliable Bell 47G-3B-4 was eventually chosen, manufactured by specialists Westland as the Sioux AH.1 for the AAC and HT.2 for the RAF. Thankfully, another diversion into unknown waters had passed Shoreham by.

Costly orphan

A rather reluctant RAF accepted the first of twenty Basset CC.1s in 1965 and their career was pock-marked with maintenance and technical problems. The fleet was withdrawn in 1974, when a 'life' of twenty-five-plus years would have been more in order. Never happy with the type, the RAF was faced with an 'orphan' after Beagle collapsed in 1970. If a 'parent' could not be found to look after design authority and product support it would be prudent to retire the Bassets. Scottish Aviation adopted the Basset and carried out modifications and overhauls until it was clear that the RAF's diminishing light transport needs and the ever-spiralling cost of making small batches of spares had brought its career to an end.

The first civil customer for a 206 Series 1 was Rolls-Royce – licence manufacturers of the type's 310hp Continental GIO-470As – on 13 May 1965. This was followed by ten more before the Series 2 was introduced. This was very early in the expected life of a design to be introducing the 'B-model' but Beagle was rapidly realising the type's limitations. Supercharged GTSIO-520Cs of 340hp were introduced and a plethora of other refinements, the most obvious being the direct-entry air stairs requiring yet another major revision of the fuselage. All this added to the costs of an already over-burdened programme. The manufacturing 'process' was shambolic: Rearsby built 206s, Shoreham fitted them out, but sometimes, so did Rearsby. Things were so hand-to-mouth that 'slave' engines were fitted at one airfield to ferry an airframe; these were then removed so that another machine could be flown.

It was clear that greater seating capacity would help sales and in late 1968 a Series 2 was converted to an aerodynamic prototype of the ten-seat Series 3, featuring a 'solid' enlarged rear fuselage grafted over the original contours. A fully engineered prototype, which turned out to be the last 206 built, had its maiden flight on 21 August 1969. This was no 'tweak'; it required major reconfiguration and restressing, fitting out and certification. Production of all variants of the 206 came to seventy-nine units, making an estimated loss in the region of £3.5 million.

The 206 assembly line at Rearsby during the summer of 1966. In the foreground is Series 1 B.039, which first flew in July 1966 as G-ATYC and was put directly into storage. Note the Pup fuselage mock-up on the right. *Beagle*

Stylish brochure for the 206, featuring artwork of the second prototype, G-ARXM. *KEC*

At last, a winner

Beagle's last product was a real winner, going on to have a legacy lasting into the 1980s and to the acclaim of the RAF – but with another manufacturer. As with the twin-engined Miles M.115, the M.114 trainer/tourer was reconfigured as the all-metal M.117 and then became the B.121 Pup. John Larroucau led the design of this machine, which left little to its Miles days. Considerable attention was paid to using existing components – including those PSC door handles – to streamline manufacture and keep the costs down. From day one the Pup could take a range of engines and power output and had the potential to be transformed into a military trainer with comparative ease. With Beagle from the start, Belgian-born Larroucau had cut his design teeth with

Avro from 1955, working on what became the HS.748 twin turboprop. At the collapse of Beagle he left to join the British Aircraft Corporation at Filton in 1970 on the Concorde project, ending his design career with Scottish Aviation at Prestwick on the reborn Jetstream 31.

The first Pup flew at Shoreham on 8 April 1967 and quickly attracted a promising backlog of orders. Again, the ad hoc nature of the business was apparent. Pup fuselages and wings were built at Rearsby for final assembly and flight test at Shoreham. But circumstances meant that eight Pups were finished off at Rearsby despite the duplication of effort. A military version, the B.121T, later the B.125 Bulldog, made its debut on 19 May 1969. Scottish Aviation took over development and the Bulldog's story is told in Chapter 33.

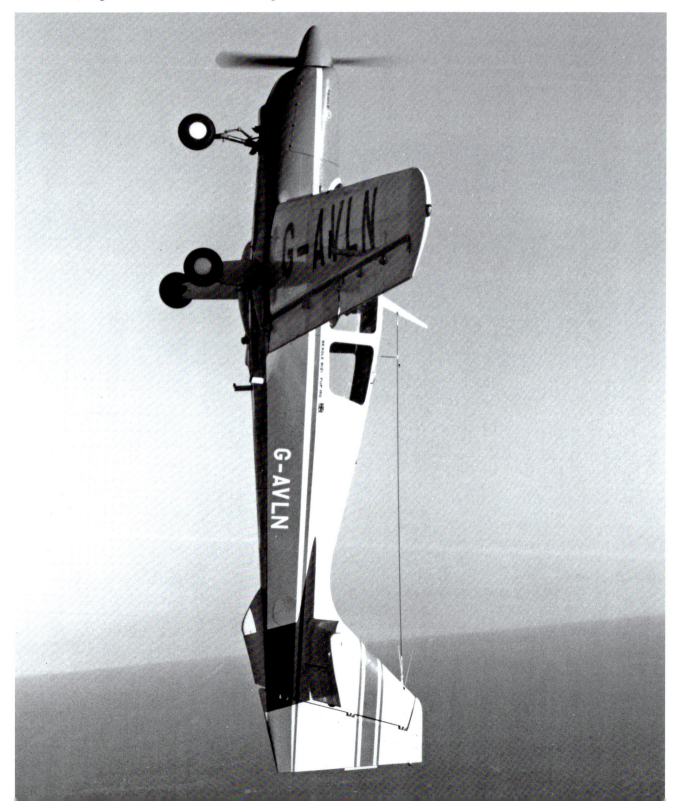

Above: Front cover of a Pup 100 and 150 brochure handed out in 1968 by agents Peter Clifford Aviation, based at Kidlington, Oxford. It featured an image of the third Pup, G-AVLN, during trials in Switzerland in 1968. *KEC*

Right: Peter Masefield showing Minister of Technology Tony Benn around Rearsby in January 1969. *Beagle*

In February 1965 Beagle approached the Labour government for £600,000 to keep the 206 Series 2 going. By then, PSC was less than enamoured with its protégée and in July it became part of the British Motor Corporation. BMC had no wish to be a 'sugar-daddy' to an ailing aviation business and Beagle was left out in the cold. This is where Tony Benn MP, Minister of Technology from 1966 to 1970, came into the plot. On 12 December 1966, the government took over Beagle and in July 1968 it became a Min Tech micro-managed company. The following year Shoreham turned to HMG asking for a further £6 million. As the Americans would say, 'Do the math'; that was £120 million in today's values, *ten times* what was sought only three years before! There was no way that Beagle could be considered a 'strategic industry' that needed protection for the nation's security. Continued support of the RAF's Basset fleet was no argument either. The inevitability of receivership came in December 1969 and Beagle was wound up the following month.

George Miles reappeared in an attempt to buy the carcass, but eventually withdrew. Shoreham aerodrome was readopted by the councils of Brighton, Hove and Worthing on 15 May 1971; Auster product support went to Hants and Sussex Aviation; and, as already

mentioned, the Bulldog embarked on a new life in Scotland. Beagle's consistently profitable sub-contract business was sold off to C F Taylor Ltd of Christchurch, which had been in that line of work since 1956. Taylor also acquired the rights to the Beagle name, which is why the winged diamond logo can be found on the sides of its premises today along with the name Beagle Technology Group. The Christchurch factory is a distant reminder of the last British major builder of light aircraft that fell on its self-blunted sword.

Beagle

From	To	Total	Name/Designation	Type	Engine(s)	Notes
1961	1963	43	Airedale	Tourer	1 x Lycoming O-360	
1961	1969	79	B.206	Light transport	2 x Continental IO-470	[1]
1962	-	5	WA.116	Gyroplane	1 x McCulloch	
1962	-	1	M.218	Tourer/Trainer	2 x Continental O-300	[2]
1964	-	1	B.242	Tourer/Trainer	2 x Continental IO-360	[2]
1967	1971	175	Pup	Tourer/Trainer	1 x Continental O-200	[3]
1969	-	1	Bulldog	Military trainer	1 x Lycoming IO-360	[4]

For the Auster-derived Husky series, Terrier, Tugmaster and 'AOP.11' (A.115) see Chapter 5. [1] Including 22 Basset CC.1 light transports for the RAF and one 'pure' Series 3 ten-seater. [2] Composite construction M.218 extensively – if not totally – rebuilt in conventional all-metal guise as B.242. [3] Includes seven airframes fitted out and flown by other concerns after the collapse. [5] Two airframes built at Shoreham, only the prototype was flown by Beagle, second example by Scottish Aviation – see Chapter 33.

Opposite: Dynamic view of Pup 150 G-AVLN in its element, February 1968. At the time of publication, this machine was still going strong, based at Sywell. *Beagle*

CHAPTER EIGHT

If at First You Don't Succeed

Beardmore
1913 to 1928

'the all-metal Beardmore Inflexible was probably the most impressive and useless aeroplane in the world…earning it the nickname "Impossible"' Harald Penrose

IF THE NAME BEARDMORE springs to mind as an aircraft manufacturer, the chances are that one word will dominate: Inflexible. Appearing in 1928, the huge tri-motor took three years to construct and boasted a wingspan that was nearly 12ft greater than that of a Boeing 707. That's certainly memorable, but Beardmore was a pioneer in shipborne aviation and that includes lobbying for the concept of a full-length flight deck for carriers and creating the first so equipped, HMS *Argus*, in 1917.

William Beardmore and Company was founded in 1886 by the man of the same name, who became Lord Invernairn in 1914. Headquartered at Dalmuir on the River Clyde west of Glasgow, it produced steel forgings, ships of all kinds, naval artillery, armour plate and motor vehicles. In 1912 Beardmore signed a licence agreement for the 120hp, 6-cylinder in-line Austro-Daimler designed by Ferdinand Porsche, later immortalised by the Volkswagen 'Beetle' and classy sports cars. This alliance was not happenstance: it was the first move to get into aviation. Samuel Franklin Cody had won the 1912 British military trials with his biplane powered by an Austro-Daimler. There was bound to be demand for this engine and the Beardmore Aero Engine Ltd of Parkhead, Glasgow, was established.

At Dumfries, motor car manufacturer Arrol-Johnston Ltd, wholly owned by Beardmore, geared up to manufacture British versions of the Austro-Daimler under managing director Thomas Pullinger. There were problems with reliability and power and Frank Halford was brought in to cure these in 1916. Before long, the engine was developing 160hp and later 230hp. To honour its protagonists, the engine was known as the BHP, for Beardmore, Halford, Pullinger and not, as is often cited, brake horse power. Galloway Engineering was founded as a subsidiary to build the BHP as the Adriatic and Armstrong Siddeley adopted it as the basis for its Puma. Beardmore produced a series of aero engines – see the table.

Beardmore came to a deal with Deutsche Flugzeug Werke of Leipzig in 1914, purchasing a DFW B.II military biplane to act as a pattern. This did not arrive until the summer and soon any plans in that direction were quashed by events. With the outbreak of war Dalmuir and later Dumfries became sub-contractors – see the table. Across the Clyde at Inchinnan an airship factory was established, where Beardmore built the rigid R27, R34 and R36 between 1919 and 1921. The airship works provided an ideal place to erect the nine Handley Page V/1500 bombers completed under sub-contract.

The first Inverness, N183, beached at Felixstowe after its delivery flight from Denmark on 18 September 1925. *KEC*

William Beardmore/Galloway aero engines

Name, Type/Format	From	Application*	Notes
Austro-Daimler, 6-cyl in-lines	1915	AW FK.8	[1]
BHP, 6-cy in-line/Adriatic	1916	Airco DH.4	[1] [2]
Atlantic, V-12	1918	HP V/1500	
Simoon, 8-cyl in-line	1922	Blackburn T.4	
Typhoon, 6-cyl in-line	1923	Avro 549	
Tornado, 8 cyl in-line diesel	1929	R101 (airship)	

* Typical, or only, use. [1] See narrative. [2] Also developed by Siddeley-Deasy as the Puma.

William Beardmore sub-contracts

Type	Total	From	To	Notes
R A/c Factory B.E.2c	120	1915	1916	
Wight Type 840 floatplane	32	1915	1916	[1]
Nieuport 12	70	1916	1917	
Sopwith Pup	50	1916	1917	[2]
Sopwith 2F1 Camel	140	1917	1918	[3]
Handley Page V/1500	20	1918	1919	[4]

Arrol-Johnstone sub-contracts

Type	Total	From	To	Notes
Sopwith 2F1 Camel	50	1918	1919	[5]

[1] Twenty completed and flown, remainder engineless spare airframes. [2] Last of batch finished as WB.III prototype. [3] 'Ship's Camel'; ten from contract transferred to Arrol-Johnstone. [4] Nine V/1500s flown, 11 despatched as airframe spares to Handley Page. [5] 'Ship's Camel'; ten 'sub-let' from Beardmore, remainder direct contract.

Shipborne experience

By 1916 both Beardmore and Arrol-Johnston were making Sopwith 2F1 'Ship's Camels' and an aviation department was set up at Dalmuir under Lt George Tilghman Richards. Cedric Lee had engaged Richards in 1911 to help exploit the patent he had acquired for an annular – circular – wing. Three distinct Lee-Richards Annular types emerged: a tractor biplane in 1911, a biplane glider in 1912 and three monoplanes during 1913 and early 1914. The first monoplane, a two-seater, was constructed at Shoreham and after considerable modification flew well. Trials ceased with the onset of the Great War.

By 1916 Richards was a member of the Royal Navy volunteer reserve and his Lee-Richards pedigree led to a posting to Dalmuir as the Admiralty's inspector of aircraft. It was not long before Richards was appointed as the company's chief aeronautical designer and he resigned his commission. The WB.I two-seat long-range bomber had a span of 61ft 6in – long wings were going to become a Beardmore hallmark. The prototype had its maiden flight at Inchinnan on 20 September 1916 and its undercarriage collapsed on landing. It was rebuilt, but did not enter production. Richards thought the B.E.2's greatest defect was the placing of the observer in front of the pilot and devised a replacement. The WB.II of 1917 put the observer in the back with a machine gun. It attracted no orders and a civil trainer/tourer version, the WB.IIB, appeared in 1920 but also remained a one-off.

Two more original designs came from Richards's drawing board in 1917; both radical and destined to remain prototypes. To give the pilot of the WB.IV exceptional view, he placed the 200hp Hispano-Suiza inside the fuselage, driving the tractor propeller via an extension shaft, the cockpit was high up in front of the upper wing. Utilising the upper wing and tail surfaces of the WB.IV, the WB.V was created around a French Puteaux 37mm cannon that fired through the propeller shaft. Two examples were flown, on 3 December 1917 and 20 February 1918, but the project was terminated.

Sub-contracting the Sopwith Pup and the Camel gave Richards great experience in the specialist world of shipborne flying. The Pup was rethought to create the WB.III, Beardmore's most successful aircraft with a production run of 100. The final Dalmuir-built Pup was modified to the new configuration with a lengthened fuselage incorporating flotation

Displayed at the Imperial War Museum in London is Beardmore-built 2F1 Camel N6812. Launched off a lighter towed by HMS *Redoubt* on 11 August 1918, this aircraft, piloted by Lt S D Culley, shot down Zeppelin L53. *Ken Ellis*

Above: The second WB.III, N6101, an SB.3F variant with foldable undercarriage. This machine entered service at East Fortune in July 1917 for use on the seaplane tender HMS *Manxman. KEC*

Right: The unfortunate WB.X G-EAQJ at Martlesham Heath in August 1920. *Peter Green Collection*

gear, full-length inter-plane struts at the centre section and no 'stagger' on the wings and wing folding. To make ditching less fraught the SB.3D version had a jettisonable undercarriage. Richards also devised the SB.3F with folding main gear, allowing ease of stowage below decks: it is thought that only two WB.IIIs were so fitted.

Revival and decline

As already mentioned, the WB.II was offered for commercial use in 1920 while Richards looked for new business. The WB.IX got as far as the construction phase, but was not completed. It was a ten-passenger amphibian to have been powered by a quartet of Adriatics driving two wing-mounted propellers via shafts and gears. Using his knowledge of airship structural techniques, Richards schemed the WB.X, which was completed as a single-seater but had the capability to carry four or five passengers within a deepened forward fuselage. During the summer of 1920 the Aeroplane and Armament Experimental Establishment (A&AEE) at Martlesham Heath was to host a competition for civil aircraft with £64,000 in prizes for the most promising designs. (That was enough to fund a dozen aircraft programmes in the 1920s.)

Construction of the WB.X encountered many problems and it was not ready as the Martlesham deadline loomed. It was taken by rail to the Suffolk airfield, assembled and tested. It flew just the once, on 16 August 1920, returning with the 185hp Beardmore's radiator, buried in the centre section, inoperative. There was no replacement to be had and the WB.X was withdrawn. Also competing was Avro with its Type 547 four-passenger triplane powered by a 160hp Beardmore. Avro test pilot Harold Hamersley, who had carried out the triplane's first flight in February 1920, is quoted in Harald Penrose's *British Aviation – The Adventuring Years* that after the WB.X's test flight it was apparent that: 'somebody [had] mislaid the centre of gravity and the [WB.X] was only safe to fly as a single-seater.' Enough was enough; Lord Invernairn closed the aviation department. Richards resigned and took up a post with Martinsyde – which see – just before that venture packed in. After that Richards tried to get the Air Ministry interested in annular wings, but to no avail.

The smallest...

After a four-year gap Beardmore returned to building aeroplanes, in 1924. Thirty-year-old William 'Bill' Stancliffe Shackleton was appointed as chief designer and his first project was a two-seat ultralight to compete in the Air Ministry's Light Aeroplane Trials to be held at Lympne in September and October. Shackleton began work in 1916 in the drawing office of Blériot and Spad Ltd at Addlestone in Surrey, which was renamed the Air Navigation and Engineering Company (ANEC) in 1919. Shackleton conceived the ANEC I single-seat ultralight, which competed in the 1923 Lympne trials, and followed this up with the two-seat ANEC II for the following year's event. More or less as the ink was dry on the ANEC II plans, Shackleton accepted the job at Dalmuir and produced the WB.XXIV Wee Bee, of very similar format to the ANEC II. The 840lb all-up weight Wee Bee (from William Beardmore's initials) was powered by a 32hp Bristol Cherub 1,095cc twin-cylinder, which gave a top speed of 87mph. The 1924 competition should have seen rival entries from the same designer, but the ANEC II had technical difficulties and was withdrawn. The Wee Bee was the event's overall winner, netting £2,000.

Commissioned from the Latvian government in 1925, the WB.XXVI fighter was very advanced. Bracing wires were dispensed with and replaced by streamlined struts. The fuselage 'floated', suspended between the top and bottom wings in a similar manner to the Bristol F.2B Fighter. The radiator for the Rolls-Royce Eagle IX was mounted on the leading edge centre section of the lower wing. It was not greeted well by its customer and was returned to Dalmuir and quietly forgotten.

...and the largest

Negotiations with Dr Adolph Rohrbach in 1924 led to the setting up of the Light-Metal Aircraft Company, an Anglo-German concern to oversee Beardmore's use of patents held by Rohrbach Metall Flugzeugbau. It was agreed to produce two large flying boats and an even larger landplane transport to champion Rohrbach's stressed skin all-Duralumin construction and high aspect ratio wings with box spars. Both projects would have input from each organisation. Responsibility for the transport lay with Shackleton's team at Dalmuir: this was designated BeRo.1 and to emphasize its strength it was called the Inflexible. The flying boats remained the domain of Rohrbach, carried the German designation Ro IV and were described as 'four-seater open-sea reconnaissance flying boats'. In Britain the two 'boats were known as the Beardmore-Rohrbach BeRo.2 Inverness.

Parts for the flying boats were manufactured in Berlin but supply of these machines would be in breach of the conditions of the 1919 Treaty of Versailles that was imposed on the defeated Germany. Rohrbach had a subsidiary, Rohrbach Metall-Aeroplan, in Copenhagen so that Allied Control Commission could be circumvented. The Invernesses were assembled, had their Napier Lion engines fitted, test flown and were delivered from Copenhagen – Britain was receiving a Danish product! The first example was ferried from Copenhagen via the island of Texel off the Netherlands to the Marine Aircraft Experimental Establishment (MAEE) at Felixstowe on 18 September 1925. The second appeared in November 1928. Neither of these impressed the evaluation teams at MAEE.

Construction of the Inflexible dragged on, taking three years; during this time the giant took on the nickname 'Impossible'. Co-ordinating such a large and technically challenging project took a huge toll on Shackleton and he had to stand down in 1926. Sqn Ldr Rollo Amyatt Wolseley de Haga Haig AFC took over the programme's management. Joining the design team was Swiss-born Helmuth Johannes Stieger. Haig and Stieger went on to set up the Monospar Wing Company, which became General Aircraft.

Shackleton sailed to Australia in January 1928, going on to design light aircraft for Larkin Aircraft of Melbourne. Returning to the UK in 1930, he teamed up with Australian Lee Murray and formed Forward View Aeroplanes Ltd. They devised the Shackleton-Murray SM.1 tandem two-seat pusher parasol monoplane and commissioned Airspeed to build it. It flew in early 1933, but remained a one-off. Shackleton went on to form his own company, W S Shackleton Ltd, which specialised in the supply of aircraft to Australia and acted as agent for American aviation companies in the UK. During the war he was involved in development work for the Ministry of Aircraft Production. Post-war, W S Shackleton Ltd became a famous aviation sales outfit, based at Baginton.

By the time the Inflexible was ready Lord Invernairn had lost all patience with aeroplanes and for the second – and final – time he axed the Beardmore aviation department. The 'Impossible' was a monster with a span of 157ft 6in, a length of 82ft including the servo-rudder on its outriggers and a loaded weight of 37,000lb – 16½ tons. It was decided that Martlesham Heath was the best place to test the giant and it was taken there by ship and road – shades of the WB.X of 1920. Sqn Ldr Jack Noakes AFC MM was in command of the A&AEE's 'B' Squadron and the honours for the debut outing fell to him. After a prolonged period of ground runs and 'straights' he took the 'Impossible' up for its maiden flight on 5 March 1928. It caused a sensation when it appeared at the Hendon display in June that year. The monster was woefully underpowered and it was dismantled in 1930 – a 7ft 4in diameter main undercarriage wheel continues to make jaws drop in the Science Museum in London.

A motor car and a biplane provide scale for the awesome Inflexible at Martlesham Heath, 1929. *Peter Green Collection*

Beardmore

From	To	Total	Name/Designation	Type	Engine(s)	Notes
1916	-	1	WB.I	Bomber	1 x BHP Adriatic	[1]
1917	-	2	WB.II	Armed recce	1 x Beardmore	
1917	1918	100	WB.III	Shipborne fighter	1 x Le Rhone	[2]
1917	-	1	WB.IV	Shipborne fighter	1 x Hispano-Suiza	
1917	1918	2	WB.V	Shipborne fighter	1 x Hispano-Suiza	
1920	-	1	WB.X	Light transport	1 x Beardmore	
1924	-	1	WB.XXIV Wee Bee	Ultralight	1 x Bristol Cherub	
1926	-	1	WB.XXVI	2-seat fighter	1 x RR Eagle	[3]
1928	-	1	BeRo.1 Inflexible	Experimental	3 x RR Condor	

All tractor biplanes except WB.XXIV and Inflexible, tractor monoplanes. **[1]** Also reported referred to as the R.E.12. **[2]** Built in two versions: SB.3D with jettisonable undercarriage and SB.3F with folding undercarriage for stowage. **[3]** Ordered by Latvian government.

CHAPTER NINE

Sand-Scratching

**Blackburn
1909 to 1960**

'Go and help Bob, he's playing with an aeroplane.' *George Blackburn, Robert Blackburn's father*

'I N 1909, in the works of the Leeds engineering firm of Thomas Green and Sons Ltd, there was a young apprentice named Harry Goodyear. [The company built agricultural rollers, lawn mowers and similar equipment.] He was a willing lad, certainly not disposed to question the instructions he was given one day by the general manager himself. "Go and help Bob," he was told. "He's playing with an aeroplane."' The general manager's name was George Blackburn and Bob was his son.

Robert Blackburn – Bob – did not keep a diary, so the tentative aerial expeditions by the 24-year-old most likely took place in April 1909, very definitely on the sands at Marske-by-the-Sea, near Redcar on the Yorkshire coast. 'It was … an inconspicuous beginning to Robert's aeronautical career. His machine taxied bravely up and down the sands, and now and then succeeded in making short hops – the occasional absence of tyre marks in the sand left no room for doubt on this point. But this was not flying and Robert Blackburn knew it. "Sand-scratching", he called it.'

Young Blackburn's first session was terminated when the monoplane hit a hole and a wing dug in: he was hurled from the craft, but only his dignity took a knock. (To avoid confusion with the company he created, Robert Blackburn is RB from here on.) When RB came back to the workshop in Leeds with his damaged monoplane, Harry was waiting for him and asked: 'Shall I go back to Greens now?' 'No,' said the pioneer, 'I'd like you to stay with me. I'm going to make a business of this!'

These extracts come from a delightful, and now very rare, sixty-page little hardback entitled *The Blackburn Story 1909–1959*,

published by the company to celebrate a half-century of endeavour. The founder's prediction was quite right: he created an enterprise that carried his name until 1963. A corporate acquisition in 1951 must have given RB great satisfaction: Thomas Green and Sons Ltd, the firm his father had managed in 1909. Still based in Leeds, the business fitted well within Blackburn's expanding agricultural offshoot.

The sand-scratching continued in 1910, but from the extensive beach at Filey, further down the coast. There RB lived with his work, occupying a small bungalow and 'hangar' at the top of Low Cliffs; his aircraft could be winched up or down an adjacent slipway. During 1912 and 1913 Bob employed Harold 'Harry' Blackburn as a test pilot: he was no relation but it is likely at this time that the boss became referred to as 'RB' and the moniker stuck.

Buccaneer S.2B XV332 over the sands of Lossiemouth's eastern beach in 1993 during its final days with 208 Squadron. Built in 1967 for the Fleet Air Arm, it was a reserve for the Iraq War in 1991 and was painted in 'desert' colours with the nose art 'Dirty Harriet'. On 5 April 1994 it was ferried to Marham for use as an instructional airframe, the last ever RAF Buccaneer flight. *British Aerospace*

Harry Goodyear started to work at 'Greens' in 1903. He might have had doubts when he was sent off to help the gaffer's son but it was a pivotal instruction for the 19-year-old. He stayed with RB until 1912, when he crossed the Pennines to join Avro. During the first half of 1914 Harry left Avro to become engineer to Bentfield 'Benny' Charles Hucks, a freelance test and display pilot, who had flown for RB during 1911 to 1912. Harry was back with Avro by July 1914, but the ties to RB were strong and he returned to Leeds in 1915. The lean post-Armistice years forced him into the motor vehicle industry. With another war looming, Harry's talents were in demand again with Blackburn and he took on a managerial role from 1937 to 1947. After that he went back to vehicles and retired in 1955.

Improve and diversify

Graduating with a degree in engineering at Leeds, RB worked in France in 1908 and it was there that the course of his life was set. He was transfixed watching Wilbur Wright demonstrating the Flyer biplane at Le Mans and studied the French pioneers at the Aero Show held in the Grand Palais, Paris. George backed his son and helped him establish a workshop in Leeds. Two of RB's brothers, Charles and Norman, also pitched in. Charles was commercial manager by the mid-1920s and Norman managed the RAF reserve school from 1924 and all aspects of the Sherburn in Elmet factory from 1939.

The first, short-lived, monoplane had a high-winged format with the pilot and engine suspended below, not unlike Alberto Santos-Dumont's Demoiselle. The second machine adopted a far more conventional layout, exhibiting the influence of Léon Levavasseur's Antoinette monoplane. Benny Hucks took this for its – and his – maiden flight, at Filey, on 8 March 1911. Although the sortie ended with a sideslip into the sand, RB was in the aviation business and to prove it, he began to trade as the Blackburn Aeroplane Company. The 'Antoinette' layout was refined and developed and single- and two-seater Mercury monoplanes were built for customers and to train would-be purchasers at Filey. The school 'followed the money' in September 1912, setting up at Hendon. But the competition was tough and the enterprise was wound down in 1913. Here was a recurrent hallmark of RB's approach: strive to improve and diversify. On a personal level, design and flying were less important to RB; others could do that, he was taking hold of a different sort of helm – steering his enterprise.

A Gnome-powered Mercury over Filey in 1911.
Blackburn and General Aircraft

The oldest airworthy British-built aircraft performing at the Shuttleworth Trust, Old Warden: the Blackburn Monoplane ordered by Cyril Foggin in 1912 and acquired by Francis Glew the following year. *Richard Hall*

The French Antoinette clearly meant a lot to RB; in 1916 he acquired a Type VII built in 1910 by Société Anonyme Antoinette at Puteaux. It had been in store at Colwyn Bay, North Wales, and was bought for the princely sum of £60. It almost certainly had been the property of Vivian Hewitt. While piloting a Blériot XI, Hewitt became the second man to fly across the Irish Sea, on 26 April 1912, routing from Holyhead to Dublin. The Antoinette was kept unflown at Brough: RB donated it to the Science Museum in 1926 and today it is displayed within the 'Flight Gallery'.

Admiralty contracts

The monoplanes became more sophisticated but they were not going to attract the War Office. As the world teetered towards a European war, biplanes were the aeroplane of choice: witness Avro's dramatic change of fortunes with the advent of the Type 504. Early in 1914 RB made two brave decisions. First, the workshop was too small so 'The Olympia', a defunct roller-skating arena in Leeds, was taken over as an ideal factory. RB was not alone in finding such a venue a practical solution, 'Tommy' Sopwith had opted for an ice skating rink at Kingston-on-Thames. Second, a float-equipped biplane – which became the Type L – should be built to compete in the *Daily Mail*'s 'Circuit of Britain' race. There were prizes of £10,000 at stake and if the Type L had obvious military intent that would also help. The race competition was due to start on 10 August but the declaration of war six days earlier brought about the demise of the event.

Besides, the pace at the skating rink had been transformed the previous May when the Admiralty placed a contract to build Royal Aircraft Factory B.E.2cs there. The following month, the business was put on a safer legal footing as the Blackburn Aeroplane and Motor Company Ltd. The link with the Royal Navy was to endure all the way to the 1970s. RB invested in tooling to support the B.E.2 order; this included machines to churn out fittings such as turnbuckles. All were inspected and tested to exacting Aircraft General Standards – the AGS hallmark. Soon Leeds-manufactured AGS stock was being supplied to other sub-contractors and this work proved to be a post-Armistice lifeline as the demand continued.

A single F.E.2b bomber was completed in 1917, but a switch was made to Sopwith designs, initially Baby floatplanes but a requirement for Cuckoos – the first British shipborne torpedo-bomber – set Blackburn's course for decades. Assembly and testing took place at nearby Sherburn and production ran to 1920, crucially keeping some

The last of nine twin-fuselage T.Bs, 1517, at the Isle of Grain in 1917. On the float is the original Blackburn Aircraft logo, a 'BA' in a circle. In the background is believed to be the Port Victoria PV.9 – see Chapter 31. *Blackburn Aircraft*

of the workforce going through an otherwise barren period. Blackburn gained a good reputation for quality and meeting deadlines. When Pegler of Doncaster announced that it could not fulfil its commitments for fifty Cuckoos on time, Olympia took over the first thirty of the batch. Increasingly, Blackburn was used as a 'hub' to oversee the management of Yorkshire sub-contractors.

As well as sub-contracting and manufacturing components, RB was determined to maintain a design office. Using the experience gained from the Type L, the company's first true military type was the twin-hulled T.B. floatplane that appeared in the summer of 1915 – but only nine were built. Occasionally this is erroneously referred to as a torpedo-bomber, from its T.B. designation. This was not the case, the initials stood for 'Twin Blackburn'. A high-flying Zeppelin hunter, it was intended to rain incendiary fléchettes down on a marauding airship.

The notion of Zeppelin-busting continued, this time not with darts but a two-pounder recoilless Davis gun. In 1915 two single-seat biplane scouts were built, designed by Harris Booth of the Admiralty Air Department. Booth joined Blackburn in 1916 and created an ungainly triplane pusher around a Davis gun, but it got no further than a prototype. He also created a rival to the Cuckoo – the Blackburd – but by the time it got into the air in mid-1918, Olympia was busy on the mass manufacture of the Sopwith. (Blackburd is *not* a typo, it is the Scottish spelling of Blackbird. RB seemed to enjoy taking the naming 'system' set up by the Technical Department of the Ministry of Munitions to the extreme, as we shall see soon with the Blackburn *Blackburn*!)

Kangaroo B9985 (later G-EADG) of the Grahame-White Air Service at Hendon in June 2019. *Peter Green Collection*

The large and very conventional three-seat twin-engined G.P. floatplane of 1916 was intended for anti-submarine patrol but failed to attract an order. Its format was revisited in late 1917 with the R.T.1 Kangaroo, which appeared in January 1918. Those initials stood for Reconnaissance-Torpedo and this was Blackburn's first in-house torpedo-bomber. The Kangaroo saw limited service, but when demobbed its passenger-carrying potential was exploited by Grahame-White and by Blackburn's own North Sea Aerial Navigation Company.

Brough – into the 21st century

While the Olympia Works and the adjacent aerodrome at Soldiers Field, Roundhay Park, were capable of handling landplanes such as the B.E.2 it did nothing for RB's vision of creating flying boats. In 1916, Mark Swann, who had been with RB since 1911 helping to build and mend Mercuries, was tasked with finding a new site. *The Blackburn Story 1909–1959* explains how Brough was chosen: 'Mark Swann, naturally, set off towards the coast. On his way, so the story goes, he happened to find himself at Brough and there [was] everything he sought: a potential aerodrome beside the wide River Humber, offering excellent facilities for launching water-borne aircraft; handy railway services on the Hull–Leeds line; and, says the legend, two good public houses! One might ponder on which of these amenities most commended itself to Mark Swann.' The Station Hotel in Brough was one of the watering holes that helped Swann in his decision. To commemorate the link, the hostelry was renamed The Buccaneer on 12 September 1982: at the time of writing it was still thriving.

A large hangar and a slipway were ready in the autumn of 1916 and the second G.P. floatplane was the first airframe assembled and tested at Brough. No sooner had this facility got up and running than it was requisitioned, although Blackburn could continue its work there. Swann had indeed chosen carefully when he picked Brough. The military ceased operations in 1919, leaving an imposing structure known as the North Sea Hangar and other buildings, all put to good use by Blackburn.

Ever keen to establish kindred enterprises, RB set up the North Sea Aerial Navigation Company on 23 April 1919. Like other manufacturers – Airco having led the way – RB had great faith in the future of air transport and, along with other types, eight war surplus Kangaroos were adapted to carry passengers, mostly for 'joyriding'. The North Sea operation went through several name changes, but from the mid-1920s it was used as an umbrella for training organisations, winding down in the 1950s. An RAF Reserve school was initiated at Brough in 1924 and this became 4 Elementary and Reserve Flying Training School (E&RFTS) in 1935. At the same time Blackburn formed Flying Training Ltd to run 5 E&RFTS at Hanworth, initiating a link that was later to lead to the Beverley airlifter. Both schools used 'home-grown' aircraft whenever possible.

From 1925 the transfer of the headquarters from Leeds to Brough began and this was achieved in 1929. (As part of rapid expansion in the run up to World War Two, the Olympia factory was reoccupied in 1935. It was vacated again by the late 1940s.)

Torpedo dynasty

Acting as the Air Board's inspector during construction of G.P. and Kangaroo biplanes was Major Frank Arnold Bumpus and RB offered him the post of chief designer in 1919. Recruiting from War Office factory liaison staff – 'try before you buy' – was a fairly common method of recruitment; for example Bob Noorduyn by Armstrong Whitworth and George Richards by Beardmore. Having secured Bumpus, RB's dream of launching flying boats down the Brough slipway could be addressed. That would need what in those days was called a naval architect and the search resulted in the appointment of another major, John Rennie, as we shall see.

Working well as a team, RB and Bumpus established a good collaboration. Bumpus enabled RB to get on with running Blackburn and its subsidiaries. In return RB promoted Bumpus to serve as joint managing director and chief engineer, a post he held until 1951. Bumpus monitored individual projects but allowed his designers 'room' to assert their concepts and skills. Like RB, Bumpus was aware that an Admiralty 'monopoly' was only *part* of a product line and he encouraged diversity, particularly into fighters and transports. Among the staff at Brough was George Edward Petty, whose prowess was quickly recognised and by the mid-1920s he was chief designer. In 1937 Bumpus took charge of the new division at Dumbarton with Helmuth Johannes Stieger as his assistant. (Stieger's 'CV' can be found in Chapter 21.)

The Blackburd had failed to excite the Air Ministry, so Bumpus was instructed to devise what became the T.1 Swift, a private venture that was a considerable advance on the Cuckoo. While its range and speed was little improved on its Sopwith predecessor, the Swift offered enhanced performance off flight decks and its steel tube fuselage was incredibly robust. In competition with the Handley Page (HP) Hanley, the T.1 was declared the winner, going into production as the Dart, after the river in Devon. Export versions stuck with the name Swift; two going to Japan, three to Spain and, in a major breakthrough, a pair to the US Navy. Two-seat Darts were used by Blackburn's in-house RAF Reserve school.

The trainer Dart gave rise to a long-term overseas business arrangement. By 1924 the Greek National Aircraft Factory at Old Phaleron, near Athens, was moribund and in need of skilled management. On 1 July 1925 Blackburn secured a five-year contract to run the facility and a torpedo-bomber based on the two-seat Dart was produced from 1926. This was the Velos (Greek for arrow, or even dart) and more were made at Brough for service with the RAF Reserve school. Old Phaleron carried out repairs and refurbishing of other types as well as assembly of two-dozen Avro 504Ns and ten Armstrong Whitworth Atlases for the Greek armed forces. Well pleased, Athens extended the contract to 1937.

The format and construction techniques established with the Swift allowed Bumpus and his team to meet other requirements. With a deepened fuselage to accommodate a wireless operator-cum-gunner and a navigator, the R-1 Blackburn was created. As a recce type the Air Ministry naming rubric for the R-1 specified a British town and

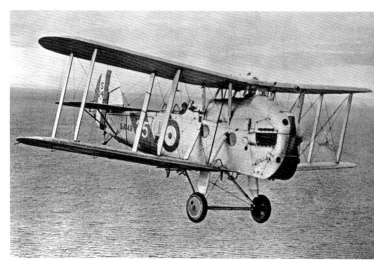

Blackburn II S1049 of 420 Flight, operating from HMS *Furious*, circa 1927. *KEC*

so some devilment was attempted. The opportunity could not be resisted to try for the absurd double use of the word 'Blackburn', even though this involved the *Yorkshire* concern highlighting a venue in *Lancashire*! Around Brough, the story was that RB wished to send up the ministerial mandarins and was both amazed and amused when the designation was approved. This double-Blackburn did not faze the Fleet Air Arm, where the stout type was nicknamed 'Bull'. Enlarging the Swift/Dart format created the massive 88ft span coastal patrol Cubaroo of 1924 – apparently named from combining its Kangaroo forebear and its 1,000hp Napier Cub engine. Scaling down the layout created the diminutive Sprat trainer of 1926. Neither achieved a production order.

Second and third generations

Intended to replace the Blackburn and the Avro Bison, the Airedale – a town in the Yorkshire dales – was a three-seat, high-winged fleet reconnaissance type. The first of two prototypes crashed at Brough in 1925 but the second was sent to Martlesham Heath in the summer of 1926. The opposition comprised biplanes: the Fairey Ferret, the ever-hopeful HP Hanley and the Hawker Hedgehog. The Aeroplane and Armament Experimental Establishment was overtly pro-biplane and Bumpus had ready plans for a biplane Airedale. In the end, the entire requirement – Specification 37/22 – was abandoned. Ahead of its time, the unfortunate Airedale bequeathed its wing-fold mechanism to the Skua, which had its debut eleven years later.

As greater endurance was expected of carrier-borne strike aircraft and reconnaissance was added to the role, the days of the single-seater were numbered. A crew of two or three was specified to help the pilot tackle the increased workload. Specification 21/23 sought a two-seater capable of torpedo strike or five-hour loiter for observation, operating from land, ships or as a floatplane. Avro pitched in with the Buffalo and HP with two versions of its Harrow biplane. Blackburn defended its niche with the Velos-inspired and Yorkshire township-named Ripon and was triumphant in 1928. The Ripon also attracted a licence from the National Aircraft Factory at Tampere, Finland, and it was used as the basis for the T.7B made by Mitsubishi in Nagoya for the Imperial Japanese Navy. After a Brough-built prototype, a staggering 205 were created in Japan. Substituting the Bristol Pegasus 9-cylinder air-cooled radial for the more maintenance-intensive 3-row, 12-cylinder water-cooled Napier Lion created the Baffin – named after the Canadian island beyond Hudson's Bay. This not only extended production but initiated a remanufacturing line, converting more than sixty Ripons to the new standard well into the 1930s.

Ripon II S1559 of the Gosport-based Torpedo Training Flight dropping a 'tin fish', circa 1933. This machine was converted to Baffin status by 1935. *KEC*

The torpedo-spotter-reconnaissance (TSR) biplane still had life in it and the Air Ministry issued Specification S.15/33 to find a new machine to serve into the 1940s. All of the experience of the Brough design office was crystallised into what became the B-6 Shark, three generations on from Sopwith's Cuckoo. Stepping stone to the Shark was the Rolls-Royce Buzzard-powered M.1/30A of 1932, which boasted an all-metal monocoque fuselage that was watertight, greatly improving crew survivability in the event of a ditching. Petty took all of the plus points of the M.1/30A, reduced wire bracing to the absolute minimum and created the multi-strutted, robust and advanced B-6. Toting a 700hp 14-cylinder radial Armstrong Siddeley Tiger IV, it first flew on 24 August 1933. The competition comprised the Fairey TSR and the Gloster TSR.38. Both the B-6 and the less complex Fairey contender – soon to be the Swordfish – were ordered.

The Shark was a spectacular success; Portugal became a customer and Boeing Aircraft Canada built them in Vancouver under licence for the Royal Canadian Air Force. The Shark production line moved from Brough to Dumbarton in 1938, with the last examples delivered in 1940. Technically superior to the Swordfish, the Shark was more demanding to manufacture in very large numbers and it was the Fairey product that endured. Blackburn's prowess as a sub-contractor again came to the fore and, as we shall see, it went on to make the majority of the 'Stringbags'. As well as new-builds, the Shark provided Dumbarton with upgrades to Mk.IV status and conversions to target tugs.

While landing on HMS *Courageous* on 30 January 1937, Shark II K8466 'engaged' the ship's island and was written off. The crew were uninjured. *Peter Green Collection*

Flying boats on the Humber

Blackburn's first flying boat was the stillborn N.1B single-seat pusher biplane aimed at replacing the Sopwith Baby. Designed by Booth, construction of the prototype was suspended in 1918 and the fuselage was put aside. (See also Chapters 36 and 38 for the Supermarine and Westland responses to the N.1B requirement.) Britain's victory in the 1922 Schneider Trophy race at Naples, Italy, inspired RB to have the N.1B dusted down for use in the 1923 contest. The fuselage formed the basis of the 450hp Napier Lion-powered Pellet. The compact 'boat – the span was 34ft, the loaded weight 2,800lb – was launched into the Humber in early September 1923 but it was caught by the tide and rolled over. Test pilot Reginald Watson Kenworthy received a drenching – it was not to be his last.

The competition was scheduled for the 28th, with the previous day set aside as the 'last possible' moment for acceptance trials. The Pellet was sent by rail to Southampton and from there by truck to Hamble. A test on the 26th revealed that the Pellet was *very* nose heavy and then the Lion overheated. Kenworthy put it down abeam Calshot seaplane station and it was towed to Cowes by a motorboat. The following day he tried again, on the River Medina, but the little 'boat started to violently porpoise, then reared into the air and crashed back into the water. Kenworthy managed to extricate himself and clambered onto the upturned wreck to await rescue.

It was another three years before a Blackburn flying boat went down the Brough slipway. The contrast with the Pellet was considerable, the Iris was powered by three 650hp Rolls-Royce Condors, had a span of 95ft 6in and an all-up weight of 27,608lb. This monster was reported to have cost £60,000. The prototype five-crew, long-range recce 'boat, with the capability of carrying up to 1,040lb of bombs, had its debut on 19 June 1926. Its wooden fuselage was removed in 1927 and substituted by an all-metal example. It was followed by another four metallic Irises and up to 1933 these were re-engineered with differing powerplants. All were tractor tri-motors other than the Mk.IV of 1931, which had Armstrong Siddeley Leopard radials – two tractors and a central pusher.

The man in charge of creating the Iris – named after the flower when seabirds or Commonwealth cities were the order of the day – was Major John Douglas Rennie. He was no stranger to large flying boats, having assisted John Porte on the design of the 123ft span, five-engined Felixstowe Fury triplane of 1918. Rennie later served with the Air Ministry and Bristol before joining Blackburn. Rennie stayed with Blackburn, based at the Dumbarton plant from 1939, until May 1946. Then the wise decision was taken not to re-enter the flying boat market and his six-engined B-49 Clydesman was shelved.

The second Perth, K3581, was delivered to 209 Squadron at Mount Batten, Plymouth, in January 1934. *Rolls-Royce*

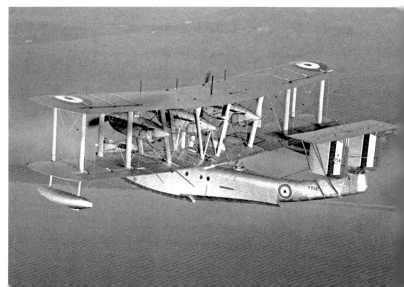

The ill-fated Blackburn B.20 on the slipway at Dumbarton, March 1940. *KEC*

The success of the Iris tri-motors encouraged an Air Ministry order for an all-metal, monoplane, long-range flying boat in the summer of 1927. With the financial boost of a government purchase, Blackburn went ahead with the military RB.2 Sydney (after the Australian city) and a broadly similar civil version, the CB.2 Nile. The Sydney first flew on 18 July 1930 but was not well regarded by the Marine Aircraft Experimental Establishment (MAEE) down the coast at Felixstowe. The Rolls-Royce F.XII engines proved troublesome and the Sydney was, after all, a monoplane. It remained a one-off and the Nile was never completed. Rennie reverted to the safety of biplanes for his next commission, the Perth (another Australian city, not the town in Scotland) which was an enlarged Iris. Four were built, the last one being accepted in March 1934.

In the mid-1930s Rennie came up with a method of avoiding the inherent drag from the deep hulls that monoplane flying boats required to place the engines as far away from water spray as possible. This format was fine in transports, such as the pioneering Short C-Class 'boats for Imperial Airways as cabin volume was an essential requirement. For a military type, such deep hulls reduced speed and range. Rennie came up with a retractable hull that provided the 'height', allowed the correct wing incidence for take-off and landing and a dramatically reduced cross section once fully airborne. Retractable wing tip floats further cleaned up the airflow.

The B-20 was pitched at Specification R.1/36, which was won by the very conventional – but troublesome – Saro Lerwick. The ingenious retractable hull was too good an opportunity to pass up and the Air Ministry ordered a B-20 for evaluation by MAEE, which had moved from Felixstowe to Helensburgh, opposite Greenock in 1939. The B-20 was built at the Dumbarton plant, further up the Clyde, and Flt Lt Henry 'Bill' Bailey carried out the inaugural flight in March or early April 1940. During a high-speed trial, with the hull retracted, on 7 April 1940 Bailey encountered severe vibration and he ordered the crew to bale out. Only one made it, Bailey and observer Fred Weeks were killed. Rennie sketched layouts for a fighter with a retractable central hull, but it remained a paper exercise.

Fighters and frustration

As noted above, both RB and Bumpus were determined to cater for more than the well-trodden shipborne and flying boat markets. Forays into fighters proved frustrating but one creation, the Lincock, had a modicum of success. Breaking into the domestic bazaar was not easy as the Air Ministry tended to 'compartmentalise' its thinking, eg.: Blackburn did torpedo-bombers, Hawker fighters, Vickers bombers, etc, and it was best left that way. To circumvent this Bumpus aimed directly at exports – the company had achieved such success with several of its designs and had experience with licensing. So, Blackburn embarked on its first fighter, the F.1 Blackcock, a generic title that would be tailored to customers. B A Duncan took charge of this all-metal, lightweight biplane. The prototype was ordered by the Turkish government and was named Turcock accordingly. It was short-lived; first flown on 14 November 1927, it was destroyed seventy days later in a crash at Martlesham Heath.

The light fighter concept was not forgotten and it was chief designer George Petty that schemed the F.2 Lincock in 1928. More word games; the Lincock was a developed Blackcock with an Armstrong Siddeley Lynx radial – but spelt with an 'i' instead of a 'y'. Despite investment in two demonstrators that gave dazzling aerobatic displays and a top speed of 159mph on the Mk.III, the type managed to solicit orders for only a pair each for China and Japan in 1930. Piaggio acquired a licence for the Lincock and completed one, as a two-seat trainer, in 1932.

A bid was made for Specification F.7/30 seeking a single-seat interceptor in competition with the Supermarine Type 224 and the Westland PV.4. All were doomed because of the Air Ministry's selection of the disastrous Rolls-Royce Goshawk engine. Petty's unusual biplane got as far as taxi trials before it was axed. The government paid for the unproven prototype but if Petty was frustrated at the wasted effort, he was not alone. As described in Chapter 36, a designer there had seen his first fighter to reach the construction stage discarded – he was Reginald Joseph Mitchell.

The Lincock I G-EBVO with what is believed to be Sqn Ldr Jack Noakes in the foreground, Hendon, July 1928. *Blackburn*

Civil diversions

Blackburn had greater success with civil aircraft, even if its first post-Armistice foray was a failure. The bizarre-looking Sidecar monoplane of 1919 remained flightless but was ahead of its time with a side-by-side cockpit: a layout that was returned to with the Bluebird and B-2. With a price of £450, when a war-weary Avro 504 was going for £80, the Sidecar was expensive. Nevertheless, it was sold to a gent with a London address but remained a one-off.

The 1924 Air Ministry lightplane trials at Lympne encouraged Blackburn to enter a conventional biplane, with side-by-side seating and folding wings. Arthur Cecil Thornton conceived the all-wood Bluebird, powered by a meagre 36hp Blackburne Thrush. As noted later, Blackburn established its own aero engine division but its products are not to be confused with the 2- and 3-cylinder Tomtit and Thrush made by Burney and Blackburne of Bookham, Surrey – trading as Blackburne with an 'e' – in the 1920s. Refitted with a 60hp Armstrong Siddeley Genet, the Bluebird took part in the 1926 competition, proving to be exceptionally reliable and the seating arrangement was well regarded.

Thus enthused, the Bluebird was committed to production and the ADC Cirrus-powered Mk.II and the improved Mk.III appeared in 1927 and 1928 respectively. By that time de Havilland (DH) had begun its domination of the market with the Moth series. Although the Bluebird's side-by-side arrangement was very sociable for touring and ideal for instruction, it was more expensive than the DH biplane and only twenty were built. Thornton continued to work in the Blackburn drawing office and was allowed, in his spare time, to create the potent Arrow Active single-seat sportsplane in 1931.

In 1928 Petty redesigned the Bluebird with an all-metal airframe, as the Mk.IV. Production of Ripons and the later Baffins meant that Brough lacked capacity to build Bluebird IVs and, other than the prototype, it was farmed out to Saunders-Roe (Saro) at Cowes on the Isle of Wight, while Boulton Paul (BP) made the wings. No sooner had Saro taken on Blackburn's biplanes than it started suffering from its own manufacturing problems while meeting orders for its Cutty Sark amphibian. Up to twenty Bluebirds were returned to Brough in 1931 as unfinished airframes and assembled on an 'as and when' basis through to 1935.

Blackburn's final two-seater biplane married Bluebird wings – sub-contracted to BP – to a new fuselage that employed the constructional techniques of the B-1 Segrave – see below. The design office had realised that the Bluebird was too costly for private owners and aero clubs and aimed the new machine, the B-2, at reservist and full-blown military schools, with a particular eye on a Portuguese requirement. The prototype flew on 10 December 1931 and was followed by a disappointing forty-one examples, the bulk of which served with the company-managed Brough and Hanworth schools.

B-2 G-ACBJ joined the Blackburn-managed reserve school at Brough in 1933 and was camouflaged by early 1940. *KEC*

Tubular spars and the Duncan sisters

Incomplete Bluebird IVs were not the only items handed over by Saro: a sleek twin called the Meteor flew into Brough in late 1930 with high hopes for the future. Other than being manufacturers of flying boats, Blackburn and Saro seemed to have little in common, but they shared venture capital funding from the Aircraft Investment Corporation (AIC), which hoped to stimulate innovation in civil aviation. Acting as a consultant to AIC was the dynamic and charismatic Sir Henry Segrave, a former Great War pilot and the holder of speed records on both land and water.

As the world economy slumped, Segrave schemed a high-speed, four-seat, twin-engined corporate conveyance or tourer, which was turned into reality by Saro's Harry Broadhurst. In 1928 Alliott Verdon Roe had bought into Saunders, which took the name Saunders-Roe. Broadhurst, the man who had perfected the variable engine mount for the Avro 504K, followed his boss to the Isle of Wight. Cantilever wing techniques learned at Woodford through a licence agreement for the Fokker F.VII were applied to the Segrave project. The prototype Saro A.22 Segrave Meteor had its maiden flight on 28 May 1930. Sixteen days later Sir Henry was at the helm of his Saro-built speedboat, *Miss England II*, on Lake Windermere. During two runs he averaged a record-breaking 98.76mph but on the third attempt the boat somersaulted and the 33-year-old knight died from his injuries.

Prior to Segrave's death, AIC had decided that the future for the Meteor lay with metal construction and Blackburn was best placed to achieve this; hence the arrival at Brough of the prototype. Designated CA.18 Segrave II, later B-1, two examples with metal-framed fuselages appeared in 1931 and 1932. Apart from an unfulfilled licence agreement with Piaggio in Italy, the twins failed to attract other interest. The concept was rethought, employing an innovation perfected by a new member of the Brough design team, Frederick Duncanson. The all-metal CA.20 Segrave II featured his patented spar and had its debut at Brough on 2 February 1934.

Former marine engineer Duncanson worked in the mid-1920s under Marcel Lobelle at Fairey on such types as the Flycatcher, before joining Gloster. It was at Hucclecote that Duncanson devised an innovative tubular spar, strengthened with corrugations; but chief designer Henry Folland showed no interest in it. Bumpus did, so Duncanson jumped ship to Brough in 1929. Hopefully, the Segrave II would find buyers but it had the added utility of acting as a test bed for the new spar. Light but strong, the Duncanson spar doubled as a fuel tank and provided buoyancy for marine aircraft – all reasons to arouse Bumpus. The Segrave II remained a one-off but the technology was used again in the B-9 twin, which was also known as the HST.10 – High-Speed Transport, 10-passenger. This was Blackburn's first machine with a retractable undercarriage and the substantially complete prototype was rolled out at Brough in July 1936. At that point the HST.10 was already a spent force; warplanes were the order of the day and the elegant, advanced twin never flew.

In 1931 Blackburn received a commission from the Air Ministry for two light transports with a crew of two and a cabin for ten passengers. Powered by a pair of 400hp 14-cylinder Armstrong Siddeley Jaguar IV radials, they were similar in every aspect other than the layout of their wings: one was a biplane, the other a monoplane. They were intended for comparative trials to help with the long-running question: One wing or two? Charged with creating the two CA.15s was B A Duncan, who had previously schemed the Turcock fighter. At Brough the project was known as 'The Duncan Sisters' after Rosetta and Vivian Duncan, an American theatre and film duo of the 1920s. The biplane flew in June 1936 and the monoplane four months later. The former had several quirks, the latter was more straightforward: neither helped to clinch the debate.

Minor, Major and Turbo

As related in Chapter 24, while working for the Aircraft Disposal Company (ADC, also known as 'Airdisco') in 1924, Frank Halford 'halved' an 80hp Renault V-8 engine. The result was a 60hp 4-cylinder that became the ADC Cirrus and transformed the prospects of British light aviation. The major benefactor was the Moth and to capitalise on this Halford moved to DH in 1926 to conceive the exceptional Gipsy. In 1930 ADC was wound down and rights to the Cirrus were taken over by the Cirrus-Hermes Engineering Company the following year. Three years later, Phillips and Powis – the company behind the Miles brothers – took on the stock, spares and rights of the Cirrus I, II and III. Keen to establish a line of aero engines, Blackburn bought the Cirrus-Hermes title in 1934 and embarked upon a new range of 4-cylinder in-lines at Brough; the Cirrus Minor and Major, which stayed in production beyond 1945. The division created another all-new engine, the Bombardier, in the late 1950s for military and civil applications. The main application for the Bombardier was the AOP.9 observation aircraft.

With the prospects for piston engines dwindling and realising that larger powerplants for civil and military use would prove very costly to develop, Blackburn sought co-operation. In October 1952 visits to Pau in the lee of the Pyrenees in southern France paid off. The British and Commonwealth rights for the entire range of gas turbines made by Société Turboméca were snapped up. Anglicising these innovative engines took much time and investment. The Artouste was transformed into an airborne auxiliary power unit and a podded and wheeled Palouste was used as a ramp-side, low-pressure starter for jets, ruining the hearing of pilots and ground crew alike for many decades! On 1 April 1959 the engine division became Blackburn Engines Ltd and in November 1961 it was absorbed into Bristol Siddeley Engines (BSE). Blackburn's turbines culminated in the all-new A129 turboshaft in 1958 and this entered series production under the BSE banner as the Nimbus, powering the Westland Scout and Wasp helicopters.

Blackburn aero engines

Name, Type/Format	From	Application*	Notes
Cirrus Minor, 4 cy in-line	1936	BA Swallow	
Cirrus Major, 4 cy in-line	1936	Miles Messenger	
Palouste 500 turboshaft	1954	Fairey Ultra Light	[1]
Turmo 600 turboshaft	1957	Kaman K-17	[1]
Bombardier 4-cy in-line	1958	Auster AOP.9	
A129 Mk.3 turboshaft	1958	Saro P.531-2	[1] [2]

* Typical, or only, use. [1] British development of the French Turboméca range. [2] Entered production as the Bristol Siddeley Nimbus.

Back to war and sub-contracts

On 2 April 1936 Blackburn Aircraft Ltd came into being, the title Blackburn Aeroplane and Motor Company having been considered 'dated' for some time. The last years of the 1930s saw three aircraft developed, all under the leadership of George Petty, powered by Bristol Perseus 9-cylinder radials and destined to be outmoded by the time they were called into combat. Named after an aggressive seabird, the Skua was a carrier-borne, catapult-launched, arrester wire-recovered fighter and dive-bomber. The prototype took to the air on 9 February 1937 and went straight into production. It entered service the following year and, as the Fleet Air Arm's first operational monoplane, it was a revelation, replacing Hawker Nimrods and Ospreys. By the time war came, the Skua was outmoded but gave brief, valiant service.

The same airframe was adapted to the ill-conceived turret fighter concept as the Roc, appropriately the name of a mythical bird. With Brough fully committed to Skua and Botha manufacture, the Roc needed to be farmed out. The Roc's four-

A pair of Rocs from 759 Squadron, Eastleigh, 1940 – nearest is L3118. *KEC*

gun, electrically operated turret was made by Boulton Paul and it made sense to transfer the entire programme to the Wolverhampton company, which in turn 'sub-let' some assemblies to General Aircraft. The first of 136 Rocs, ordered straight off the drawing board, flew at Pendeford on 23 December 1938. The type saw the briefest of front-line service before taking up secondary roles, principally as a gunnery trainer.

Blackburn sub-contracts and Hawker Siddeley work

Type	Total	From	To	Notes
R A/c Factory B.E.2c	111	1914	1918	[1]
R A/c Factory F.E.2b	1	1917	-	[1] [2]
Sopwith Baby	186	1917	1918	[1] [3]
Sopwith Cuckoo	132	1918	1920	[4] [5]
Airco DH.9A	18	1927	-	[1] [6]
AW Siskin IIIA	42	1928	1929	[1]
Fairey Swordfish I, II, III	1,700	1940	1944	[4]
Fairey Barracuda I, II	635	1942	1945	[7]
Short Sunderland III, V	250	1942	1945	[8]
Percival Prentice T.1	125	1948	1949	[7]
Handley Page HP.88	1	1951	-	[7] [9]
Boulton Paul Balliol T.2	30	1953	1954	[7]
HS Sea Harrier FRS.1	-	1981	1982	[10]
HS/BAe/BAE Hawk	-	1988	date	[7] [10]

[1] Built at Leeds. [2] A8950, an unusual single aircraft contract. [3] RNAS referred to these as 'Blackburn Babies'. [4] Built at Sherburn. [5] Includes 30 taken over from a contract issued to Pegler, Doncaster. [6] Substantially rebuilt 'stock' from 1919 for RAF. [7] Built at Brough. [8] Built at Dumbarton. [9] Design originated with General Aircraft. Blackburn designation YB.2 – full details in Chapter 24. [10] See narrative and Chapters 12 and 26.

Specification M.15/35 called for a short-range, twin-engined, shore-based torpedo-bomber or recce-bomber. This was asking a lot, but the requirement was altered, in Specification 10/36, to a four-crew twin that could take on general reconnaissance (essentially maritime recce), torpedo-bombing *and* general-purpose duties! Both Blackburn and Bristol were given contracts prior to the maiden flights of the Botha and Beaufort respectively.

The Beaufort went on to great things, but only after a tortuous evolution; the Botha remained woefully underpowered and had a brief front-line career followed by relegation to aircrew training. There was no prototype Botha as such, the first production example taking to the skies at Brough on 28 December 1938 – five days after the Roc's debut at Pendeford. The assembly line moved to Dumbarton in late 1939. Named after the inaugural prime minister of the Union of South Africa, the word 'Botha' is Afrikaans and therefore most accurately pronounced 'Boater', whereas 'Brits' – depending on their region of birth – will say it as 'Bowther' or 'Boffer'. Poorly regarded by pilots, trainee aircrew and ground crew alike, many of these had another name for the Blackburn twin – the 'Why Bother?'

The first production – and prototype – Botha, December 1938. *Blackburn*

Apart from piecemeal orders for Firebrands – see below – Blackburn spent the war building for others. The company returned to Sherburn and churned out 1,700 Fairey Swordfish from December 1940 to August 1944. Known locally as 'Blackfish', the irony of manufacturing a lumbering biplane of the sort the Firebrand was supposed to confine to the scrapheap cannot have been lost on Brough's designers. At Brough 635 Fairey Barracuda naval dive-bombers were built, while at Dumbarton 250 Sunderland Is, IIs, IIIs and Vs were constructed, with the last launched into the waters of the Clyde in October 1945. As a Fleet Air Arm specialist, Blackburn also found contracts preparing for service Grumman Avengers, Hellcats, Martlets and Wildcats, and Vought Corsairs.

On 27 February 1942 the prototype Firebrand naval single-seat fighter was flown, powered by a 2,305hp Napier Sabre III. Blackburn gained a development contract in competition with Hawker, which had put forward a navalised Typhoon. While it can mean a piece of burning wood, the accepted use of 'Firebrand' in this case was someone who causes chaos. Changing requirements drew the programme out and the Mk.II was re-engineered with a widened centre fuselage so that it could carry a torpedo; the first example appearing in the spring of 1943. By that time, the Bristol Centaurus 18-cylinder twin-row radial had been substituted and Petty and his team faced another major redesign. The Firebrand saw no service during World War Two and it was the much-developed Mk.IV that entered squadron use in September 1945, with the further improved Mk.V arriving in 1947. The 220th and last Firebrand was delivered in March 1947.

Damaged 827 Squadron Firebrand TF.5 EK661 taking the 'net' on the deck of HMS *Eagle* during the summer of 1952. *KEC*

Readjustment

By late 1947, the company had retrenched significantly; the Sherburn factory having closed with the end of Swordfish work. To help counter the blow of the end of Firebrand production a sub-contract for Percival Prentice trainers began in January 1948 with a follow-on commission for BP Balliols in 1952. As a result of RB's policy of diversification in the 1950s a variety of products kept Brough going: Rowcrop tractors, lorry bodies, conveyor belts and a newly established Light Alloy Structures Section specialised in trusses for large buildings. It was a similar story at Dumbarton, which was restructured as Blackburn (Dumbarton) Ltd on 6 October 1947. The Clydeside plant manufactured the Permanent Traditional House two-storey prefabricated dwelling in considerable numbers into the early 1950s. Aviation sub-contract work was also sought; during the 1950s Bristol Britannia fuselage 'barrels' were made at Dumbarton.

Brough's design office was far from idle and fostered hopes for a continued relationship with the Navy. A radically developed Firebrand, the B-48 strike fighter, was first flown on 1 April 1947 but no orders ensued. Unofficially known as the 'Firecrest', with an all-up weight of 15,280lb the B-48 could hardly be likened to a small European warbler! Specification GR.17/45 called for a shipborne anti-submarine aircraft, ideally powered by a turboprop. This was a major requirement that could set the firm up for a long time with the prospect of follow-on orders and exports. The interim B-54, powered by a Rolls-Royce Griffon 56 piston, was first flown on 20 September 1949. Enlarged and expensively rethought, the B-88 with an Armstrong Siddeley Double Mamba coupled turboshaft took to the skies on 19 July 1950. Fairey clinched GR.17/45 with the Gannet, changing its fortunes for the rest of the decade. An unusual sub-contract was the YB.2 aerodynamic test bed for Handley Page as part of the Victor V-bomber programme – full details in Chapter 24.

The first B-48, RT651, during the summer of 1947 prior to its appearance at the Farnborough display. *Blackburn and General Aircraft*

General and the Beverley

On New Year's Day 1949, Blackburn merged with the much smaller General Aircraft Ltd (GAL) of Hanworth. This was not a takeover, it was a mutual arrangement and without it the iconic name Blackburn might not have survived much into the next decade. GAL was developing a promising airlifter that had great potential but lacked production capacity. Building Sunderland flying boats at Dumbarton had given Blackburn staff vital experience of large airframes and the Brough factory was more than big enough. In 1959 Blackburn and General Aircraft Ltd was reorganised as the Blackburn Group, including Blackburn Aircraft and Blackburn Engines.

Most of the GAL design office made the journey north, but the head of the project, Frederick Francis 'Croak' Crocombe, departed for new ventures with Boulton Paul. Construction of the GAL.60 Universal Freighter had begun at Hanworth and the sections were brought to Brough for assembly. The prototype had its debut on 20 June 1950. Bearing in mind the disruption of the relocation, this was a swift outcome for such a gargantuan project. Brough's runway was too restrictive for testing and Blackburn acquired the nearby airfield of Holme-on-Spalding Moor in 1951. The much refined second example was flown on 14 June 1953. Under the designation B-101, an order for forty-seven Beverley C.1s was placed for the RAF, the last coming off the line in May 1958. The airlifter was named after the township to the north of Kingston upon Hull. Despite intensive sales tours, no other orders were forthcoming.

Solid success

Blackburn still held ambitions of renewing its relationship with the Fleet Air Arm. This was to come to fruition in the formidable Buccaneer. This tough machine generated its own folklore. For many years the B-103 was known by Blackburn staff and enthusiasts alike as the 'Brick'. While touring the Buccaneer production line at Brough in mid-1976 – the last six were nearing completion – the author was struck by a cartoon pinned to a work station. The first 'frame' showed an enormous ingot being delivered to the factory. The second drawing depicted several of these giant blocks, each one being 'attacked' by men with hammers and chisels. The final image was of a pristine, gleaming Buccaneer surrounded by large chunks of discarded metal.

Left: Newly camouflaged Beverley C.1 XL149 joined 84 Squadron at Khormaksar, Aden, in early 1965. Scrapped in 1977, its cockpit is displayed at the South Yorkshire Aircraft Museum, Doncaster. *RAF Museum*

Below: The Beverley forebear, Universal Freighter WF320, with a Freemans of Brough coach showing the airlifter's load-carrying capability, 1951. *Blackburn and General Aircraft*

Blackburn landplanes and floatplanes 1919 to 1936

From	To	Total	Name/Designation	Type	Engine(s)	Notes
1919	-	1	Sidecar	Tourer	1 x ABC Gnat	[1]
1920	1923	8	Swift	Torpedo bomber	1 x Napier Lion	
1921	1927	120	Dart	Torpedo bomber	1 x Napier Lion	
1922	1928	62	Blackburn I, II	Shipborne recce	1 x Napier Lion	[2]
1924	1925	2	Cubaroo	Coastal defence	1 x Napier Cub	
1924	1929	20	Bluebird I-III	Tourer	1 x AS Genet	
1925	1927	23	Velos	Torpedo bomber	1 x Napier Lion	[3]
1925	1926	2	Airedale	Fleet recce	1 x AS Jaguar	[4]
1926	1934	121	Ripon I-III	Torpedo/recce	1 x Napier Lion	[5]
1926	-	1	Sprat	Trainer	1 x RR Falcon	
1927	-	1	Turcock	Fighter	1 x Bristol Mercury	
1928	-	1	Beagle	Torpedo/bomber	1 x Bristol Jupiter	
1928	1932	8	Lincock I-III	Fighter	1 x AS Lynx	[6]
1929	-	1	Nautilus	Shipborne fighter	1 x RR F.XII	
1929	1935	56	Bluebird IV	Tourer	1 x Cirrus Hermes	[7]
1929	1935	206	T.7B	Torpedo/recce	1 x Hispano Suiza	[8]
1931	1934	5	Segrave	Light transport	2 x Cirrus Hermes	[9]
1931	1936	42	B-2	Trainer	1 x DH Gipsy	
1932	-	2	CA.15	Airliner	2 x AS Jaguar	[10]
1932	-	2	B-3/ M.1/30A	Shipborne torpedo	1 x RR Buzzard	
1932	1935	35	Baffin	Torpedo/recce	1 x Bristol Pegasus	[11]
1933	1940	269	Shark	Torpedo/recce	1 x AS Tiger	[12]
1934	-	1	F.3	Fighter	1 x RR Goshawk	[13]
1934	-	1	B-7	GP/patrol	1 x AS Tiger	
1935	-	1	HST.10	Light transport	2 x Napier Rapier	[14]

All tractor biplanes, unless noted. [1] Monoplane: completed, *believed* tested, but did not fly. [2] Like New York, so good they named it twice, this was genuinely the Blackburn. [3] Includes 12 built under licence at Blackburn-managed Greek National Aircraft Factory, Old Phaleron, Athens. [4] Monoplane. [5] Includes 12 licensed by National Aircraft Factory, Tampere, Finland. Around 64 Ripons remanufactured as Baffins from 1935. [6] Includes one under licence by Piaggio SA, Final Ligure, Italy, as P.11. [7] Includes 52 – possibly 55 – sub-contracted to Saunders-Roe. Up to 20 returned unfinished to Brough and assembled through to 1935. [8] British prototype followed by 205 licensed to Mitsubishi in Japan, designated 3MR4. [9] Prototype built by Saro as A.22 Meteor – see narrative. Blackburn designations CA.18 Segrave I and CA.20 Segrave II; later B-1. Includes two licensed by Piaggio SA, Final Ligure, Italy; as P.12. [10] One high-wing monoplane layout, other biplane. [11] Conversions of T.5 Ripons to Baffin status. [12] Production transferred to Dumbarton from 1937, flown at Abbotsinch. Includes 16 licensed by Boeing Aircraft of Canada, Vancouver. [13] Failed to get further than taxi trials. [14] Monoplane, also failed to get further than taxi trials.

The message was that Buccaneers were so strong because they weren't assembled – they were sculpted from solid metal. (This was based on fact: the wing panels were milled not pressed.) Not far away at Holme, inside the flight shed was a banner also alluding to the durability of the jet, but with a helping of Yorkshire self-deprecation: 'Buccaneer – Honed to perfection and hammered to fit'.

The Navy issued a requirement for a low level, high-speed, nuclear-capable, carrier-borne strike jet, M.148T or NA.39, in 1952 and in July 1955 Blackburn was awarded the contract for its ambitious but very capable design. Powered by de Havilland Gyron Junior turbojets, the B-103 – it did not take the name Buccaneer until August 1960 – featured

boundary-layer control (or 'super circulation') to help with the extremes of its challenging flight envelope, the rear fuselage had 'area rule' bulging and a 'petal' dive-/speed brake, advanced electronics for the low-level environment and a rotating bomb door to keep the airframe 'clean'. An incredible thirty-three months after the ink dried on the initial contract, the prototype was flown from Thurleigh on 30 April 1958 because the runway at Holme was considered too 'tight' for the inaugural sortie, although it was being lengthened. All others were towed from Brough to Holme on their own undercarriages (a few had their debut at Driffield – see the table) – tough things, Buccaneers!

Liverpudlian Barry Pemberton Laight was appointed chief engineer at Brough in 1952 and he headed the considerable design team that created the Buccaneer. In 1963 he relocated to Kingston and Dunsfold to head up the Hawker Siddeley Advanced Projects Group and was appointed as director of Military Projects in 1968. During this time he worked with Ralph Hooper on the abortive P.1154, on many aspects of the Harrier and lead-up to the Hawk. Barry Laight OBE died on 6 October 2012, aged 92.

The first S.1 was issued for work-up trials at Lossiemouth in March 1961 and the final Gyron-powered version was delivered in December 1963. As can be seen from the comparison table, the S.2 with Rolls-Royce Spey turbofans was a very different beast, requiring substantial re-engineering. The first S.2 flew on 17 May 1963 and the variant attracted the only export order: sixteen were ordered by the South African Air Force as S.50s; the last flying to Cape Town in 1966.

Buccaneer S.1 XN976 was used for armament trials at Holme-on-Spalding Moor in 1964. It is carrying Martin Bullpup radio-guided, air-to-surface missiles outboard and 2in unguided rocket pods inboard; the tail dive/speed brake is deployed. *British Aerospace*

Blackburn to 1918

From	To	Total	Name/Designation	Type	Engine(s)	Notes
1909	-	1	Monoplane	1-seater	1 x Green	
1911	-	1	Monoplane	1-seater	1 x Isaacson	
1911	1912	9	Mercury	1 or 2-seater	1 x Isaacson	[1]
1912	-	1	Type E Monoplane	1-seater	1 x Green	[2]
1912	-	1	'Foggin' Monoplane	1-seater	1 x Gnome	[3]
1913	1914	3	Type I Monoplane	2-seater	1 x Gnome	
1914	-		Type L	2-seat floatplane	1 x Gnome	
1915	1916	9	T.B.	'Zeppelin hunter'	2 x Gnome Mono	[4]
1915	-	2	AD Scout	Scout	1 x Gnome Mono	[5]
1915	-	1	White Falcon	2-seater	1 x Anzani	[6]
1916	-	1	Triplane	Scout	1 x Clerget	
1916	-	2	G.P.	Maritime patrol	2 x Sunbeam Nubian	[7]
1918	-	20	R.T.1 Kangaroo	Torpedo bomber	2 x RR Falcon	[8]
1918	-	3	Blackburd	Torpedo bomber	1 x RR Eagle	[9]

All tractor biplanes, unless noted. All built in Leeds: from 1914 with assembly and testing at Roundhay Park, Leeds, and, from late 1916, at Brough. [1] All similar monoplanes with a variety of engines fitted. Includes the Type 'B' reduced-span single-seater, the second Mercury II (as unilaterally defined by A J Jackson in *Blackburn Aircraft since 1909*). [2] Second, so-called 'Military' two-seater completed, but did not fly. [3] Ordered by Cyril Foggin. [4] T.B. – Twin Blackburn, twin-hulled floatplane. [5] Pusher designed by the Admiralty Air Department and nicknamed 'Sparrow'. [6] Monoplane, used as a company 'hack'. [7] G.P. – General-purpose, three-seat floatplane. [8] R.T. – Recce Torpedo; landplane version of G.P. [9] That name is *not* a typo, Scottish spelling of Blackbird.

Blackburn flying boats

From	To	Total	Name/Designation	Type	Engine(s)	Notes
1923	-	1	Pellet	Racer	1 x Napier Lion	[1]
1926	1933	5	Iris I-V	Long-range patrol	3 x RR Condor	[2]
1930	-	1	Sydney	Long-Range patrol	3 x RR F.XII	[3]
1933	1934	4	Perth	Long-range patrol	3 x RR Buzzard	
1940	-	1	B-20	Experimental	2 x RR Vulture	[4]

All tractor biplanes, unless noted. [1] Used fuselage of N.1B flying boat, which was abandoned in 1918. [2] One-off Iris IV with three AS Leopard IIIs, two tractor, centre engine pusher. [3] Monoplane. Construction of a civil transport version, the CB.2 Nile, suspended in 1930. [4] Built at Dumbarton. Monoplane, retractable hull flying boat – see narrative.

Buccaneer S.2B XT286 of Lossiemouth-based 208 Squadron with a full load of BAe Sea Eagle active radar homing anti-ship missiles, circa 1988.
British Aerospace

Blackburn: Skua to Buccaneer

From	To	Total	Name/Designation	Type	Engine(s)	Notes
1937	1940	192	Skua I, II	Dive-bomber	1 x Bristol Perseus	
1938	1940	136	Roc	Turret fighter	1 x Bristol Perseus	[1]
1938	1942	580	Botha	Recce/bomber	2 x Bristol Perseus	[2]
1942	1947	220	Firebrand I-V	Torpedo/fighter	1 x Napier Sabre	[3]
1947	1948	2	B-48/YA.1	Shipborne strike	1 x Bristol Centaurus	
1949	1950	3	B-54	Shipborne anti-sub	1 x RR Griffon	[4]
1950	1958	49	Beverley	Tactical transport	4 x Bristol Centaurus	[5]
1958	1964	60	Buccaneer S.1	Shipborne strike	2 x DH Gyron Jnr	[6]
1964	1977	149	Buccaneer S.2	Shipborne strike	2 x RR Spey	[6]

All piston engined other than YB.1 turboprop version of B-54 and twin-jet Buccaneer. **[1]** All sub-contracted to Boulton Paul. **[2]** 242 at Brough; 200 at Dumbarton: flown at Abbotsinch. **[3]** B-37 Mk.I and II Sabre-powered, all others Centaurus; B-45 Mk.III, B-46 Mks IV and V. **[4]** Three versions, YA.7 two-seater, YA.8 three-seater, B-88/YB.1 as YA.8 but with AS Double Mamba turboprop. **[5]** Includes prototype: started as GAL.60 Universal Freighter at General Aircraft, Hanworth, first flight at Brough. Second example also designated Universal Freighter; RAF examples called Beverley. **[6]** Prototype flown at Thurleigh; most roaded to Holme-on-Spalding Moor for maiden flight; ten S.2s first flown at Driffield 1967–68.

There was still one customer to come – the RAF. The Buccaneer suffered from the 'not invented here' syndrome, being an upstart designed for the Royal Navy, and the RAF shunned it in favour of the British Aircraft Corporation TSR.2. When that programme was cancelled in 1965 the RAF filled the void with the General Dynamics F-111K 'swing-wing' strike aircraft. The last time the RAF had opted for an US fighter was the Canadair-built version of the North American F-86 Sabre in 1955. The F-111K fell by the wayside in 1968. With nowhere else to turn, the RAF finally focused on the Buccaneer, which turned out to be its last all-British bomber.

The first S.2s were issued to Honington in October 1969 and the last Buccaneer, out of a total run of 209, was delivered on 6 October 1977. Brough basked in upgrades of S.2s and programme support all the way through to the RAF's retirement of the type in 1994. During the First Gulf War of early 1991 Buccaneers did RB proud with their own version of sand-scratching. As that conflict demonstrated, the Buccaneer was the king of low-level flying: an aircrew member paid tribute by saying that riding down on the deck in a Buccaneer was 'like a ball bearing on glass'.

Buccaneer S.1 and S.2 compared

	S.1	S.2
First flown	23 Jan 1961*	5 Jun 1964**
Engines	DH Gyron Jnr DGJ.1	RR RB.168-1A Spey
	7,100lb st	11,100lb st
Loaded weight	45,000lb	62,000lb
Max speed at sea level	645mph	667mph
Max range	1,730 miles	2,300 miles
Max weapon load	8,000lb***	16,000lb***

* First production example, XN922. ** First production example, XN974 (converted S.1, XK526, as prototype S.2 maiden flight 17 May 1963) *** In weapons bay and underwing; S.2 figure relates to S.2B.

End of an era

The 'persuasion' deployed by Harold Macmillan's Conservative government from the late 1950s made it obvious that Blackburn could not remain a stand-alone; the plan was for two major groupings that would compete for contracts. The choice was the British Aircraft Corporation (BAC) or Hawker Siddeley Aviation (HSA). As related in Chapters 13 and 26, BAC was not receptive to wooing and Blackburn climbed into bed with HSA in May 1960 and on 1 July 1963 it became the Hawker Blackburn Division. On 1 April 1965 HSA reorganised and the famous name was extinguished. Beyond the Buccaneer the Brough factory settled down to look after tasks from other elements of HSA and, in turn, British Aerospace (April 1977) and BAE Systems (January 1999). From 1968, Brough became the partner site for the Royal Navy and RAF McDonnell Douglas (McDD) F-4K and 'M Phantoms. (BAC at Samlesbury supplied the McDD production line at St Louis, Missouri, with rear fuselages while Shorts at Belfast manufactured outer wing panels for the F-4K and 'M programme.) The jets flew into Holme for strip-down and were taken by lorry to Brough for airframe refurbishment and special fit before reversing the road journey to Holme for reassembly and test. The need for Holme dwindled and it closed in 1984, with Scampton taking on the role of receipt and dispatch for Phantom reworks. From 1987 to 1990 a new programme to extend the fatigue life of seventy-five RAF Phantom FGR.2s brought further work to Brough, including the fitting of British Aerospace-built outer wing panels: the jets 'commuting' from Scampton to Brough and return by lorry.

The wind-down of Dunsfold meant that from 1992 the Humberside factory became responsible for production and development of the Hawk family. Airframes were trucked across the Pennines to Warton for completion. Brough's runway was closed to traffic in the early 1990s, but in January 2008 it was announced that Hawks were to be completed and flown out for delivery to Warton. This was a short-lived scheme as Hawk orders declined and the bulk of the process moved to Lancashire. At the time of writing, the workforce at Brough was diminishing, with 2020 quoted as the end of manufacturing on site, although this could change with the status of the Hawk programme. (See Chapters 26 and 12 for more on the first- and second-generation Hawks respectively.)

Robert Blackburn OBE, the great man who gave his name to the company, retired as its chairman in 1955. At a board meeting on 25 August that year RB expressed his pleasure that in the previous month the NA.39 requirement for a shipborne strike jet had been clinched. He added: 'All I hope is that I live to see it fly.' That was not to be; sixteen days later, he died while on a fishing trip off the coast of Devon: he was 70. A great pioneer and a prudent industrialist, he was one of a few who founded aviation companies that carried their surnames. Yet Robert Blackburn's name is seldom trumpeted in the way that de Havilland, Handley Page or Roe are. Upon his death, warm tributes were penned and it fell to Harald Penrose to explain why he was rarely 'front of house': 'Too modest to play the big man in public aeronautical affairs, he was generous in word and deed, strong willed, but of great kindness.'

A flight of Defiant Is from 264 Squadron during the spring of 1940. In the foreground is L7026 from the first production batch. It was shot down by Messerschmitt Bf 109s of Jagdgeschwader 26 over Herne Bay, Kent on 28 August 1940 – one of three Defiants lost that day. *Peter Green Collection*

CHAPTER TEN

More than Defiant

Boulton Paul
1915 to 1957

'The greatest asset was experience, as it was a time of learning by trial and error…' Gordon Kinsey

BOULTON PAUL is forever linked with the Defiant turret fighter: a superb technological achievement but a thoroughly outmoded tactical concept. As a manufacturer, it was unusual in that it built more machines designed by other companies than it did of its own types. Although the turret fighter was a failure, the complexities of the mechanisms involved allowed the business to evolve into a pioneer of powered control units, leading to fly-by-wire technology.

Having taken aircraft into its portfolio, the organisation split in 1934 with the original engineering and carpentry activities – Boulton *and* Paul – remaining at the ancestral Norwich base while the aviation side – Boulton Paul – migrated to Wolverhampton in search of a skilled workforce. For three decades there were two 'Boulton Pauls': one in Norfolk, the other in the Midlands. While the name 'Boulton Paul' is no longer extant, two present-day concerns proudly trace their history back to the two 'arms', both of which built aircraft of quality.

Starting off as an ironmonger business in 1797, Boulton and Paul Ltd – B&P from here onwards – was established a century later. Expansion and diversification was the order of day and carpentry, wire netting and even boat building were carried out. With the outbreak of the Great War, the imposing Riverside Works close to the River Wensum was constructed and was up and running by 1915. The management agreed with the War Office that B&P's mixture of skills made it ideal to manufacture aeroplanes and a contract for Royal

Aircraft Factory F.E.2s was signed. Like Blackburn, B&P took this seriously and opted to make its own fittings to ensure quality and supply. On the north-east edge of Norwich nearly 300 acres of Mousehold Heath were acquired and during the summer of 1915 large hangars were erected and a flying ground cleared. These buildings were a valuable exercise as B&P thus gained a reputation as a manufacturer of specialist structures for aerodromes and the aviation industry.

Sub-contracts and original thoughts

A wrongly connected lead on the Beardmore engine of F.E.2b 5201 provided an inauspicious start to B&P's sub-contracting on 1 October 1915. Howard Pixton, winner of the Schneider Trophy race at Monaco in a Sopwith Tabloid the year before, had been engaged to carry out the maiden flight in front of invited dignitaries. Carrying the name *City of Bombay* on its nacelle, the F.E.2 had been paid for by the Overseas Club of Bombay, which had organised fund-raising across India to acquire what was grandly called an 'Imperial Aerial Flotilla'. Try as he might, Pixton could not get 5201 fired up and it was the following day, with the guests long gone, that it took to the air.

When production shifted to F.E.2d versions, another East Anglian sub-contractor was involved, Garrett and Sons building the nacelles. In a similar arrangement, B&P made the fuselages of Felixstowe F.3 and F.5 flying boats for Phoenix Dynamo of Bradford. The F.E.2s and Felixstowes prepared B&P for its next commission, an eventual total of 1,575 Sopwith Camels, which achieved a weekly average of forty-three units. This success was rewarded with an order for 425 Sopwith Snipes, which occupied the production line into early 1919. Aircraft were not the only war work at Riverside: propellers, munitions and incredible amounts of galvanised wire were made.

John Dudley North, guiding light of Boulton Paul. *BPA*

The experience gained in manufacturing aircraft was too valuable to let it dissipate on the return of peace: B&P was determined to stay in the aviation business. In late 1917 the company made an appointment that was to last nearly forty years. Aged 24, John Dudley North was appointed designer, later taking the role of chief engineer and, from 1934, he became managing director.

After school, North was apprenticed to Harland and Wolff at Belfast, studying maritime engineering. He developed an interest in aviation and joined the Hendon-based Aeronautical Syndicate, assisting Horatio Barber on his Viking biplane. Barber wound down his business in 1912 and North found work further along the hangar line at Hendon with Grahame-White. There he excelled, creating types as diverse as an armed pusher 'Gunbus' and the Charabanc multi-passenger joyrider. In 1915 North became the works superintendent and designer for the Austin Motor Company.

As he got established at Norwich, North found the B&P ethos matched his own with great emphasis on research and experimentation. When he retired in 1954, North had put the enterprise firmly on track in a new direction, to become a leading light in powered flying controls and systems. John Dudley North CBE died on 13 January 1968, aged 75.

The influence and inspiration of North can be found throughout the Boulton Paul story, but a couple of aspects will help to highlight the diversity of his skills and aspirations. Under North's guidance the Research and Development Department was established – a costly venture, especially in an era of swingeing cutbacks – including a wind tunnel. Convinced that wooden-framed aeroplanes were coming to the end of their potential, North led the way to high-tensile steel

construction techniques with the aim of making B&P a completely 'metallised' manufacturer. Other companies adopted aluminium, but B&P stuck with steel into the 1930s.

In a research paper dated May 2009, Les Whitehouse of the Boulton Paul Association wrote about North's work on the Bittern twin – of which more anon. To give the Bittern fighter-like performance, North came up with a circular cowling to improve the airflow over the 230hp Armstrong Siddeley Lynx 7-cylinder radials as early as 1926 – the prototype began flight trials in February 1927. The team at B&P called these fairings 'Anti-Turbulence Rings' or 'North Cowlings'. Whitehouse: 'At that time North saw his cowling ideas as little different from the simple cowls which had been fitted around rotary engines from before World War One by Deperdussin and, unfortunately, no move was made to patent his ideas until he had investigated further in typical North manner – test and check everything.'

From 1924 North was heavily involved in the R.101 airship programme as a technical advisor. Also engaged on this project was Dr Hubert Charles Henry Townend of the National Physical Laboratory (NPL). Townend was investigating airflow over the hull of an airship and was examining placing huge aerofoil rings around the nose to control boundary layer turbulence and smooth out drag. In July and October 1928 Townend and NPL applied for patents on concentric rings, either circular or hexagonal, around radial engines, either ahead or behind the cylinders. Having tested and checked everything, North only applied for patents for his pioneering versions from March 1929. Hence the cylinder-hugging cowls took the name 'Townend' when they should have been 'North Rings'.

The twin-pronged national airship programme initiated in 1924 has already been mentioned in Chapter 3. The State-supported R.101 was a product of the Air Ministry's Royal Airship Works at Cardington; the other was the private-venture R.100 from the Airship Guarantee Company, a Vickers-Armstrongs subsidiary, at Howden. The Cardington team commissioned B&P to come up with girders that could form the central 'skeleton' of the R.101. Following rigorous North-style testing, B&P was awarded the contract to create the main structure – amounting to *eleven miles* of girders – plus the 'tail feathers'. This was a massive task and explains how the quite meagre fixed-wing work of the period up to 1930 was not needed to keep the aviation side of B&P buoyant. The R.101 crashed into the French countryside near Beauvais on 5 October 1930. The tragedy had nothing to do with North's structure, but Britain's global passenger-carrying airship dreams perished with the R.101 and the future for B&P was to be wing-borne.

Metallisation

In *Boulton and Paul Aircraft: The History of the Companies at Norwich and Wolverhampton*, Gordon Kinsey presents a captivating and personality-based study of the evolution of the firm's aircraft. In his chapter headed 'Metallisation' Kinsey sets out the relative simplicity of aircraft from the Great War to the mid-1930s. This appraisal holds well for every organisation active during that era. 'Unlike the present time, when an aircraft is a vast complex of mechanical, hydraulic and electronic devices, the designs of the post-World War One years were comparatively simple in structure. No computers plotted out involved calculations of stresses and loadings, and there were very few reference books to use for guidance. At the same time the requirements of the day were limited and the only calculations called for were elementary load factors and pressure distributions over a given wing or tailplane.

'The greatest asset was experience, as it was a time of learning by trial and error, but because loadings were comparatively low, failures were not always disastrous. A failed component was often still available after an incident for detailed examination and

The skeletal P.10 on display at the Grand Palais, Paris, in December 1919. Under the starboard wing is a sign declaring: 'Avion en Acier, Système Breveté' – all-metal aircraft, patented process. In the background is Handley Page W.8 G-EAPJ. *BPA*

subsequent re-design. The number of designers, draughtsmen and stressmen involved in a new design was minimal by today's standards and a small number of design office staff could usually produce working drawings in a matter of weeks. Up to this time wood and fabric had been the main materials for aircraft construction …'

The first B&P design to employ steel construction was a two-seat tourer, the P.10. It was shown off, in uncovered state, at the Salon de l'Aéronautique, held within the magnificent Grand Palais on the Champs Élysées in Paris during December 1919. A 'special commissioner' for the magazine *Flight* was clearly impressed with the B&P stand: '… where we find Mr J D North busy with paint pot and brush putting a few finishing touches on the all-metal P.10. However, we persuade him to put down the brush and explain something about the construction of the extraordinarily interesting machine. … although designed and built in a very short time [it] is the result of very long experience in rolling sheet steel into special sections, and it represents years of painstaking experiments and research work. It may be said without fear of offending anyone that the P.10 probably marks the greatest step forward in aeroplane construction of any machine at the show …'

As well as the patented steel construction, the P.10 boasted a rear fuselage covered in Bakelite Dilecto sheets – canvas impregnated with the pioneering plastic compound – and a hinged engine mount allowing access to the rear of the 100hp Bristol (Cosmos) Lucifer 3-cylinder. Despite all these attributes, the P.10 never flew: it was an advanced and therefore expensive product in a world dominated by war surplus.

Fighting bombers

With the experience gained in the mass manufacture of Camels and Snipes, it seemed that single-seat fighters would be B&P's future. The first venture was the Bobolink – named after an American song bird – of 1917, but only one example was produced. The company had another go in 1928, meeting the hotly contested Specification 9/26 with the private-venture Partridge, complete with a 'North Ring' around the cylinders of its Bristol Jupiter VII. The line-up hoping to replace the RAF's fleets of Armstrong Whitworth Siskins and Gloster Gamecocks was impressive: Avro Avenger, Armstrong Whitworth Starling and AW.XVI, Blackburn Blackcock – in the form of Turcock, Bristol 105, Gloster Goldfinch and SS.18, Hawker Hawfinch, Vickers 141 and Westland Wizard. It was the Bristol and Hawker entrants that went on to further consideration and the former's Type 105 emerged as the incredibly successful Bulldog.

The next commission set a trend with B&P – fast, agile, twin-engined types. The Bourges was named after a town in central France in the same manner that Airco and Vickers had opted for Amiens and Vimy respectively. Described as a 'fighting bomber', the Bourges was intended to carry a 900lb weapon load and two defensive gun positions courtesy of a pair of 320hp ABC Dragonfly radials. Overwhelming problems with these engines partially contributed to the protracted development, while the Air Ministry debated what was expected of the biplane and the exact format it would take. Frank Courtney, engaged as B&P test pilot, praised the Bourges, saying that it performed: 'like an over-sized Camel'. At the 1923 Hendon RAF Pageant, while flying a Bourges, Courtney was 'attacked' by Nieuport Nighthawk fighters, only to engage in aerobatics to shake them off!

The second of the trio of Bourges was badly damaged in a crash at Mousehold in December 1919. This airframe was rebuilt as the P.8 Atlantic, a long-range two-seater designed to have a crack at the *Daily Mail*'s £10,000 prize for a non-stop crossing of the Atlantic. On the first flight the P.8's port engine failed on take-off and the attempt was cancelled. A second P.8 was begun but Alcock and Brown's exploits in a Vimy on 14–15 June 1919 meant that it was used as an aerodynamic test bed.

Civil ambitions

Permission was granted in 1918 for the construction of a two-seat biplane specifically to test wing sections – typical of North's approach to design. The one-off P.6 employed as many Camel components as possible and spent its time evaluating different aerofoils or working as the company 'hack'. Further development led to the P.9 of 1919, which found limited appeal as a tourer; nine were built, including four that went to Tasmania, Australia.

Thoughts returned to the civil market in 1929 with the two-seat Phoenix parasol monoplane. Under North's guidance, detail design was conducted by William Higley-Sayers, who joined B&P in 1928 having previously been the technical editor of the *Aeroplane* magazine. Powered by a 40hp ABC Scorpion 2-cylinder, the Phoenix was initially offered with a price tag of £375 – a four-seater Austin car in 1930 retailed at around £240. Despite being declared the ideal first type for a newly qualified pilot, no sales were forthcoming. In December 1929 it reappeared as the Mk.II with a 54hp British Salmson AD9 9-cylinder radial and a redesigned forward fuselage. This did not improve its market appeal and the Phoenix was used as a runabout at Mousehold. Despite what has been written elsewhere, the Mk.II retained its wooden airframe: an all-metal Mk.III was planned in early 1930, but was not proceeded with.

The P.6 aerofoil test bed X25 also served as the company 'hack'. *BP plc*

Twins and a trio

The Air Ministry had a brief flirtation with the so-called 'engine room' layout – placing powerplants *within* the fuselage and using shafts to drive the propellers. This would enable a flight engineer to be 'hands on', capable of tinkering with the engine from the comfort of the fuselage. Specifications 9/20 and 11/20 covered this scheme; the former for what was termed a 'postal' (ie. mail-carrier) aircraft, the latter a bomber. With the fuselage filled with engines and drive shafts, stowage of mail sacks was achievable, but it is difficult to envisage just where the bombs would have been housed. B&P was contracted to build two Bodmins – named after the Cornish town – with two Napier Lions one behind the other within the fuselage, driving via shafts and gearboxes four propellers, two pushing and two pulling. The 'postal' version appeared in July 1922 and the bomber three years later; both spent their lives in trials work.

Lancashire was the inspiration for the much more conventional Bolton twin-engined recce type of 1923, yet by the following year it seems that musical instruments were in vogue with the Bugle, a revival of the 'fighting bomber' concept pioneered by the Bourges. The Bolton remained a one-off; the Bugle went through several iterations but never became operational.

A major departure, in terms of size if not structure, was the three-engined P.32 heavy bomber prototype, which first flew on 23 October 1931. To provide a gun position in the nose, the third Bristol Jupiter was mounted in the middle of the upper wing. By the early 1930s, the era of the biplane bomber was drawing to a close and, recognising this, the Air Ministry had lost interest in the P.32 and its de Havilland rival, the DH.72 Canberra, by 1934.

Mention has already been made of the single-seat, twin-engined Bittern, in relation to its 'North Cowlings'. Named after a member of the heron family found in the Norfolk Broads, the Bittern was an early example of the 'bomber destroyer' concept that was to give rise to the turret fighters. Heavy commitments to the R.101 airship meant that development of the Bittern was drawn out. The intention was to attack bomber streams from underneath while flying straight and level, thus keeping the speed up. On either side of the nose was an upwardly rotating barbette holding a Lewis machine gun that was slightly canted outwards. The two guns moved as one and the pilot's gunsight was slaved to their elevation, freeing him from needing to perform distracting contortions while making an attack. Two versions were ordered for trials, the first, with fixed guns, appearing in February 1927. No further development was undertaken, but the Air Ministry's commission had brought mechanical control systems technology to B&P.

A return was made to the civil marketplace in the early 1930s, but this time to an area where North and his team had considerable expertise: all-metal twin-engined biplanes. The elegant P.64 was designed in response to an Air Ministry requirement for a mail carrier, but with an eye to turning it into an airliner, or even a bomber. First flown on 23 March 1933, the prototype was destroyed in a non-fatal crash at Martlesham Heath on 21 October. By then Imperial Airways had approached B&P about a six/seven-seater light transport and two P.71As, based on the P.64, were produced in 1934. The airline also approached Avro about this need and the Manchester company's solution was the Type 652, which appeared in January 1935. Only a pair of the Avro twin-engine, retractable-undercarriage monoplane was ordered by Imperial, but the type became the sensationally successful Anson.

Mailplane G-ABYK showing off its octagonal 'North Cowlings'. *BPA*

Zipped up bomber

People with no knowledge of RAF bombers but with a love of the north Norfolk coast will immediately associate with Overstrand and Sidestrand: just to the east of Cromer lie a small township and a village with those names. The Air Ministry 'system' stipulated naming bombers after cities and towns in Britain and the Commonwealth. Overstrand just about slips into that rubric, yet the Sidestrand was the first to appear. Gordon Kinsey expresses a theory: Sidestrand Hall was the residence of Sir Samuel Hoare MP who served as Secretary of State for Air from November 1922 to January 1924. If you've got it, use it!

Several attempts had been made by B&P to break into the bomber market, but without success. With Specification 9/24, setting down the requirements for the first RAF bomber to be designated as 'medium', the company at last got a contract. The prototype Sidestrand flew in March 1926 and the all-metal biplane was an immediate sensation. It was capable of rolls and loops that would fool any RAF fighter attempting a practice interception, yet it was easy to fly and very stable. Despite this, only eighteen production-standard Sidestrand IIs were ordered, all going to 101 Squadron at Bircham Newton at the western extremity of Norfolk. With a top speed of around 144mph, the Sidestrand was nearly 40mph faster than the contemporary Handley Page Hyderabad heavy bomber. This improvement in performance was very welcome, but gunners, particularly those in the nose, complained that the slipstream was preventing accurate aiming.

As mentioned earlier, the second Bittern featured machine guns in barbettes that could be mechanically rotated to fire upwards. The firm was gaining knowledge in guns and powered control systems, so North decided that an enhanced Sidestrand required a nose turret. A single Lewis gun was manually elevated or depressed. A hydraulic ram, connected to the gunner's seat, raised or lowered him so he could continue to look along the barrel to the sight. The cylindrical, glazed, cupola had a vertical slot to allow the gun to train up or down. To prevent a howling gale coming through, the machine gun's barrel was connected to a long zip fastener, stitched to rubberised fabric. As the gun traversed up or down the zip would open above the gun and close up behind it. When the gun was pushed to port or starboard, switches detected the movement and a pneumatic motor propelled the turret in the required direction.

The new version also featured a fully enclosed and heated cockpit for the pilot and a limited-authority autopilot. The big rudder took a lot of 'boot' to move, so a large servo-rudder was mounted on outriggers attached to its trailing edge to lower control loads. The bomber had the first power-operated, fully enclosed turret to be fitted on an RAF aircraft. Converted from a Sidestrand, and initially known as the Mk.V before Overstrand was settled upon, the prototype had its maiden flight in August 1933. As was typical of the time, a production order for just twenty-four was placed.

Migration westwards

Overstrands were the last aircraft to be built by B&P in Norwich. Although the company had hardly been blessed with massive orders, it needed new premises if it was to expand and East Anglia was not abundant when it came to recruiting personnel with engineering skills. The search for a new headquarters for the aviation division was given impetus by indications from the Air Ministry that a massive expansion of military orders was to be launched in 1935 in response to the deteriorating state of European politics. The first inkling of the change came with the establishment of Boulton Paul Aircraft Ltd (BPA from here on) on 30 June 1934. Having been elevated to joint managing director, North appointed Henry Clarke as chief designer. Clarke had cut his teeth under Roy Chadwick at Avro before moving on to Parnall.

Wolverhampton and its commercially minded town councillors was the chosen destination. As noted at the beginning of this chapter, the rest of the Boulton and Paul organisation remained firmly rooted in Norwich. Just as it had been during the 1914–18 war, B&P handled huge contracts for military supplies in the 1930s through to 1945, including Sommerfeld track, the so-called 'tin-lino' used to reinforce grass airfield surfaces. In 1942 B&P acquired the Midland Woodworking Company at Melton Mowbray, Leicestershire, which was involved in the Airspeed Horsa assault glider programme, building nose sections for both Mk.Is and IIs.

Plans for the new factory and airfield at Pendeford, north-west of Wolverhampton, were presented in July 1935 and construction began at a brisk pace using roof trusses manufactured at Norwich by B&P. Initially there was some confusion about the exact nature of the name of the new company: was it hyphenated or not? Certainly, the main flight shed at Pendeford carried the name Boulton-Paul in large letters (and hyphen) when it was completed. Initial occupation of the site by staff that had moved from Norwich was made in June 1936.

Having gained a contract for Hawker Demons – the largest production run for the business since 1918 – the changeover from Norwich to Wolverhampton had to be as smooth as possible. In a shining example of industrial planning and logistics, the first Demon was ready on 21 August 1936 just thirteen days after the main workforce had occupied the premises.

Overstrand J9186 started life as a Sidestrand II in 1929, serving with 101 Squadron. It was rebuilt under the designation Sidestrand V in 1933 and briefly served with 101 Squadron on trials in early 1934. It carries the 'New Types Park' number 13 for its appearance at the June 1934 Hendon display. *BPA*

Turret fighters

A batch of the Pendeford-built Demons was completed with Frazer-Nash 'Lobster-Back' shields for the gunners. These turreted Demons entered service with the RAF in October 1936 and the 'bomber destroyer' again struck a chord with the Air Ministry. As turret technology improved, so it seemed that a faster monoplane in the same vein would be a formidable extension of the armoury. To this end, Specification F.9/35 was issued in May 1935 and BPA and Hawker – the latter with the Hotspur – were given development contracts.

The experience gained with the Overstrand's turret was invaluable, but designing and fitting a turret into a sleek monoplane fighter was another matter entirely and time was pressing. In the summer of 1932 Société d'Application des Machines Motrices (SAMM) engaged the gifted 40-year-old Joseph Bernard Antoine de Boysson, who was pioneering four-gun hydraulic and electro-hydraulic powered turrets. Seizing the opportunity, North ordered two early SAMM turrets in November 1935 and negotiations for a licence began. While BPA was in the thick of settling in to Pendeford, the French-built turrets arrived at Norwich in June 1936. One of these was used as a pattern to speed British manufacture.

Having rejected the Hotspur, an initial order for eighty-seven production Defiants was placed by the Air Ministry in April 1937 and a licence agreement was concluded with SAMM. The second French turret was fitted in the nose of Overstrand K8175 during the summer of 1937. By then the prototype Defiant was ready and, minus the turret, had its maiden flight on 11 August 1937: it was another seven months before it was fully equipped.

The Fleet Air Arm was also seduced by the idea and the first Blackburn Roc, a development of the Skua dive-bomber, appeared in December 1938. Blackburn vested design authority to BPA, as the specialist in power-operated turrets, and all 136 Rocs were built at Pendeford, including the prototype.

While a fusillade from four close-coupled 0.303in Browning machine guns into the side or the belly of a bomber would be lethal, the turret fighter was neutered if its quarry was escorted by fast and manoeuvrable fighters. The Defiant and the Roc had more in common than their turrets. Both lacked any fixed, forward-firing guns. Once the enemy grasped this, frontal attacks – not even needing to be head-on – were very effective. After valiant but limited operational use, Defiants achieved a career in support roles, including gunnery training, air-sea rescue and target towing, the type remaining in production into 1942.

Applications for the BPA turret – for example on the Lockheed Hudson maritime patroller – blossomed, but in 1940 the Ministry of Aircraft Production, wanting BPA to concentrate on aeroplanes,

arranged for the Birmingham-based Joseph Lucas Ltd and other sub-contractors to take over the task. A total of 1,804 turrets – including classroom versions – were built by BPA, while Lucas and others went on to churn out more than 20,000 examples. This was the launch pad for Lucas to enter aviation, specialising in turbojet control systems and ancillaries. In the 1990s, prior to a merger with an American company, Lucas developed a remotely controlled gun turret for use under the 'chin' of attack helicopters.

Specification F.9/35 was only part of the Air Ministry's quest for a turret fighter, F.11/37 sought a two-crew, twin-engined heavy fighter equipped with a remotely controlled barbette containing four 20mm Hispano cannons – a Bittern for the 1940s. The P.92 was an advanced concept with a hump-like slim line turret fitted within the upper centre section. A half-scale aerodynamic research vehicle, the P.92/2, was designed to help speed development. To keep the P.92/2 as simple as possible, it had a wooden airframe but, as 'masters of metal', BPA had long since lost such skills and Heston Aircraft was commissioned to build the one-off. The P.92 project was axed in May 1940, but the half-scale version had a stay of execution. After its maiden flight in March 1941 it had a limited flight test programme. By mid-1940 Leslie Frise of Bristol had shown that devastating fire power did not require the complexities of a turret; the exceptional Beaufighter could bring four 20mm and six machine guns to bear on a target.

A page from a company pamphlet entitled 'Salute to the RAF' produced in 1943 showing the BP turret as fitted to a Lockheed Hudson. *KEC*

Cramped in the cockpit, the pilot provides scale in this view of the P.92/2 during its time at Boscombe Down, August 1943. The 'hump' fairing for the turret is evident. *Les Whitehouse-Boulton Paul Association*

Only one complete Defiant survives, N1671 with the RAF Museum. Painstakingly restored in 2009–12, it wears the colours of its first unit, Polish 307 Squadron, with which it served from September 1940 to October 1941. *RAF Museum*

Trainers and sub-contracting

Henry Clarke left the post of chief designer in 1940 and his place was taken by J W Batchelor, but beyond the P.92 no other in-house types left the drawing board for the factory floor during the war years. After the Defiant, Fairey Barracudas occupied the Pendeford production line. Beyond that it was intended that BPA build navalised versions of the Hawker Fury and an example was commenced in 1945. While the RAF shunned the new fighter, the Fleet Air Arm remained loyal and Hawker took back the programme; the unflown 'Wolverhampton Fury' was trucked to Langley for completion. Immediately post-war, a contract to convert 270 Vickers Wellingtons to T.10 crew trainers was a lifeline for the Pendeford workforce from 1946 to 1950.

Trainers tended to be named after places of learning and Oxford's Balliol College was commemorated by BPA's response to Specification T.7/45 to replace the Miles Master and North American Harvard. Initially, the requirement wanted a turboprop, the Armstrong Siddeley Mamba or the Rolls-Royce (RR) Dart, but this was later dropped after much development work. A three-seat cockpit was requested, with another pupil overlooking the instructor and trainee at the controls; this was also relinquished. The prototype, powered by an interim Bristol Mercury 820 radial, first flew on 30 May 1947. In that year the RR Merlin 35, with plenty in stock and lots of spares to hand, was chosen as the standard powerplant. Balliols were supplied to the RAF, as deck-landing trainers for the Fleet Air Arm and to Ceylon (the present-day Sri Lanka).

Blackburn was intended as a 'second force' production line with upwards of 120 to be constructed, but in the end only thirty were built at Brough. Having chopped and changed the specification, ultimately the RAF's adoption of 'all-through' jet training courtesy of the Hunting Jet Provost in 1955 put paid to large numbers of Balliols. The last example – and the end of whole aircraft manufacture for BPA – left Pendeford for Ceylon in August 1957.

Over at Woodford, Avro had pitched its Athena at T.7/45 and lost. The Manchester company was given a 'consolation' order for an armament trainer version to keep a caucus of its workforce employed until the Shackleton and later the Vulcan gained momentum, although the contract was later truncated to just fifteen units. (See the comparison table.)

As BPA began to morph into a control systems specialist, sub-contracts played a prominent role during the realignment. Pre-war,

B&P had built the wings for Blackburn Bluebird tourer/trainers and for Saro London flying boats. In the 1950s wings for Supermarine Swift jet fighters were made and in the early-1960s BPA designed and produced the flaps for the Vickers Vanguard airliner and made the wings and engine nacelles (complete with undercarriage) for the Beagle 206 twin.

Modification of English Electric Canberras for test and specialist roles was also a major source of revenue until the mid-1960s. The belly gun pack for the Canberra B(I).8 interdictor variant was designed and manufactured by BPA. The company was also heavily involved in the Lightning F.3 programme in 1959–63, including structural modifications to development batch airframes and the evolution of the type's enlarged ventral fuel tank. With the advent of jets, Pendeford was too restrictive and the airfield at Seighford was used as a test centre.

Balliol and Athena compared

	Balliol T.2	Athena T.2
First flown	1947	1948
Engine	RR Merlin 35	RR Merlin 35
	1,245hp	1,245hp
Span	39ft 4in	40ft
Wing area	250sq ft	270sq ft
Length	35ft 11in	37ft 3in
Loaded weight	8,410lb	9,043lb
Max speed at 10,000ft	288mph	297mph
Number built	145	19
From–to	1952–54	1949–51

Delta experimentals

During the late 1940s and '50s contracts were issued by the Ministries of Supply, Technology or Defence for experimental types. These were not just to 'push the envelope' but were a method of keeping design offices going when no other work was in the offing. The ministry men considered a good selection of competing manufacturers was desirable as a form of strategic reserve, but this policy was to be reversed in the 1960s. With the merger of Blackburn and General Aircraft on 1 January 1949, Frederick Francis 'Croak' Crocombe left Hanworth and took over from J W Batchelor as chief designer at BPA. He was appointed technical director two years later, serving in that capacity to 1966.

The fourth Balliol T.2, VW900, began acceptance trials at Boscombe Down in May 1949. *BPA*

Manufacturing Beagle 206 wings at Pendeford in 1962. *Boulton Paul Association*

P.111A VT935 was retired to the College of Aeronautics at Cranfield in April 1959 (where it is illustrated in August 1963). It joined the Midland Air Museum in July 1975. *Roy Bonser*

Boulton and Paul, Norwich

From	To	Total	Name/Designation	Type	Engine(s)	Notes
1917	-	1	Bobolink	Fighter	1 x Bentley BR.2	
1918	-	1	P.6	Test bed	1 x RAF 1a	
1919	1920	3	Bourges I–III	Bomber	2 x Bentley BR.2	[1]
1919	1920	2	Atlantic	Long-range trials	2 x Napier Lion	[2]
1919	1923	8	P.9	Tourer	1 x RAF 1a	
1919	-	1	P.10	Tourer	1 x Cosmos Lucifer	[3]
1922	1925	2	Bodmin	'Postal'	2 x Napier Lion	
1922	-	1	Bolton	Bomber	2 x Napier Lion	
1923	1926	7	Bugle I/II	Bomber	2 x Bristol Jupiter	
1926	1932	20	Sidestrand	Bomber	2 x Bristol Jupiter	[4]
1927	-	2	Bittern	Heavy fighter	2 x AS Lynx	
1928	-	1	Partridge	Fighter	1 x Bristol Jupiter	
1929	-	1	Phoenix	Sportsplane	1 x ABC Scorpion	
1931	-	1	P.32	Heavy bomber	3 x Bristol Jupiter	
1933	-	1	Mailplane	Light transport	2 x Bristol Pegasus	
1934	-	2	P.71A	Light transport	2 x AS Jaguar	
1935	1937	24	Overstrand	Bomber	2 x Bristol Pegasus	[5]

Other than the Bittern and the Phoenix, all biplanes. **[1]** Second example rebuilt as P.8 Atlantic. **[2]** Extensive rebuild of second P.7 Bourges for Atlantic crossing attempt; second example built from scratch. **[3]** Not completed – see narrative. **[4]** Mks I, II and III. Four converted to Overstrands, including the prototype. **[5]** Prototype converted from a Sidestrand III.

Crocombe's career with BPA began on Specification E.27/46, which sought a delta wing research jet. P.111 VT935 had its maiden flight at Boscombe Down on 10 October 1950 and today it is displayed at the Midland Air Museum at Coventry Airport. A follow-up was the more refined, T-tailed, P.120 VT951 responding to E.27/49. Test pilot 'Ben' Gunn was in command when this machine first flew at Boscombe on 6 August 1952. Just eleven flying hours and twenty-three days later control was lost and Gunn had a miraculous escape from the black-painted delta. A large number of projects were churned out until 1954, chasing all manner of markets, but the P.120 was the final BPA design to be built.

Boulton Paul sub-contracts

Type	Total	From	To	Notes
R A/c Factory F.E.2b/d	550	1915	1917	[1] [2]
Sopwith F.1 Camel	1,575	1917	1918	[2]
Felixstowe F.3, F.5	70	1917	1919	[2] [3]
Sopwith Snipe	425	1918	1919	[2]
Hawker Demon	106	1936	1937	[4] [5]
Blackburn Roc	136	1938	1940	[4] [6]
Fairey Barracuda I/II/III	692	1942	1945	[4]
Hawker Sea Fury X	1	1945	-	[7]

[1] At least the batch of 250 F.E.2ds featured nacelles built by Richard Garrett and Sons at Leiston. **[2]** All at Mousehold, Norwich. **[3]** Fuselages/hulls only, completed by Phoenix Dynamo – see Chapter 18. **[4]** All at Pendeford. **[5]** At least 14 completed as Turret Demons, others converted after issue to service. **[6]** BP design number P.93. **[7]** VB857, not flown and trucked to Langley April 1945 and first flown there in January 1946 as third prototype – see Chapter 25.

Birth of fly-by-wire

Skills in powered control systems that had evolved from work with turrets meant that BPA was much in demand from the rest of the aircraft industry and, increasingly, for a wide range of other applications. From 1954, North determined that the design and supply of powered control units of increasing sophistication were to be the company's main concern. Hydraulic power gave way to electronically actuated powered controls – fly-by-wire (FBW).

In the early 1950s, BP began to convert the RR Tay-engined Vickers Viscount VX217 at Seighford to act as a test bed. Once transformed it was taken on a careful, phase by phase series of trials, initially with the electronic control system deactivated. During the summer of 1957 test pilot Richard 'Dickie' Mancus was flying using the 'electric' controls while George 'Loopy' Dunworth backed up with a 'parallel' mechanical input. The pair made approaches and landings on a 'virtual' runway at an altitude of 5,000ft. As such Dickie captained the world's first fully FBW controlled sortie. It fell to Ben Gunn to make the inaugural official 'hard' landing – at Defford – in VX217 on 2 January 1958. Step by step this work led to the Active Control Technology SEPECAT Jaguar of 1981 – detailed in Chapter 13.

Control specialist Dowty and BPA joined together as Dowty Boulton Paul in 1961, but eight years later the name became the Dowty Group. Several ownership and name changes have occurred since – Smiths Industries, GE Aviation Systems and by 2009 the Moog Aviation Group, still based at Wolverhampton. And what of the original Boulton *and* Paul? A famous name in window and door frames, the company was acquired by the Rugby Group, but the original name was retained for marketing. In 1999 the US-owned Jeld-Wen acquired the operation and the business name Boulton and Paul, established in 1874, faded away.

Boulton Paul, Wolverhampton

From	To	Total	Name/Designation	Type	Engine(s)	Notes
1937	1943	986	Defiant I/II/III	Turret fighter	1 x RR Merlin	
1941	-	1	P.92/2	Experimental	2 x DH Gipsy Major	[1]
1948	1957	199	Balliol T.1/T.2	Advanced trainer	1 x RR Merlin	[2]
1950	-	1	P.111/A	Research	1 x RR Nene	
1952	-	1	P.120	Research	1 x RR Nene	
1953	1954	30	Sea Balliol T.21	Advanced trainer	1 x RR Merlin	

Piston-engined monoplanes other than P.111 and P.120, delta-winged jets. **[1]** Built by Heston Aircraft at Heston. **[2]** Includes 30 sub-contracted to Blackburn at Brough.

CHAPTER ELEVEN

Fallen Giant

Bristol
1910 to 1960

'Sir George formed his company with the express intention of developing reliable aeroplanes capable of useful and profitable operation in both peace and war.' Christopher Barnes

CHRISTMAS CAME EARLY for Bristol, when the prototype Type 170 freighter-cum-airliner first flew on 2 December 1945. The big, portly twin heralded a change of direction for the company. Adjusting to peacetime was challenging and to help take the sting out of the inevitable turndown on the factory floor a range of aluminium prefabricated buildings had been devised to help resurrect Britain's bomb-damaged cities and towns. Orders began to roll in for the Type 170 while the Buckingham, Buckmaster and Brigand, although drastically cut in numbers, looked set to stay in production until the end of the decade.

The design office was busy issuing manufacturing drawings for the prestigious Brabazon transatlantic airliner. To get ready for the mammoth's debut, Filton airfield was being dramatically transformed. There was also a thriving aero engine division, busily supplying both the 'home team' and its rivals, with turboprops and turbojets in development and guided missiles on the horizon. The motor vehicle group was again attracting buyers for its luxury cars. As part of its diversification programme, Bristol's management had taken a very brave decision to become a rotorcraft pioneer, knowing this would take considerable investment and much trial and error.

As New Year's Day 1950 was celebrated the outlook for Bristol was rosy. Any predictions that within a decade the company would no longer be a major player would have been met with incredulity. Yet by the end of June 1960 the last two Britannia turboprop transports were awaiting delivery to the RAF. Nineteen Belvedere twin-rotor helicopters were under assembly, the last example due for delivery in mid-1962. Completion of a pair of Type 188 experimental jets was the only 'new' in-house work the once mighty concern had on its books.

On 1 July 1960 the British Aircraft Corporation (BAC), a Conservative government-inspired consolidation of an industry crippled by overcapacity, was officially born. The new entity comprised Bristol, English Electric of Preston and Vickers of Weybridge. This was not a union of equals, the once mighty Bristol was the junior partner – how had this come about?

Boxkite and lawyers

A trip to France in 1909 introduced Bristolian Sir George White to aviation and he was quick to see its potential. A shrewd businessman, his many activities included the Bristol Tramways and Carriage Company and he saw in aeroplanes another method of transport and profit. He set up four limited companies on 19 February 1910: British and Colonial Aeroplane, British and Colonial Aviation, Bristol Aeroplane and Bristol Aviation. White chose to trade under the

The maiden flight of the prototype Britannia, Series 100 G-ALBO, on 16 August 1952. Behind is a Type 170, perhaps of the Royal Australian Air Force. *Bristol*

British and Colonial Aeroplane Co Ltd banner until March 1920, when Bristol Aeroplane Co Ltd was activated and then, from January 1956, Bristol Aircraft Ltd came into use. For the purposes of this work, these three are all given the 'Bristol' label.

To celebrate Bristol's half-century in February 1960, John Pudney was commissioned to write *Bristol Fashion*, an affectionate and engaging romp through the company's heritage. Enhanced by the artwork of David Gentleman, this tome is well worth seeking out. Pudney described White, who was 56 in 1910, as: 'an eminent Victorian, wearing in his heyday fine glossy mutton-chop whiskers and attending aviation meetings in an ankle-length overcoat topped by a curly bowler.' He also noted that the knight of the realm was a 'self-made and steady, painstaking, opportunist'.

Tram sheds at Filton, north of the city of Bristol, were set aside as an aeroplane factory. White entered into a licence agreement with Société Zodiac of Paris for its steel tube construction Type 52B biplane, designed by Gabriel Voisin. This was no half-hearted matter: sub-assemblies and components for a batch of six Zodiacs were commenced. The first Zodiac failed to take off, it was too heavy for its 50hp Darracq pusher. Where others might have persevered in the hope of a breakthrough, White ordered the Zodiac prototype and the kits of parts to be scrapped. He set his lawyers on the French company to seek – successfully – recompense.

At the same time, former tramway engineer George Henry Challenger was instructed to make a pusher biplane on the same lines as that of Voisin's rival, the all-wooden Farman. Challenger admired the Zodiac's cast fittings and fasteners and incorporated them in his creation. Fitted with a reliable 50hp Gnome rotary, the biplane – soon to adopt its nickname of 'Boxkite' – flew well in July 1910. It was launched into production and demand was such that another tram shed, at Brislington, south of the city centre, was brought into service.

Lawyers crossed the English Channel from France, representing Société Henri et Maurice Farman, claiming – unsuccessfully – breach of copyright. The modifications that Challenger had incorporated allowed Bristol's legal eagles to assert that the Boxkite owed only layout similarities to the Farman. With more than eighty examples built, for flying schools and the military and with exports including Australia and Imperial Russia, the Boxkite was an outstanding first product.

Challenger went on to oversee the creation of a tractor biplane devised by two of White's 'mercenary' French pilots, Robert Grandseigne and Maurice Versupuy; the 1911 Monoplane, with Archibald R Low, and the Type T general-purpose military pusher biplane. Challenger and Low both departed in 1912 to join Vickers.

A Boxkite believed to be at Durdham Downs, Clifton, during the first public demonstration of the type, September 1910. *Rolls-Royce*

Casting the net wide

White surrounded himself with designer talent, encouraging each to beaver away to see who showed the greatest potential. In April 1910 he employed Eric Cecil Gordon England as a pilot (to avoid confusion with geography, GE from here onwards). Previously GE had flown some of the creations of British-domiciled Frenchman José Weiss. At Filton he was encouraged to try his hand at design and in 1911 GE reconfigured a Type T into a tractor biplane. A run of original general-purpose biplanes followed. In January 1912 Henri Coandă signed up with Bristol as a technical adviser; GE held reservations about the Romanian's methods and in February 1913 he left to go into business with James Radley. Jointly they devised a large pusher seaplane at Portholme, near Huntingdon. From 1914 to 1919 GE was general manager of the Peterborough-based Frederick Sage company. In 1919 GE joined his father, George, in the motor industry, using his aviation experience to create lightweight car bodies. He designed a single-seat glider for the *Daily Mail's* Itford trials of 1922. GE became the managing director of General Aircraft in 1934, holding that post until 1942. Retiring from industry in 1949, Eric Cecil Gordon England died in February 1976, aged 85.

French pilot/engineer Pierre Prier joined the Bristol staff in the summer of 1911. As an instructor with the Blériot school at Hendon, he came to fame as the first to fly non-stop from London to Paris (Hendon to Issy-les-Moulineaux) on 12 April 1911 in a time of three hours fifty-six minutes. His knowledge of monoplanes was soon put to good use at Filton: more than thirty single- and two-seaters appeared up to late 1912. In that year the Royal Flying Corps (RFC) 'banned' monoplanes and Prier returned to France, serving in the Great War.

As noted above, Romanian-born Henri Coandă began working for Bristol in January 1912, rising to chief engineer two years later. He had exhibited a biplane in Paris in 1910 with what would later be called a ducted fan in the nose. It is uncertain if this flew or not but was the first example of this method of propulsion. Coandă's initial designs at Filton were based on Prier's but he went on to conceive some original monoplanes and biplanes.

GE's antipathy towards Coandă has already been mentioned. Geoffrey William England, GE's younger brother, was also a keen aviator, learning to fly at the Bristol-owned school at Larkhill in September 1912. In the New Year GE was horrified to find that Geoffrey had joined Bristol and was assisting Coandă. Efforts to find Geoffrey other employment failed and GE's relations with Coandă fractured; it was then that GE departed for Huntingdon. On 5 March 1913 Geoffrey volunteered to carry out an endurance test prior to the Romanian government accepting an order for military monoplanes. Geoffrey had been flying for nearly an hour and began a steep descent. At about 600ft the monoplane broke up, the port wing collapsed and he was killed in the crash.

By 1915 Coandă had returned to France and worked on projects that later included ducted fan experiments for the Luftwaffe in Vichy France during World War Two. He returned to his native Bucharest in 1969, undertaking research and tuition within Nicolae Ceauşescu's regime. Aged 86, Henri Coandă died in Romania in 25 November 1972.

X Department

The last of White's itinerant 'circus' of designers was the gifted Lt Cdr Charles Dennistoun 'Dennis' Burney. The Royal Navy officer had come up with a new interpretation of a 'water plane'. Seconded from the navy, he was assigned in January 1912 to Bristol's chief draughtsman Frank Barnwell – of which much more anon – who had established the highly secret 'X Department' under White's instructions. This covert set up was not in a purpose-built, high-tech, design office; Barnwell had taken over a house at 4 Fairlawn Avenue in Filton.

Inspired by hydrofoil-equipped boats, Burney was convinced that the system could be adopted by aircraft to avoid drag-inducing floats. Burney came up with a biplane – the X.1 – but this was rejected by Barnwell, who was convinced that a monoplane was the solution. The sleek twin-seat X.2 was the result. The fuselage was sealed and the wing tips carried small floats, allowing the machine to settle in the water when not being propelled. The 80hp Canton-Unné engine drove a tractor propeller and a water screw on the end of each of two 'legs' via a clutch system. The two legs – Burney called them 'hydropeds' – resembled a conventional undercarriage but with a marine propeller and blade-like hydrofoils at the end, not wheels. The conventional propeller and the twin water screws brought the X.2 up to take-off speed, after which the hydropeds were declutched. On return, the X.2 would alight on the hydrofoils until it slowed down enough to settle in the water.

Sadly, the X.2 never got to make that transition on its own, although it was towed behind a fast launch during testing. Not deterred, the much larger X.3 was devised. Its water contra-rotating screws shared a centrally located shaft mounted between the hyrdopeds, eliminating the asymmetries encountered on the X.2. Trials of the X.3 commenced in June 1914 but the following month it hit a sandbank and was damaged. The project was brought to a close without it having flown freely.

The Burney X.3 during testing at Milford Haven, June 1914.
Peter Green Collection

Returning to the navy, in 1915 Burney invented the Paravane, a hydrofoil-equipped device towed behind minesweepers. For his work in mine countermeasures he was awarded the Order of St Michael and St George (CMG). Ideas poured out of Burney, one of which was the importance of passenger-carrying airships. He was appointed managing director of the Airship Guarantee Company, building the R.100 at Howden with Barnes Wallis of Vickers and Alfred Hessell Tiltman and Nevil Shute Norway, who later formed Airspeed. During World War Two Burney was again scheming weaponry for the Navy and was reunited with Norway. Cdr Sir Charles Dennistoun Burney Bt CMG died in retirement in Bermuda on 11 November 1968, aged 80.

Breakthrough Scout

White's 'stable' of designers had not been able to repeat the success of the Boxkite. That task fell to Frank Sowter Barnwell, who was set to transform the company's prospects. White died on 22 November 1916 having seen his aviation dreams more than fulfilled: he had started another industry in the city of his birth. Taking the helm was his son, George Stanley (later Sir Stanley), who retired in 1955.

With a predominance of monoplanes, Bristol had little to attract orders from the biplane-obsessed Royal Flying Corps. Instead, from 1913 it attracted repeat orders for Royal Aircraft Factory B.E.2s and a handful of B.E.8s. When production of B.E.2s ended in 1917 more than a thousand had been made. This required massive expansion of the factory on the south of the airfield, while on the northern perimeter nine 'Belfast Truss'-style hangars were erected for the War Office to process Filton's output. Some of these buildings became the basis for the Aerospace Bristol museum, which opened its doors in July 2017.

While the Burney project occupied a lot of Barnwell's time at No. 4, he was keen to extend his repertoire. He had befriended Henry Richard Busteed, who preferred to be known as 'Harry', and both were impressed with the compact Sopwith Tabloid. The 24-year-old Busteed had emigrated from his native Australia in 1911 along with another Harry – Harry George Hawker. They went their separate ways: Hawker joined Sopwith and Hawker Aircraft was named to commemorate him; Busteed learned to fly with Bristol at Larkhill and became an occasional test pilot for White. It was Busteed who came to grips with the X.2 and X.3. Busteed joined the Royal Naval Air Service (RNAS) in late 1914 and he retired from the RAF as an air commodore in 1943.

Barnwell and Busteed devised a small, single-seat biplane for sporting purposes, while knowing full well it would be ideal as a scout. They adapted the unfinished fuselage of Coandă's SB.5 monoplane, coupling it to new tail surfaces, small-span wings and an 80hp Gnome. The result was nicknamed the 'Baby Bristol' and Busteed took it for its first flight by February 1914. The 'Baby' was entered into a race at Brooklands in May, Busteed coming second to Barnwell's elder brother, Harold Barnwell, piloting a Tabloid with the advantage of an extra 20hp. A pair of improved Scout Bs followed and they were requisitioned in August 1914. They were sent to France for operational trials, where they were dubbed 'Bristol Bullets' by admiring pilots. Initial orders for the RFC and the RNAS were placed in late 1914 and production continued to 1916. The substantially redesigned Scout F appeared in 1918, but failed to attract further business.

Bristol's allegiance to monoplanes was at last rewarded in 1916, but it took the private-venture M.1 single-seat scout to break the War Office intransigence. Taking into account reports from front-line pilots, including those flying Bristol Scouts, the prototype M.1 appeared in July 1916 and was followed by four more for trials. It did not attract an order until August 1917 and that only amounted to 125 units. The high landing speed was given as one reason for the disappointing take-up.

Harry Busteed in front of the 'Baby Bristol' at Larkhill, February 1914.
Peter Green Collection

Civilianised M.1D G-EAVO was exported to Spain in late 1921. *E J Riding*

'The Captain'

Born in Lewisham, Kent, Barnwell was educated in Edinburgh and apprenticed to a Clydeside shipyard. With his elder (by one year) brother, Richard Harold Barnwell – who answered to Harold – Barnwell created a biplane glider and then a small pusher biplane with a 7hp engine. Both were tested by Harold but the latter failed to fly. By 1909 the brothers were running the Grampian Motor and Engineering Company in Stirling.

The third Barnwell type appeared in 1909, a canard biplane with a modified 40hp Hunter Tourist Trophy motorcar engine driving a pair of pusher propellers. With Harold at the helm on 10 September 1909, it flew a distance of 80 yards, but was damaged in the landing. Their fourth machine, which appeared in 1911, was a single-seat monoplane with an in-house 40hp Grampian twin-cylinder engine. Harold was awarded £50 for the first flight by a member of the Scottish Aeronautical Society. Later in 1911 the pair went south o' the border. As noted above, by January 1912 Barnwell was chief draughtsman in the covert X Department in Filton's leafy Fairlawn Avenue. Harold was instructing at the Vickers school at Brooklands by 1913 and in August 1914 he was appointed as that company's chief test pilot.

Feeling underused at No. 4, Barnwell enlisted in the RFC in late 1914. He served as a ferry and general trials pilot, initially as a second lieutenant, rising to captain. Sense prevailed and Barnwell was recalled to Filton in August 1915, where he was appointed chief designer, aged 35. His period in the RFC earned him the nickname 'The Captain', which stuck throughout his long tenure with Bristol.

Having settled in as chief designer, one of Barnwell's first moves was to hire an assistant. After studying at Bristol University, Gloucestershire-born Leslie George Frise signed up as a sub lieutenant in the RNAS in

1915. This was short-lived; the 30-year-old's engineering abilities had been drawn to the attention of Barnwell and 'LG', as Frise was known, was offered the post in September 1915. He started off with stress calculations and drawings for what became Barnwell's F.2B Fighter. The pair became a formidable force, good friends and vital to the success of the company, working side-by-side all the way through to the Beaufort.

Barnwell's wanderlust returned in 1921 and he resigned from Bristol to take up a commission in the Royal Australian Air Force. He joined Sqn Ldr Lawrence James Wackett's newly established experimental department at Randwick, Sydney. Although Wackett became known as the 'Father of the Australian Aircraft Industry', Barnwell was soon disillusioned. He returned to Filton in October 1923, taking his old post. With the advent of the *Britain First* and the Blenheim he was promoted to chief engineer in 1936.

When Bristol had reluctantly let Barnwell go in 1921, Wilfred Thomas Reid took over as chief designer. Reid had joined Bristol in 1916 from the Royal Aircraft Factory. He tackled the detailing of the all-metal MR.1 reconnaissance biplane in 1917 to take the load off Barnwell and Frise as they launched the F.2 series. He took a similar role on the Braemar triplane bomber, its Pullman airliner derivative, and the flightless Tramp project. As chief designer, Reid was in charge of the Ten-Seater, Taxiplane, Racer and Bloodhound fighter, handing over the Berkeley bomber to his former boss. With Barnwell's reinstatement, Reid was surplus to requirements and it was his turn to emigrate, going to Montreal-based Canadian Vickers in 1924. His story continues in Chapter 37.

In 1923 Barnwell retrospectively gave numerical designations to Bristol designs (both built and projected), starting with the Scout as the Type 1 through to the Type 89 advanced trainer of the F.2B for Greece. The first to be given a number from inception was the Type 90 Berkeley – his 'inheritance' from Reid. The tables only note such numbers from the Berkeley.

In *Bristol Fashion* Pudney praises Barnwell's creativity and leadership skills while pointing out that: 'this great man of the air was a very poor pilot indeed and went through life to his death happily unacknowledging [sic] the fact.' Barnwell's career included a string of 'prangs', two of which will serve as examples. In 1917 he took an F.2B to France on a fact-finding expedition with front-line pilots. He crashed and broke both his ankles, thereafter always walking with a limp. While delivering the second prototype MR.1 biplane to the Royal Aircraft Establishment at Farnborough on 19 April 1919 Barnwell hit a tree while landing. Barnwell was unhurt, but the biplane was a write-off. By the 1930s the management at Bristol had imposed a ban on Barnwell flying their products. As will be seen later, tragically this could not apply to other types.

A delightful depiction of Frank Barnwell by David Gentleman in John Pudney's 'Bristol Fashion'. A Scout is fancifully outside the window, while the great man is holding a model F.2B. The drawing is titled 'Barnwell inside No. 4' – his X Department at Filton's Fairlawn Avenue. *KEC*

With an airman supplying scale, the second Braemar, C4297, in 1919. This example was powered by four Liberty 12s, two tractors and two pushers. *Bristol*

F.2B Mk.III J8452 was part of a batch built in 1927 fitted with dual controls. Stripped down, it served as an instructional airframe at Hamble from July 1934. *KEC*

One of twelve Hispano-Suiza-powered F.2Bs supplied to the Spanish Air Force in 1924. *Bristol*

5,000-plus, eleven years

The Introduction puts forward eight vital characteristics needed to create a really great aircraft. For Bristol and Barnwell all those boxes were ticked by the F.2 family and nineteen years later by the Blenheim dynasty. Just as the 504 turned Avro from a manufacturer to an industrial giant, so did the F.2 for Bristol: both biplanes are among the most significant aircraft of the Great War – and beyond.

The concept of a heavily armed, yet fast and agile, two-seater was revolutionary. With a fixed, forward-firing Vickers gun and a flexible machine gun in the rear compartment, the 'Biff' or 'Brisfit' as it was nicknamed, was able to attack and defend itself. To enable the gunner to fire forward, over the pilot's head, the 'dropped' wing layout was adopted. The lower wing was separate from and below the fuselage. This allowed a good separation of the two wings from one another while leaving the smallest practical gap between the top of the fuselage and the upper wing. A cut out centre section on the trailing edge of the upper wing gave the pilot good upward visibility. The initial version, the F.2A, had a gap between the lower wings, but this was replaced by a centre section – so that the wing was continuous from tip to tip – on the further refined F.2B. This greatly increased the structural integrity and added to the wing area for a slight increase in weight. For all of Barnwell's innovations, engine choice was vital. The Rolls-Royce Falcon V-12, at first rated at 190hp but rising to 275hp, was the perfect marriage, although Hispano-Suizas, Siddeley Pumas, Sunbeam Arabs and Wolseley Vipers were also employed.

The prototype flew on 9 September 1916 and the initial F.2As were delivered three months later. Huge orders poured in and the type was widely sub-contracted. F.2Bs survived the immediate post-Armistice culls and continued to be manufactured until September 1919. This dovetailed nicely with a sub-contract for a batch of Parnall

Panther carrier-borne fleet reconnaissance biplanes, which lasted to 1921. But the Brisfit's reliability and adaptability meant that it was ideal for the RAF's roles of 'aerial policeman' and army co-operation, especially within the Middle East and India. The second phase of the F.2B's prodigious industrial life was dawning. Reconditioned F.2Bs to Fighter Mk.II status proved to be insufficient; new-build examples were needed. The trend continued with the beefed up Mk.III with higher operating weights finally bringing the production line to a close in July 1927. Surviving Mk.IIIs again went through the factory in 1928–30 as they were converted to the still heavier Mk.IV status.

Licences were granted to Belgium and the USA and F.2Bs were exported to Australia, Canada, Greece, Ireland, Mexico and New Zealand, among others. The type also made the translation to civil usage, the Siddeley Puma-engined Tourer finding a niche among emerging charter operators. Fitted with an in-house Bristol Jupiter radial, the market was again extended, particularly as an advanced trainer. All of the versions amounted to more than 5,000 F.2s. Reconditioning and rebuilding contracts provided further work on about 1,200 airframes: the Brisfit was an industry all of its own. Along with rival concerns, Bristol sought to capture F.2B replacement contracts with the F.2C Badger of 1918 (despite its designation, a totally new design), the Bloodhound of 1923 and the Boarhound of 1925. However, until the end of the 1920s the need continued to be met by reworked F.2Bs.

Out of the Cosmos

As well as Barnwell, there is another name that came to the fore to turn the business into a giant – Roy Fedden. During his apprenticeship with the original Bristol Motor Company, Bristolian Fedden devised a car that sparked the interest of local omnibus manufacturer Brazil Straker and Co. By the advent of 1914 the War Office was the main customer for Brazil Straker, which by then was mass producing lorries

Bristol F.2 'family' 1916 to 1927

From	To	Total	Name/Designation	Type	Engine(s)	Notes
1916	1919	4,747	F.2A, F.2B	2-seat fighter	1 x RR Falcon	[1]
1919	1924	488	F.2B Mk.II	Military GP	1 x RR Falcon	[2]
1919	1921	33	Tourer	Light transport	1 x Siddeley Puma	
1923		26	Jupiter-Fighter	Advanced trainer	1 x Bristol Jupiter	
1926	1927	121	F.2B Mk.III	Military GP	1 x RR Falcon	[3]

[1] Also sub-contracted to Armstrong Whitworth, Gloucestershire (Gloster), National Aircraft Factory 3, Liverpool, and Angus Sanderson, Newcastle upon Tyne; Austin, Birmingham; Harris and Sheldon, Birmingham; Standard, Coventry. Licensed to Curtiss, Buffalo, New York, USA (27 as O-1), US Army Engineering Division, Dayton, Ohio, USA (1 as XB-1A), and Dayton-Wright Airplane, Dayton, Ohio, USA (40 as XB-1A). [2] Additionally nearly 600 F.2Bs reconditioned to Mk.II status from wartime airframes. Includes 40 licensed by Société Anonyme Belge de Constructions Aéronautiques (SABCA), Belgium. [3] Includes 38 airframes delivered without engines and dual-control versions. Surviving Mk.IIIs upgraded to Mk.IV status 1928–29.

and other wheeled hardware. The RNAS turned to Fedden and his team to solve problems with American Curtiss OX-5 engines. The efficiency and quality of their work led to a sub-contract to make Rolls-Royce Hawk and Falcon engines; the only organisation to be given such an accolade. Most of the Brazil Straker Falcons were fitted on Bristol F.2Bs – local engine, local aeroplane.

Fedden was keen to branch out to his own designs and created a 345hp, two-row, helical-pattern, 14-cylinder radial – the original Mercury and not to be confused with his incredibly successful single-row, 9-cylinder Mercury of the 1920s. Nothing came of the innovative powerplant but the next creation, the 9-cylinder Jupiter, was destined for great things. Brazil Straker had been acquired by Cosmos Engineering in 1919, but by early 1920 that business had foundered. The second F.2C Badger was fitted with a Jupiter and Barnwell was very taken with the radial's potential.

The Air Ministry shared Barnwell's views and cajoled Bristol to take the plunge and buy the rights to the Jupiter. The ministry mandarins were recovering from the foolhardy 1917 decision to standardise on the woeful ABC Motors Dragonfly 9-cylinder and a manufacturer to fill the void made great sense. In the economic downturn of post-war Britain, this was a risk-laden venture for Bristol but it soon turned into a masterstroke. The receiver is believed to have accepted £15,000 – £825,000 in present-day values – and Fedden and his team moved into Filton's 'Belfast Truss' hangars.

Fedden and Barnwell worked closely together and Bristol engines were made available to almost all-comers; there was no merit in making the product exclusive to Bristol types. As explained in the introduction, the powerplant side of things must be dealt with fleetingly, but the tables give an indication of the scope of the Filton aero engine enterprise. As part of the consolidation of the British aviation industry, the Bristol engine division merged with Armstrong Siddeley in April 1959, becoming Bristol Siddeley Engines (BSE). This, in turn, was acquired by Rolls-Royce in October 1966. Gifted engineer Sir Alfred Hubert Roy Feddon MBE died on 21 November 1973, aged 88.

Centaurus 661 18-cylinder 2-row sleeve-valve radial, as fitted to the Airspeed Ambassador. *Bristol Siddeley*

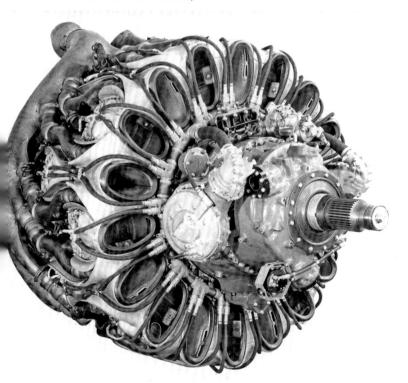

In 1910 White had registered four trading names. The Bristol and Colonial Aeroplane Company was dissolved and on 9 February 1920 the Bristol Aeroplane Company was activated. This was not an indication of dire straits, it was shrewd gambit to raise further capital and minimise the dreaded Excess Profits Duty.

Bristol piston engines

Name, Type/Format	From	Application*	Notes
Jupiter, 9-cy radial	1920	Hawker Woodcock	[1]
Lucifer, 3-cy radial	1920	B&P P.10	[1]
Cherub, 2-cy hoz opposed	1923	Avro Avis	
Orion, 9-cy radial	1926	Bristol Brownie	
Mercury, 9-cy radial	1926	Bristol Blenheim	[2]
Titan, 5-cy radial	1928	Avro 504N	
Phoenix, 9-cy radial diesel	1928	Westland Wapiti	
Neptune, 7-cy radial	1930	Bristol 110	
Hydra, 16-cy 2-row radial	1931	Hawker Harrier	
Pegasus, 9-cy radial	1932	Westland Wallace	
Draco, 9-cy radial	1932	Westland Wapiti	
Perseus, 9-cy radial	1932	Blackburn Botha	
Aquila, 9-cy radial	1934	Vickers Venom	
Taurus, 14-cy 2-row radial	1936	Bristol Beaufort	
Hercules, 14-cy 2-row radial	1936	Short Stirling	
Centaurus, 18-cy 2-row radial	1938	Hawker Sea Fury	

* Typical, or only, use. [1] Cosmos developed the Jupiter and Lucifer, rights acquired by Bristol in July 1920 – see narrative. [2] Not to be confused with the Brazil Straker Mercury of 1918, another Roy Fedden creation.

Bristol turbine engines

Name, Type/Format	From	Application*	Notes
Theseus turboprop	1945	HP Hermes 5	
Phoebus turbojet	1946	Avro Lincoln	[1]
Proteus turboprop	1947	Bristol Britannia	
Coupled Proteus Turboprop	1949	Saro Princess	[2]
Orion turboprop	1956	Bristol Britannia	[1]
Olympus turbojet	1950	Avro Vulcan	
Orpheus turbojet	1954	Folland Gnat	

* Typical, or only, use. [1] Test bed only. [2] Princess had four Coupled 610s and a pair of Proteus 600s.

Trial and error

All of the manufacturers during the 1920s and '30s worked feverishly creating prototypes to meet Air Ministry requirements, some with ministerial backing, others as private ventures. Additionally, new markets were sought and designers searched far and wide to find new construction techniques, all to provide an edge over the competition. The table 'Bristol inter-war types' gives a brief taste of these and two types deserve greater attention.

To showcase the Jupiter 9-cylinder engine, a radical single-seat racer was conceived in 1922. It was initially to be called the Blizzard but the more pedestrian Racer was settled upon. The big radial was submerged within the fuselage, with a very large 'hollow' spinner allowing airflow into the engine for cooling. The short wing was fitted with full-span ailerons and the main undercarriage was retractable. On the Racer's first outing in July 1922, test pilot Cyril Uwins was in trouble as soon as he lifted off; the ailerons were far too powerful and caused the thin wing to bend. A quick, very low-level circuit was accomplished. The wing was wire-braced for the second excursion but the fabric on the port wing ripped badly and the pitot head on the leading edge of that wing vanished. Another short circuit! While the Racer was being fitted with bracing wires, the huge propeller spinner had received several coats of paint: this was sufficient to unbalance the moulded wooden structure. It had shattered, damaging the wing surface and stripping off the pitot head as the debris departed. The ailerons were reduced in size, but by the seventh flight it was clear that the Racer was a step too far and it was quietly forgotten.

The one-off Racer G-EBDR at Filton in August 1922 with wire-braced wings. The troublesome spinner has yet to be painted. *Bristol*

The Bagshot – named after the town in Surrey – was a disaster for Bristol and underlined just how badly Air Ministry requirements were devised. A December 1924 request for a twin-engined monoplane fighter did not specify the armament. A contract for a prototype was secured in March 1925. In September, with construction well advanced, the specification was amended requiring supercharged engines, increased speed and extra fuel capacity. A month later the weaponry was revealed: a pair of 37mm Coventry Ordnance Works cannon. These 'COW-guns' fired 1½lb shells and each weapon weighed a cool 120lb, *without* the shell feed mechanism, magazine and mountings. Barnwell was astounded, suggesting either a new fuselage to bring the weight down or scrapping the whole deal. The ministry insisted on continuing. The Bagshot had its first flight in July 1927. Testing went badly, the wing flexing so much as to induce aileron reversal. Eventually the ministry accepted the one-off for structural testing: it never carried armament.

Bulldog and Bombay

The stand-out Bristol types of the inter-war period prior to the advent of the Blenheim 'family' were the Bulldog and the Bombay. After the exceptional F.2B Fighter, the company churned out a string of hopeful prototypes from 1919 to 1925 but, try as it might, it could not break back into the RAF fighter market. By 1926 the Air Ministry was changing its mind regarding fighters, seeking a higher-performance interceptor, replacing the standing patrols as epitomised by the Armstrong Whitworth (AW) Siskins and Gloster Gamecocks of the day.

Specification F.9/26 was hotly contested with a dozen types from eight concerns hoping to sweep up the entire contract or a part of it. Established procedure with the Air Ministry was to secure agreement for a prototype with fingers crossed that a production order would follow. Manufacturers were increasingly realising that there was another route: seek agreement with the ministry to submit a private venture in the belief that a design that did not adhere to the specification's strictures might have greater appeal than more cautious interpretations.

Barnwell and his team came up with two solutions, the Jupiter-powered Bulldog and the Bullpup, with a Mercury. First flown on 17 May 1927, the Bulldog was triumphant in its Mk.II form and deliveries began in 1928. Ironically, the factory floor at Filton was also busy with a sub-contracted batch of AW Siskins, RAF replacement policy being a leisurely process in the 1920s. Along with smaller numbers of Hawker Furies, Bulldogs formed the basis of British air defence in the first half of the 1930s. The RAF's endorsement of the Bulldog paid huge dividends and export orders rolled in, including Scandinavian and Baltic states, Australia and two for the US Navy. Japan took out a licence, but only two were completed in Tokyo. Later attempts at Air Ministry fighter specifications – the Type 123 biplane, the 133 monoplane (both of 1934) and the 146 monoplane (of 1938) all failed to raise eyebrows. Having waited a long time to achieve a post-F.2B mainline fighter order from the RAF, the Bulldog was the last of the line for Bristol: the manufacturer's future lay with the ground-breaking Blenheim.

All eight Bulldog IIs – A12-1 to -8 – ordered by the Royal Australian Air Force in 1929 under assembly at Filton. In the background is the fuselage of a Type 110A four-passenger biplane. *Bristol*

The wing-bending antics of the Bagshot gave rise to much toil in the Filton design and stress departments that resulted in the adoption of multiple spars and stressed-skin surfaces. This was put to good use in the Bombay bomber-transport, named after the Indian city these days called Mumbai. The prototype flew on 23 June 1935 and Uwins offered George White, Sir George's grandson, and Archibald Russell, part of Barnwell's staff, to go along for the ride. By then Barnwell had been banned from flying Bristol types because of he was such an important company asset. The prospect – remote though it may have been – that the Bombay's maiden flight might have robbed Bristol of a veteran test pilot, the future of the White 'clan' and a vital element of the design team seems to be at odds with a policy of caution.

Above: The first Short-built Bombay, L5808, had a brief career. First flown at Sydenham in March 1939, it crashed on take-off from Martlesham Heath five months later. A Hawker Hurricane and Henley are in the background. *Rolls-Royce*

Right: Type 138A K4897 was designed as a high-altitude record-breaker and was delivered to the Royal Aircraft Establishment on 23 July 1936. With Flt Lt M J Adam at the helm it reached a world record 53,937ft in a ninety-five-minute climb on 30 June 1937. *Bristol*

Middle right: Bristol's design team knew it as 'The Captain's Gig', Lord Beaverbrook called it 'Britain First' – the Type 142, precursor of the Blenheim. *Bristol*

Bottom right: New Filton House, Bristol's art deco headquarters, was completed in April 1936. Above the main door is Pegasus, the winged horse, and at the top is a head-on view of 'Britain First'. In 2013 this building was renamed Pegasus House as part of the Airbus Aerospace Park. *Ken Ellis*

Bristol was awarded a contract for eighty Bombays, later reduced to fifty. The runners-up had not wasted their time in creating two large prototypes: both became the basis for bombers, the AW.23 as the Whitley and the Handley Page HP.51 morphed into the Harrow. Using the same wing and a deeper fuselage, Barnwell came up with the Type 137 airliner/freighter but the demands of the Blenheim meant that it did not leave the drawing board. Bristol was to return to the concept in 1945. Preoccupation with mass manufacturing the Blenheim led to the Bombay being sub-contracted to Shorts in Belfast. The new Northern Ireland Shorts factory used the type as a learning curve before turning to Stirling bombers and Sunderland flying boats.

'The Captain's Gig'

Specification 21/32 was granted to Bristol to investigate via test specimens and rigs stressed-skin construction: the so-called monocoque and semi-monocoque structures. Barnwell delegated much of this exercise to Russell while he visited the USA in 1934 on a fact-finding tour of manufacturers. Upon his return Barnwell came up with the Type 142 and the larger 143, both very clean-looking twins with retractable undercarriage that might appeal to businesses and the rich – Learjets of the 1930s. This project was known as 'The Captain's Gig', from Barnwell's nickname and the craft's playboy image.

In his exceptional book, *The Bristol Blenheim,* Graham Warner – the man whose vision and determination succeeded in putting the type back in the air in May 1987 – describes a meeting at the *Daily Mail's* headquarters at Stratton House, London, on 29 March 1934. The aim was to secure an order for the Type 142. Newspaper magnate Lord Rothermere – born Harold Sydney Harmsworth – referred to the proposal as the fastest commercial aeroplane in Europe. Rothermere could see more potential it than a runabout for his reporters and photographers: 'he also wished to show the Air Ministry that a small civil transport could be made that was faster than any of the RAF's fighters and far faster than any of its bombers…'

The second Blenheim I, K7034, polished and fitted with spinners, was displayed at the Grand Salon Aéronautique in Paris, November 1936. *KEC*

Attending the gathering with Rothermere were Bristol chairman Sir George Stanley White, Barnwell, Bristol's engine guru Roy Fedden and Robert 'Blos' Lewis, editor of the *Bristol Evening World*. The local newspaper was part of Rothermere's empire and it was a chance encounter between Lewis and Fedden on a train that had started the ball rolling only the month before. Agreement was reached: 'A price of £18,600 was quoted, based on Bristol's standard figure of £2 per pound of weight for a prototype and [Rothermere] was asked to pay half of this amount upon signing the contract and the other half in 12 months … The terms were settled, the order – then just for a 'one-off', but an order that was to have momentous consequences – was confirmed, the noble chairmen shook hands, and the party adjourned for luncheon.'

When it was evaluated in 1935, *Britain First* – as Rothermere called the 142 – ruffled feathers. It was 54mph *faster* than the state-of-the-art Gloster Gladiator biplane fighter that had just been ordered for the RAF. Here was a twin with obvious potential to become a 'heavy' fighter, or a bomber. Point made, his lordship presented *Britain First* to the nation. In August 1935 an appreciative Air Ministry ordered 150 military-configured Type 142Ms off the Filton drawing boards. The incredible Blenheim had been conceived.

The first production Mk.I took to the air on 25 June 1936, and churning them out en masse became Bristol's priority. The new type made a dramatic contrast with a batch of sub-contracted Hawker Audax biplanes that were on the factory floor at the time. Realising that Bristol had achieved a new 'Brisfit', the design office busied itself with variants and extending the family. With a 'pallet' of four machine guns under the centre section, the Mk.If (F-for-fighter) was issued to the RAF in December 1938. Blenheim Is were taken off the production lines in late 1938 and the long-nosed Mk.IV became the standard both in fighter and bomber form.

Specification B.6/40 called for a twin for ground attack and dive-bombing. Bristol responded with a modified Blenheim and the prototype flew on 24 February 1941. It was initially named Bisley, after the world-famous rifle shooting range in Surrey. Two versions were offered: a day bomber with a glazed nose offset to port or a strike aircraft with a solid nose toting four machine guns. The latter was ordered but the name Bisley was dropped in favour of Blenheim V.

Blenheim IVs in production, probably at Rootes Securities, Speke, Liverpool. *KEC*

Family legacy

Frank Barnwell did not get to bask in this success. On 2 August 1938 he died while piloting a single-seat ultralight monoplane of his own design. He was making the little machine's second outing when it plunged to the ground. Despite the 'ban' at his place of work, Barnwell was determined to keep flying and he conceived the BSW Mk.1 as a personal runabout. The designation was derived from B-for-Barnwell, 'S' for its 28hp Scott Squirrel twin-cylinder and the 'W' from its place of birth, Whitchurch. In *Bristol Fashion*, Pudney relates that Uwins offered to test it, only to be told by Barnwell: 'I wouldn't insult you by letting you fly it.'

The world had been robbed of a great talent. A moving tribute to Barnwell in *Flight* magazine published nine days later declared: 'there is no designer who has had the confidence and loyalty of his entire staff to a greater degree … Service was given to him, not through fear, for Barnwell was the most gentle of men, but because everyone felt that it was a privilege to be allowed to work for him.'

The Barnwell BSW, G-AFID, nearing completion at Filton in 1938. *KEC*

Tragedy surrounded the Barnwell family. We have already been introduced to Richard Harold Barnwell, Barnwell's elder brother, chief test pilot for Vickers. While flying the prototype FB.26 Vampire single-seat 'Gunbus'-style fighter on 25 August 1917 Harold failed to recover from a spin at 2,000ft and was killed; he was 38.

John Sandes Barnwell became a proud pilot officer flying his father's creation, the Blenheim, for 29 Squadron. On the night of 18/19 June 1940, he and Sgt K L Long were flying in Mk.If L6636 from Martlesham Heath. They were observed chasing an enemy bomber and there was a vigorous exchange of fire. One of the combatants came down in the North Sea. As hours turned into days it was clear it was the Blenheim that had fallen, not the enemy. After sixteen days, the body of 20-year-old John Barnwell washed up on the Suffolk coast.

Elder brother Richard Anthony (24) died piloting 102 Squadron AW Whitley V P5082 on a raid to Bremen, Germany, on the night of 28/29 October 1940. He and his crew of four are also believed to have come down in the North Sea.

Plt Off David Usher Barnwell DFC, an 'ace' with five 'kills' and two shared to his credit, was with the Malta Night Fighter Unit at Ta Kali by early 1941. Engaging Italian Macchi MC.202s on 14 October, his Hawker Hurricane was shot down and the 19-year-old perished. A graduate of Cranwell, John Barnwell's grave is in the churchyard at Scopwick, a short distance to the north-west of the RAF College: the headstone records the passing of three brothers and their father, pilots all.

Bristol licence build and sub-contracts

Type	Total	From	To	Notes
Société Zodiac 52B	1	1910	-	[1]
R A/c Factory B.E.2a/b/c/d/e	1,167	1913	1917	[2]
R A/c Factory B.E.8	5	1914	-	[2]
Parnall Panther	36+	1919	1921	[3]
AW Siskin IIIA	83	1928	1930	
Hawker Audax	141	1936	-	
Hawker Tempest II	36	1945	-	[4]

[1] Parts for six laid down at Filton, one completed but did not fly. **[2]** Additionally, four Royal Aircraft Factory B.E.10s were started, but not completed. **[3]** Production figure estimated: includes 16 spare airframes – see Chapter 29. **[4]** Fifty Tempests laid down at Banwell, only 36 completed and flown. Unfinished remainder transferred to Hawker.

A pair of 'Beaus'

Responding to an Air Ministry requirement for a torpedo-bomber and another for a general reconnaissance bomber, Barnwell used the rugged Blenheim airframe as a starting point. The two specifications were combined into one and the resultant Beaufort featured a lengthened and deepened fuselage, including a bomb bay. (It took its name from the Dukes of Beaufort, their ancestral home being the Badminton Estate, to the east of Filton.) Two 1,130hp Bristol Taurus radials replaced the 840hp Mercuries, as the Beaufort was a much heavier beast. The prototype had its debut on 15 October 1938. Development problems – dominated by the troublesome Taurus – delayed the introduction to service until November 1939. Searches for a better engine settled on another dependable radial, the Pratt & Whitney Twin Wasp, and the first Beaufort II appeared in November 1940. Australia's Department of Aircraft Production (DAP) built Beauforts under licence.

With the advent of the Beaufort, Bristol needed to expand its production facilities yet again. The airport to the east of the seaside town of Weston-super-Mare was ideal and its borders were extended westwards from the autumn of 1940. This took it close to Oldmixon and the factory was named after this village. Another plant was established to the east, south of the RAF station at Locking, and close to Elborough, although it took the name of Banwell, slightly further east. Both sites were up and running by late 1941, using the enlarged airfield for testing. Oldmixon concentrated on Beaufighters; Banwell built Beauforts, Beaufighters and ended the war with a batch of Hawker Tempest IIs.

Barnwell and Frise had been examining the possibilities of a four-cannon fighter, as had Westland's designer, 'Teddy' Petter. Concentrated fire from 20mm guns clustered in the forward fuselage would provide unprecedented 'punch'. Fighter Command needed a two-seat 'heavy' fighter for day and night interceptions and Coastal Command was seeking a nimble, hard-hitting torpedo/strike aircraft.

A line-up of Beaufort Is from 22 Squadron, the RAF's first operational unit, at Thorney Island, spring 1940. *KEC*

Frise came up with an inspired transformation of the Beaufort. Retaining the wings, centre section, tail unit and undercarriage, he created a new slimline fuselage with a pilot and observer in tandem. Gone were the troublesome Taurus radials; in their place was a pair of beefy Hercules. This gelled as the Type 156, which was given a name that reflected the thinking behind it: the Beaufort-Fighter, or Beaufighter. A more advanced version was called the 'Sports Model' by the Filton design staff.

Just over six months after the initial layouts had been presented, Uwins took the prototype into the air on 17 July 1939 and an order for 300 was signed. Without weaponry and operational fittings the first Beaufighter had a maximum speed of 335mph at 17,000ft – the Hurricane I was capable of 316mph. From July 1940 the Battle of Britain was raging and the need to replace the Blenheim in the night fighter role had become urgent. Trials of the Beaufighter with airborne interception radar revealed a formidable potential that could be deployed with rapidity. The RAF realised that no further development was needed; the new Bristol was already a 'Sports Model'. Sub-contracting went into full swing, the 100th 'Beau' was ready for service on 7 December 1940 and in November 1942 the 1,000th appeared – an exceptional achievement.

Another powerplant was deemed prudent as 'insurance'. The Rolls-Royce Griffon was put forward, but the Merlin XX was substituted. The Merlin-engined Beaufighter II flew in July 1940. The ultimate strike version, with radar, a torpedo, Hercules engines and fuel for a long patrol, was the Mk.X. It was a heavily-laden beast on take-off – as much as 25,400lb – that's 400lb *more* than *two* fully loaded Blenheim Is!

At Fishermen's Bend in Victoria, the Australian Department of Aircraft Production replaced the Beaufort on the assembly line with Beaufighters; designated Mk.21s. Production came to a halt in Britain during September 1945, with TF.X SR919 taking the accolade as the last of the breed. That machine and others were converted into the final variant, the target-towing TT.10 from May 1948, providing Bristol with much-needed work.

Right: Leslie George Frise, whose talents ran from the Beaufighter to the Jet Provost. *Peter Green Collection*

Below: Beaufighter TF.X SR919 had its maiden flight at Oldmixon on 21 September 1945. It was the 5,564th and last of the awesome twins to be built in Britain. *Bristol*

Taking up the baton

An early task for Frise in 1919 at Filton was the design and setting up a wind tunnel; a novelty with most companies at that time. Always looking at ways to improve aircraft controllability, he invented the slotted aileron, which was patented in 1921. It was employed worldwide and became known universally as the Frise aileron. In the 1920s the combination of Barnwell and Frise pioneered the strip-steel construction method, contributing greatly to the dominance of the Bulldog.

The death of Barnwell came as a severe blow to Frise and everybody at Bristol. Promoted to chief designer, he masterminded the Beaufighter and went on to create the Buckingham and others in the 'twin' family. It is very likely that the Type 155 recce bomber was transferred to AW, where it became the Albemarle, to offload the huge pressures on Frise as the Beaufort entered flight test and the Beaufighter was initiated. As the war came to an end, promoted to chief engineer, he oversaw the Brabazon airliner, devised the Type 170 and spearheaded the helicopter division.

Bristol Boxkite to Tramp*

From	To	Total	Name/Designation	Type	Engine(s)	Notes
1910	1914	c.80	Boxkite	2-seat GP	1 x Gnome	
1911	-	1	Racing Biplane	Sportsplane	1 x Gnome	
1911	-	2	Monoplane	1-seater	1 x Gnome	
1911	-	5	Type T Biplane	Military GP	1 x Gnome	
1911	-	1	Challenger-England	1-seater	1 x ENV	[1]
1911	1912	34	Prier Monoplane	1/2-seater	1 x Gnome	
1911	1912	5	G.E.1/G.E.2/G.E.3	Military GP	1 x Gnome	
1912	1913	35	Coandă Monoplane	Trainer	1 x Gnome	[2]
1912	-	1	Coandă Hydro	Floatplane	1 x Gnome	
1912	1914	2	Burney Monoplane	Experimental	1 x ENV	[3]
1913	-	7	Coandă BR.7	Military GP	1 x Renault	[4]
1913	-	41	Coandă TB.8	Military GP	1 x Gnome	[5]
1914	-	1	Coandă PB.8	Military GP	1 x Gnome	
1914	-	1	Coandă GB.75	Military GP	1 x Gnome	
1914	1916	376	Scout A to D, S.2A	Scout	1 x Gnome	[6]
1914	-	1+	SSA	Scout	1 x Clerget	[7]
1916	-	2	Twin Tractor A	Heavy scout	2 x Beardmore	
1916	1918	130	M.1 Monoplane	Scout	1 x Clerget	
1917	1918	2	MR.1	2-seat recce	1 x Hispano-Suiza	
1918	1919	4	Scout F	Scout	1 x Sunbeam Arab	
1918	1919	4	F.2C Badger	2-seat recce	1 x Cosmos Jupiter	[8]
1918	1919	2	Braemar I, II	Long-range bomber	4 x Siddeley Puma	[9]
1920	-	1	Pullman	Airliner	4 x Liberty 12	[9]
1921	-	2	Tramp	'Spares carrier'	4 x Siddeley Puma	[10]

* For F.2 and derivatives, see separate table. See narrative for details of retrospective allocation of type numbers prior to 1923. All are tractor biplanes other than: pusher biplanes – Boxkite, Type T, PB.8; tractor monoplanes denoted as such; Braemar, Pullman and Tramp triplanes; see notes for layout. [1] Substantial redesign of Type T by Gordon England. [2] Licensed Caproni and Faccanoni, Vizzola, Italy (1 or 2). Unknown quantity under licence by Deutsche Bristol-Werke, Halberstadt, Germany. [3] Hydrofoil/floatplane hybrid, known as 'hydroped' – see narrative. [4] Licensed (probably only one) by Deutsche Bristol-Werke, Halberstadt, Germany. [5] Unknown quantity licensed to Société Anonyme des Ateliers d'Aviation Louis Bréguet, Douai, France. [6] S.2A two-seat version based on Scout. [7] Final Coandă design for Bristol. Unknown quantity licensed to Société Anonyme des Ateliers d'Aviation Louis Bréguet, Douai, France. [8] Includes experimental Badger X single-seater. [9] Tandem engines, ie. one tractor, one pusher. [10] 'Spares carrier' – also referred to as 'Postal' – suspected as ruse to circumvent cancellation. Four engines mounted in series within fuselage, driving two tractor propellers via gearing. Both completed, neither flew.

By early 1946 the never-ending demands of the war years caught up with Frise and he resigned due to ill health, handing over to Archibald Russell. He took up the post of technical director and chief engineer with Percival in 1948 (Hunting Percival from 1954), working on the incredibly successful Provost and Jet Provost. In 1956 he became special projects manager for Blackburn before retiring in the early 1960s. Leslie George Frise, the man who created the Beaufighter and the Jet Provost, among others, died on 26 September 1979, aged 80.

End of an era

With the surrender of Japan in August 1945, Filton was nearing the end of contracts for the Buckingham and the Buckmaster trainer variant. First flown on 4 February 1943, the Buckingham had been conceived as a replacement for the de Havilland (DH) Mosquito and the remaining front-line Blenheims, and there had been high hopes for it. The dazzling capabilities of the 'Mossie' and delays in the programme led to large reductions in orders and eventually only 119 Buckinghams and 110 Buckmasters were built. Last deliveries of both types occurred in 1946. (The Buckingham took its name from the county town of Buckinghamshire. Buckmaster appears to follow the same derivation as Beaufort to Beaufighter: ie. a trainer – hence 'master' – version of the Buckingham.)

The Buckingham spawned another derivative that was the last of the military twin 'family'. A slim fuselage was married to Buckmaster wings and 'tail feathers' to create the Brigand, aimed at replacing the Beaufighter as a torpedo-bomber. The prototype had its debut on 4 October 1944 but just as the Mosquito refused to be usurped, so the Beaufighter steadfastly remained in production. After a small run of torpedo-bombers, none of which entered operational service, Filton switched to building light bomber and later crew trainer versions. Like

North Luffenham-based Brigand T.5 RH797 of 238 Operational Conversion Unit with Woolfox Lodge airfield in the background, 1958. *KEC*

the Buckingham, time ran out for the Brigand. Deliveries did not begin until 1946 and continued to 1951. For the RAF, the Brigand was the last of its kind, a piston-engined attack aircraft.

Unsung hero

Planning for peace began at Filton in 1944. Frise revived the concept of the Type 137, a projected commercial version of the Bombay bomber-transport of 1935. Another likely influence was the General Aircraft Hamilcar assault glider of 1942. Designed to carry a light tank into battle, it featured a box-section fuselage with a hinged nose, allowing for straight-in loading of bulky items or vehicles. Using a modified version of the Bombay's wing structure, Frise devised the Type 170, a simple, rugged high-wing twin with fixed undercarriage. Two versions of this private venture were offered: the humbly named

A page from a brochure of Bristol 170 variants, showing the thirty-two-seat layout of the Wayfarer. *KEC*

Freighter with clam-shell nose doors and strengthened cargo floor and the Wayfarer thirty-two-passenger airliner. The prototype had its maiden flight on 2 December 1945.

Despite Douglas Dakota-derived do-it-all military transports flooding the post-war market, there was nothing like the Type 170. It was an instant success with the utilitarian Freighter version and the stretched Mk.32 car-ferry 'Super' Freighter constituting the majority of the production run. As intended, the 170 also appealed to military operators; those of Pakistan having hardpoints and a bomb aimer's position in the nose. To clear the production hall for the Britannia, the final examples were assembled by Western Airways at Weston-super-Mare; the last Freighter was completed in February 1957.

With 214 completed, the Type 170 exceeded the total of Britain's previous best-selling airliner, the Vickers Viking, which was built at Weybridge from 1945 to 1949, by fifty-one units. The Freighter was an important cash cow for Bristol and an unsung hero of Britain's post-war transports.

Rotary revolution

Planning for the eventual peace gave rise to the relatively safe Type 170 but Bristol's management also made a very bold step in 1944, establishing a helicopter department under Austrian-born rotorcraft pioneer Raoul Hafner. From 1929 Austrian-born Hafner and Bruno Nagler collaborated on helicopters. The basic R-I was followed by the improved R-II, which was tested at Aspern, near Vienna, in 1930–31.

Hafner moved to Britain in 1932, bringing along the R-II. This was probably at the behest of his backer, Scottish cotton magnate Major Jack Coates, because of the increasingly repressive regime of the Austrian chancellor, Engelbert Dolfuss. The R-II was reassembled at Heston in 1933 but it was underpowered and relegated to a test rig for Hafner's rotor hubs and control systems. This treasure – the oldest surviving helicopter in Britain – has survived and it is displayed at The Helicopter Museum at Weston-super-Mare, close to Bristol's former factory.

Hafner contracted Martin-Baker to build his first UK-based design, the single-seat AR.III gyroplane, which had its debut at Denham in 1937. With the onset of war, Hafner worked at the Central Landing Establishment (CLE) at Ringway, tasked with developing airborne forces equipment in readiness for the liberation of Europe. During January 1942 CLE became the Airborne Forces Experimental Establishment (AFEE) and that July the outfit moved to Sherburn in Elmet. At AFEE Hafner devised a one-man fully steerable rotorcraft 'parachute' using bicycle frame construction techniques, a simple twin-blade rotor and a basic plywood tail section. This was the Rotachute intended for use in commando operations; towed to a drop zone, it was released to flutter down to a landing. From this concept, the Rotabuggy emerged – a means of towing a Willys Jeep to a battleground under a large 'free-wheeling' two-blade rotor. Hafner hoped that this concept could also 'deliver' light tanks into battle. By the time of the final Rotabuggy tests, D-Day had been and gone and the project subsided.

Thanks to Bristol, Hafner at last had substantial backing and he established a small team to create the five-seat Type 171 – later named Sycamore – which first flew on 27 July 1947. (The seeds of the sycamore tree have 'rotors' that help them fall to earth.) Appealing to both civil and military operators, this was the first British helicopter to enter series production. The helicopter division left Filton in 1955 settling on Oldmixon. The last Sycamore was delivered in December 1958 and, like the Type 170, was an important contributor to Bristol's 'bottom line'.

To create a much larger helicopter, Hafner bolted the rotor systems of two Sycamores to a longer, more capacious, fuselage. This emerged as the piston-engined Type 173, aimed at the military as an anti-submarine platform or flying crane and civil operators as a thirteen-seater 'air coach'. After much ground running, the first Type 173 took off from Weston-super-Mare on 29 April 1952, heralding a long and expensive development programme. Only the RAF adopted the much-refined and rethought turboshaft-powered Type 192, as the Belvedere HC.1, from August 1961. (The twin rotor's RAF name maintained alliteration – B-for-Bristol – adopting an Italian-derived term for a gazebo or similar structure affording a magnificent view.)

Sycamore HR.14 of Aldergrove-based 118 Squadron at Upavon in June 1962. *Roy Bonser*

A trio of Belvedere HC.1s of Odiham-based 66 Squadron, the first RAF squadron equipped with the type, late 1961. *Bristol*

Bristol helicopters

From	To	Total	Name/Designation	Type	Engine(s)	Notes
1947	1958	178	Sycamore	General purpose	1 x Alvis Leonides	
1952	1956	3	173	Transport	2 x Alvis Leonides	
1958	1962	26	Belvedere	Transport	2 x Napier Gazelle	[1]

Type 171 single rotor, piston-engined. Type 173 tandem rotor, piston-engined. Type 192 tandem rotor, turboshaft-driven. [1] Preceded by three Leonides-powered Type 191/1s, none of these flew and were used as Gazelle and transmission rigs for the Type 192.

The last Belvedere had its maiden flight in June 1962; just twenty-nine of the whole twin-rotor family flew, others were relegated to ground-running rigs. As part of the consolidation of the British industry, Westland acquired Bristol's helicopter interests in February 1960. Rotorcraft pioneer Raoul Hafner died, aged 75, in a boating accident on 14 November 1980; his influence on the development of helicopters in Britain cannot be overestimated.

Crystal ball gazing

Bouncing across the thick sage grass at Shellbeach on Kent's Isle of Sheppey on 30 April 1909 in a French Voisin biplane 25-year-old John Theodore Cuthbert Moore-Brabazon become the first officially recognised 'Brit' to fly in his country of birth. (He can be seen sitting next to Wilbur Wright outside Mussel Manor, Sheppey, in May 1909 in Chapter 34.) Flying from the same turf, but this time in a Short biplane, on 8 March 1910 'Brab' qualified for Aviator's Certificate No.1. Fighting on the Western Front with the RFC, he returned to serve as a Conservative Member of Parliament. Appointed Minister of Transport in 1940, he took over the Ministry of Aircraft Production (MAP) from Lord Beaverbrook in May 1941.

Elevated to the peerage in 1942 as Lord Brabazon of Tara, he headed the inter-departmental committee that eventually took his name. The task was to recommend what sort of civilian transports would be required when peace returned. Deliberations began in December 1942 with a non-stop transatlantic airliner as the priority. Such a machine would 'wave the flag' for post-war Britain politically and commercially.

The private-venture Type 170 had been the result of careful estimations of its potential for both commercial and military applications, backed by market surveys. Filton's next fixed-wing

product was based on the machinations of a wartime ministerial committee attempting to predict the early 1950s with thinking based firmly in the 1930s. The result was the Type 167 Brabazon, which boasted a capacity for 100 passengers in spacious, luxurious surroundings, a dozen crew, and eight coupled engines driving four contra-rotating propeller assemblies providing a cruise of 250mph. With an all-up weight of 290,000lb, at the time the Brabazon was the largest and most complex commercial aircraft – anywhere.

Lord Brabazon of Tara (left) inspecting test equipment on the Brabazon I, G-AGPW, during a flight from Filton to Heathrow, 15 June 1950. *Bristol*

Brabazon Committee recommendations, November 1945

Type	Role	Spec	Emerged as	Built	Chapter	Notes
I	Transatlantic, non-stop	2/44	Bristol Brabazon I	1	11	
IA	Transatlantic, non-stop	2/46	Bristol Brabazon II	-	11	[1]
IIA	European, medium range	25/43	Airspeed Ambassador	23	3	
IIB(i)	European, medium range	8/46	Vickers Viceroy	445	37	[2]
IIB(ii)	European, medium range	16/46	AW Apollo	2	4	
III	Empire, long-range	6/45	Avro 693	-	-	[3]
IV	High speed, medium range	22/46	DH Comet	112	17	
VA	UK internal, feederliner	18/44	Miles Marathon	43	28	[4]
VB	Light transport, air taxi	26/43	DH Dove	542	17	[5]

[1] Not completed. [2] Produced under the name Viscount. [3] Four-jet transport, project terminated in 1947. [4] Three prototypes by Miles; production examples by Handley Page, including 29 adopted by the RAF as the T.11 crew trainer. [5] Including essentially similar Devon and Sea Devon for RAF and Royal Navy.

Other than Air Ministry blessing for the prototype and a second, Bristol Coupled Proteus turboprop-powered, example, there was not a whiff of an order. The new airliner had not been given a catchy, international name, instead it honoured Lord Brabazon in a piece of classically insular British 'branding'!

For all the types discussed by the committee, the likely performance, passenger numbers, powerplants, etc, were outlined, with the design offices of the UK's leading manufacturers interpreting the more specific ministry intentions. Initially those gathered around Brabazon's table came only from the Air Ministry and MAP. By May 1943 representatives from the state-owned British Overseas Airways Corporation (BOAC) and the industry, for example Geoffrey de Havilland, were invited. By the time British European Airways (BEA) and British South American Airways Corporation were established in the summer of 1946, the committee had been wound up and the two organisations faced a 'shopping list' that they had not compiled.

Brabazon's team came up with nine types – see the table – to meet the brave new world of the 1950s. The final report was issued in November 1944 at the same time as the Air Ministry established the Ministry of Civil Aviation – often referred to as the 'Ministry of Airliners' to reflect the heft of the Brabazon conclusions. Of the nine, only one failed to translate into hardware; all the others became Air Ministry specifications and were awarded prototype contracts. Three went on to success, headed by the spectacular Vickers Viscount – initially called the Viceroy – but radically enlarged from the original proposal. First into the air – in September 1945 – was the DH Dove. This was a modern interpretation of the equally successful Dragon Rapide, hitting a known and expanding need. The committee's support of a jetliner was daring and the resulting DH Comet had enormous potential. The Comet suffered from being the first in a high-risk market and never recovered from early setbacks.

White elephant

With the Buckingham high-speed attacker under test from 4 February 1943, the Bristol design department had plenty of capacity. With a proven industrial track record and its own engine division Bristol,

The Brabazon I and II under assembly in the gigantic Filton hangar. The Lancaster is believed to be Mk.III RE131, which trialled a scaled down version of the huge airliner's control system. *Bristol*

was ideally placed for the Brabazon Type I transatlantic proposal. In March 1943 Bristol was instructed to investigate concepts under the strict proviso that such work would not get in the way of any military contracts. In late 1944 the Air Ministry released the first issue of Specification 2/44, with a more detailed second iteration following in mid-1946. The turboprop Brabazon Mk.2 was enshrined in Specification 2/46 that appeared in July 1951.

Specifications 2/44 and 2/46 were off-limits to the remainder of the British manufacturers. Miles and Shorts pitched private-venture schemes but neither was considered. Both of these proposals were more radical than the Type 167. Miles offered the X-11 powered by eight coupled engines and a 'blended wing', wide-fuselage format. Shorts came up with a fairly conventional six-engined type and a flying wing powered by five pusher engines based on Geoffrey Hill's Pterodactyl theories. A project of this size was a pipe dream for Miles; the company fell over trying to develop the Brabazon-inspired Marathon feederliner in 1947. Shorts had good infrastructure and was an established builder of big aircraft but its Sunderland had already been determined by the Brabazon Committee as the basis of a family of post-war civil flying boats and was not to be diverted from this task.

At Filton the Brabazon Type I and IA projects were overseen by chief engineer Frise and executed by chief designer Archibald Russell and his team. (Later to conceive the Britannia; as head of the UK design group for Concorde, Russell's 'CV' appears in Chapter 13.) The first manufacturing drawings were ready in April 1945, but much had to be done before the 230ft-span monster could take to the air.

The preferred venue for the assembly line and flight testing, Weston-super-Mare, was ruled out as a long, heavy load-bearing runway was impossible given the character of the coastal sub-soil. So the runway at Filton needed extension westwards from 2,000ft to 8,250ft with more than a million cubic yards of excavation required. The foundations used rubble from areas of the city of Bristol that had been ravaged by the Luftwaffe. In the path of this huge concrete edifice lay the village of Charlton, the bulk of which needed demolishing; its unfortunate residents were rehoused. Elaborate rerouting of local roads was also required.

A massive new three-bay assembly hall, 1,052ft wide, with a 'footprint' of nearly 8 acres, was created, along with extensive apron space. Construction of both the hall and the prototype Brabazon commenced in October 1945. The eastern bay of the new building was ready in the autumn of 1947 and sections of the prototype were moved inside: it was another two years before all of the gigantic edifice was complete.

The Brabazon in Context

	Stratocruiser*	Brabazon I**	Britannia 101
Powerplant	4 x 3,500hp	8 x 2,500hp	4 x 2,800hp
	P&W Wasp Major	Centaurus XX	Proteus 625
Span	141ft 3in	230ft 0in	142ft 3in
Length	110ft 4in	177ft 0in	114ft 0in
Wing area	1,769 sq ft	5,317 sq ft	2,075 sq ft
All-up weight	145,800lb	290,000lb	155,000lb
Max speed	340mph	300mph	362mph
Typical Range	3,000 miles	5,500 miles	4,580 miles
Passengers	100	100	90
First flown	1947	1949	1952
Built (all variants)	55	1	85

* Boeing Model 377 Stratocruiser was a development of the Model 367 C-97 Stratofreighter, first flown in 1944. Nearly 900 were built for the USAF.
** Statistics for the Brabazon are based on flight trials of the prototype, which was never fully furnished or equipped to airline standard.

When Arthur John 'Bill' Pegg took the Brabazon for its maiden voyage on 4 September 1949 there were more concerns for the project than there were hopes. The undertaking was estimated to have cost between £12 and £15 million – an eye-watering financial commitment

for a country still enduring food and fuel rationing. What airline interest there was in the Brabazon ranged from bemusement to a sense of dread. A high-capacity version that BEA flirted with briefly would have required further investment and more delays. In 1949 BOAC opted for the opulence, capacity and ready availability of the Boeing Stratocruiser for its transatlantic routes; despite Britain's dollar-strapped economy. (See the panel for a comparison.) Inevitably the axe fell with the prototype – undeniably an incredible technical achievement – clocking up around 400 hours. It and the unfinished Mk.2 were scrapped in 1953.

Whispering Giant

The Brabazon taught Bristol much about design, powerplant choice and the need to seek a wide market. It also bequeathed a massive assembly hall and flight test hangar. All of this combined to keep the company in the airliner business. Prospects for the Britannia were far better, although engine problems dogged early testing. Once ironed out, the Bristol Proteus turboprops earned the type the nickname 'Whispering Giant'.

Pegg took the prototype for a thirty-minute debut on 16 August 1952, with the redundant Brabazon and the carcass of the Mk.2 still lingering at Filton. From the start, the Britannia attracted BOAC and the first example entered service with the national flag carrier in December 1955. Although initial interest from the USA vaporised, exports were beginning to roll in and it looked as though Bristol would need extra manufacturing capacity.

To remedy this, £360,000 was shelled out for a 15.25% stake in Northern Ireland's Shorts and a second production line was laid down at Sydenham, Belfast. A valuable licence agreement was also reached with Canadair of Montreal – see below. The Shorts assembly line was running by 1959 but by then the Britannia bubble had burst: thirty were completed in Belfast but parts for five examples had to be taken to Filton to keep the 'home' factory busy.

In 1953 Douglas flew the first DC-7 and three years later Lockheed brought out the Starliner: these were the last of the piston-engined long-range airliners. With 338 and forty-four built respectively, they mopped up most of the market – the turboprop appeal of the Britannia was not powerful enough. But it was the transition to jets that really frustrated the Britannia: DH's Comet entered service in April 1952, Boeing's 707 in November 1958 and the DC-8 in May 1959. The last Britannia was handed over to an airline in November 1959; RAF deliveries eked out production into the following year. The link with Shorts continued, the SC.5 strategic transport adopted the Britannia's wing structure and Filton designed and manufactured the wings for the ten examples built in 1964–67. To reflect this, the big airlifter was to have been called Britannic, before opting for Belfast.

Britannia formation over Upavon in June 1962; both are Short built and belong to the 99 and 511 Squadron pool at Lyneham; C.2 XN392 left and C.1 XM497 right. *Roy Bonser*

Bristol inter-war types

From	To	Total	Name/Designation	Type	Engine(s)	Notes
1919	-	3	Babe	Sportsplane	1 x Viale	[1]
1919	-	1	Bullet	Experimental	1 x Bristol Jupiter	
1920	-	1	Seeley	2 or 3 seat GP	1 x Siddeley Puma	
1921	1924	2	Ten-Seater	Light transport	1 x Bristol Jupiter	[2]
1922	1923	3	Bullfinch I, II	Fighter	1 x Bristol Jupiter	[3]
1922	-	1	Racer	Sportsplane	1 x Bristol Jupiter	
1923	1928	28	Taxiplane/PTM	See notes	1 x Bristol Lucifer	[4]
1923	1925	4	Bloodhound	2-seat fighter	1 x Bristol Jupiter	
1925	1926	3	Berkeley	Bomber	1 x RR Condor	
1924	1926	3	Brownie	Sportsplane	1 x Bristol Cherub	[5]
1925	-	1	'Laboratory'	Research	1 x Bristol Jupiter	
1925	1927	4	Boarhound	2-seat fighter	1 x Bristol Jupiter	[6]
1926	-	1	Badminton	Sportsplane	1 x Bristol Jupiter	
1927	-	1	Bagshot	Heavy fighter	2 x Bristol Jupiter	
1927	-	1	101	2-seat fighter	1 x Bristol Jupiter	
1927	1935	443	Bulldog I-IV	Fighter	1 x Bristol Jupiter	[7]
1928	-	1	109	Long-range special	1 x Bristol Jupiter	
1929	-	1	110A	Light transport	1 x Bristol Titan	
1931	1932	2	118 and 120	Military GP	1 x Bristol Pegasus	
1934	-	1	123	Fighter	1 x RR Goshawk	
1934	-	1	133	Fighter	1 x Bristol Mercury	
1935	1940	51	Bombay	Bomber-transport	2 x Bristol Pegasus	[8]
1936	-	1	138A	High altitude exp	1 x Bristol Pegasus	
1937	-	2	148/148B	Army co-op	1 x Bristol Mercury	
1938	-	1	146	Fighter	1 x Bristol Mercury	

All tractor biplanes other than monoplane: Bullfinch I, Racer, Brownie, Bagshot, 133, Bombay, 138A, 148, 146. See narrative for details of retrospective allocation of type numbers prior to 1923. [1] Two biplanes flown; monoplane version completed but did not fly. [2] One finished as Brandon ambulance for RAF. [3] Two Mk.Is, single-seat, parasol-winged fighter; Mk.II two-seat recce biplane. [4] Three 3-seat Taxiplanes; 24 Primary Training Machines (PTM) and one engine test bed Type 83. [5] Two 2-seaters and one single-seater. [6] Includes one Beaver GP version. [7] Includes: one Type 107 Mercury-powered Bullpup, 59 Type 124 Bulldog TM trainers; two licensed to Nakajima at Tokyo as JSSF – Japanese Single-Seat Fighter. [8] After prototype, sub-contracted to Shorts, Belfast.

Canadian connection

Based at Cartierville, Montreal, Canadair acquired a licence to build the Britannia in 1954. The intention was to use the airframe as the basis for two very different Royal Canadian Air Force (RCAF) requirements. A new fuselage with weapons bays was mated to Britannia wings, tail surfaces and undercarriage to create the CL-28 Argus maritime patroller to replace aged Avro Lancaster 10s. Powered by four 3,700hp Wright R3370 Duplex-Cyclone radials, the prototype first flew on 28 March 1957 and the last of thirty-three was delivered in November 1960.

The second design was a stretched airliner/freighter version, the CL-44, powered by Rolls-Royce Tyne turboprops. The bulk of the production was of a swing-tail version, allowing for the direct loading of bulky items into the rear fuselage. The prototype had its maiden flight on 15 November 1959 and thirty-nine were made for the RCAF (as the Yukon) and a handful of airlines, the last being delivered in March 1966.

The CL-44 found a niche in the transport market. Swing-tail CL-44D-4 N452T served US operator Flying Tiger Line from 1961 to 1972. *KEC*

Canadair 'Britannias'

Type	Total	From	To	Notes
CL-28 Argus 1	13	1957	1958	[1]
CL-28 Argus 2	20	1958	1960	[1]
CL-44-6 Yukon	12	1959	1961	[2]
CL-44D4	27	1960	1965	

[1] RCAF designation CP-107. [2] RCAF designation CC-106.

Only jet

Specification ER.143T had been issued for a research aircraft capable of sustaining speeds beyond Mach 2 to investigate the effects of kinetic heating and Bristol was awarded the contract in February 1953. Design of this very challenging project took the rest of the decade, with input by AW, which later also acted as sub-contractor. With no Bristol turbojets suitable, two DH Gyron Juniors, capable of 14,000lbst in reheat, were chosen. Special construction techniques, using stainless steel, had to be developed to create the futuristic-looking Type 188.

The first Type 188, XF923, during a sortie in May 1962. *Rolls-Royce*

Blenheim to Type 188

From	To	Total	Name/Designation	Type	Engine(s)	Notes
1935	-	1	'Britain First'	Exec transport	2 x Bristol Mercury	
1936	-	1	143	Exec transport	2 x Bristol Aquila	
1936	1944	1,415	Blenheim I/II	Light bomber	2 x Bristol Mercury	[1]
1937	1944	3,177	Blenheim IV	Light bomber	2 x Bristol Mercury	[2]
1938	1944	2,129	Beaufort I/II	Torpedo bomber	2 x Bristol Taurus	[3]
1939	1943	676	Bolingbroke I–IV	Coastal patrol	2 x Bristol Mercury	[4]
1939	1945	5,928	Beaufighter I–XI	Heavy fighter	2 x Bristol Hercules	[5]
1941	1943	944	Blenheim V	Attack bomber	2 x Bristol Mercury	[6]
1943	1946	123	Buckingham	Light bomber	2 x Bristol Centaurus	
1944	1951	147	Brigand	Attack bomber	2 x Bristol Centaurus	
1944	1946	112	Buckmaster	Transport	2 x Bristol Centaurus	
1949	-	1	Brabazon	Airliner	8 x Bristol Centaurus	
1945	1957	214	170 Freighter	Transport	2 x Bristol Hercules	[7]
1952	1960	85	Britannia	Airliner	4 x Bristol Proteus	[8]
1961	1963	2	188	Research	2 x DH Gyron Junior	

All piston-engined monoplanes, other than: Britannia turboprop and Type 188 turbojet. **[1]** Also Mk.If 'heavy' fighter. One completed as Mk.II general recce prototype. Also sub-contracted to Avro and Rootes Securities, Speke, Liverpool and licensed to Ikarus at Zemun, Yugoslavia (16 completed before the factory was destroyed in 1941), and Valtion Lentokonetehdas at Tampere, Finland, 1941 and 1943. **[2]** Also Mk.IVf 'heavy' fighter conversions. Also sub-contracted to Avro and Rootes Securities, Speke, Liverpool and licensed to Valtion Lentokonetehdas at Tampere, Finland, 1944. **[3]** Seven hundred licensed to Department of Aircraft Production at Mascot, New South Wales, and Fishermen's Bend, Victoria, Australia, as Mk V, VII, VIII. **[4]** Licensed by Fairchild Aircraft, Longueuil, Quebec, Canada; 457 as Mk.IVT crew trainers. **[5]** Majority built at Bristol-managed 'shadow factory' at Oldmixon, Weston-super-Mare. Also sub-contracted to Fairey and Rootes Securities, Blythe Bridge, Staffs, and 364 licensed to Department of Aircraft Production at Fishermen's Bend, Victoria, Australia, as Mk.21s. **[6]** Two built at Filton as Bisley I; remainder sub-contracted to Rootes Securities, Blythe Bridge, Staffs, as Blenheim V. **[7]** Pure passenger version – without nose doors – known as Wayfarer. Thirty-one assembled by Western Airways at Weston-super-Mare, 1953–57. **[8]** 35 built by Shorts at Sydenham 1957–60, last five completed at Filton.

Godfrey Auty flew the first of the pair on 14 April 1962, by which time Filton was firmly under the British Aircraft Corporation (BAC) banner. The second machine had its debut on April 1963 and it appropriately reached Mach 1.88 on one sortie.

Engine surge problems plagued testing and prevented the hallowed Mach 2 from being achieved. Fuel consumption was far greater than anticipated and this gave the Type 188 very little endurance – sorties of around thirty minutes were the norm. The project was abandoned in January 1964 having amassed only forty flying hours in seventy-eight flights. The Type 188 was the only Bristol jet design to see the light of day.

Awaiting Concorde

With the creation of BAC on 1 July 1960, Bristol Aircraft Ltd became the junior partner, with 20% of the business, while English Electric and Vickers had 40% apiece. From that May the name 'Bristol' was subsumed into BAC, becoming the Filton Division. While it was destined to become the design centre and final assembly site for the British half of the Concorde project, more work needed to be generated before metal began to be cut on the supersonic airliner. From Brooklands came commissions to make parts for the VC10 and tail units for the One-Eleven jetliners. Production of the forward fuselages of the Lightning T.5, the operational trainer version of the F.3 interceptor, was handed on by Warton. Laid down as a T.4, XM967 was taken by road to Filton, where it was converted to the prototype T.5 and it made its first flight on 29 March 1962. It was followed nine months later by XM966, another T.4 converted to a T.5. Between 1964 and 1969 Filton built twenty-eight Lightning two-seater forward fuselages: twenty T.5s for the RAF and export T.55s for Saudi Arabia and Kuwait.

On 5 September 1959 Fairey FD.2 WG774 was ferried from the Royal Aircraft Establishment at Thurleigh to Filton and it disappeared into the depths of the Brabazon Hangar. It was destined to be transformed into a high-speed test bed for Concorde's ogee-shaped wing. It re-flew, as the BAC 221, on 1 May 1964: it is dealt with in greater detail in Chapter 13.

As the Britannia came closer to the end of its days, from 1956 the design department spent much time on a medium-range tri-jet for BEA (Type 200) and a long-range version for BOAC, the Type 201. The airlines blew hot and cold on their requirements, with BEA seeking details in 1958 for a short-range machine. A one-size-fits-all solution was an impossibility. All of this came to naught when BEA turned to DH and its Trident. By 1959, under the inducement of Peter Masefield, even light singles and twins were being schemed; the Types 219 and 220 becoming the basis of what became Beagle.

Bristol was also part of the Supersonic Transport Advisory Committee, which was established in 1956. Russell's team came up with a variety of responses as the Ministry of Aviation evaluated the best shape, size and speed. The six-engined Mach 2-plus Type 228 and the Mach 3 Type 213 both went by the wayside. BAC sanctioned the Type 223 Mach 2-plus with four BSE Olympus turbojets in 1961. It was that combined with the French Sud Aviation Super Caravelle that became in November 1962 the Concorde – with and without the 'e'.

Four months before BAC came into being, Bristol chairman Sir Reginald Verdon Smith penned the foreword to Pudney's book *Bristol Fashion*. Soon to take a similar position at BAC, he wrote: 'In the years ahead our fortunes are to be combined with those of the very firms with whom Bristol pioneers were in keenest competition, but this combination of ability and strength affords us and succeeding generations the prospect of another half-century of work in aviation just as exhilarating, just as demanding.' From the Brigand onwards, Filton and Weston-super-Mare produced 633 aircraft, plus thirty Britannias at Belfast. The largest batches were the Type 170 transport and the Sycamore helicopter. The total output was small compared with de Havilland, English Electric or Hawker over the same period; the once giant name 'Bristol' had fallen by the wayside.

CHAPTER TWELVE

Back to the Future

British Aerospace and BAE Systems
1977 to date

'We are entering a dangerous new era of warfare, so our main focus has to be the future.
Today we offer you a glimpse of tomorrow.' Gavin Williamson, Defence Minister, July 2018

DESPITE BEING AT THE HELM of a minority government, Labour Prime Minister James Callaghan was determined to alter the nature of major British industries. Nationalising at one fell swoop a bewildering array of British shipyards and the major British aviation manufacturers was etched into the Labour manifesto. Callaghan's predecessor, Harold Wilson, had announced that intention in parliament in July 1974. The proposal was met with bitter opposition from within industry and in both Houses of Parliament. This famously boiled over during a debate of the Aircraft and Shipbuilding Industries bill on 27 May 1976. An opposition attempt to have the bill scrutinised by a special select committee was narrowly – some said unconstitutionally – defeated. The tipping point for a frustrated Michael Ray Dibdin Heseltine MP, shadow industry secretary, was the singing of *The Red Flag* on the government benches. Heseltine got up and grabbed the ceremonial mace from its stand and – interpretations differ – brandished it menacingly, or staged a mock offering of it to the Labour members. This stunt earned Heseltine the nickname 'Tarzan'. Parliament was adjourned while tempers cooled.

After a rocky ride, the Aircraft and Shipbuilding Industries Act gained Royal Assent on 17 March 1977. No time was lost and thirty-three days later British Aerospace (BAe), a nationalised statutory corporation comprising the British Aircraft Corporation (BAC), Hawker Siddeley Aviation (HSA), Hawker Siddeley Dynamics and Scottish Aviation (SAL), was formed. (Across in Northern Ireland things were unchanged at Shorts.) On New Year's Day 1978 the four entities were formally subsumed into BAe, which adopted a modified version of BAC's patriotic 'Union Jack' arrowhead logo.

What can be done can be undone. Royal Assent was bestowed on another piece of legislation, the British Aerospace Act on 1 May 1980. Another New Year's Day, this time 1981, saw British Aerospace plc set up and on 4 February the government sold a fraction over 51% of its shares in the company. In May 1985 the rest of the holdings were put on the market, save for a £1 'golden share' to ensure that BAe would remain in British control. By 1985 Callaghan was in the House of Lords. He had lost the general election of 4 May 1979 and the Conservative's Margaret Thatcher was in power, champing at the bit to change the fabric of the nation. Britain's aerospace giant had been privatised, eight years after it had been nationalised; a swift case of 'Back to the Future'.

A British Aerospace tour de force. From the top: Tornado F.3 ZE785 of 11 Squadron; Tornado GR.1 of 617 Squadron; Sea Harrier FRS.1 of 899 Squadron; Harrier GR.5 of 233 Operational Conversion Unit; the second Hawk 200 ZH200; Hawk 50 demonstrator ZA101; the EAP, ZF534. *Courtesy and copyright BAe Systems*

BAe's ambitions went well beyond all things 'aerospace'. The acquisition of Royal Ordnance in 1987 raised few eyebrows – it had the all-important 'synergy' – and munitions remains part of the BAE Systems portfolio. What *did* surprise was buying the former nationalised Rover Group in 1988. Britain's motor vehicle industry had been through trauma after trauma and it seemed an expensive way for BAe to get a good discount on company cars! Sense prevailed in 1994 when Rover was sold off to BMW. In 1991, a partnership with the French shipbuilding group Sema-Metra initiated surface vessel and submarine construction that, in the shape of BAE Systems Maritime, still functions. Other businesses, including property management, were taken on board and later jettisoned.

News that the multinational mammoth General Electric was divesting itself of its defence division, Marconi Electronic Systems (MES), focused minds at BAe. Here was a chance to expand into a true 'national champion' capable of matching the large American combines. MES brought shipbuilding, engineering, radar, communications, avionics, missiles and torpedoes among others to the party. This was not a takeover; it was a merger of equals. The result was BAE Systems, formed on 30 November 1999.

Flight magazine listed BAE Systems in September 2020 as the thirteenth largest aerospace company by revenue, with sales of $13.3 billion over the 2019 fiscal year – down from twelfth place in the 2019 survey. (The top twelve, in descending order, being Airbus [$78.9 billion] Boeing [$76.6], Lockheed Martin [$59.8], United Technologies [$46.9], Northrop Grumman [$33.8], General Electric's GE Aviation division [$32.9], Raytheon [$29.2], Safran [$28.5], L3Harris [$18.0], Rolls-Royce [$15.7], Leonardo [$15.4], Honeywell [$14.0]) In July 2019 BAE Systems had 83,000 employees; when BAe was formed in 1977 the figure was about 55,000. As highlighted above, BAE Systems is a multi-faceted, global, organisation with operations and employees in Australia, India, Saudi Arabia and the USA as well as Britain. While its pure aviation 'footprint' in the UK is unrivalled BAE Systems is not alone: Airbus UK employs around 14,000 people directly.

As Britain's largest present-day aerospace company, this chapter goes into more depth than space permits for the others: it is important to set the immediate legacy of BAE Systems.

Inheriting longevity

With the bringing together of three manufacturers in 1977, BAe inherited an impressive 'catalogue' spread across eighteen major production sites. It was inevitable that one of the management aims was to sort the wheat from the chaff among the types being built and to drastically reduce the number of factories and airfields. The table outlines the programmes that were inherited, with all but Concorde running at least into the 1990s. The Tornado and Jaguar fulfilled their promise as long-termers, especially when lucrative upgrade contracts were awarded. The Hawk was in a league of its own and via the Series 100 enhancements remains in production as this book went to press. The Harrier was to re-emerge as a joint venture by McDonnell Douglas and BAe as a true second-generation machine.

After Concorde, Filton was desperately in need of work and in the late 1970s Vickers VC10s were gathered for conversion into two- and three-point tankers for the RAF. Fourteen airframes were involved: five VC10s that had previously served with Gulf Air, four East African Airways Super VC10s and five former British Airways Super VC10s, which became K.2, K.3 and K.4 tankers respectively. The first conversion, a K.2, was flight tested in June 1982, while the first of the K.4s was airborne in 1993.

A four-year contract was secured in 1983 for depot-level maintenance of British-based United States Air Force General Dynamics F-111 swing-wing strike aircraft. Under its BAe Aviation Services subsidiary further conversion work followed, transforming retired airliners into freighters. Among these was a dozen Airbus A300B4s, the first of which had its maiden flight in January 1994. Sub-assembly work continued for other BAe/BAE Systems programmes, including the 146 and RJ family – of which more anon. With the closure of Hatfield, its Airbus wing commitments relocated to Filton. (The major wing production centre was, and still is, Hawarden, near Chester. The first A300B wing set was created there in 1971.) As noted later, this site was sold to Airbus in 2006 and in turn transferred to GKN Aerospace in 2008. Filton closed as an airfield in December 2012 but alongside GKN, Airbus and BAE Systems maintain a presence at Filton.

British Aerospace 'inheritance' programmes

Type	Last example	Chapter	Notes
BAC One-Eleven	1989	13	[1]
BAC Strikemaster	1982	13	[2]
BAC/SNIAS Concorde	1979	13	
EE Canberra	1980	18	[3]
HS Trident	1978	26	
HS Harrier/AV-8A	1983	26	[4]
HS Hawk	1997	26	[5]
HS Nimrod R.1/MR.2	1984	26	[6]
HS 125	1984	26	[7]
HS 748	1988	26	[8]
SAL Bulldog	1982	33	
Panavia Tornado	1998	13	[9]
SEPECAT Jaguar	2002	13	[10]

[1] Last British-built version flown 1982. Romanian assembly ceased in 1989. [2] Production stopped 1977, but restarted to complete a batch of ten 1980–82. [3] *Second* refurbishments for Venezuela were completed in 1980. [4] P.1127-based versions, to RAF GR.3 or T.4 equivalent. [5] Up to the Mk.60 variants but excluding the Mk.60-based, US-built T-45 Goshawk. See narrative for the programme beyond 1997. [6] MR.2 upgrade programme, first example handed over 23 August 1979. See narrative for the AEW.3 and MRA.4 sagas. [7] Up to Series 700 variants. See narrative for the programme beyond 1994. [8] Licence by Hindustan Aircraft (Aeronautics from 1964) in India completed in 1984. [9] UK-built: last GR.1 1985, last F.3 1993; GR.4 upgrade programme, first example handed over to RAF October 1997. [10] UK production completed 1984. Licence production by Hindustan Aeronautics in India completed 2002.

Corporate jet

Another champion of longevity was the exceptional 125 business jet. This began life as the DH.125 but, as described in Chapter 26, this pioneering twin-jet corporate transport first flew in August 1962, by which time de Havilland was firmly in the HSA camp. A policy of upgrades, graduation from turbojets to turbofans and airframe refinement and enlargement resulted in a superb total of 576 units when the last Series 700 was delivered in 1984.

By then the Series 800 was rolling down the production line at Hawarden, also known as Broughton. First flown on 26 May 1983, the 'Dash-800' was a major revision intended to take the type *towards*, if not *into* the 21st century. Span was increased from 47ft to 51ft 4in and the rear fuselage and the fin were redesigned. Most obvious external change was the enlarged, rakish-looking, cockpit glazing. Inside, the instrumentation was transformed; it was an 'all-glass' cockpit. Like its predecessors, the version continued to attract military customers: the US Air Force acquired six for its Combat Flight Inspection and Navigation 'flight-checker' role, as the C-29A, and the Japanese Air Self-Defence Force for search and rescue, as the U-125. This success was built upon with the Series 1000, which had its maiden flight on 16 June 1990. Switching to the Pratt & Whitney Canada PW305, the new version offered extended range and a 33in fuselage stretch to 53ft 11in. The '1000' was offered in parallel with the '800', but it achieved only a fraction of its smaller sibling's sales.

A pair of Japanese Air Self Defence Force U-125As – Hawker 800s configured for search and rescue with an under-fuselage Texas Instruments APS-134 radar and a forward-looking infrared sensor under the nose. *Raytheon*

Assembly of the prototype 125-1000 at Hawarden during September 1989. In the background are Airbus wing jigs. *British Aerospace*

First flown on 19 July 2018, the A330-based Beluga XL outsize load transport is beginning to replace the A300-based Belugas used by Airbus to fly major components – including Hawarden-built wings – around its European factories. *Courtesy and copyright Airbus*

A rejig of BAe's commercial aircraft business in February 1992 brought about three divisions – Airbus, Regional and Corporate. In the case of BAe Corporate Aircraft Ltd this was fleeting; three months later it had become simply Corporate Jets Ltd. Further rethinking of what was BAe's 'core business' was in hand and negotiations to dispose of both the regional and corporate elements began. With the bulk of 125 sales coming from the USA, a transatlantic deal looked certain. The rights to the -800 and -1000 and the outfitting and maintenance specialist Little Rock-based Arkansas Aerospace were sold to Raytheon on 6 August 1993. Defence giant Raytheon had acquired Beechcraft in February 1980 and the 125 – marketed under the 'Hawker' banner – was an ideal extension to the catalogue.

A production line was set up at Wichita, Kansas, which initially was to outfit 'green' airframes built and flown at Hawarden, while all-American production was achieved. The first Wichita-completed Hawker 800s appeared in late 1995. The Hawarden line was moved to hangars on the north side of the airfield in January 1994 and the final British-built 'green' was rolled out on 22 April 1997. About 650 Series 800s and 1000s had been flown in the UK. Added to the 576 of the pre-BAe 125s, the type had comfortably achieved a four-figure production run. From mid-1997 wings, tails and fuselages were shipped to the USA to make their maiden flights in Kansas. When BAE Systems sold off its Airbus shares and Hawarden became an Airbus UK plant in October 2006 the new management continued the 125 sub-contract.

Raytheon's Hawker Beechcraft division waved the white flag on 3 June 2012 and production ground to a halt. Launching the all-new Horizon corporate jet, which first flew on 11 August 2001 and was quickly rebranded the Hawker 4000, proved expensive and time-consuming. Sales were disappointing and the 2008 global financial collapse had put the 'biz jet' market into free fall. The Kansas line brought the final figure for the 125 family to 1,764, achieved over five decades and on two continents.

Hawarden started off as a Vickers 'shadow factory', kicking off with Wellington I L7770, which was test flown from the airfield on 2 August 1939. The Hawker 800 that was rolled out in 1997 brought to an end the manufacture of complete, ready-to-fly, aircraft at Hawarden. Today the runway resonates to Airbus Belugas carrying wings to the European Airbus plants.

All kinds of Jetstreams

As BAe was finding its feet in 1978, the former SAL plant at Prestwick was in need of a new product. The factory was a well-established sub-contractor, including work for Lockheed: fuselage 'barrels' for the C-130 Hercules airlifter and assemblies for the TriStar wide-body. The end was in sight for the Bulldog military trainer and its Bullfinch development, first flown in 1976, showed little promise. The Bulldog was an inheritance from the failed Beagle and had been a money-spinner since 1971. Just prior to BAe's formation, in December 1976, the last Jetstream T.1 had been handed over to the RAF. This had been another SAL 'rescue', this time from the collapsed Handley Page (HP). BAe management realised that it owned the rights to a twin turboprop with great potential – an announcement that the Jetstream was to be reborn was made on 5 December 1978.

Although the French Turboméca Astazou turboprop was an economic powerplant, it was of limited appeal to potential US customers. The new version kept very much to the HP creation, but opted for the very popular American 900shp Garrett TPE331. To emphasize this, the new machine was called the Jetstream 31, abbreviated to J31. A HP-built Jetstream carcass was turned into the prototype and this had its maiden flight at Prestwick on 28 March 1980. Go-ahead for the programme was approved in January 1981

British Aerospace and BAE Systems civil programmes

From	To	Total	Name/Designation	Type	Engine(s)	Notes
1982	1997	387	Jetstream 31/32	Airliner	2 x Garrett TPE331	[1]
1981	1993	222	146 Srs 100–300	Airliner	4 x Avco ALF 502	
1983	2011	650+	125-800/-800XP	Corporate	2 x Garrett TFE731	[2]
1986	1995	65	ATP/Jetstream 61	Airliner	2 x P&W Canada PW126	
1990	1997	52	BAe 1000	Corporate	2 x P&W Canada PW305	[3]
1991	1997	105	Jetstream 41	Airliner	2 x Garrett TPE331	
1992	2002	169	RJ 70/85/100	Airliner	4 x Lycoming LF507	
2001	2002	3	RJX	Airliner	4 x Honeywell AS977	

Includes examples delivered to military customers. **[1]** Not including prototype, a converted Handley Page-built example; first flown 28 March 1980. **[2]** Programme sold to Raytheon, Wichita, Kansas June 1993. Production continued at Hawarden – as a sub-contractor – initially with 'green' airframes flown to USA for fitting out; last of these April 1997. After that fuselage, wings, tail assemblies shipped for assembly in USA and from late 2006 UK 'kits' built under the aegis of Airbus UK. Marketed in the USA as the Hawker 800. **[3]** See Note [2] for Raytheon details. Rebranding of the range, in other words this was the 125-1000. Marketed in the USA as the Hawker 1000.

and a batch of ten was laid down. The first 'pure' J31 took to the skies on 18 March 1982, with deliveries beginning before the end of the year. The 200th production example was the first of the more powerful Super 31s – later redesignated the J32. Production ground to a halt in 1993, but two more were prepared as a special order for Japan Air Lines in 1996 and 1997, bringing the total to a healthy 387.

The Jetstream clearly had 'growth' in it and a new twenty-seven to twenty-nine-seat airliner, the Jetstream 41, was launched on 24 May 1989. The fuselage was 'stretched' by 16ft to 63ft 2in and the wing ran below, not through, the cabin, greatly increasing passenger appeal. The reliable TPE331s were retained, rated at 1,500shp. Although derived from the J31/J32, this programme was much more complex and costly, so BAe sought risk-sharing partners. Oklahoma-based Gulfstream Aerospace Technologies signed up to build 200 sets of wings, up to the end of the century. At Stans in Switzerland, Pilatus manufactured the tail and ailerons. Field Aircraft, at East Midlands Airport, had fitted out J31s and J32s but for the J41 its involvement was extended to 'bundling' the electrical and avionics looms and creating the interiors. ML Slingsby from Kirkbymoorside, Yorkshire, tackled the type's large composite fairings. The first J41 had its maiden flight on 25 September 1991 and was followed by 104 others. The final example was delivered to the Hong Kong government in July 1997.

By the time that BAe was up and running, April 1977, the 232nd 748 twin turboprop was getting ready for testing at Woodford. (That figure excludes the Indian licence-builds and the RAF's Andover tactical transports.) There was still plenty of 'life' in the 748, but a genuine second-generation version was thought to be able to find a wider market. Given the simple designation ATP – for Advanced Turbo Prop – the programme was launched on 1 March 1984. The same fuselage cross section was married to the beefed up centre section and inner wings of the Andover and the improved outer wing of the Series 2B 748. The Rolls-Royce Dart had had its day and 2,653shp Pratt & Whitney Canada PW126s driving six-bladed propellers were chosen. As with the 748, construction was carried out at Chadderton with assembly and testing at Woodford. The maiden flight of the prototype took place on 6 August 1986.

Initial orders failed to sustain production and by late 1993 'white tail' examples were being stored. To allow Woodford to concentrate on the RJ Avroliner and Nimrod MRA.4 – more on both below – the decision was taken to move the assembly line to Prestwick. The sixty-third and last ATP assembled at Woodford flew on 25 May 1993. The previous month, a new BAe company had been formed, Jetstream Aircraft Ltd, to look after all of the Prestwick-based twin turboprops. (This was the *second* Jetstream Aircraft Ltd: as outlined in Chapter 33 the original rescue package for the HP Jetstream programme carried that name.) The ATP was rebranded as the Jetstream 61 – the J61 – with increased power. Design studies were initiated for fifty-

Above: In 'green' (unpainted and not outfitted) state and wearing 'B Condition' ('trade plate') markings, Jetstream 31 G-31-635 at Field Aircraft, East Midlands Airport, in June 1984. It was delivered two months later to US operator Eastern Metro Express. *Alan Curry*

Right: Cover of a brochure for the Jetstream 41. *KEC*

seat J51 and seventy-seat J71 versions. The first J61 had its maiden flight at Prestwick on 10 May 1994; it was followed by just one more in July 1995, after which the ATP/J61 programme was brought to an abrupt close.

Having sold off the corporate jets business in 1993, BAe management was seeking to offload the twin-turboprop family as well. On 26 January 1995 it was announced that BAe's turboprop regional programmes were merging with the Franco-Italian Avions de Transport Régional (ATR). On 1 January 1996 this came about with the formation of Aero International Regional at Toulouse, France, with the bizarre brackets-equipped abbreviation AI(R). French Aérospatiale (these days Airbus) and Italian Aeritalia (now Alenia Aermacchi) had combined to form ATR in February 1982. The twin turboprop forty-seat ATR 42 took to the skies in August 1984 and the seventy-seat ATR 72 first flew in October 1988. The ATP was in direct competition with the ATR 72 and part of the setting up of AI(R) was an agreement to axe the British programme. The J31/32 and J41 programmes were also destined to grind to a halt. Just what BAe was to get out of the European alliance is unclear, but it cannot have been too tantalising: AI(R) was mutually dissolved in July 1998.

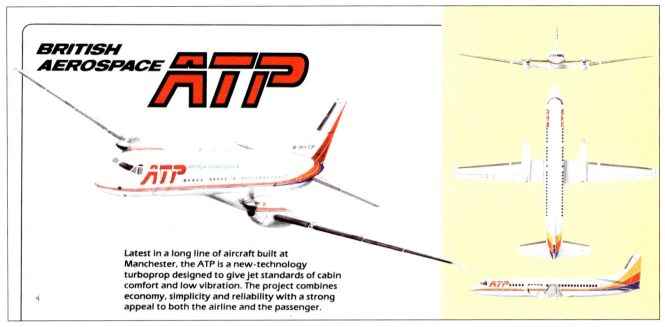

Detail of a page from a BAe Commercial Aircraft division brochure entitled 'The Quiet Family' detailing the ATP. *KEC*

After the Jetstreams had gone, the workforce at Prestwick continued sub-contracting, or 'aerostructures', for BAe/BAE Systems and with Airbus, Boeing and others. On 31 January 2006 BAE Systems sold what had been the SAL factory and its Samlesbury aerostructures subsidiary to the US-owned Spirit AeroSystems. Within what is now called the Aerospace Campus at Prestwick, BAE Systems still has a presence, supporting ATP, J31/J41, 146 and RJ operators. When the J61 line was terminated, about ten unfinished fuselages and cockpit sections were distributed to fire crews for training. This included Prestwick, where a gutted fuselage serves as a reminder of the last, short-lived, major aircraft programme built in Scotland.

Britain's last jetliner

With the throttles fully forward, Trident 2E G-BBWH climbed skyward from Hatfield on 17 April 1978. Exactly three months later it was on its way to its customer, China's Civil Aviation Administration; the final Trident had been delivered. Hopes that it would not be the last jetliner made at the Hertfordshire airfield were lifted on 10 July that year when BAe announced that it was backing what had been the HS.146 'Whisperjet', a four-turbofan airliner designed to be as quiet as possible. Back in April 1971 what was then the HSA board had approved the setting up of a design team to create a new airliner. Edward Heath's Conservative government pitched in with a pledge of funding in August 1973. The so-called 'oil crisis' of 1974 plunged the world into doubt and depression: the HS.146 was put on the back-burner.

BAE management took the bold decision to resuscitate the 146, launching the venture on 10 July 1978. Two versions were initially offered, the Series 100 capable of operating from unpaved runways and carrying seventy-two to ninety-three passengers and the stretched Series 200 with a capacity of eighty-two to 109 passengers with no 'off-road' capability. The prototype Series 100, appropriately registered G-SSSH, had its maiden flight on 3 September 1981 and the first 200 got airborne on 1 August the following year. Heading up the design team was Robert 'Bob' Edward Grigg, who had graduated from Comet to Trident and completed his career on Airbus wings.

Work on the 146 was shared across BAe: Brough built the fin, Chadderton the rear fuselage, Filton the centre fuselage, Prestwick the engine pylons while Hatfield constructed the forward fuselage

and carried out assembly and flight test. Engine pod specialist Shorts made the cowls for the Avco 502 turbofans. US company Avco's involvement was more than engine supplier; it became a risk-sharing partner with its aerostructures division building the wing boxes. This gave the new airliner the all-important high American content. Sweden's Saab made the tailplanes.

In March 1987, with sixty-three examples completed and an increasing order book, it was announced that the production rate was going to be increased by establishing a second assembly line at Woodford. A further stretch created the 103 passenger Series 300: the original prototype was re-engineered and flew in the new guise on 1 May 1987. By the end of 1991 it was clear that Woodford was in the ascendancy and Hatfield was destined for the property developers. In February 1992 came the announcement that all 146s would fly from Woodford; seven months later the closure of Hatfield was confirmed. Hatfield's iconic flight shed with its integral control tower was given listed status by English Heritage in 1998 and today provides a reminder of what had been.

The first Woodford-completed 146 flew on 16 May 1988. To remain competitive, BAe created an all-glass cockpit for the jetliner and trials began in April 1989. This led to the upgrading of the entire family and the dropping of the 146 designation. The Series 100, 200 and 300 morphed into the RJ70, RJ85 and RJ100 respectively. The first of the new family, an RJ85 for launch customer Crossair of Switzerland, had its maiden flight on 27 November 1992. The rebranding went much further than the aircraft; the creation of Avro International Aerospace was announced in January 1993 to manage the Avroliner family. There were raised eyebrows among the Woodford workforce; the hallowed name 'Avro' had been reborn and given to a Hatfield product – geographic rivalries ran deep!

Forever looking for partners, or to sell on assets, BAe began negotiations in September 1992 with the Taiwan Aerospace Corporation for a 50:50 partnership on the RJ programme. A contract was never signed and, like AI(R), it came to nought. While the four small turbofans had given the 146 an edge in the early 1980s, as the 20th century was drawing to a close the rejuvenated RJ series was far less attractive. The answer was further investment, including re-engining with the Honeywell (Garrett as was) AS977 to create the lower weight, longer range, resculptured-cabin RJX.

All three models of the RJ Avroliner cavort for the camera during the summer of 1992 in BAe house colours. Top to bottom: RJ100 G-OIII, RJ85 G-ISEE and RJ70 G-BUFI. *British Aerospace*

As the first 'all new' BAE Systems product, the prototype RJX85 had its maiden flight on 28 April 2001. The twin towers fell in New York on 11 September and fourteen days later the first RJX100 got airborne from Woodford. The world had changed and the BAe/BAE Systems on-off love affair with airliners large and small was shattered. The company had found its 'core business' – defence. On 27 November 2001 the axe fell and the 146/RJ was terminated. A 'production' RJX100 was flight tested in January 2002 and in November the final RJ, an RJ85 for Finland's Blue 1, was handed over. The first RXJ100 flew the short distance to Manchester Airport on 6 February 2003 to join the Runway Visitor Park – the RJX was a museum piece. The last of the four-jets to leave its birthplace flew away to storage at Filton on 24 June 2002; four others were scrapped. With only the Nimrod programme – see below – at Woodford, the Cheshire airfield and the Chadderton factory looked vulnerable.

Jettisoning Airbus

The escape from civilian programmes was completed in October 2006 when BAE Systems disposed of its 20% share in Airbus for £1.9 billion to the European Aeronautic Defence and Space Company (EADS) combine. EADS went on to adopt the trading name Airbus across its products from airliners to helicopters to space vehicles. For the purposes of this book this encompasses the sites at Hawarden and Filton, designing and building wings across the entire Airbus range. In 2006 this comprised: A300 last delivery July 2007; A320 family; A330, A340, A380 'Super Jumbo', which entered service in 2007; and the in-development A400 military airlifter, which had its maiden flight in December 2009.

The Airbus story originates with HSA and the British element had long had a 'shall we, shan't we' debate. By divesting itself of its Airbus division, BAE Systems had removed the last 'non-core' activity from its portfolio. While that logic could be appreciated, the sale of such a dynamic and large industrial base generated the raising of many eyebrows, particularly in the large workforce constructing the wings and the British-based supply chain. Regrets at letting the

Airbus contract go might well have been centre stage in 2012 when it was revealed that BAE Systems and EADS were in talks about a merger. These were rapidly withdrawn as shareholders and politicians on both sides of the North Sea poo-pooed the idea.

Having acquired factories near Chester and in Bristol, Airbus took over wing manufacture seamlessly; selling the Filton operation to GKN Aerospace in 2009. Ten years later the plant at Hawarden was building more than a 1,000 wing sets a year and directly employing around 6,200 people. A document commissioned by the think tank Oxford Economics in June 2017 for Airbus, entitled *The Impact of Airbus on the UK Economy*, noted that Hawarden contributed £845 million to the Welsh gross domestic product in 2015. (This is downloadable from the Airbus website and provides an overview of Airbus UK's many ventures that fall beyond the remit of this book.) At the time of writing, Airbus remained firmly committed to its British involvement but – as noted at the end of this chapter – post-Brexit things could change.

A wing destined for an A350 being moved at Hawarden, early 2019. The banner behind declares 'The World Flies on Our Wings' and shows the relative profiles of the wings for the A320, A330, A350 and A380. *Courtesy and copyright Airbus*

British Aerospace and BAE Systems military programmes

From	To	Total	Name/Designation	Type	Engine(s)	Notes
1978	1988	90	Sea Harrier FRS.1	V/STOL fighter	1 x RR Pegasus	[1]
1980	1986	11	Nimrod AEW.3	Early warning	4 x RR Spey	[2]
1985	1999	416	Harrier GR.5/7/9	V/STOL fighter	1 x RR Pegasus	[3]
1986	1999	65	Hawk 200	Light fighter	1 x Adour	[4]
1986	-	1	EAP	Concept demo	2 x Turbo-Union RB.199	
1987	date	320+	Hawk 100 series	Advanced trainer	1 x Adour	[4] [5]
1988	2009	223	T-45A Goshawk	Advanced trainer	1 x Adour (F405)	[4] [6]
1988	1999	22	Sea Harrier FA.2	V/STOL strike	1 x RR Pegasus	[7]
1994	date	667	Typhoon	Fighter/strike	2 x Eurojet EJ200	[8]
2004	2010	5	Nimrod MRA.4	Maritime patrol	4 x RR BR710	[9]

[1] Includes T.60s for Indian Navy. Also 31 conversions of Royal Navy FRS.1 to FRS.2 (later FA.2) status. [2] All converted from MR.1s – see Chapter 26. Three development batch examples and eight converted aerodynamically, with lessening installation of systems etc. [3] Joint programme with McDonnell Douglas. Includes T.10 trainer and AV-8B Harrier II, AV-8B Harrier II Plus and TAV-8B production by McDonnell Douglas in the USA 1978-1997 – see narrative. [4] Adour produced by Rolls-Royce and Turboméca. [5] Includes local assembly in Saudi Arabia at Dhahran and in South Africa by Denel at Kempton Park, Johannesburg. Also local assembly by Hindustan Aeronautics, India, which by 2010 – as Hindustan Aerospace – had become full-blown licenced production. [6] McDonnell Douglas programme based at Long Beach, California, USA, with BAe/BAe as sub-contractor – see narrative. [7] Includes T.8 trainers. See Note [1] for conversions to Mk.2 status. [8] British-German-Italian-Spanish programme under Eurofighter – see narrative. Includes seven prototypes and 38 ordered by Germany on 11 November 2020. German- and British-flown prototypes, DA.1 and DA.2, powered initially by Turbo union RB.199-34Rs; production examples with EJ200s. [9] Programme cancelled October 2010; five flown prototypes and six airframes under assembly all scrapped January-February 2011. One airframe allocated to programme was reduced to spares as 'unsuitable'.

Second-generation: Harrier

The conception and development of the Harrier up to its combat-proven GR.3 and its two-seat equivalents is dealt with in Chapter 26. That airframe still had life in it, providing the Royal Navy with a return to a fixed-wing fighter/strike capability on the new light carriers, the first of which, HMS *Invincible*, was launched in May 1977. The British government announced its backing of the navalised Harrier programme in May 1975. Side-by-side with the development of a truly shipborne Harrier was another British innovation, the 'ski-jump' mounted on the bow of an aircraft carrier. At first set at 7 degrees, later steepened to 12–13 degrees, this allowed for an increased take-off weight for the same run along the deck, permitting greater range or weapon load.

Known as the Sea Harrier FRS.1, the new machine was proofed against a corrosive maritime environment with the replacement of all magnesium airframe elements. The cockpit was repositioned to give the pilot greater visibility for air combat. The nose was enlarged to accommodate a multi-mode Ferranti Blue Fox radar in a radome that could be swung to port to help stowage on board. The prototype FRS.1 entered flight test at Dunsfold on 20 August 1978. A two-seat operational trainer, the T.8, was also developed and in addition to the Fleet Air Arm the Indian Navy ordered the Sea Harrier.

By early 1985 the Royal Navy's FRS.1s were in need of an upgrade. Initially designated FRS.2, later FA.2, this featured a longer rear fuselage, wing tip extensions and an all-weather, multi-aspect Blue Vixen radar. A Mk.1 was converted to the new status and took to the air on 19 September 1988. A mixture of reconditioned and new-build FA.2s followed over the next decade. When ZH813, the last of the eighteen new-builds, was delivered from Dunsfold on 18 January 1999 it was the last all-British fighter to enter service.

The success of the AV-8A Harrier with the US Marine Corps (see Chapter 26) encouraged closer co-operation between the UK and the USA and McDonnell Douglas (McDD) of St Louis, Missouri, partnered up with HSA. Joint UK–US studies for what was termed Advanced Harrier, or the AV-16A, were concluded in December 1973. This was to have been a jointly funded project but in March 1975 the British Labour government pulled out.

The two companies ploughed on, Dunsfold concentrating on a 'Big-Wing' of conventional alloy construction that employed leading edge root extensions and other aerodynamic improvements to improve weapon uplift. McDD proposed a more radical development with nearly 30% of the airframe of composite construction, an enlarged wing using so-called 'supercritical' lift-enhancing aerodynamics, a bigger cockpit, seven weapons stations and beefed up undercarriage. HSA – BAe from 1978 – was the junior partner in what became the AV-8B Harrier II, it and Rolls-Royce supplying up to 40% of all examples for the US, reducing to 25% for exports. Should the RAF return to the project, Dunsfold would carry out final assembly while third-party customers would be met from St Louis.

The prototype YAV-8B was first flown on 9 November 1978 with the first Harrier IIs joining the US Marines in late 1981. Alongside the single-seater, an operations-capable two-seater conversion trainer, the TAV-8B, was also manufactured. An improved version, the Harrier II Plus, first appeared in September 1992. Italy and Spain adopted the Harrier II, both opting for local assembly.

Britain returned to the fold in 1982, acquiring an Anglicised off-the-shelf AV-8B. The first example, designated GR.5, flew on 30 April 1985. The GR.5 was a stepping stone to the GR.7, a huge advance in capability and a world apart from the somewhat basic GR.1s of 1969. With the GR.7 the Harrier became a true 'night bird', with forward-looking infrared and night-vision goggles (NVG) to allow the pilot to carry out sorties in the worst of weather and in darkness. The prototype Mk.7 first flew on 10 June 1989. As well as new-builds,

Converted from a former 899 Squadron Sea Harrier FRS.1, the first production FA.2 XZ497 running down the Dunsfold flight line, March 1989. Below is a 'comms' flight Jetstream 31. *British Aerospace*

GR.5s were also upgraded to the new status. A two-seat conversion trainer with combat potential based on the GR.7 – the T.10 – was produced, with final assembly taking place at Warton. The ultimate upgrade, the GR.9, was also a Warton project: the first example flying on 30 May 2003 and entering service in October 2006. By then the birthplace of the Harrier, Dunsfold, was no more, having closed down on 29 September 2000 to await redevelopment as a housing estate.

Harrier GR.3 and GR.5 compared

	GR.3	GR.5
First flown	31 Aug 1966*	30 Apr 1985
Engines	BSE Pegasus 103	RR Pegasus 105
	21,500lb st	21,750lb st
Span	25ft 3in	30ft 4in
Wing area	201 sq ft	238 sq ft
Length	46ft 10in	47ft 1
All-up weight	23,000lb	31,000lb**
Max speed at sea level	730mph	662mph
Max weapon load	Up to 5,000lb	Up to 8,000lb

* First development batch GR.1. ** Conventional take-off.

Second-generation: Hawk

As these words hit the keyboard, the Hawk was still in production meeting export orders. Chapter 26 details that the private-venture advanced trainer first took the air in August 1974 and glories in more than a thousand units having been built. Like the Harrier, the Hawk also broke into the American market, with the T-45 Goshawk for the US Navy. The T-45 was a McDonnell Douglas-led (Boeing from 1997) programme to replace the deck-landing capable North American Rockwell T-2C Buckeye and Douglas TA-4J Skyhawk advanced trainers. Based upon the Hawk Mk.60 airframe with many modifications, the prototype first flew at Long Beach, California, on 16 April 1988. British content was high with Samlesbury building the rear fuselage and fin, Brough the wings plus Rolls-Royce's involvement in the RR-Turboméca Adour Mk.861 (US designation F405). Production of the T-45 extended to 2009 and more than 200 units.

On 21 October 1987 BAe flew the first true Hawk Mk.100 advanced trainer with weapons training and light-attack capability. It featured a new wing with a slight sweep back, four under-wing weapons pylons and the ability to carry rails on the wing tips for air-to-air missiles. A substantially enhanced cockpit included hands-on-throttle-and-stick (HOTAS), greatly reducing pilot workload. Within the elongated nose were updated avionics and room for customer options including laser rangefinders.

In parallel with the Mk.100, BAe extended the thinking to create a single-seater offering cost-effective attack or even air combat – the

A T-45A Goshawk showing its much-modified forward fuselage and arrester hook. *BAE Systems*

A Harrier GR.5 of 3 Squadron in a 'hide' during an exercise in West Germany, September 1989. *Rolls-Royce – Jack Titley*

Hawk 200. This featured a new forward fuselage housing a Westinghouse APG-66H multi-mode radar and a pair of 25mm cannon. As well as attracting new customers, both the Mk.100 and Mk.200 were intended to appeal to existing operators. The prototype Hawk 200 had its first flight on 19 May 1986 but was destroyed in a fatal crash two months later. The accident was not attributable to the aircraft and a second prototype took the air on 24 April 1987. Prior purchasers Indonesia and Oman adopted the Mk.200 and Malaysia acquired the type alongside ten Mk.108s in 1994–95. Along with three prototypes, Hawk 200 production reached sixty-five, a disappointing figure for such a costly development.

Continual evolution of the Hawk two-seater resulted in the first flight at Warton on 5 August 2002 of Mk.120 ZJ951, the Advanced Hawk Demonstrator Aircraft. Also applicable to the Mk.120 is the acronym LIFT – lead-in fighter trainer. Launch customers Australia and South Africa use the type to prepare pilots for the McDD F-18 Hornet and Saab Gripen, respectively. The Mk.120 has only 10% structural and systems commonality with the Hawk of 1974. The Mk.120 features the more powerful Rolls-Royce/Turboméca Adour 950, 'all-glass' cockpit, provision for NVG and entirely new fin, tailplane and rear fuselage. The RAF signed up for twenty-eight Mk.128s – under the designation Hawk T.2 – in 2006 and there are hopes that this will be followed up with an order for the Red Arrows aerobatic team. Saudi Arabia and South Africa opted for local assembly, but India's order for Mk.132s evolved from local assembly to licence production. Links with India extended to a joint BAE Systems/Hindustan Aerospace project for the Advanced Hawk, announced in 2017, which could take the trainer into its *seventh* decade.

A pair of Hawk 126s at Warton in March 2016, ready for handover to the Royal Saudi Air Force. *Courtesy and copyright BAE Systems*

The historic Kingston site, with its heritage going back to 1912 and Sopwith, began to wind down from 1992 and it had shut down by 1998. Harrier work was completed at Dunsfold and Warton: Dunsfold closed its doors in 2000. Production of the Hawk moved to the former Blackburn factory at Brough. Airframes were trucked across the Pennines to Warton for completion. Brough's runway was closed to traffic in the early 1990s, but in January 2008 it was announced that Hawks were to be completed and flown out for delivery to Warton. This was short-lived and the bulk of the process moved to Lancashire. In July 2017 Warton celebrated the handover of the 1,000th Hawk.

Nimrod: from the sublime to the ridiculous

Comet 4 XW626, previously involved in telecommunications trials work at Boscombe Down, touched down at HSA's Woodford airfield on 2 April 1976. It was destined for a radical transformation: the extreme nose was fitted with a huge radome for Marconi's (later GEC Avionics) new pulse-Doppler search radar. Built at Hatfield for British Overseas Airways Corporation as G-APDS in 1959, the Comet's final role was to act as a test bed for the Nimrod AEW.3 airborne early warning programme. This fusion of Nimrod and Comet gave rise to the nickname 'Nimet' or even 'Comrod' when it was rolled out in March the following year. This unusual-looking aircraft had its maiden flight on 28 June 1977.

Three months before XW626 took to the air with its new appendage James Callaghan's Labour government gave the go-ahead for the AEW.3 project. It was to replace another Woodford product, the venerable Avro Shackleton AEW.2s of 8 Squadron, which had been serving in a 'stopgap' role since 1972. With a radome in the extreme tail and another in the nose to provide 360-degree coverage, the AEW.3 was adapted from Nimrod MR.1 maritime reconnaissance patrollers. Three examples served as the development batch, with another eight airframes destined for operational use. Equipped as an aerodynamic prototype initially, the first AEW.3 had its maiden flight on 16 July 1980.

The prototype Nimrod AEW.3, XZ286, during a sortie in September 1980. *British Aerospace*

Beset with developmental problems, the majority relating to the radar system, it was 1986 before operator screens were showing uncluttered returns. All the while the costs were spiralling upwards, from an estimation of £200 to £300 million to an eye-watering £1 billion. Prolific writer Bill Gunston summed up the AEW.3's woes in *Nimrod – The Centenarian Aircraft*: 'There is nothing wrong in a defence contractor being hard-pressed by the customer to do more, and to do it faster. It is possible to cross a fine line to a point where it becomes obvious that the customer is introducing so many changes that proper management and timekeeping become impossible and eventual collapse is inevitable.' Gunston noted that GEC Avionics spokesman Peter Simmons announced on 22 September 1986 that

recent flight trials had gone well; the radar displays were free from clutter. That was of no consequence, seventy-two hours later the contract was torn up. Gunston has a point about constantly moving goalposts, but with so few airframes and such big numbers prefixed by pound signs, the programme was vulnerable from the beginning.

By the end of 1986 the 707-based Boeing E-3A Sentry had been ordered. The Shackletons trundled on until 1991 before the big American jets entered service. There was some consideration about what to do with the redundant AEW.3s; the bulk had the aerodynamic alterations, but remained as 'shells' internally. Soon all were reduced to spares or issued to fire crews. From this debacle the mandarins and the engineers appear to have learned nothing; history was going to repeat itself...

Replacing the Nimrod MR.2 – arguably the finest anti-submarine and maritime patrol aircraft of its era – was always going to be a tall order. On 25 July 1996 the Ministry of Defence announced it had selected the Nimrod 2000 over the French Dassault Atlantique 3, which would need to re-enter production, brand new P-3C Orion 2000s from Lockheed Martin or refurbished P-3As or 'Bs from Lockheed Tactical Systems with the work taking place in the UK. A contract for twenty-one Nimrod MRA.4s was drawn up in January 1997 but this was reduced to eighteen in March 2002 and then twelve in July 2004.

The programme was going to 'reuse' Nimrod MR.2 airframes, while declaring that each completed MRA.4 would involve an 80% *reconstruction* process. The MR.2's Rolls-Royce Speys were replaced by Rolls-Royce BMW BR710 turbofans and the undercarriage was entirely new. Filton provided an all-new centre section while Brough tackled the mid-fuselage barrel and forward fuselage. Brough also built the rear fuselage, design of which was sub-contracted to Dassault. It was hoped to keep the original outer wings, but the RAF demurred and new ones were manufactured at Prestwick. That these would be new aircraft was underlined by the allocation of different serial numbers: the prototype MRA.4 PA01 became ZJ516 having started life as MR.1 XV234 at Woodford in 1969, later being upgraded to MR.2 status.

BAe decided on a two-site solution for the programme. At Bournemouth's Hurn airfield, FR Aviation was to work on the remaining elements of the 'donor' MR.2s and assemble the new airframe items from the diverse sites. The resulting 'green' airframe would then be ferried to Woodford, where the task of system integration would be carried out. During February 1997 a Russian-operated Antonov An-124 freighter plied to and from the RAF Nimrod base at Kinloss and Hurn, bringing MR.2 fuselages to FR Aviation. Another MR.2 was flown under its own steam to Hurn in November 1998.

Boeing was put in charge of developing and integrating the Tactical Command and Sensor System in January 1999. FR Aviation's part in the programme was cancelled two months later and the Antonov was back in business. In November and December it ferried sub-assemblies and fuselages to Woodford. But the process was still two-site. It was announced that Woodford would act as the assembly point and that 'green' MRA.4s would fly to Warton for systems integration. By the time the first MRA.4 flew, eight other MR.2s had arrived at Woodford.

The prototype ran up to full electrical power in December 2001 but it was not until 26 August 2004 that it got airborne. Two more flew in relatively quick order: 15 December 2004 and 29 August 2005. Originally it was hoped that the MRA.4 would achieve initial operating capability in the spring of 2003, but by 2006 the new date was optimistically being put at 2012 to 2014. A new contract was issued on 18 July 2006, by which time the programme had cost £3.8 billion, 30% more than mid-1990s estimates and for half the airframes. Aircraft PA04 had its first flight on 10 September 2009 and another followed on 8 March 2010. Two days later the Ministry of Defence accepted PA04 at Woodford and the type was cleared for the RAF to commence training crews.

On 19 October 2010 the whole MRA.4 project was terminated in the government's Strategic Defence Review. During January and February 2011 scenes of mass scrapping hit the newspapers and the TV. All this was carried out at a speed reminiscent of the air-brushing from history of the BAC TSR.2. Horrifically over budget and long delayed, the MRA.4 was an example of how a requirement can be strangled from birth by naive procurement expectations, political 'salami-slicing' of budgets and inefficient management. Along with the MRA.4, the RAF's Nimrod MR.2 fleet was also axed and an island nation found itself without a dedicated maritime patrol capability. Boeing bided its time; the first 737-based Poseidon MRA.1a arrived in 2020.

At Woodford, air traffic services were stopped on 25 August 2011 and the site was ready for disposal within eighteen months. Across Manchester at Chadderton, the once vast factory closed in March 2012. Today Woodford is a housing estate with the excellent Avro Heritage Museum as a reminder of the site's heritage.

Typhoon: the last manned fighter?

Designs studies began in 1983 to provide France, Germany, Italy, Spain and the UK with what was called the Future European Fighter Aircraft. Seeking a carrier-capable machine, France pulled out in July 1985, pursuing its home-grown Dassault Rafale. Having paved the way, the Jaguar Active Control Technology test bed (see Chapter 13) allowed BAe to create an aircraft to prove advanced fly-by-wire control and canard format pathfinding for the projected European Fighter Aircraft (EFA). With *some* involvement from Aeritalia and Germany's MBB, the Experimental Aircraft Programme (EAP) was a wholly BAe-led project, with major input from other elements of UK industry. EAP had its inaugural flight, at Warton, on 8 August 1986 'clocking' Mach 1.1 during the sixty-seven-minute sortie. It was retired on 1 May 1991, its 259th and last excursion completing 191 hours twenty-one minutes of flying time, and today it is on show at the RAF Museum, Cosford.

Germany, Italy, Spain and the UK formed Eurofighter Jagdflugzeug GmbH in June 1986 with similar multinational concerns, Eurojet and Euroradar, to create EFA, later known as Eurofighter 2000 and named Typhoon in September 1998. The road to the exceptional Typhoon proved to be as long, rocky, tortuous and frustrating as any collaborative project, but the outcome has been well worth the angst. A full commitment was signed on 22 December 1997 and construction began in May 1998. The table outlines the workshare and orders for the four nations. Protocols laid down that export orders would be apportioned 'appropriately', reflecting the marketing effort or political considerations. Germany handled the inaugural customer, Austria, which received its first example in July 2007. The alpine nation announced in July 2017 that it was looking for a replacement, ideally as early as 2020. This would bring about the prospect of second-hand Typhoons on the market far earlier than Eurofighter would have liked. The British assembly line at Warton handled the Oman and Saudi Arabian orders and will process the two dozen for Qatar announced in January 2018 and due for completion by 2024. Italy will assemble the twenty-eight for Kuwait; BAe Systems began building its share of this order in mid-2019.

Seven development aircraft were built, two each by Britain, Germany and Italy and one in Spain. To speed the flight testing the first two examples were fitted with Turbo Union RB.199-34R turbofans, similar to the Panavia Tornado's powerplant. First off was Germany's DA1 on 27 March 1994, hotly pursued ten days later by Britain's DA2 from Warton. The first example with the intended Eurojet EJ200 was Italy's DA3 on 4 June 1995. During negotiations relating to the British order, there was debate about the merits of fitting a 27mm Mauser cannon, but this was retained. Deliveries of the first two-seat operational trainer T.1s and Tranche 1 F.2s to the RAF's 17 Squadron were made in 2003 and involved only a walk across the ramp at Warton. While detailed development and testing was carried out, 17 Squadron was temporarily based with BAE Systems, so that manufacturer and operator could maximise co-operation.

The nearly complete EAP during roll out from its assembly hangar on 27 October 1985 en route to the weighbridge at Warton. *British Aerospace*

Initial versions for the RAF were interim; the T.1 two-seat conversion trainer and the F.2, which was optimised as an interceptor. The current baseline versions are the T.3 and FGR.4, both upgrades from previous models and new-builds. The Mk.4 is referred to as 'swing-role' by the RAF, having the ability to adopt air superiority or precise strike duties. By August 2019 the final RAF new-build example was in flight test at Warton. Support and upgrades – the current buzzword for this is 'sustainment' – for the Typhoon will remain an important programme for BAE Systems throughout the type's operational life.

Piloting Typhoon DA2 down Warton's Runway 26 on 5 April 1994 was Chris Yeo. He and everyone else around him could not be aware that it was to be the *last* maiden flight of any significant from-new *manned* British aircraft programme to the present day. Depending on the fortunes of the Tempest – see below – it may well be that such an event will never happen again in British skies.

Eurofighter 2000 share out

Country	Workshare*	Company	Flown from	Initial/ actual order
UK	33%	BAe, now BAE Systems	Warton	250/160
Germany	33%	EADS, now Airbus	Manching	250/181
Italy	21%	Alenia, now Alenia Aermacchi	Caselle	165/96
Spain	13%	EADS, now Airbus	Getafe	100/73

* Airframe workshare as follows: UK – forward fuselage, canard, dorsal fairing, inboard flaperons, fin, rear fuselage Section 1; Germany – centre fuselage; Italy – port wing, outboard flaperons, rear fuselage Sections 2 and 3; Spain – starboard wing, leading edge slats.

F-35 and the future

A deal struck in December 1995 by BAe gave BAE Systems the equivalent of the Airbus wings programme. Britain signed up to become the only full collaborative partner in the Lockheed Martin F-35 Joint Strike Fighter (JSF) on 18 June 1997. The RAF and Royal Navy have a requirement for up to 138 of what Britain originally called the Joint Combat Aircraft, the F-35B short take-off, vertical landing (STOVL) fifth-generation stealth fighter. The prototype X-35A first took to the air on 24 October 2000 and was successful in winning the JSF requirement for the combined US Air Force (as the land-based F-35A, first flown 15 October 2006), US Marines (STOVL F-35B, first flown 11 June 2008) and US Navy (F-35C 'big-winged' catapult-launched carrier-based version, maiden flight 7 June 2010).

Left: The Typhoon assembly line at Warton, autumn 2005. On the right is F.2 line number BS008, which was delivered to the RAF as ZJ917 in December 2005 and was later upgraded to FGR.4 status. *Courtesy and copyright BAE Systems*

Below: Typhoon F.2 ZJ932 during 11 Squadron's stand-up ceremony at Coningsby in 2007. *Courtesy and copyright BAE Systems*

The BAE Systems workshare is across *all* of the F-35 programme and not restricted to the STOVL variant. This gives BAE Systems 13 to 15% of the F-35, which the company estimates will be worth £1 billion to the UK over the life of the programme. Up to 25,000 people are employed on the British JSF supply chain; of which 1,800 are working directly on the project at the Samlesbury plant.

BAE Systems designed and builds the rear fuselage and horizontal and vertical tails on all F-35s and the nozzle bay doors for the STOVL version. BAE Systems is also the lead design authority of the crew escape and life support equipment and the fuel system. Its USA-based subsidiaries works on the electronic warfare suite and BAE Systems Australia makes vertical tail components. In terms of sustainment, contracts at the main F-35 base at Marham and for integration support on the two Queen Elizabeth-class carriers all add up to classic BAE Systems 'core business'.

'A new team is already on the runway. Their timetable is clear … By 2035 I want to see Tempests flying alongside world-beating Typhoons and F-35s.' These words and the ones at the heading of this chapter were uttered by Gavin Williamson CBE, Britain's defence minister, at the Farnborough airshow in July 2018 when BAE Systems launched its Tempest 'sixth-generation' combat aircraft project. (Williamson's tenure of the defence portfolio was brief; he was banished to the back benches on 1 May 2019, only to return to the Cabinet two months later.)

The Tempest can be either manned or remotely controlled, or operated as a mix of both. By choosing the name 'Tempest' BAE Systems is adhering to the 'wind' trend established with the Panavia Tornado and handed on to the Eurofighter Typhoon, while also perpetuating Hawker designs of the 1940s: Tornado, Typhoon and Tempest.

With France, Germany and Spain teaming up to devise the Future Combat Air System to enter service in 2040; BAE Systems announced that it was looking for risk-sharing partners to come on board Team Tempest. Japan is seeking partners for its F-3 project – but is traditionally tied in with US hardware – and Turkey – fast becoming a pariah state – were included among the possible collaborators. More realistic was Sweden's Saab and Italy's Leonardo – the latter owning Westland.

On 19 July 2019 Saab announced that British defence minister Penny Mordaunt (who lost her post five days later) and her Swedish counterpart, Peter Hultqvist, had signed a memorandum of understanding to 'work on a joint combat air development and acquisition programme, including the development of new concepts to meet both nations' future requirements'. This Swedish link-up is not out of the blue. BAe and Saab co-operated during the early days of the JAS 39 Gripen (Griffon) multi-role fighter. Warton built three sets of carbon fibre-reinforced plastic wings during the developmental phase; the prototype flew at Linköping on 9 December 1988. During the 1990s BAe built other elements of the Gripen, including the undercarriage. The two companies signed an agreement in November 1995 whereby BAe's considerable marketing expertise would be applied to achieve export customers for the JAS 39. In 1998 BAe acquired a 35% share in Saab, but by March 2010 this had been reduced to 10%. Not content with announcing the 'pairing' with Sweden, on 10 September 2019, Italy signed up with Leonardo at the head of a list of avionics and weapons companies.

When BAE Systems was established, the author occasionally met up with the organisation's PR people. Each would patiently stress that the first part of the new corporate identity was *not* an abbreviation: while derived from the previous British Aerospace, the initials stood for *nothing*, emphasizing the global nature of the new concern. Expressing some puzzlement, I remarked that I had only just got used to the lower case 'e' on BAe. There has long been a debate about presenting the entire name in block capitals – BAE SYSTEMS – or as BAE Systems. For a long time now the company's website has used the latter.

With Britain's determination to commit Brexit confirmed in 2016, I bumped into an old friend who had not long retired from Samlesbury, where he worked on the F-35. Like the author, he refuses to call the Lockheed Martin product a Lightning – that belongs irredeemably to Freddie Page's English Electric wonder. As we parted, I reminded him of the BAE Systems 'abbreviation or not' conundrum. He declared that recent events had revealed what BAE stands for: Brexit Alters Everything!

An RAF F-35B leading a pair of US Marine Corps examples during the type's first appearance in the UK, Fairford, July 2016. *Lockheed Martin Aeronautics – Angel DelCueto*

CHAPTER THIRTEEN

Shotgun Marriage

British Aircraft Corporation
1960 to 1977

'The three nations are making one of the wonderbirds of aviation ... cheaper and better for us than any alternative plane.' Prime Minister Harold Wilson, on the Tornado

AMALGAMATE OR FACE being ostracised: that was the blunt message from Harold Macmillan's Cabinet to the aircraft industry. The 1950s was a Conservative decade, but only towards the end had the nettle of overcapacity been grasped. Had Labour held sway, perhaps nationalisation would have been a solution: such a device was anathema to the Tories, another means was required.

Conservative, Labour or Liberal governments had failed to address this situation since the Great War when aviation had morphed from curiosity into a vital element of the nation's defence, an increasing commercial asset and an earner of foreign currency. The companies that survived the inevitable downturn of the 1920s were kept going with piecemeal orders and the onset of another war proved the wisdom of keeping the industry diverse. With the return of peace in 1945 it was back to square one: too many companies facing a rapidly diminishing marketplace.

By the end of the 1940s a new concept, the 'Cold War', had reared its head. This postponed Labour premier Clement Attlee's reshaping of Britain's aircraft manufacturing base. The desperate need for a rethink was emphasized by the nonsensical trio of V-bombers – discussed in Chapter 24. As the nation celebrated New Year's Eve 1959 it's worth reminding ourselves of the major 'players': Auster, Blackburn, Bristol, de Havilland, English Electric (EE), Fairey, Folland, Handley Page, Hawker Siddeley (HS), Hunting, Saunders-Roe, Scottish Aviation, Shorts, Vickers and Westland – fifteen in all. Since 1935 Armstrong Whitworth, Avro,

Gloster and Hawker had been part of Tommy Sopwith's HS consortium but effectively behaved as individual concerns, each vying for business, carrying out its own research and development.

Ideally, the government wanted two combines of similar capability so that one could be played off against the other over future defence contracts and launch aid for airliner projects. As regards aero engines, conveniently by 31 December 1959 there were already two major protagonists: Bristol Siddeley Engines (BSE) and Rolls-Royce, but in 1966 the latter swallowed the former. To bring about a realignment, Macmillan's administration employed a variation of American President Theodore Roosevelt's foreign policy doctrine: 'Speak softly and carry a big stick.' To sweeten what was overtly a shotgun marriage the government offered a lucrative dowry: Operational Requirement 339 (OR.339), the Canberra successor. To meet this glittering prize, most of the 'players' mentioned above engaged in a game of musical chairs and the panel shows how they ended up in 1960.

Rolling Concorde G-BOAF into its display hall at Aerospace Bristol, Filton, February 2017. *Aerospace Bristol*

British aircraft industry rationalisation 1960

British Aircraft Corporation	Hawker Siddeley Aviation	Westland	Independent
English Electric	Hawker Siddeley [1]	Westland Helicopters [2]	Auster
Vickers	Blackburn	Bristol helicopter division [3]	Handley Page
Bristol [3]	de Havilland	Fairey	Scottish Aviation
Hunting	Folland	Saunders-Roe	Shorts [4]

[1] Already comprising Armstrong Whitworth, Avro, Gloster and Hawker: Hawker Siddeley Aviation from January 1959. [2] Westland Aircraft Ltd was renamed Westland Helicopters in 1966. [3] Bristol engine division merged with Armstrong Siddeley in April 1959 to produce Bristol Siddeley (acquired by Rolls-Royce October 1966). The helicopter division was acquired by Westland in February 1960. [4] 69.5% state-owned with Bristol and Harland and Wolff holding the remainder.

By far and away the most absorbing and instructive book on BAC is Charles Gardner's 1981 tome entitled simply *British Aircraft Corporation*. He succinctly set the scene regarding the challenges of the 1950s: 'The days of knocking up quick, cheap, private-venture prototypes in the experimental hangar were over. The development of a significant new aircraft, military or civil, would, henceforth, have to be backed by resources of the kind which many of the [contemporary] firms did not possess. Further, this expensive complication and sophistication were predictably going to increase, and, correspondingly, the ability of the industry's main customer, the government, to buy the end-product in quantity was going to decrease.'

Carrot and stick

In 1954 Denis Haviland (with one 'l') at the Ministry of Supply embarked on a study that highlighted the inefficiencies of the disparate industry and poor ministerial procurement policies. The Korean War had ground to an inconclusive end only the year before and the 'West' was reeling about how potent was Soviet fighter technology. This was no time for Haviland's paper to rock the boat; that could await someone else.

Picking up the cudgel was Winston Churchill's son-in-law, Duncan Sandys, Minister of Defence 1957 to 1959 and Minister of Aviation 1959 to 1960. His Defence White Paper of 1957 was designed to drastically reduce costs by announcing that the future was missile-shaped and that the days of piloted aircraft were on the wane. The majority of the rockets Sandys was scheming were to be nuclear-tipped: his would be an all-or-nothing war. He kept the EE P.1 while junking the Avro 730 supersonic bomber, the Fairey F.155 long-range fighter and the Saunders-Roe SR.177 jet-plus-rocket-propelled point defence interceptor and, a little later, the Hawker P.1121 private-venture interceptor. While he had got rid of a lot of future pilots and some navigators, he'd missed the point: developing such systems would be as prohibitively expensive as the winged hardware he was jettisoning. Gardner: 'Sandys killed all the advanced projects … in the 1957 pipeline. He demoralised the RAF and the industry and set British military aviation back at least several years – and some say by a decade.'

Government launch aid was available for airliners and the two state-owned operators, British European Airways (BEA) and British Overseas Airways Corporation (BOAC), could be 'influenced' in their fleet renewal plans. Big airliner programmes were few and far between and fraught with problems when dealing with these two unbending customers. Without the 'cushion' of military contracts, civil projects were effectively private ventures and a leap in the dark.

Sandys might not have read Haviland's words on dismal ministerial management and woeful prediction of complex requirements but he seems to have got the picture about too many companies – he did not cancel OR.339, leaving it dangling like a carrot. By the spring of 1958 the *notion* that the industry needed to rationalise had become *policy* and the pace of meetings between aviation chairmen and managing directors increased. HS also

convened a flurry of internal meetings. Initially it responded to OR.339 through the Avro, Gloster and Hawker design offices, a crazy waste of resources that was reduced to a single proposal by mid-1958.

Discussions trying to bring EE and Vickers together were not easy: Brooklands seemed to regard EE as 'upstarts' while Warton thought the Surrey-based men were 'old school' and there was more than a little north–south divide to attitudes. Both concerns brought balance to combining: EE with the Canberra and the Lightning programme, Vickers with its airliner prowess. On New Year's Day 1959 the lines were drawn; Vickers and EE were awarded OR.339, later redrawn as OR.343. The Ministry of Aviation bestowed project leadership on Vickers, which flabbergasted EE. But Freddie Page (Sir Freddie from 1979 – his story is covered in Chapter 18) and his team at Warton were not the only ones with current supersonic jet experience. Vickers Supermarine division was completing production of Scimitars for the Royal Navy. The Scimitar was very sophisticated and could lay claim to being a 'weapon system'. George S Henson's design team was kept intact and brought to Brooklands to pour its skills into TSR.2.

But the game of musical chairs was not over: the search was on by EE and Vickers for another partner to acquire a stature similar to HS. The OR.339 'package' came with a pre-ordained choice of engine, the BSE Olympus. This put Bristol, owners of BSE, in the frame. Like Vickers and EE, Bristol had a vibrant and Sandys-pleasing guided weapons division but its aircraft programmes were on the wane, although it was well placed for the projected Supersonic Transport (SST). Favourite in this courtship was de Havilland (DH), well versed in missiles, with its own engine division and preparing to build the Trident jetliner and the Sea Vixen Mk.2 shipborne fighter. All the while Handley Page seemed determined to plough its own furrow. DH eventually climbed into bed with HS and so a provisional agreement was hastily reached with Bristol Aircraft on 6 January 1960. The new combine had no wish to take on Filton's rotorcraft or BSE; Westland snapped up the former and BSE remained self-contained. On 1 July 1960 BAC was born; Bristol was the junior partner with 20% of the business, while EE and Vickers had 40% apiece.

Captain of industry

At the helm of this uneasy amalgamation was a man of great perception and experience. He had that all-too-rare ability to inspire and lead staff, be they on the shop floor or in the boardroom. Essex-born George Robert Freeman Edwards was known throughout his working life as 'GRE'. Gaining a degree in engineering at London University, in 1935, aged 27, he joined Vickers under Rex Pierson. (See Chapter 37 for more on Pierson.)

Edwards made a name for himself as an innovator and problem solver when he was put in charge of converting a Wellington into a minesweeper. The Royal Aircraft Establishment (RAE) reasoned that a low-flying aeroplane generating a magnetic field could mimic the 'signature' of a ship. Sufficiently high and far away, the Wellington should to be safe when the mine exploded. In December 1939 Edwards's team installed a 48ft diameter magnetic coil attached at the rear fuselage and at each mid-wing. An auxiliary power unit

Sir George Edwards (second from left) escorting the Duke of Edinburgh around the One-Eleven production line at Hurn in early 1966. The aircraft in the background is a Series 401AK destined for American Airlines. *BAC*

generated the charge in the coil. To 'spoof' the new Wellington's role it was designated DWI – Directional Wireless Installation. DWI Wellingtons had limited lives as the Royal Navy established ways of neutralising the magnetic field of ships; known as degaussing. After the DWI, Edwards took charge of special projects at Brooklands.

Succeeding Reginald Kirshaw 'Rex' Pierson as chief engineer in 1945, Edwards's initial designs stemmed from the Wellington: the Viking airliner, Valetta military transport and the Varsity crew trainer. By the end of the 1940s Edwards had qualified as a pilot and in the '60s and '70s he delighted in captaining the BAC 'runabout' Beagle 206 G-AVHO. (This machine graces the Beagle section – Chapter 7 – in its later guise as G-FLYP.) Edwards was also in charge of the aborted V1000 jetliner and the Valiant, the first of the V-bombers. The pinnacle of his design prowess was the exceptional Viscount.

Appointed managing director (MD) of the Vickers aviation division in 1953, Edwards was knighted in 1957. He was at the helm of BAC from its inception in July 1960 as executive director of aircraft, soon to be made MD. He was thrust into the maelstrom of dealing with the British government and, increasingly with counterparts in Europe. His involvement with Concorde earned him deep respect on both sides of the Channel, while his bold championing of the One-Eleven was pivotal in rescuing BAC after the TSR.2 was axed. With nationalisation looming, Edwards decided to retire as chairman in 1975 at the age of 67. He was succeeded by Warton's Freddie Page.

Along with Charles Gardner's *British Aircraft Corporation*, there is a book by *another* Gardner – Robert. This is Edwards's authorised biography, *From Bouncing Bombs to Concorde*, and is also essential reading on the life and times of BAC. Inside, Edwards describes what becoming BAC MD meant: 'I am now the wearer of the labelled pants which the Minister of Aviation can kick!' A speech in November 1960 shows Edwards's grasp of BAC's situation: 'The one thing we must not be asked to endure is the starting and stopping of jobs when there is no reason. I have seen too many cases of an order being placed for an excessive number of aircraft because the political mood at the time made it possible, with the break clause as a comfort factor against the day when the mood changed and the axe fell. … one big company with which I am acquainted has not completed a single contract since the war without the break clause being invoked …' Finally, Edwards

was seldom to be found at BAC's London head office in Pall Mall, explaining: 'a headquarters never built anything'.

Sir George Robert Freeman Edwards OM CBE died on 2 March 2003, aged 94. He had lived to see the British industry grow to be world-renowned and he had played a significant part in that achievement.

British Aircraft Corporation 'inheritance' programmes

Type	Last example	Chapter	Notes
Bristol Britannia	1960	11	
EE Canberra	1964	18	[1]
EE Lightning	1972	18	[2]
Hunting Jet Provost	1965	30	[3]
Hunting H.126	1963	30	
Supermarine Scimitar	1960	36	
Vickers Viscount	1964	37	
Vickers Vanguard	1964	37	
Vickers VC10/Super VC10	1970	37	[4]

[1] Last PR.9 delivered to RAF 1960; final new-build were B(I).12s for South Africa, dispatched in 1964. As Chapter 18 shows, extensive refurbishing and resale programme lasted to 1980. [2] Final RAF deliveries, F.6s, 1967. Deliveries to Saudi Arabia completed 1968, but one extra F.53 completed and handed over June 1972. [3] Last RAF T.3s and export versions delivered 1961, RAF T.4s and export versions delivered from 1961; final T.52 for Iraq completed 1965. [4] All built and delivered during BAC's days, but always identified as a Vickers product.

Pulling the plug

Even today, hackles rise when the TSR.2 is discussed. The number of books on the subject is vast and the ins and outs, whys and wherefores are best left with those tomes. In a nutshell: the programme sponsor and only customer, the British government, terminated the venture as it was entitled to do.

The small print on OR.339 and its later redrafting, OR.343, required an incredibly ambitious warplane. Standing for Tactical, Strike and Reconnaissance, TSR.2 was primarily to undertake long-range nuclear and conventional precision supersonic strike around the clock and in all weathers. It was also to perform low-level battlefield interdiction as well as tactical and strategic reconnaissance tasks. All this and the ability to go 'off-road', it was to have a near-STOL (short take-off and landing) capability and to tackle unpaved runways if needs be. From conception the joint venture encountered design, engineering and logistic difficulties and a string of problems from the engine supplier, BSE. This was to be expected of such a complex venture, but costs were spiralling on a programme that looked to encompass at best 110 units.

Thirteen years of Conservative rule came to an end in October 1964 when Labour's Harold Wilson took over. He had inherited a cash-strapped and ailing economy, and aviation was an obvious target for cuts. On 2 February 1965 the newly established HS Aviation had both of its V/STOL projects, the P.1154 supersonic fighter and the HS.681 transport, terminated. TSR.2 had survived, but it was only a sixty-three-day stay of execution.

TSR.2 was cancelled on 6 April 1965, the prototype having flown 192 days previously. That machine had been assembled at Warton and was moved by road to Boscombe Down. On 27 September 1964 Wg Cdr Roland Beamont lifted XR219 off the runway for a thirteen-minute, fifty-second test flight. The second of nine development aircraft, XR220, was completed at Brooklands and trucked to Boscombe Down on 9 September 1964. The low-loader jack-knifed on the apron and the fuselage fell off, requiring considerable attention from a Warton working party. With repairs complete, XR220 started ground running on 22 February 1965. The ministerial axe fell on the very day that it was planned to fly it.

The only TSR.2 to fly, XR219, on a sortie out of Warton, early 1965. *BAC*

The one and only 'flyer', XR219, became a static ballistics target at the Proof and Experimental Establishment, Shoeburyness, Essex. Airframes on the production line, the jigs and all sundries including mock-ups were scrapped or burned with great haste. Two examples managed to survive the cull: XR220 at the RAF Museum, Cosford, and XR222 at the Imperial War Museum, Duxford.

Wilson turned to the Americans and the General Dynamics F-111, which looked set to achieve a production run in excess of 1,000. The prototype 'swing-wing' F-111 had first flown on 21 December 1964 and was destined for a problematical development phase. The F-111 evolved into a very capable and mature weapons system, the final examples being completed in the mid-1970s with around 560 built. The Royal Australian Air Force, a hoped-for TSR.2 operator, became the only F-111 export customer.

The Labour government placed an order of fifty F-111Ks for the RAF in February 1967, but this was turned on its head thirteen months later with cancellation of the contract. Two aircraft were nearly complete on the Fort Worth, Texas, assembly line and long-lead items were in process for most of the others. Swingeing cancellation fees had to be paid. What caused this about face? It all comes down to a speech by Wilson on 19 November 1967: 'It does not mean that the pound here in Britain, in your pocket or purse, or in your bank has been devalued.' The Bank of England had gone through a torrid time ploughing an incredible £200 million from its all-too-meagre gold and dollar stocks to prop up a decaying pound. Devaluing Sterling by about 14% took the heat out of the crisis, but left the UK in a dismal international financial state. (Britain was not alone, France had to devalue its currency in 1969.)

With nowhere else to turn, the RAF finally focused on the HS Buccaneer. Few realised at the time, but it turned out to be the last all-British bomber to serve the RAF. Surplus Royal Navy stocks were joined by forty-nine examples ordered from new. The first Buccaneer S.2Bs – delayed Canberra replacements – were issued to 12 Squadron at Honington in October 1969.

In *British Aircraft Corporation* Gardner succinctly describes the rationale for the cancellation, it was not: '… because of a change in government policy – the defence requirement was still there and still valid – but it was cancelled because of a change in government *procurement* [Gardner's emphasis] policy, which was a different thing.' The TSR.2 was not given a chance to see if it met the RAF's needs; it was a victim of monetary circumstances and a government desperate to offload expensive commitments. If it had avoided the axe in 1965, would the more or less all-British TSR.2, with minimal requirement for foreign exchange, been better-placed to weather the British fiscal tsunami of November 1967? That's impossible to answer, but it does show how complex programmes are far more reliant on politicians than engineers.

The editor of the monthly *Air Pictorial* was sufficiently enraged that he put a cartoon by Chris Wren on the cover of the February 1965 edition; pre-empting the TSR.2 decision. Playing the part of seven Disney-like dwarfs are members of the Labour cabinet. Clockwise from the top left: George Brown, Minister of Economic Affairs, with the HS.681; Patrick Gordon Walker, Foreign Secretary, lowering the Society of British Aircraft Constructors flag to half-mast; James Callaghan, Chancellor of the Exchequer, with the Hawker P.1154; Edward Shackleton, Minister of State for the Air Force, having attacked a BSE Pegasus and Olympus; Roy Jenkins, Minister of Aviation, with a model of Concorde; Denis Healey, Defence Minister, hacking at TSR.2; and Prime Minister Harold Wilson. *via Alan Curry*

Bus-stop Jet

When BAC was formed on 1 July 1960, there was one other constituent alongside the founder members EE, Vickers and latecomer Bristol. During September, Luton-based Hunting Aircraft was acquired and it proved to be a very shrewd move. Hunting acquired Percival in 1944 and a decade later the company was renamed Hunting Percival Aircraft, before settling on Hunting Aircraft in 1957. As well as the Jet Provost – see below – Hunting had been studying a thirty- to fifty-seater twin-jet airliner, the H.107. This was a 'clean sheet' design based on a market survey with fifty-plus airlines – an exercise almost unheard of in the British industry at that point. Hunting had got as far as registering the prototype H.107 as G-APOH – said to stand for 'Pride of Hunting' – but it remained a 'paper plane'.

Hunting's technical director was the gifted Frederick 'Fred' Henry Pollicutt, who had started at Luton in 1953 as chief designer under Leslie Frise. Three years later Frise moved on to Blackburn and Pollicutt took his desk. He began his career at the RAE in 1924 before joining Bristol six years later, rising to head of the stress department and by 1950 deputy chief designer. In 1952 Pollicutt briefly took the post of chief designer at Folland before signing up with Hunting. Pollicutt's chief designer was Ken Carline, who started off with Avro in 1946 on the abortive Type 720 rocket-powered interceptor. Carline came to Hunting in 1955 and headed up the H.107 study, transferring to BAC in 1960. He travelled to the USA in 1967, working in turn for Martin Marietta, Convair and General Dynamics. In the 1970s he was seconded to Fairey SA at Gosselies in Belgium, where the F-16 Fighting Falcon was being manufactured under licence. Later jobs included Gulfstream and Fairchild before setting up his own consultancy in 1985.

Both Bristol and Vickers had pitched for BEA's requirement for a medium-range jetliner – the Type 200 and the VC11 respectively – but the deal was clinched by DH with its Trident. With the establishment of BAC, Edwards reconsidered the VC11, which had government launch aid and an agreement to purchase from Trans Canada Airlines. The VC11 was a four-jet, scaled-down VC10 but Edwards wisely listened to Pollicutt and the H.107 became the BAC 107. More than 100 airlines were quizzed and while they were interested in the proposal, they wanted up to eighty seats. So the BAC 107 was 'grown', adopting the designation BAC 111, but it soon took on the trendy name One-Eleven and the marketing department dubbed it the 'Bus-stop Jet'.

Brooklands was to make the centre section and wing skins, Filton the rear fuselage and tail, Luton the wings and associated control surfaces. Final assembly took place at Hurn, which had last been used for Varsity production a decade earlier. The BAC board approved the scheme in March 1961 and took the bold decision to lay down a batch of twenty – they were sanctioning a new airliner design without regard for the state-owned BEA or BOAC. Two months later Freddie Laker's British United Airways signed up for ten Series 200s.

On 20 August 1963 Jock Bryce took the prototype, G-ASHG, for its maiden flight from Hurn. Lt Cdr Mike Lithgow was the captain of *Hotel-Golf*'s fifty-third sortie on 22 October 1963 along with a crew of four and assistant chief aerodynamicist B J Prior and assistant chief designer C J Webb. Among the tasks for the sortie was a series of stalls; *Hotel Golf* crashed near Chicklade, Wiltshire, killing all on board. The accident investigation report, published in late March 1965, concluded: '… the angle of incidence reached a value at which the elevator effectiveness was insufficient to effect recovery … the aircraft entered a stable stalled condition. Recovery from which was impossible.' Apart from the loss of life, including members of the design team, this was a major blow to the One-Eleven. A 'fix' was quickly initiated and confidence in the type was soon restored.

In the month after the accident report was published, on 6 April, the TSR.2 was cancelled. On that day the third One-Eleven Series 200 for US airline Braniff was delivered. BAC was teetering on the abyss; the jetliner was far from being a money-spinner and would require much more investment. The BAC board members held their nerve and the One-Eleven became a major part of the corporation's recovery; indeed production continued in the UK to 1982, under British Aerospace (BAe). With the fuselage stretched by 13ft 6in with two 'plugs' fore and aft of the wing, the Series 500 'Super One-Eleven' was launched by BEA, the prototype flying for the first time on 30 June 1967.

The first production One-Eleven Series 500 G-AVMH was delivered to BEA in June 1969. *BAC*

A government-to-government agreement was reached in June 1978 with Nicolae Ceauçescu, the Romanian dictator. Rights to the One-Eleven were to be transferred to a new organisation, the appropriately named Rombac. The manufacturer of Britten-Norman Islander airframes, Intreprinderea de Reparat Material Aeronautic (IRMA, see Chapter 14) carried out assembly of BAC-supplied kits at Baneasa, Bucharest. The first Rombac-assembled One-Eleven had its maiden flight on 18 September 1982, but it was only followed by another eight, all using British-built sections. The programme ground to a halt following the overthrow of the odious Ceauçescu in December 1989. An attempt to rebrand the One-Eleven as the Airstar 2500 got nowhere. With 244 examples completed in total, the 'Bus-stop Jet' was a success for BAC, well justifying the faith placed in it.

Small mercies

The purchase of Hunting Aviation also brought the Jet Provost under BAC's umbrella: the full story of the 'JP' is told in Chapter 30. Initially this seemed like a simple 'inheritance' programme to be wound down when its contractual obligations were met: the Luton factory had 115 T.3s to complete for the RAF when BAC was established in 1 July 1960. A fortnight later the first of the higher-powered T.4s had its maiden flight and deliveries of these and export versions continued through to April 1965.

The more powerful T.4 had amended one of the Jet Provost's shortcomings but there was one other that really needed addressing: its cramped, unpressurised cockpit reflected its late 1940s origins. BAC at Warton dusted down the H.145 project, which boasted a new, bulbous cockpit, improved instrumentation and increased fuel capacity – the hallmark tip tanks were relegated to an option. The wing was beefed up and capable of taking weapon pylons. A former T.4 was re-engineered as an aerodynamic prototype of the BAC 145 and first flew on 28 February 1967. This private venture secured an order for the RAF as the T.5, with deliveries commencing in July 1969.

To meet a Royal Saudi Air Force requirement for a light-attack platform, the BAC 145 became the basis for the BAC 167 Strikemaster. This relatively simple development had a disproportionate effect on BAC's prospects. Here was a foot in the door to export markets that might also opt for the upcoming Jaguar and was a tangible way of showing off the new corporation as a global 'player'. The pace on the Strikemaster programme was such that the first Mk.80 for Saudi Arabia took to the air at Warton just eight months after the original BAC 145.

Having 'gifted' BAC a mould-breaking jetliner and paved the way for a 'second-generation' of Jet Provosts it saddened Edwards that when faced with cutbacks in the light of the TSR.2 cancellation the axe had

A trio of tip tank-equipped Jet Provost T.5s of the Finningley-based 6 Flying Training School in the late 1970s. *RAF Finningley*

to fall on the Luton division. The plant's One-Eleven work was absorbed at Brooklands, while Jet Provost T.5 and Strikemaster production was undertaken at Warton, with the wings being manufactured at Hurn. Luton closed in August 1966 but was briefly reopened to build a batch of BAC 145s for Sudan in 1969. The Strikemaster line moved again in 1979 as Warton made space for the Jaguar programme. A batch of ten Strikemasters was completed by 1982, although the final deliveries to customers did not occur until 1988.

A Strikemaster brochure, bizarrely in German, circa 1970 with a Kuwaiti Mk.83 showing off the vast array of weaponry options. *KEC*

Supersonic politics

Concorde's story is the stuff of mythology, European politics and conspiracy theories. When the prototype had its maiden flight, the incredibly challenging programme was just over a year behind schedule – such slippage is chickenfeed compared with more recent airliner projects. The astounding technological achievement, the champagne-toting imagery of its passengers and its exceptional 'fan base' among the British public in particular are all part of its legend.

Unlike TSR.2, which was reliant on domestic politics, the SST was enshrined in an international treaty signed by Britain and France on 29 November 1962. This was a national flag-waver from inception and bound by non-commercial considerations. Like any arranged marriage, there were strings attached that quickly took on the proportions of chains as the costs mounted. The small print on the inter-government agreement included a so-called 'poison pill': you pull out; you pay the other half's costs. That locked occasionally timid British governments firmly into line.

France had realised its SST ambitions – the Super Caravelle – would go nowhere without a partner to share the challenges and the costs. Like France, Britain was looking for a technological wonder to reinforce its global industrial image. Far more importantly, Conservative Prime Minister Harold Macmillan had announced in August 1961 that he was making a formal application for the UK to join the European Economic Community (EEC), or 'Common Market'. What better way to launch a charm offensive with one of the most prominent members? With the ink well and truly dry on the SST agreement of November 1962 French premier General Charles de Gaulle uttered a firm 'Non!' to British membership on 15 January 1963. (De Gaulle did a repeat performance, this time with Harold Wilson, on 27 November 1967.)

It fell to Labour's Harold Wilson to oversee Concorde through to its first flight, despite eye-watering cost escalation. Conservative Edward Heath took Britain into the EEC on New Year's Day 1973. By then the pre-production Concordes were blasting skyward and, thanks to French intransigence, European aerospace co-operation had settled with other nations on what would become the spectacularly successful Tornado.

And the conspiracy theories? The Americans were determined to finish it off and clear the way for the Mach 3 Boeing 2707. Seattle certainly got the capacity right – around 250 seats –but Boeing backed away from the whole issue in 1971, five years before

Pre-production Concorde 202 G-BBDG displayed at the Brooklands Museum. To the right is the cockpit of Vanguard G-APEJ and in the background the Sultan of Oman's VC10 A40-AB. *Brooklands Museum*

Concorde had even entered commercial service. Environmental issues were high among the reasons for cancellation and, besides, with the 747 Boeing had invented flying for the masses and had no need for another flag-waver.

New outrage erupted on 10 April 2002 when British Airways and Air France announced that after consultation with Airbus – as the inheritors of the SST's design authority – they were going to cease operating Concorde. The manufacturer and the airlines were conspiring to strangle a world icon. Since the tragic crash of Air France's F-BTSC on 25 July 2000, Airbus had spent a fortune on modifications to an active fleet of just thirteen. No sooner had Concorde been recleared for service, the Twin Towers fell in New York on 11 September 2001 and cockpit doors needed locking and armouring. Air France paid off its machines by June 2002, British Airways in November the following year. Still the grumbles roll on … Why can't the authorities allow *just one* Concorde to convey passengers in a glorified Vulcan to the Sky-like manner? Surely that's what Permits to Fly are for?

Concorde work share

As the design teams got into gear at Filton and Toulouse – see below – the heavy lifting was done at boardroom and ministerial levels. Taking the brunt of this was BAC's Edwards and Sud Aviation's chairman General Andre Puget. (Sud became Aérospatiale on 1 January 1970.) Filton had run out of steam and an early priority for Edwards was keeping it afloat until metal began to be cut on the SST: both Brooklands and Warton supplied sub-assembly work.

The completed forward section of Concorde 202 leaving the assembly hall at Brooklands ready for the journey to Filton in 1971. *Brooklands Museum*

The political agreement set the British–French workshare for the airframe at 40:60 and for the engines at 60:40. France made the centre fuselage, inner and outer wings, control surfaces and the undercarriage and supplied the hydraulics, control linkages, navigation and radio systems, and the air conditioning supply. Britain tackled the 'droop snoot' nose, forward fuselage, tail cone, fin and rudder, engine intakes and cowlings along with the electrical, oxygen, fuel, fire suppression and de-icing systems, engine controls and instrumentation, and the air conditioning distribution gear. The 38,050lb st Olympus 593 Mk.610

afterburning turbojets and the reverse thrust nozzles, or 'buckets', were the responsibility of Rolls-Royce and Société Nationale d'études et de Construction de Moteurs d'Aviation (SNECMA). Components and sub-assemblies were supplied to both national assembly lines.

In Britain, the largest amount of the airframe was created at Brooklands, providing much-needed work after the last VC10 had been completed in 1970. While Concorde was designed and assembled at Filton it was *driven* by Brooklands. The huge factory within the Edwardian motor racing track continued to supply other plants until its closure was announced in July 1986. The bulldozers arrived in 1989 and by 1990 the site had been flattened ready for redevelopment. Today the incredible Brooklands Museum is a fitting tribute to the astonishing aviation heritage of the site, including pre-production Concorde 100 G-BBDG.

Trams to Concorde

Heading up the British design team at Filton was Archibald Russell, his French counterpart being Pierre Satre, Sud's technical director. Satre had masterminded the innovative Caravelle twin-jet, which first flew in 1955 and was to remain in production until 1972. Russell had been embedded in supersonic studies since 1956 when Bristol was part of the SST Advisory Committee. His team came up with a variety of responses as the Ministry of Aviation evaluated the best shape, size and speed. The six-engined Mach 2-plus Type 228 and the Mach 3 Type 213 both went by the wayside. Under Edwards's firm guidance, in 1961 BAC sanctioned the Mach 2-plus, four BSE Olympus-powered Type 223. It was this that was combined with the French Super Caravelle in November 1962 to become Concorde.

Test pilot Brian Trubshaw (left) congratulating Archibald Russell on being granted the Daniel Guggenheim Award for his contribution to aircraft engineering. Russell had just had his first flight in Concorde 002 at Fairford, July 1971. *BAC*

Graduating from Bristol University with a degree in automotive engineering, Russell took up a post in the Bristol Tramways and Carriage Company sheds – part of Sir George White's empire. In 1925 he transferred to Sir George's aviation enterprise at Filton and remained there for the remainder of his working life. One of his first tasks was stress calculations for Frank Barnwell and Leslie Frise on the Badminton sportsplane and the Bagshot heavy fighter. The latter's wing flexed so much as to induce aileron reversal, an alarming phenomenon witnessed by Russell, who was sent up to observe the monoplane's behaviour. By the advent of the Blenheim Russell had become head of the technical office.

When Frise retired in 1946 Russell became chief designer. Russell oversaw the misguided Brabazon, the unsung Type 170 and the unfortunate Britannia while managing Raoul Hafner's helicopter division. With the setting up of BAC Russell was appointed managing director of the Filton division in 1960. Announcing that he would like to see the Concorde project through to its maiden flight, Russell was made Filton's chairman in 1968, retiring the following year. His autobiography, *A Span of Wings*, was published in 1992. Sir Archibald Russell CBE died on 29 May 1995, aged 91.

Ogee pathfinder

With Satre's experience of the Caravelle, the Frenchman was given overall responsibility on the SST with Russell functioning as his deputy. Russell was far from lacking in jet experience, more importantly *supersonic* jets. He had headed up the only jet to carry the Bristol name, the Type 188 stainless steel research aircraft. He also oversaw a dedicated Concorde test bed, which maintained its Filton design number but was always denoted as a BAC machine, the 221.

Responding to a requirement for a high-speed delta research platform issued in September 1950, Fairey created the Roll-Royce Avon-powered FD.2 and received a contract to build two examples at Hayes. Long before Concorde was ever thought of, a 'droop snoot' tilting the cockpit and nose down by 10 degrees allowed for a better view on approach to land. Test pilot Peter Twiss was at the controls on 6 October 1955 for the first flight of FD.2 WG774 at Boscombe Down. On 10 March 1956 Twiss seized the World Absolute Airspeed Record at an astonishing 1,132mph, crushing by 310mph the previous record held by a North American F-100 Super Sabre.

On 5 September 1959, WG774 was ferried to Filton and disappeared into the huge Brabazon hangar. Under Russell's guidance the FD.2 was treated to radical surgery so that it could have a new life as the BAC 221, a high-speed test bed for the ogee wing planned for Concorde. It was given an entirely new wing and long-stroke undercarriage, requiring considerable re-engineering. In its new configuration, WG774 flew from Filton on 1 May 1964. It was used by BAC for trials before transferring to the RAE on 20 May 1966. The 221 was grounded at Thurleigh after 273 sorties on 9 June 1973. Today, it is displayed at the Fleet Air Arm Museum Yeovilton, alongside Concorde 002.

Twenty in ten years

Sud chief test pilot André Turcat and his crew took 001 F-WTSS for its forty-two-minute maiden flight from Toulouse on 2 March 1969. On its fifth sortie – 21 March – his British counterpart, Brian Trubshaw, was in the co-pilot's seat, providing him with enormous experience ready for the big moment at Filton. That came on 9 April 1969 as Trubshaw piloted 002 G-BSST on a twenty-two-minute sortie to Fairford, chosen as the British test centre. It was not until 17 December 1971 that another Concorde was ferried to Fairford. *Delta-November* was the third of six aircraft used in the extensive six-and a-half-year testing programme that preceded Concorde's entry into service.

Air France and British Overseas Airways Corporation (which became British Airways on 31 March 1974) signed up for four and five examples each – later increased to seven each – on 28 July 1972. Despite interest from Pan Am and others, the two state airlines found themselves with nowhere to go other than to seek purchase and operating subsidies from their governments.

The SST's commercial life began with a simultaneous inauguration by Air France and British Airways from Charles de Gaulle and Heathrow airports, respectively on 21 January 1976. The tenth British-assembled Concorde and the final example of the combined run of twenty, G-BFKX, had its maiden flight at Filton on 20 April 1979 and was delivered to British Airways in June 1980. (Later registered G-BOAF, it made the last-ever Concorde flight, from Heathrow to Filton on 26 November 2003. Today it is displayed by Aerospace Bristol at its birthplace.)

Supersonic afterthoughts

Stephen Clarke's *1,000 Years of Annoying the French* (Bantam, 2010) might not spring to mind as an aeronautical reference, but it provides an engaging observation on the 'Brits' adding the 'e' to Concord and how Tony Benn learned about the extent of British involvement in the project. '… when the first prototype was unveiled in Toulouse [11 December 1967], Britain's Minister of Technology [and Member of Parliament for Bristol South] Tony Benn, announced that the plane would be called Concorde. The final 'e', he said, stood for 'excellence', 'Europe', 'entente' and 'England'. When a Scot wrote to him pointing out that the nose cone was made north of the border, Benn added that the 'e' also stood for 'Écosse', the French for Scotland.'

Bird's eye view of the BAC 221 ogee wing test bed as it neared completion at Filton, 1964. *BAC*

In *A Span of Wings*, Russell included a comparison of operating costs for the Boeing 707, the 747 and Concorde as calculated in 1967. For what the reader has to assume was a transatlantic flight the fuel burn was estimated at 80,000lb, 160,000lb and 160,000lb: equating to 910lb, 640lb and 2,000lb per passenger given that each airliner was carrying 87, 250 and 80 customers, respectively. For the two Boeing products, the load factor was assessed at 50%, for Concorde the number of 'bums on seats' was increased to 66% because of its speed advantage boosting its appeal. Russell's table also noted that the 120-passenger Concorde should also have its 66% load factor recorded as 160 seats because the supersonic transport offered 'two trips for [the price of] one'. He concluded: 'The killing blow came with the rocketing inflation of 1970s, and especially in the price of aviation fuel. From the first assessment of Concorde operating costs the price of fuel rose from $1.50 a barrel to $30 a barrel.'

The prototype 'Jumbo Jet' took to the skies over Seattle twenty-two days before Concorde 001 had its maiden flight from Toulouse on 2 March 1969. It was the sheer capacity of the Boeing 747 that was to make it the enduring 'Queen of the Skies' and an engine for global social change. Russell concluded that as the fuel costs spiralled ever upwards, then Concorde became: '… a first-class service only. Then the potential sales are dramatically cut and the first price [initial cost] goes up. Someone has to lose money and experience shows this has to be the taxpayer.'

Le learning curve

Collaboration with France was not limited to Concorde. On May 17 1965 an inter-government accord was signed for the development of what became the Jaguar, the Anglo-French Variable Geometry (AFVG) fighter and the Gazelle–Lynx–Puma helicopter partnership – see Chapter 38 for the latter. Leadership was vested respectively in Bréguet (part of Dassault from 14 December 1971) and BAC. France later pulled out of AFVG, leaving the way clear for another European consortium – the very successful Panavia. In May 1966 Société Européenne de Production de l'Avion d'Ecole de Combat et d'Appui Tactique (SEPECAT) was established to govern the Jaguar project.

SEPECAT translated as: 'European company building a trainer and strike aircraft', adequately explaining the requirement.

Each nation was to acquire 200 examples. Bréguet making the nose, centre fuselage and undercarriage; BAC the wings, tail unit, rear fuselage and engine intakes. Assembly was to be carried out in two sites, Toulouse-Blagnac and Warton. Initially British Jaguars were intended to replace Folland Gnat T.1 and Hawker Hunter T.7 advanced trainers, but this was changed when the incredible HS Hawk (Chapters 12 and 26) was ordered in 1972. Jaguar was developed as a ground-attack platform, enabling the RAF McDonnell Douglas Phantom force to concentrate on air defence.

The prototype, a two-seater, flew from Istres, France, on 8 September 1968 with the first British-assembled single-seater lifting off on 12 October and going supersonic during the fifty-minute sortie. On 30 August 1971 the T.2 two-seater with attack capability had its maiden flight. The final RAF GR.1 flew at Warton on 16 February 1978 and the last T.2 was delivered in November 1982. Jaguars excelled in the strike/recce role and the systems and armament were frequently upgraded, ending up with the GR.3A variant.

While Jaguar provided BAC with experience of a co-operative *military* programme, it also provided the means to leap a generation and lay the foundations for the Eurofighter Typhoon. GR.1 XX765 was ferried to Warton on 4 August 1978, where BAe undertook a complex rebuild to turn it into the ACT – Active Control Technology – demonstrator. ACT is perhaps best known as fly-by-wire, no physical linkage from the pilot's controls to the ailerons, elevators, rudder and flaps, all being moved by digitally controlled actuators. Principal 'player' in this technology was Dowty, the inheritors of Boulton Paul.

Jaguar XX765 was destined to be the world's first aircraft with a digital quadruplex control system with no physical back-up. Such systems would allow future fighter designs to be inherently unstable, permitting regimes that could not be obtained with 'conventional' controls. From the ACT Jaguar, BAe could take the leap to the EAP test bed and from there to the incredible Typhoon. Test pilot Chris Yeo was at the controls when XX765 took off in this new form on 20 October 1981. Its job done, XX765 was retired in November 1984 and today is displayed at the RAF Museum, Cosford.

The first Jaguar, French-built two-seater E.01, ground running at Istres, 1968. *BAC*

The second Jaguar International, FAE302, for Ecuador, in 1977. The country had previously been a Strikemaster customer. *BAe*

The BAC/Bréguet twosome began to disentangle early in SEPECAT's existence. Dassault took control of its rival, Bréguet, in December 1971 and did not appreciate that it was marketing Mirages in competitions that also involved the Jaguar. Increasingly BAC found itself alone in trying to find export customers for the increasingly capable Jaguar. In 1974 Warton coined the name 'Jaguar International' for a more powerful version of the GR.1 with the potential for nose-mounted radar and increased weaponry. On 19 August 1976 the first 'International' for Ecuador, a two-seater, was flown at Warton and Nigeria and Oman joined the queue. Warton took over all responsibility for the Jaguar in 1980 and France received its final example the following year.

The last export Jaguars flew from Warton in 1984, but the programme was far from over. In 1979 BAe announced a licence agreement with India's Hindustan Aeronautics at Bangalore. To ease things along eighteen refurbished RAF Jaguars were dispatched, the last of these returning to the UK in 1984. The six-phase venture began with the assembly of kits from Warton, with increasing Indian content. Sub-assemblies and components were shipped out from May 1981. The first all-Indian Jaguar, local name Shamshar (assault sword), appeared in 1988. Indian production is believed to have been concluded in 2004, but a modernisation campaign initiated in 2017 should see just over 100 examples fitted with Israeli Elta Systems radar by 2022.

Wilson's Wonderbird

There is a strong argument that the Tornado is the most significant warplane the RAF has operated since World War Two – rivalled perhaps by its predecessor, the EE Canberra. From the First Gulf War of 1991 to its stand down with the advent of the Lockheed Martin F-35 on 31 March 2019, the Tornado force was almost constantly on call, acting as what the RAF calls 'a rapid and flexible crisis response tool'. In the Introduction the eight points required to make an industrially great aircraft are outlined. Accepting that the civil market was not an option, Tornado ticked all of those boxes. At the time of writing the chances of Germany, Italy and Saudi Arabia passing their fleets on to other nations seems remote, but the Tornado has managed the 'resale' element in essence. To bridge the gap between the arrival of its Eurofighter Typhoons and the impending retirement of its Lockheed F-104S Starfighters, the Italian Air Force 'leased' former

Europe's solution to Europe's defence...

Cover of a poster-brochure of the MRCA, circa 1971. *KEC*

RAF F.3s from 1995 until 2004. Upgrades of the RAF GR.1s, especially the complex GR.4 version that first appeared in 1993, proved very lucrative for BAe and BAE Systems.

Britain (BAC), Germany (Messerschmitt Bölkow Blohm) and Italy (Aeritalia) formed Panavia Aircraft GmbH on 26 March 1969. The aim was to create what was then called the twin-engined, swing-wing Multi-Role Combat Aircraft (MRCA) to fulfil strike, attack and reconnaissance roles for the three nations into the 21st century. In Britain cynical writers claimed that MRCA stood for 'Much Reconditioned Canberra Aircraft' and from the prime ministerial announcement of the alliance, quoted at the heading, it was 'Wilson's Wonderbird'. As the Tornado entered service, such scepticism soon vaporised and the Labour premier was shown to be spot on.

MRCA became Tornado in March 1976 and four months later Britain, Germany and Italy signed up for 809 examples, providing a sustainable run without the need for further customers. Each nation had a final assembly line for its domestic requirements and if any of the triumvirate secured export orders, it would build them: British Aerospace clinched Saudi Arabia in September 1985. Work split included the front fuselage and entire tail to Britain, the centre fuselage and wing pivot section to Germany and the outer wings to Italy.

The first Tornado was flown at Manching in West Germany on 14 August 1974 followed by the British prototype at Warton, seventy-eight days later. The tri-national theme was maintained; initial deliveries were of 'twin-stick' versions in July 1980 to the ground-breaking Tri-National Tornado Training Establishment at Cottesmore. There it was possible to have a British trainee and a German instructor flying in an Italian-owned and liveried aircraft, and all other combinations.

Forward cockpit of a Tornado GR.1. *BAe*

A pair of 31 Squadron Tornado GR.1s carrying ALARM anti-radar missiles, circa 1995. *Sgt Rick Brewell – RAF PR*

The Foxhunter was subject to delay and, for a while, F.2s were not fitted with the radar, carrying ballast instead. This 'modification' was nicknamed 'Blue Circle' to sound like a top-secret device, but was actually from the well-known brand of cement reputed to be in the nose! The definitive F.3 had its inaugural flight on 20 November 1985 and the type entered service the following summer.

Italian production was completed in 1984, and the last German machine was handed over in 1992. Although the bulk of the Tornado programme was a BAe/BAE Systems enterprise, the conception was wholly a BAC achievement. The final RAF GR.1s and F.3s departed Warton in 1992 and 1993, respectively, with deliveries to Saudi Arabia concluding in 1998. The first reworked GR.4 began test flying on 29 May 1993, and this and fleet sustainment up to withdrawal from service in the spring of 2019 provided forty-five years of employment at Warton and the many organisations making up the supply chain. Incredibly, the Tornado IDS provided Britain's strike capability for thirty-seven years and was never found lacking.

From the dark days of the cancellation of the TSR.2 and teetering on the abyss, by 1977 BAC had turned itself into a potent, world-class business providing British Aerospace with an exceptional reputation and product base.

All three countries ordered what was termed the Interdictor/Strike (IDS) model, but Britain had also opted for the Air Defence Variant (ADV), which was also adopted by Saudi Arabia. The ADV was conceived as a stand-off interceptor, with the ability to loiter up to 350 miles away from its base to tackle incoming Soviet bombers long before they got close to British airspace. Capable of acquiring and attacking multiple targets, the ADV was equipped with the advanced GEC-Marconi Foxhunter radar. At 61ft 3½in long, the ADV was 6ft 5¼in longer than the IDS but otherwise boasted 80% airframe commonality. The prototype of the interim F.2 version flew on 27 October 1979 and a small number entered service at Coningsby from November 1984.

British Aircraft Corporation

From	To	Total	Name/Designation	Type	Engine(s)	Notes
1963	1989	244	One-Eleven	Airliner	2 x RR Spey 506	[1]
1964	-	1	Type 221	Experimental	1 x RR Avon 28R	[2]
1964	1965	2	TSR.2	Strike/recce	2 x BSE Olympus	[3]
1965	1972	117	Jet Provost T.5	Trainer	1 x BSE Viper 201	[4]
1967	1982	151	Strikemaster	Light attack	1 x BSE Viper 535	[5]
1968	2002	543	Jaguar	Trainer/attack	2 x RR/Turbo Adour	[6]
1969	1979	20	Concorde	Airliner	4 x RR/Snecma Olympus	[7]
1974	1998	795	Tornado IDS	Strike/recce	2 x Turbo Union RB.199	[8]
1978	-	1	Petrel	Light aircraft	1 x Continental O-240	[9]
1979	1993	197	Tornado ADV	Air defence	2 x Turbo Union RB.199	[8]

[1] All but 12 built at Hurn, last example flown 1982. Five assembled and flown from Brooklands 1966 and another 7 in 1969–70. Includes licence assembly by Rombac at Bucharest, Romania, last one completed 1989. [2] Radical re-engineering of a Fairey FD.2 at Filton for Concorde wing research – see narrative. [3] Only one flown, second machine commenced ground runs before programme was cancelled. Two unflown examples survived to become museum pieces, all others scrapped. [4] Includes two T.4s used as aerodynamic prototypes for T.5. Five BAC 145 T.55s for Sudan at Luton 1969; all others for RAF and built at Warton. [5] Production, all at Warton, stopped in 1977, but was restarted at Hurn to complete a batch of ten 1979–82. [6] Warton production, 297 plus three prototypes, completed 1984. By Bréguet: five prototypes, and 200 production examples at Toulouse. Includes licence assembly of Warton-built kits from 1981 by Hindustan Aeronautics at Bangalore, India, followed by full licence manufacture from 1988. [7] Ten built at Filton and another ten at Toulouse. Each comprised three prototype/pre-production and seven production examples. [8] See narrative. [9] Apprentice project, referred to as the BAC Petrel and improved version of the Procter Petrel all-metal homebuild.

CHAPTER FOURTEEN

Perpetual Motion

Britten-Norman
1950 to date

'Absolutely delightful, it flies like a fully developed aircraft that has been in service for a couple of years.'
Desmond Norman, after the first flight of the prototype Islander

BEST KNOWN as a former Fleet Air Arm base, Lee-on-Solent does not spring to mind as a centre for manufacturing, yet it is the home of Britain's newest aircraft factory. Since 2010 Britten-Norman has been headquartered at what is now called Solent Airport and has begun to once again constructing the incredible BN-2 Islander in the nation of its birth. There was a time when Islanders were being churned out at the rate of one a fortnight but the goal for 2020 onwards is one every three months. The design may have evolved from mass production to niche status, but fifty-five years on from its maiden flight, there is still demand for the robust, adaptable, enduring twin, particularly in high-value special mission roles. With close on 1,300 BN-2s built, Britten-Norman (BN) is an unsung British success story and unique in still being named after the men that created it.

The present-day company has diversified into specialist divisions. As well as the manufacturing subsidiary BN Aircraft, there is BN Aviation, which provides overhaul, refurbishment and conversion of existing airframes, and BN Defence, which supports the British military Islander/Defender fleet and other overseas commitments. In the spring of 2019 William Hynett, BN's chief executive, noted that since 2010: 'BN Defence has created over 60 jobs on the [Solent Airport] site and we now intend to utilise the airfield as our primary base for our UK civil operations as well, creating or safeguarding another 50 jobs. To date we have invested £20 million into the local community …'

A Defender AL.2 delivered to the Army Air Corps in 2009. Responsibility for Britain's military Islanders and Defenders was transferred to the RAF on 1 April 2019: the AL.2 was redesignated R.2. *BNG*

Desmond and John

Nigel Desmond Norman met up with Forrester Robin John Britten at the de Havilland Technical School at Hatfield in 1946: the pair became firm friends and business partners. After RAF national service, Norman continued in the Royal Auxiliary Air Force, flying Gloster Meteor F.8s with 601 (City of London) Squadron from North Weald. Britten was destined for a career in the Royal Navy, attending the naval college at Dartmouth. Determined to get 'into' aviation, he enrolled at Hatfield and in early 1948 gained his flying licence.

In 1949 the pair began construction of a single-seat parasol monoplane at Bembridge on the Isle of Wight. Their initials were part of the craft's designation, BN-1. Norman made its first 'hops' on 4 August 1950 but it was badly damaged when its 40hp JAP J-99 failed on take-off during a later flight. It was substantially rethought and rebuilt with a Lycoming 'flat-four' and was tested in the new guise at Bembridge on 26 May 1951. Today this little aeroplane is displayed at Solent Sky in Southampton.

The BN-1, G-ALZE, in its original guise at Bembridge 1951.
Peter Green Collection

After the BN-1, Britten and Norman developed the revolutionary Micronair rotary atomiser for aerial crop-spraying. To exploit this device, Crop Culture (Aerial) Ltd was established in 1955, carrying out spraying contracts in many countries. Alongside this company, Britten-Norman Ltd was also set up in 1955. Two years later, Britten and Norman completed a commission on behalf of the Ultralight Aircraft Association (later the Popular Flying Association and today's Light Aircraft Association) to build a Druine D.5 Turbi two-seat monoplane, appropriately registered G-APFA. Among other enterprises, they also dabbled in hovercraft, forming Cushioncraft in 1961. A range of hovercraft was produced, including the eleven-passenger CC.2. The pair gave up their holdings in Crop Culture in 1963 and Cushioncraft was sold to the British Hovercraft Corporation (BHC) in 1972.

World-beating Islander

Through Crop Culture, BN was given a contract to run Cameroon Air Transport in 1960, based at Douala in the West African country and using Piper Apache and Aztec twins. Britten and Norman were intrigued to find that to increase capacity they would have to make the leap from six seats to thirty; or go back in time and acquire de Havilland Dragon Rapides. They began a market survey and came up with a nine-passenger, no-nonsense, fixed-undercarriage, high-wing twin, which they designated BN-2. The Lycoming from the BN-1 was used to power a rudimentary wind tunnel set up by Britten in the garden of his Bembridge home as the design was firmed up. The two men were determined to keep costs to a minimum, centring everything on the Isle of Wight. There was an abundance of skilled personnel that had previously worked for or were employed by Saunders-Roe (Westland from 1960 and BHC from 1966) at East Cowes. Although Britten and Norman had other schemes, they determined to concentrate on the BN-2; in philosophy BN was the antithesis of Beagle.

The first metal was cut in September 1964. With Britten as second pilot, Norman flew the prototype BN-2 on 13 June 1965 and four days later it was in the static at the Paris Salon at Le Bourget. In August the following year the twin was named Islander. Despite Norman's praise after the maiden sortie quoted with the title, the decision was taken to substitute the 210hp Rolls-Royce Continental O-200s with 260hp Lycoming O-360s and to increase the span by 4ft to 49ft. While recruiting staff in 1965, the talented Ronald Edward 'Dickie' Bird was recruited as chief designer. Bird had previously been with Beagle and Auster – see

The third Islander, G-AVCN, at the BN factory at Bembridge in May 1967. The number on the nose was for its appearance at that year's Paris Salon. As this book went to press, *Charlie-November*, the oldest surviving Islander, was nearing the end of a restoration at its birthplace by the Britten-Norman Aircraft Preservation Society. *BN*

Chapter 5 for his background. The first production BN-2 took to the air on 20 August 1966 and deliveries began a year later.

A purpose-built factory was completed in December 1966 as orders rolled in. The plan was to be *capable* of constructing aircraft from components upwards but *ideally* to place sub-contracts for the 'heavy lifting' – the building of airframes – and use Bembridge for assembly and fitting out to customer requirements. To this end an agreement was reached with BHC to manufacture what became 236 airframe sets from 1968 to 1973.

A higher-weight variant – the BN-2B – was introduced and during 1971 a new and very important development was launched; the military-configured Defender. This had under-wing weapons pylons, an optional parachute door and the capability to fit a nose-mounted radar. Pylons were also available for civilian operators, including the fitting of Micronair pods for aerial spraying. At first a novelty, military versions became the backbone of orders from the late 1980s.

Romanian-built BN-2A-6 G-BFCV fitted with a Micronair rotary atomiser and fluid tank for aerial spraying in 1978. *BN*

By the 1970s Islanders were being delivered all over the globe and it was clear that a turboprop version was required as piston engine fuel, Avgas, was not universally available. The first turbine Islander, fitted with Lycoming LTP-101s, had its maiden flight on 6 April 1977, but was frustrated by BN going into liquidation four months later – of which more anon. When ownership transferred to Pilatus, a turboprop version was seen as a priority and the BN-2T Turbine Islander, appropriately registered G-BPBN, took to the air on 2 August 1980 powered by a pair of Allison 250-B17s. An incredible milestone took place on 7 May 1982 when the 1,000th BN-2 was delivered. The advent of a turboprop version was particularly important for military operators and exemplified by the breakthrough sale of turbine Defender AL.1s in 1989 to the Army Air Corps (AAC) for surveillance work in Northern Ireland. Repeat orders were placed for Series 4000-based Mk.2s in 2009. (From 1 April 2019 operation of the AAC Islander and Defender fleet was transferred to the RAF and redesignated as follows: AL.1 to R.1 and AL.2 to R.2.)

Specialist variants included a bulbous-nosed version for the Ministry of Defence's Airborne Stand-off Radar (ASTOR) requirement, the prototype flying in March 1984. In parallel with this, BN created an airborne early warning version with a Thorn-EMI radar in the nose. In an agreement with the American Westinghouse Corporation, the Defender AEW test bed was taken to the USA and converted into the Multi-Sensor Surveillance Aircraft (MSSA). Fitted with an AN/APG-66 radar, similar to that in the General Dynamics F-16 Fighting Falcon, the MSSA test bed began trials from Baltimore, Maryland, in the autumn of 1991. Despite extensive trials nothing came from any of these initiatives.

The Islander AEW G-TEMI was first flown in July 1984. The registration denotes its nose-mounted Thorn-EMI radar. This machine became the Westinghouse MSSA test bed in 1991. *PBN*

From the early 1990s the Islander/Defender was given a major rethink, especially optimising it for special missions work. The wing was enlarged, the undercarriage beefed up, the fuselage stretched forward by 2ft 6in, the tail surfaces redesigned and the entire nose profile altered, including a much deeper windscreen. The prototype, designated Defender 4000, flew for the first time on 17 August 1994. The BN-2 of 1965 had an all-up weight of 4,750lb, while the Defender 4000 came in at 8,500lb – such was the adaptability of the airframe.

Put it in the tail…

The first production standard BN-2, G-ATWU, was wheeled into a quiet hangar at Bembridge and it reappeared in the summer of 1970 in a radical new guise. Britten and Norman wanted to double the number of passengers and could achieve this by stretching the fuselage, from 35ft 8in to 43ft 9in. They examined powerplant options and decided that *another* Lycoming O-540 would be best – they were proposing a tri-motor. The most obvious place to put the additional engine was the nose, but this would mean a much longer, stalky nose and main undercarriage. This would ruin the BN-2's hallmark 'step-in' low floor level and put the engines out of reach, requiring gantries for access. Perhaps inspired by the Douglas DC-10 three-engined wide-bodied jetliner that appeared in 1968, BN mounted the third engine at the top of the fin and rudder, with the tailplane and elevator at the rear of this nacelle and an extra fin above it. The prototype had its maiden flight on 11 September 1970 and stunned crowds at that month's Farnborough airshow. Despite this dramatic transformation, the tri-motor boasted 75% commonality with the twin. Deliveries of the seventeen-passenger Trislander began in March 1971.

This machine remained a niche purchase and the last of eighty-one was delivered in September 1984. For short 'hops', classically defined by the inter-island services of Aurigny Air Services linking the Channel Islands of Alderney, Guernsey and Jersey, the Trislander was a natural.

Trislander G-AZLJ of Aviation West, 1985. *KEC*

Derek Kay's *The Last Grand Adventure in British Aviation?* is an absorbing read on BN's ups and downs and its day-to-day routines. He summed up why sales of the Trislander were limited: 'Although it was a highly economic, utilitarian workhorse for many areas of operation, there was no doubt that [it] lacked passenger appeal. Its long narrow cabin … in nine seat rows, without aisle or cabin attendant facilities, precluded operations on all but the shortest routes.' Its *three* engines, one difficult to reach, did not endear it to maintenance staff or the accountants, and the lack of a turboprop version limited the marketplace. In August 1982 the rights to the Trislander were acquired by the Miami-based International Aviation Corporation and eleven kits were shipped over but nothing came of the scheme.

Manufacturing travelogue

With orders blossoming for the Islander, in 1968 BN signed a licence production agreement for 212 airframes with Romania's Intreprinderea de Reparat Material Aeronautic – IRMA – at Baneasa, Bucharest. BN-2s built in Bucharest were ferried in 'green' – basic state – to Bembridge for fitting out to customer requirements. This deal came about as a 'sweetener' arranged by the British Aircraft Corporation (BAC). The Romanian state airline, Transporturile Aeriene Romane (Tarom), had signed up in February 1968 for six One-Eleven Series 424 jetliners with a view to more to follow, provided the country's own aircraft industry could benefit. Tarom became a loyal One-Eleven customer and in 1975 Romania, BAC and Rolls-Royce began negotiations that led to the rights to the twin-jet being transferred to an organisation called Rombac, with IRMA carrying out final assembly. This arrangement involved a further extension of the BN–IRMA alliance. BN's relationship with IRMA was only severed in 2010, by which time more than 600 BN-2s had been built.

The outfitting stage could take a long time, restricting cash flow, and it was one of the reasons why the receiver was called in to Bembridge on 22 October 1971. Restructured as Britten-Norman (Bembridge) Ltd the following month, on 31 August 1972 a bid was accepted from the Fairey Group and Fairey Britten-Norman (FBN) was born. The jigs from BHC at East Cowes were moved to the Fairey SA factory at Gosselies and by early 1973 Islanders and Trislanders were being made in Belgium as well as Romania. This relocation was a costly exercise and delays in setting up an assembly line for F-16s for the Belgian Air Force put Fairey SA and FBN into financial jeopardy. The receiver was called in on 3 August 1977, by which time around 260 BN airframe sets had been manufactured.

By the time Gosselies ground to a halt, a *third* overseas production line had flown its first Islander, on 18 February 1976. This event took place on the other side of the world in Manila in the Philippines. At the instigation of President Ferdinand Emmanuel Edrain Marcos, the Philippine Aerospace Development Corporation (PADC) had been formed to increase his country's technology base. A deal was struck covering 100 Islanders and phased licence construction began with the supply of fourteen 'green' airframes, followed by twenty kits and then jigs for full-blown manufacture. Creation of an amphibious floatplane version – the so-called 'Sealander' – was also mooted. By the mid-1980s the PADC venture had petered out, with just under fifty aircraft flown, all for local use.

Several companies examined picking up the pieces but it was Switzerland's Pilatus that acquired the assets of BN (Bembridge) Ltd on 24 January 1979 as Pilatus Britten-Norman (PBN). Pilatus was building the exceptional PC-6 Porter workhorse and the PC-7 military trainer, both turboprops. Under PBN, Bembridge handled only Romanian-built airframes. As related earlier, Pilatus initiated the much-needed turbine version of the BN-2, heralding a new era for the design.

Beyond BN

Britten and Norman left the concern they had founded on 1 March 1976. By then Britten and Denis Berryman – a designer with BN – were firming up plans for a family of low-cost, rugged, light twins; ranging from fixed undercarriage two-seat trainers to retractable four-seaters. John was very proud to be appointed High Sheriff of the Isle of Wight in 1976 and this inspired the name of the new machine: Sheriff. Tragically, Forrester Robin John Britten CBE died at his Bembridge home on 7 July 1977; he was just 48.

John's brother, Robin, stepped in and Aircraft Designs (Bembridge) Ltd and later Sheriff Aerospace were formed at Sandown to continue the project. In May 1981 the prototype was registered as G-FRJB – incorporating Britten's initials. Wight Aviation, a BN sub-contractor, had been engaged to build fuselages and wings for a production batch. However, in March 1983 the plug was pulled on the programme and early in 1984 a receiver was called in. The unfinished prototype is today displayed at the East Midlands Airport Aeropark.

Desmond Norman was at the helm of a new design on 14 May 1969. Extending BN design philosophy to a four-seat tourer/trainer, there were high hopes for the BN-3 Nymph. It was deliberately uncomplicated with a view to being offered for licence production overseas. With a 'nod' to the light aircraft of the 1920s and '30s, the Nymph was offered with optional wing-folding to help keep hangar fees down. The Trislander was shortly to appear and take up lots of design time and investment, so the prototype Nymph was 'parked', hopefully to be resuscitated one day.

Norman formed NDN Aircraft – from his initials – in 1977. While Britten was aiming at the civil market, Norman had his eyes on military trainers. Taking off from Goodwood on 26 May 1977, Norman was at the controls of the piston-engined NDN-1 Firecracker. It was followed in 1983 by three turboprop examples, the first taking to the air on 1 September 1983. In association with Hunting, the NDN-1T was aimed at the RAF's requirement to replace the Jet Provost, but was unsuccessful.

Capitalising on his knowledge of agricultural aviation, Norman developed the large, turboprop-powered NDN-6 Fieldmaster crop-sprayer with support from the National Research Development Corporation. The NDN-6 was built around a titanium hopper, which

The first of three NDN-1T Turbo Firecrackers used by Specialist Flying Training for military contracts from 1984. *NDN*

Britten-Norman and Britten *and* Norman

From	To	Total	Designation/Name	Type	Engine(s)	Notes
1950	-	1	BN-1	Lightplane	1 x JAP J-99	
1965	date	1,290+	BN-2 Islander	Light transport	2 x Lycoming O-540	[1]
1969	-	1	BN-3 Nymph	Tourer	1 x Lycoming O-235	[2]
1970	1984	81	BN-2 Trislander	Airliner	3 x Lycoming O-540	[3]
1980	date	as above	BN-2T Islander	Light transport	2 x Allison 250-B17C	[4]
1977	1983	4	NDN-1 Firecracker	Trainer	1 x Lycoming AE1O-540	[5]
1981	1988	6	NDN-6 Fieldmaster	Agricultural	1 x P&W PT6A-34	[6]
1984	-	1	NAC-2 Freelance	Tourer	1 x Lycoming O-360	[7]
1984	-	1	SA-1 Sheriff	Tourer/trainer	2 x Lycoming O-320	[8]

[1] Manufacture sub-contracted to British Hovercraft Corporation at East Cowes 1968 to 1973. Licensed from 1969 to 2010 to Intreprinderea de Reparat Material Aeronautic (IRMA) in Romania. Built from 1972 to 1978 by Fairey SA at Gosselies, Belgium. Licence assembly/production by Philippine Aerospace Development Company, Manila, 1975–88. Two BN-2As assembled by Globetrotter Engineering at Eastleigh, Southampton mid-1981. See narrative for more. BN-2, BN-2A and BN-2B; also includes Defender variants. Production figure includes BN-2T turboprop versions. [2] Nymph rebuilt as pre-production NAC-1 Freelance G-NACI, 1984. [3] Trislanders built at Bembridge and Gosselies. [4] Not including initial turbo-powered version – with Lycoming LTP101 – converted from BN-2A in 1977. Also includes Defender variants. Production total included within the figure given for the BN-2 piston versions. [5] One piston version followed by three NDN-1T Turbo-Firecrackers in 1983. [6] Five production examples designated NAC-6. Two reworked by Brooklands Aircraft at Old Sarum as Firemaster 65s. [7] Production version – see note [2] – sets for at least another five laid down but not completed. [8] Prototype not completed – see narrative.

The first and second NAC-6 Fieldmasters during a brief lease to France Aviation, 1988. *NAC*

The one-off BN-3 Nymph G-AXFB. 1969. *BN*

was an integral part of the forward fuselage and also acted as the engine bulkhead. The prototype first flew on 17 December 1981 from Sandown, again piloted by its designer. A new entity, the Norman Aeroplane Company (NAC) was established in 1985, with a factory at Rhoose, Cardiff Airport. Five NAC-6 Fieldmasters were produced before NAC went into receivership in August 1988. The following year Brooklands Aircraft at Old Sarum re-engineered two examples as Firemaster water bombers. A scoop on the end of a rig that deployed from the rear fuselage – like a giant arrester hook – allowed the aircraft to skim a lake and top up its tank without landing. Nothing further came of this, or a plan to build the type in Turkey from 1998.

In 1984 the BN-3 Nymph was dusted down and relaunched as the NAC-1 Freelance, again with folding wings. It was followed by a production-standard example, NAC-2 G-NACA, in 1988 as part of an initial batch of six. Like the Fieldmaster, the Freelance never recovered from the winding up of NAC in 1988.

Farewell to Bembridge

By the mid-1990s Pilatus was looking to divest itself of PBN. In 1991 it flew the prototype PC-12 at Stans, Switzerland. This revolutionary single-turboprop ten-seater impinged upon the Islander/Defender market as well as the private owner and business sector. Like the Islander, the PC-12 is still in production, with more than 1,500 built. Pilatus sold PBN in July 1998 to an investment management company, but it was quickly handed on to yet another organisation, only for the receiver to be called in again on 3 April 2000. Within a month PBN had become BNG – the Britten-Norman Group – having been acquired by aviation-minded, Omani-based, Alawi Zawawi Enterprises.

The restructuring that was mentioned in the beginning of this chapter was initiated and much-needed diversification introduced. In 2010 the company moved lock stock and barrel to Lee-on-Solent. At the same time, the jigs and unfinished airframes were brought back from Romania to the new base in Hampshire to enable in-house manufacturing.

Awarded a CBE in 1970, Nigel Desmond Norman died on 23 November 2002, aged 73. Along with John Britten, the duo created a brand that still carries their names. The Islander is an exceptional and enduring aircraft and its success remains a target that many other designers still strive to emulate.

CHAPTER FIFTEEN

Iberian Radical

Cierva and Weir
1926 to 1973

'Cierva combined the talents of inventor, mathematician, practical engineer and experimental test pilot.' Peter W Brooks

AFTER FRENCHMAN LOUIS BLÉRIOT became the first person to fly the Channel, on 25 July 1909, he began to market his Type XI monoplane across Europe and further afield. The appearance of a Blériot XI in Spain during 1910 had a pivotal effect on Spaniard Don Juan de la Cierva Codorníu. (To avoid confusion with the companies that went on to carry his name, he will be referred to from here on as Juan.) Along with his brother, Ricardo, and some friends Juan constructed a pair of gliders, neither of which was successful. In 1912, Juan, Ricardo and Pablo Diaz designed the two-seat BCD-1 El Cangrejo (Crab), which flew in August 1912, becoming the first Spanish-built aircraft to fly. This was followed by the BCD-2 monoplane of December 1913 and, responding to a government competition, the C.3 tri-motor bomber, but this crashed on its maiden flight on 8 July 1919.

Juan studied engineering in Madrid, graduating in 1917. He investigated slow flight and concluded that rotating 'wings' were the answer. His initial patents featuring a windmilling rotor were lodged in July 1920 and the word 'Autogiro' was registered by him. A halfway house to the helicopter, the Autogiro's rotor was unpowered, acting as a circular 'wing'. The engine drove a conventional propeller, providing forward motion. If all else failed, the machine could auto-rotate to earth like the seed of a sycamore tree.

Juan's first Autogiro, retrospectively designated C.1, used the fuselage from a 1911 Deperdussin monoplane and featured contra-rotating rotors. It was tested in October 1920 but did not fly. On 17 January 1923 Lt Alejandro Gómez Spencer made the world's first controlled gyroplane flight in Autogiro No. 4 (or C.4), which featured hinged rotor blades and started intensive trials and developments. The C.5 – the first to carry the C-series designation from the start – appeared in 1923. The C.6, based on the fuselage of an Avro 504K, of 1926 was followed by the much-refined C.6bis.

Cierva dished out an incredible brochure to support sales of the W.11 Air Horse – the illustrations would have done credit to the *Budgie the Helicopter* books of an altogether different era! *KEC*

A line-up in front of the trans Channel C.8L-II G-EBYY at Hamble in 1928. Left to right: 'Bud' Taylor, A V Roe, Arthur 'Dizzy' Rawson and Juan de la Cierva. *KEC*

Spanish–Scottish alliance

With the C.6, Juan gained the attention of governments and manufacturers. Vickers made approaches for him to come to the UK but it was an invitation from the British Air Ministry to come to the Royal Aircraft Establishment (RAE) to which he responded. The C.6A was assembled at Farnborough on 1 October 1925 and was to have been flown by experienced pilot Captain Joaquín Loriga, but he was ill and RAE engaged freelance test pilot Frank Courtney to carry out the trials. Courtney achieved his first sorties in the C.6A on the 12th, thus making the inaugural sustained rotary winged flight in Britain. Air Ministry and industry interest was high and Juan made plans to move to England.

With Scot James 'Jimmy' George Weir as its chairman, the Cierva Autogiro Co Ltd was created on 24 March 1926. At first the company was based at Hamble, where a close relationship with Avro was fostered before an independent factory was established at Hanworth, Middlesex, in 1931. Weir was a director of G and J Weir Ltd, a huge engineering combine based at Cathcart, Glasgow: as the Weir Group this concern is still a major industrial force. Weir qualified as a pilot in a Blériot at Hendon in 1910 and served in the Royal Flying Corps from 1914; leaving what became the RAF in 1920. He was fascinated by rotary-wing flight and became a staunch supporter of the Spanish pioneer. Air Commodore James George Weir CMG CBE died on 7 November 1973, aged 86: an advocate of aviation and rotorcraft throughout.

As Juan settled in Britain he did so as a gifted and pioneering designer; he was not a pilot and had been a spectator whenever his creations flew. He was determined to master his own machines and he qualified as a pilot at Hanworth in January 1927. In his superb book *Cierva Autogiros – The Development of Rotary-Wing Flight*, Peter Brooks notes that from 1927 he took over the testing of his designs, leading to his debut with a new type, the C.17, in October 1928.

During 1928 Avro Hamble-built C.8L Mk.II G-EBYY, powered by a 180hp AS Lynx IV, was used for an extensive tour of British aerodromes. With Henri Bouché, editor of the French magazine *l'Aéronautique*, as his passenger, Juan flew from Croydon to Le Bourget, Paris, on 18 September. This was the first-ever rotary-wing crossing of the English Channel: Juan had managed to emulate his hero, Blériot. After demonstrations in Paris, Juan picked up test pilot Arthur 'Dizzy' Rawson and they went on to Brussels and then Berlin in early October. This adventure helped to 'normalise' the Autogiro in the eyes of potential operators. The Channel-crossing C.8L stayed on in France and today is displayed at the Musée de l'Air et de l'Espace at Le Bourget, Paris.

A colour-enhanced postcard of Avro-built C.30A G-ACWF. This machine was used by the Cierva Autogiro Company at Hanworth from 1934 for training and demonstration. *KEC*

For everyday pilots

To keep costs to a minimum, several early designs used the fuselages of light aircraft, including the Avro 504 and Avian. The Comper C.25 was based on the Swift sportsplane, reflecting Juan's belief that the Autogiro was the natural evolution from wing-borne to rotor-borne types. The first of Juan's designs intended for 'club' use – by everyday pilots – was the two-seat C.19. He flew the prototype in July 1929 and it became the first Cierva type to enter series production. Much development work lay ahead to render the Autogiro truly a 'people's aeroplane'. Initially fitted with conventional aircraft controls, flying an Autogiro at low speed in experienced hands was no problem, but not so with novices. The answer was what Juan called 'direct control', the ability to tilt the rotor disc to suit the flight regime. By allowing the rotor hub to tilt in all directions and providing a control stick that could be accessed from the cockpit, the responses of the C.19 were greatly enhanced. Juan began testing this on a C.19 Mk.V from March 1932.

The following year Juan commenced development of a mechanism to achieve a 'jump' take-off by spinning up the otherwise free-wheeling rotor directly from the engine. This spin-up was disengaged once level flight was achieved. In August 1933 the prototype of the most prolific of his designs, the C.30, was trialled by Juan. By October that year Alan Marsh was able to wind up the rotor on the C.30, after which it would leap 10 to 12ft into the air and he could then commence his climb-out. This work produced the patented Autodynamic rotor in the summer of 1936.

In collaboration with Don Rose, Juan wrote the influential *Wings of Tomorrow*, which was published in New York in 1931. It was a detailed examination of his steps to the Autogiro, its aerodynamic challenges and its possibilities for the future. At a fog-shrouded Croydon Airport, Juan boarded the already delayed KLM flight to

Amsterdam on 9 December 1936. Douglas DC-2 PH-AKL of KLM took off but its pilot became disoriented and the airliner hit houses on the perimeter and crashed in flames. Two of the sixteen on board survived; by a miracle nobody on the ground was killed. Among those who perished was the 41-year-old Spaniard; one can only guess at what might have been achieved by Señor Don Juan de la Cierva Codorníu had he survived. Frank Courtney's autobiography *Flight Path* highlights the irony of Juan's death: 'He had devoted his life to the creation of an aircraft that could not stall, and he lost it in a plane that stalled on take-off.' This was a massive blow to the Cierva company, but its founder's work continued.

Licence agreements

The Cierva Autogiro company granted licences in France, Germany and the USA and its concepts were copied in other countries. Avro, Comper, de Havilland, Parnall and Westland all built Cierva designs. Avro was the most persistent, manufacturing the most prolific version – the C.30 – which was widely exported and adopted by the RAF as the Rota. The final evolution was the 'jump-start' C.40; with side-by-side seating under a semi-enclosed cockpit, it was ideal for training. James Allan Jamieson Bennett took charge of the design of the C.40. Starting his career in the chemical industry, Bennett joined G and J Weir, transferring to Cierva and later heading up the nascent Fairey helicopter branch from August 1945.

The British Aircraft Manufacturing Company (BAMC), neighbours of Cierva at Hanworth, secured a contract for two development examples and five for the Air Ministry as Rota IIs. BA had engaged Oddie, Bradbury and Cull Ltd (OBC) of Southampton, the specialist rotor blade builder, to construct the wooden monocoque fuselages for the C.40s as well as the blades. After completing the prototype C.40 in 1938, BAMC ceased trading and OBC finished the batch.

For the larger manufacturers, Autogiros only appealed if they could break into the multi-seat market, but none were successful. de Havilland spent a lot of time and money on the C.24 cabin two-seater. The one-off G-ABLM flew in September 1931 and today is displayed at the DH Aircraft Museum, London Colney. Westland devoted considerable effort to the C.29 five-seater and the CL.20, jointly designed by Frenchman Georges Lepère. Neither of these flew.

Weir and Cierva

James Weir persuaded the family company, G and J Weir, to get directly involved in the rotorcraft business. The Weir W.1 (Cierva C.28) was a collaborative design between Juan and F L Hodgess and was first flown at Hanworth, by Juan in May 1933. The W.2 of June 1934, schemed by Hodgess, is displayed in the National Museum of Scotland in Edinburgh. From 1936 multi-talented engineer Cyril Pullin, who won the Isle of Man TT motorcycle race in 1914, was engaged as Weir's designer. His W.3 of June 1936 included a 'jump-start' mechanism and initiated an evolution that resulted in the twin-rotor W.6 pure helicopter, which flew on 20 October 1939. With the deliveries of the final C.40s in 1939, Cierva suspended operations the following year. Brooks records how much developing the Autogiro had cost by 1940: '… something like £750,000 (of mainly James Weir's money – currently [1988] worth about $24.5 million) is believed to have been spent …'

In 1943 the activities of Cierva and Weir were merged – under the Cierva name – and Pullin commenced development of the W.9. It featured a radical jet efflux pipe in the tail to counter torque – most other designers adopted a tail rotor – that gave it the nickname 'Drainpipe'. The prototype thrashed itself to pieces during ground-running in late 1944. Rethought and rebuilt, it was flown successfully in June 1945. By then Cierva had bigger fish to fry; scheming the world's largest helicopter – the W.11 Air Horse. Powered by a 1,620hp Rolls-Royce Merlin driving *three* rotors mounted on outriggers, the W.11 could carry twenty-four passengers, or a jeep, or a crop-spraying rig. Two prototypes were ordered against Specification E19/46. Cierva needed a partner for this venture and moved to Southampton's Eastleigh airfield, sharing Cunliffe-Owen's facilities. The first Air Horse flew at Eastleigh on 8 December 1948 but was involved in a fatal accident on 13 June 1950. Even before this the W.11 had failed to find any market and was doomed.

The de Havilland-built C.24 cabin Autogiro, G-ABLM, tested by Juan de Cierva in September 1931. *de Havilland Heritage Centre*

Cierva and Weir autogiros and helicopters

From	To	Total	Name/Designation	Type	Engine(s)	Notes
1926	-	2	C.6C and 'D	1-seater	1 x Clerget	[1]
1926	1928	5	C.8V, 'L, 'W	1-seater	1 x AS Lynx	[2]
1927	-	1	C.9	1-seater	1 x AS Genet	[3]
1928	-	1	C.10	1-seater	1 x AS Genet	[4]
1928	-	1	C.11	2-seater	1 x ADC	[5]
1928	1929	2	C.17 Mk.I and II	2-seater	1 x Avro Alpha	[6]
1929	1932	34	C.19 Mk.I to V	2-seater	1 x AS Genet	[7]
1931	-	1	C.24	Cabin 2-seater	1 x DH Gipsy	[8]
1932	-	1	C.25	1-seater	1 x Pobjoy R	[9]
1933	-	1	C.28	1-seater	1 x Douglas Dryad	[10]
1933	-	1	C.29	Cabin, 5-seater	1 x AS Panther	[11]
1933	1936	83	C.30, 'P, 'A	2-seater	1 x AS Civet	[12]
1934	-	1	Weir W.2	1-seater	1 x Weir	
1935	-	1	CL.20	Cabin, 2-seater	1 x Pobjoy Niagara	[13]
1936	-	1	Weir W.3	1-seater	1 x Weir Pixie	
1937	-	1	Weir W 4	1-seater	1 x Weir Pixie	[14]
1938	-	1	Weir W.5	Twin-rotor (H)	1 x Weir Pixie	[15]
1938	1939	7	C.40	'Cabin', 2-seater	1 x Salmson 9N	[16]
1939	-	1	Weir W.6	Twin-rotor (H)	1 x DH Gipsy Six	[17]
1944	-	1	W.9	2-seater (H)	1 x DH Gipsy Queen	
1948	-	2	W.10 Air Horse	Triple-rotor (H)	1 x RR Merlin	
1948	1949	2	W.14 Skeeter	Light (H)	1 x Jamieson FF.1	[18]
1961	-	1	CR Grasshopper 1	2-seat (H)	2 x Walter Minor	[19]
1969	1971	1	CR Grasshopper 3	5-seat (H)	2 x Cont O-300-A	[19] [20]

Based upon: *Cierva Autogiros – The Development of Rotary-Wing Flight*, Peter W Brooks. British-built examples only. All single-rotor unless noted. All Autogiros, ie. with 'free-rotating rotor': helicopters denoted as (H). **[1]** Built by Avro, based on Type 504 fuselage: Types 574 and 575 – latter rebuilt as C.8R (Avro 587). **[2]** Built by Avro, based on Avro 504 fuselage: Types 586, 611 and three 617s. **[3]** Avro 576. **[4]** Built by Parnall, wrecked on first flight. **[5]** Built by Parnall, also wrecked on first flight. **[6]** Built by Avro, based on Avian fuselage: Types 612 and 620. Type 620 converted to float-equipped Hydrogiro. **[7]** Built by Avro as sub-contract to Cierva – no Avro Type numbers. Mk.V single-seater. **[8]** Built by de Havilland. **[9]** Built by Comper, based on Swift fuselage. **[10]** Built by Weir as the W.1. **[11]** Built by Westland, failed to fly. **[12]** Prototype C.30 built by National Flying Services, Hanworth. Single C.30P Mk.II built by Airwork, Heston. Seventy-eight built by Avro; British military variants – from new and impressed, known as Rota Is. **[13]** Joint Cierva and Georges Lepère design. Built by Westland; six production examples laid down, but not finished. **[14]** Wrecked before proper flight achieved. **[15]** Single-seater. **[16]** First built by British Aircraft Manufacturing Co, Hanworth. Six by Oddie, Bradbury and Cull, Southampton, five of which for the Air Ministry, as Rota IIs. **[17]** Two-seater. **[18]** Development taken over by Saunders-Roe 1951 – see Chapter 32. **[19]** Co-axial, contra-rotating rotors. **[20]** Two others built, second example used for ground-running only; neither flew.

Nicknamed the 'Drainpipe', Cierva W.9 PX203 being tested in the summer of 1945. *KEC*

Alongside the Air Horse, Pullin opted for lower risk with the W.14 Skeeter two-seater, which could appeal as a trainer. The first example flew on 10 October 1948. Still reeling from the repercussions of the W.11 crash and its huge cost, Cierva cut its losses and sold the W.14's design rights and most of its assets to Saunders-Roe (Saro) on 22 January 1951. Saro desperately wanted to diversify and helicopters seemed to be the way forward. This was a wise decision; the Skeeter was a success, leading to the Scout and Wasp. The Isle of Wight-based company had also become a sub-contractor to Vickers on the Viscount programme, and the Cierva factory at Eastleigh was very conveniently sited.

Grasshoppers

There is a postscript to the Cierva story. Its pre-war chief technical officer, Jacob Shapiro, joined Frank Whittle's Power Jets in 1940 but returned to Cierva in 1943. He surfaced again in 1960 as designer for Rotorcraft Ltd at Feltham, creating the twin-engined, two-seat Grasshopper. This was Britain's first co-axial helicopter. Two sets of contra-rotating rotor blades, one above the other, were driven by two shafts, one inside the other, from a common gearbox. What was added in complexity was offset by a smaller rotor diameter and the ability to dispense with a tail rotor. The prototype first flew in the spring of 1961. It was given more powerful engines in 1962 but was soon shelved.

Cierva Rotorcraft Grasshopper G-ARVN during early trials by Basil Arkell in 1961. *Servotec*

By the late 1960s, Cierva – which had remained an independent research entity – took an interest in the Grasshopper – establishing Cierva Rotorcraft Ltd. A five-seater version using Shapiro's co-axial dynamic system was the result. Only the prototype Grasshopper 3 flew, in 1969, although two others were nearly complete when the project folded in 1973. All of the Grasshoppers are held by The Helicopter Museum at Weston-super-Mare as remnants of a fascinating, if abortive, episode of British rotorcraft technology.

In his book *Cierva Autogiros*, Brooks sums up Cierva's relentless determination: 'Towards the end of his life, he seems to have become so preoccupied with the development of the Autogiro, because his name had become inseparably linked with it, that he regarded this type of machine as an end in itself. Initially, like most people, he had probably looked upon it as a step toward the ultimate development of the helicopter.'

The first Grasshopper 3, G-AWRP, during early trials at Redhill, 1969. *Cierva Rotorcraft*

CHAPTER SIXTEEN

Temperamentally Swift

**Comper and Heston
1929 to 1948**

'…in many ways a clever designer, and yet he somehow always just failed to "get there".' Flight *magazine 22 June 1939*

TRUTH TO TELL, even combined, the output of the Comper and Heston companies does not reach this book's coverage definition – the construction and flying of at least five original, individual, types and a grand total of at least 250 machines built – by a long way. However, well conscious of the regard in which the Comper Swift is held, the author decided that he would very likely be lynched if he did not include it.

Nicholas Comper's zeal for aviation, particularly its lighter side, drove him throughout his life. Having established his own business, he followed a path trod by others before him – and since – striving to keep a grip on the drawing board, the flight test office *and* the boardroom. Typically, he excelled in the first two but the latter was his undoing. (We will refer to him as Nick from here on, to differentiate the man from the companies that carried his name.)

From the summer of 1914, aged 17, Nick was an apprentice

draughtsman at the Aircraft Manufacturing Company, Hendon (Airco) working under the chief designer, Geoffrey de Havilland (GDH). Among his tasks was the testing to destruction of turnbuckles for use on the DH.2 single-seat pusher scout. Nick left in 1915 to enlist in the Royal Flying Corps and in July 1916 he was a second lieutenant pilot, joining 9 Squadron equipped with Royal Aircraft Factory B.E.2s (designed by GDH). He returned to Britain in April 1917. Nick took a commission and studied aeronautical engineering at Cambridge from 1920. Placements during his course are variously reported to have included the Royal Aircraft Establishment at Farnborough and/or the National Physical Laboratory at Teddington.

'New build' Comper Swift G-LCGL, completed in 1993 and fitted with a Pobjoy Niagara 1A. *Andy Wood*

Merseyside and Middlesex

In November 1926, Nick was posted to the Marine Aircraft Experimental Establishment at Felixstowe and straight away formed the Felixstowe Light Aeroplane Club, although no full-scale types were built. Nick formed Comper Aircraft in March 1929 – with himself as managing director and chief designer – and resigned his RAF commission the following month. Hooton Park on the Wirral was chosen as the base because Comper's first chairman, G H Dawson, owned the aerodrome and, as previously mentioned, Pobjoy located there. Nick set about creating one of the most charismatic sporting aircraft of the era, the CLA.7 Swift, its designation paying homage to its Cranwell heritage. The prototype had an ABC Scorpion and Nick took it for its maiden flight in January 1930. Many in the production run of forty-one adopted the locally built Pobjoys. Nick had devised a racy looker for the sporting flyer. His attention to detail included a compartment in the upper rear fuselage that could take a selection of golf clubs, if not a full set and a bag. In the nose, Nick managed to find a space for a bespoke suitcase that slid into a locker above the port undercarriage.

Nicholas Comper in front of one of his creations, the Mouse, in 1933.
Peter Green Collection

The CLA.3 parasol monoplane, G-EBMC, at Hendon in 1926.
Peter Green Collection

Swift G-ABWE with faired-over wing struts, wheel spats and a cowled Pobjoy. This machine was owned by Richard Shuttleworth from June 1932 to August 1935. *KEC*

Having graduated, Nick was posted to the RAF College Cranwell in October 1922 as a lecturer. There he formed a model aircraft club and, in January 1923, the Boys' Wing Glider Club, which became the Cranwell Light Aeroplane Club (CLAC). With Nick as the chief designer, CLAC built a small biplane, the CLA.2, to compete in the 1924 light aeroplane trials at Lympne. One of the apprentices helping construct this machine was the 17-year-old Frank Whittle. Nick carried out the first flight of the CLA.2 on 14 September 1924. The CLA.3 monoplane followed in 1925 and two CLA.4 biplanes in 1926; all were entered for the Lympne contests of those years.

Captain Douglas Rudolf Pobjoy became the Boys' Wing Education Officer in 1924. He was developing a 7-cylinder radial intended for light aircraft. Impressed with Comper and CLAC, Pobjoy wanted to install the engine in the CLA.4, but it was 1928 before it was ready for testing. Pobjoy's establishment of Pobjoy Airmotors at Hooton Park in 1928 was one of the reasons that Nick set up his own company there the following year. (Pobjoy relocated his works to Rochester, Kent, in 1933 to begin a long-lasting co-operation with Shorts.)

A Swift fuselage was used as the basis for the Comper-built Cierva C.25 Autogiro; this was wrecked on its first test in the hands of Juan de la Cierva in March 1932. Repaired, the Spaniard successfully flew it the following month but it was not followed through.

In the spring of 1932, Nick moved the company to a brand-new factory at Heston, racking up the costs both in terms of overheads and in physically transporting the Swift 'production line' to Middlesex. The firm was kept going with the occasional injection of cash from supporters – the largest influx coming from Richard Ormonde Shuttleworth. He was a Swift owner (G-ABWE – 1932 to 1935 – and G-ACBY – during 1933) and had twice flown examples to and from India. Shuttleworth – a very rich young man – sank an incredible £7,000 into Comper. That sum would buy thirteen Pobjoy-engined Swifts at 1931 list prices.

Sporting it may have been, but as a single-seater the Swift lacked sociability, and orders were drying up. Comper needed to find other, larger, markets – ideally two-seat tourer/trainers. Nick came up with no fewer than three types in quick succession. The Streak low-wing single-seater was envisaged as a replacement for the Swift that *may* have attracted established owners to upgrade. A two-seat version, the Kite, had a climb-in, fighter-like, cockpit that would not appeal to inexperienced passengers or flying training organisations. Both of these included the complication and added cost of a retractable undercarriage, as did the Mouse, Nick's really big gamble.

Above: The one-off Comper Streak, G-ACNC, aimed at the single-seat sportsplane market. *KEC*

Right: The Comper Mouse, G-ACIX, at Martlesham Heath in 1934. *Peter Green Collection*

Bottom right: A poor, but very rare, image of the Comper Fly at Heston in 1939. It is carrying the serial number T1788 on the boom. The device above the centre section is an anti-stall parachute container. *Peter Green Collection*

The Mouse was a three-seater under a sliding glazed canopy. Again this was more suited to a military machine as it made access difficult for more genteel aviators, especially those wearing skirts. There was a rear luggage compartment with space for a trio of Comper specially crafted luggage. This innovation was panned by a Heston air taxi operator, who complained he would have to send these out to clients so that they could pack them and then he would have to try and retrieve them afterwards. Convinced that the Mouse would find a welcoming market, Nick commenced a batch of a dozen, including the prototype, which he flew for the first time on 11 September 1933. The Streak, the Kite and the Mouse did not get beyond the prototype stage.

Swept away by the winds

Comper Aircraft folded in August 1934 and was re-formed on the 10th as Heston Aircraft – of which more anon. There was no place for Nick in the new line-up and by December he was consultant engineer for Austrian Oskar Asboth's helicopter project, trying to interest Blackburn Aircraft in it: nothing came of the negotiations. Nick formed Comper Aeroplanes Ltd in December 1936, promoting concepts for long-range airliners.

An association with another Swift owner, Captain Gerard William Reginald Fane (G-AAZF 1930 to 1937), Nick designed the CF.1 Scamp, a two-seat, high-wing, twin-boom pusher with tricycle undercarriage. In March 1938 Swift Aircraft Ltd was formed and construction of the Scamp commenced courtesy of the Chelsea College of Aeronautical Engineering at Brooklands. Cost considerations meant that the Scamp had to be finished as a single-seater and in this form it was called the Fly. Fane took over the project, establishing C F Aviation in August 1939 and Fane Aircraft in April 1940. The Fly failed to get airborne during trials at Heston in June 1940. Fane commissioned an entirely new machine with a simplified layout hoping to attract interest as an air observation post (AOP): but

Lance Wykes's Taylorcraft –Chapter 5 – had that all sewn up. Powered by a Continental A80 pusher, the Fane F.1/40 had its maiden flight at Heston on 21 March 1941 and thereafter faded into history.

Badly injured in a street altercation in Hythe, possibly caused by a misinterpretation of Nick's well-established ability to be a prankster, 42-year-old Flt Lt Nicholas Comper died of medical complications on 18 June 1939. His obituary in the *Times* summed up his endeavours: 'It was his true boast that he never produced a bad aeroplane, although the markets for each successive design were continually being swept away from him by the winds of the world depression.' *Flight* magazine for 22 June 1939 caught his dilemma: 'One felt that he was solely cut out for a designer, and should never have attempted to enter the commercial sphere, for which he was temperamentally quite unsuited. So long as he confined himself to the technical aspect he did very well. But in a managing director's chair he never seemed to fit quite happily.'

Comper

From	To	Total	Name/Designation	Type	Engine(s)	Notes
1930	1934	42	Swift	Sportsplane	1 x Pobjoy R	[1]
1933	-	1	Cierva C.25	Autogiro	1 x Pobjoy R	[1] [2]
1933	-	1	Mouse	Tourer	1 x DH Gipsy Major	[3]
1934	-	1	Kite	Tourer	1 x Pobjoy Niagara	
1934	-	1	Streak	Sportsplane	1 x DH Gipsy Major	
1939	-	1	Fly	Army co-op	1 x Praga	[4]

See the narrative for details of the Cranwell Light Aeroplane Club designs. **[1]** First 20 Swifts and the C.25 built at Hooton Park, all others at Heston. **[2]** Cierva licence: based on a Swift fuselage. **[3]** Production batch, reported as a dozen, laid down and offered in varying degrees of completion in March 1935 – assumed reduced to spares. **[4]** Comper Aeroplanes Ltd design, in association with Gerard Fane. Flight trials failed in June 1940.

Out of the ashes

None of Nick's designs featured in Heston Aircraft's business plan. The prototype Mouse, the design rights, and eleven incomplete airframes were offered for sale in March 1935 but there were no takers. Previously with Saunders-Roe and Hawker, George Cornwall was appointed chief designer. To emphasise the new beginning, Heston's badge featured a phoenix – the regenerating bird of Greek mythology – and this was the name of its first design, the elegant, five-seater Phoenix monoplane retractable. The prototype was flown for the first time by company test pilot Edmund Gwyn Hordern on 18 August 1935. It was followed by another five examples up to 1937. A combination of the relatively high cost of the Phoenix and the ever-darkening prospect of a peaceful future militated against sales.

The second Heston Phoenix, G-AEHJ, in 1938. *KEC*

Edmund Hordern (left) with the Duke of Richmond and Gordon – Frederick Gordon-Lennox – in front of the Hordern-Richmond Autoplane, G-AEOG, at Heston in October 1936. *via John Swain*

Test pilot Hordern had worked for British Klemm, later renamed British Aircraft Manufacturing Company, at Hanworth carrying out the maiden flights of the Swallow and the Eagle lightplanes. He joined Heston in 1935, taking a directorship. While he was at Heston, Hordern and the Duke of Richmond and Gordon – Frederick Gordon-Lennox – commissioned the company to build a two-seater twin to their specification. This was the Hordern-Richmond Autoplane, which he flew on 28 October 1936. The pair formed Hordern-Richmond Aircraft in 1938 but the prototype remained a one-off.

The failure of the Phoenix might have sunk Heston, but it was embarking upon a diversification scheme in which the design and construction of aircraft was of lesser importance. From 1937 Heston struck up a relationship with Vickers and its subsidiary, Supermarine. Sub-assemblies for the Wellesley bomber were followed up in 1938 with increasingly large contracts churning out Wellington leading edges and engine nacelles. Building wing-tip floats for the Supermarine Walrus and Sea Otter was also a lucrative task. Heston became the specialist in photo-reconnaissance conversions of Spitfires, as well as a major Civilian Repair Organisation centre. By 1946 Heston was sub-contracting for de Havilland, taking a leading role in the Sea Hornet programme, including creating the folding wings and the reprofiled nose section for the radar-equipped NF.21 version.

One-offs

In early 1937 the Air Ministry released Specification T.1/37 bizarrely requesting a replacement for the venerable Avro Tutor biplane trainer. Heston pitched in with the Cornwall-designed JA.3, Miles with the M.15 and Parnall entered the private-venture Type 382. All resembled an enlarged Miles Magister then entering widespread use by the RAF. Heston and Miles were awarded contracts for prototypes and the Heston T.1/37 first took to the air on 17 November 1938. With more pressing matters looming, the requirement was quietly shelved.

By the autumn of 1938 Lord Nuffield, founder of the Morris Motors empire, agreed to underwrite the design and construction of an aircraft to take the World Absolute Speed Record for Britain. Famed aero engine manufacturer, Napier, was looking for a way to promote Frank Halford's incredible 24-cylinder, H-format Sabre. This monster had first bench-run in 1937 and a crack at a record or two seemed an ideal way to achieve this.

Heston built two examples of a sleek all-wooden monoplane, designed by Napier's consultant Arthur Hagg and Cornwall. (Hagg was previously with de Havilland and was shortly to join Airspeed.) Top speed was estimated to be 480mph. The hugely complex Sabre suffered many delays and it was well into 1940 before the first Heston-Napier Type 5 Racer was ready. With World War Two into its tenth month, any record breaking was academic and perhaps it was then being touted as a lightweight fighter prototype. On 12 June 1940 Sqn Ldr G L G Richmond took the Racer up for its maiden sortie but the Sabre I 'Special' encountered problems. After just seven minutes, the aircraft was back on the ground, wrecked beyond repair and Richmond hospitalised. Work on the more advanced second Type 5 had already been halted; Britain had more urgent priorities.

Heston

From	To	Total	Name/Designation	Type	Engine(s)	Notes
1935	1937	6	Phoenix	Tourer	1 x DH Gipsy Six	
1936	-	1	H-R Autoplane	Tourer	2 x Continental A40	[1]
1938	-	1	JA.3, T.1/37	Trainer	1 x DH Gipsy Six	[2]
1940	-	1	Heston-Napier Racer		1 x Napier Sabre	[3]
1941	-	1	JA.8, P.92/2	Experimental	2 x DH Gipsy Major	[4]
1947	-	2	JC.6, A.2/45	Observation	1 x DH Gipsy Queen	
1948	-	1	Youngman-Baynes	Research	1 x DH Gipsy Queen	[5]

[1] Built for Horden-Richmond Aircraft. [2] Second example *believed* not completed. [3] Second example not completed. [4] Built under sub-contract for Boulton Paul. [5] Sub-contract from Alan Muntz and Co; substantially re-engineered Percival Proctor IV.

Delayed and ill-fated, the Heston Racer in early 1940. *Peter Green Collection*

Not content with the success of the Auster AOP series, the Air Ministry issued Specification A.2/45 in search of much larger aircraft to do the same task. Prototypes were ordered from Auster and Heston, which came up with an all-metal, twin-boomed pusher, the JC.6. It was ironic that such a layout was adopted, given Nick Comper's Scamp and the Fly but, other than the format, the designs were unconnected. The first of two prototypes was flown at Heston in September 1949 but, wisely, the contest was cancelled in March 1950.

The unconventional Heston A.2/45 in 1949. *KEC*

Heston's final 'new' aircraft was a sub-contract from the design consultancy Alan Muntz and Company, which was also based at the Middlesex aerodrome. Muntz had been charged with converting a Percival Proctor IV into a test bed for the Youngman high-lift flap system. Robert Talbot Youngman had been head of Fairey's technical department for most of the war years and he had spent a lot of time pondering how to lower the landing speed of naval aircraft. He came up with a double-slotted flap and the Ministry of Supply wanted it testing initially on something relatively simple.

With the Percival design number P.46 and the military serial VT789, a Proctor fuselage and 'tail feathers' were supplied to Heston. Chief designer for Muntz was the glider and light aircraft expert Leslie Everett 'Barron' Baynes. Although the resulting Youngman-Baynes High-Lift aircraft resembled a Proctor, it featured a completely new wing with full-span, double-slotted, electrically actuated flaps. The fuselage was deepened and the undercarriage extended. The one-off had its debut at Heston on 5 February 1948. It was used at Farnborough for research until mid-1950, when it was acquired by its initiator, Robert Youngman, who flew it, civil registered as G-AMBL, until 1954.

With the departure of the Youngman-Baynes test bed, Heston's work with whole airframes was more or less over. The company remained a sub-contractor into the 1950s, but increasingly concentrated on support equipment, including aircraft steps and gantries, and it changed its name to Hestair to reflect this.

CHAPTER SEVENTEEN

Founding Father

de Havilland
1920 to 1960

'…if any article of equipment can be simplified or made smaller, or of easily worked materials, more of it can be made for a given number of man-hours. This is where the Mosquito scored heavily.' Sir Geoffrey de Havilland

TAKING TO THE SKIES from Hatfield on 22 June 1937 in a light aircraft might seem a fairly unremarkable event. The pilot was Geoffrey de Havilland, the man who had put his name to the company that had created the DH.94 Moth Minor he was flying. There were high hopes that this new type would be the successor to the incredibly popular Moth biplane family. The sortie was not a 'jolly' for the 55-year-old; he was taking the prototype DH.94 on its maiden flight and it was to be the last time he would take on the role of test pilot. By the author's estimates, the DH.94 was the twenty-second time he had launched into the unknown with a totally unproven machine.

A pioneer aviator from 1909, Geoffrey de Havilland had progressed quickly from novice to a designer who also tested his own handiwork, to being a captain of industry and a leader in the boardroom. While he took a close interest in the conception of new machines, Geoffrey had long since handed over the mantle to a gifted design department. Now he was leaving the testing to others. Following in his footsteps in the family enterprise were his three sons: Geoffrey Raoul (27), Peter Jason (24) and John (19).

To differentiate between the man and the company that came to bear his name, Geoffrey – Sir Geoffrey from 1944 – is referred to here as GDH. His eldest son, who also answered to Geoffrey, and was known to many personnel at Hatfield as 'Young DH', is denoted as 'Geoffrey DH'.

The prime movers behind the Mosquito. Left to right: Charles Clement 'CC' Walker, chief engineer; Geoffrey de Havilland; R M Clarkson, chief aerodynamicist; Ronald Eric Bishop, chief designer. *British Aerospace*

Any aircraft can 'bite' or malfunction and testing something as apparently benign as a Moth Minor was not without its risks, as was revealed two years later. John Cunningham – who was at the helm of the Comet jetliner for its first flight in the summer of 1949 – started his career with DH in 1938 as an assistant test pilot to Geoffrey DH. On 11 April 1939 the pair investigated the DH.94's spinning characteristics with the centre of gravity set well aft. Try as they might they could not recover from a spin and both took to the silk; the stricken aircraft plummeting past them to crash near Wheathampstead, Hertfordshire. In his book *Ominous Skies*, fellow test pilot Harald Penrose writes that they both lunched in a nearby hostelry with hardly a mention of their first use of parachutes.

As well as dominating this chapter, the exploits of GDH can be found in Chapter 31 when he was designer and test pilot for Mervyn O'Gorman, superintendent of what became the Royal Aircraft Factory at Farnborough, from 1911 to 1913. GDH took on a similar, far more satisfying and productive, role for George Holt Thomas and his Aircraft Manufacturing Company (Airco) at Hendon 1914 to 1920. These two periods receive short treatment here and it is hoped that readers will appreciate that GDH's contribution to 'The Factory' and Airco was so pivotal that it would be a crime to gloss over them in their respective chapters.

Aviation has benefitted from the vision and zeal of many families. Britain has had its share, names such as Barnwell (of Bristol), Miles and Short among others, but there has been no dynasty like de Havilland.

'The Factory' and Airco

A lot of books have been written about de Havilland, its personalities and its aircraft. Two stand out far beyond the others. Launched in 1961 GDH's autobiography, *Sky Fever*, is an insight into a pioneer, a strong-minded leader of men and a determined industry mogul. Cecil Martin Sharp was DH's publicity manager, among other roles, and his *D.H. – A History of de Havilland*, is an exceptional tome, full of facts but highly readable. Originally published in 1960, the much-expanded edition to commemorate the centenary of GDH's birth in 1982 is a treasure.

After studying at Crystal Palace Engineering School from 1900 to 1903, GDH joined engine manufacturers Williams and Robinson Ltd at Rugby. During this period he created his own motorcycle, including the engine. From 1905 GDH worked in the design office of Wolseley Tool and Motor Car Company, moving to the Motor Omnibus Construction Company in 1906, both in London. He befriended Frank Hearle,

employed by the rival Vanguard Motor Bus Company as an engineer. With financial help from GDH's grandfather, the pair combined their talents and jacked in their jobs, so that they could build a flying machine.

They created what became known as Biplane No. 1, a single-seater powered by a 45hp four-cylinder engine driving a pair of pusher propellers via belting. As well as the airframe, GDH designed the engine and both were manufactured on commission by the Iris Motor Company. In May 1909 GDH and Hearle transported the No. 1 to a shed at Seven Barrows, close to the de Havilland family home at Crux Eaton, near Highclere, Hampshire. On its first flight in December it got to a height of about 15 to 20ft and crashed; GDH was only slightly hurt. Undaunted, he devised a two-seater biplane with the engine from No. 1, but this time driving a single pusher propeller. On 10 September 1910 Biplane No. 2 flew for about a quarter of a mile at Seven Barrows. GDH was in the aeroplane business.

In January 1911 he demonstrated it at the Balloon Factory at Farnborough. This was so successful that No. 2 was purchased for £400 and designated F.E.1, GDH engaged as designer/pilot and Hearle took up a post as an engineer. (The Balloon Factory was renamed the Royal Aircraft Factory on 26 April 1911.) GDH went on to create, among others, the F.E.2 and the exceptional B.E.2 before he was shunted to the Aeronautical Inspection Directorate (AID) in 1913. Realising that AID was not for him, GDH began to look for a new job and was snapped up by Airco in May 1914. Between 1915 and 1920 Airco manufactured the DH.1 to DH.18: of these the DH.4, DH.6, DH.9 and DH.9A achieved four-figure runs.

Going it alone

Airco was one of the casualties of the return to peace and in 1920 Thomas bowed to the inevitable and sold the company to Birmingham Small Arms, which was only interested in the industrial capacity, not the products. GDH established his own business – de Havilland Aircraft (DH) – on 25 September 1920, initially taking on unfinished work from Airco. One of those backing the new venture – to the tune of £10,000 – was Thomas, who wished his protégé the success he deserved.

The 38-year-old GDH inspired other talent from Airco to join him at Stag Lane, Edgware, which became the DH factory and aerodrome. Charles Clement 'CC' Walker had been with GDH at Farnborough and worked alongside him at Hendon; he became chief engineer, retiring from the board in 1954. Francis Edward Noel St Barbe championed the marketing of the Moth 'family', establishing contacts across the globe that helped to swell the order books.

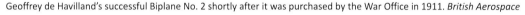
Geoffrey de Havilland's successful Biplane No. 2 shortly after it was purchased by the War Office in 1911. *British Aerospace*

Stag Lane aerodrome and factory, looking east towards Hendon.
British Aerospace

Loyal partner from the days of Biplane No. 1 in 1909, Frank Trounson Hearle left 'The Factory' in 1912, initially for the British Deperdussin Company and then Vickers. He joined up with GDH again in 1917 at Airco, where he took charge of the experimental department. At Stag Lane he started as works manager, taking a directorship in 1922. Hearle was determined that DH should make its own powerplants and from 1927 DH had its own engine shop: he deserved the accolade of 'Father of the Gipsy'. Not content with an engine division, he secured British rights to the American Hamilton controllable-pitch propellers, leading to another thriving and expanding DH enterprise.

Within nine years Stag Lane was full to overflowing and Hearle masterminded the relocation to Hatfield, which began in 1930 and the new production lines started 'rolling' two years later. (Stag Lane finally closed its doors as an aerodrome in July 1934 but the Gipsy engine division stayed there until 1945.) Hearle's dynamism was rewarded in 1938 with the managing directorship and the massive expansion of the war years fell largely on his shoulders. He was chairman of the aircraft division from 1950 to 1954, retiring in 1956. Frank Trounson Hearle CBE died in 1965, aged 79.

Finding a direction

Work began at Stag Lane with the completion of two unfinished DH.18 eight-passenger transports from Airco's Hendon factory and three more from scratch in 1921. Devised by GDH during his final months at Hendon was the DH.27 Derby heavy day bomber, two of which were ordered to compete against the Avro Aldershot in 1922. The latter won the day with seventeen being built over the next two years. If that sounds like a derisory figure, it was generous for that decade and enough to keep the workforce going and – probably – make money. The DH.29 Doncaster long-range experimental for the Air Ministry in 1921 broke a mould – it was GDH's first monoplane. A second example, known simply as the DH.29, was touted as an airliner, but failed to attract interest. As will be seen from the tables, these were the first of a series of military 'hopefuls' destined to remain prototypes. Despite the fact that GDH had created the exceptional DH.4 and DH.9, they were the products of the once mighty Airco and DH had no track record as a manufacturer.

By the late 1920s DH's future was firmly embedded in light aviation and airliners, and the lack of military contracts was of little consequence. An Air Ministry contract for a pair of twin-engined survey biplanes was met by the DH.67 but the plans were revised and then shelved by the company because its priorities were to build Moth biplanes and big DH.66 Hercules airliners. This embarrassing

situation was solved by 'CC' Walker, who came to an agreement with Gloster to take over DH's military commitments, at least in the short term. The DH.67 project was handed over and Gloster's Henry Folland completely redesigned it as the AS.31.

As well the DH.67, the unfinished DH.72 tri-motor heavy bomber was taken by road to Hucclecote for assembly and testing. This had been languishing at Stag Lane, taking up valuable factory space and annoying the Air Ministry. Like the DH.67/AS.31, the fuselage of the DH.72 was of light alloy tube construction and DH was in the early stages of adopting the technique. Gloster was well versed in the process and had both design and manufacturing capacity. The DH.72 was the first to carry the name Canberra – after the Australian administrative capital.

The DH.77 interceptor monoplane of 1929 was the product of George Carter, who had joined the DH design office in 1928. The advanced DH.77 flew from Stag Lane on 11 July 1929. A plethora of types fought for Specification F.20/27, including Gloster's SS.19 biplane (a stepping stone to the Gauntlet) and the DH.77, but the requirement went unfulfilled. The DH.77 was handed over to Gloster for further testing and going with it was Carter.

Chief designer for DH was Arthur Ernest Hagg, who had worked in the Airco drawing office. He cut his teeth at Stag Lane devising the DH.29's differential ailerons, which became a standard application on DH's types. (Conventional ailerons traverse up or down symmetrically; the down-going aileron creates a lot of drag – adverse yaw requiring a lot of rudder to balance. With differential ailerons, the upward deflection moves a greater distance than the downward travel of its opposite number, greatly reducing adverse yaw.)

Hagg oversaw designs all the way through to the Albatross airliner, although he had resigned before it took to the air. *Flight* magazine for 4 March 1937 caught the bewilderment at Hagg's departure from DH: 'Those in the aircraft industry who knew that Mr Hagg had fairly recently become interested in boat-building probably jumped to the conclusion that he was forsaking his old love for new. This *Flight* is very glad to state, is not the case, and Mr Hagg will continue to be connected with the industry … Of his future plans nothing may, however, be said at the moment.' The Albatross was not to be Hagg's last airliner, he joined de Havilland subsidiary Airspeed to create the Ambassador and his full 'CV' can be found in Chapter 3.

The prototype DH.93 Don, with mocked up turret, at Hendon in June 1937. It carries the 'trade plate' identity E.3 and the '1' on the nose was its 'New Types Park' identifier for the Society of British Aircraft Constructors display.
British Aerospace

By the late 1930s the agreement with Gloster was moribund and DH again pitched for an RAF need. Specification T.6/36 sought a three-seat, all-wood, crew trainer including a gun turret. With a potential purchase of 250, this was tempting and the prototype DH.93 Don (as in a university lecturer) appeared in June 1937. Beset with weight problems, the type was robbed of its turret and relegated to communications duties.

Only thirty-five were completed and another dozen were delivered engineless: by the spring of 1939 the entire fleet was serving as flightless instructional airframes. It was a costly exercise: real military money was made with the Tiger Moth and its Queen Bee drone derivative, and the Dominie crew trainer based on the Dragon Rapide.

Masters of light aviation

A quick way of assessing if a book or an article on DH is worth its salt is the appearance of the word 'gypsy', in which case beware. With the first 'y' and a capital 'G' the word is generally used to denote nomadic people. Its variant spelling – with an 'i' – is used in the common name for *Lymantria dispar*, the gipsy moth. This version was adopted by ardent lepidopterist (one who studies moths and butterflies) GDH for his company's engine range.

While it is true that the single-seat Humming Bird was DH's first light aircraft, it was a dead end. Designed for the 1923 trials at Lympne, the DH.53 was a triumph of economy of airframe, with an empty weight of 326lb and austerity of power, less than 30hp. Such machines were challenging to design and, in many cases, to pilot, but they had little relevance in the marketplace.

The true father of the Moth dynasty was the DH.51, a practical and affordable two/three-seater that had its first flight in the hands of GDH on 1 July 1924. Its 120hp V-8 Aircraft Disposal Company (ADC) engine, a war-surplus 80hp Renault upgraded by Frank Halford, was part of its downfall. The key to a real 'people's plane' was a reliable, cheap and easy to manufacture engine. The answer was the Cirrus and then the Gipsy, the latter set to transform DH and the world of light aviation and this evolution is charted below. The last of the trio of DH.51s built survives in airworthy trim at the Shuttleworth Collection. While it might not turn many heads at Old Warden it is a vitally important 'missing link': the DH.51 was the template for the DH.60 Moth.

At Stag Lane on 22 February 1925 GDH took a small biplane, registration G-EBKT, for its maiden flight; this was the prototype DH.60 Moth, propelled by an ADC Cirrus I. Very soon the word 'Moth' was going to become both a 'brand' and a generic name for a light aircraft. G-EBKT's debut was just seven months after the DH.51 had appeared, but a lot of thinking had gone on since then. The DH.51 had a span of 37ft and an empty weight of 1,342lb; the DH.60 was a scaled-down version at 29ft and 764lb respectively. The engine was also 'shrunk', the DH.51's V-8 was rated at 120hp; the DH.60's

While this panorama may be showing its age of ninety years or so – it is believed taken in 1927 or 1928 – it is fascinating. In the foreground is twelfth DH.53 Humming Bird G-EBQP, to the left Boulton and Paul P.9 G-EBEQ and to the right Westland Woodpigeon II G-EBIY. *KEC*

The last of three DH.51s, G-EBIR, built in 1925, is kept in airworthy trim by the Shuttleworth Collection at Old Warden. *Roy Bonser*

A line-up of a DH.60G and DH.60X Moths of the London Aeroplane Club at their base and birthplace, Stag Lane, circa 1928. *KEC*

ADC was a 4-cylinder in-line of 60hp. The DH.51 could take three people in tandem, the DH.60 settled on two. Surrounding the two seats was a plywood box, at the corners of which were anchored four spruce longerons running forward to the firewall and rearwards to the rudder post. The sides and bottom of the fuselage were flat ply. Simplicity itself: a cabinetmaker's delight. The DH.51 had two-bay wings (two pairs of inter-plane struts connecting the wings outboard of the centre section) while the DH.60 had single-bay wings that folded to save on hangarage or even allow it to be trailered home. Like the centre section struts of the DH.51, they supported an aerofoil section fuel tank. The Moth's undercarriage comprised telescopic tubes with rubber blocks to absorb countless touch-and-goes.

With the Moth, Sir Sefton Brancker, the charismatic and dynamic Director of Civil Aviation, had found an aircraft he could use for his plan for Air Ministry-sponsored aero clubs. The first Moths were delivered five months after the prototype flew and they were in the vanguard of the civilian flying school revolution. Affordable tuition and hire-by-the-hour for cross-countries allowed aero clubs to blossom all over Britain. This was not completely down to the DH.60; the Gipsy engine was employed in a barrage of other types that can be found within the pages of this book, many of which earned their keep at aero clubs. The pool of pilots generated by these organisations provided an ever-increasing number of professionals for air taxi and airline operators and as instructors at the clubs; plus an immeasurably valuable 'second force' as war approached. (The 53-year-old Sir Sefton Brancker KCB AFC was killed on 5 October 1930 when the airship R.101 crashed near Beauvais, France. His contribution to aviation in British aviation was immeasurable and tragically cut short.)

By February 1929 Stag Lane was building three Moths every workday, with increasingly healthy export orders and – as the table on Moths shows – a queue of countries wishing to sign licensing agreements. DH had struck the mother lode. A policy of steady improvements allowed DH to keep the market invigorated – Francis St Barbe was establishing dealerships, encouraging owners to 'trade up' and finding new customers. Races, rallies and long-distance flights all kept the little biplane in the news.

The year 1928 was a busy one for the Moth family. The Cirrus III-powered DH.60X appeared – the suffix coming from the split axle undercarriage that gave a distinctive 'X' shape when viewed from the front. The DH.60G Gipsy Moth appeared with DH's home-grown 85hp Gipsy I and the split axle gear. In 1930 DH created the Gipsy III, with *inverted* cylinders offering a radically improved view over the cowling. This turned the Gipsy Moth into the DH.60GIII Moth Major, making its debut in 1932. The 'Major' also boasted a steerable tail skid that was made available to the rest of the line-up.

Steps to the Tiger

Intended for 'outback' locations and hot climates, the DH.60M – 'M' for metal – of 1928 had a welded steel tube fuselage and provided easier access to the cockpits. From this basis a dedicated military trainer arrived in 1931 – the DH.60T Moth Trainer. This had new wings, a beefed up structure and deeper cockpit doors: it was the stepping stone to the Avro 504 of the 1930s, the DH.82 Tiger Moth. Comments from client air forces and critiques from the Aeroplane and Armament Experimental Establishment at Martlesham Heath gelled with the Tiger Moth (the *second* use of the name – see below), which first flew on 26 October 1931.

Five Tiger Moths of the Wittering-based Central Flying School rehearsing for the June 1932 RAF display at Hendon. In April 1932 they had returned to Stag Lane to have their engines 'plumbed' for inverted flying. *KEC*

Newark Air Museum's superbly restored Tiger Moth has its port side uncovered to reveal its structure. *Ken Ellis*

Trainers need to be able to get instructor and trainee in and out quickly, be that on the ground or when taking to their parachutes. The DH.82's upper wing was 'staggered' forward to give better overhead clearance for the two cockpits – much improved for the instructor, less so for the pupil. This altered the centre of gravity, which was negated by giving the wings a *slight* sweep back. The opportunity was taken to make the upper rear fuselage of plywood, in place of fabric covering. The Tiger Moth, which stayed in production for fourteen years, also spawned the DH.82B Queen Bee radio-controlled target drone in 1935. Although having a DH.82 designation, it was a hybrid, using the simpler (and more expendable) wooden fuselage of the Moth Major with Tiger Moth wings and tail 'feathers'.

Cabins and monoplanes

As the 1920s drew to a close, the demand for enclosed cockpits or cabins was increasing. There were still plenty of diehard cap-and-goggles flyers but there was an almost untouched market for those who would like to wear normal attire and travel with a degree of shelter and warmth. The DH.75 Hawk Moth of 1928 was a four-seat cabin monoplane for air taxi or 'bushplane' work but with an eye to the private owner. It was not a success, but just as the DH.60 had been a scaled-down DH.51, so the DH.75 was 'shrunk' to create the three-seat DH.80 Puss Moth in 1929. It was an instant success, as was the follow-up DH.85 Leopard Moth of 1933.

By the mid-1930s the difficult task of replacing the DH.60 family was being pondered. The biplane DH.87 Hornet Moth of 1934 is seen as a retrograde step by some writers. This was far from the case; a large number of potential customers remained biplane advocates and a cabin 'version' of the DH.60 would be ideal. The Puss and the Leopard featured a pilot forward and two passengers behind; the Hornet offered side-by-side seating, more sociable and allowing the DH.87 to function as a trainer.

For those that wished to keep the open cockpits, but adopt a monoplane layout, the DH.81 Swallow Moth appeared in the summer of 1931. Eventually fitted with a cabin, the two-seater seems to have been flown exclusively by GDH and it was quietly retired the following February, being declared as only experimental. Lessons learned and with the economy in far better trim, GDH's refined thinking on a 'Moth replacement' was given form by Phil Smith (destined to head up design of the DH.110 jet). That was the DH.94 Moth Minor with which this chapter began. The onset of World War Two put an end to the prospects of both the Hornet Moth and the Moth Minor. By the time peace returned, the strategy at Hatfield did not include light aviation; a golden era had quietly closed.

British operator Airwork established an Egyptian subsidiary, Misr Airwork, at Almaza, Cairo, in 1930. The company acted as sales agents for DH in Egypt; alongside the trio of Moths is newly delivered Puss Moth SU-ABE. *Peter Green Collection*

de Havilland Moth family

From	To	Total	Name/Designation	Type	Engine(s)	Notes
1925	1930	1,381	DH.60 and 'X Moth	Trainer/Tourer	1 x ADC Cirrus	[1]
1927	-	2	DH.71 Tiger Moth*	Racer	1 x DH Gipsy	
1928	1932	780	DH.60G Gipsy Moth	Trainer/Tourer	1 x DH Gipsy	[2]
1928	1932	695	DH.60M Moth	Trainer/Tourer	1 x DH Gipsy	[3]
1928	1930	8	Hawk Moth	Light transport	1 x As Lynx	
1929	1932	285	Puss Moth*	Tourer	1 x DH Gipsy Major	
1931	1932	64	Moth Trainer		1 x DH Gipsy	
1931	-	1	Swallow Moth*	Tourer	1 x DH Gipsy	
1931	1945	9,522	DH.82 Tiger Moth	Trainer	1 x DH Gipsy Major	[5]
1932	1935	144	DH.60GIII Moth Major	Trainer/Tourer	1 x DH Gipsy	[6]
1932	1948	154	Fox Moth	Light transport	1 x DH Gipsy Major	[7]
1933	1936	132	Leopard Moth*	Tourer	1 x DH Gipsy Major	
1934	1939	165	Hornet Moth	Tourer	1 x DH Gipsy Major	
1935	1944	380	Queen Bee	Target drone	1 x DH Gipsy Major	[8]
1937	1942	95	Moth Minor*	Trainer/Tourer	1 x DH Gipsy Minor	[9]

All biplanes, unless marked*. Light aircraft with the Moth name only, does not include the 7,000lb all-up DH.61 Giant Moth (DH.60 Moth was 1,350lb) – see the biplanes table. **[1]** Licensed by: General Aircraft, Sydney, New South Wales (NSW), Australia (9); Valtion Lentokonetehdas, Helsinki, Finland (10); Veljekset Karhumäki, Keljo, Finland. Three assembled by Qantas, Longreach, Western Australia (WA) from UK-made parts. **[2]** Two assembled by DH Technical School 1932 and 1933. Licensed by: Larkin Aircraft Supply, Melbourne, Victoria, Australia (32); Morane-Saulnier, Villacoublay, France (40); Moth Aircraft Corp, Lowell, Massachusetts, USA (18). **[3]** Licensed by: Haerens Flyvemaskinefabric, Kjeller, Norway (100); Moth Aircraft Corp, Lowell, Massachusetts, USA (159). Three assembled by DH Aircraft Pty, Bankstown, NSW, from UK-made parts. **[4]** Twenty-five assembled by DHC, Downsview, Canada, from UK-made parts. **[5]** Includes eight initially designated DH.60T Tiger Moth; three assembled by the DH Technical School 1934, 1935 and 1937. Manufacture switched to Morris Motors at Cowley (3,214) in 1940, after 3,065 built at Stag Lane/Hatfield. Production by sister organisations: DH Aircraft Pty, Bankstown, NSW (1,277); DHC, Downsview, Canada (1,683 – all but 30 DH.82Cs); DH Aircraft New Zealand, Rongotai, New Zealand, assembled 25 from UK-built parts and built another 132. Under licence: Haerens Flyvemaskinefabric, Kjeller, Norway (37); Oficinas Gerais de Material Aeronautico (OGMA), Alverca, Portugal (91); Svenska Järnvagsverkstäderna, Stockholm, Sweden (23). See biplanes table for Queen Bee drones. **[6]** Includes Moth Major. One assembled by DH Technical School 1935. **[7]** Ninety-eight built at Stag Lane/Hatfield. Production by sister organisations: DH Aircraft Pty, Bankstown, NSW (two – one in 1937 and other in 1938); DHC, Downsview, Canada (54 – two of which were sub-contracted to Leavens Brothers Air Services, Toronto, 1947–48). **[8]** Hybrid of Moth Major fuselage with Tiger Moth flying surfaces. Includes 60 sub-contracted to Scottish Aviation at Glasgow. [9] Forty-two built by DH Aircraft Pty, Bankstown, NSW, plus others completed from British-built parts.

Moth Minor G-AFOZ at Leicester East in 1968: it was written off in 1975. *Roy Bonser*

'Tek Kollege'

As an extension to the company's well-established apprentice scheme, the de Havilland Aeronautical Technical School – mostly referred to as the 'DH Tech' – was formed at Stag Lane in 1928. At first premises and courses were a little ad hoc but accommodation and staffing was soon sorted out. The school moved to Hatfield in 1932 and in June 1949 relocated to bespoke premises at Astwick Manor on the north-west edge of the airfield. Schools were also established at the former Airspeed plants at Portsmouth and Christchurch, and at Hawarden, Leavesden and Lostock, near Bolton – the main de Havilland Propellers factory – but on a smaller scale.

As training exercises, students assembled and flight-tested aircraft taken from the production lines: a DH.9J in 1931 from stored 'stock'; two Gipsy Moths 1932 and 1933; three Tiger Moths in 1934, 1935 and 1937; a Moth Major in 1935 and Druine Turbi G-AOTK – a two-seat French monoplane, in 1958. This 'hands on' concept was extended to building and flying an original design. The two-seat TK.1 biplane was first flown by test pilot Hubert Broad on 14 November 1933. Piloted by Geoffrey DH, the TK.1 came fifth at 124mph in the 1934 King's Cup, staged at Hatfield. The designation 'TK' has its origins in the drawings prepared for the TK.1 by Dutch student Juste van Hattum: he labelled the documents 'Tekniese Kollege No. 1' and it stuck. By the mid-1950s van Hattum was an authority on sailplanes – full-size and model – in his native Netherlands. Apart from the TK.2, the Air Registration Board was 'persuaded' to allocate registrations that ended in 'TK' to the college's aircraft, a tradition that continued with the Turbi in 1958.

The sleek TK.2 single-seat, long-range racer of 1935 was also competed by Geoffrey DH. He won the Heston to Cardiff races of 1937 and 1938 at 161mph and 187mph, respectively. The diminutive (19ft 8in span) TK.4 was conceived as the smallest possible airframe that could be harnessed to a Gipsy Major II; it still manged to accommodate a retractable undercarriage. It had its maiden flight in the summer of 1937. While preparing for a speed record attempt, DH chief test pilot Robert John 'Bob' Waight was killed in the TK.4 on 1 October 1937. He was succeeded by Geoffrey DH in the post.

The TK.5 was an experimental single-seater to examine canard layouts. It was a pusher with the main wing located at the rear, with fins and rudders close to the wing tips. Either side of the nose was a

de Havilland Aeronautical Technical School

From	To	Total	Designation	Type	Engine(s)	Notes
1933	-	1	TK.1	2-seat biplane	1 x DH Gipsy	
1935	-	1	TK.2	Long-range racer	1 x DH Gipsy Major	
1937	-	1	TK.4	One-seat racer	1 x DH Gipsy Major	
1939	-	1	TK.5	Canard test bed	1 x DH Gipsy Major	[1]

TK.1 flown at Stag Lane, all others at Hatfield. [1] Single-seat canard-format test bed, flight attempted by Geoffrey DH but it failed to get airborne.

A publicity shot of students and staff of the 'DH Tech' with the nearly complete TK.4 G-AETK at Hatfield in the spring of 1937. *de Havilland*

canard foreplane with elevators. Try as he might, Geoffrey DH could not coax the TK.5 into the air during trials in late 1939; it was soon scrapped. (Projects TK.3 and TK.6 were not built.) In 1965 the 'DH Tech' was renamed the Hawker Siddeley Aviation (Hatfield) Apprentice Training School.

Power for the people

Frank Hearle had insisted that DH needed an engine division to sustain growth and give some degree of independence from other suppliers. Vital to this was Major Frank Bernard Halford, who devised the incredible Gipsy engine and also brought the company into the jet age. After service in the Royal Flying Corps, Halford became the 'H' in Beardmore, Halford, Pullinger, moving on to ADC in 1920. As related in the story of the DH.51, above, its 120hp ADC was too large for a genuine light aircraft. Halford had the solution; he sliced the Renault V-8 down the middle into a four-cylinder in-line with a new crankcase to create the 60hp Cirrus. From 1925 the DH.60 Moth and the Cirrus was a perfect combination – for the time being. (ADC was wound down in 1930 and the remainder of the Cirrus saga is told in Chapter 9.)

Halford was taken on as a consultant to DH and tasked with devising a Cirrus replacement that could form the basis of a 'family'. The result was the Gipsy, which was ground run at Stag Lane in the spring of 1927. The engine's maiden application was another DH departure: the single-seat, high-performance DH.71 monoplane, the first to carry the name Tiger Moth. Two examples, both initially Cirrus II-powered, were intended only for high-speed research, a spot of racing and to act as the Gipsy's test bed. After less than a month of flying, the first DH.71 was fitted with a prototype Gipsy, rated at 135hp. On 24 August 1927 Hubert Broad clinched a category world record for a 100km close circuit of 186mph. Their trials work complete, both DH.71s were withdrawn from use by the end of 1928. Members of the Gipsy series were still in production in 1964: a grand total of 27,654 units were manufactured.

Halford stayed on as a consultant with DH, while taking up a similar arrangement with Napier to develop a range of larger engines. These included the 16-cylinder H-format Rapier (first appearing in 1929) and the Dagger (1934) and Sabre (1939), both 24-cylinder H-format monsters. By 1941 Halford was back with DH, creating his H-1 turbojet, which began running in April 1942 and became the Goblin. Turbine engines come with phenomenal development costs and in February 1944 the de Havilland Engine Company was formed, with Halford as its chairman. Gipsies had been manufactured by a division of DH, but financial separation was needed to prevent a financial disaster pulling the entire enterprise down. The Goblin led to the Ghost before much time and effort was poured into the Gyron, which failed to secure an

application: the Gyron Junior powered Blackburn Buccaneer S.1s.

When Stag Lane ceased building aeroplanes, the engine division remained at the site. It moved to Leavesden in 1945, taking the place of the Mosquito production line. de Havilland's engine interests were merged with Bristol Siddeley in 1961, which five years later became a part of Rolls-Royce. Frank Bernard Halford CBE died on 16 April 1965, aged 71.

de Havilland engines

Name, Type/Format	From	Application*	Notes
Gipsy, 4-cy in-line	1928	DH Tiger Moth	[1]
Ghost, V-8	1929	DH Hawk Moth	
Gipsy Major, 4-cy inv**	1932	DH Dragon	[2]
Gipsy Six 6-cy inv**	1934	DH Dominie	
Gipsy Queen, 6-cy inv**	1938	Percival Proctor	[3]
Gipsy King, V-12 inv**	1938	DH Albatross	[4]
Gipsy Minor, 4-cy inv**	1938	DH Moth Minor	
Goblin turbojet	1943	DH Vampire	[5]
Ghost turbojet	1950	DH Venom	[6]
Gyron turbojet	1953	Short Sperrin	[7]
Gyron Junior turbojet	1958	Blackburn Buccaneer S.1	
Gnome turboshaft	1959	Westland Whirlwind	[8]

Based upon *D.H. – A History of de Havilland* by Martin Sharp. * Typical, or only, use. ** Inverted in-line. [1] Inverted 4-cylinder from Gipsy III. [2] Gipsy Major I licensed by General Motors-Holden in Australia. Production continued post-war, for the DHC Chipmunk, Saro Skeeter and others, last examples 1958. [3] Production continued post-war, for the DH Dove and Heron, last examples 1964. [4] Also known as the Gipsy 12/Twelve. [5] Initially Halford H-1 of 1942. Widely licensed, including Allis-Chalmers in the USA as the J36. [6] Licensed to Svenska Flygmotor, Sweden, as the RM2. [7] Sperrin test bed only, Gyron intended for the cancelled supersonic Hawker P.1121. [8] Anglicised General Electric T58.

Challenging airliner market

Completing a pair of DH.18s removed from Airco after its demise became the first manufacturing activity for the newly founded DH in 1920. The format that GDH had adopted for the big biplane – pilot in an open cockpit to the rear with a passenger cabin between him and the engine – proved to be a winning formula. Three new DH.18s followed, helping to keep the workforce occupied while new machines came off the drawing boards. The DH.50 first appeared in 1923 as a scaled-down DH.18 with a four-seat cabin. It proved particularly important in helping to open up the Australian 'outback' market, mostly through licence agreements. The need to replace the DH.50 brought about the six-passenger DH.61 Giant Moth of 1927, which with an all-up weight of 7,000lb and a span of 52ft was far removed from the diminutive statistics of the rest of the Moth family.

Siddeley Puma-engined, float-equipped DH.50 A8-1 delivered to the RAAF in 1926 for use by the nation's governor general. *British Aerospace*

Hagg turned the pilot-and-cabin arrangement into a true Moth with the DH.83 Fox Moth, which first took to the skies on 29 January 1932. He married the wings, tail 'feathers' and undercarriage from the Tiger Moth to a boxy four-seat cabin in the centre section. The pilot could keep an eye on his passengers – and they vice versa – via a small hatch below his instrument panel. Aimed at air taxis and small airlines, the Fox Moth was also an early 'bushplane' but could be equally at home with a private owner and his family. de Havilland Canada (DHC) capitalised on the appeal of the type and the availability of locally made DH.82C Tiger Moth components to build a batch from 1946, with the last completed two years later.

Immaculate Fox Moth G-ACEJ at Old Warden in the summer of 1976. *KEC*

Imperial Airways Hercules G-EBNA *City of Teheran* at Shaibah, Iraq, 1929. *Peter Green Collection*

The DH.34 ten-seater biplane was a conventional rethink of GDH's first monoplane, the DH.29. With no frills, it was a reliable workhorse and Dobrolet, a Soviet operator, was one of the purchasers. Named after the town near the de Havilland family home at Crux Eaton, the DH.54 Highclere of 1924 was an attempt to refine the DH.34, but it remained a one-off.

While DH was struggling to be recognised by the RAF as a manufacturer of merit, the order from Imperial Airways for what became eleven DH.66 Hercules tri-motors was particularly important. Imperial was taking over the Cairo, Egypt, to Baghdad, Iraq, air mail-with-passengers service from the RAF and the airline's requirements were for a rugged, easily maintained transport. Two pilots and a radio operator, up to seven passengers and a generous bay for large consignments of mail and packets were the payload. A steel tube fuselage 'skeleton' with ply-encased cabin and mail/baggage bay taxed the production schedule at Stag Lane, but the second batch of 1929 was a far smoother process. A 79ft 6in span biplane, with a biplane triple fin and rudder tail was the result, the first example flying on 30 September 1936. The pilots sat out in the open, but were later afforded an enclosed cockpit.

Dragons, large and small

In November 1932 Hubert Broad eased a twin-engined biplane off the turf at Stag Lane on its debut flight. This was the DH.84 Dragon, designed to help airlines operating at the Fox Moth level to increase capacity without overstretching things. There was nothing fancy about the DH.84, it was a big 'Moth' and the concept could be adapted to smaller, or larger, types. The prototype was granted its certificate of airworthiness thirty-four days after its maiden flight and handed over to an eager Edward Hillman of Essex-based Hillman's Airways in January 1933. Introducing an airliner to service was far easier in those days!

Hagg turned to a joint British and Australian requirement for a ten-seat, long-range airliner. In just four months he came up with the elegant DH.86 biplane, powered by four of the new Gipsy Queen six-cylinder in-lines. This was first flown on 14 January 1934 and a very creditable production run of sixty-two was achieved. The nose section was originally very like the profile of the Rapide, but a two-pilot cockpit with a 'stepped' windscreen was quickly introduced. Often referred to as the 'Express' or 'Dragon Express', the DH.86 never aspired to an official name.

Below left: Built for the RAAF as A34-59 at Bankstown in 1943, this Dragon was imported into the UK in 2001. Lovingly restored, it flies as G-ECAN in the colours of Railway Air Services. *KEC*

Below: Jersey Airways DH.86 G-ACYF *Giffard Bay* on delivery 16 February 1935. The airline famously used the beach at St Helier, tides permitting, for its operations. *KEC*

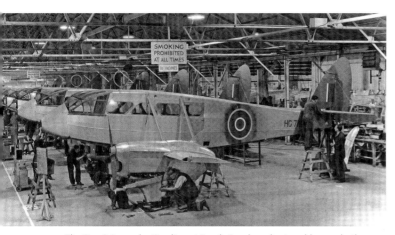

The Dominie production line at Brush Coachworks, Loughborough: the example in the foreground was delivered to the RAF in March 1944. *Brush*

Edward Hillman clamoured for extra seats and increased speed, and he was not alone in these demands. Hagg scaled-down the DH.86 to create the new twin, the DH.89, which first flew on 17 April 1934. This retained the ruggedness of the Dragon while offering two more seats, greater payload, speed and range, and it was a much cleaner design than its somewhat angular forebear. Wanting to stress the family links while emphasising its enhanced performance, the DH marketing team called the new machine the Dragon Rapide. At first glance the Rapide should have cancelled out the Dragon, but DH had wisely perceived two separate markets – see the comparison table. The fledgling DH.84 was not eclipsed by the DH.89; the former remained in production in Britain until 1936. It also enjoyed a renaissance in 1943 to meet an urgent Royal Australian Air Force (RAAF) need for crew trainers. A similar RAF requirement was met by the Rapide and large numbers of the Dominie version began in 1939.

While the Rapide was a scaled-down 'Express', the DH.90 Dragonfly of 1935 was a scaled-down Rapide but it adopted a new construction technique. The fuselage of the five-seat tourer/air taxi was a monocoque plywood shell, giving a much smoother look. The cockpit was no longer a single-seat 'pulpit'; it had side-by-side seating and dual controls. The pointed nose cone doubled as a luggage bay. All of these thoughts were translated to the DH.92 Dolphin, intended as a Dragon Rapide replacement. A ten-seater, the prototype originally had the distinctive Rapide-like 'trouser' fairings around the main undercarriage, but it later boasted retractable undercarriage. First flown in September 1936, the Dolphin was found to be very overweight. The design office was overcommitted with the upcoming Moth Minor tourer, Albatross airliner and Don crew trainer for the RAF and Rapide sales were still buoyant. With what seems like undue haste, the Dolphin was pushed to one side and dismantled before the end of 1936.

DH.84 Dragon and DH.89 Dragon Rapide compared

	Dragon	Rapide
First flown	12 Nov 1932	17 Apr 1934
Engines (2x)	DH Gipsy Major 1 130hp	DH Gipsy Queen 3 200hp
Passengers	6	8
Loaded weight	4,200lb	5,500lb
Cruise	109mph	132mph
Range	460 miles	578 miles
Production	115 + 87	391 + 336 + 2*
From – To	1932 to 1936**	1934 to 1947

* First at Hatfield, Herts, to late 1942 and then by Brush, Loughborough, early 1943 to mid-1946. DH assembled another two from spares stock at Witney in 1947. ** Production restarted in Australia with 87 built at Bankstown, New South Wales, during 1943.

Glittering prize

Six years before the Mosquito – the 'Wooden Wonder' – took to the air, DH flew the first of five 'special order' piston twins that were also destined for fame – the DH.88 Comets. An oft-held fallacy is that the DH.88s pioneered the construction methods used in the Mosquito. The precursor of the composite 'Mossie' was another 'looker' from Hagg's drawing board, the DH.91 Albatross.

In March 1933 Sir MacPherson Robertson offered a glittering prize of £10,000 for the winner of an air race from Britain to Melbourne, Australia, to mark the centenary of the establishment of the State of Victoria. The flag would go down at 0630 hours on 20 October 1934 at Mildenhall.

The contest attracted a lot of interest and DH offered a twin-engined, long-distance racer specifically for the event. It invited orders at £5,000 each, with a deadline of 28 February 1934. Three orders, conditional on the DH.88s being ready in time, were placed for an event that was only *nine months* ahead. By July 1934 the production lines at Stag Lane had all moved to Hatfield. Hagg's DH.88 team stayed on so that they could concentrate on the job in hand, taking the airframes to Hatfield only at the last moment.

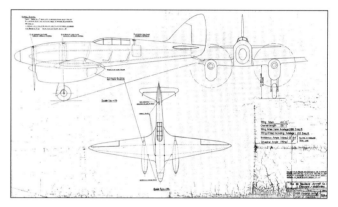

General arrangement of the DH.88 Comet, issued by the Stag Lane drawing office, 1934. *British Aerospace*

Designing and manufacturing against the clock precluded radical departures in technique so Hagg adopted the DH.86 'Express' as the state-of-the-art and combined this with his passion for the craft of boat-building. He created a breathtakingly beautiful aeroplane that any shipwright could appreciate. The Comet's fuselage was mostly conventional, much of it being flat-sided and ply covered. The long, elegant wings were covered by a skin of two layers of spruce planking, laid diagonally for immense strength, as found in yachts of quality. This process was also used to achieve the complex curves of the forward fuselage.

Hubert Broad piloted G-ACSP, the first of the trio, on its maiden flight on 8 September, just six weeks prior to the start. The three were: G-ACSP *Black Magic*, owned and flown by Jim and Amy (née Johnson) Mollison; the unnamed G-ACSR, owned by Bernard Rubin and piloted by Owen Cathcart-Jones and Ken Waller; and G-ACSS *Grosvenor House*, owned by Arthur Edwards of the Grosvenor House Hotel and flown by C W A Scott and Tom Campbell Black. Two other DH.88s were later commissioned: a mailplane for the French government and G-ADEF *Boomerang* for Cyril Nicholson.

It was *Grosvenor House* that clinched the race. Scott and Campbell Black crossed the finishing line at 0534 on 23 October after a gruelling 70 hours 54 minutes 18 seconds, travelling 11,333 miles and averaging 158.9mph, setting a new point-to-point record. Today, a much rebuilt and 'restored' G-ACSS is airworthy with the Shuttleworth Collection at Old Warden.

As well as the significant prestige and publicity DH received from the DH.88, the main lesson it left for the next generation was the value of good project management under an extreme deadline. Using a 'tight' design team secreted away from the main factory to knuckle down and deliver was a procedure that paid dividends when it came to the Mosquito.

Beautiful birds

Well satisfied with the DH.66 Hercules tri-motor, Imperial Airways was receptive to a DH proposal for an advanced, high-performance, long-range airliner using an innovative construction technique – the DH.91 Albatross. This was a big leap and the Air Ministry pitched in with an order for two four-engined 'mail carriers' capable of transatlantic performance on 21 January 1936. Frank Halford devised the inverted 12-cylinder Gipsy Six of 525hp for the new machine. The one-piece wing used the DH.88's diagonal spruce ply planking for the outer skins. The cylindrical fuselage was a lamination of cedar ply with an inner layer of balsa, providing strength with the ability to be moulded into shapes unobtainable in wood by any other manner. The fuselage 'sandwich' was formed on a jig, bulkheads were made in a similar manner, and cut-outs were made for the tailplane and cabin windows prior to assembly. The undercarriage was anchored under the inboard engines and retracted *inwards* – another challenging element. The tail was originally a twin fins and rudders arrangement, set about a third of the way out on the elevators; this was changed to an elegant 'endplate' layout.

'Bob' Waight took the first of the two mailplanes for its maiden flight on 20 May 1937. The second machine joined the programme and during overload tests broke its back, at the trailing edge of the wing, towards the end of its landing run on 27 August 1938. With the forward fuselage pointing skywards, the Albatross must have been an ominous sight: was this a step too far? Local strengthening was all that was required: an application of ply and resin. (The Mosquito prototype suffered in a similar manner, at Boscombe Down in 1941.) Imperial Airways was not shaken and stuck to its order for five of a twenty-two-passenger version; these and the two mailplanes entered service from October 1938.

The looming war blunted any chances of other sales, but although the Albatross was a very advanced machine, the appeal of the all-metal, US-designed Douglas DC-2 and DC-3, which had entered service in September 1933 and June 1936 respectively, had rendered wooden airliners – no matter how eye-catching – obsolete. By the time the Albatross entered flight test, its designer, Arthur Hagg, had left DH and it was his successor, Ronald Bishop, who tackled the all-metal challenge to the Americans. Although there were very few lessons from the Albatross that applied to the new airliner, it had proved the structure that was to make the Mosquito a reality.

The prototype Albatross during an early test flight in mid-1937 and wearing the 'trade plate' identity E.2: it was later registered G-AEVV. *KEC*

The prototype Flamingo, G-AFUE, during route proving for Guernsey Airways in mid-1939. *KEC*

Stages in the creation of a DH.91 Albatross fuselage. Steel bands were wrapped around the ply-balsa-ply 'sandwich' to apply pressure while the adhesive cured. Once dried the windows and apertures were cut out. *Both British Aerospace*

de Havilland 'non-Moth' biplanes 1922 onwards

From	To	Total	Name/Designation	Type	Engine(s)	Notes
1920	1921	5	DH.18A and 'B	Light transport	1 x Napier Lion	[1]
1922	1923	2	Derby	Heavy bomber	1 x RR Condor	
1922	-	11	DH.34	Airliner	1 x Napier Lion	
1923	1924	2	DH.37	Tourer	1 x RR Falcon	
1923	1924	3	DH.42	Fighter-recce	1 x AS Jaguar	[2]
1923	1929	38	DH.50	Light transport	1 x Siddeley Puma	[3]
1924	1925	3	DH.51	Tourer	1 x ADC	
1924	-	1	Highclere	Airliner	1 x RR Condor	
1925	1926	2	Hyena	Army co-op	1 x AS Jaguar	
1926	1928	3	Hound	2-seat GP	1 x Napier Lion	
1926	1929	11	Hercules	Airliner	3 x Bristol Jupiter	
1927	1929	9	Giant Moth	Light transport	1 x Bristol Jupiter	
1931	-	1	Canberra	Night bomber	3 x Bristol Jupiter	[4]
1932	1937	202	Dragon	Airliner	2 x DH Gipsy Major	[5]
1934	1937	62	DH.86	Airliner	4 x DH Gipsy Six	
1934	1947	729	Dragon Rapide	Airliner	2 x DH Gipsy Queen	[6]
1935	1938	67	Dragonfly	Light transport	2 x DH Gipsy Major	
1936	-	1	Dolphin	Airliner	2 x DH Gipsy Six	

Note: Details of GDH's first biplanes given in the narrative. His designs for the Royal Aircraft Factory appear in Chapter 31 and for the Aircraft Manufacturing Company in Chapter 2. **[1]** Two incomplete airframes from Airco, finished at Stag Lane, followed by three new examples. **[2]** One DH.42 Dormouse, fighter-recce two-seater; two DH.42A Dingo army co-op. **[3]** Licensed by: Aero, Prague, Czechoslovakia (7); Larkin Aircraft Supply, Melbourne, Victoria, Australia (1); Queensland and Northern Territories Aerial Services (QANTAS) at Longreach, Queensland, Australia (7); West Australian Airways at Perth, Western Australia (3); Société Anonyme Belge de Constructions Aéronautiques (SABCA), Belgium (3). **[4]** Began at Stag Lane but completed at Hucclecote by Gloster. **[5]** One hundred and fifteen built at Stag Lane/Hatfield. Production restarted by DH Aircraft Pty, Bankstown, New South Wales, in 1943 creating another 87. **[6]** RAF crew trainers named Dominie. Total of 391 produced at Hatfield 1934–42 and two completed from spares by DH Repair Unit, Witney, 1947. Total of 336 Dominies sub-contracted to Brush, Loughborough, 1943 to 1946.

Bishop designed the all-metal, stressed-skin DH.95 as a seventeen-passenger, medium-range airliner. Like the Albatross, it was named after an imposing bird, the Flamingo, at the suggestion of GDH. The prototype first flew on 22 December 1938 and in the summer of the following year it entered trial service with Guernsey Airways. Sixteen were manufactured up to 1941, including a purpose-built military transport version, the Hertfordshire (named after Hatfield's county), the first of an otherwise cancelled batch of thirty. Thoughts about resuscitating the Flamingo post-war were stymied because the DC-3 – in the form of surplus C-47 Skytrains – was crowding out the market and DH needed to focus all of its attention on the forthcoming Comet jetliner.

Shrouded in tarpaulins, the Mosquito prototype at Hatfield, December 1940. *British Aerospace*

'Wooden Wonder'

Hatfield's industrial prospects changed completely on 25 November 1940 when an all-yellow twin-engined type was put through its maiden flight by Geoffrey DH – the DH.98 Mosquito. This revolutionary private venture capitalised on the moulded laminate construction pioneered by the company and was followed by 7,780 other examples. Following the experience of the DH.88 Comet, the prototypes had been designed and built in great secrecy away from Hatfield at nearby Salisbury Hall, London Colney, in a staggering eleven months from the go-ahead. Salisbury Hall is now the home of the de Havilland Aircraft Museum and pride of place is held by the Mosquito prototype, W4050, back at its birthplace. Salisbury Hall was also where the Airspeed Horsa assault glider was conceived. The hall served as an early example of an institution made famous by Lockheed's 'Skunk Works' at Burbank, California, USA, which had its origins in the summer of 1943.

From 1936 *the* man to bounce ideas off about what sort of weaponry the RAF would need for a future conflict was ACM Sir Wilfrid Rhodes Freeman. His post was Air Member for Research and Development and he was not restricted to theories and strategies; he was able to get an idea into the air. Having perfected the rationale for what was to become the Mosquito, GDH wrote to Freeman on 20 September 1939 – seventeen days after Europe had been plunged into war. Part of GDH's case ran as follows: 'We believe we can produce a twin-engined bomber which would have a performance so outstanding that little defensive equipment would be needed. This would employ the well tried out method of construction used in the Comet and the Albatross and being wood or *composite construction* would not encroach on the labour and material used in expanding the RAF. It is especially suited to really high speeds because all surfaces are smooth, free from rivets, overlapped plates and undulations and it also lends itself to *very rapid initial and subsequent production*.' The italics are the author's: here is the word 'composite' long before it became commonplace and forethought about the ease and speed of manufacture. Freeman was 'sold' but the Air Ministry was sceptical as it was a radical proposal. GDH decided to go ahead no matter what and a team began to gather at Salisbury Hall.

de Havilland 'non-Moth' monoplanes 1922 to 1939

From	To	Total	Name/Designation	Type	Engine(s)	Notes
1921	1922	2	Doncaster	Long-range trials	1 x Napier Lion	[1]
1923	1924	15	Humming Bird	Ultralight	1 x Douglas	
1929	-	1	DH.77	Fighter	1 x Napier Rapier	[2]
1934	1935	5	DH.88 Comet	Long-range racer	2 x DH Gipsy Six	
1937	1939	7	Albatross	Airliner	4 x DH Gipsy Twelve	
1937	1939	35	Don	Crew trainer	1 x DH Gipsy King	[3]
1938	1941	16	Flamingo	Airliner	2 x Bristol Perseus	[4]

[1] Second example configured as airliner. [2] See narrative and Chapter 22. [3] Twelve delivered in 1939 without engines, becoming instructional airframes. [4] Includes one prototype Hertfordshire, to RAF specification; at least two scrapped when contract for 30 was terminated in 1939.

British Overseas Airways Corporation used Mosquitos on the diplomatic shuttle service from Leuchars to Stockholm, Sweden. Hatfield-built FB.VI HJ720 was handed over to the airline from new in April 1943 with the civil registration G-AGGF. It crashed into high ground near Leuchars on 17 August 1943. *British Airways*

Mosquito B.20s on the DH Canada production line at Downsview, Ontario, 1944. *National Aviation Museum of Canada*

The diagonal planking employed on the wings of the Comet and Albatross could not take the loads expected on the Mosquito's upper wing skin. The two-spar, tip-to-tip wing had span-wise stringers and a double plywood sandwich covering. During the celebrations of the fiftieth anniversary of the Mosquito's maiden sortie, *Flight* magazine's Mike Ramsden, a former 'DH Tech' pupil, outlined how the fuselage was made in: '… halves by stretching two skins of birch plywood over concrete moulds … three 45-degree plies were stretched cold over the mould, into which the bulkheads and other structural members had been slotted. Steel straps stretched the plywood to its double curvature shape. Before the second skin was applied balsa fillings were inserted to stabilise the structural sandwich.' Prior to joining together, each half-shell was: 'fitted with its wiring, plumbing and equipment … The Mosquito's designers separated the installations for ease of production so that the electrics were in one fuselage shell and hydraulics in the other. Of course, the fuselage had to be made in halves anyway, because [of] the double curvature limitation of plywood: but this limitation was turned to manufacturing advantage.'

Legend has it that DH's chief designer, Ronald Eric Bishop, penned the first sketches of the Mosquito's layout while sitting on a loo in Salisbury Hall. He joined DH at Stag Lane in 1921 as an apprentice and two years later was a fixture in the drawing office. He worked on the trailblazing DH.51 and the blossoming Moth family. In the late 1920s cutbacks found him out of a job and contemplating employment with Junkers in Germany: he was brought back into the fold, becoming Hagg's deputy. He was appointed design director in 1946 and was deputy managing director by 1953, retiring in 1964. Ronald Eric Bishop CBE, the man who created the Mosquito and the Comet jetliner among others, died on 11 June 1989, aged 86.

To clear factory space at Hatfield, Tiger Moths were manufactured by Morris Motors at Cowley through to 1944, and Brush Electrical at Loughborough built Dominies until 1946. On 15

November 1950 the last of 6,439 British-built Mosquitos, a radar-equipped, night fighter NF.38, was rolled out at Hawarden. Reconditioned examples for export continued to be money-spinners for another two years. The final version was the ugly, stretched, TT.39 target tug, a conversion of the B.XVI. From its first appearance, the Mosquito met the eight-point criteria given in the introduction.

This chapter starts with a quote from GDH, taken from his autobiography *Sky Fever*, which highlights the strategy behind the Mosquito. More of his words on the subject sum up the industrial and tactical rationale of a war-winner: 'It could carry a great load of bombs per man-hour of work than the big bombers, and, of course, at a much higher speed, and only needed a crew of two instead of five to eight. To attain this result we had had to fight hard, we were constantly urged during design, for example, to equip it with rear defence, but we consistently refused because it would have led to a heavier and slower aircraft. For rear defence we relied entirely on high speed … The proof that we were justified was demonstrated by the performance of the Mosquito in actual war operations.'

Last of the pistons

As with the Mosquito before it, the DH.103 Hornet began as a private venture. It bore only a familial likeness to its predecessor; it was an entirely new design taking in all of the lessons learned since 1940. The fuselage employed the same production technique as the Mosquito, while the laminar flow wing combined wood and metal; the lower wing skin was aluminium and the top surface was plywood. The Hornet was the first aircraft in Britain – if not the world – to employ wood-to-metal bonding.

The prototype Hornet had its maiden flight at Hatfield on 28 July 1944 and during trials reached 485mph. Entering service in May 1946, the shapely Hornet was the fastest and the last of all of the RAF's piston-engined fighters. Also produced for the Fleet Air Arm (FAA) as the Sea Hornet; the final Hornets left the factory at Hawarden in 1952.

A rocket- and bomb-armed Hornet F.1 of Butterworth-based 33 Squadron over Malaya in 1953. *KEC*

The three de Havilland brothers discussing the finer points of a Mosquito's tailplane: left to right, Peter, John and Geoffrey. *de Havilland*

de Havilland licence* and construction for other concerns

Type	Total	From	To	Notes
Cierva C.24*	1	1931	–	[1]
Airspeed Oxford I/II	1,515	1939	1942	[2]
DH Canada Chipmunk	1,066	1949	1960	[3]

[1] Two-seat cabin Autogiro – see Chapter 15. [2] Up to 1940 production was a sub-contract. DH acquired Airspeed in 1940 and those manufactured beyond that date were technically not sub-contracted, but built at a sister plant. [3] Production by the parent company for RAF and exports; unknown number assembled by Aero Engineering and Marine Ltd (previously Martin Hearn Ltd) at Hooton Park, circa 1950–51. Licence production (66) by Oficinas Gerais de Material Aeronáutico (OGMA) at Alverca, Portugal.

To strive, to seek

Geoffrey Raoul de Havilland, the first of three sons of Louie and Geoffrey de Havilland, was born in 1910. When he was just eight weeks old he was flown, cradled in his mother's arms, in his father's Biplane No. 2 at Seven Barrows. He joined DH as an apprentice at Stag Lane in 1928 and learned to fly, going on to instruct and carry out production flight tests at Hatfield. With the death of DH chief test pilot 'Bob' Waight in the 'Tech School' TK.4 on 1 October 1937, Geoffrey DH replaced him. Bob was 28 when he died; Geoffrey was just a year younger at the time. As described elsewhere, he piloted the Mosquito and the Vampire on their maiden flights.

Middle son, Peter Jason, was born in 1913; he went on to a long career within the company, working in sales in the 1950s. The third son, John, was born in 1918. He was apprenticed to the DH Aeronautical Technical School at Hatfield 1937 to 1939 and learned to fly at the Hatfield-based London Aeroplane Club. John followed in the footsteps of his elder brother and by 1943 was involved in testing Mosquitos fresh from the Hatfield factory. On 23 August 1943 John was flying FB.VI HJ734 with John Scorpe alongside as observer. Up at the same time was George Gibbins in Mk.VI HX897 accompanied by the DH flight test foreman G J 'Nick' Carter. The two aircraft collided at about 500ft, the shattered wreckage falling to the ground near St Albans; all four were killed. Aged 24, John was buried in the churchyard of St Peter's at Tewin, west of Hertford.

In early 1946 Geoffrey DH was preparing to test a swept-wing, tail-less derivative of the Vampire that was initially conceived as a test bed for a jetliner concept. This layout was abandoned for what was to become the more conventional Comet in March 1946 but development of three DH.108 prototypes continued. The first example was trucked to Woodbridge, where the long runway and lack of prying eyes facilitated testing. Geoffrey DH carried out the maiden flight on 15 May 1946 and began to explore its characteristics.

The second DH.108 was more refined with slightly increased sweep back. It also had powered flying controls to help in the progress of the similarly equipped Comet. Geoffrey DH piloted this

The first of three DH.108s, ready for flight test, May 1946. *British Aerospace*

de Havilland from the Mosquito to Sea Vixen

From	To	Total	Name/Designation	Type	Engine(s)	Notes
1940	1950	7,781	Mosquito	Multi-role	2 x RR Merlin	[1]
1943	1958	3,364	DH.100 Vampire	Fighter	1 x DH Goblin	[2]
1944	1952	388	Hornet	Fighter	2 x RR Merlin	[3]
1945	1968	542	Dove	Light transport	2 x DH Gipsy Queen	[4]
1946	1947	3	DH.108	Research	1 x DH Goblin	
1949	1965	112	Comet	Airliner	4 x RR Avon	[5]
1949	1958	1,619	Venom	Fighter	1 x DH Ghost	[6]
1950	1964	149	Heron	Light transport	4 x DH Gipsy Queen	[7]
1950	1961	1,069	DH.115 Vampire	Trainer	1 x DH Goblin	[8]
1951	1966	151	Sea Vixen	Naval fighter	2 x RR Avon	[9]

Note: Published works on DH differ wildly about production figures, none more so than on Vampires and Venoms. The best analysis on those two types is David Watkins's *Vampire – The Complete History* and *Venom – The Complete History*, published by Sutton in 1996 and 2003 respectively. **[1]** Includes Sea Mosquito. Built by DH at Hatfield, Leavesden and Hawarden. Production by sister organisations: Airspeed, Christchurch (122); DH Aircraft Pty, Bankstown, New South Wales – NSW (212); DHC, Downsview, Canada (1,034). Sub-contracted to: Percival, Luton (245) and Standard Motor, Ansty (1,066). **[2]** Includes Sea Vampire. Built at Christchurch, Hatfield and Hawarden. Sub-contracted to English Electric, Samlesbury (1,311) and Fairey, Ringway (67). Produced by sister company DH Aircraft Pty, Bankstown, NSW (80) and under licence by: Aeronautica Macchi, Varese, and Societa per Azioni Fiat, Turin, Italy (circa 120); Flugzeugwerk Fabrique Federale de Aviations (FFA), Emmen, Flug und Fahrzeugwerke (FFW), Altenrhein and Pilatus, Stans, Switzerland (100); Hindustan Aircraft, Bangalore, India (247); Société Nationale de Constructions Aéronautiques de Sud-Est (SNCASE), Marignane, France as the FB.52 and SE.532/SE.535 Mistral (434). **[3]** Includes Sea Hornet. Built at Hatfield and, from 1948, Hawarden. **[4]** Includes Devon and Sea Devon. Built at Hatfield and Hawarden. Final example assembled from Hawarden-built parts at Baginton, Coventry. **[5]** Comet 1s powered by DH Ghost 50s. All Comets 1s, 2s and the sole Mk.3 built and flown at Hatfield. Airframe sets for around another 30 Mk.1s abandoned. At least seven Mk.2s and a Mk.3 laid down at Hatfield but scrapped mid-1950s. At least ten Mk.2s laid down at Hawarden but scrapped in the mid-1950s. Two Mk.2 fuselages built by Shorts at Sydenham, but not completed. Comet 4s built at Hatfield until 1957 when production moved to Hawarden. Last two airframes became aerodynamic prototypes for the HS Nimrod – see Chapter 26. **[6]** Includes Sea Venom and two-seat all-weather fighter variants. Built at Hatfield, Christchurch and Hawarden. Sub-contracted to: Brooklands Aviation, Sywell (5); Fairey, Ringway (37) and Marshall of Cambridge, Teversham (83). Licence-built by: FFA, Emmen, FFW, Altenrhein and Pilatus, Stans, Switzerland (250); SNCASE, Marignane, France as the SE.201, SE.202 and SE.203 Aquilon (116). **[7]** Includes Sea Heron. Built at Hatfield and Hawarden. **[8]** Includes Sea Vampire trainers and DH.113 Vampire NF.10 night fighter. Built at Hatfield, Christchurch and Hawarden. Sub-contracted to Fairey, Ringway (30) and 2 by Marshall of Cambridge, Teversham, 1954. Also built by DH Aircraft Pty, Bankstown, NSW (110). **[9]** Built at Hatfield (2 prototypes) and Christchurch and Hawarden (119 FAW.1s and 29 new-build FAW.2s.)

machine for the first time on 23 August 1946; it was soon achieving speeds that could set a world record. On 7 September 1946 a Gloster Meteor F.4 of the RAF High Speed Flight gained a world speed record of 616mph along a calibrated course off Tangmere. Geoffrey DH began to practise a similar circuit profile over the Thames Estuary: it was beginning to look as though the Meteor would not hold the laurels for long. On 27 September 1946 Geoffrey DH took off from Hatfield for a final trial run before transiting to Tangmere for a crack at the record. As the evening drew on it was clear that he was overdue and after extensive searching wreckage of the DH.108 was found off Gravesend and the 36-year-old's body was washed ashore at Whitstable. The DH.108 had reached Mach 0.875 in a dive from 10,000ft and suffered structural failure.

Geoffrey Raoul de Havilland OBE was buried alongside his brother, John, at Tewin. Their mother, Lady Louie de Havilland, was buried there in July 1949; she took the deaths of her sons badly and never recovered her health. The headstone of the de Havilland brothers carries the following: 'They gave their lives in advancing the science of flight. To strive, to seek, to find and not to yield.'

'Colonials'

Major Hereward de Havilland, GDH's younger brother, saw the wisdom of stronger ties with Australia and in March 1927 de Havilland Aircraft Proprietary (Pty) Ltd was established. This was the start of a string of 'colonial' companies: Canada (in 1928), India (1929), South Africa (1930) and New Zealand (1939). Of these DH Australia (DHA) and DHC developed indigenous designs. Based at Bankstown, Sydney, New South Wales, DHA followed up limited production of the G.2 assault glider with a DH.104 Dove-based 'bushplane', the Drover. Powered by three Gipsy Major 10s, the prototype first flew on 23 January 1948 and the last of twenty examples was completed in 1956. DHA was absorbed within Hawker Siddeley (HSA) in 1960 and three years later the Australian interests of Bristol and Fairey were

amalgamated with DHA as Hawker de Havilland. In 2009 the company was renamed Boeing Aerostructures Australia.

At Downsview, Ontario, DHC designed a two-seat basic trainer, the Chipmunk; the prototype first flying on 22 May 1946. The Royal Canadian Air Force received 158 but in 1949 the parent company hit the jackpot with an order from the RAF to replace the Tiger Moth. With export orders and a small number of civilian deliveries, UK-manufactured Chipmunks reached a very neat 1,000 units.

On 16 August 1947 DHC flew the first of what is regarded as the ultimate 'bushplane', the Beaver. At Hatfield, there were high hopes of emulating the success of the Anglicised Chipmunk with a British production line. The Series 2 demonstrator, powered by a 550hp Alvis Leonides radial, was imported in 1953, but attracted no orders. There was a consolation prize when the Army Air Corps ordered Beavers. Although built in Canada, the forty-six examples were assembled and fitted out at Hawarden between 1961 and 1967. The Beaver was followed by its 'big brother', the Otter, from 1951 at Downsview.

Peter Masefield's (see Chapter 7) much-modified DHC Chipmunk G-AOTM was built for the RAF in 1953, but was disposed of three years later. The so-called 'Masefield Tourer' was created at Filton in 1960. *Beagle*

DHC turned its hand to specialist short take-off and landing (STOL) transports, initially with the twin-piston Caribou in 1958 and the refined, twin-turboprop Buffalo from 1964. By adapting the fuselage of the Otter and harnessing it to a pair of turboprops the highly successful Twin Otter appeared in 1965. DHC was absorbed into HSA in 1960 but the parent company became wary of the development costs of the four-turboprop STOL airliner, the DHC-7, or 'Dash 7'. DHC was acquired by the Canadian government in June 1974. Nicknamed the 'Quad Otter', the DHC-7's maiden flight took place in 1975 and the twin-turboprop Dash 8 appeared in June 1983.

de Havilland Australia indigenous production

Type	Total	From	To
DHA G.2 assault glider	8	1942	1943
DHA.3 Drover 'bushplane'	20	1948	1956

de Havilland Canada indigenous production to 1974

Type	Total	From	To	Notes
DHC-1 Chipmunk trainer	218	1946	1956	[1]
DHC-2 Beaver 'bushplane'	1,692	1947	1967	
DHC-3 Otter 'bushplane'	466	1951	1967	
DHC-4 Caribou transport	307	1958	1973	
DHC-5 Buffalo transport	c.75	1964	ongoing	[2]
DHC-6 Twin Otter airliner	115	1965	ongoing	[3]

[1] Majority (1,066) built by the parent company in the UK, plus 60 under British licence by Oficinas Gerais de Materiel Aeronáutical (OGMA) in Portugal – see narrative and table. **[2]** Production completed in 1986 with a total of 122. **[3]** Series 100 production ended in 1968 at 115. Twin Otter continued to 1988 with another 729 units. (Production started again from 2009 by Viking Air with the Series 400.) Additionally, DHC built 100 CSF-2 Tracker patrol/anti-submarine aircraft under licence from Grumman 1956–60.

All this is way beyond the remit of the book, but it's worth hanging on in there. DHC was privatised in 1986 and it was snapped up by Boeing before being sold on to Bombardier Aerospace in 1992. Changing marketplaces and development problems with the CSeries twin-jet airliner forced Bombardier to reassess its priorities and it began to divest itself of some of its products. The type certificates for the Twin Otter were acquired by Viking Air, part of the Longview Aviation Capital group, and manufacture restarted in 2009. A decade later Longview acquired the rights to the Dash 8, keeping the Downsview production line going. In a case of history repeating itself, in July the name de Havilland Canada was reborn for the new Dash 8 venture, Longview calling it 'one of Canada's most iconic aircraft brands'.

Vampire, Venom, 'Vixen

As the Mosquito entered mass production, Hatfield's design office was already at work on another world-beater. Gloster had pioneered jet-propelled flight in Britain and the first Meteor twin-jet fighter took to the air in March 1943. DH's response to Specification E.6/41 was the single-engined, twin-boom Vampire jet fighter. This was initially known as the Spider Crab but, thankfully, common sense prevailed. The wings and tail were all-metal, but the fuselage 'pod' used the same wooden composite structure as the Mosquito: even in the jet age, wood still had a place.

Geoffrey DH took the prototype, LZ548, into the air for the first time on 29 September 1943 at Hatfield. In Martin Sharp's *D.H. – A History of de Havilland*, Geoffrey DH's assessment of the Vampire is quoted: 'So smooth, it was like driving a quiet car off into the sky. I found myself tapping the instruments to make sure the needles weren't sticking.'

Screened off from prying eyes, the prototype Vampire, LZ548, under construction at Hatfield in 1943. *British Aerospace*

Like the Mosquito, the Vampire was destined for a long production run. The 'pod-and-boom' layout permitted radical changes to the cockpit area, creating a side-by-side two-seater with relative ease. Night fighter and trainer variants had a very Mosquito-esque forward fuselage. With Hatfield dominated by the 'Wooden Wonder', Vampire manufacture was initially entrusted to English Electric at Samlesbury. The Vampire was also sub-contracted to Fairey and Marshall and it was extensively licence-built. Production returned to the fold in the late 1940s at Hatfield, Christchurch and at the 'second force' factory established at Hawarden (both from 1951). It was 1961 before the final Vampires were completed, at Hawarden: a pair of T.55 trainers for Syria that were embargoed and eventually scrapped.

While the Venom shared the same 'pod and boom' layout of the Vampire, it was an altogether different beast. Powered by the Ghost 103 turbojet, the Venom FB.1 had 50% more thrust, was nearly 50mph faster, had twice the range and a greater weapon load than the early Goblin-powered Vampires. The prototype Venom had its maiden flight on 2 September 1949. It followed the same progression as the Vampire, with two-seat radar-equipped versions and licence manufacture, in France, Italy and Switzerland.

John Cunningham was at the controls of the prototype DH.110 on 26 September 1951 for its first sortie. The twin-engined, twin-boom, all-weather fighter was initially aimed at both the RAF and the FAA. While sharing the same format as the Vampire and the Venom, the DH.110 was a much larger, wholly new design. The development programme was brought to a tragic halt on 6 September 1952 when the second example disintegrated while displaying at Farnborough, killing John Derry, Tony Richards and twenty-nine members of the crowd as wreckage and the engines ploughed into the public area.

Philip 'Blinkers' Smith was in charge of the conception of the DH.110. He enrolled at the 'DH Tech' in 1934 and joined the company in 1937, going straight on to the Moth Minor team. He worked through the war years on the Mosquito and Vampire before taking charge of the Dove – of which more below. When the naval DH.110 was transferred to Christchurch, Smith turned to airliner developments, including the Trident and early Airbus A300B work. Phil Smith CBE retired in 1980.

By the time of the Farnborough tragedy, the RAF had dropped the DH.110 in favour of the Gloster Javelin, which flew in November 1951. For some time the project looked certain to be axed, but two years later, the Navy confirmed its intention to go for the DH.110. The programme office was moved to Christchurch, where 'Tam' Tamblin – see below – led the design team that substantially rethought the airframe to adapt it to shipboard operations. The prototype navalised version, known as the Mk.20X, had its maiden flight on 20 June 1955.

Vampire NF.10 WM705 of 151 Squadron over its base, Leuchars, circa 1952. Built at Hawarden in 1951, it was issued direct to the unit. *Graham Pitchfork*

Carrying the deck code 'V' on the fin, signifying HMS *Victorious*, Sea Vixen FAW.2 XS587 of 893 Squadron at Yeovilton in July 1967. It was built at Hawarden in 1965. *Roy Bonser*

Named Sea Vixen, the first FAW.1s appeared in early 1957, production moving in 1963 from Christchurch to Hawarden. The improved FAW.2 had its debut on 1 June 1962. It offered increased range thanks to the ingenious forward extension of the tail booms to provide extra tankage. Both the Mk.1 and Mk.2 Sea Vixen toted home-grown armament, respectively the Firestreak and Red Top infrared homing missiles, built by DH (from 1960, HS) Dynamics. A total of twenty-nine Sea Vixen FAW.2s were manufactured, while another sixty-seven FAW.1s were brought up to the new standard up to 1968. The conversion contract and other upgrades up to the type's withdrawal in 1974 provided valuable work. The 'Vixen was DH's last warplane.

Replacing the Rapide

By the end of 1945 DH had evolved beyond the wildest dreams of the newly knighted GDH. Airspeed had been acquired in 1940, largely for its factory and workforce at Christchurch. Not far from Hatfield, DH was running a 'shadow factory' at Leavesden to ease Mosquito capacity problems. When the company completed the move to Hatfield in 1932, the facility seemed vast: but by 1945 it was clear that DH needed another production facility. A search for a suitable venue, ideally with skilled personnel locally and with lower payroll and site costs than southern England, was started. In 1948 the massive assembly plant at Hawarden, near Chester, previously run by Vickers, was acquired and the final Mosquitos completed there. (Today, in the hands of Airbus UK, Hawarden is the main British wing manufacturing centre.)

Post-war there was to be no return to light aircraft: military jets, prestige airliners and smaller transports were the way forward. No time was lost in creating a new civil type; twenty-three days after the Japanese surrender the prototype Dove, a monoplane with retractable undercarriage intended to replace the Dragon Rapide, flew on 25 September 1945. Along with its military version, the Devon, the Dove was a phenomenal success; the last of 542 was delivered in 1968.

The ninth production Dove, ZS-BCB, was delivered to Suid Afrikaanse Lugdiens (South African Airways) in December 1946. Lockheed Lodestar in the background. *SAA*

Heron 1 G-ANXB was delivered to British European Airways for its 'Highlands and Islands' services in March 1955. Today it is preserved at the Newark Air Museum. *BEA*

A four-engined growth version of the Dove, the Heron, had its debut on 10 May 1950. Initially with fixed undercarriage, it adopted retractable gear in 1952. The last one was handed over in 1964, bringing the total built to 149. The Heron was nicknamed 'Tam's Tram' after the man who led its design, William 'Tam' Tamblin. He began his career with DH as part of the Salisbury Hall Mosquito wing crew, and he was involved with all the major variants. After perfecting the Heron, Tamblin took up the post of chief designer of the Christchurch division, bringing the DH.115 Vampire trainer to production.

Comet: triumph and tragedy

Determined to re-enter the airliner business, DH bravely took a leap of faith to create the Comet, the world's first jetliner to enter production. Interest from airlines was intense: This was high risk, but DH was in the vanguard of a potentially massive marketplace. Cunningham captained the maiden flight of the prototype, G-ALVG, on 27 July 1949. Powered by DH Ghost 50s, this machine was a humble thirty-six-seater, but there was potential to 'grow' the airframe. The Comet 2 was to adopt the more powerful Rolls-Royce Avon 500.

Range was a critical factor and the Mk.1s were incapable of flying the Atlantic without a refuelling stop. A solution was proposed by Flight Refuelling Ltd (FRL) in 1950 and it fell to former DH designer Arthur Hagg to lead negotiations with Bishop. Hagg had taken up a part-time post with FRL as consultant technical director. He outlined fitting the jetliner with a nose-probe for in-flight refuelling from a fleet of converted Avro Tudor 1 piston-engined airliners. The idea got as far as Cunningham flying *Victor-Golf* tucked up behind FRL's Avro Lincoln B.2 tanker, RA657, to assess wake turbulence in late 1950 and early 1951. This got no further as the modified Comet would incur weight and centre of gravity penalties, and the planned Avon-engined variant offered better range.

British Overseas Airways Corporation (BOAC) took the first-ever fare-paying passengers on a scheduled jetliner service in Comet 1A G-ALYP on 2 May 1952. The Hatfield production line was swelling, including exports for Canada and France. Hawarden was gearing up as a second assembly line and Shorts at Belfast was building fuselages. On 10 January 1954 BOAC Comet 1 *Yoke-Papa* disappeared off Elba, Italy, with the loss of all on board. This was tragedy enough but eighty-eight days later another, G-ALYY, crashed into the sea off Naples. There had been accidents to Comets before – see the table – but they were not attributable to the design: what had happened to these two?

A salvage operation was initiated and the Royal Aircraft Establishment (RAE) was put on full alert: Britain's world-beating jetliner was under intense scrutiny. A massive and fast-paced analysis brought together two elements at Farnborough; the resident Accidents Investigation Branch and the RAE's Structures Department worked to find the cause and, if possible, a cure.

On 14 April, just *four days* after *Yoke-Yoke* had plunged into the Mediterranean, its sister ship, G-ALYS, touched down at Farnborough to start 'live', ground-based, trials. The prototype Comet, G-ALVG, was already on site and was quickly used for metal fatigue experimentation. Arriving by road, G-ALYU was placed inside a huge water tank on 19 May, beginning four months of intensive pressurisation trials. An unfinished Mk.2 went into a similar tank at Hatfield. Meanwhile, *Yoke-Papa* had been retrieved from the deep and was reassembled in a hangar. Mk.1A G-ANAV flew in from Hatfield on 24 May and carried out a variety of tests until it was grounded in mid-August. Up to 1957 another *four* Comet airframes were brought by road to Farnborough to join the diagnostic effort. The investigation process was unprecedented at the time.

Cracking under a cabin window led to catastrophic failure of the structure of G-ALYU in the tank, replicating the misfortunes that had befallen its sisters. With much redesign – including the profile of the windows – and structural strengthening Comets returned to service and were put back into production. The type's vast sales potential had suffered a mortal blow and Boeing and Douglas reaped the rewards with the 707 and DC-8 respectively. The Avon-engined Comet 4 series, with capacity for 100 passengers, attracted some interest, but when the last example was delivered in February 1964 the total of all Comet variants came to a disappointing 112.

The Comet disasters were not stand-alone events: jetliner development has been a rocky road ever since. On 3 March 1974 a Turkish Airlines Douglas DC-10 tri-jet crashed near Paris, killing all 346 on board: a cargo door was incorrectly secured. Faith in the DC-10 was recovering when an American Airlines example crashed following the separation of the port engine pylon on 25 May 1979 – 273 people perished. The DC-10's image appeared permanently tainted.

Such tragedies were not confined to the 20th century: on 29 October 2018 a Lion Air Boeing 737 MAX crashed followed by another, of Ethiopian Airlines, on 10 March 2019, killing 189 and 157 respectively.

The first Comet C.2 for the RAF was not completed and instead was used for pressure testing in a tank at Hatfield in late 1955. *Hawker Siddeley*

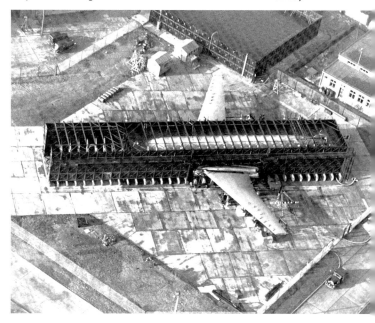

Comet 4C OD-ADR, one of four for Beirut-based Middle East Airlines – at Hatfield ready for delivery in December 1960. In the background is an Avro Ashton flanked by a pair of EE Canberras. *de Havilland*

The MAX was grounded seventy-two hours after the second incident with examples rolling straight off the production line and into storage. Software was the core of the problem and it was not until 18 November 2020 that the US Federal Aviation Administration allowed the type to return to service. Boeing had suffered swingeing damage in terms of expenditure/compensation and reputation.

Return to jetliners

Despite the traumas and the cost of the Comet programme, DH was not through with airliners. The prototype three-engined Trident got airborne at Hatfield shortly after noon on 9 January 1962. The first of the spectacularly successful DH.125 executive jets took to the skies for its debut on 13 August 1962. As design of the Trident crystallised in the late 1950s, DH needed to find partners to fund and manufacture the tri-jet. A consortium of DH (as the lead partner), Fairey and Hunting was established in January 1958. With an eye to history, the name of the organisation chosen as the legal entity was The Aircraft Manufacturing Company – Airco.

Having secured an order from the state-owned British European Airways for the Trident, DH was in a powerful position to be courted by the two groups intending to amalgamate to meet the Conservative government's wishes to restructure the industry. English Electric and Vickers were keen to take DH on board, but Hatfield preferred HSA and the deal was struck in January 1960. Three years later the great name of de Havilland disappeared amid the corporate reshuffle.

In his autobiography, *Sky Fever*, GDH records his great pride that his company had a family atmosphere. Despite being the 'Founding Father', he declared that no relative or friend: 'has ever suggested I should use any influence on his behalf, and they have retained their jobs on merit alone. Geoffrey and John, for example, were obvious pilots of great skill; and Peter, my surviving son [he died in 1977], after doing some years of very useful flying, joined the sales side where his knowledge of French was, and is today, a big asset.' Sir Geoffrey de Havilland OM CBE AFC died on 21 May 1965 aged 83; his ashes were scattered at Seven Barrows, where the adventure began.

Comet 1 accident chronology

Date	Aircraft	Fatalities	Location and circumstances
26 Oct 1952	G-ALYZ	0	Failed to get airborne at Rome-Ciampino. *Yoke-Zulu* had its maiden flight on 23 Sep 1952 and had clocked just 81 hours, 31 minutes flying time
21 Jan 1953	G-ALYY	1	Landed short at Entebbe, Uganda. Nobody on board injured but a woman working on the approach lights was killed. *Yoke-Yoke* repaired by late February – see 16 Jul 1953 and 8 Apr 1954
3 Mar 1953	CF-CUN*	11	Failed to get airborne at Karachi, Pakistan, while on delivery
2 May 1953	G-ALYV	43	Crashed six minutes after take-off from Calcutta-Dum Dum at Jugalgari, near Calcutta, India, after encountering a severe tropical thunderstorm
25 Jun 1953	F-BGSC**	0	Overshot on landing at Dakar, Senegal
16 Jul 1953	G-ALYY	0	Mistook Juhu aerodrome for Bombay-Santa Cruz and undershot. Substantially damaged but repaired – see 21 Jan 1953 and 8 April 1954
25 Jul 1953	G-ALYR	0	Taxiing accident at Calcutta-Dum Dum. Not repaired, shipped to the UK
10 Jan 1954	G-ALYP	35	Crashed off Elba, Mediterranean Sea – between Corsica and Piombino on the Italian mainland
8 Apr 1954	G-ALYY	21	On charter to South African Airways. Crashed off Stromboli, Sicily, Mediterranean Sea. See also 21 Jan 1953 and 16 Jul 1953

All owned by British Overseas Airways Corporation, except for: * Canadian Pacific, ** Union Aeromaritime de Transport, France

CHAPTER EIGHTEEN

Life in the Fast Lane

English Electric
1920 to 1926
1939 to 1960

'Mach 1.95 was stabilised briefly by gentle reheat throttle reduction and then maximum throttle acceleration was resumed in smooth, precise control conditions with no problems.' Roland Beamont on flying P.1B XA847, November 1958

WHEN THE PROTOTYPE Canberra twin-jet bomber had its maiden flight on Friday, 13 May 1949 it was envied across the world. On seeing the newsreels, intelligence officers, industrialists and journalists would have had problems establishing just what this 'English Electric' was. As the Canberra looked like a jet-age Mosquito, pundits might be forgiven for thinking it was a de Havilland product, or perhaps Hawker or Supermarine. After a bit of research the realisation dawned that this was the first original design from an organisation that had previously been a sub-contractor. This ground-breaking aircraft came from a group well versed in making engines, switchgear, locomotives and even domestic appliances. English Electric (EE) was a 'new kid on the block' at a time when well-established manufacturers were viewing the future with foreboding.

Two of the most successful military jet programmes that Britain has ever embarked upon – the Canberra and the Lightning – were created by EE. Both were radical and high-risk yet they had

The first of two Lightning T.55Ks for Kuwait under test from Warton with 'B condition' ('trade plate') markings in the summer of 1968. *British Aerospace*

long-term, lucrative production runs with upgrade and refurbishing contracts to keep the coffers topped up and a large workforce active for decades. The Canberra also achieved the 'Holy Grail' – being adopted by the Americans. These two exceptional machines laid the foundations for a dynasty that is still at the top of its game with the Eurofighter Typhoon.

The second COW Biplane at Larkhill in 1912. *Peter Green Collection*

Four into one

An amalgamation of mostly engineering and electrical businesses, EE was established on 14 December 1918. Combining their assets and talents were: Coventry Ordnance Works (COW) specialising in armaments; Dick, Kerr and Co and the United Electric Car Company, both of Preston and engaged in manufacturing trams and locomotives; and Phoenix Dynamo of Bradford, makers of electric motors.

During the Great War COW, Dick, Kerr and Phoenix had also built aeroplanes but by the time EE was up and running, they had completed their contracts, or were in the process of closing down such operations. COW had taken over the business of the Wright brothers in 1911. *These* Wright siblings were Howard Theophilus and Joseph Warwick, trading as Warwick Wright Ltd of Battersea. Between 1908 and 1910 they had created more than twenty different aircraft, mostly to the commission and design of clients.

Working with the Wrights was William Oke Manning and he and Howard Wright transferred to COW. They designed a pair of two-seat biplanes to compete at the Larkhill military aeroplane trials in 1912, but were unsuccessful. The following year a seaplane *may* have been built for the Admiralty, but this is poorly documented. Howard Wright departed COW in 1912, eventually becoming the chief designer for J Samuel White at Cowes. From 1918 COW became a successful sub-contractor, making Royal Aircraft Factory B.E.2s, B.E.8s, B.E.12s, R.E.7s, R.E.8s and Sopwith Snipes, until 1919.

Dick, Kerr and Co constructed an assembly shed and slipway at Lytham and produced at least forty Felixstowe F.3 twin-engined flying boats from 1918 to 1919. The company secured a contract in 1919 to complete a Fairey N.4 four-engined flying boat. The hull was made by the Airco-owned May, Harden and May at Hythe. Assembly was nearly complete when it was halted and the 'boat languished indoors at Lytham until it was removed by road in 1921, bound for the Isle of Grain in Kent: it did not fly until July 1923.

Phoenix Dynamo at Bradford manufactured Maurice Farman Longhorns, Short Bombers and a pair of Armstrong Whitworth FK.10 quadruplanes during 1916 and 1917. Short 184 floatplanes and Felixstowe F.3 flying boats were built between 1916 and 1918. These were taken by road to Brough and flown off the River Humber. In late 1917 the decision was taken to set up an in-house design department

and Manning was employed to create what became the P.5 Cork biplane flying boat. After leaving COW, Manning had enlisted in the Royal Navy Volunteer Reserve in 1914 and, as a lieutenant, was posted to the Port Victoria marine aircraft trials establishment on the Isle of Grain. This experience made him ideal for Phoenix Dynamo's ambitions. The first P.5 was flown on 4 August 1918 from Brough and it was followed by another in June 1919. With no further orders, Manning spent his time scheming a vast passenger-carrying flying boat, which he named the Eclectic: it did not see the light of day.

Short-lived venture

Perhaps the availability of Manning – or the man himself – persuaded EE's management to enter the aircraft manufacturing business. Appointed chief designer in 1920, Manning began to tackle two flying boat projects: a replacement for the Cork – the Kingston – and an experimental machine of radical layout – the Ayr. Manning recruited Henry Knowler, previously with Vickers, as his assistant. In 1923 Knowler became chief designer for S E Saunders.

While the flying boats were nearing completion, in the summer of 1922 Manning was diverted by a trip to Itford Hill, north of Newhaven in Sussex, to watch the newly introduced sport of gliding. He came back fired up with the notion of a glider-like single-seater using the least power possible. The Air Ministry was approached and it accepted the offer to build a prototype. This was embodied in

Peter Hillwood piloting the rebuilt Wren No. 4 at Warton in 1956. *English Electric*

Specification 4/23 as a 'training machine' capable of thirty minutes' endurance. A price of £600 was agreed upon and it was given the serial number J6973 and the name Wren. It was built in the former Dick, Kerr works in Preston and Sqn Ldr Maurice Wright achieved the Wren's first sustained flight on 8 April 1923 from the sands at Lytham St Annes – to the west of the disused Dick, Kerr flying boat factory. The first EE type had taken to the air.

Manning hoped that the Wren could become a cheap to operate type for private owners and two more, referred to as Mk.IIs, were made. These were entered into the *Daily Mail*-sponsored light aircraft trials at Lympne in October 1923 and came away with a useful £750 in prizes for fuel efficiency. After long periods of storage, the two Lympne Wrens were brought to Warton in late 1954. There, with advice from Manning, they were combined to create an airworthy example for the Shuttleworth Collection. Restoration complete, EE test pilot Peter Hillwood conducted the first sustained flight since the 1920s along Warton's generous runway on 25 September 1956. Today, on rare occasions the Wren delights the audience at Old Warden with short 'hops' care of its 7hp, 400cc ABC twin-cylinder engine.

The Dick, Kerr factory and slipway at Lytham was dusted down and used to assemble the prototype Kingston. Launched into the Ribble estuary on 22 May 1924, it hit something floating in the water during take-off and sank: the crew survived. Despite this inauspicious start, six more Kingstons followed. Intended as an experimental, it was hoped that the Ayr would become the basis for a coastal reconnaissance type. Manning married a very conventional hull to a pair of radical wings. The upper example featured a swept leading edge outboard of the centre section and substantial 'N' struts supported its otherwise cantilever structure. The lower wing was fully swept back with considerable dihedral and was attached to the lower fuselage at the chine. As well as providing lift, in the water the lower wing stabilised the machine, doing away with wing-tip-mounted floats. Launched from Lytham in March 1925, the Ayr failed to get airborne. It was scrapped and construction of a second example was halted. When the last Kingston was handed over in March 1926, the EE management closed – for the second time – the Lytham factory. The company concentrated on its extensive core businesses.

After EE, Manning worked for a while with the Italian manufacturer, Fabbrica Italiana Automobili Torino (FIAT), as a consultant, before working for Simmonds Aircraft at Weston, Southampton, in a similar capacity. In the mid-1930s he penned *Airsense: For those Engaged in or Interested in Flying*, which became a best-seller. He was engaged at the Royal Aircraft Establishment, Farnborough, by 1940. Two years later Manning joined Flight Refuelling Ltd and he played a major role in the development of the probe and drogue tanker–receiver system. William Oke Manning died on 2 March 1958, aged 78.

The ill-fated prototype Kingston, N168, at Lytham in 1924. The extended rear of the engine nacelles contained a position for a gunner. *KEC*

Sub-contracting

Much to the consternation of many in the aircraft industry, the government's response to massively increasing the output of armaments of all kinds was to introduce the 'shadow factory' scheme in 1935. The established manufacturers believed they were best placed to manage these state-financed plants. This stance was not wholly based on self-interest; a similar system during the Great War had been riddled with problems. That was not Whitehall's view. Well-run aviation companies needed to concentrate on designing, developing and fostering new machines, not be diverted by humdrum factory processes. The Air Ministry also had a jaundiced view of some constructors and their ability to meet their own commitments, let alone others. Some 'trusted' concerns did get to run 'shadows': Bristol-at Oldmixon, Weston-super-Mare, and Fairey at Stockport, for example.

For the aviation sector electrical and vehicle industries were favoured to run the new factories: taking on proven, in-service types and churning them out with co-operation from the 'parent' design house. Ideally, the 'shadows' would be sited in areas that did not denude the workforce of established aviation manufacturers. Instead they would be located nearby, or adjacent to, the contractor's 'caucus' area, where key personnel could be diverted to the new, temporary, enterprise and recruitment could target former employees and 'kindred' local firms. A good example was vehicle manufacturer Rootes Securities, which ran two very efficient factories, at Speke in Liverpool and Blythe Bridge, in Staffordshire.

It was the 'shadow' plan that brought EE back into the 'fold' in 1938. This had nothing to do with its previous dalliance with aircraft, it was the company's managerial prowess and the abundant, skilled workers around Preston that were called upon to expand the factory at Strand Road, Preston, and build Handley Page (HP) Hampdens. Samlesbury, to the east of Preston, was chosen as the assembly site and airfield and construction began in April 1939: today it is the giant BAE Systems plant. The first EE-built Hampden had its maiden flight on 22 February 1940 and production ran to the spring of 1942. By then EE had geared up for the four-engined HP Halifax, the first example getting airborne on 15 August 1941, and by the middle of the following year Samlesbury was completing one every day.

With Hatfield dominated by assembly of the 'Wooden Wonder', de Havilland (DH) Vampire manufacture was entrusted to EE, setting the Lancashire company on the way to becoming a centre of jet excellence. Geoffrey de Havilland Junior was at the helm of the first EE-built Vampire F.1, TG274, for its maiden flight from Samlesbury on 20 April 1945. Initially Vampire contracts came from the Ministry of Aircraft Production (MAP), but from 1946 EE worked directly for DH. Vampire construction ran until 1952, making EE immune from the post-war cutbacks experienced by other organisations.

English Electric sub-contracts

Type	Total	From	To	Notes
Handley Page Hampden I	770	1940	1942	
Handley Page Halifax	2,145	1941	1945	[1]
de Havilland Vampire	1,376	1945	1952	[2]

[1] Mks II, III, VI and VII. [2] Mks I, II, F.3, FB.5, F.20.

From Sabres to fridges

Frank Halford – creator of the de Havilland Gipsy family of engines – also conceived the 24-cylinder, H-format Napier Sabre. This monster began bench-running in 1937 and went on to power Hawker Typhoons and Tempest Vs and VIs. Much was expected of the Sabre and a factory with one million square feet of floor space was built at Walton in north Liverpool in 1940 to parallel and eventually relieve the main D Napier and Son plant at Acton, London. Achieving mass production proved as problematical as the engine's development. The first Liverpool-built 2,300hp Sabre II was delivered in February 1942, way behind schedule.

MAP determined that Napier could not continue to manage the plant. Two days before Christmas 1942, EE acquired D Napier and Son, much to the relief of the ministry. At this point EE had no independent design house, so had no need to 'vertically integrate' by adding an aero engine concern to its portfolio. Napier was not snapped up for that reason. EE was a large and varied conglomerate, building marine and locomotive powerplants, which Napier also made. The Sabre went on to be a successful, if high maintenance, engine. Post-war, Napier's aero engine division was given a remarkably free rein by EE. The Nomad, Naiad and Oryx failed to enter quantity production, the Eland turboprop remained a niche choice and only the Gazelle turboshaft made the leap to quantity production. The Liverpool factory went on to sub-contract Avon turbojets for Rolls-Royce and built engines for Deltic locomotives in the early 1960s. It also turned its hand to fridges and other domestic appliances. In order to separate the aero engine side of Napier's business, EE set up Napier Aero Engines Ltd in 1961. To nobody's surprise, the following year EE sold it on to Rolls-Royce.

Napier aero engines 1942 to 1962

Name, Type/Format	From	Application*	Notes
Sabre 24-cy H-format piston	1940	Hawker Tempest V	[1]
Nomad turbo-compound diesel	1949	Avro Lincoln	[2] [3]
Naiad turboshaft	1949	Avro Lincoln	[2] [3]
Eland turboprop	1952	Fairey Rotodyne	
Oryx turboshaft	1953	Percival P.74	[4]
Gazelle turboshaft	1955	Westland Wessex	

* Typical, or only, use. [1] First ran 1937, development protracted. [2] Test bed only. [3] Programme cancelled 1955. [4] Failed to fly – see Chapter 20.

Independent force

Sir George Horatio Nelson took the helm of EE in 1933 and was determined to make it an industrial giant with global influence. In April 1945, choosing the occasion of the maiden flight of the first EE-built Vampire, Nelson announced that the company was to become an aircraft manufacturer in its own right; sub-contracting was not enough. EE's personnel had excelled in the mass production of complex aircraft, including jets – a legacy not to be ignored. This was a very brave move: EE was entering an overcrowded, and very likely, dwindling, marketplace. To muscle its way in to the 'establishment' EE needed to invest in technology and innovate.

The men who created the Canberra standing in front of the prototype, 1949. Left to right: F D Crowe, chief draughtsman; D L Ellis, aerodynamicist; H C Harrison, production design; A E Ellison, assistant chief designer; W E W Petter, chief engineer; R P Beamont, chief test pilot; D B Smith, administration; F W Page, assistant chief designer; H S Howat, Ministry of Supply technical officer. *British Aerospace*

In July 1944 EE signed up the gifted 36-year-old William Edward Willoughby Petter as chief engineer. He had previously worked for Westland and brought with him his thoughts on a jet bomber. The impetuous 'Teddy' did not make himself overly popular at the family-run Westland, based at Yeovil. Petter's Lysander was a remarkable machine; the twin-engined Whirlwind and Welkin less so. Frustrated, Petter found the challenge of starting from scratch at Preston intriguing. (His full 'CV' can be found in Chapter 38.)

Three months prior to Petter's arrival, his 'office' had been established in a former garage in Preston's Corporation Street that had been commandeered as a training centre for EE's employees. Among the recruits was Frederick William Page as chief draughtsman. The first of several wind tunnels was introduced. Petter's initial thoughts had a pair of engines buried within the fuselage, alongside one another, but the layout soon evolved to wing-mounted powerplants. Britain's newest design department was rewarded by an order for a quartet of prototypes in January 1946. Specification B.3/45 was drawn up for a high-speed, high-altitude unarmed twin-jet bomber. Just over three years later the paperwork was transformed into hardware.

A dedicated flight test airfield was needed, and in 1947 EE acquired the former United States Army Air Force Base Air Depot 2 at Warton, west of Preston on the banks of the River Ribble. Britain's first-ever jet bomber, the EE A.1 VN799, started taxying at Warton on 8 May 1949 with Wg Cdr Roland Prosper Beamont taking increasingly long 'hops' down the runway. That Friday – the 13th – offered perfect weather. Petter was far from happy with the portents of the date but Beamont would have none of it. At 1046 hours he eased the vitally important prototype into the air for a twenty-seven-minute and very successful inaugural flight. The entire envelope was cleared in just thirty-six sorties.

Revolutionary Canberra

In 1950 the A.1 was given the name Canberra, after the Australian administrative capital. This was a shrewd move as the Royal Australian Air Force ordered forty-eight, to be built under licence. The Canberra propelled EE to the status of dominant military jet manufacturer and was to alter the fortunes of much of the British industry. (The twin-jet was not the first Canberra: that was the DH.72 tri-motor bomber.)

After the prototypes, nominally designated B.1s, the mainstay of production was the B.2 and this airframe proved to be exceptionally adaptable. By reconfiguring the forward fuselage, photo-recce and trainer versions were easily achieved. With its offset, fighter-like

The original EE design office, the former garage in Corporation Street, Preston, 1945. *British Aerospace*

Cover of a Canberra brochure from the early 1960s with images of Lightnings superimposed. It was promoting the two machines as a perfect combination: 'backbone and spearhead'. *via Dean Wright*

Australia's Prime Minister, Robert Gordon Menzies, during the Canberra naming ceremony at Biggin Hill, 19 January 1951. *Peter Green Collection*

canopy the B(I).8 interdictor looked like a huge departure but was essentially another exercise in altering the nose section to suit the role. Hardpoints on the wings allowed for bombs or rockets and a special pack, created by Boulton Paul, provided the clout of a quartet of forward-firing cannon. The gun pack was mounted in the rear of the bomb bay, the forward portion of which could still accommodate three 'thousand-pounders'.

As the comparison table reveals, it was the 'strategic' photo-recce Canberra PR.9 that was the most extreme. After an interim conversion of a PR.7 by sister company Napier at Luton in 1955, design authority was handed over to Shorts at Sydenham. The result was a high-flying, big-winged version with powered flying controls and a navigator/camera operator in an extended nose section. This was a substantial programme aimed at an order for forty-three units, only to be cut back to twenty-three four months before the prototype PR.9 first flew, on 27 July 1958.

Canberra B.2 and PR.9 compared

	B.2	PR.9
First flown*	24 Apr 1950	27 Jul 1958
Engines	RR Avon 101	RR Avon 206
	6,500lb st	11,250lb st
Wing area	960sq ft	1,045sq ft
Max loaded weight	46,000lb	55,000lb
Max speed at 40,000ft	570mph	560mph
Initial climb	3,800ft/min	12,000ft/min
Service ceiling	48,000ft	60,000ft-plus

* First full production example.

Throughout its production life and beyond, when refurbishing airframes became a very important venture, EE and the British Aircraft Corporation (BAC) rigorously promoted and demonstrated the Canberra. The most crucial presentation was made in February 1951. Beamont piloted B.2 WD932 in a fly-off at Andrews Air Force Base, Maryland. Martin's tri-jet XB-51 was the rival, but a Douglas A-26 Invader (twin-piston), North American B-45 Tornado (four-jet) and

Canberra PR.9 XH132 after its conversion at Sydenham to SC.9 status, May 1961. The nose carried infrared trackers for the Ferranti Red Top missile, as fitted to the Lightning F.6. *Shorts*

Above: During delivery to the USA on 31 August 1951 Canberra B.2 WD940 set a new transatlantic record. Allocated the USAF serial 51-17352 and painted with 'stars n bars', it was used for a press release photo in July 1952 on a sortie out of Baltimore with the then unfinished Chesapeake Bay Bridge as a backdrop. *Martin*

Left: Built in 1951 as a B.2, WD955 was converted to T.17 electronic countermeasures status in the mid-1960s. At the tender age of 33 it returned to Samlesbury as the first of a small batch to be upgraded to T.17A; the final refurbishing contract carried out by EE/BAC/BAe. *British Aerospace*

North American AJ-1 Savage (twin-piston plus single turbojet) were flown for comparative purposes. Each of the five was to make one flight, performing a set sequence of manoeuvres within ten minutes: all four US types ran out of time. After Beamont had taken the Canberra through the entire sequence, Beamont found that he still had three and a half minutes in hand, so he freelanced with two extra routines, landing with time to spare. While its XB-51 was thoroughly outclassed, Glenn L Martin Company was in a win-win situation, it built the Canberra under licence as the B-57. With Beamont in command, B.2 WD940 was delivered to the USA on 31 August 1951 to act as a pattern for Martin. Flying from Aldergrove to Gander, a new point-to-point world record of four hours, eighteen minutes at 481mph was set. Not only had the USAF got an aircraft that exceeded its requirements, it had acquired a record-breaker. The first B-57A flew on 20 July 1953. The 'B-model' featured a fighter-like canopy but, unlike the B(I).8, the pilot and weapons system operator sat in tandem. Production was relatively swift and the final example – a B-57E – was handed over in March 1957.

The Canberra more than fulfilled the eight vital characteristics that make an industrially great aircraft, as outlined in the introduction. From the British production run, 143 Canberras were exported from new to: Ecuador, France*, India*, New Zealand, Peru*, South Africa* and Venezuela*. (Those marked * topped up with refurbished examples or airframes handed on from RAF stocks.) After the cancellation of the TSR.2 in 1965 the Canberra – the last new-build examples having been handed over in 1964 – took on new importance with conversions to other roles and the refurbishing of former RAF airframes to meet continued overseas demand. Venezuela put some of its surviving airframes through a *second* refurbishment process between 1978 and 1980 to extend their operational lives. Support of the UK military fleet was also an important source of cash flow and employment. The final conversion programme was the T.22 Buccaneer crew trainer, the first of which appeared in 1973. The last major programme for the RAF was the upgrade of surviving electronic countermeasures T.17 variants to T.17A status. This was completed when WJ981 flew out of Samlesbury on 29 June 1988 on return to the RAF; this flight also marked the official closure of the airfield after forty-eight years of use.

Supersonic spearhead

Hand-in-hand with the conception of the Canberra, EE's design department was working on an exceptionally challenging task. The Ministry of Supply expressed its faith in the new team on 12 May 1949 by placing a contract for two supersonic research aircraft to meet Experimental Requirement 103 (ER.103), designated P.1A by EE. It was apparent that a successful ER.103 could form the basis of a supersonic fighter and this requirement was formalised as Specification F.23/49. This was firmed up with an agreement on 5 August 1953 that launched the P.1B: the name Lightning was adopted in 1958.

Petter and his team benefitted from Britain's first transonic wind tunnel, which the go-ahead leadership at Warton saw as vital to EE's future. A relatively non-British, very American, approach was taken with the new jet. The P.1As were what today would be called 'proof-of-concept' airframes, with the more definitive P.1Bs emerging from an extended pre-production batch – EE was committed to the long run.

Beamont carried out an uneventful thirty-three-minute maiden sortie on 4 August 1954 in the first P.1A, WG760, from Boscombe Down. With this event, British industry made a massive leap forward in capability. On WG760's third outing Beamont took it to 30,000ft and clocked Mach 1.02. The machine did not have afterburning, that was available from January 1956. By November 1958, P.1B XA847 began sorties to give the Lightning Mach 2 service clearance – hence the Beamont quote at the beginning of this chapter.

Powered by two Armstrong Siddeley Sapphires, the P.1As allowed the concept to be proved before the P.1Bs adopted the refined layout and the intended Rolls-Royce Avons. The engines were stacked one on top of, and slightly behind, the other. An annular nose intake fed air into the turbojets and the intercept radar was mounted in a 'bullet' fairing within the airflow: all of this minimising the fuselage cross section. The wing sweep was so extreme that the ailerons were at the wing tips.

As part of the preparation for the P.1 project, Shorts was commissioned to build a slow-speed, highly swept jet, the SB.5, which first flew on 2 December 1952. The SB.5's wings could be adjusted for sweep (but *not* in flight) and the tailplane could be placed at the top of the fin or low set on the rear fuselage. The definitive format for the P.1A was finalised as 60 degrees of sweep with the low-set tailplane. (Both of the P.1As and the SB.5 are now part of the RAF Museum's collection.)

By the time the first production F.1 had its maiden flight on 29 October 1959, the Lightning was the sole survivor of the Duncan Sandys Defence White Paper of 1957 – detailed in Chapter 13. While the Canberra could be adapted to a wide variety of roles, the Lightning's development was essentially a step-by-step improvement in capability, range and performance with the increased size of the under-fuselage fuel tank being an obvious change. First flights of the main variants were as follows: F.2, 11 July 1961; F.3, 16 June 1962; and F.6, 6 October

The second P.1A, WG763, first flown on 18 July 1955. *English Electric*

Fabulous advert from the early 1960s for the 'Incomparable Lightning'. Note the pointed hand and 'missile' logo with the English Electric Aviation Group lettering. *KEC*

THE INCOMPARABLE **LIGHTNING**

THE ENGLISH ELECTRIC AVIATION CO. LTD., MARCONI HOUSE, STRAND, LONDON, W.C.2.

A MEMBER OF THE ENGLISH ELECTRIC AVIATION GROUP

1964. The Lightning's thin wing, housing the outward-retracting main undercarriage, offered little scope for hardpoints, but ingenious solutions were found for both additional fuel and weaponry. Over-wing fuel tanks dramatically altered the appearance and under-wing pylons, mounted close to the wing tips, could also carry bombs or rocket pods. The side-by-side two-seat trainer with full operational capability involved an entirely new forward fuselage. The prototype T.4, based on the F.1, took to the air on 6 May 1959 and the F.3-based T.5 had its production debut on 17 July 1964.

The third P.1A was used as a structural test airframe in a jig at Warton, from 1956. *English Electric*

Like the Canberra, the Lightning was a long-term programme for EE and BAC with upgrades and equipment refits providing additional work at Warton. Saudi Arabia and Kuwait were export customers in the late 1960s for F.6-based F.53s and T.55s. Both were high-value contracts that included training, operation and support. Kuwait received the final single-seater in September 1969 but another F.53 was completed as an attrition order and was test flown on 29 June 1972 – allowing Lightning production to encompass three decades.

Taking the lead

Petter left EE in February 1950, going to pastures new at Folland, as both managing director and chief designer. There he conceived the Midge 'bantam' fighter, which evolved into the Gnat. While the *theory* of the Lightning was Petter's, its *reality* lay entirely with his successor, Frederick William Page. His career began in 1938 as an apprentice at Hawker, under Sydney Camm at Kington-upon-Thames. Aged 28, Page joined EE in 1945, becoming assistant chief designer four years later. He had a methodical, scientific, approach to his work while embracing the radical with none of the emotional fireworks of Petter. In August 1955, Page promoted two of the A.1 team of 1949 as designers-in-charge of the Canberra, A E Ellison, and the P.1, Don Crowe.

In his unpublished memoirs, Page set down a telling judgement of the upper echelons of aviation industry management: 'It has always seemed odd to me that, particularly in UK, financial, commercial and business school people with little or no practical experience or training in the industry are considered to be suitable for the top boardroom posts whereas engineers have been regarded with suspicion. Perhaps it is because most city types and politicians

are geared to short-term thinking and buzzwords but aeronautical engineers must be creative and think long term.'

Page managed to buck the trend he was describing. In 1959 he was appointed chief executive of EE's aircraft division. He did not stop there; he was co-chair of SEPECAT, the Jaguar organisation, and then chairman of Panavia, overseeing the Tornado programme. In 1967 he was appointed as the chairman of the military division of BAC. Upon the retirement of Sir George Edwards in 1975, Page became its overall chairman and continued in this role with the advent of British Aerospace in 1977. He retired in 1982. Warton's dominance in military hardware could not have been achieved without the apprentice who started work on Hurricanes and applied the long-term view of a humble engineer. Sir Frederick William Page CBE, the father of the Lightning and guiding light of the Tornado, died on 29 May 2005, aged 88.

The experience of the Canberra and especially the Lightning put EE in pole position for the next major UK military requirement, the potentially glittering prize of GOR.339 – the TSR.2. The government was dangling this potentially lucrative programme at a rearranged industry – amalgamation was the name of the game. To prepare for this, EE set up English Electric Aviation Ltd on 9 January 1959 as a separate entity, as the remainder of the Preston-based group would continue in its diverse electrical and mechanical pursuits. From a crude design office in a former garage just fifteen years before, EE found itself negotiating *as an equal* with giants that had been in the aviation business for a century. On 1 July 1960 EE became part of the new BAC combine along with Vickers and Bristol. The shotgun marriage to conceive a state-of-the-art strike bomber was destined to be a rocky ride.

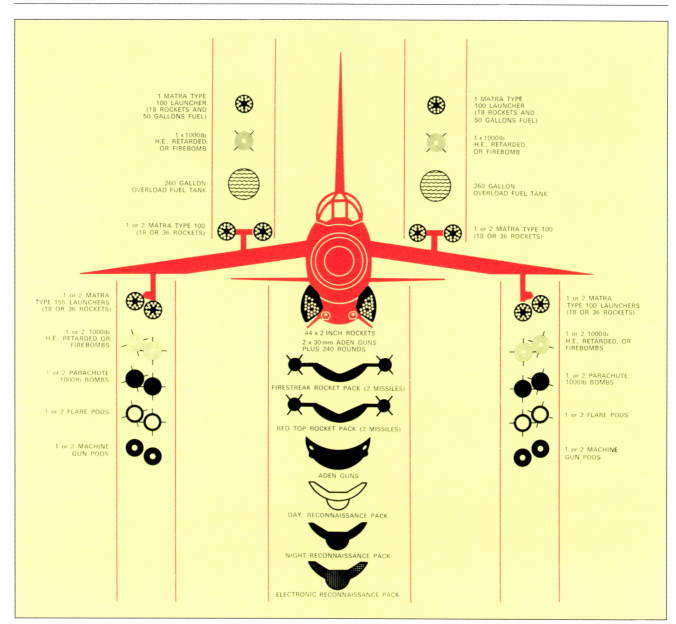

A page from a 1969 brochure, entitled *Lightning – the World's Finest Interceptor*, showing the weaponry that could be carried by an F.53 series. *KEC*

English Electric

From	To	Total	Name/Designation	Type	Engine(s)	Notes
1923	-	3	Wren	Ultralight	1 x ABC	
1924	1926	6	Kingston I II	Patrol flying boat	2 x Napier Lion	
1925	-	1	Ayr	Exp flying boat	1 x Napier Lion	[1]
1949	1964	1,693	Canberra B.2 etc	Bomber	2 x RR Avon	[2]
1955	1964	212	Canberra B(I).8	Interdictor	2 x RR Avon	[3]
1958	1960	23	Canberra PR.9	Photo-recce	2 x RR Avon	[4]
1954	1955	2	P.1A	Research	2 x AS Sapphire	
1957	1959	23	P.1B	Fighter	2 x RR Avon	[5]
1959	1972	266	Lightning	Fighter	2 x RR Avon	[6]
1959	1969	52	Lightning T.4/T.5	Advanced trainer	2 x RR Avon	[7]

Based upon: *English Electric Aircraft and their Predecessors*, Stephen Ransom and Robert Fairclough. [1] Ayr failed to fly. [2] Basic 'bomber' airframe – Mk.1 to Mk.7, Mk.12 and Mk.13. Includes new production export orders. Large number of conversions to other variants – again, see table. Sub-contracted to: Avro, Woodford (75 B.2); Handley Page, Radlett (75 B.2); Shorts, Sydenham (60 B.2, 40 B.6). Licence production: Government Aircraft Factory, Fisherman's Bend, Melbourne, Victoria, Australia (48 B.20) and by Glenn L Martin Co, Baltimore, Maryland, USA (403 as the B-57). [3] 'Fighter' forward-fuselage version. Includes new production export orders. Sub-contracted to: Shorts, Sydenham (12). [4] All built by Shorts, Sydenham. [5] Three prototypes and 20 pre-production – or DB, development batch – examples. [6] Interceptors for RAF and export: F.1/1A, F.2 (conversions to F.2A), F.3, F.6 and F.53. [7] Operational trainers for RAF and export: T.4, T.5 and T.55.

CHAPTER NINETEEN

Fleet Requirements

Fairey
1915 to 1960

'One gradually became very attached to the "Stringbag". It was utterly reliable and had no vices…'
Stanley Yeo, Swordfish pilot, 837 Squadron

LIKE ROBERT BLACKBURN, Charles Richard Fairey does not spring to mind in the same way that Alliott Verdon Roe, Geoffrey de Havilland, Frederick Handley Page or Thomas Sopwith do. While the company that carried his name, Fairey Aviation, is very well known, the scope and importance of its products is far less appreciated. Like Roe, Fairey was a prize-winning maker of flying models and determined to take part in the new-fangled world of full-scale powered flight. Like Sopwith, Fairey was a keen yachtsman and he devised several vessels. Also like Sopwith, Fairey created a group of organisations, for example Fairey Marine, established in 1946, which became a prodigious builder of cabin cruisers. Then there was Fairey Engineering, Fairey Hydraulics, Fairey Surveys, Fairey (guided) Weapons and the Belgian Avions Fairey. Unlike those mentioned above, Fairey did not pilot his creations and this may be a reason why he is not as well known; time to correct that.

Known as Richard, or 'Dick' to close associates, Hendon-born Fairey trained as an electrical engineer. Fascinated by aeroplanes, he became adept at creating flying models. While working at Finchley power station, Fairey met Edgar Isaac Everett, proprietor of Colindale electrical and mechanical engineers Everett Edgcumbe and Company. Everett was building a tractor monoplane and Fairey helped him complete it. Trials during early January 1911 at what became Hendon aerodrome met with failure; it only managed 'hops'. Later that year Fairey won a competition staged by the Kite and Model Aeroplane Association and managed to capitalise on his model-making skill, selling the rights to one of his monoplanes to the well-known London department store Gamages for a princely £300 – four times the average annual salary.

Lt John William Dunne was the gifted designer of tail-less, swept-back biplanes for the Blair Atholl Syndicate at Eastchurch, Kent. He contacted the 24-year-old Fairey declaring that the Gamages model infringed his patents. Things were resolved amicably. Recognising talent and enthusiasm, Dunne offered Fairey a job. At Eastchurch, Fairey worked alongside Harris Booth, who had cut his teeth at the National Physical Laboratory at Teddington and taught Fairey structures and stressing. Booth was later employed by the Admiralty Air Department and joined Blackburn in 1916.

Built by Blackburn at Sherburn in late 1941, Swordfish I W5856 was restored to flight by British Aerospace at Brough. It was reflown on 12 May 1993 and posed for the camera with Brough in the background before joining the Royal Navy Historic Flight at Yeovilton. *British Aerospace*

Eastchurch was also the base of the Short brothers and, in late 1912, Fairey accepted Horace Short's offer of the post of stress calculator. Fairey quickly advanced to chief stressman, works manager and chief engineer. Shorts relocated to Rochester in 1914 but Fairey was determined to go his own way by then, establishing the Fairey Aviation Company in July 1915. (To differentiate between the man and the business that came to bear his name, Richard is referred to here as CRF.)

The Short brothers clearly held CRF no malice, awarding him a sub-contract for a dozen Short 827 floatplanes. Finding space in a lorry factory at Hayes, Middlesex, Fairey initially used an airstrip at Harlington, west of Heston, for assembling and testing landplanes and Hamble Spit on the banks of the Solent for floatplanes. After the 827s, an order for 100 Sopwith 1½ Strutters was obtained. CRF embarked upon his first design, the F.2 'heavy' fighter, which reflected his experience with large Short biplanes, but it remained a one-off.

Under CRF's guidance the company weathered the post-Armistice downturn, diversifying to make car bodies for Daimler, under the name Fairey and Charles. This was not enough to avoid voluntary liquidation in 1921 but the business came bouncing back. Increasingly, CRF's involvement took the form of overseeing his design and factory staff and planning the expansion of his enterprise. The inadequacies of Harlington were solved by adopting Northolt for flight testing from 1917, but the Air Ministry would not renew the lease after 1929 and in the summer of 1930 Fairey acquired land further west at Harmondsworth to create the Great West Aerodrome (GWA). Most aircraft built at Hayes would be towed through the streets to the GWA, under police escort. GWA served until 1944, when it was singled out as the potential site of the next London Airport in place of Croydon. Today the former Fairey flight test centre lies swallowed within the concrete vastness of Heathrow. Fairey moved to Heston in 1945, although it was far from ideal. Two years later White Waltham in Berkshire was adopted and this was still in use when Westland acquired Fairey.

Hoped for large orders for the Hendon twin-engined heavy bomber put pressure on capacity at Hayes and GWA and a new facility was established at the former Crossley vehicle plant at Heaton Chapel, Manchester, in late 1935. Flight testing was initially from Barton, which was then Manchester's Airport, switching to the newly opened Ringway – today's Manchester Airport – in the summer of 1938. Also in that year Fairey began running a 'shadow factory' at the Errwood Park site, alongside Heaton Chapel, going on to build Bristol Beaufighters and Handley Page Halifaxes in quantity.

Fairey sub-contracts

Type	Total	From	To	Notes
Short 827 floatplane	12	1916	–	[1]
Sopwith 1½ Strutter	100	1916	1917	[1]
Bristol Beaufighter I/VI	500	1941	1943	[2]
Handley Page Halifax	662	1942	1945	[2] [3]
Tipsy M (Primer)	2	1948	1949	[4]
de Havilland Vampire	67	1952	1955	[5] [6]
de Havilland Vampire T.55	30	1954	1955	[5]

Based upon: *Fairey Aircraft since 1915*, H A Taylor. **[1]** Built at Hayes. **[2]** Built at Errwood Park, flown at Ringway. **[3]** Mk.IIIs, Vs and VIIs. **[4]** Tipsy M first flown at Gosselies, Belgium, in 1938. Built as the Fairey Primer by the parent company at Hamble. **[5]** Assembled at Ringway. **[6]** FB.9s for the RAF and 16 FB.52s for export. Does not include a large number of fuselage 'pods' manufactured for use in the Vampire programme as a whole.

With the outbreak of war in 1939, CRF's stature within the industry made him an ideal candidate for a difficult job; he began what turned out to be a five-year stint in the USA based at Washington DC, becoming Director-General of the British Air Commission. This was vital work, co-ordinating the needs of the British war machine and liaising at diplomatic level and across the American aircraft and aero engine manufacturers. As will be seen later, CRF's absence from Hayes had a detrimental effect on his company's production schedule. The task also had a serious effect on his health. After heart surgery, CRF returned to Britain in July 1945, taking command of Fairey again early the following year. Sir Charles Richard Fairey MBE died on 30 September 1956, aged 69 – six months after 'his' Fairey Delta 2 jet had shattered the world airspeed record. A no-nonsense boss, patron of marine craftsmanship on or over the water and unafraid to challenge norms, CRF had forged a diverse empire.

Floatplane family

Former marine engineer Frederick Duncanson was taken on to run the drawing office in 1917. Duncanson stayed with Fairey, working from 1924 under Marcel Lobelle, until 1927 when he moved on to Gloster as assistant designer. Duncanson later joined Blackburn, where his tubular spar concept was turned into reality. Taking its name from the passenger liner *Campania*, which had been converted into a seaplane carrier, the Fairey Campania took the company from a one-off to series production and set a format that was not challenged until the 1930s. A two-seat, single-engined patrol floatplane, the prototype Campania flew on 16 February 1917 and was the first British aircraft commissioned for carrier operation. Campanias took off from the flight deck care of trollies underneath the floats, which were tethered by a cable so that they could be retrieved for continued use. The floatplanes alighted alongside the *Campania*, and the later *Nairana* and *Pegasus,* to be brought on board by crane. Via the N9 and N10 of 1917, the Series III general-purpose floatplane family was born.

Conceived as a bomb-carrying patroller, the first Series III appeared in late 1917 and by the arrival of the IIID in 1920 it had evolved into a two/three-seat general-purpose floatplane/landplane. With commitments in Malta, Egypt and the Middle East and from an increasing number of ship's flights, there was a constant need for such an aircraft within the Fleet Air Arm (FAA) and the RAF. There was no requirement for a leap in performance, what was demanded was reliability and ease of maintenance. The Series III was also a huge export success.

The Series III concept lent itself to other uses. The Fremantle of 1924, intended for a round-the-world flight, was an extension of the Series III family. Named after the Australian port, it was a classic example of the Air Ministry's policy of sharing out 'one-offs' to keep design offices busy and stimulated. H A Taylor, author of the superb *Fairey Aircraft since 1915*, while discussing the Ferret of 1925 believes it was: 'Generally considered to be the missing 'E' variant'

Crowds lined the seawall at Stranraer as Fairey IIID N9777 took on fuel during the 950-mile King's Cup race on 12 August 1924. The floatplane was piloted by Fairey test pilot Norman Macmillan with Ernest Tips as crewman. *KEC*

Gordon I K2645, built in 1932, flying through a striking landscape in Iraq, circa 1937. *KEC*

Flycatcher N9619 cavorting on a sortie out of Leuchars in October 1930. The Scottish airfield was home to the RAF Training Base, which specialised in ship-based tuition. *KEC*

of the Series III. In many ways the Ferret was up against its well-established siblings, but it was a landmark as the first Fairey type with an all-metal structure while adhering to the proven fabric covering.

The Series III had morphed from wooden airframes to mixed steel tube and wood, and in 1927 adopted all-metal construction. The final development abandoned the faithful Napier Lion for the Armstrong Siddeley (AS) Panther radial as the Series IIIF Mk.V for the RAF and the Mk.VI for the FAA. The prototype, a converted IIIF Mk.IV, appeared in April 1929. By then it was high time to drop the 'Series III' label and the new version was called Gordon by the RAF and Seal by the FAA. The RAF were reviving memories of 19th-century warrior Major-General Charles George Gordon and the Navy was sticking to its naming convention of maritime wildlife. It could be argued that the Swordfish, of which more anon, was an extension of the Series III/Gordon/Seal lineage, using the same construction technique and philosophy. Such thoughts could be extended to the post-war Gannet, a Series III for the Cold War.

Fleet fighters

The first Fairey type to reach three figures was not an in-house design; it was a substantial rethink of the Sopwith Baby single-seat patrol floatplane, and to distinguish it the type was referred to as the Hamble Baby. Warplanes throughout time have suffered relentlessly increasing weight and the Sopwith Baby, introduced in 1916, was getting a reputation as challenging to fly from anything other than tranquil waters. Among many innovations, CRF devised the variable camber wing, an early version of the flap and it was introduced on the Hamble Baby. Hinged from the rear spar, this trailing edge flap ran from the wing root to the aileron. A hand wheel in the cockpit allowed the pilot to adjust the incidence of the trailing edge, which increased the lift available on take-off and landing. After modifying a Kingston-built Baby, Fairey was rewarded with a production order, including a sub-contract to Parnall, and a lucrative patent.

The 27ft 9in span of the Hamble Baby contrasted dramatically with the 139ft of the N.4 flying boats, *Atalanta* and *Titania*, tackled with limited success from 1918. With the four Rolls-Royce Condors, arranged in tandem as two tractors and two pushers, the ponderous 'boat was the largest of its kind when it was conceived and it was the 1920s before either of them flew. Fairey never revisited flying boats – floatplanes were its forte.

The single-seater format of the Baby was revisited with the Flycatcher fleet fighter, first flown on 28 November 1922. This was a demanding requirement, the biplane requiring easy conversion to wheeled undercarriage for operation from land or carriers, or floats or even amphibious floats, fitted with wheels. With a tubular steel forward fuselage but otherwise conventional wooden structure, 195 Flycatchers were manufactured up to 1930, making it Fairey's second most successful design of the era behind the Series III. The all-new and all-metal Flycatcher II of 1926 failed to attract an order.

Shot in the arm

In March 1923 the prototype Fawn, initially intended for army co-operation, had its debut. The Air Ministry chopped and changed its requirements and it was accepted as the RAF's first all-new light bomber – replacing the venerable Airco DH.9A. Inconsistent ministerial whims infuriated CRF and influenced his later thinking. A change of 'policy' to no longer place fuel tanks within the fuselage, to reduce the risk of fire, required a costly redesign. Streamlined tanks were positioned, port and starboard, on top of the inboard upper wing. A cynic at the time observed that these were: 'perfectly positioned to rain ignited petrol down upon the crew'. When production ended in 1926 a total of seventy-four Fawns had been built in four versions.

The Schneider Trophy was hosted by Britain in 1923 and CRF was wide-eyed at the sleek American Curtiss CR-3 biplanes, one of which won at a sizzling 177mph – 32mph faster than the 1922 victor. A fact-finding tour of the USA led to CRF concluding a licence agreement for the Curtiss D-12 V-12 that powered the CR-3s, Curtiss-Reed adjustable-pitch propellers and patented wing sections. Tired of Air Ministry meddling, Fairey created a private-venture day bomber that would make the Fawn look pedestrian. The first Fox took to the air on 3 January 1925. It did everything the Fawn could do, but was nearly 50mph faster – an incredible leap in performance.

As the Fox wasn't officially sanctioned, it was going to be difficult to get it accepted. The Chief of the Air Staff, ACM Sir Hugh Trenchard, visited Northolt on 28 July 1925 and watched the Fox being put through its paces. The story goes that Trenchard was so impressed he ordered a squadron of them there and then. Reporting later to the Secretary of State for the Air, Sir Samuel Hoare MP, Trenchard said: 'The industry needs a shot in the arm. I've just administered one, and I want you to defend my action in parliament.' Trenchard got his way: Fairey built twenty-eight of the revolutionary bombers, but no more.

Fox I J9026 was used for most of its life on Rolls-Royce Kestrel trials from Martlesham Heath, 1927 to 1934. *KEC*

Illustrated on the cowling of a Buccaneer S.2, the head of a red fox was adopted by 12 Squadron, the only RAF unit to fly the Fairey Fox. Approved by King George VI in February 1937, the badge had the appropriate motto 'Leads the Field'. *Roy Bonser*

Fairey was not finished with sleek aerodynamics and the Curtiss D-12. On 9 November 1925 the Firefly, a single-seat fighter clearly from the same mould as the Fox, had its maiden flight. Predictably, this private venture went nowhere. All was not lost; Specification F.20/27 sought an interceptor and soon the Rolls-Royce F.XI engine – the nascent Kestrel – was stipulated. The result was a considerable refinement over its already advanced predecessor. The part steel tube, part wood Firefly II appeared in February 1929 but was then transformed to an all-metal airframe, flying again on 6 January 1930. Taylor's *Fairey Aircraft since 1915* describes a classic case of 'How to Win the Sale' when test pilot Christopher Staniland took the Firefly II to Belgium in July 1930 to demonstrate it in competition with the Czech Avia BH.33 and the French Dewoitine D.27. 'Staniland and the Fairey representatives showed their confidence in the [Firefly II] by permitting it to be flown in turn by sixteen Belgian fighter pilots … The culminating trial involved a demonstration, using recording gear, of a powered dive … the Firefly was the only aircraft whose pilot and sponsors agreed to make this test …' A contract for twenty-five was signed with local production to follow. Avions Fairey was about to be born, as will be detailed below.

Fairey is believed to have lost a fortune developing the Fox and the Firefly. Estimates vary, but a middle-of-the-road value of £20,000 would equate to £1,100,000 in present day values. That 'twenty grand' is best understood as Fairey Aviation's 'fighting fund' for *all* of 1925. The company was fighting entrenched thinking from Whitehall and the rest of the industry by circumventing procedure *and* using a foreign engine. (Fairey intended to build the D-12 in Britain as the Felix, but with such a small order for the Fox I, it was not economical.) It is likely that Hawker's Sydney Camm was enthused by the thinking that had brought about the Fox: his ground-breaking Hart had its debut in June 1928. Even the Air Ministry began to take notice of the initiative, realising that, occasionally, manufacturers might be more in tune with cutting-edge technology than Whitehall. In 1955 CRF declared: 'I think that we can claim that the remarkable Fairey Fox of 1925 altered the whole trend of design of military aircraft.'

Cosmopolitan talent

The Fox was untrammelled by blinkered thinking; using the best engine for the job and careful attention to streamlining paid dividends in performance. A good example was a stowage bay for the gunner's Lewis machine gun and fairing that tucked it out of the slipstream when not in use. The Fox was the result of a potent, but brief, pairing of chief designer Marcel Jules Odilion 'Bluebelle' Lobelle and Pandia Antonio Ralli, head of the technical department. These two gifted men worked under chief engineer Major Thomas Morgan Barlow. He had been chief technical officer at the Aeroplane and Armament Experimental Establishment (A&AEE), Martlesham Heath, and had served with the Royal Naval Air Service.

Lobelle was not the only Belgian influence on Fairey, as we shall see. Born at Courtrai, he was badly wounded during the capture of Ostend in October 1914 and spent a lot of time in hospitals in Britain. He eventually elected to stay in the country but it may have been as late as 1928 before he was naturalised.

Joining Martinsyde as a draughtsman in August 1917, Lobelle rubbed shoulders with Sydney Camm, who worked in the stores. In 1918 he was tempted to Byfleet in Surrey, where Walter Barling was transforming W G Tarrant Limited's Tabor 'Berlin bomber' from a four-engined biplane into a six-engined (four tractors and two pushers) *triplane*. Assembled at Farnborough, the Tarrant Tabor crashed with fatal consequences during its maiden take-off on 26 May 1919.

Wholly disenchanted by his time with Tarrant, Lobelle moved to Fairey not long afterwards and in 1924 was appointed chief designer; his creations running from the Fox all the way to the Barracuda. In the summer of 1940 Lobelle was offered the post of technical director and chief designer at the Slough-based sub-contractor R Malcolm Ltd. Following investment from Noel Mobbs (Sir Noel from 1948), the firm was restructured as ML Aviation in October 1946, taking the initials from Mobbs and Lobelle. The company developed an incredible range of products, including the famous 'Malcolm hood' clear-vision fighter canopy, weapons dispensers, ejection seats, target drones, target-towing winches and, from 1954, the ML Utility inflatable wing aircraft: all stemming from Lobelle's fertile mind. ML Aviation was absorbed into Cobham plc in 1997. Marcel Jules Odilion Lobelle, creator of the Swordfish, died on 30 August 1967, aged 74.

Trained as an electrical engineer at Lausanne in Switzerland, Ralli took up a post with Fairey in 1916, soon heading the technical department. He was regarded by all around him as having outstanding ability, specialising in high-speed aerodynamics and airscrews. Ralli and Lobelle became a tightly knit team. Aged just 41, Pandia Antonio Ralli died in 1930 amid much sadness at Hayes. His place as head of the technical department was taken by David Leonard Hollis Williams from Hawker. Williams departed in 1934 bound for General Aircraft, handing the baton on to Robert Talbot Youngman, the pioneer of Fairey-Youngman flaps. In late 1942 Williams returned to the fold, this time as chief engineer – his 'CV' can be found in Chapter 21.

Belgian offshoot

As mentioned above, determined marketing and piloting resulted in a contract for twenty-five Firefly II fighters for the Belgian Air Force to be built at Hayes. Belgium was keen to expand its own aircraft industry and Fairey was happy to not just grant a licence, but to set up a subsidiary venture. Société Anonyme Belge Avions Fairey was established on 12 September 1931 at Gosselies, near Charleroi. The number of Firefly IIs completed at Gosselies is open to debate – see the biplanes table – but what is certain is that these paved the way for the very advanced Fox II.

In the same manner as the Firefly I evolved into a Rolls-Royce powered Mk.II, the Fox was rethought in response to Air Ministry Specification 12/26 for a high-speed day bomber. Development took its time, fitted with a Rolls-Royce F.XI (later Kestrel), the prototype all-metal airframe Fox IIM took to the air on 25 October 1929. By then Hawker had secured the contract with the Hart but, released from Air Ministry strictures, Fairey could offer the Fox II wherever it wished. The Hayes production line benefitted from an order for six floatplane versions from Peru and a dozen landplanes for Belgium. The latter were the vanguard for 120 from Gosselies, including a pair of Mk.VIs supplied to Switzerland. The first Belgian-built Fox had its debut on 21 April 1933 and the last was rolled out in May 1939.

Civilian registered as G-ADIF, the first Fantôme, June 1935.
Peter Green Collection

Lobelle surpassed himself with his final biplane aimed at a Belgian requirement. The Fantôme (phantom) and the Féroce (literally, fierce) were one and the same; if adopted by Belgium it would have carried the latter name. An elegant single-seat biplane fighter powered by a 925hp liquid-cooled Hispano-Suiza 12, it could pack considerable punch with a 20mm Oerlikon cannon firing through the propeller hub. The prototype flew for the first time from the GWA on 6 June 1935 and three other airframes were sent to Gosselies for fitting out. Two of these were supplied to the Soviet Union, while the other was ordered by the British Air Ministry, for evaluation. By 1940 Gosselies was involved with a fighter of very different capabilities, having taken a licence for the Hawker Hurricane. Only one had been completed and flown before the German blitzkrieg was unleashed on Belgium: the Gosselies factory was bombed on 10 May 1940.

Gosselies reopened in October 1946 and by the beginning of the new decade was a sub-contractor in turn on Gloster Meteors, Hawker Hunters and Lockheed F-104 Starfighters for the Belgian and other European air arms. In 1964, after Fairey Aviation had been acquired by Westland, the enterprise took on the name Fairey SA, continuing its sub-contracting activities with Dassault Mirage 5s. The Fairey Group acquired Britten-Norman (Bembridge) Ltd on 31 August 1972 and Fairey Britten-Norman (FBN) was born, building Islanders and Trislanders. Troubles with the General Dynamics F-16 Fighting

Falcon European programme and heavier than anticipated costs incurred to re-establish Islander production in Belgium took a heavy toll on the fortunes of Fairey SA and FBN. The latter called in the receiver on 3 August 1977. The Belgian government intervened to save Fairey SA, setting up Société Nationale de Construction Aérospatiale SA (SONACA) to ensure the F-16 business. Today, SONACA remains active in aerospace structures work.

There is another Belgian connection for Fairey. In 1915 Ernest Oscar Tips, a 22-year-old, born at Temse near Antwerp, escaped to Britain. Along with his brother, Maurice, Tips had designed and built an unsuccessful biplane in 1909. In Britain he approached CRF and was put in charge of the erecting department at Hamble. Tips returned to his native Belgium, becoming the manager of Avions Fairey in 1931. He also resumed his design ambitions and, under the tongue-in-cheek Tipsy brand, created a series of light aircraft that were built in association with Avions Fairey. These were the single-seat S.1 and S.2 monoplanes of 1934 and 1936 respectively; the two-seat tourer Tipsy B of 1937 and Tipsy M trainer of 1938. Both the S.2 and the B were licence built in small numbers in Britain. In 1940 Tips was again in Britain, taking on the role of chief engineer at the Fairey-run Burtonwood Repair Depot, near Warrington. In 1943 he became chief experimental and research engineer at Hayes and Heston before returning to his homeland in 1945.

In 1948 Fairey turned to its Belgian sister company for the expertise it lacked in light aircraft. The Tipsy M was adapted to meet RAF Specification 8/48 to replace de Havilland (DH) Tiger Moths. Called the Primer by Fairey, two were built at Hamble as a 'reverse' sub-contract. The competition was won by DHC, who entered its Canadian sister's superb Chipmunk.

At Gosselies, the Tipsy B was redesigned as a cabin monoplane and the single-seat Junior was launched in 1948; both entered limited production. The final Tips creation was the diminutive single-seat Nipper, which first appeared in December 1957 and was made in some numbers. Tips retired from his management role at Gosselies in 1960 and the rights to the Nipper were acquired by Nipper Aircraft in Britain in 1966. A total of thirty-five were manufactured on that company's behalf by Slingsby at Kirkbymoorside, the first examples using Belgian-built fuselages.

Engine diversion

Although plans to produce the Curtiss D-12 engine in Britain as the Felix failed to materialise, CRF still held hopes to have a powerplant division. In 1931 former Royal Flying Corps pilot and Air Ministry liquid-cooled engine specialist Captain Graham Forsyth was appointed as chief engine designer. The P.12 Prince, a 670hp 12-cylinder vee-format, ran for the first time in 1934, but failed to find an application. This was followed in 1938 by the mammoth 2,240hp P.24 Monarch, consisting of two self-contained 12-cylinder blocks forming a 'double', H-format, engine driving co-axial propellers. The P.24 was intended to provide twin-engined power in a single-engined airframe.

A Monarch was fitted to a Fairey Battle test bed and flown on 30 June 1939. Because of this, some sources have floated the idea that the P.24 was intended to transform the Battle; this was not the case. In the USA, Republic considered the P.24 as a possible powerplant for its in-development P-47 Thunderbolt. To this end the Battle test bed was shipped to the USA in December 1941. In the meantime the prototype Thunderbolt had its maiden flight on 6 May 1941 powered by a 2,000hp Pratt & Whitney R-2800 radial. Nothing more came of the American venture. Only a handful of P.12s and P.24s were built, an exceptionally costly exercise for Fairey. The P.24 was intended to be able to run as a 'single' powerplant, with one side shut down. It is ironic that Fairey had created an engine of the same concept as the AS Double Mamba turboprop that powered its Gannet just over a decade later.

Heaton Chapel-built Battle I K9370 fitted with the awesome Fairey P.24 engine and co-axial propellers at Wright Field, Dayton, Ohio, in 1942. Note the US Army Air Force markings on the rudder and under the wings. *USAF*

Irreplaceable Swordfish

Through the III Series, the Gordon and the Seal, Fairey had accrued vast experience of biplane workhorses and so the steps that led to the redoubtable Swordfish were relatively easy. Specification G.4/31 whipped up an incredible fight to replace the Gordon and the Westland Wallace. This contest is detailed in Chapter 37 as Vickers was the ultimate winner. Lobelle's entrant for G.4/31 followed the Series III/Gordon lineage and provided the basis for a two- or three-seater that met a Greek navy need for a torpedo strike and spotter-reconnaissance aircraft. A private-venture prototype known as the TSR.I, or the 'Greek Machine', first flew on 21 March 1933. Originally with an AS Panther radial, a Bristol Pegasus radial was substituted in June – this was a masterstroke.

Lobelle adopted a similar airframe when the Air Ministry released Specification S.9/30 for a spotter–reconnaissance type with a Rolls-Royce Kestrel and a central float with wing-tip 'outers'. A contract was given to Fairey for a prototype, which flew on 22 February 1934. Thankfully S.9/30 was not taken further: the Kestrel was unlikely to thrive in harsh oceanic conditions.

Staniland was lucky to escape from the TSR.I on 11 September 1933 when it entered a flat spin from which recovery was deemed impossible. Lobelle designed another version, aimed at the more refined S.15/33. This had a longer fuselage, spin recovery strakes in front of the tailplanes and a Pegasus IIIM3 of 690hp. This was the TSR.II: a perfect piece of evolution, matching benign flying characteristics with an engine that was simple, robust and reliable. An order was placed in the spring of 1935 and the first production Swordfish took to the skies on the last day of 1935. Nobody could have predicted that 2,000-plus would follow all the way to 1944. The quote by a Swordfish pilot at the header of this chapter explains why a radial-engined, open cockpit biplane – nicknamed 'Stringbag' because its profusion of flying wires – could hold its own in what had become the jet age. Lobelle's Swordfish didn't need more speed or sleeker looks to operate from thrashing carrier decks in atrocious weather across inhospitable seas; its crews needed it to be 'utterly reliable' and have 'no vices'. In order to help Fairey concentrate on the Barracuda and Firefly the vast majority of Swordfishes were 'Blackfish'; built by Blackburn at Sherburn in Elmet.

The two-seat, all-metal, catapult-capable Seafox fleet reconnaissance biplane had its debut on 27 May 1936. It was designed *and* built at Hamble – a first for Fairey – and was the only production aircraft to utilise the 16-cylinder H-format Napier Rapier. The Seafox's ability to look over the horizon was quickly eclipsed by radar and it might well have been Fairey's last biplane. When tackling Specification

Five Swordfish of the Gosport-based Torpedo Training Unit, May 1937. *KEC*

Albacores of 817 Squadron, based at Hatson, 1942. *KEC*

S.41/36 of early 1937, Lobelle drew up monoplane and biplane formats for what became the Albacore. The prototype flew on 12 December 1938 and featured all the refinements that the Swordfish lacked. Had war not broken out the Albacore – named after a tunny, or tuna, fish – would have carried out its task, replacing Swordfish across the fleet.

As Swordfishes continued to roll out of the Sherburn factory in November 1942 when the last Albacore was assembled at Hayes, the general conclusion is that the latter was a failure. With a production run of 800 and a successful operational career, that cannot be the case. It might well have been that Sherburn would have switched to Albacores as Hayes geared up in 1943 to churn out Fireflies. Moving the jigs and retraining workers would have been expensive and time-consuming; the Albacore did not offer sufficient increase in performance and reliability to merit this: the Swordfish prevailed.

Monoplane debut

Fairey's first monoplane was a challenging commission from the Air Ministry's Directorate of Technical Development. It was intended as an ultra-long-range record-breaker, but to throw the Treasury off the scent it was referred to as a 'Postal' aeroplane. Eventually the RAF came clean and designated it, prosaically, the Long Range Monoplane. Williams produced a clean-looking monoplane with a span of 82ft. Sqn Ldr Arthur Jones-Williams was allocated as the RAF's pilot for the record attempt and he took J9479 for its maiden flight on 14 November 1928 and conducted most of the testing. On 24 April 1929 Jones-Williams and Flt Lt N H Jenkins took off from Cranwell on the first non-stop flight to India, landing at Karachi after fifty hours, thirty-seven minutes and 4,130 miles. The pair embarked again on 16 December 1929, this time bound for South Africa. The large monoplane impacted on high ground to the south of Tunis in North Africa, killing its crew. A second, improved, example flew on 30 June 1931. Sqn Ldr O R Gayford and Flt Lt G E Nicholetts departed Cranwell on 6 February 1933 and landed at Walvis Bay, north of Cape Town after 5,341 miles and fifty-seven hours, twenty-seven minutes in the air, capturing the record that Jones-Williams and Jenkins had tried to achieve.

Manoeuvring the 82ft span of the second Long-Range Monoplane, K1991, out of a hangar, circa 1932. Fox IA in the background. *KEC*

Fairey chief test pilot Norman Macmillan took the prototype Night Bomber for its maiden flight on 25 November 1930. In terms of design, it was a major departure: with a span of 101ft 9in, it turned out to be the largest type ever built by the company. The Air Ministry was hoping to place a three-figure order for what would be the RAF's first cantilever monoplane heavy bomber, so it was worth the risk. It was October 1934 before the Night Bomber was named Hendon.

A dual-control Hendon, very likely K5092, at Marham in May 1938.
Peter Green Collection

Under the naming convention of the time, this was after the town and 'coincidentally' CRF's birthplace, *not* the aerodrome as some authors claim. The Hendon set the format for all the monoplane 'heavies' that served with the RAF through World War Two. The fuselage was deep enough for a bomb bay that could accommodate two of the RAF's latest weapon, the 1,000-pounder. There were three turrets, manually operated, in nose, dorsal and tail positions.

The prototype overran while landing on 15 March 1931 and was badly damaged: nobody was hurt. During rebuild it was given a comprehensive and costly redesign: Rolls-Royce Kestrels replaced the Bristol Jupiter radials, the wing's aerofoil section was changed and rods instead of cables (which stretched) actuated the flying controls. This transformation is believed to have cost in the region of £11,000: Fairey was offering production Hendons for £12,760 each. Despite the changes, evaluation at the A&AEE favoured the Handley Page Heyford and 124 were eventually ordered. Fairey received a consolation 'prize' for fourteen Hendons, which were built at Heaton Chapel and almost certainly not economically viable: follow-on orders for sixty-two were cancelled.

Battle and Fulmar

Named after the town in Sussex where nearby in 1066 Britain succumbed to invasion, the Battle is widely regarded as a dismal failure. The prototype had its maiden flight on 10 March 1936 and half of the production run was sub-contracted under the 'shadow' scheme to Austin Motors from 1938. The Battle was a modern, monoplane rethink of the incredibly successful Hawker Hart and Hind line of biplane light bombers. That concept worked – albeit largely untried – in the late 1920s and early '30s but was eclipsed by rapidly changing technologies. When war broke out in September 1939 the RAF had slightly more than 1,000 Battles on charge, numerically an impressive strike force, and there was nothing to put in its place. Branding the Battle a disaster is to decry the incredible valour shown by the aircrew that did what they could to face the German blitzkrieg of May 1940 and avert another invasion of Britain.

The Battle lent itself to other tasks; as mentioned earlier it served as an engine test bed, but it found greater application as a two-cockpit trainer and as a target tug. Lobelle also transformed the airframe into a carrier-borne, all-weather fighter, the pioneering Fulmar. There was an interim step in this evolution: Specification P.4/34 was looking for a light day bomber with dive attack potential. Cleaning up the Battle, giving it shorter wings and inward retracting undercarriage (the Battle's wing accommodated bulky bomb 'cells', the P.4/34 carried its single 500-pounder under the centre section) produced a relatively nimble performer. The first of two P.4/34s flew on 13 January 1937. While the RAF requirement vaporised, the Danish navy was keen on licence manufacture but that was curtailed by the German invasion of 9 April 1940.

Above: The prototype Battle, K4303, over the Great West Aerodrome, 1936. *Fairey*

Right: The first Fulmar, N1854, was kept on as a 'hack' by Fairey and was displayed at the Farnborough airshow in September 1962. It was flown for the last time on 18 December 1962, when it was donated to the Fleet Air Arm Museum. *Roy Bonser*

Heaton Chapel-built Barracuda II P9926 serving as a torpedo trainer with 785 Squadron at Crail, 1944. *KEC*

An urgent FAA requirement was enshrined in Specification O.8/38 for a two-place fleet fighter. The Navy had woken up to the need to defend its vessels, having abandoned the concept when it withdrew the Flycatcher in 1934. P.4/34 was perfect as the basis for this need: eight machine guns were put into the wings to create a formidable opponent. (Battle crews had to content themselves with *one* fixed forward-firing machine gun and another flexibly mounted in the rear compartment.) The FAA leapt at this design and in 1938 named it Fulmar, after an oceanic gull. The Fulmar programme was fulfilled by the Heaton Chapel plant and the P.4/34 prototypes meant that there was no need for another prototype. The first production Fulmar, N1854, took to the air at Ringway on 4 January 1940 and survives at the Fleet Air Arm Museum at Yeovilton.

Barracuda and Firefly

Lobelle's final design to enter production with Fairey was the Barracuda, ordered in quantity in March 1939 but only entering service in the summer of 1942. Specification S.24/37 sought a three-crew, carrier-borne aircraft capable of torpedo strike, dive-bombing and reconnaissance – effectively *another* Swordfish replacement! The Barracuda, named after a vicious tropical fish, was intended to be powered by the Rolls-Royce Exe, a 24-cylinder X-format engine that was not proceeded with. The Merlin 30 was substituted – no mean feat in terms of redesign and all of the 'plumbing' associated with it. Large Fairey-Youngman flaps were fitted behind the trailing edge of the wing. The prototype flew from the GWA on 7 December 1940, while manufacture was to take place at Heaton Chapel. During the long development phase, the tailplane was moved to a high-set position on the fin. In late 1944 the Barracuda gained another

powerplant, the Rolls-Royce Griffon 30, to create the radar-equipped Mk.V. The first production examples appeared in November 1945 and orders were drastically reduced.

By the time the prototype Barracuda flew its designer, Lobelle, had moved on to pastures new. As noted earlier, CRF was in the USA for much of the war. Heaton Chapel was slipping in the timetable; it was not until the summer of 1942 that Barracuda deliveries began. At Hayes, manufacture of Albacores was tardy and the Firefly was well behind schedule. This was a serious concern to the Ministry of Aircraft Production, which took the extreme sanction of installing G E Marden as a 'supremo' to sort things. Among the 'fixes' was a system of 'project teams' instigated by Williams, who had returned to Fairey in late 1942 as chief engineer. This was an American procedure, with all members of the design team remaining dedicated to the progress of the aircraft until such time as it was 'signed off' and rolling out of the factory. Prior to this, glitches in test flying or on the production line were normally referred back to a designer or engineer who was already engaged on another, also pressing, project.

After an angst-ridden start, including suffering from problems with the Rolls-Royce Griffon and self-generated production delays, the Firefly – the company's second use of that name – became a truly multi-role workhorse for the FAA and, later, export customers well into the 1950s. It was conceived by Herbert Eugene Chaplin MBE – inevitably nicknamed 'Charlie'. Originally with Parnall, Chaplin began with Fairey as a draughtsman in 1930, taking the reins as chief designer in 1940; retiring in 1957. The Firefly I prototype had its maiden flight on 22 December 1941. The very last, a U.8 drone, was flown – by an on-board pilot – from Ringway on 3 March 1956.

A Firefly FR.5 of 810 Squadron taking the wire on the deck of HMS *Theseus* during the Korean conflict, 1951. *Dave Dawes*

Naval revival

On 5 July 1945 Fairey flew an all-new prototype, the Spearfish. Despite its 'fish' suffix, it was a successor to the Barracuda, not the 'Stringbag'. With its weapon load contained in a bomb bay and a remotely controlled gun barbette supplying rearward defence, the all-up weight of the Spearfish was 21,882lb, contrasting with the Barracuda II's maximum of 14,100lb. Only four of these monsters were built and more than a hundred were cancelled.

With new variants of the Firefly and a healthy amount of reconditioning and conversion of older examples to tackle, and the Barracuda V in limited production, there was enough to keep Hayes and Heaton Chapel busy. Nevertheless, the need for a new long-term type was pressing. With Fairey's prowess in creating naval aircraft, it was not surprising that the three-seat carrier-borne anti-submarine Gannet beat the Blackburn YB.1 in the 1951 fly-off. The Gannet combined search and strike roles in one airframe and, thanks to its AS Double Mamba turboprop, could loiter on 'half' of the engine, increasing time on-station. The prototype flew on 19 September 1949 from Aldermaston, presumably for privacy. With the outbreak of the Korean War in June 1950 several programmes were determined as 'Super-Priority' and the Gannet became one of these. The first production AS.1 had its maiden flight on 9 June 1953 and both Hayes and Heaton Chapel manufactured Gannets. The improved AS.4 had its debut on 13 April 1956. Trainer versions of the AS.1 and AS.4 were the T.2 and T.4, respectively. Australia, Indonesia and West Germany also ordered both anti-submarine and trainer variants.

Gannet AS.1s – with a T.2 fifth from the camera – lined up at Culdrose in 1955. They belonged to 817 Squadron, Royal Australian Navy, and were awaiting embarkation on HMAS *Melbourne* after working up on type. *RNAS Culdrose*

Gannet AEW.3 XL472 of Brawdy-based 849 Squadron at Yeovilton, September 1967. *Roy Bonser*

The airborne early warning radar picket version, the AEW.3 was essentially a new design. An all-new fuselage accommodated two radar operators, while the bulky AN/APS-20 search radar was housed under the centre section. The fin and rudder were also new and the AEW.3 sat on a taller undercarriage. The first example served as an aerodynamic prototype and had its maiden flight on 20 August 1958,

Fairey biplanes

From	To	Total	Name/Designation	Type	Engine(s)	Notes
1917	-	1	F.2	'Heavy' fighter	1 x RR Falcon	
1917	1918	62	Campania	Carrier floatplane	1 x RR Eagle	[1]
1917	1918	190	Hamble Baby	Scout floatplane	1 x Clerget	[2]
1917	-	2	N9/N10	Carrier floatplane	1 x RR Falcon	[3]
1918	1919	115	IIIA, 'B, 'C	Carrier bomber	1 x Sunbeam Maori	
1918	1922	2	N.4	Patrol flying boat	4 x RR Condor	[4]
1920	1923	6	Pintail	Fighter floatplane	1 x Napier Lion	
1920	1926	247	IIID Mk.I, II, III	Military GP	1 x Napier Lion	
1922	1930	195	Flycatcher	Shipborne fighter	1 x AS Jaguar	
1923	1926	75	Fawn	Day bomber	1 x Napier Lion	[5]
1924	-	1	Fremantle	Long-range special	1 x RR Condor	
1925	1926	3	Ferret	Shipborne recce	1 x Bristol Jupiter	
1925	1929	28	Fox I	Day bomber	1 x Curtiss D-12	
1925	-	1	Firefly I	Fighter	1 x Curtiss D-12	
1926	-	1	Flycatcher II	Shipborne fighter	1 x AS Jaguar	
1926	1932	622	IIIF	Military GP	1 x Napier Lion	[6]
1929	1933	88	Firefly II/III	Fighter	1 x RR F.XI	[7] [8]
1929	-	1	Fleetwing	Shipborne recce	1 x RR.FXI	[7]
1929	1939	141	Fox II, III, VI, VIII	Fighter	1 x RR Kestrel	[9]
1931	-	290	Gordon/Seal	GP/Recce	1 x AS Panther	[10]
1934	-	1	G.4/31	Military GP	1 x Bristol Pegasus	
1933	1934	1/1	TSR.I/S.9/30	Naval prototypes	1 x RR Kestrel	[11]
1934	1944	2,392	TSR.II/Swordfish	Torpedo strike	1 x Bristol Pegasus	[12]
1935	1937	4	Fantôme/Féroce	Fighter	1 x Hispano-Suiza 12	[13]
1936	1938	65	Seafox	Shipborne recce	1 x Napier Rapier	
1938	1942	800	Albacore	Torpedo strike	1 x Bristol Taurus	

Based upon: *Fairey Aircraft since 1915*, H A Taylor. **[1]** Includes 12 sub-contracted to Barclay, Curle and Co, Glasgow. **[2]** Also sub-contracted to Parnall – 140; 74 of which were completed as Baby Convert landplanes. **[3]** RNAS serials as designations: N10 became Series III (Fairey III) prototype. **[4]** N119 *Atalanta*, hull built by May, Harden and May, Hythe; remainder by Dick, Kerr, Lytham (Chapter 18); not flown until 1923. N129 *Titania*, hull built by 'Fyffes' at Glasgow (Elders and Fyffes?), completed at Hamble 1923; not flown until 1925. **[5]** Airframes built as 'spares' not included. **[6]** Mks I, II, III, IVC steel tube/wood construction; Mks. IIIM and IVM all-metal. Includes three Fairey Queen target-drones. Does not include airframes finished as Gordons on the Hayes production line. **[7]** Rolls-Royce F.XIS later named Kestrel. **[8]** About 63 built by Avions Fairey at Gosselies, Belgium. **[9]** Twenty-one built at Hayes, including 6 Mk.IV floatplanes for Peru; remainder by Avions Fairey at Gosselies. **[10]** Production split: 186 Gordon/104 Seal. Does not include in-service conversions from IIIF to Gordon. **[11]** TSR.I with Bristol Pegasus. Swordfish predecessors, see narrative. **[12]** Blackburn built 1,699 Swordfish from December 1940, all others by Fairey. **[13]** See narrative.

from Northolt. The pace of the programme was such that a fully equipped machine joined the trials fleet just five months later. Gannet AEW.3s were taken by road to White Waltham from Hayes for assembly and testing. The final Mk.3 was delivered to the FAA in June 1963, under the aegis of Westland. This was the last Fairey-designed aircraft to serve with the Royal Navy, the first having been built forty-six years earlier.

Delta swansong

As it turned out, the last Fairey fixed-wing types were experimental deltas. Since it was set up in 1915, the company had not picked up a research-based contract for a specific aircraft. The FD.1 was a low-speed vehicle for an ambitious project to create a vertically launched turbojet-with-rocket-boost interceptor, similar to the Luftwaffe's purely rocket-powered Bachem Ba 349 Natter of 1944. Fairey engaged in trials with scale model rockets to explore the concept, including launches at the Woomera range in Australia from 1949. Built at Heaton Chapel, the dumpy-looking FD.1 was put through taxi runs at Ringway in May 1950 before it was moved by road to Boscombe Down, where it made its first flight on 12 March 1951. By that time the vertical launch element had been dropped from the project. The jet was used for delta wing research until a landing accident on 6 February 1956 put paid to its brief career.

Specification ER.103 of 1947 gave rise to a pair of FD.2s – most often referred to as 'Delta 2s'. Long before Concorde, the FD.2s had a nose section that drooped 10 degrees to give the pilot a better view while landing: this innovation had been suggested by Chaplin. In charge of the Delta 2 was Robert Lickley, as technical director and chief engineer

and previously with the Royal Aircraft Establishment. The Gannet programme rightly took precedence and it was not until 6 October 1954 that the first FD.2 took off. Peter Twiss flew the iconic delta to an average of 1,132mph on 10 March 1956, smashing the previous speed record by 310mph. (The first FD.2 was converted into the BAC 221 ogee wing test bed, flying in 1964. Today, both the BAC 221 and the second FD.2 are preserved, at Yeovilton and Cosford, respectively.)

Derived from a project for a 'vertical riser', the FD.1 research delta VX350, mid-1951. *Fairey*

The second 'Delta 2', WG777, on display at Finningley, 1968. *KEC*

The Gannet was profitable for Fairey, but during the 1950s the company failed to achieve another long-runner. Specifications such as ER.103 were intended to 'push the envelope' with research projects that would benefit the industry in general in keeping it abreast of the state-of-the-art. The Air Ministry, Ministry of Supply and the like also used such contracts to keep underused design offices 'alive' to avoid any one manufacturer assuming a monopoly of expertise. By the 1970s such awards became rare with the onus transferring to industry to fund its own initiatives.

Breaking the world record brought huge prestige to Fairey, but it did not translate into a flush order book. The lessons learned from both of the deltas gave Fairey the experience to come up with the large, twin-engined delta F.155 long-range fighter, but the Sandys Defence White Paper of 1957 put paid to the project. All now depended on the Rotodyne compound helicopter.

High-risk rotorcraft

As World War Two was drawing to a close Fairey decided that it needed to try new regimes and helicopters were an obvious target. It was not alone in this; Bristol, Saro and Westland also took this route. In August 1945 the 42-year-old James Bennett approached Fairey with his concept of a tip-jet-driven autogyro. He had worked with G and J Weir on rotorcraft in the early 1930s, before transferring to Cierva in 1936 and designing the C.40 Rota II. During the war he was engaged by the Airborne Forces Experimental Establishment and for a while with the US Army Air Technical Service Command. Bennett was put in charge of setting up a rotorcraft division at Hayes. He left Fairey in 1952 for American helicopter manufacturer Hiller. Among other posts, he was Professor of Aerodynamics and later Deputy Principal at the College of Aeronautics, Cranfield, from 1954 to 1969. Professor James Allan Jamieson Bennett died on 27 February 1973.

Fairey's winged logo was given three 'blades' to emphasize the new departure into rotorcraft. A high-risk strategy was devised that required a step-by-step programme paving the way for a daring end product, a huge rotorcraft. This could be a military transport, but the more tempting prize was to break into the civil market with a vertical take-off and landing short-range airliner. Bennett devised the initial phase; the FB-1 (Fairey and Bennett) Gyrodyne compound helicopter, which flew untethered for the first time on 7 December 1947. Hardly the snappiest of names, Gyrodyne is a *compound* word, based upon gyration – the act of rotation – and aerodyne – a machine that flies courtesy of aerodynamic forces. The Leonides piston engine drove the rotor blades *and* a tractor propeller mounted on the end of the starboard stub wing. Compound rotorcraft use the main rotor for lift and *some* of the propulsion, and sometimes employ stub wings to offload the rotor and use propellers, or even jet efflux, for the bulk of the thrust. The concept has the potential to provide speeds otherwise unobtainable in a fixed-wing helicopter and is still viable: Sikorsky flew its S-97 Raider in 2015, combining co-axial main rotors with a tail-mounted pusher propeller. The S-97 is a hopeful in a US requirement for a scout/attack helicopter.

Jet Gyrodyne XJ389 during its first transition at White Waltham, March 1955. For early sorties the access door was not installed to allow test pilot John Dennis ease of escape. *Fairey Aviation*

Fairey monoplanes

From	To	Total	Name/Designation	Type	Engine(s)	Notes
1928	1931	2	Long Range Mono	'Postal'	1 x Napier Lion	
1930	1937	15	Hendon	Heavy bomber	2 x RR Kestrel	[1]
1936	1940	2,201	Battle	Day bomber	1 x RR Merlin	[2]
1937	1943	602	Fulmar	Shipborne fighter	1 x RR Merlin	[3]
1940	1945	2,572	Barracuda I, II, III	Torpedo bomber	1 x RR Merlin	[4]
1941	1956	1,702	Firefly	Shipborne fighter	1 x RR Griffon	[5]
1944	1947	30	Barracuda V	Torpedo bomber	1 x RR Griffon	[6]
1945	1947	4	Spearfish	Torpedo bomber	1 x Bristol Centaurus	
1949	1957	309	Gannet	Anti-submarine	1 x AS Double Mamba	[7]
1958	1963	44	Gannet AEW.3	Early warning	1 x AS Double Mamba	

Based upon: *Fairey Aircraft since 1915*, H A Taylor. **[1]** Prototype Hayes-built, production at Heaton Chapel – flying from Barton – 1936–37. **[2]** 1,029 sub-contracted to Austin Motors, Longbridge, 1938–40. Includes dual-control and target tug versions built from new. **[3]** Includes two P.4/34 prototypes. **[4]** Also sub-contracted to Blackburn (700), Boulton Paul (692) and Westland (18). **[5]** Also sub-contracted to General Aircraft, 132 of 'base-line' Mk.Is. **[6]** Does not include conversions from Mk.IIs. **[7]** Variants: AS.1, T.2, AS.4, T.5.

Along with the Gyrodyne, White Waltham airfield sprouted a series of ground rigs that led to the next step, the Jet Gyrodyne. This time the Leonides powered a pair of pusher propellers on stub wings *and* it drove a pair of compressors that blasted air into and along the main rotors to Bennett's patented pressure jets at the tips, which blew the blades around. For landing and take-off the bulk of the power went to the rotor, but for forward flight the blades almost 'idled' (like those of an autogyro) while the stub wings and the propellers provided lift and thrust. This was cutting edge technology, involving intense and complex experimentation. Leading the Jet Gyrodyne and the Rotodyne project was Dr G S Hislop, as chief designer helicopters, and chief engineer helicopters Graham Forsyth. Although the Jet Gyrodyne first flew in January 1954, it was not until March of the following year that a full transition from one flight phase to another, and back, was achieved.

Prior to the 90ft diameter rotor, 33,000lb all-up weight, twin 2,800shp Napier Eland turboprop-powered Rotodyne appearing, Fairey took the technology to the other end of the scale. The simplistically named tip-jet driven Ultra Light Helicopters were built to tempt the Army and the FAA, but did not attract orders. The first of these flew on 14 August 1955 and featured a 28ft 3½in rotor, an all-up weight of 1,800lb and tiny 252lb thrust Blackburn-built Turboméca Palouste turboshaft.

With a Ministry of Supply research contract signed in July 1953 to help develop the prototype, the very impressive Rotodyne first flew on 6 November 1957. Testing went well, but although British European Airways (BEA) and others flirted with Fairey, no orders were forthcoming. A further ingestion of £4 million from the Conservative government of the day kept the prototype in the air. But on 26 February 1962 the plug was pulled. The one and only Rotodyne was scrapped:

One of the diminutive Ultra Light Helicopters, G-APJJ, flying in Royal Navy markings, 1957. *Fairey Aviation*

elements of its rotor pylon and fuselage are held by The Helicopter Museum at Weston-super-Mare.

The Rotodyne was ahead of its time, vastly expensive, monstrously noisy and aimed at a tenuous market. BEA had expressed interest in a developed version of the Rotodyne, the Type Z, which could carry fifty-five passengers 250 miles at 200mph, making London to Brussels or Paris just about possible with minimal diversion reserves. In 1960 BEA was using Vickers Viscount 800s to ply these routes, at a cruise of 320mph. The Rotodyne would only be more attractive by flying city centre to city centre, not Heathrow to Zaventem or Le Bourget. That would require massive investment in top-value land and the infrastructure for a 'mini-airport'. BEA would be pioneering a new form of aviation at incredible financial and technological risk, when its conventional routes were doing fine. The entire Rotodyne project is estimated to have cost £11 million – a cool £275 million in present-day values. Parallels with Concorde are inevitable. Like Concorde, there has been nothing like the Rotodyne since.

A 1960 advert proclaiming: 'In the Rotodyne we see the promise of tomorrow's airbus systems. Air travel every day, everywhere.' *KEC*

Fireflash 'beam-riding' air-to-air missile. His experience as a 'rocketeer' led to him being snapped up by de Havilland Propellers (later Hawker Siddeley Dynamics) in 1956. Costigan's autobiography, *Adventures of an Aircraft Designer*, was published in 1980. It is well worth seeking out, especially for its insights into the contribution of more 'lowly' design office members. He also pays tribute to 'the Old Man' – Sir Richard Fairey – as 'a brilliant engineer who had the courage of his convictions.' Costigan considers CRF's death in September 1956 as the end of an era: '… from then, I think, the firm began to die too. … denuded of the verve and drive of its great Founder [the company] started to decline …'

With the writing on the wall, the Fairey group was restructured on 31 March 1959 and a new Fairey Aviation Ltd was born. This ring-fenced the diverse constituents of the Fairey enterprise and eased a sale of the aircraft business. Westland took over on 6 February 1960 and, other than honouring government contracts and investment in the project, had no interest in taking the Rotodyne further. Westland was already supplying the only other

Joseph 'Joe' Costigan began his aeronautical career as a fitter at Vickers, Brooklands, working on Wellesley components before moving to Hawker at Kingston as a jig maker. Aged 24, he took up the post of junior draughtsman in 1936 with Fairey but left the following year for a brief stint with Miles at Woodley. He returned to the fold in 1939 and stayed for seventeen years. He ended up as chief designer with the research and development department, based at Heston, his tasks including the vertical launch delta rocket 'models' at Woomera and the

likely – but wholly disinterested – Rotodyne customer, the RAF, with a practical heavy-lift helicopter, the Belvedere. When it swallowed Fairey, Westland was attracted by the skilled workforce and abundant shop floors at Hayes. Before long Scouts, Wasps and Pumas were coming off the production line at Hayes, taken by road and assembled inside the Rotodyne hangar ready for flight test. Apart from a brief renaissance with Britten-Norman in the 1970s, in terms of aircraft manufacture, the name of Fairey was extinguished.

Fairey jets and rotorcraft

From	To	Total	Name/Designation	Type	Engine(s)	Notes
1947	1948	2	Gyrodyne	Compound helicopter	1 x Alvis Leonides	[1]
1951	-	1	FD.1	Research	1 x RR Derwent	
1954	-	1	Jet Gyrodyne	Compound helicopter	1 x Alvis Leonides	[2]
1954	1956	2	FD.2	Research	1 x RR Avon	[3]
1955	1958	5	Ultra Light	Helicopter	1 x Palouste	[4]
1957	-	1	Rotodyne	Compound helicopter	2 x Napier Eland	

Based upon: *Fairey Aircraft since 1915*, H A Taylor. **[1]** Second example converted to Jet Gyrodyne in 1954. **[2]** Rebuilt second Gyrodyne. **[3]** First FD.2 converted to BAC 221 ogee wing test bed, flying in 1964 – see Chapter 13. **[4]** Blackburn-built Turboméca Palouste turboshaft powering tip-jets.

CHAPTER TWENTY

Bantamweights

**Folland
1937 to 1959**

'In a world of increasing complications … we at Follands have recognised that there is room for a simple, efficient and versatile fighter of high performance.' Folland advert for the Gnat, 1955

CREATING THE ROYAL AIRCRAFT FACTORY S.E.5a, arguably the best British single-seat fighter of the Great War, was just the beginning. Pipe-smoking Henry Phillip Folland – 'Harry' to friends and colleagues – went on to conceive a stream of superb fighters: the Nieuport Nighthawk and for Gloster the Grebe, Gamecock, Gauntlet and Gladiator. Folland went his own way in 1937 and popular belief is that he set up Folland Aircraft, but it was his employers that took the shrewd move of renaming their business in his honour. Ironically, the last Henry Folland design to fly was not a fighter; it was an ugly test bed that earned the nickname 'Frightful'. Folland Aircraft did get into the warplane business in 1954 when 'Teddy' Petter's Midge bantamweight jet fighter had its maiden flight. Celebrations were quickly muted, less than a month later Henry Folland, the great fighter perfectionist, died, leaving the little jet to bring Henry's name to a new generation.

Phantom flying boat

Established in February 1936, British Marine Aircraft Ltd (BMA) was unusual for an entrant into the industry. To generalise, the British norm has often been to create a design with potential, acquire a ramshackle workshop and endure hand-to-mouth funding. Not so BMA. With deep pockets, a delegation of board members travelled to Bridgeport, Connecticut, to talk to Sikorsky Aircraft about a licence to build the S-42-A four-engined, long-range, flying boat then pioneering trans-Pacific routes for Pan American Airways. Rights were secured to market the S-42-A in the British Empire, with the exception of Canada. With this was an initial flow of components and sub-assemblies that would lead – presumably – to

The Midge hitching a ride from Hamble to Boscombe Down on 11 August 1954: it had its maiden flight later that day. Folland

indigenous manufacture in due course. This agreement was reported to have cost £130,000 before any hardware crossed the Atlantic. The spending did not stop there: the 118ft span S-42-A – which was to be designated BM-1 – needed a big 'home' and land was acquired at Hamble on the Solent, with an enormous factory, hardstanding and slipway completed in July 1936. Within six months, BMA had a keel laid and other sub-assemblies were coming together, but at a painfully slow pace. The board had rapidly come to a conclusion about BMA's prospects. Imperial Airways and other Empire operators were unlikely to entertain an expensive *American* flying boat from an unproven manufacturer when they could turn to long-established *British* companies, particularly Shorts. BMA had plans for a big 'boat and nowhere to go, and in April 1937 it announced a loss of £222,000. The BM-1 was abandoned and all of the management were ousted.

A new board was convened, determined that something could be salvaged. While there wasn't a gleaming flying boat standing at Hamble, there was a state-of-the-art aircraft factory and a country rearming at a frenetic pace. Henry Folland, aged 48, was snapped up and appointed as technical director to take BMA into more prosperous waters. Folland began his career in 1912 at the Army Aircraft Factory at Farnborough, which took the name Royal Aircraft Factory that April. His time there, crowned by the S.E.5, is charted in Chapter 31. In 1917 Folland moved to Nieuport and General Aircraft (N&G), where he created the Nighthawk. N&G closed in November 1920 and Gloucestershire Aircraft (which traded as Gloster from 1926) acquired the Nighthawk's design rights. In January 1921 Folland signed up with Gloucestershire and his incredible output can be found in Chapter 22. All was well until 1934, when Gloster was subsumed into Thomas Sopwith's Hawker Siddeley (HS) conglomerate. Folland was increasingly troubled that the company would merely become an outstation for Sydney Camm's military biplanes: he left in 1937.

Henry Phillip Folland, creator of a fighter dynasty. *Gloster*

Upon joining BMA, Folland was flattered in October 1937 when the company was renamed Folland Aircraft. Having produced nothing 'marine', the Hamble company *had* to change its identity and with a man as renowned as Folland on the payroll it was an obvious choice. Folland set about finding sub-contracts and touting a 'problem solver' consultancy for the wider industry. All the while Folland responded to Air Ministry specifications in the hope of an order, forever mindful that the new business did not have the capital to turn blueprints into hardware. Like Comper, Folland falls below the book's criteria for inclusion – see the introduction – but the Gnat programme alone permits a breach. (To differentiate between the man and the company that came to bear his name, Henry is referred to here as HPF.)

'Booted' Spitfires

During the late 1930s there was plenty of work available for a contractor that could be relied upon and had a proven guiding light such as HPF trouble shooting. Examples of Folland's commissions included Bristol Blenheim and Beaufort nose sections; Supermarine

Seafire outer wings and thousands of Spitfire ailerons; and Vickers Wellington and Warwick engine nacelles. Hamble was an easy target for Luftwaffe bombers and dispersal sites were set up at Southampton's Eastleigh airfield – close by but still vulnerable – and at Staverton in Gloucestershire.

An instance of 'problem solving' that occupied much of HPF's time was the transformation of the Spitfire into a floatplane. Early in 1941 thoughts were gelling around a need for a fighter capable of defending areas and installations beyond the range of land-based equivalents and where carriers would not be available or could not risk exposure. Trials with a Spitfire I fitted with Blackburn Roc floats in the spring of 1941 were unsuccessful.

The third Folland-developed Spitfire V (Type 355) EP754, during trials in Egypt, 1943. *Peter Green Collection*

A Mk.V was taken off the production line in Southampton and handed over to Folland in August 1941, and given the Supermarine designation Type 355 Special. As well as the stylish 'sea-boots', creating the 'Special' involved removing the undercarriage and associated 'plumbing', the wing was strengthened to accept the floats and the Merlin engine was given a four-bladed propeller. A completely new tail section boasted a larger rudder and a ventral fin to help compensate for the massive increase in side area. Trials began in November 1942 and continued sporadically into the summer of 1943. By that time, two more Mk.Vs had been transformed by Folland. In September all three 'booted' Spitfires were shipped to Egypt for further testing. In December 1943 a Spitfire IX was handed over to Saunders-Roe for conversion to floatplane status with a view to potential use in the Pacific. After trials in the summer of 1944, the concept was shelved.

Frightful finale

Specification 43/37 brought about a remarkable aircraft – a dedicated test bed that could easily have different piston engines attached to the firewall. Despite this being uncharted territory for HPF – and any other designer in the country for that matter – he responded with the Fo 108, which turned out to be his last creation to take to the air. A dozen 43/37s were ordered. In wartime, this was a luxury requirement and it is likely that Folland was chosen for the task because it would not be diverting drawing board time from other, more pressing, needs. Construction began at Eastleigh in early 1940 and the prototype, powered by a Napier Sabre, first flew in the summer and was followed by another. The other ten of these all-metal monocoque, fixed undercarriage, monoplanes were completed at Staverton, where Gloster test pilots Gerry Sayer and Michael Daunt shared testing.

Daunt was flying the fourth example on 19 May 1942 when the tailplane failed, followed by the propeller parting company with the Bristol Centaurus engine. Wisely electing to bale out, Michael came down in a field and it was six months before he was fully recovered.

The prototype Folland 'Frightful', P1774, probably at Staverton, August 1941. *D Napier and Sons*

Describing the Fo 108 as 'bloody dangerous', Daunt dubbed it the 'Folland Frightful' – and the nickname stuck. While pilots loathed the machine, flight test observers had nothing but praise for it as it had a purpose-designed, spacious cabin behind and below the cockpit, whereas normally they were squeezed in wherever possible.

Specification E.28/40 was issued in February 1941 for a pair of aircraft to explore higher weight operations from carriers, using high-lift devices to the full, and Folland was awarded the contract for his Fo 116. Construction began but was cancelled in late 1942: this was not the time for complex experimental types. In 1943 HPF schemed the Fo 117 four-cannon fighter. If it had gone ahead, manufacture would have been carried out by English Electric (EE) at Samlesbury. It is interesting to speculate that had the Fo 117 progressed, EE might well not have been chosen as the de Havilland (DH) Vampire sub-contractor, thereby robbing the Lancashire company of the jet experience that gave rise to the Canberra.

Midge and Gnat

Like many firms, Folland diversified during the downturn of the late 1940s, creating specialist furniture and electric trucks among other ventures. Its reputation as an efficient sub-contractor meant that work soon returned to Hamble. Vickers ordered Viking airliner sub-assemblies, while DH entrusted Dove and later Chipmunk wings to Folland. Bristol engaged HPF to design all the control surfaces for the massive Brabazon; Folland built these huge units and the ground-support items – stairs, access platforms, etc.

Having suffered from ill health for some time, HPF retired in July 1951, but kept his seat on the board. Henry Phillip Folland OBE died on 5 September 1954, aged 65. HPF's deputy from October 1950 had been William Edward Willoughby Petter, previously with EE and seeking an outlet for his concept of a simple, small, jet warplane. Teddy Petter took over as managing director and chief engineer, and

Frederick 'Fred' Henry Pollicutt, latterly with Bristol, was appointed as chief designer. Pollicutt's tenure at Folland was short: he decamped to Luton to join Hunting in 1953 and had a major role in the British Aircraft Corporation One-Eleven jetliner. Pollicutt's departure from Hamble *may* well have been down to Petter, who was renowned for not being easy to get on with. (Petter's life and times are outlined in Chapter 38.) Alan Constantine, from EE, took Pollicutt's place.

Work began on the interim Fo 139 Midge, fitted with an Armstrong Siddeley Viper, to enable testing to get started while the more powerful Bristol Orpheus became available for the definitive, cannon-armed Gnat. The project was a private venture and a huge risk for the small company. Petter's philosophy was that large numbers of small, nimble, cannon-armed Gnats were a more cost-effective way of countering massed formations of Soviet bloc fighters and bombers than a few, overly complicated, missile-armed interceptors. The Gnat would also lend itself to nations with smaller budgets, either as direct export customers or through manufacture under licence.

The fourth Gnat F.1, XK741, for Ministry of Supply evaluations at Boscombe Down, carrying drop tanks and unguided rocket clusters underwing. *Folland*

With its span of just 20ft 8in reduced by 16in through the removal of the wing tips, the Midge was roaded otherwise intact to Boscombe Down for its maiden flight on 11 August 1954. After a couple more sorties it was ferried the short distance to Chilbolton, where Folland had established its test centre. The first Gnat had its inaugural sortie, also from Boscombe Down, on 18 July 1955. In that year the Ministry of Supply (MoS) ordered a dozen Gnat F.1s: the first taking to the air in May 1956. The chances of RAF purchasing policy being overturned were remote, but the Gnat was a concept that required a thorough evaluation. The MoS contract also provided a much-needed financial injection to help fend off the heavy costs – the Gnat might have been small but any military programme is expensive. Also, exports were very unlikely unless the home country had adopted the type. Finland took delivery of thirteen Gnats during 1958–60 and Yugoslavia received a pair in mid-1958. Both nations harboured plans to build the type, but things went no further.

Sabre Slayers

The real bonanza was a licence deal with India, signed on 15 September 1956. Folland's predecessor, British Marine, had nearly come unstuck with a licence arrangement; two decades later Hamble had achieved a very lucrative deal, transforming its prospects. A batch of thirty Gnats began to be delivered to the Indian Air Force in the summer of 1957. Hindustan Aircraft Ltd (HAL) of Bangalore received fifteen 'kits' to start off its production line and the first of these was flying in India by 1959. The first Gnat built entirely by HAL took to the skies on 26 May 1962. The diminutive fighters acquitted themselves well against North American F-86F Sabres during the Indo-Pakistan War of 1965, earning the nickname 'Sabre Slayers'.

Figures for how many Gnats HAL constructed up to 1974 vary, but 235 is believed to be accurate. As the last examples came off the Bangalore line the design rights were signed over to HAL (which had become Hindustan Aeronautics Ltd in 1964) on 19 July 1974. HAL was now free to develop the Gnat as it wished. The result was the Ajeet

(literally, invincible) which was much refined, including a 'wet wing' holding fuel, banishing the pylon-mounted drop tanks that were more or less a permanent feature of the F.1s. Optimised for ground attack, Ajeets had two weapons stations under each wing. During 1975 two Gnats were converted to Ajeet status and the first new-build example flew on 30 September 1976. Production amounted to ninety, plus a pair of trainers, and was completed by 1985.

Red Arrows and aerostructures

While the RAF had little interest in the single-seat Gnat, it was enthused by a two-seat advanced trainer version to replace the venerable DH Vampire T.11. With an elongated forward fuselage with tandem seating under a one-piece canopy and permanent wing-mounted 'slipper' tanks to extend endurance, the first Gnat T.1 had its maiden flight on the last day of August 1959. Two months later HS acquired Folland. The contract for T.1s was attractive, but not the main reason behind the purchase. Hamble was a major supplier for HS, for example it had manufactured Hunter tail planes from 1955. Before long, Folland was clearing space to build the wings for the HS.748 twin turboprop and by the mid-1960s was a major contributor to the Harrier programme.

The arrival of HS disillusioned Petter and he retired to Switzerland in December 1959; where he died nine years later. Replacing him as chief designer was Maurice Joseph Brennan, latterly of Vickers and before that Saunders-Roe. Brennan saw the Gnat T.1 through to full production before departing for HS at Woodford. (He is profiled in Chapter 32.) Famed as the first mount of the RAF Aerobatic Team, the Red Arrows, the last Gnat T.1 was delivered in May 1965. Dunsfold became the test centre for Gnats from 1959, but it was not until 22 April 1965 that Chilbolton was given up when pre-production T.1 XM706 was returned to the RAF after modifications.

By 1971 Hamble was hard at work on structures for the Airbus A300 and A310, among other programmes. In March 1977 it became a British Aerospace sub-site but in January 1989 it was sold off, becoming Aerostructures Hamble Ltd. After several name changes, the site continues in the aerostructures business under the aegis of General Electric subsidiary GE Aviation.

An official Indian Air Force release of a 'scramble' during the Indo-Pakistan war of 1965. Gnat IE1078 was one of the airframes supplied from Hamble as a 'kit' for assembly by Hindustan Aircraft at Bangalore, 1960. *Indian Air Force*

Gnat T.1s of the Red Arrows, complete with Central Flying School badges, lined up during the team's second year, 1966. *KEC*

Folland

From	To	Total	Name/Designation	Type	Engine(s)	Notes
1940	-	12	Fo 108 43/37	Engine test bed	1 x Napier Sabre	
1954	-	1	Midge	Development proto	1 x AS Viper	
1955	1985	384	Gnat F.1	Fighter	1 x Bristol Orpheus	[1]
1959	1965	105	Gnat T.1	Advanced trainer	1 x Bristol Orpheus	

[1] Thirty delivered direct to India, plus four as full knocked-down kits. Hamble made 11 airframe sub-sets to start licence production by Hindustan Aircraft (later Aeronautics) Ltd (HAL), Bangalore, India. Total HAL Gnats reported as 235. Production of HAL Ajeet version reported as 90 plus two two-seaters.

CHAPTER TWENTY-ONE

From Air Taxis to War Chariots

General Aircraft
1931 to 1949

'Twelve Locust tanks and a 4.2in mortar troop were flown in under flak attack when airborne and on landing…'
5th Airborne Armoured Recce Regiment diary, Operation Varsity, the Rhine Crossing, March 1945

HELPING TO DESIGN an aircraft with a span of 157ft 6in and a loaded weight in the region of 37,000lb would be great experience for anyone interested in structures – especially so in 1926. Swiss-born Helmuth Johannes Stieger – John to colleagues – joined the aviation department of William Beardmore and Company, which was creating the giant Inflexible monoplane. Adopting German engineer Dr Adolph Rohrbach's stressed skin all-Duralumin construction techniques, the Inflexible's gestation had been so tortuous that it was nicknamed the 'Impossible'. With a span nearly 12ft greater than that of a Boeing 707, the Inflexible was coaxed into the air in March 1928. By then Beardmore's owner, Lord Invernairn, was sick of the venture and lost no time in closing down the aviation branch of his Glasgow-based manufacturing empire. Stieger and others were looking for jobs.

An engineering graduate of Imperial College London, Stieger came up with a lightweight structure that he hoped would revolutionise cantilever wings, making monoplanes far lighter and stronger and needing only one spar – hence the brand name Monospar. Based on the proven Warren girder linear triangular bracing system, found on many bridges, Stieger employed 'pyramidal', 'diamond' or 'box' tube cross sections to counter torsional – twisting – forces. This form of spar could also be used as a 'keel' upon which a fuselage could be anchored. Stieger turned to friends and colleagues to establish the Aero Syndicate Ltd in 1929 to exploit his patents. These included Sqn Ldr Rollo Amyatt Wolseley de Haga Haig AFC, previously with Beardmore, and Frederick Francis 'Croak' Crocombe, also tutored at Imperial College.

Tarrant Rushton on D-Day -1, 5 June 1944: Handley Page Halifax tugs await the call to start engines while a pair of Airspeed Horsas are at the head of thirty-two Hamilcars ready to reinforce the beachhead. *KEC*

Monospars

The Air Ministry was very interested in Stieger's technique and ordered a wing section – called ST-1 by Stieger – for trials. The ministry was so impressed that it commissioned Gloster to construct a one-piece 63ft Monospar wing to be fitted to the Royal Aircraft Establishment's Fokker F.VIIA/3m test bed in place of its one-piece, all-wooden structure. This wing, believed to have been the ST-2, was worth £4,100 to Gloster. The structure was fitted to the Dutch-built tri-motor at Hucclecote and it had its maiden flight on 16 December 1931. Beating the Fokker into the air by a couple of months was the ST-3, a three-seat cabin monoplane designed by Stieger and powered by a pair of Salmson radials. A diamond-shaped Monospar 'girder' also acted as a keel for the twin's fuselage structure. The ST-3 was also made by Gloster, under the designation SS.1 – Stieger, Salmson, 1. In another era, the role of the ST-3 would be called a proof-of-concept aircraft: it validated Stieger's claims, proving it was time to capitalise on the invention.

Above: A treasure among treasures at the Newark Air Museum is Monospar ST-12 VH-UTH. Delivered to Australia in 1936, it was returned to the UK in 1961. As this book was published, it was nearing the end of a painstaking restoration. *Ken Ellis*

Left: A near head-on view of a Monospar ST-25 Universal, showing the thinner wing section inboard of the engines and the 'carry-through' upper element of the spar. *Peter Green Collection*

Evolving for war

During 1936 Stieger departed GAL, heading north to become deputy to Major Frank Bumpus, who was setting up Blackburn's new division at Dumbarton. At Hanworth, the role of chief designer was taken by Crocombe. Things went well enough that in 1938 GAL was able to expand, picking up the neighbouring premises of the defunct British Aircraft Manufacturing Company. A two-seat, side-by-side twin-boom pusher trainer, the GAL.33, was flown in 1937 but failed to attract orders. Crocombe returned to the twin-boom pusher layout with the GAL.47 in 1940 to meet the emerging need for an air observation post: this also remained a one-off.

During 1937 CW Aircraft of Slough flew the prototype Cygnet, a two-seat, side-by-side, tourer/trainer. This attractive-looking 'tail-dragger' broke the mould for British light aircraft: it featured a semi-monocoque fuselage and was all metal-skinned. CW ran out of cash in March 1938 and GAL bought up the design rights. Crocombe and Williams refined the Cygnet, giving it twin fins and rudders, generous flaps and tricycle undercarriage with rudder bar-actuated ground steering. Williams took the Cygnet II for its first flight in 1939 and it was clear that GAL had a potential winner on its hands, but the coming war altered priorities. A private-venture, tandem, open-cockpit military trainer based on the Cygnet airframe, the Owlet, was flown in September 1940, but failed to attract any interest.

The Aero Syndicate gave way to the Monospar Wing Company in 1930 and on 27 February 1931 General Aircraft Ltd (GAL) was set up with Stieger as manager and chief designer. Premises were acquired at Croydon but GAL relocated to Hanworth two years later. In 1934 GAL underwent voluntary financial restructuring and Eric Cecil Gordon England became managing director, until 1942. (England was an early designer and test pilot for Bristol – see Chapter 11 for his details.)

Also arriving, as chief engineer, was David Williams, a former RAF pilot who joined the Hawker drawing office in 1923. He moved to Fairey two years later, his work including the Long Range Monoplane and the Hendon bomber. Williams returned to Fairey in 1942, as chief engineer, and took part in solving that company's production logjam. He left for Westland in 1952, becoming technical director and setting up Yeovil's helicopter division. He retired in 1962 as assistant managing director. Plt Off David Leonard Hollis Williams died on 2 April 1974, aged 74.

Stieger embarked upon a series of twins to meet the corporate, taxi and private owner markets, all having a keel and a tip-to-tip wing spar to his formula. Inboard of the engine nacelles the wing section thinned and the spar split into two, the lower element dipping to the cabin floor, while the top component ran through the cabin, behind the front seats. The prototype four-seat Monospar ST-4 took to the air in May 1932 and orders – domestic and export – began to roll in. A version with retractable undercarriage and an additional passenger seat, the ST-6, flew the following year, but failed to catch on. The breed continued to be refined with the ST-25 of 1935 initially marketed under the name Jubilee to celebrate King George V's quarter century on the throne. In the following year the Jubilee gave way to the ST-25 Universal with twin fins and rudders to improve engine-out control. The name Universal was chosen to emphasize the aircraft's multi-tasking ability: the name was used again in 1949 on a transport of altogether different proportions. Stieger scaled up his twin 'formula' to create the ten-passenger, retractable undercarriage ST-18 Croydon powered by 450hp Pratt & Whitney Wasp Juniors. First flown in early 1936, it remained an expensive one-off.

The last Cygnet II built, G-AGBN, at Biggin Hill in January 1975. Today it is part of the National Museum of Flight Scotland at East Fortune. *KEC*

Based on the Cygnet II, the Owlet military trainer, G-AGBK, of 1940 remained a one-off. *KEC*

Airspeed and GAL were awarded contracts to each build a prototype to meet the bizarre Specification S.23/37 of October 1937 seeking a 'special observation aircraft', which was referred to as the 'Night Shadower' or 'Fleet Shadower' by the Fleet Air Arm. The wording of S.23/37 included: 'The primary object will be to maintain continuous visual contact with the ship being shadowed without the aircraft betraying its own presence. The engine and airscrew should be designed to enable the aircraft to fly as silently as possible. This feature is of vital importance. The type of aircraft visualised is a three-seat pusher.' There was no need for this slow-flying machine to be armed: quietness would be its protection. What the Air Ministry got was a pair of four-engined, fixed undercarriage, machines each looking remarkably like the other. First off the mark was the GAL.38, which had its maiden flight on 13 May 1940, followed by the AS.39 on 17 October 1940. Sense prevailed in February 1941 when the entire programme was axed – the answer was conventional long-range patrollers and radar-equipped ships.

GAL's answer to the bizarre Specification S.23/37, Fleet Shadower P1758. *Peter Green Collection*

In 1935 GAL succeeded in becoming a sub-contractor, building Hawker Fury II biplane fighters during 1936 to 1937. It went on to be a major supplier and set up an outstation at Lasham to ease the load on Hanworth. Work included Blackburn Skua and Roc sub-assemblies, a leading role in the Sea Hurricane conversion programme and a batch of Fairey Firefly Is built and flown from 1943 to 1945. Designated GAL.59, GAL created in 1947 and 1948 the ugliest-ever version of the de Havilland Mosquito, the TT.39 target tug, a conversion of the B.XVI bomber. All this was important bread and butter for GAL, but the wartime types for which it was to become most famous were a radical change in direction.

Silent wings

Crocombe and his team responded to Specification 10/40 for a troop-carrying glider, capable of depositing a pilot and seven fully equipped troops into a minimal-sized landing zone (LZ). This was a brave venture for a business that had little experience of wooden airframes, let alone gliders, but it prove to be a gifted decision. The prototype Hotspur flew in March 1941. The concept of airborne forces warfare was evolving rapidly and Hotspurs proved too small for the task. Instead the type became the standard trainer for the men of the Glider Pilot Regiment. Mass production of Hotspurs, and the later Hamilcar, was handed on to sub-contractors.

An ingenious 'fix' to the Hotspur's lack of capacity appeared in 1942 in the form of the Twin Hotspur. By joining a pair of Hotspur fuselages with a centre section and an extended tailplane/elevator, fitting standard wings port and starboard, a sixteen-troop transport was created. To keep the changes to a minimum, both fuselages retained their cockpits, but only the port element had controls. The Airspeed Horsa, capable of taking twenty-eight soldiers, was in production in 1942 and nothing more came of the Twin Hotspur. (This was not a unique design solution: Heinkel had carried out such an exercise in 1941, joining two He 111H bombers to form a *five*-engined heavy glider tug, the He 111Z 'Zwilling', and North American devised the F-82 Twin Mustang fighter.)

Believed to have been taken at the Central Landing Establishment, Ringway, in late 1941, Hotspur II BT480 with a Pegasus winged horse logo on the nose. In the background are Westland Lysanders, a DH Tiger Moth and Avro Manchesters. *KEC*

Austrian-born Robert Kronfeld became an important protagonist of the sport of gliding: among his exploits he became the first person to fly a glider across the English Channel, on 20 June 1931. In May 1933 Kronfeld took over GAL's neighbours at Hanworth, the British Aircraft Company, manufacturers of gliders and light aircraft, renaming it Kronfeld Ltd in 1936. Kronfeld commissioned GAL to build a two-seat tandem parasol pusher to his design the following year. This remained a prototype and Kronfeld Ltd ceased trading.

With the advent of war in 1939 Kronfeld adopted English citizenship and became a leading light at the Airborne Forces Experimental Establishment in 1942. In this capacity, Kronfeld renewed his acquaintance with GAL. The company had been contracted to build a series of two-seat gliders with different wing planforms to investigate the slow-speed characteristics of the swept back, tail-less format. Three GAL.56s with a 'conventional' fuselage and the much more advanced GAL.61 with the pilot seated within a thick centre section were completed –see the table. The first GAL.56 featured a sweep back of 28 degrees and a planform that was termed 'Medium V'. Kronfeld took it for its first flight, towed aloft behind an Armstrong Whitworth Whitley, from Farnborough on 13 November 1944. He declared it to be a nightmare and the famed test pilot Captain Eric 'Winkle' Brown was equally scathing when he tried it. Despite this, the trio of GAL.56s continued trials. Kronfeld was flying the first GAL.56 on 12 February 1948 when it entered an inverted spin. His observer managed to extricate himself, but 43-year-old Sqn Ldr Robert Kronfeld AFC's body was found in the wreckage. The entire programme, including the unflown GAL.61, was terminated in 1949.

Flying tanks

With the experience of the Hotspur, GAL was in a good position to tackle the exceptionally challenging Specification X.27/40, which emerged as the 110ft span, 37,000lb all-up weight Hamilcar. To prove the design a half-scale piloted model, the GAL.50, was tested in 1941. The real thing had its maiden flight on 27 March 1942. Towed behind a Handley Page Halifax or a Short Stirling, the Hamilcar could take a Mk.VII tank – all 15,780lb of it – into battle. Once landed, the nose swung open, out came a ramp and the payload trundled on its way. Unlike the other British 'war chariot', the Airspeed Horsa, Hamilcars were intended to be towed out of the LZ and used again. Trials were carried out with under-wing, rocket-assisted take-off (RATO) gear to facilitate recovery.

The architect of the forthcoming ultimate war chariot was 'Croak' Crocombe who, as related above, at the age of 28 was a founder member of the Aero Syndicate. Upon the departure of Stieger in 1936 he took the post of chief designer and the fruits of his drawing board culminated in the massive GAL.60 in 1948. Perhaps the merger of GAL and Blackburn was not to his liking as he decamped to Boulton Paul, becoming its chief designer in 1951. Frederick Francis Crocombe retired in 1966 and died in August 1987, aged 85.

We shall take a diversion into the labyrinthine realm of Air Ministry naming conventions and the origins of Hotspur and Hamilcar. The 14th-century warrior Sir Henry Percy was nicknamed 'Harry Hotspur'. (The name Hotspur had been used as recently as 1938 for Hawker's abortive turret fighter.) Hamilcar Barca was a 3rd-century BC general from Carthage (present-day Tunisia) and the father of the more famous Hannibal.

By adding two 965hp Bristol Mercury 31 radials, the Hamilcar X was born in February 1945. Designed for the Pacific theatre, the Mk.Xs were supposed to be self-launching, and given long, surfaced runways and reasonable temperatures they could achieve this. In the Far East they would have been tug-assisted; the two Mercuries would *help* during the take-off process and the Hamilcar X would then glide behind the tug. The engines would restart to help manoeuvring into tight jungle LZs. Given sufficient space and RATO, empty Hamilcar Xs could power themselves out to fight another day. One can't help but wonder if the format of the Hamilcar – as a glider; the powered Mk.X came too late – influenced Leslie Frise when he was formulating the Bristol 170 Freighter, which first flew on 2 December 1945.

The prototype Hamilcar X during trials in 1944. *KEC*

Joining the 'Big League'

The design staff at Hanworth realised that heavy gliders – even self-recovering ones – were costly assets and that most ended up as matchwood on the battlefield. However, the capacious fuselage of the Hamilcar, plus its ease of loading, was a major step forward. Crocombe decided to explore how this concept could be made into a durable powered aircraft. Early studies centred around two- and four-engined giants with twin tails and a narrow, boom-like fuselage that could accommodate troops. Underneath this was a large, detachable streamlined freight pod. The aircraft would fly low – *very* low, 10ft or so – above the LZ and release the pod, which would grind to a halt and its contents would then be offloaded. Then the 'mother-ship' would climb away and drop parachutists for good measure. This remained a project, but the knowledge gained would pay dividends.

One of the many stipulations in Specification C.3/46 for a four-engined heavy freighter, troop carrier, parachute platform, supply-dropper and glider-tower issued in July 1947 was that 'speed is not a primary requirement' – that was just as well as this was a very demanding requirement. GAL snapped up the contract for a prototype, designated GAL.60. To emphasize its civilian applications as well as its military intentions it was named Universal Freighter in 1949. Gone was the droppable pod, a cavernous double-deck fuselage was what was required. Unlike the Hamilcar, the nose did not swing open, there were clam-shell doors at the rear allowing easy access for bulky loads. Powered by four 2,020hp Bristol Hercules 730s, this massive craft had a span of 162ft, a wing area of 2,916 sq ft and plodded along at a cruise of 162mph. The GAL.60 could lift *nine* Jeeps, or other vehicles up to 25,200lb: even a bulldozer could be taken into a moderate, unprepared airstrip.

Construction started in 1948, but it was abundantly clear that a production order would require massive investment by the still-small company. Apart from Mosquito conversion work and the like, GAL had little other revenue coming in. More importantly, it had no experience of how to make big, complex, aircraft. What to do? The word was put out that it was looking for a partner, or a buyer. Up at Brough, Blackburn had finished building the Firebrand naval strike fighter and had a batch of Percival Prentice trainers on the go as a sub-contract. Blackburn was in contention with Fairey for a shipboard anti-submarine aircraft but if it lost the contest (it did, the Gannet became spectacularly successful) then the Humberside company faced slim pickings. Manufacturing Sunderland flying boats at Dumbarton had given Blackburn staff vital experience of large airframes and the Brough factory was more than big enough. On New Year's Day 1949, Blackburn merged with the much smaller GAL – this was not a takeover, it was a mutual arrangement – to become Blackburn and General Aircraft. The unfinished GAL.60 was taken in sections by road to Brough and began assembly in the spring of 1949, ready for its first flight. As the Beverley C.1, the GAL.60 was to keep Brough busy for nearly a decade. In the space of just eighteen years, General Aircraft had been transformed from a struggling light aircraft manufacturer into an enterprise that merged with a long-established major 'player'.

General Aircraft commissions and sub-contracts

Type	Total	From	To	Notes
Kronfeld Monoplane	1	1937	-	[1]
Hawker Fury II	89	1936	1937	
Fairey Firefly I	132	1943	1945	

[1] To the commission of Robert Kronfeld Ltd; two-seat tandem parasol pusher light aircraft – it remained a prototype.

General Aircraft

From	To	Total	Name/Designation	Type	Engine(s)	Notes
1932	1935	29	ST-4	Light transport	2 x Pobjoy R	[1]
1933	-	2	ST-6	Light transport	2 x Pobjoy Niagara	[2]
1934	1935	12	ST-10, ST-12	Light transport	2 x Pobjoy Niagara	[3]
1934	-	2	ST-11	Light transport	2 x DH Gipsy Major	
1935	-	1	Croydon	Airliner	2 x P&W Wasp Jnr	
1935	1937	59	Jubilee/Universal	Light transport	2 x Pobjoy Niagara	[4]
1937	-	1	GAL.33 'Cagnet'	Trainer	1 x Cirrus Minor	
1938	-	1	GAL.41	Research	2 x Pobjoy Niagara	[5]
1939	1941	8	Cygnet II	Trainer	1 x Cirrus Major	
1940	-	1	Fleet Shadower	Naval recce	4 x Pobjoy Niagara	
1940	-	1	Owlet	Trainer	1 x Cirrus Major	
1940	-	1	GAL.47	Observation	1 x Cirrus Major	
1941	1943	1,012	Hotspur I–III	Assault glider	nil	[6]
1941	-	1	GAL.50	Scale test bed	nil	
1942	-	1	Twin Hotspur	Assault glider	nil	
1942	1946	323	Hamilcar I	Assault glider	nil	[7]
1943	-	2	GAL.55	Trainer glider	nil	
1944	1947	3	GAL.56	Research glider	nil	[8]
1944	1945	12	Hamilcar X	Transport	2 x Bristol Mercury	[9]
1948	-	1	GAL.61	Research glider	nil	[10]
1949	-	1	GAL.60	Transport	4 x Bristol Hercules	[11]

[1] Two converted to ST-6 status. [2] Retractable undercarriage version of ST-4; conversions of ST-4s not included. [3] ST-12 with DH Gipsy Major. [4] From 1936 produced as the Universal with twin fins and rudders. One converted to Cirrus Minors as GAL.26. [5] ST-25 with pressure cabin fuselage. [6] Also sub-contracted to a group led by Harris Lebus, Tottenham, and including Waring and Gillow, Lancaster; Mulliners, Birmingham; and William Lawrence and Co, Nottingham (996); and Slingsby, Kirkbymoorside (about eight). [7] Also sub-contracted to the Hamilcar Production Group, led by Birmingham Carriage and Wagon Co (300). [8] Tail-less research gliders with three different wing formats: 'Medium V' with 28-degree sweep back; 'Medium U' with 28-degree sweep back; 'Maximum V' with 36-degree sweep back. [9] Twelve built from scratch, also ten conversions of Hamilcar gliders. [10] Completed and handed over to the Royal Aircraft Establishment, but not flown. [11] Named Universal Freighter in 1949 – taken on by Blackburn and taken to Brough for completion – see Chapter 9.

CHAPTER TWENTY-TWO

Fighter Factory

Gloster
1917 to 1959

'…the Javelin had got into some sort of stabilized stall, [it] dropped almost vertically like a brick at more than a mile a minute…'
Test pilot 'Bill' Waterton on the loss of WD808, 1953

HAVING RAISED MORE than a glass or two to celebrate victory over Japan, the workforce at Gloster's assembly line at Hucclecote returned to the job in hand. Eight days later, on 23 August 1945, Meteor F.III EE358 was accepted by 74 Squadron at Colerne – the first peacetime handover of the jet fighter. A myth lingers that the RAF had only a handful of Meteors by the end of the war: this was far from the case, EE358 was the 103rd Meteor built.

The twin jets turned heads wherever they appeared but in the summer of 1945 they were far from new. Gloster was Britain's most experienced manufacturer of jet aircraft, having started in 1941. Propelled by Frank Whittle's pioneering technology, on 15 May 1941 the E.28/39 became the first British jet to fly. That put its designer, George Carter, and the company into a powerful position to turn that knowledge into an operational fighter that might help shorten the war.

Capitalising on this, Carter and his team conceived the Meteor, which had its maiden sortie on 5 March 1943. No time was lost and the development programme quickly morphed into full-blown production. On 23 July 1944 the RAF entered the jet age when 616 Squadron accepted its first F.I at Manston. Four days later the new type was engaging the barrage of V-1 'Doodlebug' flying-bombs and the Meteor became the first – and only – Allied jet in combat during the war.

Gloster did not have a monopoly in first-generation jet fighters: de Havilland (DH) wasn't far behind: its Vampire appeared in September 1943 and entered RAF service in April 1946. DH was an industrial giant with an expanding product line by 1945, while Gloster was beginning to shake off the image of a sub-contractor and was keen to use the Meteor as a launch pad to the 'big league'. The company's marketing department took every opportunity to exploit the Meteor's achievements. There was vast export potential and Gloster had the edge on DH and indeed, the rest of the world. A fighter factory since the 1920s; the post-war course was obvious, it would specialise in jets: with the Meteor, it had command of the future.

Fighter Collection chief pilot, Pete Kynsey, testing Gladiator II at Duxford on 1 May 2013. It carries the colours of 72 Squadron's 'B' Flight. *Col Pope*

Airco's legacy

George Holt Thomas – the founder of the Aircraft Manufacturing Company and other ventures – left two legacies when his empire collapsed in 1920 (Airco). Geoffrey de Havilland, Airco's designer, established his own enterprise that grew into a giant. Sub-contractors for Airco were widespread and in 1915 the Cheltenham-based woodwork specialist H Martyn and Co Ltd was signed up to make assemblies for Farmans and DH.2s. These were followed by fuselages for DH.4s and whole DH.6s, the latter being test flown from Hucclecote. The quality was excellent and talks about setting up a new business resulted in Airco and Martyn going into a 50:50 partnership as the Gloucestershire Aircraft Company on 5 June 1917. Holt Thomas had planted the seed.

The post-war order slump did not deter the young company and it took the brave move to elevate itself from sub-contractor to design house. The 'Gloucestershire' name was eventually regarded as too provincial and as a mouthful for export customers. On 11 November 1926 the name was changed to Gloster Aircraft. For the purposes of this chapter, the business will be referred to as 'Gloster' throughout.

At Cricklewood, the Nieuport and General Aircraft Company (N&G) had developed the promising Nighthawk fighter. It was designed by the man who had created the Royal Aircraft Factory S.E.5 – Henry Phillip Folland – but was powered by the disastrous ABC Dragonfly radial. Gloster became a Nighthawk sub-contractor, but N&G folded in November 1920. Scrabbling to keep going, Gloster followed the accepted course of diversifying, turning to sub-assemblies for the automotive industry. That was a stopgap, as a creditor of N&G Gloster managed to secure a vast stockpile of Nighthawk airframes, parts and the design rights. This was a masterstroke: this was the basis of a new aviation business.

Creating a family

In January 1921 Folland signed up with Gloster, initially as a consultant, but he soon accepted the post of designer. (Folland's story is detailed in Chapter 20.) He began to modify and refine the Nighthawk under the 'brand' Mars (this confusing name was dropped by 1923). The best way to get noticed was to achieve some speed records by attending European aviation events in a high-speed machine. The result was the Mars I, using Nighthawk sub-assemblies. This initially featured a streamlined fuel tank ahead of the pilot that

Folland's 'flag waver', the Mars I, G-EAXZ, was commonly known as the 'Bamel', in 1924. *Peter Green Collection*

also supported the upper wing centre section, in place of what would usually have been a draggy arrangement of struts. This 'hump' gave rise to its nickname. During its construction Folland referred to the covered fuselage and the skeletal rear fuselage as 'half bare, half camel' and the words 'bare' and 'camel' were fused into 'Bamel'. First flown at Hucclecote on 20 June 1921, the Bamel – radically modified throughout its career – was soon clocking speeds over 200mph. Gloster's potential was very firmly demonstrated.

Initial recognition of the Nighthawk's potential was not from Britain, but from the Imperial Japanese Navy in 1921. An order for fifty was a lifesaver for Gloster, the aircraft dropping the Mars designation for the name Sparrowhawk. Japan remained loyal to the company, taking a licence for the Gambet in 1927. This machine was an unwanted prototype version of the Grebe for shipboard use. (A gambet is a bird akin to a sandpiper.) After lengthy development, the RAF also adopted the Nighthawk and a carrier-based version, the Nightjar in 1922.

Folland needed a test bed to validate his differing aerofoil concept from 1923. In general, biplanes used the same aerofoil on both wings. Folland believed that a thick-section upper wing and a thinner-section lower component could create lighter airframes through reduced span without sacrificing lift and giving lower stalling speeds. This technique he termed the High Lift Biplane (HLB). By mating a 'thick' and a 'thin' wing to a two-seat Sparrowhawk, fuselage Folland created the Grouse. This experimentation paid dividends; the Grouse led to the Grebe and the Gamecock.

Nightjar H8539 at Farnborough in 1922. The devices inboard of the mainwheels are the arrester wire 'jaws' used for deck landing. *KEC*

A pair of Hawkinge-based Grebe IIs of 25 Squadron, circa 1925. Folland's 'thick and thin' aerofoils are apparent. *KEC*

Between them, the Grebe and the Armstrong Whitworth (AW) Siskin heralded an important era for the RAF when they entered service in 1924: they were the force's 'new generation' fighters, not inherited from the Royal Flying Corps. Prior to the Grebe order, Gloster needed to seek additional business and accepted a contract to rebuild Airco DH.9As – a job that carried several firms through the doldrums of the early 1920s. Other work included more than 500 sets of wings for the Westland Wapiti general-purpose type from 1929 to 1932.

The HLB wings gave the Nighthawk series a new life and in 1923 Gloster flew a Grouse development that the Air Ministry referred to initially as the Nighthawk (Thick Winged) before settling on definitive name Grebe (an aquatic, diving, bird). A trio of prototype Grebes was followed by a large order for 109 fighters plus twenty-one dual-control Mk.IIIDCs. The latter, along with a similar version of the Siskin, established the notion of the advanced trainer, acknowledging that the step from basic trainer to front-line fighter was becoming more and more challenging. Anxious to spread work across the industry, the Air Ministry contracted Avro to build the upper wings, Hawker the lower ones and DH the ailerons. The same thinking resulted in Gloster manufacturing a batch of Siskins.

Also named after a bird, in this case a fighting cock, the Gamecock was an improved version of the Grebe, from February 1925. As well as the more powerful Bristol Jupiter VII radial, the rotund Gamecock had its machine guns mounted within the fuselage, either side of the cockpit. The Grebe carried its guns Sopwith-style on the upper decking in front of the pilot. Large orders were again shared out by the rest of the industry, followed by licence production in Finland. The Gamecock was the last RAF fighter of wooden construction.

In 1927 Gloster acquired a large stake in the London-based Steel Wing Company (SWC) and eventually became the sole owner. This was probably brought on by both Folland and the Air Ministry deciding that the future was all-metal, signing a hefty £10,000 contract for a 'metallised', high-altitude version of the Gamecock, the Goldfinch. Folland used the occasion to experiment; flying an SWC-inspired rolled steel box-spar section that was graphically described as a 'triple-barrelled shotgun' and the patented Gloster Lattice Girder technique. Folland rang the changes, the Goldfinch testing both upper and lower wings with the 'shotgun' spar, followed by a pair of lattices. He ended up with lattice for the thick top wings

and box-type for the thin, lower, wings. In the summer of 1927 pilots at Martlesham were very keen on the Goldfinch. When it came to issuing an all-metal, high-flying, day and night fighter specification – F.9/26 – Gloster was in a strong position. Although the prize went to the Bristol Bulldog, Folland and his design office had learned a tremendous amount – one of the intentions of the Air Ministry.

The progression from Nighthawk to Gamecock allowed Gloster to expand its activities. As well as SWC, from the mid-1920s a propeller division was set up, specialising in variable-pitch blades. In 1936 this business was sold on to a partnership of Rolls-Royce (RR) and Bristol, with the composite word Rotol chosen as its trade name. Folland's department was expanded, including assistant designer Frederick Duncanson, recruited from Fairey and later to develop his tubular spar with Blackburn. Until 1928 the Hucclecote site had been leased: it was purchased in its entirety in 1928 and within two years the Cheltenham factory had been vacated.

Schneider troubles

Folland's experience honing the 'Bamel' into a clipped-wing racer provided the best of backgrounds when Hucclecote was contracted to build a pair of 585hp Napier Lion-powered Gloster II biplane floatplanes for the 1924 Schneider Trophy competition. In *Gloster Aircraft since 1917*, Derek James notes that the Air Ministry paid £3,000 for each of these. The first example was written off and for a variety of reasons the contest was postponed. Two much more sophisticated Gloster IIIs, fitted with 700hp Lions, appeared in August 1925 and were dispatched to Baltimore, Maryland. One was damaged and withdrawn, but Hubert Broad took the other to 199mph to come second.

In 1927 each of three Gloster IVs for the competition in Venice, Italy, cost, according to James, £8,250. Powered by 900hp Lions, the trio – all to slightly varying specifications – represented the pinnacle of biplane aerodynamics, although Folland was still of the belief that the format outclassed monoplanes. A Supermarine S.5 was the winner, beginning what was to be a 'hat-trick' for Britain. The Gloster V biplane remained on the drawing board and in 1929 Folland produced his first monoplane – the Gloster VI with a metal semi-monocoque fuselage and wooden wings. The two floatplanes – each costing £12,500 – suffered technical problems and did not compete in the 1929 race, staged from Calshot. All of the efforts were

Gloster VI N249 on it beaching trolley at Calshot, 1929. *KEC*

vindicated afterwards when Flt Lt George Stainforth piloted Gloster VI N249 for recorded runs along the Solent on 10 September 1929 at an average of 336mph, a world record. The glory was fleeting, forty-eight hours later Sqn Ldr Augustus Orlebar took a Supermarine S.6 to 357mph. The final Schneider Trophy, held at Calshot in 1931, was an all-Supermarine affair.

Prototypes and commissions

The table 'Gloster piston-engined types' reveals a range of prototypes, none of which were rewarded by production orders. Except for private ventures, where the risk was all on the company, the Air Ministry paid for the machines for evaluation by the Aeroplane and Armament Experimental Establishment at Martlesham Heath. For such contracts, estimating costs needed very careful assessment. Margins were wafer thin and an aircraft needing modification or rectification could be a heavy drain on income. While the Air Ministry was of the belief that such competitions helped to keep designers and some of the workforce of each manufacturer going; maintaining sufficient drawing office staff to respond to requirements and modifications was expensive, when perhaps overheads could have been pared back.

Two of the 'hopefuls' given in the table deserve further comment. The Gorcock – a male red grouse – research machine of 1926 was the company's first type with a steel tube fuselage and wooden wings, while the third example was all-metal. The four-engined – two pulling, two pushing – TC.33 was the largest Gloster to take to the air. In the late 1920s through to the mid-1930s the Grebe and the Gamecock and the lucrative licence arrangement with Nakajima for the Sparrowhawk/Gambet were cash cows but even so, in 1932 Hucclecote needed to turn to making car bodies and milk churns to survive.

Chapter 21 details the link between Gloster and John Stieger – founder of General Aircraft – and the ST-3 light twin and the Monospar wing. This was not the first time that Gloster's expertise in wing structures was sought. In 1929 the Italian Ugo Antoni requested the company build and fit a variable camber wing of his own design to a Breda 15 light aircraft. Testing went well until the Breda crashed in December 1933.

In the late 1920s DH had an embarrassment of work and some of it was discomforting the Air Ministry by continued delays. After conceiving the Short-Bristow Crusader Schneider floatplane, George Carter was recruited at Stag Lane. He created the DH.77 single-seat interceptor, which first flew at Stag Lane on 11 July 1929. The DH.67 twin-engined survey type had been through several rethinks but was forever stalled. Design authority was vested in Gloster and Folland kept only the format in his complete rethink, as the AS.31. The first of two appeared in June 1929. The unfinished DH.72 tri-motor heavy bomber was taken by road to Hucclecote for assembly and testing. There it was completed, with some redesign; it debuted on 28 July 1931.

The 'Empire' pounces

The late 1920s was a barren time for Gloster and the Air Ministry was lobbied about amalgamation. In February 1934 Hawker began *takeover*, not *alliance*, talks and the deal was quickly accepted. The following year Hawker's 'Tommy' Sopwith and Fred Sigrist were busy and their company and AW came together on 25 June 1935; the massive Hawker Siddeley Aircraft (HSA) was born. The constituent businesses all continued to trade under their own names. The enterprise was reorganised in 1948 as the Hawker Siddeley Group and again in January 1959 when it became Hawker Siddeley *Aviation*. To prevent confusion between the 1935 to 1948 HSA and the HSA of 1959 onwards, throughout the book the earlier HSA is referred to as the Hawker Siddeley (HS) consortium.

Sub-contracts – really inter-factory work share – were immediately available. Hawker was desperate for production capacity for its military biplane family and handed on Hardy, Hart and Audax assembly and, from 1938, Henley target tugs. The biplanes kept Hucclecote busy until the Gauntlet and Gladiator took their place on the factory floor. Despite this salvation there was disquiet, particularly from Folland, that Hucclecote had been downgraded and that original designs were a thing of the past. According to Folland, the Hawker head designer, Sydney Camm, did not hide this opinion. As will be seen, Camm had worked *under* Folland and may well have been wary of his mentor's experience encroaching on what he saw as his domain.

The very distinctive Hucclecote watch tower and flight office in 1994, before the entire site was redeveloped. *Ken Ellis*

Gauntlet II K7804 operated by 3 Group's Meteorological Flight, Mildenhall, 1937. Recording instrumentation is carried under the lower wing tips. *KEC*

With Europe accelerating into hostilities, Hucclecote was expanded considerably. Fellow HS consortium member AW was heavily occupied making Whitley bombers and the entire Albemarle programme was transferred to Hucclecote. The venture remained AW-managed and A W Hawksley Ltd – a play on Armstrong Whitworth Hawker Siddeley – was created for administrative purposes. It was late 1940 before Albemarles began rolling out of the Hucclecote 'shadow' factory. In November 1940 Gloster was ready to mass produce Hawker Hurricanes, churning out 2,750 over four years; the first entering flight test on 20 October 1939. Hucclecote also made all of the metal stressed-skin wings for Hurricanes coming off the Kingston line. From 1941 Gloster took on manufacturing the Typhoon in its entirety; the first example flying on 27 May 1941.

Gloster sub-contracts and work for Hawker Siddeley

Type	Total	From	To	Notes
Airco DH.6	150	1917	-	
Bristol F.2B	461	1917	1918	
AW Siskin IIIA	74	1927	1929	
de Havilland DH.77	1	1929	-	[1]
de Havilland DH.72 Canberra	1	1931	-	[2]
Monospar ST-3 (SS.1)	1	1931	-	[3]
Hawker Hardy	47	1934	1936	
Hawker Hart Special	72	1935	1936	
Hawker Audax (India)	25	1935	-	
Hawker Henley	200	1938	1940	
Hawker Hurricane	2,750	1939	1942	
AW Albemarle	600	1940	1944	[4]
Hawker Typhoon	3,285	1941	1945	

[1] Built at Stag Lane; designed by George Carter – see Chapter 17 and narrative. [2] Began at Stag Lane, but completed at Hucclecote – see Chapter 17 and narrative. [3] Gloster designation SS.1 – Stieger, Salmson 1; light twin to the commission of the Monospar Wing Company – see Chapter 21. [4] Built at Hucclecote under the aegis of A W Hawksley Ltd – see Chapter 4.

Last of the breed

After his success with the Grebe and the Gamecock, Folland was determined to retain the company's role as supplier of the RAF's fighters. When it came to replacing the Bristol Bulldog, Folland's answer was the Gauntlet of 1933, destined to be the last RAF open cockpit fighter. Despite being powered by a draggy Bristol Mercury radial, the new fighter had the edge on Camm's sleek V-12-powered Hawker Fury, by about 30mph at 15,000ft. While there might have been rivalry, or even suspicion, between the Kingston and Hucclecote design offices, the benefits of membership of the HS consortium were obvious. Access to Hawker's construction techniques and volume production expertise gave rise to a major revision of the Gauntlet: the Mk.II had 'dumb bell'-shaped spars and a revised fuselage structure.

Folland realised that the Gauntlet still had more to offer and it provided the basis for Gloster's answer to Specification F.7/30, which sought an RAF interceptor for the second half of the 1930s. The private-venture SS.37, which was refined into the Gladiator, won out against a host of competitors – see the table – including monoplane prototypes from Bristol and Supermarine. The bulk of the hopefuls had opted for the Air Ministry's favoured RR Goshawk V-12. Featuring evaporative, or 'steam', cooling, the engine proved to be a road to nowhere and only about twenty Goshawks were completed.

When the Gladiator entered service the writing was already on the wall for its kind; it was the last RAF front-line biplane. Nevertheless, it provided a vital stepping stone to the next generation. Hawker and Supermarine seized the initiative with the private-venture Hurricane and Spitfire multi-gun monoplane interceptors, cutting through the Air Ministry's inertia. The Gladiator gave the pilot the luxury of a canopy; four machine guns; single-bay inter-plane struts in place of twin-bay; plus cantilever main undercarriage and split flaps on upper and lower wings. The result was the pinnacle of biplane achievement and was well greeted by the squadrons.

Folland's final design for Gloster was an F.5/34 contender, the specification that eventually gave rise to the Hurricane and the Spitfire. The first of two Bristol Mercury radial-engined prototypes flew in December 1937, by which time both the rival Hawker and Supermarine designs were a reality. George Carter took over from Folland and he conceived the elegant twin-engined F.9/37 heavy fighter, with the prototype making its maiden flight on 3 April 1939. After another example powered by another problematic engine, the RR Peregrine, nothing further came of the project and Carter turned to face far greater challenges.

All fifteen of the former RAF Gladiator IIs ordered by the Portuguese Air Force parked out on the Hucclecote turf – now a housing estate – in the summer of 1939. *Gloster*

The first F.9/37, the Taurus-engined L7999, during the summer of 1939. *Gloster*

Battling the Gladiator: Specification F.7/30 competitors

Aircraft	Status	Format	First flown	Engine
AW AW.35	PV	Biplane	18 Mar 1935	AS Panther
Blackburn F.3	AM	Biplane	See notes	RR Goshawk
Bristol Type 123	PV	Biplane	12 Jun 1934	RR Goshawk
Bristol Type 133	PV	Mono	8 Jun 1934	Bristol Mercury
Gloster SS.37*	PV	Biplane	12 Sep 1934	Bristol Mercury
Hawker PV.3	PV	Biplane	26 Jun 1935	RR Goshawk
Supermarine Type 224	AM	Mono	19 Feb 1934	RR Goshawk
Westland PV.4	AM	Biplane	23 Mar 1934	RR Goshawk

Notes: PV – private venture; AM – Air Ministry contract. The F.3 failed to get airborne. * Gloster submitted an improved SS.37 in June 1935 that included enclosed cockpit, altered landing gear and tail unit; this was snapped up and the Gladiator received a production contact on 1 July 1935.

Jet pioneer

Henry Folland was increasingly disturbed by the changed nature of Gloster and he left in 1937, bound for British Marine Aircraft – Chapter 20. In his place came Wilfred George Carter, like Folland one of Britain's most important designers but, unlike his predecessor, largely unsung. Aged 17, Bedford-born Carter was apprenticed in 1906 to a local engineering works, with maritime turbines in its portfolio. In 1915 he joined Sopwith at Kingston, soon becoming chief draughtsman and later designer under Herbert Smith. In 1920 Sopwith was wound up and Carter returned to his native Bedford to seek employment.

Meanwhile, 'Tommy' Sopwith had relaunched his enterprise as H G Hawker Engineering, appointing Bertram Thomson as chief designer, but he left for Saunders in 1923. At this point Carter returned to the fold, taking Thompson's seat and starting off on the Woodcock II fighter and the Horsley bomber. Appointed as Carter's assistant was the 30-year-old Camm – his full story belongs to Chapter 25. Carter had become unhappy with life at Hawker by 1925, differences of opinion regarding procedure with the forthright Fred

Sigrist playing a part. Carter was back on the train to Bedford.

Carter's availability was made known to aero engine maestro Roy Fedden, who was putting together a team to compete in the Schneider Trophy floatplane races. Lt Col Whiston Alfred Bristow employed Carter and between them they created the Short-Bristow Crusader, which first flew on 4 May 1927. With the aircraft in the air, Carter was soon to be unemployed … back to Bedford. He was out of the industry only for a short while, taking a post at DH to conceive the DH.71 monoplane interceptor. When the development of this was handed over to Gloster, Carter followed the trend, joining up in 1930. His first task was to 'tweak' the DH.72 and see the huge biplane through its trials. With the Hawker buyout Carter found himself working for his former assistant, Camm. This relationship did not go well but the following year, the establishment of the HS consortium allowed great job mobility and Carter was transferred to Woodford, helping the mercurial Roy Chadwick on the Manchester bomber.

In 1937 Folland headed for Hamble and Carter returned to Hucclecote as chief designer. With the Meteor programme gaining more and more traction, from the summer of 1943 Carter's assistant, Richard Walker, took on responsibility for the jet 'family'. Six years later Walker was promoted to chief designer, with Carter becoming technical director and later consultant. Wilfred George Carter CBE MBE retired in 1958: he died on 27 February 1969, aged 79. Tim Kershaw, in his excellent *Jet Pioneers: Gloster and the Birth of the Jet Age*, sums up Carter perfectly: 'His honours were few and his fame is slight. He deserves more.'

Lighting the 'torch'

Through risky trials and frustrating errors, Sqn Ldr Frank Whittle and his Power Jets team were creating an aviation gas turbine against many odds. In March 1938 the unit began its first ground runs, fraught with potential self-destruction, but proving beyond doubt that the young engineer had created a viable alternative to piston engines.

Gloster piston-engined types

From	To	Total	Name/Designation	Type	Engine(s)	Notes
1921	-	1	Mars I/Gloster I	Racer	1 x Napier Lion	[1]
1921	1922	51	Sparrowhawk I–III	Naval fighter	1 x Bentley BR.2	[2] [3]
1922	1923	54	Mars VI Nighthawk	Fighter	1 x AS Jaguar	[2]
1922	1923	22	Mars X Nightjar	Shipborne fighter	1 x Bentley BR.2	[2]
1923	-	1	Grouse I/II	Research/trainer	1 x Bentley BR.2	[4]
1923	-	1	Gannet	Ultralight	1 x Carden	
1923	1927	133	Grebe I/II	Fighter	1 x AS Jaguar	
1924	-	2	Gloster II	Floatplane racer	1 x Napier Lion	
1924	1930	111	Gamecock I/II	Fighter	1 x Bristol Jupiter	[5]
1925	-	2	Gloster III	Floatplane racer	1 x Napier Lion	
1926	1928	3	Gorcock	Research	1 x Napier Lion	
1926	1927	2	Guan	Research	1 x Napier Lion	
1926	-	1	Goral	Military GP	1 x Bristol Jupiter	
1926	-	1	Goring	Day bomber	1 x Bristol Jupiter	
1926	-	3	Gloster IV/'A/'B	Floatplane racer	1 x Napier Lion	
1927	-	1	Goldfinch	Fighter	1 x Bristol Jupiter	
1927	1932	151	Gambet	Shipborne fighter	1 x Bristol Jupiter	[6]
1927	1930	2	Gnatsnapper	Shipborne fighter	1 x Bristol Mercury	
1929	1938	246	SS.18/Gauntlet	Fighter	1 x Bristol Mercury	[7]
1928	1929	2	Gloster VI	Floatplane racer	1 x Napier Lion	
1929	1931	2	AS.31 (DH.67)	Survey	2 x Bristol Jupiter	[8]
1932	-	1	TC.33	Bomber-transport	4 x RR Kestrel	
1932	-	1	TSR.38	Torpedo strike	1 x RR Kestrel	
1934	1939	747	SS.37/Gladiator	Fighter	1 x Bristol Mercury	[9]
1937	1938	2	F.5/34	Fighter	1 x Bristol Mercury	
1938	1940	2	F.9/37	Fighter	2 x Bristol Taurus	

Based upon: *Gloster Aircraft since 1917*, Derek James. Other than the Gloster VI, F.5/34 and F.9/37, all are biplanes. **[1]** Also known as the 'Bamel'. **[2]** Modified Nieuport Nighthawk airframes. **[3]** Originally designated Mars II–IV. Contract also included airframe 'kits' for another 40 – thought to have been used for attrition repairs. One Sparrowhawk I modified as Grouse I/II. **[4]** Modified Sparrowhawk I. **[5]** Also licensed by Finnish National Aircraft Factory, Helsinki, 15 under the name Kukko, 1929–30. **[6]** Total of 150 licensed by Nakajima, Japan, as A1N1 and A1N2, 1929–32. **[7]** Seventeen Mk.IIs licensed to Flyvertroppernes Vaerksteder, Copenhagen, Denmark. **[8]** Design originated with de Havilland – Chapter 17 – detailed design and construction vested with Gloster. **[9]** Includes Sea Gladiator.

Whittle had made his point so much so that on 21 January 1940 Specification E.28/39 was issued to Gloster for a pair of experimental aircraft to test the jet concept and provide the basis for a fighter.

By that time, Carter's office was involved in development of the F.9/37 twin-engined fighter, but it was clear that no production commitment would be forthcoming. Otherwise the team was involved in integrating changes and adjusting working drawings for the Hurricane's production schedule at Hucclecote. This excess capacity was to change Gloster's fortunes and aviation across the globe. Carter's capability was well established, his drawing office team was well respected, and Gloster's prowess as a major manufacturer – even if for other firm's designs – was obvious. After several meetings, the methodical Carter and the headstrong Whittle – the latter nineteen years younger – began to bond. Carter's days making and designing marine turbines and his determination that the jet was the future helped to cement a vital partnership.

Unpainted, the first E.28/39, W4041, ready for taxi trials at Hucclecote in early April 1941. The striping along the rear fuselage is heat-sensitive paint. *Gloster*

E.28/39 was further amended in late December 1940, dropping the need for armament. By then Carter was already well on with conceiving a twin-jet, cannon-armed fighter and the single-engined prototypes were pathfinders and no longer needed to prove their worth as potential warplanes. The contract price was £18,500 each, plus £1,800 to cover test rigs and mock-ups. An astounding fifteen months after the paperwork was signed, the first E.28/39 was ready for testing. It had been determined that Cranwell was the best place for trials; the Lincolnshire aerodrome was a classic flying field with usable long grass runways in most directions. Prior to taking the E.28/39 by road to Cranwell, Gloster test pilot Philip Edward George 'Gerry' Sayer carried out initial taxi trials on home turf at Hucclecote. Sayer and Carter had worked closely on the layout of the cockpit and other elements of the prototype.

Kershaw details Sayer's report for three runs on 8 April 1941: 'The aeroplane left the ground on each of these three runs. The actual flights being about six feet off the ground and varying in distance from 100 to 200 yards along the ground.' While these were certainly more than 'hops', a maiden flight is generally defined as a circuit. Even so, with the great occasion having been 'exported' to Cranwell, these were important moments in Hucclecote's history.

Having got the prototype rigged, 15 May 1941 looked likely as the big day, but most of it was spent hoping that the weather would co-operate. Finally a westward take-off was possible. At 1948 hours the throttle was eased forward, its pilot long since accustomed to the lag before the power kicked in. The prototype touched down on the turf seventeen minutes later and, as the engine wound down, he was met by euphoria from the small team; the greatest smile coming from the man who had battled against the odds to create the powerplant – Frank Whittle. The testing urgently needed to validate the concept so that the baton could be handed over to Carter's twin-engined fighter. (The first E.28/39, W4041, is today displayed inside the Science Museum in London.)

Runaway success

Carter's twin-jet emerged as the F.9/40, destined to become the spectacularly successful Meteor. Cranwell had been the venue for the maiden flight of the E.28/39 and the large grass aerodrome was again chosen for its successor. On 5 March 1943 Michael Daunt was at the helm of the Halford H1-engined DG206 for its truncated debut at Cranwell. He encountered considerable directional stability problems – 'snaking' – and the sortie lasted just 210 seconds. Despite this, the pace of the programme increased: he flew DG205 on 12 June 1943 and forty-two days later DG202; both of these fitted with Whittle W2B/23s. (DG202 is today part of the RAF Museum's collection.) The first pre-series Meteor I EE210, complete with cannon in the nose, flew on 12 January 1944.

Early operational experience with the Meteor F.III gave rise to the F.IV in mid-1945 and this became the staple of the production line. As well as the RAF ordering the type in quantity, it was with the Mk.IV that Gloster started its long run of exports; Argentina placing an order for 100 in May 1947. The Mk.IV had its limitations and from 1947 Walker, under Carter's guidance, set to on creating the ultimate day fighter version that had the potential to expand into other roles, including ground attack and reconnaissance. This was how the Meteor gained the vital characteristics for a great 'Industrial' aircraft, as outlined in the Introduction. The result was the exceptionally clean-looking F.8, which had its maiden flight on 12 October 1948 and became the backbone of RAF air defence up to the mid-1950s.

Design work on the F.8 was extensive; it was not a mere 'tweak' but a major refinement to keep it competitive well into the 1950s when swept-wing, second-generation types – the Hunter and the Swift – were to take over. The F.8 gave new impetus to the programme and the variant was built in greater numbers than any other Meteor – including under licence in the Netherlands. While the F.8 took the limelight, in 1948 a private-venture trainer version also flew and opened up further markets for Gloster. For many air arms, including the post-war RAF, the ability for pilots to spend time in a two-seater was desirable.

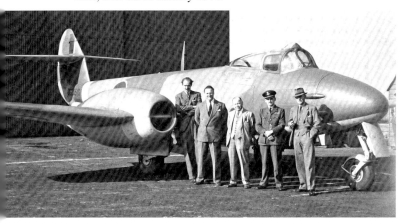

Left: At 6ft 8in Gloster test pilot John Crosby-Warren (left) dominates this line-up. The others are: Michael Daunt, Gloster chief test pilot; F McKenna, Gloster general manager; Gp Capt Frank Whittle; George Carter, Gloster chief designer. Behind is DG205/G, the second F.9/40 prototype to fly, the first with Whittle engines and the aircraft in which Crosby-Warren was killed in April 1944. *Gloster*

Below: Meteor F.8 manufacture in top gear at Hucclecote in 1950. *Gloster*

By removing the cannon, an elongated cockpit accommodating two pilots in tandem – instructor in the rear, pupil in front – was devised and the T.7 was born. The T.7 and F.8 were a persuasive package and the Meteor became a runaway success. Following Argentina's lead, export customers queued up with Australia, Belgium, Brazil, Denmark, Ecuador, Egypt, France, Israel, the Netherlands, Sweden and Syria all placing orders; some taking reworked RAF examples.

In 1948 Hucclecote was heavily involved with the T.7 and the F.8 and was formulating its response to Specification F.44/46 for an all-weather and night fighter based on the Meteor. The biggest drain on the company's design resources was the definitive day/night fighter that would emerge as the Javelin. Something had to give and in 1949 it was decided to hand over the interim Meteor night fighter's design responsibility and production to sister organisation AW.

On 9 April 1954 test pilot Jim Cooksey strapped himself into the last Gloster-built Meteor, F.8 WL191, and piloted it off the small runway at Hucclecote for the short 'hop' south-west to the test airfield at Moreton Valence, the centre of Gloster jet testing since October 1943. Conversions to new roles – for example the TT.20 target tug – and refurbishing second-hand airframes for export kept the Moreton Valence and AW workforce heavily engaged for years to come.

Jet diversion

While the Meteor and the Javelin are well known, there was one other post-1945 Gloster type. Specification E.1/44 originated in May 1944 for an experimental single-seat jet with the potential to become a fighter. Changes in the specification and the priority of the Meteor delayed the programme and it was not until mid-1947 that the first prototype was completed. While on a Queen Mary articulated transport on its way to testing at Boscombe Down, the first E.1/44 was wrecked when the vehicle crashed after a downhill 'runaway'.

The second machine was finished and successfully trucked to Boscombe, where it was flown on 9 March 1948, and the third followed in 1949. Both performed well enough, but the E.1/44 was not followed up; Gloster was close to saturation with Meteors and the Vampire had cornered the single-engined jet fighter market.

The second E.1/44, TX148, at Moreton Valence in early 1949. *Gloster*

A trio of Wattisham-based Meteor NF.14s – WS805 closest to camera – of 152 Squadron, 1954. *KEC*

Delta finale

Richard Walter Walker became chief designer in 1948, with George Carter taking the role of technical director until 1954. Walker's major assignment was the Javelin, twin-engined delta-winged, all-missile armed, all-weather fighter. While the Meteor was a first generation jet, the Javelin represented what later would be called a 'weapon system'; a complicated mixture of aerodynamics, powered flying controls, sophisticated weaponry and radar. The Javelin had all the potential to be an even bigger money-spinner for Gloster, by overall value if not by unit.

Gloster jets

From	To	Total	Name/Designation	Type	Engine(s)	Notes
1941	1943	2	E.28/39	Experimental	1 x Power Jets W.1	
1943	1944	8	F.9/40	Experimental	2 x RR W.2B/23	[1]
1944	1950	903	Meteor I–V	Fighter	2 x RR Derwent	[2]
1947	1949	3	E.1/44	Fighter	1 x RR Nene	[3]
1948	1956	716	Meteor T.7	Advanced trainer	2 x RR Derwent	
1949	1954	1,697	Meteor Mk.8–10	Fighter/Recce	2 x RR Derwent	[4]
1950	1954	578	Meteor NF.11–14	Night fighter	2 x RR Derwent	[5]
1949	1958	433	Javelin	All-weather fighter	2 x AS Sapphire	[6]

Based upon: *Gloster Aircraft since 1917*, Derek James. **[1]** Meteor prototypes; variety of engines. Sixth example served as F.II prototype. **[2]** Includes 46 built by sister company Armstrong Whitworth – Chapter 4. **[3]** First example written off in a road accident on its way to Boscombe Down July 1947 – it did not fly. **[4]** F.8, FR.9 and PR.10. Includes 430 built by sister company Armstrong Whitworth – Chapter 4. Includes 300 built by Fokker at Schiphol, Netherlands and 30 Fokker-built kits assembled by Avions Fairey at Gosselies, Belgium. **[5]** All built by sister company Armstrong Whitworth – Chapter 4. **[6]** Includes 133 built by sister company Armstrong Whitworth – Chapter 4. FAW.7s upgraded to FAW.9 status 1960–61.

Aged 15, Walker was employed in the drawing office of a Bradford engineering business from 1915, before serving as an engine fitter in the RAF in 1918–20. With a diploma in engineering, he joined the RAE in 1924 as a stress calculator. A brief spell with Blackburn in 1925 was followed quickly by enrolling with Hawker, under George Carter. Kingston sent him to Sweden in 1933 to prepare the way for that country's licence production of Harts and Ospreys. He was back in the UK in 1935, as assistant designer. Among his tasks was the development of the Hurricane's metal-skinned wing. Walker renewed his acquaintance with Carter in 1937 when he transferred to Gloster, going on to take a major role in the conception of the E.28/39 and the Meteor. Appointed technical director in 1954, with the end of the Javelin and Gloster, he joined AW. He needed to move again in 1966 when Bitteswell ceased building aircraft, heading to Avro. Richard Walter Walker retired in the late 1960s and died on 10 April 1982, aged 82.

An ambitious design, the Javelin suffered from a protracted development period, with many specification changes and more than its fair share of accidents. Chief test pilot 'Bill' Waterton carried out the prototype's first flight from Moreton Valence on 26 November 1951. During this aircraft's ninety-ninth sortie, on 29 June 1952, Waterton encountered elevator flutter but did not abandon it, bringing it back for a very risky forced landing. He was awarded the George Medal for this heroic act. Eight days after Waterton's horrific incident the Ministry of Supply announced that it was buying the Javelin in quantity and that it had been given so-called 'super priority' status. Between 1953 and 1956 three Gloster test pilots lost their lives in accidents with Javelins. AW shared in the manufacture, building 133 at Bitteswell.

Development ran from the FAW.1 to the Mk.9 and, with the exception of the T.3 dual-control trainer, all featured radar or armament changes, upgraded engines and aerodynamic refinements. Walker worked on so-called 'thin-winged' variants to extend the production run but the venture was cancelled in July 1956. Gloster needed a drastic change of direction and quickly – the civil sector was the only answer. One hopeful project was the twenty-eight-seat twin-turboprop Accountant from Southend-based Aviation Traders (Engineering) Ltd (ATEL). Gloster had been engaged to help with design and construction and to provide a market survey. It had an option to handle production if the Accountant caught on. The prototype, G-ATEL (for Aviation, an early example of a 'fixed' registration) was first flown on 9 July 1957 from Southend and demonstrated at the Farnborough airshow that September. This was more than a year ahead of the rival Handley Page Dart Herald but with no sales interest, the one-off Accountant was retired in 1958. ATEL went on to produce the radical car ferry conversion of the Douglas DC-4, the Carvair.

Gloster's work on the Accountant was far from a wipe out; its experiences were handed on to Avro, which was formulating its own twin turboprop, the 748 launched in 1960. Gloster and AW were combined as Whitworth Gloster Aircraft on 1 October 1961, with Bitteswell as the headquarters. Test pilot 'Dickie' Martin flew Javelin FAW.8 XJ128 out of Hucclecote to Moreton Valence on 8 April 1960. This was the final maiden flight of the long line of Gloster fighters. Upgrades to FAW.9 status occupied the company for a while, but on 6 April 1964 the disposal of Hucclecote was announced and the name Gloster disappeared.

Javelin FAW.2 XA813 of Waterbeach-based 46 Squadron in its element, 1961. *RAF Museum*

CHAPTER TWENTY-THREE

Hendon's Showman

Grahame-White
1911 to 1922

'The fact that I have embarked upon the construction of aeroplanes does not mean that I am giving up flying myself…'
Claude Grahame-White, 1911

'WE WEREN'T REALLY CLASSED as anything more than entertainers in those days. We didn't mind because that was the only way to make flying pay. There was no money in selling aeroplanes.' John Dudley North recalling his early days as a designer for Claude Grahame-White at Hendon, as explained to Harald Desmond. Aged just 24, in 1917 North began an association with Boulton and Paul that was to last near four decades. Like several others, North's time with Grahame-White was brief; staff turnover was frequent.

Gifted pilot, visionary designer, spirited performer, fiercely competitive, cunning entrepreneur, determined industrialist, galvanizing public speaker, engaging personality, dogged anti-bureaucrat, prolific author and considerate employer are all used to describe Claude 'Whitey' Grahame-White; a man well-known as an aviator and showman, but not regarded as an 'aero industrialist'. Landlord to George Holt Thomas of the Aircraft Manufacturing Company (Airco), Grahame-White did not reach the heights of Airco in terms of the number of aircraft manufactured. Indeed, the output of the Grahame-White Aviation Company (GW) falls below the

'radar' of this book, the definition for inclusion being: the construction and flying of at least five original, individual, types and a grand total of at least 200 machines built. Just over 2,000 sub-contracted or licensed aircraft were made by GW, but only one of many original types reached three figures. Despite this, it would be a crime not to include this exceptional enterprise. (To distinguish between the man and the business, the former is referred to as Grahame-White, the latter as GW.)

Designer–pilot–entrepreneur Claude Grahame-White seated in a 'Boxkite' at Hendon, 1912. *Peter Green Collection*

The recreated Grahame-White boardroom at the RAF Museum, Hendon. *Ken Ellis*

A Boxkite and the GW Lizzie competing during an air race at Hendon, circa 1913. *Peter Green Collection*

Grahame-White was apprenticed, aged 16, to a Bedford engineering company in 1885. This was the start of an incredible range of occupations that included: working in a Yorkshire woollen mill; establishing the Yorkshire Motor Vehicle Company hiring out charabancs (remember that word); 'exploring' southern Africa and car salesman. Fascinated by the cross-Channel flight of Louis Blériot on 25 July 1909, Grahame-White attended the aviation meeting at Reims in France the following month and was 'sold' on aeroplanes. He enrolled at the Blériot school at Pau in the south of France and was granted the Aéro Club de France certificate No. 3 on 4 January 1910. Ordering six Blériot XI monoplanes, he set up a school at Pau while scouting for a British base. His first flight in Britain was at Brooklands, just nine days after he got his French 'ticket'. Back at Pau, he qualified for his Royal Aero Club aviator's certificate – No. 6 – in a Blériot on 26 April 1910. From here on, Grahame-White's flying exploits sadly get short shrift so as to keep to the task in hand: profiling him as the head of an aircraft manufacturing business.

Assembly of the Blériot XIs began in Edgar Isaac Everett's shed at Hendon in 1910, a stone's throw from the site of the aerodrome Grahame-White was soon to run. (Another 'name' was associated with this shed; Richard Fairey helped Everett during the early days of his monoplane in 1911 – Grahame-White and Fairey did not meet at this time.) Initially Grahame-White centred his activities on Brooklands, but he had been 'taken' by the possibilities at Hendon. Everett leased his shed to Grahame-White and during 1910 he acquired a ten-year lease on 207 acres of land – the London Aerodrome was born, GW and a flying school followed. Sheds were built and several operators, including the Blériot School and the Blackburn School, took up residence. More and more individuals and organisations came to fly from Hendon, with a string of 'firsts' and record flights achieved. Grahame-White was determined that Hendon would be a place to which the public would throng. On 8 June 1912 the first Aerial Derby was staged and a crowd of 45,000 turned up.

In September 1910 Grahame-White began the first of two tours of the USA, the second taking place in August the following year. He won a string of cash prizes and became equally well known in the States as he was at home. During the second trip to America, Grahame-White designed an aircraft that took into account his experiences. He commissioned renowned boat-builder William Starling Burgess of Marblehead, Massachusetts, to make the Baby two-seat, scaled-down, Farman-like biplane. It was easily dismantled

for road or rail transport and featured steel fittings for robustness and ease of replacement. The Baby was brought across 'The Pond' for display at the Olympia Aero Show in London during March 1911. At least one more, known as the New Baby, was also manufactured. Some sources give the 'Babies' as being British creations, but *the* reference, Graham Wallace's *Claude-Grahame-White – A Biography* records that: 'the Babies had been built in America'.

End of a 'Golden Age'

With the collapse of Horatio Barber's Aeronautical Syndicate at Hendon in April 1912, Grahame-White and Frederick Handley Page picked up most of the stock, while Airco took on the premises. It was at this point that GW employed John Dudley North as designer; he had been assisting Barber with his Viking biplane. Prior to the arrival of North, GW had produced mostly Farman-derived machines on a 'workshop' basis, the Grahame-White School of Flying using at least a dozen 'Bi-Rudder Buses', as they were nicknamed.

North's first creation for his new employer was the Popular, a boxkite-format two-seater with a span of 28ft aimed at schools and private owners. In *British Aircraft 1809 to 1914*, Peter Lewis records the Popular's intention: 'At the time … the majority of aeroplanes cost about £1,000. [The Popular's] price of under £400 was a praiseworthy attempt to place on the market a machine at a reasonable price without compromising standards of safety, economy and comfort'. As the table shows, like many GW types, the Popular remained a one-off.

The Popular biplane, intended as an affordable private owner type. *Peter Green Collection*

The Type VI gun-carrier was shown off at the 1913 Olympia exhibition. This capitalised on North's experience with Horatio Barber, who had schemed a variant of the pod-and-boom layout, permitting a nose-mounted gun a wide arc of fire. The tail surfaces were carried on a triangular cross section frame attached to the rear of the crew nacelle. An Austro-Daimler engine was fitted within the nacelle, driving the pusher propeller through an extension shaft. Control cables for the elevator and rudder ran *through* the propeller boss and along the upper element of the 'boom'. No interest was shown in the Type VI but on 27 November 1913 the armed potential of an aeroplane was vibrantly demonstrated. A Hendon school Boxkite was the platform for the first airborne firing of a Lewis machine gun. Belgian army officer Lt Stellingwerf hit specially prepared targets at the famous Bisley range in Surrey.

Visitors came to Hendon events in their tens of thousands and many wanted to take to the air – Grahame-White became the 'king' of 'joy-riding'. In previous employment, he had hired out charabancs for trippers in Yorkshire. The French word 'charabanc' – for coach – was fashionable in the early 20th century and in 1913 GW commissioned North to create a multi-seat joy-rider. Sticking to the tried and tested Farman layout, the 62ft 6in span biplane had a nacelle intended to carry a pilot and four passengers. Ever keen for headlines, Grahame-White began the Charabanc's career in fine style on 22 September 1913 when Frenchman Louis Noel and *seven* passengers squeezed in and set off for a sortie out of Hendon that lasted just over seventeen minutes – a world record uplift and endurance. The following month Noel surpassed this, taking *nine* 'punters' up for seconds short of twenty minutes. The Charabanc remained very busy through to the summer of 1914, but the 'Golden Age' of Hendon, its displays, races and a 'trips around the 'drome' were coming to a close.

Hendon at war

Hendon was commandeered under the Defence of the Realm Act (benignly abbreviated as DORA) on 4 August 1914 and it became a Royal Naval Air Station (RNAS), while Grahame-White was given the naval rank of flight commander twenty-seven days later. On 12 February 1915 Grahame-White was part of a massed raid – thirty-four aircraft – on the enemy coast; his Farman F20 was forced down into the sea and Hendon's showman was lucky to be rescued. A posting to France resulted in Grahame-White resigning his commission. He was not avoiding combat – he'd just risked everything over the North Sea – but was astounded that the RNAS should take him away from the far more important task of building aeroplanes.

The Airco and the British Caudron Company factories at Hendon were put on a war footing. GW was ready for orders, accepting a contract for Royal Aircraft Factory B.E.2cs in October 1914. Grahame-White took things into his own hands and began construction of an assembly hall in December 1915 without permission, opening for business in 1916. He eventually received a government loan of £320,000 and by 1917 the GW factory had spread to over 50 acres.

Early in 1914 North prepared two machines hoping to secure War office contracts. The Type XI Warplane was a classic tandem two-seat pod-and-boom layout that began testing in May 1914. Unconcerned by superstition, the Type XIII was intended as an entrant in the *Daily Mail* Circuit of Great Britain contest but was reconfigured as a two-seater scout. No interest was aroused and the XIII ended its days teaching RNAS pilots at Hendon. North was tempted to join Boulton and Paul and left in May 1915. His place at GW was taken by H V Hedderwick, who went on to conceive the Type XVIII bomber and the Airco DH.6-inspired 'Two-Seater'. By 1917 N Martineau was the GW designer. The major 'home-grown' workhorse of the Great War was the Type XV, a refined development of the well-worn Boxkite formula that served from Hendon and more widely with the RNAS and Royal Flying Corps.

War Office woes

Creating buildings without permission and barraging the War Office with suggestions and outrage, Grahame-White was not flavour of the month with 'the establishment'. The Graham Wallace biography is fantastic reading. It describes that, when berated by the Director of the Air Department about late handover of B.E.2cs, Grahame-White unleashed a broadside: 'If you *will* continue to alter the drawings and your inspectors *will* reject every blessed part we make, at the rate we're going the war'll be over before a single plane is delivered!'

During the summer of 1918 GW was approached regarding manufacture of Handley Page V/1500 bombers: ever dynamic Grahame-White initiated new buildings, only to find the requirement cancelled without warning. The company was told to tool up for ABC Dragonfly-engined Sopwith Snipes instead. Wallace takes up the story: 'Hardly had [GW] got the factory organised for the production of the Snipes when the Supply Department [of the Air Ministry] countermanded the order and told Grahame-White to prepare to turn out 500 Nieuport Nighthawks with complete sets of parts for a further 1,500 machines. [Grahame-White] had just got ahead with this assignment when, to his baffled amazement, this contract was cancelled and replaced by one for 500 Avro 504s!'

Despite permanently facing financial oblivion, Grahame-White was determined to celebrate the Armistice, granting '…two days' holiday on full pay for his entire stage of 3,000 men and women'.

Grahame-White sub-contracts and licences

Type	Total	From	To	Notes
Morane-Saulnier 'G'	1	1914	-	[1] [2]
Morane-Saulnier 'H'	24	1915	-	[1]
Royal Aircraft Factory B.E.2c	26	1915	1916	
Henri Farman F.20	100	1916	-	[3]
Bréguet V Concours	10	1916	-	[4]
Airco DH.6	700	1916	1917	
Avro 504J and 'K	900	1916	1919	

[1] Licensed from Société Anonyme de Aéroplanes Morane-Saulnier, Villacoublay, Paris, France. [2] Designated GW Type XIV. [3] Contract 'sublet' from Airco, Hendon. [4] Licensed from Société Anonyme des Ateliers de'Aviation Louis Bréguet, Douai, France. Designated GW Type XIX.

Last throws of the dice

In common with most of the British aircraft industry, GW found itself with vaporising contracts and it turned to the manufacture of vehicle bodies and furniture. A sideline of taking Rolls-Royce armoured cars, stripping them down to their chassis and turning them into luxury cars proved briefly lucrative. It was April 1919 before commercial flying was allowed to recommence, yet *still* Hendon remained impressed under DORA. Grahame-White was vigorously petitioning for the release of the aerodrome, let alone compensation for 'services rendered'. The showman circumvented this by opening the lavishly appointed London Flying School on GW-leased land that was *not* part of the wartime requisition on 1 July 1919.

By 1919 GW had another designer, Frenchman E Boudet (quoted in some sources as M Boudet, but this may be the abbreviation for 'Monsieur'), who was tasked with meeting the needs of post-war civil operators. The three-engined – two pulling, one pushing – Ganymede bomber was re-engineered into a twelve-seat airliner powered by a pair of tractor Napier Lions. Boudet created the fighter-like Bantam, which was also marketed as the 'Air Mail' capable of carrying 100lb of mail sacks at 100mph. The asking price of £800 was not unreasonable but with surplus aircraft available in their

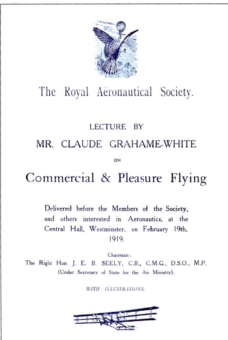

Above: The first Bantam at the 1919 Hendon Aerial Derby. It carries the interim civil registration K-150. *Peter Green Collection*

Top: Still wearing its military serial C3481, the Ganymede bomber after conversion to airliner status at Hendon in 1919. *Peter Green Collection*

Left: Cover of an illustrated brochure issued during a lecture on the future of commercial and pleasure flying given by Grahame-White at Westminster's Central Hall on 19 February 1919. A graphic of '24-seater passenger machine' triplane is featured at the bottom. *KEC*

Below: The Limousine nearing completion at Hendon in 1919; the pilot sat in the upper fuselage under the centre section. *Peter Green Collection*

thousands for a tenth of that price, it is not surprising that only three Bantams were built. The Limousine was an attempt to recreate the Charabanc, this time with a completely enclosed, glazed, passenger compartment. It had a brief life; it was destroyed by fire in 1920.

With government loans outstanding, claims for compensation unresolved, looming excess profits taxes and the original aerodrome still in the hands of the military, something had to give. Grahame-White was in the USA when the axe fell. The Treasury appointed a receiver and the GW empire was wound up: remaining staff were dismissed and all property was seized. Lawyers were unleashed on both sides, but eventually Grahame-White accepted a reported £500,000 for Hendon and it was transferred to the Air Ministry in 1922. It was the end of a great aviation adventure: Grahame-White became a property developer, with particular success in California. Claude Graham-White, pioneer and aeronautical showman, died in Nice, France, days short of his 80th birthday on 19 August 1959.

Lasting tribute

Within the RAF Museum are two buildings that provide unique testament to Grahame-White and his incredible endeavours. Constructed in 1915, the watch office gave views over the comings and goings of the aerodrome and was the nerve centre of the GW organisation. It was last used as a control tower in 1957. The imposing factory, with offices overlooking the shop floor, was completed in 1917 as the UK's first purpose-made aircraft manufacturing plant.

Part of the deal that brought about today's Beaufort Park on the former aerodrome site was the relocation of the watch office and the factory to the southern-most edge of the RAF Museum site: no trivial undertaking. The structures need recording, dismantling, relocating and re-erecting using the maximum amount of original materials while meeting modern regulations and visitor requirements. The first element to be resited was the factory and aircraft exhibits were rolled into it in February 2003; it opened to the public later in the year. Attention to detail is superb, including the replica Thomas Crapper and Company cisterns and plumbing in the loos! While the watch office was smaller, in terms of challenges it was a far bigger project. It was adapted and extended so that it linked to the factory, with the space in between telling the story of Grahame-White, Hendon, aircraft manufacture in the area and the history of the museum itself. The watch office was formally opened on 17 March 2011. Grahame-White's personal office is breathtaking, the fireplace containing offcuts of aircraft-grade wood in a typical example of Edwardian waste not, want not!

Grahame-White

From	To	Total	Name/Designation	Type	Engine(s)	Notes
1910	-	1	Biplane	1-seater	1 x Gnome (?)	[1] [2]
1912	-	1	Type IX	1-seater	1 x Anzani	[3]
1912	1914	12?	Boxkite	Trainer	1 x Gnome	[1] [4]
1912	-	1	Type VIII Hydro-Biplane	2-seater	1 x Anzani	[5]
1913	-	1	Type VI	Military GP	1 x Austro-Daimler	[6]
1913	-	1	Type VII Popular	Trainer/Tourer	1 x Gnome	[6]
1913	-	1	Type X Charabanc	Light transport	1 x Austro-Daimler	[6] [7]
1913	-	1	Lizzie	Sportsplane	1 x Gnome	[5] [8]
1914	-	1	Type XI Warplane	Military GP	1 x Gnome	[6]
1914	-	1	Type XIII Scout	2-seat scout	1 x Gnome	[5]
1914	1915	135	Type XV	Trainer	1 x Gnome	[1] [9]
1915	-	1	Type XVIII	Bomber	1 x Sunbeam Maori	[5]
1916	-	1	Type XX	Scout	1 x Clerget	[5]
1917	-	1	Type XXI	Scout	1 x Le Rhône	[5]
1917	-	1	Two-Seater	Military GP	1 x RR Hawk	[5]
1918	-	1	E.IV Ganymede	Bomber	3 x Sunbeam Maori	[10]
1919	-	3	E.6 Bantam/Air Mail	Sportsplane	1 x Le Rhône	[5]
1919	-	1	E.7 Limousine	Light transport	2 x RR Eagle	[5]
1919	-	1	E.9 Ganymede	Airliner	2 x Napier Lion	[5] [11]

Sources differ between Roman and Arabic numerals for GW pre-1919 designations: Graham Wallace's *Claude Grahame-White – A Biography* adopts the former. Production figures for most types are unknown but most GW designs are thought to have reached prototype stage only. **[1]** Pusher boxkite-format biplane. **[2]** Peter Lewis *British Aircraft 1809 to 1914* refers – no other details. **[3]** Tractor monoplane. **[4]** Also known as the 'Bi-Rudder Bus'. **[5]** Tractor biplane. **[6]** Pusher biplane. **[7]** Also known as 'Aero Bus'. **[8]** Based on Morane-Saulnier 'G' fuselage, also known as 'The Teatray'. **[9]** Also known as Admiralty 1600 Type. **[10]** Biplane, two tractor, one pusher. Converted in 1919 into the E.9. **[11]** Substantial redesign/rebuild of E.IV, with 12-seat central cabin.

CHAPTER TWENTY-FOUR

Dogged Independence

Handley Page
1909 to 1970

'Mr Handley Page is to be reckoned amongst the earliest subjugators of the air' Flight magazine, 21 September 1916

HAVING TOILED LONG HOURS alongside his boss through the winter of 1914, George Volkert had created a pile of pages of stress calculations and layouts. In February 1915 the Admiralty inspected the bundle of paperwork and authorised a contract for a quartet of prototype bombers, along with an advance of £20,000. Volkert's employer and mentor, Frederick Handley Page, scurried off to the bank to wave the cheque and demand an overdraft – there was a war on and he was going to help win it. Handley Page began a frantic search for factory premises; his little company was housed in a ramshackle set of sheds at Barking, in London's East End with a dozen people on the payroll. By the end of 1915 a former Rolls-Royce (RR) garage in Cricklewood had been taken over and the number of employees had reached 150.

Since it was formed in 1909, Handley Page Ltd had built a handful of aeroplanes of original design and to the commission of others. The company had annoyed the War Office with a much-delayed sub-contract for five Royal Aircraft Factory B.E.2s, which

Publicity image of a crew scrambling into Victor B.1 XH592, newly delivered to 15 Squadron at Cottesmore in the spring of 1959. Its cockpit section survives, at the Midland Air Museum, Coventry. *Handley Page*

was reduced to just three early in 1914 when Handley Page declared such small batches were not viable. This lack of experience and the B.E.2 frustrations did not faze the Royal Navy: it had faith in the little firm. Within the blink of an eye, Handley Page's enterprise had ceased to be a hand-to-mouth workshop and was on its way to becoming an industrial giant. (See Chapter 36 for a wager between Frederick Handley Page and Noel Pemberton Billing.)

Fredrick Handley Page in his monoplane *Bluebird* in April 1910. *KEC*

Straight out of college, aged 21, Volkert had been appointed designer by Handley Page in 1912. The first aeroplane he worked on from scratch was the elegant Type G biplane that appeared in late 1913. Powered by a 100hp Anzani, the two- or three-seater had a span of 40ft and a loaded weight of 1,775lb. This contrasted starkly with the machine that the Royal Navy ordered, soon to be designated the O/100. Eventually fitted with a pair of 250hp RR Eagles, it had a crew of four, a span of 100ft and a loaded weight of 14,000lb. Within the O/100's centre section Volkert had drawn one of the first-ever weapons bays, which would hold sixteen 112lb bombs, suspended vertically.

Handley Page and Volkert had been entrusted with developing Britain's long-range hammer blow against Imperial Germany. The O/100 evolved into the O/400 and the four-engined V/1500, and for decades to come 'Handley Page' was a generic name for any very large aeroplane. Volkert was destined to create heavy bombers all the way through to the Halifax of World War Two and had a say in the gestation of the Victor, part of the RAF's Cold War nuclear deterrent force.

Outstanding individualist

In 1906, at the age of 18, Cheltenham-born Frederick Handley Page began work with an electrical engineering company in London. Enthralled by aviation, in 1907 he joined the Aeronautical Society of Great Britain, which became the Royal Aeronautical Society and Handley Page was its president from 1945 to 1947. Through the society he met up with the French pioneer José Weiss, whose signature wings with a curved leading edge inspired Handley Page's early monoplanes. The temptation to try out ideas in his employer's time was too much and Handley Page was sacked.

Far from deterring him, he founded Handley Page Ltd on 17 June 1909 at Barking. (To differentiate between the man and the business that came to bear his name, Frederick Handley Page is referred to here as Handley Page and the company is abbreviated to HP.) While developing a canard glider with the Weiss wing, Handley Page actively pursued commissions, including one from G P Deverall Saul for a bizarre quaduplane. Handley Page was 22 when he made tentative hops in a powered aircraft of his own design, a monoplane called *Bluebird* in May 1910.

Gaining a reputation as a shrewd and pugnacious businessman, Handley Page preferred the 'brass tacks' of industry to the 'romance' of aviation. Throughout his career he was determined to teach others and it was while lecturing at London's Northampton Institute that he spotted Volkert's potential. After his student had qualified with a degree in mechanical engineering in 1912, Handley Page offered him the post of designer.

The pinnacle of Handley Page's commitment to education was to co-found, with aero engine supremo Sir Roy Fedden, the College of Aeronautics at Cranfield in 1946. Today, as Cranfield University, the campus remains at the cutting edge of aerospace study. Research and development was also part of Handley Page's credo. Hand in hand with the evolution of the O/400, a pioneering wind tunnel was introduced in 1916. From the late 1920s Handley Page introduced the post of experimental designer – Gustav Lachmann in a separate office in Edgware – to work in parallel with the drawing office to keep the company up to date with potentially profitable innovations.

Sir Frederick Handley Page CBE died on 21 April 1962, aged 76. To the end he staunchly advocated that the business he founded could still go it alone. The 3 May 1962 issue of *Flight* paid fulsome tribute, including Handley Page's exceptional skills as a public speaker: 'Official policy – no matter what government was in office – was the favourite target of his barbed but never spiteful wit ...' Lord Brabazon caught the man's dogged determination to remain independent: '... he was an individualist of outstanding personality and a pioneer of all sorts of great machines.'

Handley Page commissions and sub-contracts

Type	Total	From	To	Notes
Saul Quadruplane	2	1909	-	[1]
Thompson/Type B	1	1909	-	[2]
Sonaca Biplane	1	1912	-	[3]
Royal Aircraft Factory B.E.2a	3	1913	1914	
English Electric Canberra B.2	75	1953	1955	

[1] Pusher quadruplanes to the commission of, and designed by, G P Deverall Saul. First machine a single-seater, second a two-seater. Limited success in flight trials; first example flew well under tow. [2] Tractor biplane to the commission of, and designed by, W P Thompson, founder of Planes Ltd. [3] Tractor biplane to the commission of, and designed by, T Sonaca.

Bloody paralysers

'What we want here is a bloody paralyser to stop the Hun in his tracks.' The words were those of Commander Charles Rumney Samson sent in a terse situation report from Flanders in late September 1914. Samson was leading a force of Royal Naval Air Service (RNAS) aircraft and Royal Navy armoured cars to try to prevent Antwerp being taken by the forces of Imperial Germany: the Belgian port fell to the invaders in the second week of October. On the receiving end of Samson's vitriol was the navy's Director of the Air Department, Commodore Murray Fraser Sueter, and he took it to heart. Long-range heavy bombers could catch the German *Hochseeflotte* – high seas fleet – at its moorings and revolutionise naval warfare. It was Sueter who approached Handley Page with a

With the famous creek in the background, the Handley Page 'factory' at Barking in June 1909. In front of the main shed is the first Deverall Saul quadruplane. *Handley Page*

An O/400 of 115 Squadron at Lympne in July 1918 en route to Roville-sur-Chênes, France, in readiness for operations. *KEC*

request for such a 'Bloody Paralyser' and it was this requirement that Volkert turned into the O/100 and O/400.

George Rudolph Volkert was born in Fulham in 1891 and started at Barking on 15 shillings a week – £39 per year; not bad for a newly qualified youngster, the average annual salary in 1912 was around £60. Volkert was chief designer for HP in three sessions: 1912 to 1921, 1924 to 1931 and 1935 to 1948, and during that time he could hold claim to being the 'father of the British bomber'.

By 1921 HP – like the rest of the British industry – was in the doldrums and Volkert took the opportunity to be a part of the British Aviation Mission to Japan. In his place HP appointed S T A Richards, who took the initial lead in developing the 'W' series of airliners. Volkert's sojourn in Japan generated a distinctive entry in the *London Gazette* for 9 May 1924: 'The King has been pleased to give and grant unto George Rudolph Volkert Esq His Majesty's Royal licence and authority to wear the Insignia of the Sixth Class of the Order of the Rising Sun, which Decoration has been conferred upon him by His Majesty the Emperor of Japan, in recognition of valuable services rendered by him.'

During the early 1930s Volkert toured American aircraft and motor vehicle factories on a fact-finding mission. This paid great dividends as Britain geared up its industrial base to counter German expansionism. Techniques gleaned included sub-assemblies complete with wiring and 'plumbing' that could be built at other sites and brought to a centralised assembly line. This placed heavy emphasis on well-calibrated jigs and exceptional skills in planning the 'flow' of the construction process. The O/400 programme during the Great War had suffered badly from 'mismatches' from suppliers. As well as streamlining production, this scheme greatly aided the dispersal of production sites in the face of Luftwaffe bombing. This experience was first tried out on the Harrow and the Hampden before being employed with great success on the Halifax.

In 1948, Volkert handed over to Reginald S Stafford but remained a consultant to HP. Volkert was appointed technical director to the Reading division in 1953, lending his expertise to the project that emerged as the Herald. George Rudolph Volkert CBE died on 16 May 1978, aged 87, having made an incalculable contribution to HP and British 'heavies'.

The prototype O/100 was moved from Cricklewood to Hendon and flown for the first time on 18 December 1915. It was the largest British-built aircraft of its time and given that Volkert had 'frozen' the design only ten months previously and that HP was such a 'young' organisation, it was a tremendous achievement. In his book *Handley Page Aircraft since 1907*, Christopher H Barnes superbly sums up the occasion: 'there stood at Hendon, ready to fly, an aeroplane whose span was not much less than the total distance covered by Orville Wright's first flight at Kitty Hawk, twelve years earlier to the day'. The first O/100 featured a glazed cockpit in the extreme nose: this was abandoned for what was then a conventional open cockpit with a gunner's 'pulpit' in front of it. O/100s became operational in March 1917 and later in September that year the much-improved O/400 took

to the air. The ultimate 'Bloody Paralyser', the V/1500, appeared too late for wartime service, but reflected the command that Volkert had of large airframes. Four-engined – arranged in tandem, two pulling, two pushing – the V/1500 had a 126ft span and a 30,000lb all-up weight capable of carrying a 7,500lb bomb load 1,300 miles.

Just how many O/400s were built and by whom is a debate that will probably never be settled. Across the industry during the Great War the output of sub-contractors and suppliers to the 'subs' was poorly documented, or relevant documents failed to survive. As mentioned above, quality control and keeping to delivery schedules was a perpetual problem and contracts were hastily cancelled, or passed on to other concerns. The table 'Handley Page types to HP.46' gives insights into sub-contractors for the O/400, including ambitious transatlantic plans that at one point reached to more than 1,000 units.

Up until 1924, HP designs were allocated a letter of the alphabet; the twin-engined 'Bloody Paralyser' being the Type O and not, as is still to be found in publications, the '0' (as in zero). With 'Z' looming, in 1924 a numeric system, prefixed HP, was introduced and retrospectively applied to earlier creations: for example the O/100 and O/400 became the HP.11 and HP.12 respectively.

Off the shelf

After the Armistice of 11 November 1918, British manufacturers witnessed orders vaporising with little ministerial regard for the impact this cliff edge would have on what had become a strategic resource. HP fared better than most, construction of O/400s and V/1500s continuing into peacetime. Even so, it needed to build car bodies to tide it over while Handley Page went on the offensive to find new opportunities. In 1919 he bought out the Bognor Regis-based Norman Thompson Flight Company, makers of a range of flying boats from 1912. This *may* have been with a view to move into the marine aircraft market, but – in the light of his next purchase – was more likely about acquiring stock.

Post-war manufacturers did not just face a drought of orders. New designs to meet the burgeoning civil market faced competition from cheap and abundant surplus airframes, engines and components. Massive stocks were held at the National Aircraft Factories (NAF) and other sites and the government was very keen to move these on as quickly as possible. Established in 1917 by the Ministry of Munitions, the state-funded NAFs built aircraft and components under the management of non-aviation enterprises in a similar manner to the 'shadow factory' scheme of World War Two. There were three NAFs: No. 1 at Waddon, near Croydon, run by civil engineers Holland, Hannen and Cubitt; No. 2 at Heaton Chapel, Stockport, administered by Crossley Motors and No. 3 at Aintree, Liverpool, handled by the Cunard Steamship Company. The largest of the trio was at Waddon and it was there that the Aircraft Disposals Board (ADB) was set up to organise the mass auctioning of assets.

Handley Page realised that if this was left to the government the deluge of material unleashed on to the market was likely to result in the demise of much of the established industry. Additionally, ADB would have no idea of the true value of what it was selling off, letting items go for next to nothing. Very worryingly, flight-rated parts, engines or aircraft, would have no 'paper trail' to prove their airworthiness, rendering the certification process meaningless. Having found the means to finance the deal, Handley Page formed the Aircraft Disposal Company (ADC, known as 'Airdisco') on 4 March 1920. For a down payment of £1 million, plus 50% of the profits going to the government, ADC became the sole agent for the onward sale of the contents of the NAFs.

This deal raised the hackles of many of HP's rivals and colleagues. In his excellent biography of Roy Chadwick, *Architect of Wings*, Harald Penrose describes the reaction of Avro: 'John Lord [managing director] obtained an interim injunction restraining the Handley Page-inspired Aircraft Disposal Company from selling any aeroplanes or goods as Avro products unless of Avro manufacture because various other companies had produced the patented 504K components during the war, but there was no objection to these machines being sold as "Avro type".' It was soon appreciated that Airdisco was inspecting, cataloguing, documenting and reasonably pricing the stock and that its release would be gradual and controlled. Firms were given the right to buy back their products at substantial discount and HP itself was a beneficiary of this, acquiring O/400s for its airline – see below. What really settled doubts was ADC's intention that the industry would receive a small percentage of each transaction; this was a book-keeping nightmare but a very welcome injection to firms trying to recover from the post-war slump.

By carefully managing the liquidation of mountains of war-surplus material, Handley Page created a parallel industry that generated new business – not to mention unexpected cash flow. As detailed in Chapter 17, a good example of the benefit of ADC was the large holdings of Renault V-8s that Frank Halford used as the basis for his Cirrus in-line four-cylinder engine that led to the Gipsy family. Handley Page used ADC as the 'vehicle' for his acquisition of the moribund Martinsyde Aircraft Company in the spring of 1923 – see Chapter 27. Topping up the holdings through purchases such as Martinsyde merely delayed the inevitable. In 1925 it was restructured as ADC Aircraft Ltd and five years later, with the shelves empty, the venture was closed down.

Swords into ploughshares

On the day that civil flying was permitted after the Great War – 1 May 1919 – an O/400 flew a demonstration service from Cricklewood to Manchester and on 14 June Handley Page Transport (HPT) was founded. As noted above, another HP enterprise, Airdisco, allowed the new airline access to O/400s lying inert in storage and no fewer than twenty-eight examples were eventually registered to HPT. With their internally braced structures – wires criss-crossing the box-like fuselage – the O/400s were not ideal as passenger transports, but were well suited to freight. Although there was demand for regular services to the Continent and within Britain, the pioneer airlines vying for the business found it tough going. Sir Herbert Hambling led a committee looking into the future of British international services that recommended a single airline, subsidised or state-owned, and in March 1924 Imperial Airways came into being. The new organisation absorbed British Marine Air Navigation, Daimler Airway, HPT and Instone Airline. HP had got rid of a loss-making subsidiary and gained a potential customer.

By 1920 Cricklewood aerodrome was proving too small for large aircraft. HPT staged its last service from there in May 1921, moving its base to Croydon. Local councils were increasingly unhappy about flying from Cricklewood: noise was a factor, but more importantly the space was needed for housing. HP began a search for a new airfield and factory site, ideally within easy commuting distance of its established workforce. While ferrying an Avro Avian from Woodford to Cricklewood in March 1928, HP test pilot Jim Cordes 'discovered' Radlett when decaying visibility dictated a precautionary landing. Eleven miles north-west of Cricklewood, with great road and rail connections, it was perfect. Within six months limited test flying was taking place there and construction of hangars had begun. Cricklewood was closed as an aerodrome in November 1929, but remained as a factory.

Both Volkert and Richards were adamant that modified O/400s represented only an interim solution for the airliner market. The secret was to capitalise on the experience of the big bombers and create bespoke types for the new era. Expertise in large aircraft worked both ways: an airliner could become the basis of a bomber, or vice versa. The result was the 'W series' of two- and three-engined airliners. The prototype W.8 had its maiden flight on 4 December 1919 and the following year it entered service with HPT. Improved versions, the W.9 and W.10, attracted orders from Imperial Airways. The Belgian airline Sabena also signed up, including a licence

The first SABCA-built W.8e O-BAHN ready for delivery to Sabena, early 1925. *Peter Green Collection*

production deal. The airliner-becomes-bomber concept gave rise to the Hyderabad and the Hinaidi, of which more anon.

In 1928 Imperial Airways released its requirement for its European and Middle Eastern routes and the RAF announced Specification C.16/28 for a bomber-transport. Here was an opportunity to meet both needs with essentially the same design. Apart from fabric covering of the control surfaces and the rear fuselage, the HP.42 was of all-metal construction. The wings were supported by substantial Warren girder struts instead of a mass of flying wires. The prototype took to the air on 17 November 1930, with the other seven following in quick succession. Although the production run was just eight, the HP.42 took on fame akin to that of the 1970s Concorde – it was *the* airliner to be seen in. Although Dutch designer Anthony Fokker declared that the HP.42 featured a 'built-in headwind', speed was not the overriding factor: comfort and reliability was what mattered. In its European format, the HP.42 carried forty passengers in a sumptuous cabin with on-board catering, a generous baggage hold and superb views care of the low-slung fuselage. The pilots had the luxury of an enclosed cockpit.

The bomber-transport HP.43 followed a similar layout but had a utilitarian, box-like, fuselage and a three-engined format. The prototype first flew on 21 July 1932 but no production order was forthcoming. Sadly, the small run of the HP.42 was not to be recouped by a similar order from the RAF. The fuselage of the HP.43 was used as the basis for the HP.51 monoplane, which appeared in 1935. This also remained a one-off, but when much revised led to the Harrow – as detailed below.

The 'magic' slot

Seeking a way to increase wing loading, Handley Page began experiments in mid-1918 with slots on the leading edges of wings. He patented fixed and movable slots, both partial and full span, in 1919. An Airco DH.9 was acquired in February 1920 to test his theories: fixed full-span slots were fitted on both the upper and lower wing and the machine was later designated HP.17. Trials began in March 1920 and were very encouraging; the Air Ministry requested further experimentation. Handley Page came up with a parasol monoplane conversion of an Airco DH.9A with a thick section, semi-cantilever, wing featuring movable, full-span, leading-edge slots. Known as the X.4B, later the HP.20, it was first flown on 24 February 1921. Handley Page had perfected a revolutionary aerodynamic device with wide –and lucrative – application.

Born in Dresden, Germany, Gustav Victor Lachmann enrolled in the Imperial German cavalry in 1916 at the age of 20. The following year he transferred to the air service and was injured during training when the aircraft he was piloting stalled and spun in. While convalescing, Lachmann experimented in ways to lower the stalling speed and in February 1918 he lodged papers with the German patent office for a slotted wing. Lachmann went on to study mechanical engineering and aeronautics at Darmstadt Technical University, graduating in 1921.

Lachmann heard of Handley Page's experimentation with the HP.17 and the two men seemed poised for a head-on collision about who was first. Both realised that only the lawyers would gain and they came to an amicable arrangement over the marketing of leading edge slots. As well as enhancing safety worldwide, the invention was a lifesaver for HP, generating a staggering £750,000 in royalties from forty-five countries before the patent expired in the 1930s.

Lachmann became a consultant to HP from 1922, while taking a doctorate in engineering at Aachen Technical University in Germany. He took the post of chief designer at the relaunched Albatros Flugzeugwerke in 1925 but left a year later to act as a consultant to the Japanese aircraft industry. He returned to HP in 1929 as experimental designer, becoming chief designer in 1931. He rejoined the experimental department in 1935 when Volkert again became chief designer.

Superb night-time image – taken at 1846 hours – of HP.45 G-AAXD *Horatius* of Imperial airways outside the terminal at Croydon, winter 1932. *Imperial Airways*

James Cordes showing off the Gugnunc's slow-flying ability, thanks to the full-span slots, at Cricklewood, summer 1929. *Rolls-Royce*

Lachmann's work with HP came to a grinding halt in late 1939 when he was declared an enemy alien and was shipped off to Canada. More than 12,000 people had this status revoked in 1941 and Lachmann was one of these, returning to Britain to spend the rest of the war in an internment camp at Ramsey on the Isle of Man. Godfrey H Lee, Lachmann's former deputy, was running the HP experimental department and he was permitted to keep in touch, tapping Lachmann's thoughts as trials of the swept-wing, tail-less Manx – see below – began. It was 1949 before Lachmann came back to HP full-time and he became a British subject the following year. Elevated to the board in 1953 as director of research, Lachmann experimented with boundary layer control and laminar flow until he retired on the last day of 1965. Ever loyal to HP, he continued as a consultant, sadly not for long: Dr Gustav Victor Lachmann died on 30 May 1966, aged 70.

Ensconced inside the hi-tech Wilton Gallery of the Science Museum in London is the oldest surviving HP type, the Gugnunc. This apparently unassuming biplane is central to the HP slot saga. Ever keen to capitalise on its invention, in 1929 HP decided to have a crack at the Guggenheim Fund's 'Safe Aircraft Competition', to be held at Mitchel Field, Long Island, New York, later in the year. Powered by a 150hp AS Mongoose radial, with full-span slots on the upper wing and long-travel undercarriage, the HP.39 Guggenheim Competition Biplane, as it was officially known, first flew on 30 April 1929. Quickly it was dubbed 'Gugnunc', one of a host of words created for the *Daily Mail's* children's strip cartoon *Pip, Squeak and Wilfred*. Shipped to the USA in late September, it transpired that only the Gugnunc and the Curtiss Tanager were in contention. The competition was dominated by bitter legalities: Handley Page sued Curtiss for the full-span slots on the Tanager, which appeared to breach his patents, and Glenn Curtiss invoked a 1920 commerce act retrospectively preventing the importation of the Gugnunc. Returned to Britain, the HP.39 entered service with the Royal Aircraft Establishment (RAE) at Farnborough on 16 October 1930 and was passed on to the Science Museum four years later.

Biplane 'Heavies'

Developed from the W.8 airliner, the prototype Hyderabad bomber had its maiden flight in October 1923. It was the last British 'heavy' with a primarily wooden airframe. When 99 Squadron received its first example at Bircham Newton in December 1925, there was some relief that the unit was once again operating a twin. For the previous sixteen months, 99 had been flying the huge, single-engined Avro Aldershot. Prior to that, 99 Squadron was equipped with the reliable and well-liked Vickers Vimy.

It is reasonable to conclude that the Vimy, originating in 1917, was well outclassed by the Hyderabad. Not so; only in speed did the HP bomber win out: at its maximum 109mph it was 9mph faster. The Vimy had a range of 900 miles and a bomb load of 2,500lb, eclipsing the Hyderabad by 400 miles and 1,400lb respectively. What sort of 'progress' was this? British foreign policy assumed there would not be a major war for all of the 1920s and well into the '30s. The Hyderabad did not need long range, or high performance; it was there to present a deterrent and keep aircrew proficient in the art of bombing. None of the nations across the English Channel or the North Sea had anything that rivalled it.

On 29 March 1927 the replacement for the Hyderabad was flown for the first time. This was the Hinaidi, an improved version of its predecessor: indeed, the prototype was adapted from a Hyderabad airframe. The Hinaidi IIs that began to appear in 1930 had all-metal structures. Hyderabad is a city in central southern India; Hinaidi is a town near Baghdad in Iraq. Three transport versions of the Hinaidi were built for service in India. Originally given the name Chitral – after a city in present-day northern Pakistan – this was changed to Clive, in honour of Major-General Robert Clive, the 18th-century 'Clive of India'.

With its distinctive format, the Heyford always attracted a lot of attention. First flown on 12 June 1930, it was the RAF's last biplane bomber, but it had many of the attributes of the next generation of monoplanes. Its sleek-looking airframe was all-metal and fabric covered. The Heyford was very agile, often surprising intercepting fighters with its evasive manoeuvres during exercises. Within the Air Ministry's naming 'system', the choice of 'Heyford' was *presumably* based upon the Oxfordshire settlements of Lower and/or Upper

A Heyford of 9 Squadron – with another landing in the background, at Scampton in early 1936. The Type 'C' hangar behind is still under construction. *Rolls-Royce*

Heyford – the latter adjacent to the RAF station of the same name that was conveniently home to the Heyfords of 99 Squadron, 1928 to 1934.

There was purpose in mounting the lower wing *below* the fuselage, allowing an almost unrestricted field of fire for the nose and dorsal gunners. A conventional biplane layout would have had the top wing *above* the fuselage, hugely diminishing the field of fire, but the Heyford's was level with the top. There was also a retractable, manually operated ventral gun position, known as the 'dust bin', to cover the vulnerable 'behind and below' aspect. The centre section of the lower wing was where the bulk of the impressive war load – 2,600lb – was contained in small bomb bays called 'cells'.

Steps to the Halifax

Mention has already been made of the HP.42-derived tri-motor HP.43 bomber-transport. In 1935 the fuselage of the unwanted HP.43 was fitted to monoplane wings, once again hoping for a production contract. By then the RAF needed *bombers*, not hybrid bomber-transports. The HP.51 was radically altered into a 'stopgap' heavy bomber capable of carrying 3,600lb of bombs with gun turrets fore and aft. Despite this, the resultant Harrow was still expected to be able to accommodate twenty ready-for-action soldiers. The name Harrow – after the north London township and place of learning – had first been applied to the biplane torpedo bomber prototypes of 1926. One hundred Harrows were ordered straight off the drawing board and the prototype had its maiden flight on 10 October 1936. Construction, using Volkert's American-inspired 'streamlined' assembly techniques, preceded mass manufacture of Hampdens at Radlett. Although Harrows were issued to front-line units, by 1940 the type was relegated to transport duties: examples with the turrets faired over were nicknamed 'Sparrows'.

Named after either the Canadian or New Zealand town, the prototype Hampden first flew on 21 June 1936 and entered front-line service in August 1938. Unlike the Armstrong Whitworth Whitley and

A Hyderabad showing off its twin-unit main undercarriage and uncowled Napier Lion IIs. *KEC*

Harrow K6962 shortly after being accepted by 115 Squadron at Marham, summer 1937. *KEC*

the Vickers Wellington, it had the advantage of Volkert's 'streamlined' philosophy, enabling the most efficient use of sub-contractors. Production was handed over to English Electric at Samlesbury from the beginning of 1940 to allow HP to get the Halifax assembly line rolling. The Hampden combined simplicity – shunning power-operated turrets – with aerodynamic elegance. It was the fastest of the trio of medium bombers with which the RAF entered the war: 70mph ahead of the Whitley, 19mph better than the Wellington and only 12mph slower than the lightweight Bristol Blenheim.

A version of the Hampden powered by the troublesome 24-cylinder, H-format, 955hp Napier Dagger VIII entered limited production as the Hereford – named after the county town. The prototype, converted from a Hampden, took to the air in October 1938. The Hereford's disappointing performance and reliability meant only a handful saw operational service. Manufacture of Herefords was entrusted to Shorts at Belfast, the first example appearing in May 1939. If nothing else, the Dagger-engined variant prepared the Northern Ireland workforce to tackle mass production of the Stirling 'heavy'.

As the Hawker Hurricane was to the Supermarine Spitfire, so it was that the Halifax spent its time in the shadow of the Avro Lancaster. In 'ops' Lancasters flew nearly twice as many sorties and

Right: Ground crew working on Rootes-built, Merlin-engined, Halifax V LK911 of 76 Squadron at Linton-on-Ouse, 1943. *KEC*

Below: English Electric-built Hampden I AE148 of Upper Heyford-based 16 Operational Training Unit, 1941. *KEC*

dropped just under three times as much tonnage as their HP stablemates. But the Halifax had a glittering career that encompassed strategic bombing to the end of the war; action over the high seas with Coastal Command, demanding countermeasures sorties with 100 Group, hazardous clandestine 'special duties', airborne forces glider towing, paratroop and supply dropping, transport and training.

Like the Avro Manchester, the Halifax was conceived as a heavy twin, powered by RR Vultures. Thankfully HP avoided the traumas of having to re-engineer its design after production had started: Avro struggled morphing the Manchester into the Lancaster. The prototype Halifax initially flew with four RR Merlins on 25 October 1939. Pulling out all the stops, the first examples were handed over to Bomber Command that December. Despite a series of 'rolling' modifications, Merlin-engined Halifaxes had disappointing performance. This was corrected with the Bristol Hercules-engined Mk.III, which entered front-line service in October 1943 and transformed the type's prospects.

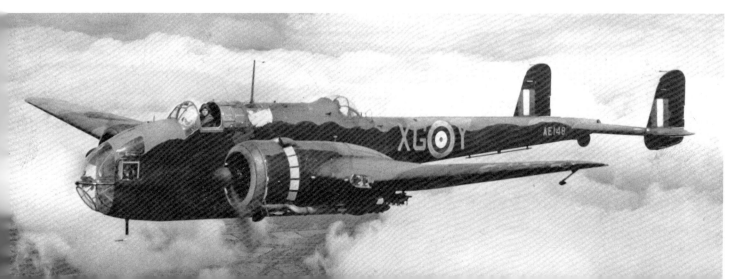

Once again, Volkert segmented the design so that it was readily transportable as sub-assemblies for dispersed production. 'Shadow factories' managed by English Electric, Fairey and Rootes Securities accounted for 4,877 of the 6,179 Halifaxes built. Proof that the Halifax had been wholly 'industrialised' was the great success of the so-called London Aircraft Production Group, a consortium of coach and lorry manufacturers including the London Passenger Transport Board, Park Royal Coach Works, Express Motor and Body Works, Chrysler Motors, and Duple Bodies & Motors. Sub-assemblies were brought to Leavesden, where a total of 710 were put together with minimal integration problems. When Halifax manufacture ended at Leavesden, de Havilland used it as an additional Mosquito completion site.

Tail-less twin

When Volkert returned to head up the HP design department in 1935, Lachmann settled back into his post as head of experimentation at the Edgware outstation. There he began to examine layouts for tail-less aircraft that might form the basis of a long-range, high-speed bomber. This took place long before the Tail-less Aircraft Advisory Committee was first convened in the summer of 1943. Lachmann conceived an all-wooden, twin-engined, pusher with tricycle undercarriage, with the outer sections of the wing swept back and fins and rudders at the tips. Radlett was busy with Hampden production and approaching Halifax testing, and its personnel had no current wood-working skills. Construction was sub-contracted in 1938 to glider and light aircraft specialist Dart Aircraft of Dunstable. It seems that the project, eventually designated HP.75, overstretched the little company and it was delivered late and overweight to Radlett in November 1939.

As recorded earlier, Lachmann – along with thousands of others – was carted off in late 1939 to Canada as a potential 'fifth-columnist'. HP chief test pilot Jim Cordes began fast taxi trials of the HP.75 on 29 February 1940. From the start Jim referred to the rotund test bed as the 'Manx' after the tail-less cats found on the Isle of Man. The following year Lachmann was brought back across the Atlantic and put in an internment camp on the Isle of Man. So Manx was even more appropriate and it was adopted as its official name. A shuttle of visitors, headed by Godfrey Lee, kept the HP.75's designer abreast of developments, picking his brains for 'fixes' to the many problems encountered. It was not until 25 June 1943 that 'Jamie' Talbot took the Manx for its first, fully fledged, maiden flight. By early 1945 Lachmann wanted to test what he termed a 'rider-plane' – what today would be called a foreplane – on the extreme nose of the Manx. Percival at Luton was contracted to build this and it was delivered to Radlett in June 1945, but never fitted to the HP.75. The Manx was flown for the final time in April 1946, by which time some of the iterations of HP's response to Specification B.35/36 – the nascent Victor – included tail-less, swept-wing jets.

Halifax legacy

Despite being eclipsed by the Lancaster in the later phases of the bomber war, the Halifax was remarkably adaptable and C.VIII special transport and A.IX airborne forces versions kept the Radlett production line busy until the last example was delivered in November 1946. There were plenty of refurbishment and change-of-role programmes, including exports to foreign air arms. Airlines and freight hauliers at home and abroad appreciated the workhorse's robustness. During 1948 Shorts converted a dozen Mk.VIIIs into ten-passenger airliners for British Overseas Airways Corporation (BOAC), under the fleet name Halton.

Using the Halifax VII wing structure as a starting point, the HP drawing office came up with a four-engined transport that would suit emerging RAF needs and, hopefully, those of the airlines. In September 1945 RAF Specification C.3/44 was written around the HP.67 multi-role airlifter, soon to be named Hastings. The airliner – the Hermes – was more sophisticated with a pressurised fuselage and the ability to be 'stretched' and turbine powered.

Sticking to the proven 14-cylinder, two-row, sleeve-valve Hercules radials of the later Halifaxes, it was the Hermes that was first to take to the air, from Radlett on 2 December 1945.

A congratulatory telegram from Winston Churchill to Sir Frederick Handley Page on the fortieth anniversary of his first flight. It was sent on 17 July 1949 from the post office at Westerham, close to Churchill's house, Chartwell. *Handley Page*

The Manx, wearing the 'B Condition' (or 'trade plate') identity H0222, at Radlett in late 1944. *Handley Page*

British Overseas Airways Corporation Halton G-AHDN *Flamborough*, converted from Halifax VIII PP234 by Shorts, 1947. *Short Brothers and Harland*

SIR FREDERICK HANDLEYPAGE C/O HYDROPHID LONDON

= ON THE OCCASION OF YOUR 40 TH ANNIVERSARY I SEND YOU MY CONGRATULATIONS ON THE FINE ACHEIVEMENT OF YOUR COMPANY AND MY GOOD WISHES FOR YOUR CELEBRATIONS THIS EVENING AND FOR THE CONTINUED SUCCESS OF YOUR GREAT UNDERTAKING = WINSTON CHURCHILL

Former Air Safaris Hermes IV G-ALDL in the airliner 'graveyard' at Stansted in May 1962: it was scrapped before year end. *Roy Bonser*

Line-up of Hastings C.2s of 24 and 36 Squadrons at their Colerne base in April 1967. Second from the right is WD477, which was built at Radlett in 1951. It was retired in January 1968. *Roy Bonser*

Marathon T.11 XA260 served all of its military life at Boscombe Down, 1952 to 1959. *Handley Page*

Porpoising violently from take-off, it crashed, killing test pilot Jamie Talbot and observer 'Ginger' Wright. The likely cause was that the elevator was overbalanced, something that extensive ground handling should have discovered. It *may* be that Talbot came under pressure from 'Sir Fred' – Handley Page – to get the prototype into the air before the year's end to prove the company was back in the airliner business.

It was 2 September 1947 before the refined Hermes 2 had its debut but HP had lost a lot of time, the 'tail-dragger' looking very dated against the tri-gear Lockheed Constellations and Douglas DC-6s on offer across the Atlantic. Further redesign created two versions featuring tricycle undercarriage: the Hercules-powered Series IV in 1948 and the Series V with Bristol Theseus turboprops the following year. During 1949–50 BOAC took delivery of twenty-five Hermes IVs, but only two Series Vs were completed. With a production total of twenty-nine, the Hermes had proved to be an expensive cul-de-sac.

That was not the case with the Hastings, which replaced the Avro York in RAF service. Perhaps mindful of the disaster that befell the first Hermes six months before, the prototype Hastings was taken by road to Wittering for its uneventful maiden flight on 7 May 1946. The RAF order went to 146 units, the bulk being C.1 tactical airlifters, plus forty-two long-range C.2s and four VIP-configured C.4s. The Royal New Zealand Air Force took a quartet of C.3s: the last of these being completed in 1953.

Reading interlude

Swift action in 1948 allowed HP to take on the assets of the collapsed Miles Aircraft at Woodley, near Reading. The main aim was to provide additional design and manufacturing capacity, and Handley Page (Reading) Ltd was created in July 1948. Before the liquidators were brought in, Miles had started testing a new airliner. This was the Marathon, designed to meet the arcane vision of the UK's Brabazon committee, which had been tasked with predicting post-war airliner requirements. (See Chapter 11 for full details of the Brabazon recommendations.)

Four-engined, all-metal and with complex systems, the Marathon was in a league into which Miles should never have strayed. It took a company of HP's stature to put the Marathon into production: much work was needed before it could be considered anywhere near viable. British European Airways had provisionally ordered the type, but wisely abandoned the idea. The Ministry of Supply had bankrolled twenty-five Marathons in advance of orders and the jigs were also government-funded. A handful of Marathons were delivered to commercial operators, the others were rolled out at Woodley, tested and parked up. In 1951 the ministry decided that the best way to divest itself of its liabilities was to turn the Marathons into navigation trainers and pass them on to the RAF. The first Marathon T.11 was ready in 1952 and another twenty-eight followed. It was no secret that the RAF was not happy with the troublesome Marathon; the type was phased out by 1958.

Under Edwin W J Gray, a separate design office was maintained at Woodley; its creations carrying the prefix HPR – the 'R' for Reading. Gray's team pitched for a potentially lucrative RAF requirement to replace the Percival Prentice trainer. Powered by an Armstrong Siddeley Cheetah XVIII radial, the first of two HPR.2s had its maiden flight on 1 May 1950. The contract went to trainer specialist Percival, with its superb Provost.

Three's a crowd

During World War Two, Bomber Command operated three different heavy bombers: in order of entry to service, the Short Stirling, Handley Page Halifax and Avro Lancaster. Immediately after the end of the war, Britain embarked upon a programme to create a fleet of sophisticated, long-range, high-flying, jet-powered heavy bombers. Intended to enter service in the early 1950s, it transpired that it was mid-decade before the so-called 'V-bombers' became operational. Capitalising on Winston Churchill's famous 'V-for-victory' gesture, it was a certainty that the new jets would have names beginning with 'V'. To bridge the gap, the RAF would have to rely upon the Avro Lincoln, essentially a 'super' Lancaster, and the revolutionary English Electric Canberra twin-jet.

The term 'Cold War' was first voiced on 14 April 1946 by American statesman Bernard Baruch to define a new era of global tension. In short order Berlin was blockaded from June 1948, the

USSR exploded an atomic bomb in July 1949; and the Korean conflict broke out in June 1950. Bomber Command was forced to supplement its arsenal with war-weary Boeing B-29 Superfortresses – RAF name Washington B.1 – from the summer of 1950.

The V-bomber programme evolved as two requirements – frequently amended, updated, revised – Specification B.35/46 for an advanced long-range bomber and B.9/48 for a less challenging equivalent to enter service earlier. Based upon Operational Requirement OR.229 issued in December 1946, B.35/46 was released in January 1947 and among its stipulations was the ability to carry a 10,000lb 'special' – atomic – weapon 1,724 miles. This was the 'Holy Grail', potentially decades of work for the winner – Armstrong Whitworth, Avro, Bristol, English Electric, HP, Shorts and Vickers entered the fray. Vickers – with proven bomber heritage – was unsuccessful but clinched B.9/48 which emerged as the interim Valiant. It was no surprise that Avro and HP – builders of Bomber Command's wartime backbones – were awarded the high-risk option, the Type 698 and the HP.80 that became the Vulcan and Victor respectively

Prior to World War Two, a need such as B.35/46 would result in a 'fly-off': two, maybe three Air Ministry-financed prototypes, perhaps even a smattering of promising private ventures. After Boscombe Down had had its say, a winner – singular – would be announced. There had been examples of two types being chosen for the same requirement, but for such a costly project as B.35/46 the duplication of effort would be crippling. Across the Atlantic, US procedure would also be a fly-off, with the runners-up becoming sub-contractors on the programme. That way, everyone was a winner: the losing prototype would become a museum piece, but the defeated design house would have gained valuable knowledge ready for the next contest.

Why did economically crippled Britain decide upon the jaw-dropping solution to operationally employ *three* V-bombers? The trio was seen as having built-in 'redundancy' should one of them fail, but it left the RAF with a massively expensive and disproportionate infrastructure to support the varied fleet. (See also Chapter 34 for the Short Sperrin, two of which were completed to the 'parallel' Specification B.14/46 but were relegated to test and trials work prior to first flight in August 1951.)

The Canberra – also considered risky in its day – went unopposed into production. It was built in Britain by Avro, HP and Shorts, as well as English Electric. This sub-contracting was not to speed entry into service: the contracts for 75 Canberra B.2s each to Avro and HP were to tide the factories over until Vulcan and Victor production geared up, ensuring that the skilled workforce was not dispersed. In Northern Ireland Shorts made just over a hundred B.2s and B.6s and the radically different PR.9, all to pump-prime the province's economy. The duplication of jigs and associated paraphernalia was both time-consuming and astoundingly expensive: in theory Warton could have handled the *entire* venture but employment needs were also in play.

While Canberras spread the work around, other than the PR.9, sub-contracting did not engage the relevant design offices. Although intended for the same task, the Victor and Vulcan were *very* different beasts and the knowledge acquired would add to the overall experience of the whole industry. This was the rationale that meant there was no winner between the Avro and HP, and why it was that Woodford *and* Radlett did not *both* manufacture Vulcans or Victors.

By taking a mammoth risk and adopting both the Type 698 and the HP.80 the Labour government of 1945 to 1952 and the following Conservative administration ensured tens of thousands of jobs. Employment was secured not just at Radlett and Woodford, but at

Victor B.1s in the flight shed at Radlett. Second from the right is XA917, the first production example, which hit the headlines on a sortie out of Radlett on 1 June 1957. With John Allam at the helm in a shallow dive from around 40,000ft, XA917 clocked 675mph – Mach 1.02 – becoming the largest aircraft at the time to go supersonic. *Handley Page*

Valiant, Vulcan and Victor compared

	Valiant B.1	Vulcan B.1	Victor B.1	Vulcan B.2	Victor B.2
First flown	18 May 1951	30 Aug 1952*	24 Dec 1952	19 Aug 1958	20 Feb 1959
Entered service**	Feb 1955	Jul 1957	Jan 1958	Oct 1960	Feb 1962
Engines x 4	RR Avon 204	BS Olympus 104	AS Sapphire 202	BS Olympus 201	RR Conway 201
	10,500lb st	13,000lb st	11,500lb st	17,000lb st	19,750lb st
Loaded weight	140,000lb	170,000lb	205,000lb	200,000lb	223,000lb
Max speed at 40,000ft	550mph	620mph	645mph	645mph	647mph
Max range***	4,500 miles	3,000 miles	3,500 miles	3,200 miles	3,500 miles
Service ceiling	54,000ft	55,000ft	57,000ft	60,000ft	64,000ft
Max weapon load	21,000lb	21,000lb	35,000lb	21,000lb	35,000lb

* Avon-engined prototype; first Olympus-powered example flew 3 Sep 1953. ** Front-line service, operational conversion unit status achieved earlier. *** Internal tankage (including wing-mounted tanks on Valiant and Victor), without in-flight refuelling.

the Bristol, Coventry and Derby engine works and across the entire country through a large number of specialist suppliers. Upgrade, refurbishing, role change and product support contracts continued for decades after the assembly lines had closed. While the V-bombers were an example of social engineering the programme was proof that the industry needed rationalising.

Crescent-winged perfection

Volkert retired as chief designer in 1948 and the baton was handed on to Reginald S Stafford. The HP.80 was going to be a massive task and Stafford wisely split the process into three elements. He handled the managerial and 'political' side, thereby freeing his talented teams to get on with the job in hand without constant, time-consuming, diversions. Stafford began with HP in his 20s as a junior in the design office and whenever he could, he flew as an observer on test flights. Among the sorties he went on, in 1927 he was aboard the Harrow biplane torpedo-bomber and nine years later, pencil in hand, he was chronicling the behaviour of the prototype Hampden. Under Volkert's careful eye, he prepared drawings to turn the Hampden into a torpedo-bomber and took part in the massive task of changing the Halifax from two to four engines. In 1953 Stafford was rewarded with a seat on the board as technical director. He was responsible for the installation of RR Conways in the Victor B.2 when the Sapphire was discontinued. A strong advocate of the Jetstream, the twin turboprop was his last project. Reginald S Stafford died in September 1980, aged 77.

While Stafford 'rode shotgun' over the HP.80 project, Charles F Joy, previously HP's chief draughtsman, was in charge of airframe and systems. Under Stafford's management, Joy went on to design the HP.115 slender delta test bed and the Jetstream. He was with the company up to its collapse in 1970; he died in April 1989, aged 78.

Although he always batted away the praise, it was Godfrey Lee who was the man who shaped the Victor. He started work at HP in 1937 as a stressman, going on to become Lachmann's deputy in the experimental department. When his boss was interned in 1939, Lee took over and liaised with him over the trials of the tail-less Manx. By 1945 he was assistant chief designer under Volkert and was part of a delegation touring Germany absorbing as much as he could of swept-wing technology. Lee compiled the brochure for the HP.72, the precursor of the Victor, in 1947 and remained as the guiding light all the way through to the exceptional B.2. Appointed chief aerodynamicist, Lee conceived the HP.100 supersonic bomber in the mid-1950s and went to head HP's concepts for the supersonic transport in the 1960s: neither of these left the drawing board. Godfrey H Lee, the father of the Victor, died in June 1988, aged 84.

The V-bomber programme was so challenging that additional sub-scale research platforms were ordered to help pave the way for the Vulcan and the Victor – in the case of the former this took the form of the Type 707 'mini-delta' series. In March 1948 Specification E.6/48 called for a test bed for the crescent wing proposed for the

The HP.88 crescent wing test bed undergoing trials in mid-1951. *Blackburn and General Aircraft*

Victor. General Aircraft was awarded the contract and came up with a scale wing and tail grafted on to the fuselage of a Supermarine Attacker, powered by a RR Nene 3 turbojet. Most of the design was completed at Hanworth, but with the merger of General Aircraft and Blackburn on 1 January 1949 the project was relocated to Brough.

The parent company designated the aircraft HP.88, Supermarine called the Attacker fuselage – with modified Swift wing roots – the Type 521 and Blackburn referred to it as the YB.2. The hybrid had its maiden flight from Carnaby, near Bridlington, on 21 June 1951. The jet was ferried to Stansted on 6 August so that HP could take it over as the Victor programme gained momentum. Twenty days later, Douglas 'Jimmy' Broomfield perished when VX330 broke up in the air. The HP.88 had been flown for just over fourteen hours in thirty-odd sorties. The first Victor had its maiden flight at Boscombe Down on 24 December 1952, having gained little real advantage from its scale-wing test bed.

Faster, higher, further, greater weapon load, longer life, veteran of *two* conflicts – the Falklands and the First Gulf War. These, and others, are the attributes the Victor holds over its comrade the Vulcan – see the comparison table. In a repetition of the Lancaster and the Halifax 'rivalry', it was the delta-winged V-bomber that got the plaudits over the crescent-winged wonder. Long before 'auto-land' systems came about, the Victor revealed a trait that its pilots enjoyed throughout its long service life. Barnes describes a sortie in the prototype on 21 July 1953 with the Chief of the Air Staff, ACM Sir John Baker, on board. Chief test pilot Hedley Hazelden: 'demonstrated the Victor's ability to land itself "hands off". This had been predicted by Stafford before the maiden flight and was due to the high tail being out of the wing downwash with flaps down, so that ground effect started the round-out and runway reaction brought the nose level when the throttles were closed.' The Victor programme did not have a good start. The prototype suffered a structural failure on 14 July 1954, killing all four on board. The second example got airborne on 11 September that year and HP went all out to return some pace to the project.

Handley Page to HP.46

From	To	Total	Name/Designation	Type	Engine(s)	Notes
1910	1911	2	Early monoplanes	1-seater	1 x Green	[1] [2]
1911	1912	2	Two-seat monos	2-seater	1 x Gnome	[1] [3]
1913	-	1	Type G	2-seater	1 x Anzani	
1915	1917	46	O/100	Heavy bomber	2 x RR Eagle	
1917	1918	c.550	O/400	Heavy bomber	2 x RR Eagle	[4]
1917	-	3	R/200	Naval recce	1 x Hispano-Suiza	
1918	1919	63	V/1500	Heavy bomber	4 x RR Eagle	[5]
1919	-	11	O/7	Airliner	2 x RR Eagle	
1919	1924	19	W.8	Airliner	2 x Napier Lion	[6]
1921	-	1	X.4B/HP.20	Research	1 x Liberty 12	[1] [7]
1922	1924	10	Hanley/Hendon	Torpedo bomber	1 x Napier Lion	
1923	1929	46	Hyderabad	Heavy bomber	2 x Napier Lion	
1923	-	3	Type S/HP.21	Shipborne fighter	1 x Bentley BR.2	[1]
1923	-	3	Sayers Motor Glider	Ultralight	1 x ABC	[1] [8]
1924	1926	15	W.8e/f and W.9	Airliner	3 x AS Jaguar	[9]
1924	1925	3	Handcross	Day bomber	1 x RR Condor	
1926	-	4	W.10	Airliner	2 x Napier Lion	
1926	-	1	Hamlet	Light transport	3 x Bristol Lucifer	[1] [10]
1926	-	2	Harrow	Torpedo bomber	1 x Napier Lion	
1927	1931	41	Hinaidi I/II	Heavy bomber	2 x Napier Lion	
1928	1930	3	Clive	Transport	2 x Bristol Jupiter	
1928	-	1	Hare	Day bomber	1 x Bristol Jupiter	
1929	-	1	Gugnunc	Research	1 x AS Mongoose	
1930	1936	124	Heyford	Bomber	2 x RR Kestrel	[11]
1931	-	8	HP.42/HP.45	Airliner	4 x Bristol Jupiter	
1932	-	1	HP.43	Bomber-transport	3 x Bristol Pegasus	[12]
1935	-	1	HP.46	Torpedo bomber	1 x RR F.XIVS	

Based upon: *Handley Page Aircraft since 1907*, C H Barnes. **[1]** Monoplane, all others biplanes. **[2]** Using José Weiss wing layout: *Bluebird* and Type D. **[3]** Using José Weiss wing layout: Type E and F. **[4]** Who-built-what and how many O/400s is a subject that could fill a book – Jack Bruce in *Aeroplanes of the Royal Flying Corps (Military Wing)*, sums up the problems superbly. Including sub-contracts to: Birmingham Carriage Co, Birmingham (102); Clayton and Shuttleworth, Lincoln (50); Metropolitan Wagon Co, Birmingham (100); National Aircraft Factory 1 (70 – almost certainly 'absorbed' in the form of sub-assemblies by HP at Cricklewood); Royal Aircraft Factory, Farnborough (24); plus one built by Harland and Wolff, Belfast, but assembled by HP. Standard Aircraft Corporation of Elizabeth, New Jersey, USA, built sub-assemblies for shipping to the UK; *at least* nine examples assembled and flown in the USA. Barnes gives the number of US-built O/400s as 107, the bulk being introduced into the British programme. **[5]** Including sub-contracts to: Alliance Aircraft Co, London (10); William Beardmore and Co, Dalmiur (20); Harland and Wolff, Belfast, bulk assembled by HP (23). **[6]** Including three under licence Société Anonyme Belge de Constructions Aéronautiques (SABCA), Belgium. **[7]** Based upon a DH.9A fuselage. **[8]** Designed by William Higley Sayers. **[9]** Including 12 under licence Société Anonyme Belge de Constructions Aéronautiques (SABCA), Belgium. **[10]** Re-engined with 2 x AS Lynx, then 3 x AS Mongoose. **[11]** Prototype designated HP.38. **[12]** Converted to HP.51 – see 'Handley page types HP.47 to Jetstream' table.

Victor B.2 XH675 was converted to a K.2 tanker by Hawker Siddeley at Woodford and first flew in that guise on 4 March 1977. While serving with Marham-based 57 Squadron it was involved in in-flight refuelling trials with the third prototype Tornado, P.03 XX947, in 1978. *Flight Refuelling*

Handley page types HP.47 to Jetstream

From	To	Total	Name/Designation	Type	Engine(s)	Notes
1935	-	1	HP.47	Military GP	1 x Bristol Pegasus	
1932	-	1	HP.51	Bomber-transport	2 x AS Tiger	[1]
1936	1942	1,582	Hampden/Hereford	Bomber	2 x Bristol Pegasus	[2]
1936	1937	100	Harrow I/II	Bomber	2 x Bristol Pegasus	
1939	1946	6,179	Halifax	Heavy bomber	4 x RR Merlin	[3]
1939	-	1	Manx	Research	2 x DH Gipsy Major	[4]
1945	1948	2	Hermes	Airliner	4 x Bristol Hercules	[5]
1946	1952	151	Hastings I–II	Transport	4 x Bristol Hercules	[6]
1949	1951	27	Hermes IV–V	Airliner	4 x Bristol Hercules	[7]
1950	1952	40	HPR.1 Marathon	Feederliner	4 x DH Gipsy Queen	[8] [9]
1950	-	2	HPR.2	Trainer	1 x AS Cheetah	[8]
1951	-	1	HP.88	Research	1 x RR Nene 3	[10]
1952	1959	52	Victor B.1	Heavy bomber	4 x AS Sapphire	
1959	1963	34	Victor B.2	Heavy bomber	4 x RR Conway	
1955	1956	2	HPR.3 Herald	Airliner	4 x Alvis Leonides	[8] [11]
1958	1968	48	HPR.7 Herald	Airliner	2 x RR Dart	[12]
1961	-	1	HP.115	Research	1 x BS Viper	[13]
1967	1970	38	Jetstream	Light transport	2 x Turboméca Astazou	[14]

Based upon: *Handley Page Aircraft since 1907*, C H Barnes. All piston-engined monoplanes unless noted. **[1]** Converted from HP.43 biplane – see 'Handley page types HP.46' table. **[2]** Both designated HP.52. Includes one HP.53 built to Swedish order, reconfigured as Hereford. Including sub-contracts to: English Electric, Samlesbury (770); Canadian Associated Aircraft Ltd, Montreal (160). Hereford: 2 x Napier Dagger. All 150 built by Short and Harland, Belfast. **[3]** HP.57 – B.I, HP.59 – B.II, HP.63 – B.V, all Merlin-engined. HP.61 – B.III, B.VI, B.VII and HP.70 – C.VIII and HP.71 – A.IX, all Bristol Hercules-engined. Including sub-contracts to: English Electric, Samlesbury (2,145); Fairey Aviation, Ringway (662); London Aircraft Production Group – London Passenger Transport Board, Park Royal Coach Works, Express Motor and Body Works, Chrysler Motors, Duple Bodies and Motors, assembly and test at Leavesden; (710) and Rootes Securities, Speke (1,070). **[4]** Sub-contracted to Dart Aircraft, Dunstable, completed at Radlett, 1940. **[5]** HP.68 – Hermes I, HP.74 – Hermes II. **[6]** HP.94 – C.4, HP.95 – C.3. **[7]** Tricycle undercarriage. HP.81 – Hermes IV (25); HP-82 – Hermes V (2) with Bristol Theseus turboprops. **[8]** Built at Woodley. **[9]** Not including three prototypes by Miles – Chapter 28 – production by HP. Twenty-eight completed as Marathon T.11 crew trainers for RAF. One converted Marathon II with AS mamba turboprops and later to HPR.5 status with a pair of Alvis Leonides Majors. **[10]** Victor wing planform jet test bed, based on Supermarine Attacker fuselage. Sub-contracted to General Aircraft, later Blackburn, Brough, with designation YB.2. **[11]** Both Leonides Major-engine prototypes converted to Dart Herald status. **[12]** Turboprop production version. Initial airframes laid down at Woodley, completed at Radlett. **[13]** Lowspeed, slender, delta jet test bed. **[14]** Twin-turboprop light transport; one example completed 1968 as Series 3M with Garrett TPE331 turboprops. Some unfinished airframes transferred to Jetstream Aircraft and production recommenced by Scottish Aviation at Prestwick – see Chapter 33 for details.

The first production B.1 had its maiden flight on 30 January 1956. Mk.1s underwent a change of role as the Valiant tanker force was phased out by early 1965. The Victor's incredible lifting capability, 35,000lb, made it a perfect 'flying petrol station'. Two-hose Victor tankers began to appear in mid-1965, shortly followed by three-pointers: in 1966 the Mk.1 Victor dropped the bomber role.

The Mk.1 Victor was just the starting point; Lee began design of the incredibly potent Mk.2, spurred on by an order for fifty-one, later reduced to thirty-four. Apart from adopting RR Conway turbofans, the Mk.2 had a greater span, a re-engineered wing and even greater performance. By the late 1950s the V-bombers relinquished the high-level attack profile, adopting a low-level transit followed by a 'pop up' to release weapons. To help the Mk.2 in this regime, HP again turned to Germanic influence: the trailing edge of the wing featured the very distinctive Küchemann drag-reducing anti-shock bodies, nicknamed 'carrots'. These were the brainchild of German-born aerodynamicist Dietrich Küchemann CBE, who began working for the RAE in 1946, taking up UK citizenship in 1953. The first production B.2 had its maiden flight on 20 February 1959. The final Victor came off the Radlett line in 1963 and conversions to the highly capable SR.2 strategic reconnaissance variant started operations in May 1965. HP hoped to secure a contract to convert B.2s and SR.2s to K.2 tankers, and retired examples had begun to congregate at Radlett in readiness for this, but the company collapsed and the task was transferred to Hawker Siddeley.

Four, then two

Management at HP realised that although the Victor was a reliable cash cow, the company could not depend on a single product – but space at Radlett was severely restricted as the bombers went through.

With the dismal Marathon out of the way, the Woodley plant had both design and manufacturing capacity. Miles had schemed a scaled-up version of the Marathon, the M.73, and these plans were dusted down, given considerable improvement and the HPR.3 Herald was born. Aiming to replace the venerable Douglas DC-3 – a potentially huge market – Handley Page himself and Reading chief designer Gray insisted the HPR.3 had four engines – drastically limiting the Herald's appeal. Thankfully, the ability to adopt a twin-engined format had been planned into the wing.

Built at Woodley, but moved to Radlett for its debut, the prototype Herald flew on 25 August 1955 powered by a quartet of Alvis Leonides Major radials. Two months later, the brave decision to commit to series production was taken and long-lead items for twenty-five Heralds were ordered. Twenty-one months previously, Fokker had flown the prototype F27 Friendship, propelled by two well-proven RR Dart turboprops. The Dutch company had a head start and had opted for the powerplant of the future, the turbine. In June 1960 HP's arch-rival Avro put its twin-Dart Type 748, aimed at the same market, into the air.

The prototype Herald went back into the workshop and emerged as the slightly stretched Dart-powered HPR.7, flying for the first time on 11 March 1958. By then, the decision had been made to pull out of Woodley and consolidate on Radlett. Seven Heralds were built at Woodley, the last one in December 1961. The fiftieth and final Herald had its maiden flight in August 1968. Fokker completed its last F27 – the 586th – in 1987. Avro's 748, known as the HS.748 from 1963, had run to 382 units when manufacture ceased at Woodford in January 1989. Both enjoyed further success as the 'second-generation' Fokker 50 (213 built) and the British Aerospace ATP (sixty-five completed) respectively. HP had really missed the boat.

Above: The prototype HPR.3 Herald, G-AODE, at Woodley in 1955 in the colours of Queensland Air Lines, one of several operators who placed orders and then withdrew. *Handley Page*

Left: Escorted by a Victor B.1, the prototype Herald G-AODE in HPR.7 guise with RR Dart turboprops, 1958. *Handley Page*

It transpired that the HP.115 was the last of a distinguished line of research airframes from HP, including the HP.17, HP.20 and Gugnunc leading-edge slot pioneers, the Manx tail-less test bed and the unfortunate HP.88 crescent wing hybrid.

Out in the cold

Governmental pressure to rationalise the UK's sprawling industry brought about the British Aircraft Corporation (English Electric, Vickers and Hunting) in 1960 and Hawker Siddeley Aviation (HSA – a combination of Armstrong Whitworth, Avro, Gloster and Hawker since 1935) expanded to take in Blackburn, de Havilland and Folland during 1963. Several overtures were made by HSA to HP to buy it, but Handley Page was always against the sale. After Sir Frederick's death in 1962, the prospect was explored again by HSA, but the HP board considered the offers derisory and opted for continued independence.

In the early 1960s, HP was no great catch. The Herald was a disappointment, Victor support work was ongoing and there was the prospect of a contract to convert some of the B.2 fleet into tankers. But none of this was long-term; it was hardly surprising that HSA was not prepared to pay much for a rival that was dying on its feet.

Gap in the market

Recognising that a watershed had been reached, the HP board made a very brave decision – worthy of Sir Frederick. A gap in the market would

Slender delta

While the Victor B.2 and the turboprop Herald entered production, the design office had got its teeth into Specification ER.197D, issued in December 1959. This was seeking a simple jet-powered, low-speed test bed to explore the characteristics of a slender delta wing. The HP.115 had fixed undercarriage, a 'podded' cockpit and, innovatively for those days, the Viper jet engine placed above the rear fuselage, with the fin and rudder mounted above it. Built at Radlett, it was roaded to its base for its entire flying career, the RAE at Thurleigh, and first flew on 17 August 1961. Very quickly, the HP.115 moved from theoretical research to practical trials, as it was ideal to investigate the slow-speed characteristics of the upcoming Concorde programme. Retired in 1974, XP841 is on show at the Fleet Air Arm Museum, Yeovilton, tucked under the wing of Concorde 002 in the 'Leading Edge' exhibition.

Herald, HS.748 and Fokker F.27 compared

	Herald Srs 200	HS.748 Srs 2	Fokker F27 Mk.200
First flown	11 Mar 1958*	24 Jun 1960	24 Nov 1955
Last delivery	1968	1989	1987
Number built	50	382**	586
Engines x 2	RR Dart 527	RR Dart 555	RR Dart 526
	2,105shp	2,280shp	2,320shp
Typical passenger load	56	48	44
Cruising speed	274mph	281mph	298mph
Typical range	1,110 miles	812 miles	1,197 miles
Max take-off weight	43,000lb	51,000lb	44,996lb

* Prototype, with four Alvis Leonides piston engines, first flew 25 August 1955. ** Includes Andover tactical transports for the RAF.

The HP.115 slender delta research aircraft, XP841, touching down at Farnborough after its debut display, September 1961. *Roy Bonser*

be exploited, creating a small twin turboprop for business, 'feederliner', general transport and military use. The new type would have the potential to 'stretch' to take more passengers and accept bigger powerplants. While sub-contractors were needed, for example Scottish Aviation built the wings, no risk-sharing partners were to be sought. Some monies were forthcoming from the government, but HP was going to fund the whole project, including a brand new assembly hall. If all went smoothly, the potential was excellent: if not, HP was 'betting the farm'.

The prototype HP.137 Jetstream had its maiden flight on 8 August 1967. While its French-built Turboméca Astazou turboprops had some virtues, they did not have great market appeal in the USA and any 'growth' versions of the HP.137 would need new powerplants. Certification delays plus the first examples being over projected weight strained the already tight finances.

Almost out of the blue, HP won the United States Air Force's (USAF) CX requirement for light transport, ambulance and general duties, securing an initial order for eleven, designated C-10A. These would have American Garrett TPE-331 turboprops, structural changes and a freight door. The Series 3M, the aerodynamic prototype for the C-10A, was flown for the first time on 21 November 1968. It was already way behind the delivery schedule anticipated by the

Americans. Overstretched, Handley Page Ltd went into liquidation on 8 August 1969. Nine days later, the dramatically slimmed down Handley Page Aircraft Ltd was formed and by the end of the year a total of forty-five Jetstreams had been completed, with about half of these delivered. The USAF cancelled the C-10A programme in October 1969, with the first machine nearly ready for test and the others under assembly. On 27 February 1970 one of the most famous names in the British aviation threw in the towel.

Hawker Siddeley took over the K.2 tanker contract and the stored Mk.2s were ferried to Woodford, where the first conversion began testing in March 1972. At first the Jetstream seemed doomed but quick actions secured the design rights and some of the airframes. As detailed in Chapter 33, in 1972 Scottish Aviation took on the Jetstream for an RAF crew trainer requirement. From 1982, under the British Aerospace banner, the design was stretched and re-engined as the Jetstream 31 and the even bigger Series 41. When the programme was halted in 1997, production totalled 385 and 104 units respectively. In the mid-1960s HP decided that the HP.137 was worth betting the farm over and designed adaptability into the airframe. Sadly it fell to other enterprises to prove the HP board's faith in an aircraft that took a great name to the wall.

Former Cal-State Airlines Jetstream 1 N1035S was demonstrated at the 1972 Paris Salon at Le Bourget by Jetstream Aircraft during the campaign to relaunch the type. *Daniel Ford*

The hulks of C-10As 68-10384 and -10385 in Coley's yard, Hounslow, July 1972. *Ken Ellis*

CHAPTER TWENTY-FIVE

Masterclass

**Hawker
1920 to 1959**

'Undoubtedly he was the greatest designer of fighter aircraft the world has ever known.'
Sir Thomas Sopwith about Sydney Camm, 1966

DURING 1920 the Sopwith Aviation Company had built fewer than fifty aircraft and its finances were being sorely stretched. Thomas Sopwith had gone down the route of several other aircraft manufacturers; his business was now making motorcycles, car bodies and kitchen implements but he knew the inevitable was coming: Excess Profit Duty. As Chapter 35 shows, 'Sopwith' and 'Camel' had become household names and Kingston-upon-Thames had spawned thousands of warplanes during the Great War. His Majesty's Exchequer had concocted a levy on what it considered to be disproportionate riches generated when the nation's back was to the wall. None of this took into account the financial risks involved in developing aircraft, often despite the whims of the War Office, or the swingeing readjustments needed as factories went from glut to famine almost overnight – suppliers still needed paying. (Chapter 2 on Airco – another doomed enterprise – provides an insight into Excess Profit Duty.)

During negotiations with the Treasury, 'Tommy' Sopwith's offer to spread payments over three years was shunned. No time was allowed to present fully audited accounts for the tax year ending April 1920; these would have shown substantial losses that, along with the figures for 1918 to 1919, would have gone a long way to negating the tax demand. Sopwith had a choice: pay the Chancellor and let his creditors down, or liquidate his company, settle the debts and leave the tax office to fight over what crumbs were left. As the closing paragraphs of Chapter 35 show, Sopwith went for the second option, sending what was left of his workforce home on 10 September 1920 and calling in the receivers the following day. So determined was Sopwith to meet his obligations to his suppliers that he put his mansion, Horsley Towers, up for sale. Ironically, it took three years to conclude the winding up of Sopwith Aviation, by which time the Treasury was left with a fraction of what it might have gleaned had it accepted the instalments proposal.

Above: Battle of Britain Memorial Flight Hurricane PZ865 *The Last of the Many* over Brooklands in the early 1980s. *British Aerospace*

Left: A Castrol advert of 1936 featured a stylised Hurricane carrying out aerobatics over the iconic racetrack. *KEC*

As one door closes, another opens … sixty-five days after Sopwith Aviation began the wind-up procedure – on 15 November 1920 – H G Hawker Engineering Co Ltd was established with the aims of general engineering, manufacturing motorcycles and, maybe, aircraft. Among the directors was Sopwith (aged 32), his right-hand man Frederick Sigrist (36) and Harry George Hawker (31). With wrangling over the Sopwith company's tax liabilities likely to go on for a long time, and given Tommy Sopwith's preference to work behind the scenes, the new firm was destined to have a new title. The obvious choice was another household name – Hawker – the charismatic, popular designer–pilot–adventurer who had been with Sopwith since 1912.

The lives of Tommy Sopwith and Fred Sigrist are detailed in Chapter 35 and both crop up in this chapter. The man that Hawker was named after is *briefly* profiled, although his time as a director was tragically short.

Man behind the name

Early employment for Harry Hawker included working in a cycle shop, a car dealership and chauffeuring. With this experience it is hardly surprising that by 1911 Hawker and his friend Harry Busteed had designed, built and raced motorcycles in their native Australia. Both were also fascinated by new-fangled flying machines. Busteed was hell-bent on travelling to Britain to become a pilot and had booked his passage. Harry decided to join him, as did Eric Harrison and Harry A Kauper. Each of this quartet made their mark in aviation: Busteed is detailed in Chapter 11; Harrison became the chief instructor at the Bristol school at Brooklands; Kauper took a job with Sopwith and by 1916 had perfected the Sopwith-Kauper gear, an efficient synchronizing (or 'interrupter') mechanism allowing a machine gun to fire 'through' a spinning propeller.

Kauper encouraged Hawker to go for an interview with Sopwith's general manager, Sigrist, on 29 June 1912. This meeting changed the fortunes of the 23-year-old-Australian and Sopwith's prospects. With tuition from Sopwith himself, Hawker showed that he was a 'natural' and was awarded Aviators' Certificate No. 297 at Brooklands on 17 September 1912. The following month Hawker flew a Sopwith-modified Wright biplane to have a crack at the British Empire Michelin Cup, which offered £500 for the first flight lasting more than five hours: he stayed aloft for an incredible eight hours, twenty-three minutes.

A rare occasion, Harry Hawker caught behind a desk. *Peter Green Collection*

Sopwith was getting ready to build aircraft from his own drawing office, located initially in a former ice skating rink at Kingston-upon-Thames. By February 1913 Tommy Sopwith was handing over the testing of the new machines to Hawker and increasingly the Australian was contributing to the design process. In late 1915 the 1½ Strutter appeared, launching a family of fighters: Pup, Triplane, Camel, Dolphin, etc. Along with the Royal Aircraft Factory S.E.5a, the Camel was the best British fighter fielded during the Great War and Hawker had considerable input in its creation. Harald Penrose, in *British Aviation – The Great War and Armistice*, quotes engine designer Wilfred Owen Bentley, who sheds light on the Australian's role: 'I had the highest admiration for Harry Hawker. He knew exactly what the fighting pilots wanted, and saw they got it. He was a delightful person, but found it difficult to get along with [Herbert] Smith [chief designer]. In fact they were often at loggerheads, and seemed to have little time for each other.' Penrose added his own thoughts: 'Perhaps it irritated Smith that the great Sopwith test pilot could criticize and condemn if need be, the projects which were [Smith's] final responsibility …'

Household name

The *Daily Mail's* £10,000 prize for the first British non-stop flight over the Atlantic – the so-called Ocean Race – tempted several British manufacturers. Sopwith created the large Atlantic biplane in very short time. Hawker's attention to detail could be found all over it, including a jettisonable main undercarriage to help improve fuel consumption and a lifeboat that formed the rear fuselage fairing, its keel cleverly blending into the tail. A good friend of Hawker, Lt Cdr K Mackenzie Grieve, was navigator and radio operator for the attempt.

After testing in February 1919, the Atlantic was dismantled for the sea voyage to St John's, Newfoundland. At Quidi Vidi airstrip, 'Freddy' Raynham and Charles Morgan were readying their Martinsyde Raymor, which took its name from its crew. 'Jack' Alcock and Arthur Whitten Brown were busy trying to find a suitable launch site for the Vickers entrant, the Vimy. Hawker and Grieve departed on 18 May, dramatically overflying Quidi Vidi to drop the undercarriage in a graphic display of finality. (Raynham and Morgan crashed on take-off later that day.)

As the hours turned into days, British newspapers became full of dread until a radio message came through on the 25th from the Danish freighter *Mary* that Hawker and Grieve had been picked up. With the ceiling decaying to below 1,000ft and the Rolls-Royce (RR) Eagle VIII close to seizing, Hawker put his hopes in finding the maritime equivalent of a needle in a haystack – and there was the *Mary*! He carried out a textbook ditching, greatly aided by the lack of undercarriage. The crew put out a lifeboat – a huge risk in those waters – and brought the pair to safety. Back in Britain the aviators were given a tremendous welcome and the *Daily Mail* presented them with £5,000 for sheer pluck. On 15 June Alcock and Brown's Vimy ended up on its nose in an Irish bog and the world's press had successful heroes to write about.

At the end of June 1920 Brooklands was holding a race meeting and Sunbeam was competing with a 450hp car. Hawker, a passionate Sunbeam owner, asked if he could take the new machine for a run prior to the main event. Up on the famous banking, clocking something like 125mph, he suffered a blow-out and crashed. The Atlantic could not claim him, nor could the Brooklands circuit: Hawker survived.

On 12 July 1921 Hawker was testing the one-off Nieuport Goshawk G-EASK at Hendon prior to racing it. At 2,500ft the biplane was seen to make a violent turn, enter a steep dive, start to burn and crash: Hawker was thrown clear, dying minutes later. It was determined that the cover of the bottom carburettor had come unscrewed and that fire had broken out. The autopsy carried out on 32-year-old Harry George Hawker MBE AFC discovered that he had advanced degeneration of the spine caused by tuberculosis – also known as 'Potts Disease' – which very likely would have taken his valiant life before long. Sir Thomas Sopwith paid fine tribute: 'I got on with [him] very well indeed. He was a beautiful pilot. He used his head.'

H G Hawker Engineering Co Ltd was renamed Hawker Aircraft in 1933: the company will be referred to simply as 'Hawker' throughout.

Back in business

By February 1921 Herbert Smith – the designer who was irritated by Harry Hawker – was on a boat bound for Japan, where he had accepted a contract to establish an aviation division for Mitsubishi. Hawker's first chief designer was Bertram Thomson, who conceived the parasol monoplane Duiker in 1923: it was twelve years before another Hawker-built monoplane appeared, the Hurricane. Named after an African antelope, the Duiker was intended for army co-operation and Raynham carried out its maiden flight in July 1923. The all-wood Duiker came in for a lot of criticism at Martlesham Heath, the most damning being its lack of directional stability.

Thomson's next design, the Woodcock, fared no better when it was evaluated in August 1923. The RAF was looking for its first dedicated – not adapted – night fighter. Agility was not a requirement; stability was what was needed in the days when flying in the dark was full of risk. Thomson left in 1923, finding work with Saunders on the Isle of Wight.

Replacing him was George Carter, who had joined Sopwith in 1915 in the drawing office, going on to become chief draughtsman under Herbert Smith at £3 per week. (£156 a year: the annual salary of a train driver in 1914 was approximately £192.) Upon the collapse of Sopwith in 1920, Carter returned to his native Bedford. With Thomson's departure, Carter was tempted back and his first assignment was to correct the Woodcock's failings. The Mk.II appeared early in 1924. It was no longer a two-bay biplane; a more robust single-bay layout conveyed excellent visibility and it was declared a good gun platform. The Woodcock II was ordered by the RAF and the Danes signed up a licence agreement: the Kingston team was back in business.

By 1925 Carter was unhappy with life at Hawker, with differences of opinion regarding procedure with the forthright Sigrist playing a part. After conceiving the Horsley, he was back on the train to Bedford. He went on to design, among others, the Meteor jet fighter for Gloster and his full 'CV' can be found in Chapter 22.

Design is an art, not a science

Alongside the Thames in Windsor's Alexandra Gardens is a full-scale model of a Hurricane honouring the birthplace of the fighter's creator, Sydney Camm. Aged 30, he started work at Hawker as Carter's assistant in 1923 and was still on the payroll when he died forty-three years later. In all of that time, although he drew up several multi-engined types, Camm, and Hawker, only produced single-engined machines.

While serving a carpentry apprenticeship, Camm caught sight of a model of a Wright Flyer biplane in a shop window – and was hooked! Soon he was building elastic-powered aircraft with the Windsor Model Aeroplane Club. Camm regularly cycled to Brooklands and Hendon and attended the annual Olympia Aero Show in London. He made meticulous notes of the structural details and in 1919 compiled these in the book *Aeroplane Construction*. (Crosby Lockwood, London, republished in 2008.) Throughout the 1920s and '30s, this tome was to be found on the shelves of design offices the world over.

With the coming of the Great War, Camm began work at the Martinsyde factory at Woking as a carpenter. George Handasyde saw his potential and Camm was elevated to the stores, where his self-taught knowledge of components was invaluable. By the end of hostilities he was a draughtsman and in 1920 he had a major hand in creating the Semiquaver racing biplane – Chapter 27 explains.

Martinsyde folded in 1920 but Handasyde set up on his own, taking Camm with him as assistant designer. Along with Raynham, Handasyde and Camm created a glider for the October 1922 trials at Itford. From this, the trio developed an ultralight monoplane, powered by a 750cc Douglas motorcycle engine, for the following year's light aeroplane contest at Lympne.

Through an introduction by Raynham, Camm signed up with Hawker in November 1923 as assistant designer. When Camm took

Woodcock II J7971 of 17 Squadron at Upavon, 1927. *Peter Green Collection*

Portrait of Sir Sydney Camm CBE on the occasion of receiving his knighthood, 1953. *British Aerospace*

over from Carter in 1925, he was 32. He was rewarded with a directorship in June 1935, accepting the post of chief engineer in 1950. Three years later he was given the title director of design and a seat on the board of the Hawker Siddeley Group. Awarded a CBE in 1941, he was knighted in 1953 – Tommy Sopwith also kneeling to the royal sword that year.

Taking the post of chief designer in the late 1950s was Roland Henry 'Roy' Chaplin, who had joined Hawker in 1926 and for much of that time was Camm's assistant. Along with Ralph Hooper, these two brought the P.1127 into the world – all the while with Camm 'hovering' above them. A heart condition forced Chaplin to retire in 1962. Roland Henry Chaplin OBE died on 13 December 1988, aged 89.

Tommy Sopwith was not alone in finding Camm to be both infuriating and stimulating, sometimes with only moments separating the two sensations, but recognised him as a kindred spirit. Camm readily adopted the company credo of carefully evolved aeroplanes, minimising risk and maximising commonality. Camm was an advocate of 'if it looks right, it is right'. He frequently declared that: 'Aircraft design is an art, not a science.'

Hawker was always happy to launch private ventures to make sure it was at least one step ahead of its rivals. Camm spent a lot of time talking to Air Ministry officials to get a 'feel' for the next requirement and maintained a close liaison with the engine manufacturers, particularly RR, for the same reason. The astounding success of the Hart family was mostly down to the ubiquitous nature of the airframe and its construction technique. Along with this was a willingness to undertake small runs of sub-variants and to be amenable to a wide range of engine choices. This philosophy continued with the Hurricane's 'extended family' and, in terms of variants, was central to the Hunter's dominance.

On 11 March 1966 Camm studied drawings of modifications to the P.1127, before leaving the office early. The following day he was enjoying a round of golf at Richmond Park when he collapsed and died; Sir Sydney Camm CBE, a doyen of warplane design, was 72. The quote at the beginning of this chapter was part of Sir Thomas Sopwith's eulogy at Camm's memorial service. Another snippet from Sopwith's speech encapsulates the nature of the man: 'He had a wonderful character – forceful to a degree when he was right but always ready to listen to another point of view on the rare occasions that he was wrong.'

Pounds not ounces

In late 1923 the decision was taken that Hawker should enter the Light Aeroplane Competition for two-seaters, to be held at Lympne in September the following year. Carter realised that his newly appointed deputy's experience with the Handasyde ultralight made Camm ideal for the project. In his seminal *Hawker Aircraft since 1920*, Francis K Mason explains that Carter: 'simply couldn't get used to thinking in terms of ounces instead of pounds'. Throughout his time with Hawker, Camm hammered home his mantra of keeping the weight down to the absolute minimum. Each with an empty weight of 373lb and a span of 28ft, the two Cygnets that competed in 1924 were classic examples of how to avoid the unnecessary. The first example, G-EBMB, is now part of the RAF Museum's collection.

Camm perfected the Carter-initiated Horsley: with a span of 56ft 5¾in it was the largest aircraft ever built by Hawker. It was the company's next production success, achieving three figures – an incredible run for the 1920s. Initially, it was to have been called Kingston – after Hawker's adopted town. Instead the Air Ministry's so-called naming 'system' was usurped and the biplane honoured Horsley Towers, a huge early 19th-century manor house set in nearly 3,000 acres of land alongside the hamlet of East Horsley in Surrey. Tommy Sopwith successfully bid a whopping £150,000 (£16.5 million in present-day values) for the place in 1918 and he poured money in to modernise it. As noted earlier, when Sopwith Aviation was liquidated Tommy was forced to sell his pride and joy.

Cygnet G-EBMB is displayed at the RAF Museum, Cosford. *Ken Ellis*

A trio of Hucknall-based Horsleys of 504 (County of Nottingham) Squadron, 1929. *KEC*

Initially conceived as a day bomber, the Horsley was adapted as a torpedo carrier. The prototype first flew in 1925. As was commonplace in the 1920s, it went through an evolution and after ten all-wooden Mk.Is; the Mk.IIs featured a metal-framed forward fuselage. The final thirty-six Horsleys had an all-metal, fabric-covered structure, but oddly these never received the more logical Mk.III designation. The big biplane enjoyed some export success in Denmark, where it was called the Dantorp, and Greece.

State-of-the-art trainer

Here is a good place to mention the Tomtit, Hawker's only foray into the trainer market from scratch. The RAF was looking to replace its venerable Avro 504Ns and Camm came up with a machine that encompassed the state-of-the art of the late 1920s. The all-metal biplane employed Camm's tubular construction – of which more anon – Handley Page slots on the leading edges of the upper wing and the Reid and Sigrist blind flying panel. Sqn Ldr George Reid DFC served with the Royal Naval Air Service in the Great War and stayed on with the RAF, retiring in 1926. Reid devised a range of quality aircraft instruments and with backing from Hawker board member Fred Sigrist formed Reid and Sigrist Ltd in 1927. The panel allowed the pupil to go 'under the hood' to simulate flying in cloud or at night with just the instruments for reference. The prototype Tomtit flew in November 1928 and attracted an order for twenty-five units from the RAF: Avro's Tutor took the lion's share. There was an attempt to sell the Tomtit to civilian operators, but its military specification meant that it was expensive. Hawker came to the obvious conclusion that trainers were not its forte.

In April 1949, to celebrate his new job as a test pilot for Hawker, Neville Duke bought himself an aeroplane. It *had* to be a Hawker and he discovered that the only surviving Tomtit, G-AFTA, was available for sale: to clinch the deal he had to sell his beloved MG sports car. Duke transferred *Tango-Alpha* to his employers in July 1950 and continued to display it as part of Hawker's small 'circus' of former products. Today, the Tomtit flies with the Shuttleworth Collection at Old Warden.

Squaring tubes

Unlike other firms outlined in this book, Hawker built only a few prototypes that failed to reach production status; while some firms seemed to specialise in creating one-offs doomed to rejection. Hawker also did very little sub-contract work: in the doldrums of the mid-1920s it built undercarriages for Fairey Fawns but for most of its existence it was the one handing out patronage to other manufacturers. Camm's brilliance, along with Sopwith's and Sigrist's enlightened management, gave rise to a succession of dynasties of types that are defined in the Introduction as having the eight vital characteristics that make a great 'industrial' aircraft: the Hart 'family', the Hurricane–Tornado/Typhoon–Tempest progression, the exceptional Hunter, and it bequeathed the P.1127 to its successor, Hawker Siddeley. This repeated attainment of the mother lode transformed Hawker from the remnants of the Sopwith funeral pyre through to the largest aviation-based British business of the 1930s through to 1977.

Keen to ditch mixed construction as soon as possible, during 1924 Camm and Sigrist reviewed the techniques employed on the shop floor at Kingston. Steel and Duralumin was the future and a patented system was developed that allowed for cheap, efficient, rapid manufacture. Tubular structures with internal wire bracing offered the least complex method of building up fuselages, but welding was time-consuming, inaccurate and very difficult to repair. The answer was to take standard tubes and use a cold system of dies – swaging – to form a square or rectangular cross section at the ends. The tubes were fastened to one another using simple fish plates with bolts, or rivets. Camm also came up with an ingenious two-part spar created from steel strip rolled into hexagons, which were connected by a riveted plate to form a dumbbell shape. Ribs were made of uncomplicated pressed aluminium.

This system transformed the construction process and was used for all Hawker designs into the early 1940s. All of this came together on the Heron fighter prototype of 1925, which was rejected by the RAF but paved the way for a revolution. All of this metallic innovation from a man trained as a carpenter!

'Hawker Air Force'

Arguably the most important aircraft to enter RAF service in the early 1930s, the Hart's influence cannot be overestimated. Its airframe was morphed into a family, including its own replacement – the Hind. It also spawned the Demon two-seat fighter; the Audax army co-operation version and its replacement, the Hector, the Hardy 'colonial' general-purpose type for the RAF and the Osprey spotter for the FAA.

Vickers-built Hart Trainer K5892 of 7 Service Flying Training School, Peterborough, 1939. *KEC*

Audax K3084 of 4 Flying Training School, Habbaniya, Iraq, after a landing accident, circa 1939. *KEC*

Westland-built Hectors of 59 Squadron at Old Sarum, mid-1937. *KEC*

There was also a plethora of export versions with all manner of engine options. (Audax is Latin-based – audacious; Hector was the son of the King of Troy; and Hardy commemorates Vice-Admiral Sir Thomas Hardy, flag captain to Lord Horatio Nelson and *possibly* the recipient of a request for kiss while on the deck of HMS *Victory*.)

Camm changed the thinking of the Air Ministry when the Hart two-seat day bomber was revealed. To achieve the exceptional aerodynamics, he needed to abandon the long-accepted radial engines – while bowing to customers that insisted on them. He embraced the ground-breaking, supercharged, RR Kestrel vee-format 12-cylinder, which gave the Hart a top speed of 184mph, a good 28mph faster than the RAF's premier fighter of the day, the Armstrong Whitworth Siskin. It could also show a clean pair of heels to the Siskin's replacement, the Bristol Bulldog.

After a fierce competition with Avro and de Havilland, Hawker's prototype Hart, first flown in 1928, earned its first contract with the RAF. That was for fifteen, but was followed by another 444 – an unheard of post-1918 figure. Two sub-variants were created, the Hart (India) and the Hart (Special) optimised for service in the Northwest Frontier and in the Middle East and East Africa respectively. The Hart Trainer was introduced from April 1932, and 473 were built from new with upwards of seventy conversions of standard bomber versions.

A Hart is a stag (male) red deer and the name Hind, a female red deer, was chosen for the type's replacement, which appeared in September 1934. The Hind featured refinements adopted as the rest of the Hart family developed, but the most obvious was a supercharged Kestrel V giving it an extra 115hp over its predecessor. When the last Hind was rolled out in June 1938, a total of 528 had been manufactured for the RAF, including twenty from-new trainer versions. Combined production of Harts and Hinds surpassed all other bomber types taken on charge by the RAF since 1919, other than the venerable, much-rebuilt and revived Airco DH.9A. No wonder that, from the late 1920s, the RAF was often referred to as the 'Hawker Air Force'.

The first of a trio of Furies for the Portuguese Air Force, delivered in 1934. *Hawker Siddeley*

Camm's concept was ripe for development and a single-seat fighter was quickly on the drawing boards. The result was the Hornet, which began testing at Brooklands in 1929. Further refinement led to the Fury, which took the air on 25 March 1931. With the Fury, the RAF had a real interceptor. The more sedate Bulldog had been labelled as such, but the greater speed, excellent climb and superb agility of the Hawker put it in a league of its own. The Fury was the first RAF fighter to exceed 200mph in level flight and it was the darling of RAF events across Britain. Initially called Norn, a shipboard version of the Fury – the Nimrod – entered service with the FAA in 1932.

The design office did not rest on its laurels: Camm argued that the best replacement for a Fury was a more improved Mk.II and work started in 1934. Fitted with a 540hp Kestrel VI, the most obvious outward changes were the dapper mainwheel spats and a tailwheel replacing the skid. Top speed on the Fury II was 223mph, an increase of 16mph on the Mk.I. The Fury I's climb to 10,000ft was achieved in an impressive four-and-a-half minutes, but the new model could get there fifty seconds faster. These small advances helped to keep the Fury 'cutting edge' while the next generation was contemplated.

Corporate growth

Such was the growth of the company – renamed Hawker Aircraft in 1933 – that its chief, Thomas Sopwith, masterminded dramatic corporate expansion. In May 1934 the ailing Gloster was acquired, providing Hawker with much-needed production capacity. The biggest coup occurred on 15 June 1935 when the Armstrong-Siddeley Development Company was snapped up. This brought Coventry-based Armstrong Whitworth Aircraft (AW) and the sister Armstrong-Siddeley Motors (ASM), Air Service Training (AST) at Hamble, Avro in Manchester and Midlands-based High Duty Alloys into the fold. From near oblivion in 1920, Tommy Sopwith had become Britain's most prominent aircraft mogul.

All of the businesses constituted Hawker Siddeley Aircraft (HSA), but continued to trade under their own names, although there was increasing 'cross-fertilisation' in development and manufacture. By November 1937 HSA was the world's largest aeronautical business. This was not the end of the 'collecting', in January 1955 Avro Canada and other Canadian aviation businesses were snapped up. All of the enterprises were gathered under the 'umbrella' of the Hawker Siddeley Group, which had been formed in 1948.

Expansion for what looked like another world conflict was making Brooklands, also home to Vickers, a very crowded place.

Hawker settled on Langley in 1936 as its new assembly line and airfield and it was ready in June 1939. The last Brooklands-built Hurricanes rolled off the production line in 1941. The post-war choice of Heathrow – the former Fairey aerodrome – as the new London Airport condemned Langley – the airspace was going to become very busy. The search ended with the acquisition of Dunsfold in 1948: Langley closed its doors a decade later. In August 1952 the Hunter was declared a 'Super-Priority' venture and to meet the surge in orders Hawker took over the factory at Squires Gate, Blackpool, which had previously produced Vickers Wellingtons during the war. Among the final Hunters to depart Squires Gate in mid-1956 were Mk.50s destined for the Swedish Air Force.

Battle of Britain saviour

While the ink was drying on the Fury II drawings, in 1934 Camm and his team came up with the ultimate Fury evolution. Tiring of unrealistic Air Ministry specifications, the Hawker board had prepared the way for a private venture. A Fury II fuselage with an enclosed canopy was married to a monoplane wing of relatively deep section. A fixed, spatted, undercarriage was proposed, but this was soon abandoned in favour of a wide-track, retractable arrangement. Four machine guns, two in each wing, were chosen but they gave way to a breathtaking four on either side. Also busy throwing its own resources into the pot was RR with the PV.12 engine, the nascent Merlin. Hopes were high that, just as the Fury had broken the 200mph 'barrier', the Fury Monoplane, as the new design was referred to at Kingston, would go beyond 300mph. All of this was but a short step away from the Hurricane.

Because Camm had conceived the Hurricane as an extension of the Hart's construction philosophy, when 'George' Bulman took the prototype, K5083, for its maiden flight on 6 November 1935 it was a low-risk programme. Not content with creating the Hurricane as a private venture, four months before the debut of the prototype, the Hawker board had taken another incredible decision: it was going to tool up to produce 1,000 units. So it was that on 1 July 1940 – nine days before the Battle of Britain began – Fighter Command's order of battle comprised twenty-nine Hurricane, nineteen Spitfire, eight Blenheim and two Defiant squadrons. A month later Hawker had delivered a total of 2,309 Hurricanes, nearly double that of the Spitfire. Owen Thetford, in his exceptional book *Aircraft of the Royal Air Force since 1918*, summed this up 'During [the Battle of Britain], Hurricane pilots shot down more enemy aircraft than all other defences, air and ground, combined.' PZ865, a Mk.IIc still airworthy with the Battle of

Hurricanes under assembly, showing the internal structure, first employed on the Heron biplane of 1925. *KEC*

Above: Loading Gloster-built Hurricane I V6756 of the Merchant Ship Flying Unit onto a Catapult Aircraft Merchantman, Iceland, circa 1942. *KEC*

Left: Early Hurricanes Is of 56 Squadron at North Weald, early 1939. *KEC*

on 6 October 1939, but this programme was brought to a halt in July 1941. The Vulture was troublesome and RR needed to concentrate on expanding the Merlin family. The plan had been that Avro – a Hawker Siddeley consortium member – would make the Tornado and one was completed and flown at Woodford. Avro's experience of the Manchester twin-Vulture bomber was expected to smooth the Tornado's path but events had already quashed this. The Vulture had stymied the Manchester and in January 1941 Avro had begun testing a four-engined evolution with Merlins – the Lancaster.

The Sabre-engined prototype Typhoon had its maiden flight on 24 February 1940 and became the RAF's first fighter to exceed 400mph. The Mk.Ia featured the dozen machine guns but it was the Mk.Ib with four 20mm cannon that became the standard model. Halfway through production, the cumbersome framed cockpit and car-like access door were replaced by a Perspex teardrop-shaped canopy offering greatly enhanced visibility.

Structural problems and protracted development of the Sabre engine delayed entry into service. A series of fatal accidents in which the tail section separated looked set to cancel the Typhoon. Hawker developed a 'fix' and the Typhoon went on to become a famed close-support aircraft. The thick wing profile allowed the fitting of rails under the wings for eight 60lb rocket projectiles. These, coupled with the cannon, made the Typhoon a formidable presence over the battlefield.

Ground crew getting Typhoon Ib EK139 *Dirty Dora* of 175 Squadron ready for another sortie at Colerne, May 1944. *Peter Green Collection*

Britain Memorial Flight, was completed in July 1944. Called *The Last of the Many*, it marked the end of Hurricane production.

Two designs add a postscript to the Hurricane story: the Henley and the Hotspur. Named after the famous town on the banks of the Thames, the Henley was a response to Specification P.4/34 for a light bomber. Camm's team used as many Hurricane sub-assemblies as possible, including the outer wings and tail 'feathers'. The first of two prototypes flew on 10 March 1937 but within a year the Henley had been relegated to target tug status: 200 were manufactured by Gloster.

The 14th-century warrior Sir Henry Hotspur lent his name to two very different types. First off was Hawker's interpretation of Specification F.9/35 for a turret fighter to replace the Demon. Based upon the Henley, the prototype Hotspur had its maiden flight on 14 June 1938, but by then Boulton Paul had made all the headway with the unfortunate Defiant. The Hotspur remained a one-off. The second use of 'Harry Hotspur's' name was by General Aircraft's assault glider.

Typhoon, Tempest and another Fury

Even before the Spitfire had entered squadron service, the Air Ministry began the process of replacing both it and the Hurricane, issuing Specification F.18/37 in March 1938. Twelve machine guns or six 20mm cannon were the armament options, and the RR Vulture or Napier Sabre, both 24-cylinder monsters, were preferred to power it. Hawker won the contract and Camm decided to build prototypes with both engines. The Vulture-powered Tornado was the first into the air,

Hawker: Duiker to Hector

From	To	Total	Name/Designation	Type	Engine(s)	Notes
1923	-	1	Duiker	General recce	1 x Bristol Jupiter	[1]
1923	1926	64	Woodcock I/II	Fighter	1 x Bristol Jupiter	
1924	-	2	Cygnet	Ultralight	1 x Bristol Cherub	
1924	-	1	Hedgehog	Shipborne recce	1 x Bristol Jupiter	
1925	1928	15	Danecock	Fighter	1 x AS Jaguar	[2]
1925	-	1	Heron	Fighter	1 x Bristol Jupiter	
1925	1932	119	Horsley/Dantorp	Torpedo bomber	1 x RR Condor	[3]
1926	-	1	Hornbill	Fighter	1 x RR Condor	
1927	-	1	Hawfinch	Fighter	1 x Bristol Jupiter	
1927	-	1	Harrier	Light bomber	1 x Bristol Jupiter	
1928	1936	1,031	Hart	Light bomber	1 x RR Kestrel	[4]
1928	1931	36	Tomtit	Trainer	1 x AS Mongoose	
1928	-	1	F.20/27	Fighter	1 x Bristol Jupiter	
1928	-	1	Hoopoe	Shipborne fighter	1 x Bristol Mercury	
1929	-	1	Hornet	Fighter	1 x RR F.XI	[5]
1929	1937	261	Fury I/II	Fighter	1 x RR Kestrel	[6]
1930	1935	87	Nimrod I/II	Fleet fighter	1 x RR Kestrel	[7]
1931	1938	259	Demon	2-seat fighter	1 x RR Kestrel	[8]
1931	1935	137	Osprey I–IV	Shipborne recce	1 x RR Kestrel	
1931	1936	693	Audax	Army co-op	1 x RR Kestrel	[9]
1934	1936	47	Hardy	General purpose	1 x RR Kestrel	[10]
1934	-	1	PV.3	Fighter	1 x RR Goshawk	
1934	-	1	PV.4	GP/dive-bomber	1 x Bristol Pegasus	
1934	1938	581	Hind	Light bomber	1 x RR Kestrel	[11]
1935	1938	69	Hartbees	Light bomber	1 x RR Kestrel	[12]
1936	1937	178	Hector	Army co-op	1 x Napier Dagger	[13]

Based upon: *Hawker Aircraft since 1920*, Francis K Mason. **[1]** Monoplane, all others biplanes. **[2]** Version of the Woodcock, also built under licence by Danish Royal Naval Dockyard, Copenhagen, as LB.II Dankok (12). **[3]** Two Dantorp versions for Danish military, with AS Leopard. **[4]** Day bomber, two-seat fighter, trainer, Indian theatre, comms and 'special' sub-types. Includes sub-contacts to Armstrong Whitworth (456), Gloster (72) and Vickers (226). Also under licence by Swedish State Aircraft Factory, Trollhättan (42) with licensed Bristol Pegasus. **[5]** Regarded as the Fury prototype. **[6]** Includes one-off High Speed Fury for trials. Engine variants for exports, including Pratt & Whitney Hornet for Persia. Includes sub-contract to General Aircraft (89 Mk.II). **[7]** Initially known unofficially as Norn. **[8]** Includes sub-contract to Boulton Paul (106), batches converted to turret fighter, others from new. **[9]** Engine variants for exports, including Pratt & Whitney Hornet and Bristol Pegasus for Persia. Includes Indian theatre sub-types and sub-contracts to Avro (244), Bristol (141), Gloster (25) and Westland (43). **[10]** Prototype converted from a Hart; all production sub-contracted to Gloster. **[11]** Engine variants for exports, including Bristol Mercuries for Latvia and Persia. General Aircraft converted 124 to trainers for the RAF. **[12]** Audax development to meet South African requirement for close support of ground forces. Hawker referred to this as Hartbees – an African antelope: other possible spellings: Hartbee, Hartebeeste. Majority under licence by South African Air Force Depot, Pretoria (65). **[13]** Prototype converted from a Hart, all production sub-contracted to Westland.

Originally referred to as the Typhoon II, the Tempest was, essentially, a thin-winged version of its forebear. With an elegant, elliptical, laminar-flow wing and a longer fuselage, the Tempest was 30mph faster than its older brother and could carry a similar warload. Typically, Camm decided to explore powerplant options for his new fighter. The Mks I, V and VI stayed with the Typhoon's Sabre, while the Mk.III was fitted with a RR Griffon. The aerodynamics of the Tempest were so clean that it could take the more practical Bristol Centaurus radial, with little penalty in performance – this was the Mk.II.

Only the Mk.V saw combat in World War Two, becoming the fastest British-built fighter of the conflict. It earned fame as the champion V-1 flying-bomb killer, bringing down 638, about half of the 'doodlebugs' destined for England that were destroyed by the RAF. The Mk.VI, a tropicalised Mk.V, served in the Middle East from December 1946. Intended for use in the Far East against Japan, the Tempest II entered RAF service in August 1945.

Invasion-striped Tempest V JN766 of 486 Squadron, RNZAF, June 1944. *Peter Green Collection*

Sea Fury T.20S D-CABY, converted in 1963, and a North American AT-6 Texan of contractor Deutsche Luftfahrt Beratungsdienst at Cologne in June 1967. *Roy Bonser*

Production of Napier Sabre-powered Tempests came to an end in the autumn of 1947 and it was June 1948 before the last Centaurus-equipped Mk.II rolled out at Langley. As Hawker prepared to enter the jet age it was the Fury, the ultimate development of the piston fighters, that carried the firm through the transition; indeed it was still making money into the 1960s.

Originating with a joint RAF–FAA Specification F.2/43, Hawker chose to reuse the Fury 'brand': the prototype flying on 1 September 1944. It was a lighter version of the Tempest made possible by the simple expedient of removing the centre section and anchoring modified outer wings to revised wing roots. Anticipating large RAF orders, the naval variant was vested with Boulton Paul but when the air force lost interest and the Admiralty became the only customer, that scheme was scrubbed.

The first true Sea Fury was airborne in February 1945 and, after a batch of interim Mk.Xs, production FB.11s entered service in May 1948. A batch of T.20 two-seaters followed. Australia and Canada were supplied through Royal Navy stocks. Egypt, Iraq, the Netherlands and Pakistan also ordered the type; the last new-built example going to Pakistan in 1954. Hawker was quick to capitalise on the secondary market, buying back and refurbishing former FAA machines for other customers, including Burma, Cuba and a German civilian target tug contractor, the last being delivered in the early 1960s.

Shaping the Hunter

As early as December 1944 Hawker was considering single-seat jet fighter configurations. The result was the Sea Hawk and, to Camm's acclaim, the company's first stab at a jet fighter remained in production until October 1962. FAA requirement N.7/46, already looking for a Sea Fury replacement, was written around Hawker's P.1040 proposal – Camm once again was ahead of the game. To keep the jet pipe short and the powerplant near the centre of gravity, a bifurcated exhaust arrangement was patented. The Y-shaped jet pipe allowed the RR Nene turbojet to vent either side of the fuselage, behind the trailing edge of the wing. Classically keeping costs down, Tempest outer wings were to be fitted. The first example was flown on 2 September 1947 from Boscombe Down. With its straight wing permitting easy folding and the cockpit offering unrestricted views forward, the navy was very impressed with what was surely the most beautiful of Britain's 'first-generation' jets.

At Hamble, AST carried out major modifications to the prototype and in mid-1950 it emerged as the P.1072 with an ASM Snarler solid-state rocket in the rear fuselage. Both AST and ASM were HSA members, proving the capabilities of Sopwith's consortium. The maiden flight with the Snarler used 'in anger' took place on a sortie out of Bitteswell on 20 November 1950. Limited testing continued into 1952, when the project was shelved.

Line-up of Sea Hawk FGA.6s of the Fleet Requirements Unit, Hurn, August 1962. *Roy Bonser*

Hawker: Hurricane to P.1127

From	To	Total	Name/Designation	Type	Engine(s)	Notes
1935	1944	14,533	Hurricane	Fighter	1 x RR Merlin	[1]
1937	1940	202	Henley	Target tug	1 x RR Merlin	[2]
1938	-	1	Hotspur	Turret fighter	1 x RR Merlin	
1939	1941	4	Tornado	Fighter	1 x RR Vulture	[3]
1940	1945	3,333	Typhoon	Fighter-bomber	1 x Napier Sabre	[4]
1942	1947	950	Tempest V, VI	Fighter	1 x Napier Sabre	[5]
1943	1948	438	Tempest II	Fighter-bomber	1 x Bristol Centaurus	[6]
1944	1954	801	Fury/Sea Fury	Shipborne fighter	1 x Bristol Centaurus	[7]
1947	1962	528	Sea Hawk	Shipborne fighter	1 x RR Nene	[8]
1948	1951	69	Sea Fury T.20	Advanced trainer	1 x Bristol Centaurus	[9]
1948	1949	2	P.1052	Research	1 x RR Nene	
1950	-	1	P.1081	Research	1 x RR Nene	
1951	1960	1,852	Hunter	Fighter	1 x RR Avon	[10]
1955	1960	92	Hunter	Advanced trainer	1 x RR Avon	[11]
1958	-	1	P.1121	Fighter	1 x DH Gyron	[12]
1960	1963	6	P.1127	V/STOL research	1 x BS Pegasus	[13]

Based upon: *Hawker Aircraft since 1920* and *Hawker Hunter – Biography of a Thoroughbred* (Patrick Stephens, 1981), both by Francis K Mason. **[1]** Includes Sea Hurricane conversions. Includes sub-contacts to Austin Motors, Longbridge (300) and Gloster (2,750). Also under licence by Canadian Car and Foundry, Fort William, Ontario (1,077). **[2]** After two prototypes, all production (200) by Gloster. **[3]** Production planned for Avro; only one completed. **[4]** Three prototypes and 15 produced by Hawker; remainder sub-contracted to Gloster. **[5]** Includes Tempest I (Sabre IV) prototype. **[6]** Includes sub-contract to Bristol: 36 completed. **[7]** Production of naval version initially planned for Boulton Paul at Woodford; only one completed and flown at Langley. Includes seven prototypes and 50 Mk.X for Fleet Air Arm (FAA); all others FB.11 or export equivalent. Does not include former FAA airframes refurbished for export. **[8]** Three prototypes and 35 F.1s by Hawker, remainder under sub-contract to Armstrong Whitworth. **[9]** Includes export equivalents, eg. T.61 for Pakistan. Does not include former FAA airframes refurbished for export. **[10]** Includes sub-contract to Armstrong Whitworth for F.2s, F.5s and F.6s, total 278. Also under licence by Fokker-Aviolanda, Amsterdam, Netherlands: F.4s (96) and F.6s (93); Avions Fairey at Gosselies, Belgium: F.4s (112) and F.6s (144). Does not include airframes refurbished for export and/or converted to two-seaters; or conversions to FGA.9, FR.10, GA.11 or special Mk.12 for RAF/FAA. **[11]** Does not include airframes refurbished for export. **[12]** Air superiority fighter project, cancelled 1958; unfinished prototype is part of the RAF Museum collection. **[13]** Detailed in Chapter 26.

The first production Sea Hawk F.1 flew from the newly activated Dunsfold in November 1951. By then Hawker was beginning to test the Hunter, a much more complex and challenging programme. Accordingly, the bulk of Sea Hawk manufacture was handed over to another HSA company, AW at Bitteswell. As well as FAA contracts, AW supplied the export customers, the naval air arms of India, Netherlands and West Germany, with a mixture of new-build and refurbished examples. The Indian Navy paid off the last few Sea Hawks in 1983 when its first Sea Harrier FRS.51s were delivered – exceptional loyalty to the Hawker 'brand'!

Attractive though the Sea Hawk was, its unswept wing was performance limiting: thankfully its configuration meant that sweeping the wings would be relatively easy. Two prototypes, designated P.1052, were ordered for trials. To keep things simple, the tailplanes remained unswept. The first example, VX272, flew from Boscombe Down on 19 November 1948. Deck-landing trials on HMS *Eagle* were carried out in May 1952, which explains why VX272 is today held by the Fleet Air Arm Museum at Yeovilton, Somerset.

'Wimpy' Wade flying the P.1081 VX279, July 1950. *Hawker*

Through this very straightforward step, knowledge of swept wings grew steadily at Kingston. The design office was already working on the next member of the jet family. The Royal Australian Air Force was interested in an improved P.1052 and the result was the P.1081, a 'halfway house' to the layout adopted by the Hunter. The second P.1052 was given an entirely new rear fuselage, featuring a straight jet pipe exhausting at the extreme rear and swept vertical and horizontal tail surfaces: it flew on 19 June 1950. Trials were going well but six months later interest from Australia waned.

Exceptional Hunter

Comparisons are dangerous things but the Hunter could be called the Spitfire of its day. There are so many similarities: initiated as a private venture, a stunning-looking machine, a long service history and an incredible number of roles, variants and exports. The two thoroughbreds also shared a dodgy start that threatened the programme's progress.

There was a lot riding on the Hunter; it was to be the spearhead of Britain's airspace defence and guard the UK's interests worldwide for the bulk of the 1950s. Should the Hunter falter, the plan was that the Supermarine Swift would pick up the slack, or the other way around. The Air Ministry wished to hedge its bets still further and the Hawker jet was to have powerplant options; the preferred RR Avon and the AS Sapphire.

Duke first flew the Avon-powered prototype Hunter, WB188, from Dunsfold on 20 July 1951. Modified with a reheated Avon as the one-off Mk.3, Duke took the all-red WB188 to a new record of 727mph on 7 September 1953 and on the 29th clinched the 100km closed-circuit record at 709mph while operating from Tangmere. (Part of the RAF Museum's collection, WB188 is displayed on loan at the Tangmere Military Aviation Museum.)

The prototype was followed by an example with provision for guns on 5 May 1952 and the initial Sapphire example and prototype F.2 on 30 November 1952. Sapphire-powered Hunters were manufactured exclusively by AW at Bitteswell. Declared a 'super priority' programme by Churchill's Conservative government of the day, the first F.1 flew in May 1953. It was christened *State Express* to reflect how much the industry was gearing up for mass production. As Chapter 36 explains, the Swift fell by the wayside, but the Hunter also suffered from teething problems. Hasty acquisition of Canadian-built North American Sabres was needed to tide Fighter Command over.

Gun or no gun

Much thought had been put into making the Hunter a formidable interceptor. Powered controls made it very agile. Turnarounds were to be kept to a minimum by two 'firsts' for the RAF: a single-point refuelling system and a self-contained four-cannon pack that slotted in and out of a bay in the lower nose. The gun 'cassette' was a brilliant concept, but it was the main issue in the Hunter's tardy entry into full service. The Hunter's 30mm cannons were derived from a wartime Luftwaffe Mauser. The British version was conceived by the Armament Development team at the Royal Small Arms Factory at Enfield, from which came the abbreviation ADEN.

During the Hunter's design phase, which was initiated in the summer of 1948, there was feverish debate about the need for guns at all. Unguided 'dumb' rockets were considered more efficient. Thankfully, the Hunter was allowed to swerve around this debate. The 'gun or no gun' argument has raised its head periodically all the way to the present-day Eurofighter Typhoon, which ironically packs a Mauser cannon.

The Hunter F.4 production line, Langley, circa 1954. *British Aerospace*

The Hunter evolved to take an incredible array of armament. From the rear: DH Firestreak and Fairey Fireflash air-to-air missiles; 5in unguided rocket pylons; 2in and 3in unguided rocket pods; 3in unguided rockets (left) and 2in unguided rockets (right); 5in unguided rockets with warhead options; four 30mm ADEN cannon pack with ammunition lined up in front; napalm tanks, 100-gallon drop tanks, 230-gallon drop tanks; 500lb and 1,000lb bombs; practice bombs and their dispensers. *Hawker*

Delays to the Hunter programme occurred when it was decided to install an air brake underneath the lower rear fuselage, but this was a simple 'fix' compared with the tribulations of the cannon. ADENs were carried aloft for the first time on 5 May 1954. During trials above 10,000ft, pressing the gun button could result in it all going quiet as the Avon 113 flamed out. To compound the angst at RR and Hawker, this did not happen to Sapphire-powered examples. After a lot of detective work, it was discovered that the gases emitted by the gun muzzles were still combustible as they flowed backwards, into the turbojet intakes. This surged the Avon, often to the state of flame-out – relights were possible, but the height loss could be nerve-racking. With an Avon 115 installed the F.4 addressed the flame-out issue and improved the interceptor's range. In parallel, the Sapphire-powered F.5 was introduced.

As the shell cases of ADEN cannon flew clear, the links that formed the ammunition belt were also expelled and could cause considerable damage as they bounced along the lower fuselage. Streamlined fairings under the forward fuselage were fitted to collect the spent links. These bulbous additions became known as 'Sabrinas', after a well-endowed 1950s actress. The ADEN gun went on to be a great success; versions equipped the Gloster Javelin, English Electric Lightning, HS Harrier and Hawk and SEPECAT Jaguar.

Exports, new and rebuilt

The F.4 and F.5 paved the way for the ultimate Hunter pure fighter, the F.6, which was delivered to front-line units from October 1956. From the outside it was distinguished by a 'saw-tooth' on the leading edge of the wing; inside it was fitted with a much more powerful Avon 200 series. With the advent of the F.6, production was standardised and the Sapphire version was dropped. A combat-capable operational trainer,

the T.7, was first flown on 8 July 1955 and the FAA adopted its own version, the T.8. With the Lightning due to come on strength in the early 1960s, withdrawn F.6s were converted into FGA.9s, optimised for ground attack to take over from obsolete de Havilland Venoms. The F.6 was also adapted as the FR.10 for tactical reconnaissance.

A quartet of test and trials Hunters salute their birthplace – Dunsfold. Clockwise from the top: T.7 XL564 of the Empire Test Pilots School (ETPS); hybrid F.6 XE601 of the Aeroplane & Armament Experimental Establishment; T.7 XL614 also of ETPS; T.7 WV383 of the Royal Aircraft Establishment. *British Aerospace*

The Hunter was adopted by the US Mutual Defense Assistance Program as part of its 'off-shore' funding to NATO allies. A large number of RAF F.4s came under this arrangement, as did licence manufacture by Fokker-Aviolanda for the Netherlands and Avions Fairey for Belgium. With three production lines in Britain, Hawker also had the capacity to meet a burgeoning export market. Denmark, India, Sweden and Switzerland all placed substantial orders. The last Hunter, a T.66 for India, was tested at Dunsfold on 21 October 1960. Following in the footsteps of the Sea Fury and Sea Hawk secondary market, refurbishing Hunters became a major occupation for Dunsfold and Bitteswell. India and Switzerland placed repeat contracts that were met by rebuilt examples bought back by Hawker from previous customers. An impressive list of new export customers added to a lucrative trade in 'refurbs' that lasted into the early 1970s.

Upwardly mobile

With political pressure mounting for the consolidation of the British industry, Hawker Siddeley Aviation was formed in January 1959 and three other organisations joined: Folland (in February 1959), de Havilland (January 1960) and Blackburn (May 1960). In his 72nd year, Sir Thomas Sopwith was presiding over an international aviation colossus. As with the set up in the 1930s, all of these concerns traded under their original names, but not for much longer as policy became centralised. The holding company morphed into two bodies on 1 July 1963: Hawker Siddeley Aviation looking after aircraft design and manufacture, and Hawker Siddeley Dynamics specialising in propulsion systems, missiles and space technologies. On All Fool's Day 1965 all of the constituent bodies ceased using their historic names and blended under the Hawker Siddeley banner.

The final design that Sir Sydney Camm presided over was also the most radical of the jet family and the last to carry the Hawker name. In fame it was to eclipse the Hunter, and like Sopwith's Camel of 1917, it became a household name – the Harrier. The prototype P.1127 was laid down in May 1959 and rolled out at Dunsfold in July 1960. The story of the P.1127, Kestrel and Harrier belongs with the next chapter.

As well as attending airshows, Hawker-operated Hurricane II PZ865 *The Last of the Many* was also occasionally used as a 'chase-plane'. This work included shadowing P.1127 XP831 during its early excursions from Dunsfold. *Hawker Siddeley*

CHAPTER TWENTY-SIX

Unequal Partners

**Hawker Siddeley
1960 to 1977**

'…the US military are not given to buying their aircraft from overseas unless these aircraft are pretty special.'
Test pilot John Farley AFC on the Harrier

AS THE 1950s DREW TO A CLOSE, the British aircraft industry was involved in a game of musical chairs. The Conservative government was determined to rationalise the manufacturing base and intended that by 1960 there would only be 'seats' available for two major 'players'. The 'special case' of Shorts would remain, bolstering the fragile employment prospects of Northern Ireland. There was no 'policy' as such for helicopters and Westland emerged having picked up the 'orphans' Fairey and Saunders-Roe, plus Bristol's rotary-wing division. So takeovers and mergers were the order of the day. Chapter 13 has already outlined this rationale and the emergence of the British Aircraft Corporation (BAC) – English Electric and Vickers with Bristol – less the 'choppers' and the engine division – and Hunting.

There was no doubt that the other grouping would be Sir Thomas Sopwith's Hawker Siddeley Aviation (HSA), perhaps without any additions. In May 1934 Sir Thomas began a spending spree when Hawker acquired the ailing Gloster. The following year the Armstrong Siddeley Development Company was bought, bringing Avro and Armstrong Whitworth among others into the conglomerate, which was called Hawker Siddeley *Aircraft*. In 1948 the many elements of this empire were brought under the banner of the Hawker Siddeley Group. Throughout Sopwith allowed a largely unfettered management system. Avro, Armstrong Whitworth (AW), Gloster and Hawker continued to trade under their own names and ran separate design offices, competing for Air Ministry requirements and seeking civilian markets however they could. There were instances of building one another's aircraft: for example Gloster constructed the majority of the Hawker Typhoons. This loose arrangement was tightened throughout the 1950s and in the next decade was brought to an end.

The Hawker Siddeley Group was a vast organisation, far more than 'just' an aircraft manufacturing consortium. In January 1959 it went through a major revision: Hawker Siddeley *Aviation* (HSA) was born with missile, rocket and aero engine divisions as well as the aircraft factories. At the same time, Hawker Siddeley Industries was created, with railway, engine, generator and nuclear interests, and a diverse Canadian combine. HSA boasted the following major factory and/or airfield sites: Avro – Chadderton and Woodford; AW – Baginton and Bitteswell; Gloster – Hucclecote and Moreton Valence; Hawker – Dunsfold and Kingston.

A line-up at Wittering in 1994 celebrating the twenty-fifth anniversary of the Harrier entering RAF service. Left to right: Development batch GR.1 XV279, first flown in 1967; GR.3 ZD688, built in 1986, in the colours of 20 Squadron; T.4; Sea Harrier FRS.1; T.8 in 899 Squadron colours; T.4, GR.5, GR.7, Sea Harrier FA.2. *RAF Wittering*

British aircraft industry rationalisation 1960

British Aircraft Corporation	Hawker Siddeley Aviation	Westland	Independent
English Electric	Hawker Siddeley [1]	Westland Helicopters [2]	Auster
Vickers	Blackburn	Bristol helicopter division [3]	Handley Page
Bristol [3]	de Havilland	Fairey	Scottish Aviation
Hunting	Folland	Saunders-Roe	Shorts [4]

[1] Already comprising Armstrong Whitworth, Avro, Gloster and Hawker: Hawker Siddeley Aviation from January 1959. [2] Westland Aircraft Ltd was renamed Westland Helicopters in 1966. [3] Bristol engine division merged with Armstrong Siddeley in April 1959 to produce Bristol Siddeley (acquired by Rolls-Royce October 1966). The helicopter division was acquired by Westland in February 1960. [4] 69.5% state-owned with Bristol and Harland and Wolff holding the remainder.

There were two other leading contenders that the Ministry of Aviation had an eye on: de Havilland (DH) and Handley Page (HP). As Chapter 24 shows, the latter was more or less determined to plough its own furrow. Realising that rationalisation was inevitable, DH had its own ideas. Charles Gardner, in *British Aircraft Corporation – A History*, sums up the character of the firm very well, it was: 'then, as until the end, a law unto themselves as the "only true aristocrats" of the business.' The ministry held hopes that DH would join the Vickers–English Electric camp and steered negotiations in that direction.

Management at DH argued that the Aircraft Manufacturing Company (Airco – reprising the name of the firm that Geoffrey de Havilland had designed for during World War One – see Chapter 2) was sufficient to act as a third 'force'. Formed in January 1958 by DH, Airco was a combination of DH, Fairey and Hunting to build the DH.121 jetliner – of which more anon. The Air Ministry rejected the 'Airco alone' proposal out of hand – DH *had* to find a partner, ideally with Vickers and English Electric. Negotiations came to halt in November 1959 and DH bosses turned to HSA for sanctuary.

Three months earlier, HSA had snapped up a 'minnow' – Folland. As well as DH, Blackburn was being courted as another element of HSA. On 17 December 1959 DH issued a statement that it would be merging with HSA with effect from January 1960. Blackburn signed up in May 1960 and the game of musical chairs was complete – for the time being. By then the 'carrot' that had been dangled to force rationalisation on the industry – Operational Requirement 339, leading to the supposedly lucrative TSR.2 – had gone to BAC. The table that appeared in Chapter 13 covering the rationalisation process in 1960 bears repetition here.

HSA was reorganised on 1 July 1963 and from then on the constituent 'famous names' began to slip into division status and their names quickly dissolved as Hawker Siddeley became the 'brand'. Management at DH had hoped for a degree of autonomy within the new enterprise, also suggesting that the name Hawker de Havilland be adopted. This was not acceptable to Sir Roy Dobson and the remainder of the HSA team. Although both HSA and DH referred to the coming together as a merger, it was a buyout – the 'aristocrats' had joined the masses.

In his autobiography, *Sky Fever*, published in 1961, Sir Geoffrey de Havilland was brief but upbeat about the onset of HSA, noting that this was: 'not a coming together of strangers.' He'd known Sopwith – chairman of the conglomerate – since 1910 and Dobson – its managing director – from 'the early days'. Sir Geoffrey concluded: 'Many of our people know many of their people and although amalgamations are sometimes "difficult", I feel confident that in this case the result is going to be highly successful.'

Sum of the parts

Sir Geoffrey was right, but in 1960 the aircraft side of HSA was largely composed of programmes that were either winding down, just starting up or were still on the drawing boards. With Hawker, production of the Hunter at Dunsfold stopped in 1960 and new Sea Hawks for the Indian Navy lasted at Bitteswell only until 1962. Both of these jets would go on to enjoy a long and profitable life in the 'secondary market' – refurbished and reroled. The revolutionary P.1127 vertical/short take-off and landing (V/STOL) fighter had begun tentative flight test, but this was a high-risk project.

Of the remainder of the 'established' HS group, AW was building the Argosy freighter, but it met a niche requirement and was unlikely to last long on the Bitteswell assembly line. AW's design office at Whitley was working on the HS.681 STOL and potentially V/STOL military transport but its prospects were not good – it was axed in February 1965. Bitteswell had proven to be an efficient manufacturing, refurbishing and overhaul facility and that was where its future lay: the other AW plant at Baginton was closed in the mid-1960s.

By the end of 1960 Avro at Woodford had completed eighteen of eighty-nine Vulcan B.2s with no prospect of repeat orders: the final example was delivered in 1964. Support for the V-bomber fleet, including major overhauls and changes of role, ensured the Vulcan remained a reliable cash cow into the 1980s. Manufacture of the Shackleton maritime patroller had finished in 1959 but, like the Vulcan, updating the fleet helped to keep the workforce at Woodford and Bitteswell employed. The first of a dozen airborne early warning versions of MR.2s appeared in 1971. When HP went into liquidation in 1970, HSA took over the contract to convert redundant Victor Mk.2s into K.2 tankers. These were ferried from Radlett to Woodford and flight testing began in March 1972. The prototype Avro 748 twin turboprop transport had its maiden flight, from Woodford, in June 1960; it had good prospects, but Avro had a poor track record with commercial aircraft; the DH marketing department would be useful in this task. Avro's vast factory at Chadderton offered great capacity for the manufacture of sub-assemblies within HSA. Gloster had flown the last new-build Javelin in 1958 and Hucclecote and Moreton Valence were involved in the upgrade of FAW.7s to FAW.9 status; but both facilities were soon to close.

Folland had been a long-established HSA sub-contractor and was a logical acquisition, providing extra production capacity for other ventures – for instance the 748. Hamble was busy building Gnat T.1 advanced trainers for the RAF and managing a valuable licence agreement with India. Experience gained with the Gnat paid dividends with its successor in RAF service, the Hawk.

Blackburn was completing Gyron Junior-powered Buccaneer S.1s and was preparing for the much-improved S.2, which appeared in 1964. Upgrade programmes kept the Buccaneer a money-spinner into the late 1980s. Brough also offered HSA additional capacity and it was still functioning in that form when this book went to press.

As can be seen from the 'Hawker Siddeley 'inheritance' programmes' table, DH brought an impressive number of types to HSA, including five from its Canadian subsidiary. Of the British machines, the Dove, Heron and Comet were running out of steam. The Sea Vixen FAW.2 carrier-borne strike aircraft for the Fleet Air Arm included new-built examples, the last of which was rolled out in 1966, and upgrades. It was 1962 before the prototype Trident jetliner got airborne. It had an up-front order from British European Airways (BEA) and hopes for exports. Hatfield also brought additional, experienced, design capacity to HSA. The DH Propeller subsidiary had for some time been a misnomer, propellers being a fraction of its turnover; it was renamed HS Dynamics to better reflect its activities in missiles and rocketry. The DH engine division was swallowed by Bristol Siddeley.

Hawker Siddeley 'inheritance' programmes, 1960

Type	Last example	See Chapter	Notes
AW* Argosy	1966	4	
Avro* Vulcan B.2	1964	6	
Blackburn Buccaneer	1977	9	
DH Dove/Devon	1968	17	
DH Comet	1965	17	
DH Heron	1964	17	
DH Sea Vixen	1966	17	
DHC Beaver	1967	17	[1]
DHC Otter	1967	17	[1]
DHC Caribou	1973	17	[1]
DHC Buffalo	1986	17	[1]
DHC Twin Otter	ongoing	17	[1] [2]
Folland Gnat	1985	20	[3]
Hawker* Sea Hawk	1962	25	
Hawker* Hunter	1960	25	

* Existing HS Group constituent. [1] de Havilland Canada sold to the Canadian government in June 1974. [2] Twin Otter production completed in 1988, but restarted by Viking Air in 2009. [3] Last Gnat T.1 delivered to RAF 1965. Licence production of Gnat F.1 and more developed Ajeet by Hindustan Aeronautics (HAL), Bangalore, India, continued until 1985. Design rights transferred to HAL July 1974.

The prototype 748 (originally G-APZV) was re-engineered to act as the prototype for the Andover C.1, as G-ARRV, from late 1963. *HSA*

Enduring airlifter

Avro's mixed propellant – rocket and turbojet – Avro 720 interceptor project was axed in 1956 and the gloom and doom fostered by the Defence White Paper of the following year prompted the decision to get back to commercial products. The design office conceived the robust 748 twin-turboprop aimed at a broad civilian and military customer base.

Avro was the fourth company to enter this marketplace: all using the incredible Rolls-Royce (RR) Dart. Fokker was the pioneer with the F27 Friendship, which appeared in 1955 and was destined to remain in production in its original form until 1987. HP saw the error of its ways and re-engineered its Herald from four piston engines to Darts, getting that prototype into the air in 1958. Chapter 22 makes a comparison of all three types, the Herald running to a dismal fifty units. What was the fourth? As Chapter 22 shows, Southend-based Aviation Traders took a brave move into original design to create the twenty-eight-seat Accountant. The prototype first flew in the summer of 1957 but remained a one-off and was retired the following year. Aviation Traders had engaged Gloster to help with design, construction and to conduct a market survey. Gloster's investment in the Accountant was not wasted: its experiences were handed to Avro to aid the formulation of the 748.

After overseeing the evolution of the Vulcan into the definitive B.2, Avro chief designer Roy Ewans and his team turned their talents to creating the 748. Ewans had joined the staff of the Royal Aircraft Establishment (RAE) at Farnborough in 1939. Briefly employed by Blackburn, he moved to Woodford in

1949, working for the man he was later to succeed, Stuart Davies, but he was tempted to the newly created BAC in 1961. Five years later Ewans crossed the Atlantic to Fairchild Industries at Germantown, Maryland. Fairchild was planning a 'shrunk' fifty-seat version of the Fokker F28 Fellowship twin-jet (which first flew on 9 May 1967) but it remained on the drawing board. Ewans was snapped up by Sweden's Saab in the late 1970s to lead the team creating the 340 twin-turboprop, initially developed in conjunction with Fairchild. John Roy Ewans retired to his native Cornwall shortly before the first flight of the Saab 340 (25 January 1983): he died on 22 January 2012, aged 95.

The prototype 748 had its maiden flight on 24 June 1960 and from the start generated worldwide interest. Deliveries from Woodford began in June 1962 and UK production ended in January 1989 with the 382nd example – including the Andover tactical airlifter version. The design was improved, evolved and vigorously marketed: nobody at Woodford rested on their laurels. Not since the Vickers Viscount (445 units) had Britain basked in such numbers for a transport. Hindustan Aircraft (Hindustan Aeronautics from 1964) of India took up a licence in 1961; eventually building eighty-nine. Re-engineered with a 'beaver' tail, the prototype

Cover of a 1972 brochure extolling the virtues of the HS748 as a military transport. *KEC*

HS.748-2B N118CA, delivered to Spokane, Washington State-based Cascade Airways in 1981. *BAe*

appeared in tactical airlifter guise in July 1965 and the RAF ordered the variant as the Andover C.1. HSA and its successor, British Aerospace (BAe), inherited a profit-maker in the 748. The Woodford design office had looked at jet-powered successors, but the 748 was the last Avro type to take to the air. Chapter 12 charts the much revised 'second-generation' 748 – the short-lived ATP.

Crucial 'Jump Jet'

The last deliveries of new-build Hunters took place in 1960 and for the first time since the debut of the Hart biplane in 1928, Hawker – HSA from January 1959 – did not have a successor ready for delivery. The late 1950s had been a torrid time for the industry, as described by Gardner: 'The military procurement system was demonstrably wrong, as the ever mounting list of cancellations was to show. Design and development resources were kept employed on sophisticated products, some of which went as far as the flight stage before being axed. Nothing is more wasteful of the nation's best brains and expensive facilities than to tie them down for years on aircraft and weapons that are aborted. Hawker, in particular, suffered heavily, having two potentially world-beating supersonic designs by [Sydney] Camm [the P.1121 and P.1154] stillborn…'

The private-venture P.1121 supersonic air superiority and strike fighter was intended to be next on the assembly line at Kingston-on-Thames. The design process was essentially complete and a prototype was under assembly when the Conservative Defence White Paper of 1957 put paid to the project. (To add to the woes, the P.1154, a supersonic strike fighter based on P.1127 technology, was cancelled in February 1965 by the Labour government.) As Hawker became HSA, metal was about to be cut on the private-venture P.1127 V/STOL fighter project. Ahead of its time, it could only be taken so far by HSA's finances. It needed to prove itself quickly and go into production – it was crucial to the future of the new consortium.

The story of the P.1127 and the Harrier begins with exceptional co-operation between Hawker/HSA and the engine division of Bristol/Bristol Siddeley under the guiding eyes of Sir Sydney Camm and Sir Stanley Hooker, respectively. At Kingston, Roy Chaplin was

chief designer and Ralph Hooper was senior project engineer. At Bristol, Michel Wibault and Gordon Lewis were the creators of the BE53, which became the Pegasus vectored-thrust turbofan. Wibault had developed an all-metal construction technique in the 1920s, which was adopted by Vickers – see Chapter 37.

From the mid-1950s manufacturers the world over were striving to achieve an aviation 'Holy Grail' – a viable means of making military and civil aircraft no longer reliant on runways while having the performance of conventional fixed-wing jets. Camm was set against a trend that had been established by Shorts with the experimental SC.1 of 1958. This had no fewer than *five* RR RB.108 jets, four providing lift, one giving propulsion.

'Parallel' thinking by Lewis and Hooper came up with the notion of vectored thrust more or less at the same time and independently. Lewis was inspired by Wibault's Gyropter scheme of 1956, which employed centrifugal blowers one either side of a jet engine. Hooper was influenced by the Y-shaped – bifurcated – jet outlets of the Sea Hawk carrier-borne fighter: what if they could rotate? The result was the Pegasus with tandem swivelling nozzles flanking the engine core. When these faced aft they provided thrust in a conventional manner; rotated downwards they gave sufficient lift to hover. Air bled from the turbofan to 'puffers' in the nose, tail and wing tips provided greater controllability.

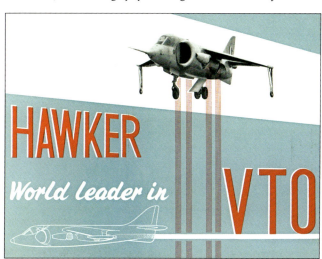

A 1962 brochure highlighting the P.1127 and the possibilities it offered. The rear cover declared: 'Any field…an airfield'. *KEC*

Working hand-in-hand, Hawker and Bristol Siddeley bit the bullet and initiated the world's first practical V/STOL warplane – the P.1127 – at their own risk. The prototype, XP831, was laid down in May 1959 and rolled out at Dunsfold in July 1960. A special gridded area was readied for careful, step-by-step, ground runs and hovers from late 1960. With Bill Bedford at the controls, XP831 made the first tethered hover on 21 October 1960. On 12 September 1961 the first transitions from vertical take-off to a conventional landing and from a 'normal' take-off to a vertical landing were achieved. Today, XP831 is displayed at the Science Museum in London.

Aged 15, Ralph Spenser Hooper began an apprenticeship with Blackburn in 1942, moving to Hawker in 1946 and working in the design office under Camm. He was appointed the P.1127 project engineer in 1957. With the retirement of Chaplin in 1962, Hooper was

promoted to chief designer, becoming an executive director and chief engineer in 1968. He went on to head the Hawk advanced trainer programme and was awarded an OBE in 1978. Taking over from Hooper as chief designer was another former Blackburn man, John Fozard, who joined Hawker in 1950. Fozard was senior project designer from 1955 and from 1962 to 1964 he led the P.1154 project. From 1965 he was chief designer for the Harrier programme and in 1968 was promoted to deputy chief engineer. Retiring from BAe in 1989, Fozard eventually became director of the National Air and Space Museum in the USA. John Fozard OBE died on 17 July 1996, aged 68.

The two private-venture P.1127 prototypes were followed by four similar machines ordered by the government as the pace of the project began to quicken. Both the US and NATO expressed interest and the next phase was the proof-of-concept Kestrel FGA.1, the first of nine of which flew on 7 March 1964. With funding and pilots from the air arms of Britain, USA and West Germany, the Tripartite Evaluation Squadron, part of the RAF's Central Fighter Establishment, took Kestrels through operational trials during 1964 and 1965. Afterwards six of the Kestrels, designated XV-6A, were taken to the USA, where assessments by the US military continued. This was the beginning of a transatlantic relationship that blossomed with the Marine Corps ordering the Harrier – as the AV-8A – and McDonnell Douglas taking the lead role in the 'second-generation' Harrier – as detailed in Chapter 12.

Despite looking very much like its forebears, the Harrier GR.1 was a much more sophisticated machine, the result of nearly a decade of evolution. In July 1969 at Wittering, 1 Squadron became the world's first operational V/STOL strike fighter unit. As the Pegasus grew in power, so Harriers were upgraded to GR.1A status with Mk.102 engines and the definitive first-generation variant, the GR.3, was fitted with a Pegasus 103. The GR.3 carried a laser-ranging and marked-target seeker in an elongated nose. From 1969 a conversion trainer, the T.2, began testing and it was followed by the T.4, the two-seat equivalent of the GR.3. As well as the US Marines, the Spanish Navy adopted the Harrier, calling it the Matador. Manufacture of the first-generation Harrier came to an end in 1983 under the aegis of BAe. While it may not have achieved the production figures that the Hunter had reached, the Harrier had redefined tactical air support.

Frustrated tri-jet

The big bargaining chip that DH brought to HSA in 1959 was the DH.121 jetliner for the state-owned BEA. Or so it seemed: history proves that it was the 125 executive jet that was a real money-spinner. In 1956 BEA was looking for a three-engined jet for its European routes, hauling about 100 passengers just over 1,000 miles: Avro, Bristol and DH responded with broadly similar designs.

By the late 1950s Bristol was not in a position to fund such a programme on its own – developing the Britannia turboprop had sapped already meagre resources. A rare pairing of rivals took place; HS dropped the Avro 740 and threw its weight – and finances – behind the Bristol 200, but it would be assembled at Woodford. DH was in a similar position to Bristol; it was still recovering from the Comet disasters. Negotiations began with Fairey, HP, Hunting and Saunders-Roe (Saro) to form a joint company to construct the DH.121, with final assembly at Hatfield. HP and Saro opted out but DH, Hunting and Fairey formed the Aircraft Manufacturing Company (Airco) in January 1958, buying in to the tune of 67½%, 22½% and 10% respectively.

As a Comet customer, BEA decided in 1958 that DH was the best bet and, with governmental approval, signed up for twenty-four DH.121s, soon to be called Trident. The order was small, no other customers had been sought, but it was hoped that the airline would want more in due course. This was going to be a sophisticated aircraft, for example the Smith's 'Autoland' system was part of the requirement, allowing for 'hands off' touchdowns in all weathers. BEA began to ring the changes with its needs, making design costs spiral upwards and the DH.121's appeal to other operators decline as it became smaller, lighter and less powerful.

In December 1959 DH became a part of HSA and suddenly Airco was unworkable. Hunting was destined to join BAC, while Fairey was absorbed by Westland – the partnership was dissolved in February 1960. The workshare became an all-HSA affair, the former DH and Airspeed factory at Portsmouth built the forward fuselages while Folland tackled the wings and tailplane. If demand warranted it, a second assembly line would be set up at Hawarden. Portsmouth closed in 1968 and manufacture of the forward fuselages moved to Brough.

The prototype Trident, G-ARPA, taxiing past the Hatfield control tower and flight shed on the day of its first flight, 9 January 1962. *Hawker Siddeley* Today, that building is called 'The Hangar' and used as a gymnasium, among other purposes, and the taxi-track is a main road. *Ken Ellis*

Leading the Trident design team was Tim Wilkins, an industry veteran. He served an apprenticeship with Vickers before starting in DH's drawing office in 1928. Two years later he moved to Cierva and then HP, returning to Stag Lane – this time to stay – in 1932. He served as chief designer Ronald Bishop's right-hand man for more than two decades, from the Mosquito to the Comet. Appointed chief designer in 1954, four years later he joined the board as technical director. Alongside the Trident, he was in charge of the HS.125 executive jet, drawing the first layouts before handing the project on to Joe Goodwin. Wilkins transferred to HS Dynamics in 1963, taking the grand title of chief executive, space. Charles Timothy Wilkins OBE – father of the Trident and the HS.125 – retired in 1970 and died in 1979, aged 66.

There was no dedicated prototype Trident, as the first machine was destined to serve with BEA after trials: it had its maiden flight at Hatfield on 9 January 1962. The Trident entered service on 11 March 1964, by which time Boeing had flown its 727. Bigger, more powerful and with greater range, the Seattle product oozed development potential – see the comparison table. By the summer of 1965 Boeing's order book for its tri-jet stood at 388 from twenty-three airlines and BEA was knocking on the government's door asking for permission to spend dollar reserves on a fleet of 727-200s for 1968!

A 'hot-and-high' version, the Trident 1E was followed by the more powerful Series 2E, which entered service with BEA – forbidden from ordering Boeings! – in July 1967. The Trident attracted small orders from a variety of operators and the Civil Aviation Administration of China, which was destined to take thirty-five Tridents, keeping the production line going until 1978. The final version, also in response to BEA's needs, was the Series 3B, which could carry 146 passengers. This required major, costly, re-engineering: the Trident 1's length of 114ft 9in was extended by 16ft 3in. The extra weight needed a *fourth* engine: a RR RB.162 boost jet, rated at 5,230lb st housed in the extreme tail for use on take-off. The prototype first flew on 12 November 1969. As Chapter 12 describes, another airliner was to originate at Hatfield; but the HS.146 responded to the needs of *many* airlines, not just one.

Trident and Boeing 727 compared

	Trident 1C	Boeing 727-100
First flown	9 Jan 1962	9 Feb 1963
Last delivery	1978*	1984*
Number built	117*	1,832*
Engines x 3	RR Spey 505	P&W JT8D-1
	9,850lb st	14,000lb st
Typical passenger load	103	131
Cruising speed	610mph	596mph
Typical range	1,485 miles	3,430 miles
Max take-off weight	115,000lb	160,000lb
* All versions		

Corporate success

The year 1962 was a busy one for debuts at Hatfield: on 9 January Trident jetliner and on 13 August the DH.125 corporate jet. Both had jet engines mounted on the rear fuselage and 'T'-format tail surfaces: one ran to 117 units, the other clocked an incredible total of just over 1,000. The success of the Dove – 542 examples built between 1945 and 1968 – fostered a jet version. Commonplace these days, in 1960 the market *seemed* to have potential, but was the world ready for small jets to shuttle bosses and the rich around the world?

Prior to the 125, only two companies had ventured into the arena: Lockheed with the four-engined JetStar in 1957 and North American's twin-jet Sabreliner in 1958. The bazaar was going to get very crowded: the Dassault Mystère 20 from France and from the USA the Aero Commander Jet Commander and the iconic Lear Jet 23 all appearing in 1963; the following year it was the turn of Germany's HFB 320 Hansa Jet and the Italian–American Piaggio-Douglas PD-808, and in 1966 the US Grumman Gulfstream II.

The six-to-eight passenger HS.125 offered generous cabin height and the ability to adapt relatively easily to other roles. Military applications were envisaged from the start, from personnel transports to more specialist roles, such as the RAF navigator trainer, the Dominie T.1, ordered in 1963. DH technical director Tim Wilkins was involved in the initial layouts of the 125 when the Bristol

Siddeley Orpheus was the chosen powerplant. A structural engineer on the DH Blue Streak ballistic missile project until it was cancelled in 1960, C J 'Joe' Goodwin, assisted by Bill Hampton, turned the 125 into reality with more practical Armstrong Siddeley Vipers.

Originally it was intended to call the HS.125 the Jet Dragon in honour of the 1930s Dragon and Dragon Rapide biplane transports but this name was dropped in favour of the more corporate-sounding numbers – one, two, five. The USA was the primary sales target and initially the 'DH' was kept in the designation for American-bound examples as it was believed that 'de Havilland' was a stronger brand. Ironically when Beech became the US distributor in the early 1970s, the Kansas-based organisation called it the Beechcraft Hawker, reasoning that was far more vibrant than the 'French-sounding' de Havilland.

Generating brand loyalty is important to manufacturers of corporate jets but image-conscious customers can be fickle if an aircraft starts to look dated or lag behind in performance or equipment. Well aware of this, HSA regularly rang the changes with the 125. The Series 400 – succeeding the Series 1, 2 and 3 – was the first major revision, with improved aerodynamics and a built-in airstair. By the 1970s the market wanted a larger cabin – not

Excavator manufacturer J C Bamford's appropriately registered HS.125-600B G-BJCB heading a line-up at Hawarden in 1977. Behind is a Dan-Air HS.748. *HSA*

HS.125s and Sea Vixens on the production line at Hawarden in mid-1965. In the background are the two Comet 4Cs that became Nimrod aerodynamic prototypes. *Hawker Siddeley*

necessarily more seats – and the 24in longer Series 600 (there was no Series 500) appeared in the summer of 1971. The 'Dash 600' was an interim solution as the Viper turbojet was showing its age and was not going to meet forthcoming US noise regulations. The American Garrett TFE731 turbofan was the chosen successor. As well as the new engines, the prototype HS.125-700 featured further aerodynamic refinements and first flew on 28 June 1976. This version provided BAe with another winner and it was 1984 before the next major revamp, the Series 800 appeared – its story is told in Chapter 12.

Mighty Nimrod

The final Avro Shackleton MR.3 maritime patrollers were delivered from Woodford in 1958; these and the 'tail-dragger' MR.2s were destined for a long service life. Throughout that time the airframes and the systems were upgraded, mostly at Bitteswell. From the early 1960s BAC and HSA began to address replacing the Shackleton, with the design offices coming up with solutions based on the VC10 or Trident jetliners, respectively. Speed is not a high priority for maritime patrol aircraft, what is essential is long range and a high-capacity fuselage to take a large crew, complex systems and search radars and bulky weapons. This made the choice of a modified airliner ideal and Lockheed had led the way with its very successful P-3 Orion of 1958, based on its four-turboprop Electra. In October 2019 the RAF took delivery of the first of its next-generation maritime patrollers, the Boeing Poseidon MRA.1, also a development of an airliner, the 737-800 twin-jet.

Studies at Woodford eventually settled on the Comet 4C, two of which were languishing without customers at Hawarden – along with the jigs. The RR Avons were to be replaced by more powerful Speys within a revised centre section to accommodate the larger turbofans. The Speys allowed the HS.801, as the project was designated, to shut down the two outer engines when at height, greatly extending endurance. The Comet fuselage was shortened by 6ft and a fin fillet was added to enhance directional control. Other modifications included a huge fairing underneath the lower forward fuselage housing a weapons bay, a hardpoint under each wing, a fin-mounted electronic countermeasures pod and a magnetic anomaly detector boom protruding from the tail. Within the capacious fuselage were operator stations for search radar, anti-submarine and surface vessel monitoring and attack systems and communications.

Nimrod MR.1s on the Woodford production line, 1974. *HSA*

Built as an MR.1 in 1969, Nimrod XV241 in full MR.2 guise. Note the electronic support measures pod on the wing tip and the in-flight refuelling probe. *BAe*

The 1960s witnessed the arrival of fixed-price contracts – HSA would need to keep expenditure strictly under control. By utilising modified existing jigs and tooling, airframe costs could be kept to a minimum. At the end of 1965 a production order was signed that eventually amounted to a pair of aerodynamic prototypes, thirty-eight MR.1s and a trio of specialist intelligence-gathering R.1s. The HS.801 was given the biblical name of a skilled hunter but there was also a link with the Shackleton. Explorer Sir Ernest Henry Shackleton CVO OBE sailed in the converted schooner *Nimrod* for his 1907 to 1909 Antarctic expedition.

One of the two Comet 4Cs at Hawarden was completed and on 25 October 1965 it was ferried to Woodford, where it was transformed into a Nimrod aerodynamic prototype but retaining its Avon turbojets. The other Hawarden Comet was completed with the new centre section and Speys: in this interim configuration it had its maiden flight on 23 May 1967. The first from-new Nimrod MR.1 took to the air on 28 June 1968 and in October the following year the type entered RAF service. From 1975 the Nimrod entered the digital era with the start of the extensive MR.2 upgrade. Beyond that lay the abortive AEW.3 and MRA.4 programmes; that sad story is charted in Chapter 12.

Airbus: on a wing and a prayer

The logic that brought about the Jaguar, Tornado and Typhoon international warplane collaborations applied just as well to airliners. Other than in the USA, large jetliners had become beyond the resources of individual companies, let alone single nations. By the mid-1960s the governments of Britain and France had begun to investigate the possibility of a 300-seater twin-jet. Soon West Germany was expressing interest and in 1966 the word 'Airbus' was being bandied about. The three nations announced protocols on 26 September 1967 that brought into being the European Airbus programme – Sud Aviation led the airframe, RR commanded the powerplant. Having committed a lot of time and investment in the project, HSA was to build the wings and control surfaces for what was called the A300. Cost projections increased but France and Germany remained stalwart while the British Labour government wobbled. A smaller, 250-passenger, version was proposed – the A300B.

The first Airbus A310 wings being loaded into Aerospacelines Super Guppy 201 F-BPPA at Manchester Airport, 17 May 1981. *Airbus Industrie*

Frustrated and more than a little bewildered, the French and Germans announced in April 1969 that they, in the form of Airbus Industrie, were going it alone. To the unending acclaim of its board members, HSA declared that it was staying on – not just as a sub-contractor, but as an investor. Praise needs also to be apportioned to Paris and Bonn (as the German capital was in those days): they could have cut Britain completely adrift, but HSA's experience in creating the Trident's very advanced wing was too good to ignore. In July 1969 the first contract for wing supply – *less* flaps etc – was drawn up. This required massive investment by HSA with most of its sites taking part: Hatfield (design), Hawarden (final assembly) plus Filton, Chadderton and Hamble building sub-assemblies.

The first A300B wing set was loaded into an Aerospacelines Super Guppy freighter at Manchester Airport on 23 November 1971 and ever since all of the wings for the Airbus airliners and the A400M military transport have originated in the UK. As Chapter 12 reveals, BAe and BAE Systems continued with the venture until 2006, when it was sold to the European Aeronautic Defence and Space Company (EADS) combine. Thankfully, the Europeans stuck with it and, through Airbus UK, the work goes on – at least for now.

As of the end of January 2021 Airbus was giving the following statistics for deliveries and orders (in brackets) across the 'family': A300/A310 – 816 (816 – production complete); A320 all versions and the Canadian-developed A220 – 9,855 (16,208); A330/A340/A350 – 2,296 (3,101); A380 – 251 (246). Thanks to the vision of the HSA management, this has been by far the largest – and the most profitable – aviation programme ever undertaken in Britain.

A new Hunter

In 1972 HSA accepted a fixed-price contract for 176 examples of its P.1182 advanced jet trainer, straight off the drawing board. This was the start of a programme that continues to this day – the 1,000-plus selling Hawk. The RAF was replacing Folland Gnat T.1 advanced trainers and Hawker Hunter FGA.9 and T.7 weapons trainers. For the latter role, the RAF had specified a podded ADEN cannon under the centre section and four wing hardpoints. The prototype Hawk had its maiden flight from Dunsfold on 21 August 1974.

With such a large order, HSA was already in a buoyant position and early plans were made to push the trainer vigorously for export: the RAF was not the only air arm keen to replace the Hunter. The eighth machine off the production line, in May 1976, was a demonstrator funded by HSA. Appropriately civilian registered as G-HAWK, extensive tours were undertaken and *Whisky-Kilo* was used to develop additional features to increase the Hawk's export

The Airbus A300/A310 assembly line at Toulouse, France, in 1984. In the foreground is A300B 9K-AHI, destined for Kuwait Airways. *Airbus Industrie*

appeal. The RAF received its first examples in November 1976 and two years later the weapons trainer version became operational. In 1980 the RAF Red Arrows aerobatic team's started its first display season on the new type – a most potent marketing tool. BAe was given a contract in 1983 to convert eighty-eight RAF T.1s to T.1A status with the capability to carry Sidewinder air-to-air missiles for a back-up air defence role.

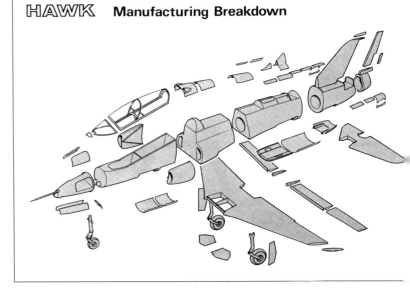

Diagram of the manufacturing breakdown of a Hawk airframe from a 1978 British Aerospace brochure. *KEC*

The bulk of the Hawk was manufactured at Kingston, while Brough made the wings and the tailplane: final assembly and flight test was carried out at Dunsfold. Demand was such that between 1979 and 1982 a batch of RAF T.1s was assembled at Bitteswell. The first overseas customer was Finland and the deal included assembly of British-built airframes from 1980: a similar arrangement was made with Switzerland in 1990. In the late 1980s a more powerful version, the Mk.60 with a RR-Turboméca Adour Mk.861, appeared. The 'first-generation' Hawk remained in production until 2009, by which time

Hawk Mk.64 145 on test out of Dunsfold in late 1985 prior to delivery to the Kuwait Air force. *BAe*

final assembly was conducted at Warton. The story of the American T-45 Goshawk and today's Mk.100 Hawks is told in Chapter 12.

Ultimate rationalisation

Using a 'carrot and stick' process, the Conservative government had achieved something that needed to have been done in the late 1940s, or perhaps even the 1930s – the rationalisation of the aircraft industry.

Both BAC and HSA had trouble settling in but by the mid-1970s both businesses were in good trim with healthy product lines and prospects. It fell to the Labour government to carry out the ultimate reshuffle: two into one by nationalisation. The Aircraft and Shipbuilding Industries Act gained Royal Assent on 17 March 1977. The result was British Aerospace, comprising BAC, HSA, HS Dynamics and Scottish Aviation – its brief corporate existence is told in Chapter 12.

Hawker Siddeley

From	To	Total	Name/Designation	Type	Engine(s)	Notes
1960	1988	351	HS.748	Airliner	2 x RR Dart	[1]
1960	1963	6	P.1127	V/STOL development	1 x BS Pegasus	
1962	1978	89	Trident 1 and 2	Airliner	3 x RR Spey	
1962	1977	365	HS.125 1 to 400	Corporate	2 x AS Viper	[2]
1964	1965	9	Kestrel FGA.1	Evaluation	1 x BS Pegasus	
1965	1968	31	Andover C.1	Tactical transport	2 x RR Darts	[3]
1966	1986	236	Harrier GR.1, GR.3	V/STOL fighter	1 x BS Pegasus	[4]
1967	1977	51	Nimrod MR.1, R.1	Maritime patrol	4 x RR Spey	[5]
1969	1983	33	Harrier T.2, T.4	Advanced trainer	1 x BS Pegasus	[6]
1969	1975	28	Trident 3	Airliner	3 x RR Spey	[7]
1974	1997	527	Hawk T.1 to Srs 60	Advanced trainer	1 x Adour	[8]
1976	1984	215	HS.125 Srs 700	Corporate	2 x Garrett TFE731	[9]

[1] Includes licence production by Hindustan Aircraft (Aeronautics from 1964), Kanpur, India 1961 to 1984 (89). See Chapter 12 for the ATP development. [2] Two prototypes built at Hatfield, remainder at Hawarden. Series 1, 2 and 3 were followed by the Series 400. Includes Dominie T.1 navigation trainer for RAF (Series 2). See Chapter 12 for Series 800 and BAe 1000 developments. [3] Not including prototype, modified from a HS.748 airframe. [4] Includes six development batch GR.1s; AV-8A Harrier Mk.50 for US Marine Corps; AV-8A Matador Mk.50 and AV-8S Matador Mk.55 for Spanish Navy. [5] Includes two aerodynamic prototypes modified from Comet 4s – see narrative. Three MR.1s fitted out from scratch as R.1 strategic reconnaissance platforms – and one MR.2 converted to R.1 status. Upgrades to MR.2 status – 32 from 1975. See Chapter 12 for AEW.3 and MRA.4. [6] Includes T.2, T.4 and T.8 operational trainers for RAF and FAA; Mk.52 company-owned two-seat demonstrator; TAV-8A Harrier Mk.54 for US Marine Corps; TAV-8A Matador Mk.54 and TAV-8S Matador Mk.58 for Spanish Navy. [7] RR RB.162 boost jet in the tail. [8] At least 39 T.1s assembled at Bitteswell, 1979 to 1982. Valmet of Finland assembled 46 Mk.51s from kits 1980 to 1985; F+W at Emmen, Switzerland, assembled 19 Mk.66s from kits 1990–91. Includes Mk.50 company-owned demonstrator. See Chapter 12 for T-45 Goshawk, Hawk 100 onwards and Hawk 200 light fighter. [9] See Chapter 12 for Series 800 and BAe 1000 developments.

CHAPTER TWENTY-SEVEN

Two into One

Martinsyde
1908 to 1924

'In the time that the splendid S.E.[5a] took to attain 15,000ft the brilliant Martinsyde would be a mile higher.'
Harald Penrose

SCOTSMAN GEORGE HARRIS HANDASYDE and Londoner Helmut Paul Martin worked in the motor industry: their businesses brought them together in 1908 but it was their fascination with aeroplanes that sealed the partnership. Known to colleagues as 'Handy', Handasyde was an irascible, perfectionist engineer who had designed and built a car in Edinburgh in 1906. Along with Vernon Trier, Martin had established carburettor manufacturers Trier and Martin Ltd. The aircraft company that carried the names of Handasyde and Martin falls below the parameters outlined in the Introduction but it richly deserves inclusion.

Originally based in a makeshift workshop near Hendon, Handasyde and Martin briefly moved to the 'factory' established by Frederick Handley Page alongside the creek at Barking. By the outbreak of war premises at Woking had been secured and test flights were carried out at Brooklands. The association was known as 'Martin and Handasyde' or 'Martin-Handasyde'. The inversion of alphabetic sequence emphasised Martin's role as the main investor, both in finance and facilities from Trier and Martin. Martin also carried out some of the early maiden flights; Handasyde was the designer and manager. As well as combining their talents, their trading name eventually morphed from two into one. By 1912 the nicknames 'Martinsyde' and 'Tinsydes' were in general use and the former stuck, although it was not until 24 March 1915 that a limited company of that name was registered. (From here on, all types will be referred to as Martinsydes.)

The first three creations were to Martin's commission and were clearly influenced by Frenchman Léon Levavasseur's elegant Antoinette monoplanes. The fourth Martinsyde, a two-seater, was ordered by Thomas Sopwith, given the name *Dragonfly* and exhibited at the 1911 Olympia Aero Show in London. This machine seems to have caught the War Office's attention as four similar examples were ordered in 1912, although only two were handed over. An improved version was entered in the military trials held at Larkhill in August 1912. The run of monoplanes was broken early in 1914. Intended to compete in June's London Aerial Derby race, a pusher biplane was created but it was not ready in time and *may* not have flown at all.

Refuelling the second of two F.4-derived ADC Nimbuses, G-EBOL, during the July 1926 King's Cup Air Race. Piloted by Frank Courtney, it was retired with engine trouble. *Esso Petroleum*

Classic Antoinette lines of the 1912 Military Trials monoplane. *Peter Green Collection*

A commission from merchant banker Edward Mackay Edgar was challenging for Handasyde and his small team. More used to powerboat racing, Edgar was backing London-born aviator Gustav Wilhelm Hamel in the *Daily Mail's* transatlantic crossing competition. Announced in 1913, the newspaper was giving away £10,000 – a fortune in those days – for the first non-stop crossing of the Atlantic. The proven Antoinette format was scaled up: the 1912 Military Monoplane had a span of 42ft 6in and an empty weight of 1,100lb, whereas the 'Atlantic' measured 66ft and 2,400lb, respectively. Two pilots sat side-by-side in a forward fuselage that was waterproofed in the hope that it would float in the event of a ditching. Hamel's Morane-Saulnier went missing over the English Channel on 23 May 1914 and the 25-year-old pioneer died. The Martinsyde project ground to a halt, but the company was not through with transatlantic attempts.

Elephants and Buzzards

With the outbreak of war, Anthony ('Tony') A Fletcher was brought in as a designer and Martinsyde expanded, anticipating contracts from the War Office. The first result was the diminutive S.1 single-seater

scout, which appeared in 1915 and was the company's first type to enter series production. Fletcher used this as the basis for a trainer, but it remained a one-off. Experience gained from the S.1 gave rise to the G.100 and G.102 scout/light bombers, which gained fame through their nickname 'Elephant'. Handasyde was not an easy man to get on with and early in 1916 Fletcher left to start a design department for the London and Provincial (L&P) Aviation Company, which was running a flying school at Hendon. Fletcher came up with a tractor biplane for L&P but the venture was terminated and in October Handasyde took his former colleague back. The pair created the F.1 two-seat reconnaissance biplane, but it failed to get beyond the prototype stage. Fletcher again resigned in 1917 and we'll take up his story later.

The F.1 had potential and Handasyde was on the hunt for another designer. He appointed Frenchman Emile Bouillon, who had been a draughtsman for Bréguet and, until January 1917, in the same capacity for Hewlett and Blondeau of Luton. Bouillon and Handasyde revised the F.1 into the F.2, but again without success. The Frenchman departed and from this point Handasyde appears to have reverted to the role of chief designer. Joining as a draughtsman in August 2017 was 24-year-old Marcel Lobelle, who was destined to create the Fairey Swordfish

G.100 'Elephant' 7282, 1915. *Peter Green Collection*

among others. Harald Penrose quotes the youngster's opinion of his boss in *British Aviation – The Great War and Armistice*: 'I had the greatest admiration for Handasyde, and though insulting and rude he was a brilliant man.' Lobelle jumped ship in 1918 to work on the ill-fated Tarrant Tabor bomber: his full story is in Chapter 19. Toiling in the Martinsyde stores in late 1917 was Sydney Camm, who remained loyal to Handasyde into the early 1920s.

Handasyde turned his talents to the powerful F.3 fighter and when it appeared in late 1917 it raised eyebrows. Penrose's description quoted at the chapter header is based on its performance during trials. The F.3 found great favour when evaluated at Martlesham Heath in November 1917. Comments in the report included: '… for its size and weight [it] has extraordinary good manoeuvre [sic] and can turn almost as quick as a Camel. She answers very quickly to rudder, elevation [sic] and aileron controls … I am confident that the enemy has not at present got a machine which could out-manoeuvre the Martinsyde … A great point is that it turns so quickly and can be made to climb at the same time.'

A stepping stone to the F.3 was the RG fighter prototype, which had a 285hp Rolls-Royce Falcon V-12 and Handasyde was determined to use the promising engine in his new creation. There was considerable demand for the Falcon and by the turn of 1918 the Woking factory was crowded with more than forty engineless F.3s. The most pressing customer for the Falcon was the Bristol F.2B two-seater and Handasyde was forced to find another powerplant: he wisely chose the 300hp Hispano-Suiza. In this guise the fighter was designated F.4 Buzzard and orders flooded in. The incredible potential of the new Martinsyde was not realised: supply and manufacturing problems meant that only small numbers of F.3s became operational. With the Armistice, large numbers of Buzzards were cancelled. The Martinsyde factory was well ahead in terms of airframes and its management was lumbered with finding other markets for the high-performance warplane.

Out in the cold

With the return of peace, the *Daily Mail's* £10,000 transatlantic challenge returned and Handasyde conceived his second ultra-long-range type. Using as many Buzzard components as possible, he came up with a Falcon-powered two-seater that was named Raymor in honour of its crew, 'Freddy' Raynham and Charles Morgan. On 18 May 1919 the aircraft was assembled and ready at Quidi Vidi, St John's, Newfoundland. The two aviators turned skyward to watch as

Harry Hawker and Lt Cdr K Mackenzie Grieve overflew the airstrip and provocatively dropped the jettisonable undercarriage of their single-engined Sopwith Atlantic before setting course for Britain. Later that day, Raynham and Morgan tried to take-off, but the undercarriage snagged in a rut and the Raymor slithered to a halt, badly damaged. Hawker and Grieve eventually arrived in Britain, courtesy of a passing ship as they had been forced to ditch. Taking off on 14 June in a twin-engined Vickers Vimy from the same field that had defeated the Raymor, John Alcock and Arthur Whitten Brown flew 1,890 miles in fifteen hours fifty-seven minutes and force-landed in Ireland – the *Daily Mail's* prize was theirs.

Working away at his drawing board, Handasyde came up with further F.4 derivatives. The two-seater F.6 could be a military trainer or a private owner machine – three were completed. Similar to the Raymor, the Type A was offered as a two-seat general-purpose machine or as a four-passenger light transport: the latter fared better, but only eight found customers. The single-seat Semiquaver was aimed at the well-to-do pilot wanting a high-performance aerial sports car – only the prototype was built. Just as a semiquaver is half a quaver, Handasyde's diminutive biplane was a scaled down F.4.

A modification to the Semiquaver involved another British manufacturer and merits a postscript. Dutch-born engineer A Holle had patented a long, high aspect ratio, flexible, spar-less wing, which he called the Alula – Latin for winglet. Blackburn was commissioned to build such a wing, in wood with fabric covering. This was fitted to an Airco DH.6 fuselage, creating a strut-braced parasol monoplane. Trials commenced from Sherburn in Elmet in January 1921 and did not go well, despite fitting a new wing of thicker section. It was decided to try the concept on a higher-performance machine and to attach the wing directly to the fuselage, cantilever fashion. The 300hp Semiquaver was chosen and it was fitted with another Blackburn Alula wing, this time covered in a skin of mahogany strips. Flying from Northolt in late 1921, the Semiquaver is reported to have reached an incredible 179mph. It is thought to have been evaluated at the Isle of Grain and Farnborough: nothing further came of the venture.

Right: Semiquaver G-EAPX with Alula wing, believed to be at Northolt in 1921. *KEC*

Below: An F.4 Buzzard and three Airco DH.9s of the Irish Air Corps at Baldonnel in the early 1920s. A quartet of F.4s was supplied to the newly established air arm in 1922 by the Aircraft Disposal Company. *KEC*

By the time the Alula Semiquaver was streaking over west London, Martinsyde was in the throes of winding down. The firm went into receivership on 2 November 1920, but continued as a legal entity while the accountants had a field day shuffling the paperwork. In February 1924 the design rights and a huge quantity of airframes, spares and sundries were acquired by the Aircraft Disposal Company (ADC). Martinsyde was finally put out of its misery on 12 July. The sale was full of irony: since its formation in March 1920, ADC had been selling off F.3s and F.4s at knock-down prices. In 1924 ADC flew the first F.4-derived ADC.1 fitted with an Armstrong Siddeley Jaguar radial – seven of these were sold to the Latvian Air Force. In the following year ADC offered a version powered by its own Nimbus in-line to private owners, but only two were completed.

Beyond Martinsyde

Tony Fletcher's on-off relationship with Handasyde ended in 1917. He went to Kilburn and the woodworkers R Cattle Ltd. There he was told to set up an aviation department, which traded as Central Aircraft. Fletcher conceived the Centaur II twin-engined transport and Centaur IV trainer biplanes. Only two and nine were completed, respectively, during 1919 and 1920. Fletcher was to be found in the Westland drawing office in the mid-1920s, helping with the Widgeon two-seat tourer, which entered limited production. By 1928 he was assisting with the ABC Robin cabin monoplane and in the 1930s was at Heston, initially assisting Nicholas Comper on the unsuccessful Mouse, Kite and Streak. Still at Heston, he assisted on the Hordern-Richmond Autoplane – another one-off, see Chapter 16.

As Martinsyde began the liquidation process in late 1920, Handasyde left to set up his own business, the Handasyde Aircraft Company. Going with him was the 27-year-old Sydney Camm, who had assisted with the design of the Semiquaver. Along with Raynham, Handasyde and Camm created a glider for the October 1922 trials at Itford. From this, the trio used it as the basis of an ultralight monoplane for the following year's light aeroplane contest at Lympne. Having no production facilities, both of these were commissioned from the Air Navigation and Engineering Company (ANEC) of Addlestone. Handasyde responded to a request for a 'bush' aircraft

The prototype Handasyde H.2 at Brooklands in late 1922. The pilot sat in an open cockpit in front of the leading edge of the wing with the passenger cabin behind and below. Note the four-wheel undercarriage.
Peter Green Collection

on behalf of the Australian government and again he engaged ANEC to build two – perhaps three – examples of his H.2 cantilever monoplane. The prototype had its maiden flight at Brooklands on 9 November 1922, but the contract was cancelled the following year.

Camm signed up with Hawker in November 1923 at the beginning of a stellar career. By 1929 Handasyde had taken on the job of redesigning Frederick 'Cully' Koolhoven's FK.41 cabin monoplane for the British market. (See Chapter 4 for more on Koolhoven.) Between 1929 and 1930 a total of forty-one were made by Desoutter Aircraft at Croydon. Handasyde was appointed chief designer for the British Klemm Aeroplane Company at Hanworth in 1934 – the business was renamed as the British Aircraft Manufacturing Company the following year. There he created three elegant light aircraft: the Eagle cabin monoplane (forty-two built from 1934 to 1938), the Cupid two-seat sportsplane (one only, 1935) and the Double Eagle cabin twin (three constructed 1936 to 1937). George Harris Handasyde OBE, unsung creator of fine aeroplanes, died in 1958, aged 81.

Martin and Handasyde sub-contracts

Type	Total	From	To	Notes
Royal Aircraft Factory B.E.2c	12	1915	-	
Royal Aircraft Factory S.E.5a	258	1917	1918	

Martin and Handasyde types

From	To	Total	Name/Designation	Type	Engine(s)	Notes
1908	1909	2	Monoplane	1-seater	1 x JAP	[1]
1910	1912	5	'Antoinette' monos	2-seater	1 x Antoinette	[2]
1912	1913	2	Military Trials Mono	2-seater	1 x Austro-Daimler	[3]
1914	-	1	Pusher Biplane	1-seater	1 x Antoinette	[4]
1914	-	1	Transatlantic	Long-distance	1 x Sunbeam	[5]
1914	1915	69	S.1	Scout	1 x Gnome	
1914	-	1	Trainer		1 x Anzani	
1915	1917	272	G.100/G.102	Scout	1 x Beardmore	[6]
1916	1917	2	F.1, F.2	2-seat recce	1 x Beardmore	
1917	-	2	RG	Fighter	1 x RR Falcon	
1917	1918	c.44	F.3	Fighter	1 x RR Falcon	
1918	1919	c.300	F.4 Buzzard	Fighter	1 x Hispano-Suiza	[7]
1919	-	1	Raymor	Long-distance	1 x RR Falcon	[8]
1919	1920	8	Type A I and II	Light transport	1 x Hispano-Suiza	
1920	1921	3	F.6	Sportsplane	1 x Hispano-Suiza	
1920	-	1	Semiquaver	Sportsplane	1 x Hispano-Suiza	[9]
1922	-	2	Handasyde H.2	Light transport	1 x RR Eagle	[10]
1923	-	1	Handasyde Mono	Ultralight	1 x Douglas	[11]
1924	1926	11	ADC.1 and Nimbus	Fighter/Sportsplane	1 x AS Jaguar	[12]

Unless noted, all tractor biplanes. [1] First machine, failed to fly. [2] First example single-seater. Second machine known as the '4B', third as Military Monoplane. [3] Second machine based on the 'Military'. [4] Referred to as the 'Racing Pusher', completed, but *may* not have flown. [5] See narrative. [6] Nicknamed 'Elephant'. [7] Large numbers cancelled 1918. Sub-contracts by Boulton Paul known to have been cancelled. Hopper and Co and Standard Motor also sub-contracted – output unconfirmed. [8] See narrative. [9] Converted to Alula wing test bed, 1921 – see narrative. [10] Built by Air Navigation and Engineering Co (ANEC). *Perhaps* three examples completed. [11] Version of Itford trials glider, 1922. Built by ANEC. [12] Designed and marketed by the Aircraft Disposal Company (ADC). Nimbus was a sportsplane, powered by the ADC Nimbus 6-cylinder, based on Siddeley Puma.

CHAPTER TWENTY-EIGHT

Mavericks

Miles
1929 to 1948

'*...starting with no knowledge, no money and no assets other than enthusiasm and determination, they were able to build up an organisation...that built over 7,000 aeroplanes.*' Don Brown on the Miles brothers

THINK OF LIGHT AEROPLANES of the inter-war period and three names dominate: de Havilland, Miles and Percival. Each has attracted ardent followers ever since, none more so than Miles. The Mosquito transformed de Havilland (DH) into an industrial giant, ultimately morphing into the Hawker Siddeley conglomerate as a maker of warplanes and jetliners. Like DH, with the return to peace Percival did not revert to light aeroplanes; instead it embraced military trainers and general-purpose twins. Percival was absorbed by the Hunting Group, which in turn became an important element of the British Aircraft Corporation.

The Miles brothers, Frederick George and George Herbert, were very different in character and while both complemented and checked one another, neither could be regarded as conservative in their methods: the word 'maverick' is often used to describe their approach to aviation and business. They created prototypes to prove their worth almost as the ink dried on the drawing board, but often they went into production. Don Lambert Brown, in *Miles Aircraft since 1925*, notes that building could commence *before* design in the early days: '... work proceeded concurrently with construction and there were occasions where there was some doubt as to which came first! [Frederick George] Miles, in particular, was prone to go ahead with the manufacture of welded metal fittings, leaving the drawings and calculations to follow after ...'

Like DH and Percival, as Britain rearmed and plunged into war, Miles offered its expertise in trainers and the fertile minds of the brothers strayed to fighters and heavy bombers, adopting novel formats. As aircraft got more complex and costly, this approach became hugely risky. Mass-producing the Master and Martinet, including a 'shadow' factory at South Marston, was challenging and taking the Monitor twin-engined target tug from the drawing board to manufacture was tortuous. In the immediate post-war years energy was poured into reverting to light aeroplanes and entering the airliner market. Characteristically overreaching, Miles folded in 1947 and its assets were liquidated the following year. The brothers found other outlets for their talents but their days as captains of industry had been brief.

A famous gathering at Woodley, 1947 with Southern Martlet G-AAYX behind. Today, the Martlet is part of the Shuttleworth Collection at Old Warden. Left to right: Don Brown, long-term associate of the Miles brothers and author of *Miles Aircraft since 1925*; Harry Hull, master woodworker, the man who built the first Hawk; George Miles; F G Miles; 'Blossom' Miles. *Miles Aircraft*

Frederick George was known to many of his associates simply as 'Miles', but also as 'FG' to avoid confusion with his brother. To distinguish between them and the firm that carried their name, George Frederick is denoted here as 'FG', George Herbert as 'George' and the company as 'Miles'. Fifty-odd years after the demise of Miles, Peter Amos produced three huge, painstaking tomes on all-things Miles. The previously cited book by Don Brown – who had 'been there, done that' from the early days – is a concise and personal view, but it is a rare and consequently an expensive candidate for the bookshelf. Within single covers, Julian Temple's *Wings over Woodley – The Story of Miles Aircraft and the Adwest Group* is an engaging and balanced view and well worth tracking down.

Gifted brothers

Leaving school at the tender age of 13, FG tried his hand at several ventures in and around his native Portslade-by-Sea. His money-making schemes began with motorcycles, graduating to a delivery service using a converted Ford Model T ambulance. As is often the case with people who are attracted to motive power – aviation also held a fascination. The pivotal moment occurred in 1922 when, aged 19, FG took a 'joyride' in an Avro 504.

Pondering how to get himself flying, the persuasive and inspiring FG tempted pioneering aviator Cecil 'Pash' Pashley back to Sussex, where he had built an aircraft of his own design in 1914. To formalise this, the Gnat Aero and Motor Company was formed and a barn used by the short-lived Sussex County Aero Club at Shoreham was leased. Pashley taught FG to fly and on 19 May 1926, he went solo. By mid-1926 George joined in the activities and FG embarked upon the construction of a single-seat biplane, the Gnat, in premises at the rear of their father's laundry business in Portslade.

Right: The Southern Aircraft sheds at Shoreham in 1931: Martlet G-AAYX on the left with 'Metal' Martlet G-ABJW to the right. *Shuttleworth Collection*

Below: The Gnat biplane under construction at Portslade, 1926. Cecil Pashley is standing by its nose. *KEC*

In mid-June 1926 a move was made to a nearby field and the present-day Shoreham Airport was born. That year also saw FG start up the Southern Aero Club and by this point no further reference was made to the Gnat biplane. A large job lot of material was acquired when Avro closed down its Hamble plant in 1927 and among this was a single-seat Avro Baby. FG fitted a 60hp ADC Cirrus in place of the 35hp Green and enlarged the cockpit to take two people: the Baby was flown by FG in this guise on 13 November 1927. Southern Aircraft Ltd was established in 1929 to reflect the intention to build aeroplanes.

The first of FG's impressive list of prototype maiden flights was not in a design of his own. Engaged by Parnall (Chapter 29) for testing duties, on 26 June 1929 he flew the prototype Elf two-seater biplane; he continued testing for Parnall until 1932. Within a month of his debut on the Elf, FG was aloft in the Hornet Baby, a much-improved sporting biplane based on the Avro Baby, powered by an ABC Hornet. As the Hornet owed its origins to Avro, FG sought permission from the original creator. He was given Avro's blessing, but there could be no connection with what today would be called the design authority: out went all reference to 'Baby', Martlet was chosen.

The first from-scratch Miles type was the diminutive M.1 Satyr. Construction was contracted to Parnall and FG took it aloft on 31 July 1932. This 21ft span biplane was named after a well-endowed male spirit of nature from Greek mythology. The Satyr remained a one-off and its development stretched the funds – while FG had plenty of ideas, he needed investment and a factory.

A month after flying the Satyr, FG married Maxine Frances Mary 'Blossom' Freeman-Thomas – née Forbes-Robertson and the former Viscountess Ratendone. He'd taught her to fly – she went solo on 25 July 1930 – and they quickly became soulmates and work partners. In *Blossom – A Biography of F G Miles*, Jean Fostekew describes Mrs FG's aeronautical attributes: 'she was not only a pilot, but a designer, draughtswoman, aerodynamicist, stress engineer and director of [an aircraft] manufacturing company.' Blossom died on 6 April 1984, aged 84.

Eight years younger than FG, George joined his brother at Shoreham in mid-1926, initially helping to maintain the 504K that was being used for instruction and 'flips' around the 'drome. Tutored by FG, George went solo in June 1928. While George was introverted when compared with his flamboyant older brother, this was not the case when it came to design. George was responsible for the most radical of the types produced under the Miles banner and was behind the plethora of projects of the wartime era and the late 1940s.

The first Miles type conceived by George was the Monarch three-seat cabin monoplane of 1938. By then his official title was manager, repair and service department, but like his elder sibling, George's responsibilities were wide, including design, production test flying, problem-solving and forecasting future requirements and technologies. George was appointed as technical director and chief designer in 1941, as FG took a greater role in management and strategy.

After the collapse of Miles, George signed up with Airspeed at Christchurch in 1949, replacing Arthur Hagg as chief designer. Among the projects that George worked on was the DH Vampire trainer. George resigned and joined his brother's newly established firm, F G Miles Ltd, at Shoreham in December 1951 – see below.

Third element

While the Miles siblings dominate the story, there is another person whose role was vital to the enterprise. Until 1943 it was his family name that was on the documents of every Miles type as the constructor: Phillips and Powis Aircraft (Reading) Ltd (P&P). With Jack Phillips, Charles Owen Powis had developed a motorcycle and small car-building organisation, along with other enterprises. They set up P&P in 1928 as a large flying school, aircraft dealership and maintenance organisation at their own aerodrome at Woodley. FG met up with Canadian-born Powis in August 1932. Enthused by FG, he agreed to team up; FG acting as chief designer and manager with P&P providing production facilities. FG had found the facilities and funding he needed.

The first Peregrine wearing the 'B Condition' ('trade plate') marking U9 on an early test flight, 1936. *Miles Aircraft*

Powis was a very competent pilot and he regularly helped out on the flying side of the business. With FG away on a business trip to the USA in 1936, Powis carried out the maiden flight of the first Miles twin, the Peregrine, on 12 September 1936. This was a double 'first' as Powis had never flown a twin before! He resigned his post in May 1937 and by 1940 was an RAF squadron leader. Charles Owen Powis, the man who turned Miles from a design bureau into a manufacturer, died in Kenya on 2 February 1990, aged 86.

Ground-breaking Hawk

The first Woodley product was the ground-breaking M.2 Hawk of 1933. It was a well-priced all-wood, two-seat, wing-folding, monoplane trainer/tourer in a world dominated by the DH Moth and similar biplanes. From the Hawk's airframe a 'family' could be created leading all the way to the Magister military trainer and the M.18 'second-generation' version. 'Thinned down' single-seaters for racing produced the Hawk Speed Six and the Sparrowhawk, while widened fuselages and enclosed cockpits created tourers, for example the Falcon Major.

Breaking the family concept in almost every way was a side-by-side two-seat pusher that was inevitably referred to as the 'Pusher'. Don Brown explains that he and George were keen on the format, especially after seeing the Airspeed-built Shackleton-Murray SM.1, but FG was less than enamoured. In the first of his trilogy, Amos quotes Geoffrey Wikner – Edgar Percival's cousin – who was working in the design office in 1935 and was given the task of turning the Pusher into reality. Wikner thought that FG flew the machine, and Amos estimates this was in January 1936. In his book Brown is less specific: '… the aircraft showed little inclination to take-off and [FG] lost no time in dropping the project …'

Carrying the Miles logo behind the firewall, G-ACTI was the thirty-sixth Hawk to be completed and was handed over in the spring of 1934 to a Woodley-based private owner. *KEC*

The second Hawk Speed Six, G-ADGP, at Baginton in August 1966. *Roy Bonser*

Peregrine and Percival Q.6 compared

	Peregrine*	Q.6
First flown	12 Sep 1936	14 Sep 1937
Number built	2	27
Engines x 2	DH Gipsy Six II 205hp	DH Gipsy Six II 205hp
Undercarriage	Retractable	Retractable**
Passengers	6/7	6/7
Cruising speed	160mph	173mph
Range	560 miles	750 miles
Empty weight	3,350lb	

* prototype. ** Six with retractable gear, remainder fixed with 'spatted' fairings.

Not content to design an ever-increasing dynasty of light aeroplanes, FG was keen to prove his machines whenever the occasion presented itself. He entered the prototype Sparrowhawk in the King's Cup air race, staged at Hatfield on 7 September 1935. At 163mph, FG came eleventh overall, but won the speed prize. That race produced a 1-2-3 for Miles types, a boon for the marketing department. Also attracting headlines was the Mohawk of 1937, a special commission for American solo transatlantic flyer Charles Lindbergh for his personal use when visiting Europe. Each new model stuck to the proven construction technique, part of a step-by-step evolution. Although several machines disappointed in the number sold, the investment each time was minimal.

The already mentioned Peregrine adhered to the Miles philosophy but as the firm's first twin introducing the complication of retractable undercarriage, it was an expensive leap. The prototype was extensively demonstrated, but failed to attract orders and was dismantled in late 1937. Experimentation with boundary layer drag reduction at Woodley attracted the interest of the Royal Aircraft Establishment (RAE) and a new Peregrine with a 'blown' wing was delivered to Farnborough in April 1939. Cash raised from this special commission must have gone some way towards recouping the outlay of an otherwise costly programme. Percival fared much better with its Q.6 twin – see the comparison table.

Private-venture gamble

After the Hawk, the most important design overseen by FG was the private-venture Kestrel, a visionary response to the then unaddressed need for an advanced military trainer. The warplanes entering service in the late 1930s offered dramatically increased performance along with advances such as retractable undercarriage, split flaps and variable-pitch propellers. Using similar thinking to the DH team that came up with the Mosquito, FG envisaged an easy-to-build monoplane with the speed and attributes of upcoming fighters and bombers. An approach to the Air Ministry was shunned, but Miles went ahead anyway as a private venture: Rolls-Royce (RR) supplied a Kestrel V-12 and the new machine took its name from the engine, conveniently also a bird of prey.

FG was at the helm of the Kestrel on 3 June 1937: less than a year after he had come up with the concept. Suitably impressed, the Air Ministry performed a U-turn and Specification 16/38 was drawn up around a fully militarised Kestrel, renamed Master as in school master. During 1937 the Hawk Trainer was also adopted by the RAF as the Magister (from the Latin for teacher) and it attracted large orders. On 11 June 1938 an order for an astonishing 500 was placed, worth £2.2 million, and this shot P&P from a 'batch' manufacturer into a full-blown industrial complex that pioneered a moving assembly track. With RR winding down production of the Kestrel,

Miles test pilot Bill Skinner in the prototype Kestrel in June 1937. The '2' is its 'new types' number for that year's Hendon display. *Miles Aircraft*

South Marston-built Master III W8513 of 9 Pilot's Advanced Flying Unit, Hullavington, circa 1942. *KEC*

the ubiquitous Bristol Mercury was adopted for the Master II, which first appeared in late 1939, and the Master III with the Pratt & Whitney Wasp Junior the following year. Both of these radials ruined the type's attractive lines while increasing its practicality. The Master also formed the basis of the Martinet target tug of 1942.

In mid-1940 Miles came up with a conversion of the Master with machine guns in the wings. The 'Master Fighter' was intended to bolster the RAF's Hawker Hurricanes and Supermarine Spitfires as the Battle of Britain loomed. This idea was revived forty-three years later when British Aerospace was given a contract to convert Hawk T.1 jet trainers to missile-equipped back-up air defence fighters for the RAF – see Chapter 12. Similar thinking gave rise to the so-called 'Utility Fighter' conceived by FG during the summer of 1940. Officially sanctioned, the M.20 was powered by a 1,300hp RR Merlin XX and toted eight machine guns. It used many Master 'stock' sub-assemblies and parts, was kept simple with spatted undercarriage and featured a 'teardrop' clear-vision canopy. Detail design was entrusted to Walter Capley and the first of two prototypes was airborne sixty-

five days after the go-ahead. The successful conclusion of the Battle of Britain and the increasing momentum of Hurricane and Spitfire deliveries meant that the Master and Utility fighters were not needed.

Production of the Master and Martinet topped 4,000 units, making FG's Kestrel a very cost-effective private venture. The Woodley assembly line could not meet the capacity needed and a 'shadow factory' was established at South Marston. A similar venture was set up at Doncaster in 1943, but only a small number of Master IIs were assembled in Yorkshire. All of this created pressures that put FG in the boardroom and away from the drawing board and the flight test shed. In 1943 the share structure of P&P was reallocated and the company was renamed Miles Aircraft.

The change of name coincided with contracts for the Monitor twin-engined, high-speed target tug for the RAF and Fleet Air Arm for 200 and 300 units, respectively. Ministry of Aircraft Production (MAP) funding allowed for further expansion of the Woodley site. The prototype had its maiden flight in April 1944 but it was May 1945 before the initial production example was sent to Boscombe Down for trials. Two months earlier the first of a series of cancellations condemned the Monitor to ever-diminishing prospects and only twenty-two were completed when the line ground to a halt in 1946. With the war over, conversions of the potent – and surplus – Bristol Beaufighter Mk.X offered a much higher-performance target tug. These provided much-appreciated work at Oldmixon during the inevitable peacetime downturn, while at Woodley unflown Monitors were a portent of disaster.

Monitors and Martinets under assembly at Woodley, 1945. *Adwest Group*

Paving the way

In July 1941 an elegant, two-seat retractable undercarriage monoplane took to the skies at Woodley: it looked like a tourer with little wartime application. This was the M.28 and a classic example of how the brothers approached projects – it was not aimed at any current requirement. It was completed as a private venture in an era when resources – including time – were supposed to be carefully shepherded by the MAP. The M.28 revived plans that George had schemed in 1939 for trainer/tourer and he piloted his creation on its first flight. The following day FG flew it, only to disgrace himself – he completely forgot the undercarriage tucked up in the wings and belly-landed the prototype!

Six M.28s were built, paving the way for the fixed undercarriage Messenger, which was aimed initially at an airborne observation post (AOP) requirement. From October 1944 Messengers were made at Banbridge in Northern Ireland and the type became the backbone of post-war light aircraft production for Miles. George flew the LR.5 – so designated because it was conceived at the Liverpool Road annexe – in June 1945. It had been created 'under the radar' by members of the design team in their spare time. It would not have looked out of place on a 1970s flight line, but unfortunately its flying characteristics were poor and it was quietly set aside.

Immaculate Messenger G-AKVZ in the early 1970s, believed to be at Biggin Hill. Built as Mk.I RH427 for the RAF in 1946, it served briefly from Wyton before being civilianised in 1949. *KEC*

Tandem wings

George spent a lot of time pondering tandem-wing layouts, especially for operation from aircraft carriers. On tandem-wing machines both the fore and aft wings contribute to lift. They are not to be confused with types, such as the Eurofighter Typhoon, that are fitted with foreplanes that act as control surfaces, providing little lift. George envisioned a fleet fighter with a pilot in the extreme nose with a commanding view, a pusher powerplant, a centre of gravity much further aft than previously achieved and of much reduced span: ideal for deck operations. Actions speak louder than words and he started to design and build a prototype at the Liverpool Road facility, away from the gaze of men from the ministry! Using as many parts raided from the production line as possible, in *six weeks*, he had the M.35 Libellula ready for testing. (The tandem-winged dragonfly insect is generically known as *Libellula*.) Tenuous flight trials began in May 1942 but they could not remain covert for long. Needless to say, George was hauled over the coals by MAP for his flagrant departure from procedure.

The incredible M.39B Libellula, the second Miles 'dragonfly' to fly. *Miles Aircraft*

George started to churn out tandem-wing concepts, including six- and eight-engined strategic bombers and the shapely M.39 twin, a rival to the DH Mosquito featuring a swept rear wing that carried the tractor engines. Once again, George elected to build what today would be called a proof-of-concept aircraft, without sanction from authority. Designated M.39B, it was a five-eighth scale version of the proposed bomber. George flew this much more advanced machine – it had flaps and retractable undercarriage – on 22 July 1943. It was far less of a handful to fly than the crude M.35 had been. The M.39B was evaluated by RAE and jet-powered versions were schemed, but it remained an aeronautical cul-de-sac.

X-planes

Another scale aerodynamic prototype was flown in February 1942: again it was not part of a specific war effort-related project. In the mid-1930s George revisited a concept for airliners with wide fuselages that blended into thick wings in which the engines could be 'buried'. In 1924 Westland had flown a blended-wing prototype – the Dreadnought – but it had come to grief on its maiden flight. The concept had a wide, stubby fuselage that permitted short span, wide-chord wings as the blended centre section also provided lift. At Miles these studies were referred to as the 'X' project. In modern parlance this format is known as the blended-wing body and is still the subject of study by Airbus and Boeing.

Ignoring the war raging across Europe and the Far East, George designed a scale test bed, the twin-engined 'X Minor', using whatever could be adapted from the stores and the production line. The result looked vaguely like his notions of the 1930s, but its 33ft span prevented the DH Gipsy Major in-lines from being hidden within the wing and the 'blend' was abrupt and not gradual. Accordingly, the 'X Minor' could not have contributed much useful data and Miles could be accused of squandering resources that could have been channelled towards victory.

Head-on view of the 'X Minor' test bed, giving a hint of what a blended wing format would look like. *Miles Aircraft*

Miles types to 1939

From	To	Total	Name/Designation	Type	Engine(s)	Notes
1926	-	1	Gnat Aero Gnat	2-seat biplane	1 x 2-cylinder	[1]
1929	1931	7	Southern Martlet	1-seat biplane	1 x AS Genet	[2]
1932	-	1	Satyr	1-seat biplane	1 x Pobjoy R	[3]
1933	1936	56	Hawk	Trainer/tourer	1 x Cirrus III	[4]
1934	1936	101	Hawk Major/Trainer	Trainer/tourer	1 x DH Gipsy Major	
1934	1935	3	Hawk Speed Six	Racer	1 x DH Gipsy Six	[5]
1934	1937	36	Falcon	Cabin tourer	1 x DH Gipsy Major	[6]
1935	1936	4	Merlin	Cabin tourer	1 x DH Gipsy Six	
1935	1940	5	Sparrowhawk	Sportsplane	1 x DH Gipsy Major	[7]
1935	-	1	Hawcon	Wing research	1 x DH Gipsy Six	
1935	-	1	'Pusher'	Two-seater	1 x ADC Cirrus III	[8]
1935	1936	6	Nighthawk	Crew trainer	1 x DH Gipsy Six	
1936	1938	51	Whitney Straight	Tourer	1 x DH Gipsy Major	
1936	1938	2	Peregrine	Light transport	2 x DH Gipsy Six	
1937	1941	901	Kestrel/Master	Trainer	1 x RR Kestrel	[9]
1937	-	1	Mohawk	Tourer	1 x Menasco	
1937	-	1	Hobby	Racer	1 x DH Gipsy Major	
1937	1948	1,393	Magister	Trainer	1 x DH Gipsy Major	[10]
1938	1939	45	Mentor	Crew trainer	1 x DH Gipsy Six	
1938	1939	11	Monarch	Cabin tourer	1 x DH Gipsy Major	
1938	1942	4	M.18	Trainer	1 x DH Gipsy Major	
1939	-	1	M.15 T.1/37	Trainer	1 x DH Gipsy Six	
1939	1943	1,350	Master II and III	Trainer	1 x Bristol Mercury	[11]

Based upon *Miles Aircraft – The Early Years*, *Miles Aircraft – The Wartime Years* and *Miles Aircraft – The Post-War Years* by Peter Amos. [1] Built under the aegis of the Gnat Aero and Motor Company, Portslade: did not fly. [2] Originally known as the Hornet Baby. Includes single 'Metal' Martlet, 1931. [3] Built by Parnall, Yate. [4] Including cabin, single-seat and three-seat versions. [5] Three built 1935–36; unfinished example completed 1940 for Royal Aircraft Establishment. [6] Includes Falcon Major and Falcon Six. [7] Prototype converted into Sparrowjet, 1953 – see table 'Miles types from 1940'. [8] May, or may not, have flown – see narrative. [9] M.9 Kestrel, production as M.9A Master, also small number converted to M.24 Master Fighter status. [10] Includes 33 kits supplied to Kayseri Tayyare Fabrikasi, Turkey and 80 examples built from new by Turk Hava Kurumu Ucak Fabrikasi, Ankara, 1944–48. Civil versions known as Hawker Trainer III. [11] M.19 Master II with Mercury, M.27 Master III with P&W Wasp Junior. South Marston built 488 Mk.IIs and all – 602 – Mk.IIIs. Ten Mk.IIs *believed* assembled at Doncaster 1941–42, plans to mass manufacture there were shelved.

In December 1942 the Brabazon Committee began its deliberations about the commercial aircraft needed in the post-war world. As detailed in Chapter 11, Bristol was given the task of creating a transatlantic airliner, which resulted in the unfortunate Type 167 Brabazon. The brothers were outraged to discover that they had not been considered for such a project. Typically, FG and George launched off devising the eight-engined, blended-wing X.11, committing a large amount of time theorising and formulating a detailed proposal: all to no avail.

As explained in the Introduction, this book tries to steer clear of designs that did not make it into hardware, but one by Miles *has* to be mentioned. We have mentioned conspiracy theories that surround Concorde and TSR.2 and there are two such musings that concern Miles, both of which flare up regularly. One is the M.52 'wonder plane' and the other the deliberate extinguishing of Miles in 1947–48 by financiers or even rival manufacturers.

Wooden mock-up of the M.52 supersonic project. The cockpit also served as the centre body for the annular jet intake. *Miles Aircraft*

The M.52 was a prestige pure research jet intended to break the so-called 'sound barrier'. Its parameters were outlined in Specification E.24/32 issued on 26 August 1944 to Miles. At that point both DH and Gloster were well into developing the Vampire and Meteor respectively and would seem to be the most likely homes for such a project, but both were heavily engaged in production programmes.

MAP had recognised that Miles was heavily involved in research and development – even if a lot of it was unofficial – and that it had perhaps been badly dealt with over the X.11, hence the award of the E.24/32. Between them the ministry, Power Jets, the RAE and Miles expended a lot of time and money on an ever-ballooning project. For the ministry and the RAE this was their stock-in-trade and for Frank Whittle's Power Jets, development of the W.2/700 turbojet could only benefit from the programme. But for Miles, it was a massive distraction that – even if it came to fruition – was unlikely to set the company up financially, or introduce an entirely new product line. Spectacular amounts of investment and major revisions of its frugal management structure would be required for that.

E.24/43 was cancelled in February 1946, just as Miles was plunging into post-war realignment and striving for markets. It is significant that Vickers – a company with well-established research capabilities and sufficient infrastructure – was given a follow-on project to drop scale rocket-propelled M.52 models from a modified Mosquito. The first launch took place on 30 May 1947 and the last on 9 October 1948. Vickers benefitted from radio control, telemetry, rocket handling techniques and ballistics experience, providing valuable background for its burgeoning missile programmes. Tony Buttler has written the calm, balanced and in-depth *Miles M.52 – Britain's Top Secret Supersonic Research Aircraft*, published by Crécy; it will put conspiracy theorists out of their misery!

Miles types from 1940

From	To	Total	Name/Designation	Type	Engine(s)	Notes
1940		2	M.20 'Utility Fighter'	Fighter	1 x RR Merlin	
1941	1947	6	M.28	Communications	1 x DH Gipsy Major	
1942	1946	1,795	Martinet	Target tug	1 x Bristol Mercury	[1]
1942	-	1	M.30 'X Minor'	Research	2 x DH Gipsy Major	
1942	-	1	M.35 Libellula pusher	Research	1 x DH Gipsy Major	
1942	1950	91	Messenger	Communications	1 x DH Gipsy Major	[2]
1943	-	1	M.39B Libellula	Research	2 x DH Gipsy Major	
1944	1945	22	Monitor I/II	Target tug	2 x Wright Cyclone	[3]
1945	1947	54	Aerovan	Light transport	2 x Cirrus Major	
1945	-	1	LR.5	Tourer	1 x Cirrus Minor	
1945	1955	148	Gemini/Aries	Tourer	2 x Cirrus Minor	[4]
1946	1947	2	Marathon	Airliner	4 x DH Gipsy Queen	[5]
1947	-	1	Boxcar	Transport	4 x Cirrus Minor	
1947	-	1	Merchantman	Transport	4 x DH Gipsy Queen	
1949	-	1	Marathon II	Airliner	2 x AS Mamba	[6]
1953	-	1	Sparrowjet	Racer	2 x Turboméca Palas	[7]
1957	-	1	HDM.105	Research	2 x Cirrus Major	[8]
1964	-	1	Student	Trainer	1 x T'méca Maboré	
1964	-	3	Boxkite	Film replica	1 x Continental A65	[9]
1965	-	2	S.E.5A	Film replica	1 x DH Gipsy Queen	[10]

Based upon *Miles Aircraft – The Early Years*, *Miles Aircraft – The Wartime Years* and *Miles Aircraft – The Post-War Years* by Peter Amos. **[1]** Includes new-build Queen Martinet radio-controlled target drones. Two trainer M.37 versions produced 1946. **[2]** Majority built at Banbridge (flying from Long Kesh) and, from February 1946, Newtownards, both Northern Ireland. At least nine completed under the aegis of Handley Page at Woodley, 1948–50. **[3]** Programme cancelled March 1945; final examples remained at Woodley and *may* not have been flown. **[4]** Six completed by Wolverhampton Aviation post-1947, one completed by F G Miles Ltd at Redhill in 1950 and two M.75 Aries with Cirrus Majors, one each in 1950 and 1955. **[5]** Production of 40 units carried out by Handley Page as HPR.1s at Woodley 1950–52 – see Chapter 24. **[6]** Turboprop prototype nearly ready upon closure 1947. First flown under the aegis of Handley Page 23 July 1948. **[7]** M.77, twin-jet conversion of first Sparrowhawk – see table 'Miles Types to 1939' – by F G Miles Ltd, Redhill. **[8]** Joint project with Hurel-Dubois – hence HDM – of France, conversion of Aerovan – see narrative. **[9]** Near replica of 1910 Bristol pusher biplane for use in *Those Magnificent Men in Their Flying Machines* by F G Miles Ltd at Ford. Third example not flown. **[10]** External replica of Royal Aircraft Factory biplane fighter by F G Miles Ltd at Ford for use in *The Blue Max*.

Dire straits

Miles entered peacetime with the M.52 project consuming vast amounts of time, Martinet and Monitor production winding down – the latter rapidly after cancellation – and no new military orders to provide vital cash flow. The Messenger had made an easy transition to a civilian tourer and was attracting customers. In anticipation of this, a new factory was built at Newtownards in North Ireland from February 1946, but this ambitious plant was not completed. A twin-engined Messenger, the Gemini, had its maiden flight on 26 October 1945 and also found favour. This 'family' involved relatively little outlay, but FG and George were about to unleash a barrage of prototypes.

The abortive LR.5 has already been mentioned. The Aerovan light utility twin had its debut on 26 January 1945. The Boxcar and Merchantman of 1947 were scaled-up, four-engined types exploiting the Aerovan format. The Boxcar featured an ingenious mid-fuselage that doubled as a trailer that could be detached and towed behind a car. The aircraft could be flown without the 'container' by fixing the rear fairing behind the cockpit, creating a dramatically foreshortened fuselage. The Merchantman attracted some interest from operators, but none of this was translating into cash flow. The Aerovan and its growth versions were of all-wood construction and while stretching did not quite empty the depleting coffers. Ironically, the wood-and-glue nature of these types contributed to the downfall of Miles.

The four-engined Marathon was an all-metal, full-blown airliner designed to meet the complex and constantly changing needs of customers such as British European Airways. This was a league into which Miles should never have strayed. The prototype flew on 19 May 1946 and nineteen months later Miles went into receivership. It took an organisation the size of Handley Page to put the Marathon into production.

The surge of prototypes would have bean counters at companies the size of DH, Hawker or Vickers wincing. Miles was teetering on the brink and vulnerable. In late January 1947 deep, relentless, snow began

to cover the country, the Thames froze over and Britain was paralysed. Deliveries of everything from milk to aero engines were disrupted or abandoned. Wartime rationing was still in place but food shortages reached crisis levels. Constant sub-zero temperatures played havoc with the electricity supply. At Woodley power cuts stopped production and the gluing up of sub-assemblies, requiring strict temperature control, had to be junked or postponed, wrecking output schedules.

That the company was struggling with a throwback process involving glue and wood in its airframes showed how archaic Miles had become. It needed desperately to refinance and further overdraft facilities were secured. The company was not alone in this; many firms were in similar dire straits as the weather gripped tighter. The country was cash-strapped and Clement Attlee's Labour government was monitoring expenditure and credit to prevent a national collapse. Miles spiralled out of monetary control and the receiver was called in. This is where the conspiracy merchants drop in. Miles was one of hundreds of concerns screaming for rescue: there was only so much the banking system could do. Why not nationalise it? Miles could hardly be regarded as a strategic resource. Even if the cash was forthcoming, if Miles was that exposed to crisis, it was heading towards doom anyway. The lights went off for the last time in early 1948.

Gemini G-AKHB, built in 1947 at Baginton in February 1961, when it was owned by a Rugby-based engineering company. *Roy Bonser*

The Boxcar with the roadable container that acted as the centre element of the fuselage. When 'unloaded' the rear fairing was attached to the rear of the cockpit, producing a tadpole-like appearance. *Miles Aircraft*

Aerovan G-AJOF was repurchased by F G Miles Ltd in 1957 and converted into the HDM.105 high aspect ratio wing test bed. It was initially flown with 'B Condition' serial G-35-3 before taking up the appropriate G-AHDM. *F G Miles Ltd*

Back at the drawing board

FG set up F G Miles Ltd at Redhill in June 1951 and George came on board in November. They moved to Shoreham – where they had started off in the late 1920s – the following year. The brothers were much sought after as consultant aeronautical engineers and became experts in plastics, actuators and electronics. Competition pilot Fred Dunkerley contracted FG to convert the prototype Sparrowhawk into a jet-powered racer. After an extensive transformation, George carried out the maiden flight of the Sparrowjet on 14 December 1953 – his first time piloting a jet. Hawker and Rolls-Royce turned to F G Miles Ltd in 1956 to design a reverse thrust system for the Hunter F.6.

Two ventures got airborne in 1957, the HDM.105 on 31 March and the M.100 on 14 May. The former was an Aerovan with a new high aspect ratio wing pioneered by the French Hurel-Dubois concern. The brothers hoped this would lead to more efficient transport types and sold the concept to Shorts, where it emerged as the Skyvan in 1963. The M.100 was a jet that had been designed from the start as a 'family', ranging from a trainer – called Student – or four-seat executive transport – the Centurion. The prototype Student was the only example to see the light of day and can be found today in the Museum of Berkshire Aviation at Woodley.

The brothers hankered after recreating the success of the Messenger and Gemini and took a modular approach to create the M.114 Merlin two-seater single and the M.115 Martlet four-seat, retractable, twin. These had many sub-assemblies in common and utilised a lot of glass fibre-reinforced plastic sections. This technique was very advanced for 1960 and had the potential to blow away the rivals. But F G Miles Ltd was a *design* house that had expanded into sub-contract work: it needed to find a partner with *production* capacity. So began the tempestuous involvement with Beagle that is charted in Chapter 7.

Both walked away from the Beagle farce and set up shop at Ford, Sussex, in 1963 and engaged in a series of projects, including the design and construction of replicas for use in movies. The brothers were involved in extensive sub-contracting work, including engine nacelles for the French Sud Caravelle jetliner, and had interests or ownership of a number of specialist companies. In 1975 the Hunting Group acquired the majority of the brothers' varied assets. Frederick George Miles died on 15 August 1976 having enjoyed seventy-three eventful, energetic, innovative and extremely full years. George Herbert Miles died on 18 September 1999, aged 88, ending an aviation dynasty like no other.

George Miles, designer and test pilot of the Student, G-35-4, outside the airport building at Shoreham, 1957. *F G Miles Ltd*

The last of three Elves, G-AAIN, is kept in airworthy trim by the Shuttleworth Collection at Old Warden. *KEC*

CHAPTER TWENTY-NINE

Weighty Decisions

Parnall
1916 to 1945

'All problems are soluble in beer.' Harold Bolas

FROM 1820 PARNALL AND SONS of Bristol expanded its shop-fittings and weights and measures instruments business. It did so well that it was tempting to the much larger rival, W T Avery Ltd, and in 1898 it acquired Parnall. Avery is a brand still to be found on weighing machines today. Having made its purchase, the bigger company wisely let the Parnall name continue under its own banner and management well into the next century. While such a background might not seem a likely path to aircraft manufacture, the design and mass production of delicate devices was exactly the sort of expertise that the War Office was looking for in a sub-contractor from 1914.

Parnall falls short of the inclusion criteria noted in the Introduction but appears as a good example of a 'middle-league' manufacturer that created some noteworthy types thanks to a charismatic, but largely unsung, designer.

As can be seen from the licences and sub-contracts table, Parnall was awarded significant work during the war, so much so that in 1916 the board took the plunge and set up a design department. The following year, Harold Bolas was taken on as chief designer. Bolas and his creations will be examined in due course, but before that the somewhat convoluted evolution of the Parnall enterprises should be examined. One of the 'and Sons' of the company was George Parnall, who resigned from the family firm in 1919. George was very keen on aviation and he was unhappy when the firm opted out just when it had made a breakthrough with orders for the Panther shipborne

fighter. He set up George Parnall and Company in 1920 as a shop-fittings manufacturer and retailer, still in Bristol and competing with the original Parnall firm – that must have made family gatherings a bundle of fun! As well as display cabinets and the like, George was determined to re-enter the aircraft business. He relocated the business to Yate, to the north-east of Bristol, in 1925, initially flying from Filton until an aerodrome could be established alongside the factory.

As the table shows, the George Parnall aviation department was hardly awash with orders through the 1920s but in 1932 George relented to pressure from Avery and sold the shop-fitting side back to his family. The Panther turned out *not* to be the end of Parnall and Sons in aviation. The same virtues that had taken the firm into sub-contracting in the Great War applied to the new world conflict. From 1939 it took on sub-assembly work, including flaps for Fairey Barracuda dive-bombers and fuselage 'barrels' for Airspeed Horsa assault gliders. The association blossomed again from 1952 when Parnall and Sons manufactured a batch of fuselage 'pods' for de Havilland Venom jets.

To return to George Parnall, the failure of the G.4/31 general-purpose military biplane to attract orders in the heavily contested fly-off triggered a decision to sell up. (Vickers was the ultimate beneficiary of G.4/31 – see Chapter 37.) In May 1935 George Parnall and Company was taken over by Nash and Thompson Ltd, makers of complex servo-controlled mechanisms and power-operated gun turrets – the latter rapidly becoming much in demand. Nash and Thompson had been established by Archibald Frazer-Nash and Esmonde Gratton-Thompson in 1927 and Parnall's large factory and skilled workforce were very attractive propositions. Nash and Thompson wished to maintain aviation as part of its portfolio and, having acquired the Hendy Aircraft Company, amalgamated it with the Yate design office under the name Parnall Aircraft Ltd.

Good judgement

Lancashire lad Harold Bolas graduated from Manchester University and in 1910 – aged 22 – was taken on by the Aeronautical Inspection Directorate (AID), part of the state-run Balloon Factory at Farnborough. As Chapter 31 shows, it was renamed the Aircraft Factory in 1911 and the Royal Aircraft Factory the following year. Bolas became a stress engineer under Stanley William Hiscocks, who was destined to become chief engineer of the Aircraft Manufacturing Company in 1917. With the coming of war in 1914, Bolas was commissioned into the Royal Naval Air Service (RNAS) and his superiors exercised good judgement by posting him to the Admiralty's Air Department (AD). There he worked on the AD Flying boat and the Navyplane, both of which were contracted to Pemberton Billing Ltd at Southampton. That company changed its name in 1916 to Supermarine and Bolas co-operated on the completion of both types with Reginal Joseph Mitchell.

Harold Bolas in front of the prototype Elf, G-AAFH. *via Ken Wixey*

Bolas was released from the RNAS in 1917, taking the post of chief designer for Parnall. His first creation for his new employer was the Panther, his last the Parasol experimental. Bolas was tempted to the USA in 1929, joining Captain R J Goodman Crouch, latterly of the Royal Aircraft Establishment (RAE) and the RNAS. Crouch was managing the Whittlesey Manufacturing Company's new aviation division at Bridgport, Connecticut, which was beginning to build Avro Avians under licence. Bolas accepted the post of chief engineer with a remit to set the concern up as a manufacturer of original aeroplanes. The so-called 'Wall Street crash' of October put paid to all of that and only about ten Avians were finished before the venture folded.

This did not put off Bolas and Crouch and in 1932 they inaugurated the Crouch-Bolas Aircraft Corporation of Pawtucket, Rhode Island. There they made the revolutionary Dragonfly biplane twin with high-lift wing sections and large two-bladed propellers that 'washed' most of the lower and upper surfaces. They had created a machine that in later times would have the label STOL – short take-off and landing. The Dragonfly was tested and demonstrated extensively, but failed to attract orders.

With Britain engaged in another war, Bolas came home to his native Lancashire. By 1941 he was managing Civilian Repair Organisation member Lancashire Aircraft Corporation factory in Burnley, which built Beaufort and Beaufighter sub-assemblies and repaired examples of the Bristol twins. (The name Lancashire Aircraft Corporation was revived in 1958 as the manufacturer of Edgar Percival's EP.9.) Parnall's experience with Cierva autogiros – see the sub-contract table – had not been encouraging but by 1943 Bolas was with Rotol, the propeller manufacturer run in partnership by Rolls-Royce and Bristol. He was tasked with examining how Rotol could expand its remit into rotor blades. This led in 1945 to a post with the revived Cierva at Eastleigh heading up the technical and stress office, working on the ill-fated Air Horse transport and the Skeeter light helicopters. When Saunders-Roe absorbed Cierva in 1951, Bolas was still engaged on transmissions and rotor blades. As the quote at the head of this chapter reflects, he was a man of ready wit and his designs reflected considerable versatility: Harold Bolas died on 8 July 1956 aged 78.

Parnall and Sons licences* and sub-contracts

Type	Total	From	To	Notes
Short 827 floatplane	20	1915	1916	
Short Bomber	6	1916	-	
Avro 504B	80	1916	1917	[1]
Avro 504A, 'J or 'K	450+	1917	1918	[2]
Fairey Hamble Baby floatplane	140	1916	1917	[3]
Cierva C.10*	1	1926	-	[4]
Cierva C.11*	1	1926	-	[4]
Hendy 302	1	1930	-	[5]
Miles Satyr	1	1932	-	
Percival Gull	24	1932	1933	[6]

[1] Total *perhaps* as high as 110 and *possibly* the additional 30 was for RNAS 504Gs. [2] Final contract, for 150, only partially completed. [3] Substantial revision of Sopwith Baby – see Chapter 19. At least 74 completed as Baby Convert landplanes. [4] See Chapter 15. Both types wrecked on first flight. [5] See also Heck in main table. [6] This figure *may* have been 22.

Naval specialist

Parnall's first original type was officially named Scout but was known in the firm as the 'Night Flyer' and more often the 'Zepp Chaser' from its anti-Zeppelin airship role. This was the brainchild of Parnall production test pilot Keith Davies. By 1912 Davies was working for AID at Farnborough and it is very likely that he was the 'conduit' by which Bolas – another AID employee – joined Parnall. The Zepp Chaser remained a one-off, but that was not the case for Parnall's second, and the first for Bolas, the Panther.

The last of six prototype Panthers built by Parnall, N96, at Filton in 1919 showing how its fuselage folded for deck stowage.

Responding to the Admiralty's N.2A requirement for a two-seat, deck-landing reconnaissance type that eventually took the name Panther, Bolas produced a robust biplane with a wooden monocoque fuselage. This choice might seem overly complicated, but it was intended to be ditched and recovered virtually unscathed and the shell-like fuselage allowed for a degree of water resistance. It also permitted a 'break' behind the observer's position so that the rear fuselage could hinge to starboard, dramatically cutting down deck space.

The prototype had its maiden flight in April 1918 but development was protracted. However, the Panther was important; as the first British type specifically designed for operation from carriers, the Admiralty was determined that it should succeed. A staggering 312 were ordered, only for that number to be butchered with the coming of the Armistice. To add insult to injury after half a dozen or so Parnall-built examples, the production contract was transferred to Bristol in 1919. It was this experience that convinced the Parnall board to get out of the aeroplane business. Ironically, Bristol turned to Parnall to complete an unknown number of Panthers in what could be described as a 'sub-sub-contract'.

Right: The second Peto, N182, folded and stowed within HMS *Furious*, January 1930. *Peter Green Collection*

Below: The third prototype Plover, N162, in 1923. *KEC*

The eventual success of the Panther put Parnall in a good position when the Fleet Air Arm was looking for a carrier-borne fighter. This emerged at Yate as the all-wooden Plover – a shoreline-feeding bird – in 1923. As could happen in the 1920s, although Fairey's mixed-construction Flycatcher took the bulk of the prize, the Plover entered limited service and in all thirteen were made.

Specification 16/24 was met by Bolas with a relatively unremarkable biplane for an incredible task. The navy wanted a small, two-seat spotter for operation from a submarine. Launched in 1919, HM Submarine M2 was laid up in 1926 and work began to fit it with a hangar in front of the conning tower ('sail' in submariner terms) and a catapult running along the deck towards the bow. The hangar doors were water-tight and a crane was installed to bring the biplane back on board. Bolas came up with the Peto – Latin for 'I enquire' – a small biplane with folding wings and Saunders-built floats. All metal fittings on the two Petos ordered were made of stainless steel to avoid corrosion.

The prototype first flew, in landplane guise, on 4 June 1925, well ahead of the transformation of the submarine. M2 was ready in April 1928 and, operating from Valletta harbour, Malta, engaged in trials early in 1930. The Peto was damaged on that cruise and rebuilt, while the second example was written off in June 1930. M2 sank off Portland Bill on 26 January 1932 with the biplane sealed in its hangar: all sixty souls on board perished, including the crew of the Peto.

HM Submarine M2 moored at Gibraltar with the first Peto, N181, in flying trim outside of its hangar and on the catapult, January 1930.
Peter Green Collection

Experimentals

In the early 1920s the Air Ministry had an interest in what it called 'Postal' or 'Special Transports'. This was a ruse to try out new formats and three manufacturers responded with a ministry favourite: the so-called 'engine room' layout, with the powerplant inside the fuselage, driving propellers via clutches, shafts or belts. Bristol came up with the Tramp, Boulton and Paul the Bodmin and Parnall the Possum. Westland went its own way with the ill-fated Dreadnought 'all-wing' design. The Possum triplane appeared in 1923 with a Napier Lion driving a pair of tractor propellers – like the others, it was a short-lived novelty.

Two simply named Parasols were delivered to RAE at Farnborough in 1930. They had been commissioned for variable-incidence wing research and Bolas determined that a parasol format would be best to achieve this.

In 1931 a one-off all-metal flying boat was delivered to the Marine Aircraft Experimental Establishment at Felixstowe. The single-seat Prawn was designed to validate a concept that might lead to a high-performance seaborne marine fighter. To achieve this it needed a sleek fuselage without draggy floats or high-mounted engine. Developed as an auxiliary power unit for the airship R.101, a 65hp liquid-cooled Ricardo-Burt S55/4 driving a four-bladed propeller was installed in the nose. For take-off and touchdown the engine was pivoted upwards by about 30 degrees. Once the little machine was in the climb the little four-cylinder was lowered to a conventional position. With such an odd thrust line and a mere 65hp, the Prawn was doomed to remain flightless.

Civil diversions

With little in the way of orders from the Air Ministry, Parnall decided to enter the 1923 *Daily Mail*-sponsored single-seat light aeroplane trials, staged at Lympne in October. Bolas came up with the adaptable Pixie, which could be configured as a monoplane (Mk.I) or a biplane (Mk.II) with relative ease. While the Pixie was not among the winners at Lympne, an order for two as 'trainers' from the Air Ministry provided some consolation. The following year's competition was for two-seaters and the Pixie III appeared, also in one- or two-winged form, although both were known as Pixie IIIs: this version had no luck at the trials either.

So that the Pixies were readily convertible, Bolas did not use bracing, or 'flying', wires to support the biplane versions, adopting robust struts. He carried this idea through to the Imp sportsplane of 1927. This was a racy looker with unswept lower and swept upper wings. The upper wing was supported by a metal tube frame at the centre section and substantial 'I'-section struts outboard. The Imp did not enter production. Single-seaters were a niche market and Bolas turned in 1929 to a classic two-seat tourer format with the Elf in the hope of greater interest. For this Warren girder struts – a series

The Prawn with its engine pivoted upwards in take-off or touch down guise. *KEC*

Parnall

From	To	Total	Name/Designation	Type	Engine(s)	Notes
1916	-	1	'Zepp Chaser'	Scout	1 x Sunbeam Maori	
1918	1920	69+	Panther	Shipborne recce	1 x Bentley BR.2	[1]
1920	1921	3	Puffin	Shipborne fighter	1 x Napier Lion	
1922	1923	13	Plover	Shipborne fighter	1 x Bristol Jupiter	
1923	-	2	Possum	'Postal'	1 x Napier Lion	[2]
1923	1924	6	Pixie I, II, III	Ultralight	1 x Douglas	[3]
1926	-	1	Perch	Military GP	1 x RR Falcon	
1926	-	2	Peto	Sub-borne recce	1 x Bristol Lucifer	[4]
1927	-	1	Pike	Naval recce	1 x Napier Lion	
1927	-	1	Imp	Sportsplane	1 x AS Genet	
1928	1929	2	Pipit	Shipborne fighter	1 x RR F.XI	
1929	1932	3	Elf	Tourer	1 x Cirrus Hermes	
1930	-	2	Parasol	Research	1 x AS Lynx	
1930	-	1	Prawn	Research	See note	[5]
1935	-	1	G.4/31	Military GP	1 x Bristol Pegasus	
1935	1936	6	Heck 2C	Tourer	1 x DH Gipsy Six	[6]
1939	-	1	Heck III (Type 382)	Trainer	1 x DH Gipsy Six	

Based upon *Parnall Aircraft since 1914* by Kenneth E Wixey. Scout and Panther: Parnall and Sons; Puffin to G.4/31: George Parnall and Co; Heck and Type 382: Parnall Aircraft. Unless noted, all tractor biplanes. **[1]** Main production contract switched to Bristol 1919, but unknown number completed by Parnall by agreement. Bristol production at least 36, plus 16 spare airframes. **[2]** Triplane; engine mounted within fuselage, driving two tractor propellers via extension shafts. **[3]** Pixie I and II single-seat monoplanes; Pixie III two-seater monoplane convertible to biplane. **[4]** Two-seat, submarine-borne reconnaissance floatplane. **[5]** Single-seat monoplane flying boat, 1 x 65hp Ricardo-Burt. **[6]** Prototype Heck built by Westland – Chapter 38.

of 'vees' – were employed to brace the wire-free wings and greatly aided the wing-folding process. Only three examples were built and, as seen at the chapter header, the last of these, G-AAIN, is cherished today by the Shuttleworth Trust at Old Warden.

Bowing out

Basil Balfour 'Hendy' Henderson set up Hendy Aircraft Ltd at Shoreham in 1928 and helped F G Miles on the one-off 'Metal' Martlet. His first original design was the Hobo single-seater of 1929, which helped him to pioneer his closely paralleled 'I'-shape wooden spars forming a cross-braced box girder arrangement. This was easy to build yet offered exceptional strength. Piloting the Hobo on its first flight was Edgar Percival. The next Hendy was the Type 302 cabin monoplane and Parnall was engaged to make it. For more on the involvement of Henderson and Percival, see Chapter 30. After building the 302, Parnall picked up a contract from Percival for a batch of his Gulls.

The Heck evolved from the 302 as a high-performance cabin tourer and the first example was built in 1924 by Westland. With the coming together of Hendy and Parnall under Nash and Thompson, the Heck was put into production at Yate, but only six followed. Using the Heck's wings and tail surfaces, a tandem, open-cockpit trainer emerged in the hope of an order for Air Ministry Specification T.1/37. The prototype appeared in 1939, but ultimately nothing came of the requirement.

That was the end of the road for Parnall Aircraft and it bowed out of aircraft manufacturing. The factory at Yate continued to expand as demand for gun turrets became almost insatiable. Other war work was also carried out, including a large contract for Supermarine Spitfire wing leading edges and sub-assemblies for Avro Lancasters. Post-war the turret business withered away and a new company was set up in 1945, Parnall (Yate) Ltd building domestic appliances – almost a full circle from the days of making weighing machines.

Hendy 302 G-AAVT, built by Parnall in 1930. *Peter Green Collection*

CHAPTER THIRTY

Luton's Legacy

Percival and Hunting
1933 to 1960

'...a jovial but determined Australian pilot with ambitious ideas...' Harald Penrose on Edgar Percival

GOOD LUCK TALISMAN or clever marketing tool? Edgar Wikner Percival's soft felt trilby hat was a fixture whenever he flew. If this particular headgear was due to superstition, it cannot have had its origins in his formative flying years: then he would have donned a military leather flying helmet. Within the company he founded, it was accepted that the cabin of each new variant of the Gull family allowed sufficient space for the famous hat. Apocryphal or not, it was a good line for Percival's sales agents: good performance, exceptional range and roomy.

Within eight years of the formation of Percival Aircraft its leading light left for pastures new. By then the well-capitalised company was into wartime mass production in a prestigious purpose-built factory. There were rumours that Edgar Percival had been ousted in a boardroom reshuffle, or that his occasionally tempestuous nature had got the better of him. More likely he was frustrated that with the dawning of 1940 the era of shapely high-performance civil monoplanes was gone and that the efficient, relentless, churning out of military hardware was the inevitable agenda. Fifteen years after his departure, Edgar Percival was back, with an innovative utility aeroplane.

The exact nature of his leaving Luton will probably never be ascertained. That is not the only ambiguous element in the incredibly varied life of Edgar Percival. From the very year that Percival Aircraft was created – 1933 – through to the late 1970s Edgar

Percival defended his role in the origins of the Gull. This could take the form of scathing letters to the aeronautical press but, at least once it ramped up to talk of solicitors in 1960, concluding in a carefully worded retraction in the second edition of a book on the history of British civil aviation.

It's time to examine the legacy of the man in a trilby. As with other chapters, in order to distinguish between the man and the company he gave his name to, Edgar Wikner Percival is referred to as 'EWP', and his original business 'Percival'. For further reading, David Gearing's *On the Wings of a Gull*, is a detailed, yet highly readable, tour-de-force of Percival, Hunting and its legacy.

Cover of a 1952 Percival brochure. Left to right: Sea Prince, Prentice, Cheetah-engined Provost, Leonides-engined Provost. The reference to Toronto relates to the subsidiary, Percival Aircraft (Canada) Ltd, set up in 1947. *KEC*

Edgar Wikner Percival and his hallmark trilby in the cockpit of a Mew Gull. *Hunting*

Fighting 'Huns' and Turks

Born on a vast farm near Albany, New South Wales, Australia, EWP exhibited various skills from early on. He had a rapport with horses and could quell the most rebellious of beasts; he was good at fixing agricultural machinery and – thanks to a nearby airstrip – was bitten by the aviation 'bug'. Aged 17, amid engineering studies in Sydney, he had built and flown at least one glider.

Enlisting in the Australian Army in 1915, EWP was put on a ship heading for Egypt. As soon as he could, he transferred from the Australian Imperial Force to the Royal Flying Corps (RFC) and trained as a pilot at 3 School of Military Aeronautics at Aboukir. Briefly in Britain, by May 1916 he was on the Western Front in France, flying Morane BBs with 60 Squadron RFC. Suffering from a chronic inner ear problem, he was brought back to 'Blighty' to recuperate. Back in action by the summer of 1917, this time in Palestine, EWP was engaged in fighting the forces of the Ottoman Empire with 111 Squadron. The unit flew a rag-tag of machines including Bristol Scouts and M.1 monoplanes, Nieuport 17s and Royal Aircraft Factory S.E.5as. EWP was still in Palestine when the RFC became the RAF on 1 April 1918.

Demobbed, EWP was again on a ship, Australia-bound, in the spring of 1920. He was not alone, coming with him were an Avro 504K and an Airco DH.6, which he'd acquired from a surplus sale. At Richmond, Victoria, he set up the first of several aviation businesses and prospered. But Australian skies were not sufficient for EWP: his ambitious ideas would take place in Britain.

Family trait

EWP was not the only family member smitten with aeroplanes. His cousin, Geoffrey Neville Wikner, designed three light aircraft in his native Australia, before coming to Britain by 1934. He is mentioned in Chapter 28 for his involvement with the Miles 'Pusher' in 1935. By the following year Wikner had teamed with 'Jack' Foster to form Foster Wikner Aircraft at Eastleigh building the Wicko light aeroplane. The prototype was flown by Wikner from Stapleford Tawney in September 1936 and was followed by nine more.

Wikner served with the Air Transport Auxiliary during the war, carrying out more than 1,000 ferry flights. In 1946 he purchased a former RAF Handley Page Halifax III, which was inevitably named

Waltzing Matilda. With fourteen fare-paying 'crew' (one source quotes twenty-one in total on board), Wikner piloted the bomber from Hurn on 25 May 1946 and arrived at Mascot, New South Wales, on 20 June. Geoffrey Neville Wikner died in 1990, aged 86: his book, *The Flight of the Halifax*, is well worth seeking out.

Gull origins

The 1928 King's Cup air race was staged from Hendon on 20 July and one of the competitors was EWP, flying an Avro Avian. That event and others provided the means to generate the contacts needed to begin the manufacture of a new sort of aeroplane. By the following year EWP was at Shoreham, piloting the Hendy Hobo single-seater on its maiden flight. This machine was designed by Basil Balfour 'Hendy' Henderson who, along with Horace Albert Miles (no relation to the Miles brothers), had patented a wooden cantilever wing. The gospel according to EWP – and there is no reason to doubt him – is that the format and detailing of the next Hendy product, the two-seat Type 302, was totally down to him. EWP paid Henderson and Miles as design sub-contractors on the project, which he financed and oversaw. Parnall was chosen to build the 302 and the agreement was made directly by EWP, not through Hendy. Ken Wixey, in his *Parnall Aircraft since 1914*, makes no mention of this, although he notes EWP as the 302's first owner. EWP carried out the maiden flight of the 302 and it looked every inch the Gull progenitor. (See Chapter 29 for more on Hendy and the 302.)

Articles and books attributing Henderson as the designer were countered by EWP. In the same manner, writers declaring Rowland Henry Bound – Percival's chief draughtsman from the start of the company – as the creator of the production-standard Gull received broadsides from EWP. In both cases, while others might carry out the detail work – in part or in whole – EWP was initiator, financer and overseer, so in every way it was *his* project.

EWP approached Saunders-Roe at East Cowes with a proposal for a three-engined mailplane with the potential to become a small airliner. A joint venture was initiated and the resulting Mailplane was first flown from Somerton, near Cowes, in early 1932. Striving to set up on his own to create the definitive Gull, EWP sold his share in the Mailplane. Design rights were vested in Saro associate Spartan Aircraft, and the much modified Cruiser airliner entered limited production in 1932 – see Chapter 32.

A flock of Gulls

Taking everything that he had learned from the Type 302, EWP conceived the Gull. Lacking premises, he sought a sub-contractor to make the prototype. British Aircraft Company (BAC), a glider specialist at Maidstone, was his choice and in March 1932 EWP again presided over the maiden flight. As much a businessman as a pilot and designer, EWP bit the bullet and committed to constructing a batch while he whipped up orders. Although BAC had done a good job on the prototype, the company was not capable of series production and EWP signed up with Parnall in 1932 for two dozen. The investment paid off, the two/three-seat Gull was soon in demand.

Percival Aircraft was formed at Gravesend in 1933 and the first Gull built in the Kent factory was ready in the summer of 1934. By that time Bound had left and he was replaced as chief draughtsman by Arthur A Bage. Kicking off his long career with Frederick Koolhoven at British Aerial Transport in 1919, Bage progressed through the drawing offices of Boulton and Paul, Gloster and Handley Page before he joined Percival: EWP had chosen wisely. Bage detailed all the Percival types through to the Proctor crew trainer. Differences with EWP erupted in May 1939 and Bage walked out. He returned three months later and the nature of his departure is probably explained by his appointment as chief *designer*.

A 1936 Percival advert extolling the achievements of the Gull family and the Gull's ability to 'Treat continents like counties'. Illustrated is the prototype Vega Gull carrying the erroneous registration G-AEAD that it wore briefly: it was actually G-AEAB. *KEC*

Above: Alex Henshaw and Mew Gull G-AEXF in their element at a British air race in 1937. *KEC*

Top: Jean Batten (centre) and her Gull Six G-ADPR en route to New Zealand in record time, October 1936. *KEC*

On 22 March 1934 EWP was at the controls of another prototype, the diminutive Mew Gull single-seat racer. Six were produced, their shape altering with the needs and whims of each owner. The achievements of the Mew Gulls – a 'mew' being another name for a common gull – could fill a book, but are crowned by the exploits of Alex Henshaw and G-AEXF. Piloting this machine Henshaw won the 1938 King's Cup, held at Hatfield over a 1,066-mile course, at 236mph. Alex turned his mind to long-distance record-breaking, setting his sights on an out-and-back flight to the Cape of Good Hope, South Africa. Taking off from Gravesend on 5 February 1939, he reached the Cape, some 6,000 miles distant, in forty hours. He stayed in Cape Town a mere twenty-seven hours before coming back – he was eleven minutes *slower* on the return leg! He broke a string of point-to-point records in many classes. (Today, a much rebuilt G-AEXF, owing very little to the original, is part of the Shuttleworth Collection at Old Warden.)

As regards the Gull family, the next step was the four-seat Vega Gull, which appeared in November 1935. This attracted the RAF, ordering a dozen for communications duties from late 1938. Other than orders for Vega Gulls for use by Air Attachés in Berlin and Buenos Aires in 1937, this was the first major contract with the British military. It was not the last; the Vega Gull-based Proctor fully militarised crew trainer appeared in 1939, changing the prospects of the company.

Luton and war

By 1936 it was clear that Percival had outgrown Gravesend and EWP hunted for a new home. Luton council was busy establishing a municipal airport and there were deals to be done. In September EWP secured a ninety-nine-year lease and the construction of a purpose-built assembly hall commenced. Percival moved in during January 1937 and Luton Airport (today London Luton Airport) officially opened in July 1938. Percival's first twin, the Q.6 six-passenger monoplane, available with retractable or fixed undercarriage, had its maiden flight on 14 September 1937. It was followed by another twenty-six: very likely there would have been more had not the war intervened.

As noted earlier, in late 1940 EWP left Percival and his later career will be examined in due course. The growth of Percival was such that the engineering firm Hunting and Son acquired it in September 1944, leaving it to trade under its well-known name. Hunting was determined to enter the aviation business and did not rule out other purchases. To this end a holding company, Hunting Aviation Management Ltd, was inaugurated in November 1944.

A proctor is a university teacher and that name was chosen for the winner of Specification 20/38 seeking a three-seat communications aircraft. The first Proctor I flew on 8 October 1939 and was followed by Mk.II and Mk.III radio trainers. In 1943 Arthur

A Hills-built Proctor line-up in early 1944. In the foreground is Mk.IV NP229, beyond that Mk.IIIs. *Percival*

A Prentice bound for the Argentine Air Force, posing for the camera on a sortie out of Luton in 1949. *Percival*

A superb Q.6 trio in 1938. Top to bottom: King Ghazi I of Iraq's YI-ROH, the prototype G-AEYE and Sir Philip Sassoon's G-AFFD. *Fox-Delta* survives and is under restoration to fly again. *Percival*

Bage redesigned the Proctor by lengthening and deepening the fuselage, creating a generous four-seater that could also take the increasingly bulky radio sets used by the heavy bomber force. From 1941 manufacture of the Proctor was sub-contracted to woodworkers F Hills and Son at Trafford Park in Manchester; the final examples being completed in the summer of 1945. The Proctors needed to move out as space was needed, Percival itself having become a sub-contractor, building more than 1,000 Airspeed Oxford crew trainers and then 245 de Havilland (DH) Mosquitos.

Percival sub-contracts

Type	Total	From	To
Airspeed Oxford I, II, V	1,355	1939	1944
de Havilland Mosquito	245*	1944	1946
*195 B.XVI, 50 PR.34.			

Next generation

With the return of peace, Percival set to reconditioning demobbed Proctors but, in a brave move, created a civil version of the RAF's Mk.IV, the Mk.V. Cheap war surplus stocks, everything from jerkins and boots to motorcycles and Douglas Dakotas, were flooding the market and giving post-war economies the world over real problems in re-establishing peacetime industry. Despite this the Proctor V did well and 147 were built, greatly assisting the transition to the next generation.

Specification T.23/43 had been bubbling for some time as a replacement for the venerable DH Tiger Moth basic trainer. Originally requiring a wooden airframe, by mid-1945 T.23/43 was to be all-metal, fully aerobatic, capable of cold weather operation and easily adapted for instrument or radio training. The ambitious 'spec'

also wanted a three-seater, with an instructor and pupil side-by-side and another trainee observing from the rear: this overpopulated option was not used in service.

Percival proposed the portly-looking P.40 that, with an all-up weight of 4,200lb, was a giant against the Tiger's dainty 1,700lb. Five prototypes were approved in the face of strong opposition. Called Prentice, an archaic version of 'apprentice', the first example flew at Luton on 31 March 1946 and after some aerodynamic tweaks deliveries to the RAF started in November 1947. Blackburn was awarded an order for 125 to tide the Brough factory through a low spot and Hindustan Aircraft in India took out a licence.

Percival, to Prentice

From	To	Total	Name/Designation	Type	Engine(s)	Notes
1932	1937	47	Gull	Tourer	1 x DH Gipsy Major	[1]
1934	1937	6	Mew Gull	Racer	1 x DH Gipsy Six	
1935	1939	89	Vega Gull	Tourer	1 x DH Gipsy Six	
1937	1939	27	Q.6	Light transport	2 x DH Gipsy Six	
1939	1948	986	Proctor I to V	Trainer/Comms	1 x DH Gipsy Queen	[2]
1946	1953	534	Prentice	Trainer	1 x DH Gipsy Queen	[3]

Based upon *On the Wings of a Gull – Percival and Hunting Aircraft* by David W Gearing. **[1]** Prototype built by British Aircraft Co, Maidstone. Initial production (24, *perhaps* 22) by Parnall at Yate. **[2]** Includes 812 Mk.Is to IVs sub-contracted to F Hills and Sons, Trafford Park/Barton. Other than three conversions from MK.IVs, the Proctor V was a from-new tourer, built from late 1945. **[3]** Includes 125 sub-contracted to Blackburn, 15 assembled by Hindustan Aircraft, Bangalore, India from Percival-built kits and 35 new-build under licence by Hindustan.

Versatile twin

Percival needed more than trainers in its portfolio and it embarked on a private-venture, twin-engined, five-passenger, general-purpose, high-wing monoplane. The Merganser (a diving duck) was first flown on 9 May 1947 but deemed to be too small and underpowered for the market. All this was rectified with the larger Prince with Alvis Leonides radials, which took to the air on 13 May 1948. This had great potential, attracting orders as a corporate transport, survey platform and mini-airliner. It was also ordered by the Fleet Air Arm as the Sea Prince crew trainer and communications type. The RAF was also tempted, adopting the Pembroke transport version. This endorsement generated export contracts, including the Luftwaffe. A civil version of the Pembroke, the President, only brought in a handful of orders. The Prince/Pembroke family was a good earner, the last one being handed over in 1959.

Bage left Luton in 1948, bound for Avro at Woodford: he retired in 1963 and died in 1987. Taking over from Bage, with the title of technical director and chief engineer, was Leslie George Frise, the man who had designed the exceptional Bristol Beaufighter, among others. The story of this huge talent is described in Chapter 11.

The company was renamed Hunting Percival Aircraft on 25 April 1954. This was a midway position for dropping the 'Percival' element and on 5 December 1957 the business became Hunting Aircraft Ltd.

Merganser G-AHMH in 1947. *Percival*

The first Pembroke C.52 for the Royal Swedish Air Force parked near Luton's control tower in late 1954. *Percival*

Tip-drive and blown flaps

Percival was tempted by rotary-winged flight and established a helicopter division in 1950, headed up by deputy chief designer D J Moore. The Ministry of Supply was favouring tip-driven helicopters and Fairey was expending vast amounts of time and money on the Gyrodyne system. Rotor tip power required the development of a gas generator that would probably not have any other industrial application. Creating such a powerplant was full of risk, but D Napier and Son was looking for new projects after its Eland turboprop failed to find a market. Napier's test department shared Luton with Percival, so a tie-up was inevitable. Both pitched for EH.125D, a requirement for a tip-jet driven experimental helicopter with potential to become a ten-passenger transport.

The rotund P.74 was rolled out on 2 December 1955. It was behind schedule; the two 754shp Napier Oryx gas generators were delayed and the transmission and main rotors had to be rethought. Ground runs revealed that it was never going to get airborne and the ministry pulled the plug in February 1956.

The curious-looking P.74, XK889, minus its main and tail rotors, 1953. *Percival*

The P.74 was the company's first dedicated research contract and its next one turned out to be the last new type it completed, the H.126 jet-flap research test bed. Jet-flaps bled air out of the trailing edge of the wings to either replace a conventional jet exhaust or complement it. In May 1959 two H.126s were ordered, although the second one was never completed. Powered by a Bristol Siddeley Orpheus 805 turbojet, the H.126 was propelled via two outlets low down on each side of the fuselage, a rear exhaust and through two ducts under each wing. It first flew on 26 March 1963 and had a relatively short trials life including evaluation in the USA by NASA. The oddly shaped one-off is displayed at the RAF Museum, Cosford.

Covered in tufting to highlight slow-speed airflow, the H.126 in 1963. *Hunting*

Trainer evolution

The RAF was disappointed with the Prentice, largely because too much had been asked of it at the expense of performance. Percival had been given a clear run with the type, having beaten the opposition at the blueprint stage, but when it came to its replacement there was a fly-off between the P.56 and the Handley Page HPR.2. The prototype Provost (mentor, or overseer) first flew on 23 February 1950 and won an RAF order in February 1951. Deliveries began in the summer of 1953 and exports took the final production figure beyond 400. The last Provosts were handed over to the Irish Air Corps in 1960.

With the Provost, the RAF had taken the first step to revolutionise its training regimen. Students went from the Provost through to the DH Vampire T.11 jet, but the aim was for what was known as 'all-through' tuition. Trainees would start on a basic jet, graduating to the two-seat Hawker Hunter for the advanced phase. Practical thinking from Frise and his team used as much of the Provost as possible, including the wings and tail 'feathers'. Choosing the AS Viper turbojet was a marriage made in heaven. Originally intended as a 'throw away' engine for the Australian Government Aircraft Factory Jindivik target drone, the Viper proved to be exceptionally reliable and adaptive.

The prototype had its maiden flight on 26 June 1954. Luton's pre-emptive thinking paid off handsomely. A batch of ten Jet Provost T.1s was evaluated by 2 Flying Training School at Hullavington. Two parallel courses were carefully monitored, one set of pupils doing their 'basics' on piston-engined Provosts, the others on what universally became known as 'JPs'. The experiment was a resounding success, Plt Off R T Foster becoming the world's first military pilot to go solo on a jet on 17 October 1955. The RAF was sold on the idea and ordered production-standard T.3s in 1957, followed by further improved T.4s in late 1961. It also appealed to overseas air arms; the last JPs left Luton, bound for Iraq, in April 1965.

It was the Jet Provost programme that most attracted the British Aircraft Corporation (BAC) to take a 70% stake in Hunting Aircraft in September 1960 for £1.3 million – when Hunting acquired Percival in 1944 it paid £192,000. In January 1964 the remaining Hunting holding was bought out and the factory became the Luton Division of BAC. As Chapter 13 explains, Hunting's further development ideas for the 'JP' and turning its H.107 short-range twin jetliner design study into the winning One-Eleven played a significant role in keeping BAC afloat after the TSR.2 had been cancelled. It was ironic that in order to survive that blow the Luton plant was a casualty and its doors were closed on 31 July 1966. Local car builder Vauxhall took over the plant.

Provosts and Princes/Pembrokes under construction at Luton in the mid-1950s. *Hunting*

Jet Provost T.1 XD693 and Provost T.1 WV625 both of 2 Flying Training School at Hullavington and part of the 'all-through' evaluation of 1955. *Percival*

Hunting Percival, Hunting and Edgar Percival

From	To	Total	Name/Designation	Type	Engine(s)	Notes
1947	-	1	Merganser	Light transport	2 x DH Gipsy Queen	
1948	1959	207	Prince/Pembroke	Light transport	2 x Alvis Leonides	[1]
1950	1960	464	Provost	Trainer	1 x Alvis Leonides	
1954	1956	14	Jet Provost T.1, T.2	Trainer	1 x AS Viper	[2]
1958	1965	461	Jet Provost T.3, T.4	Trainer	1 x AS Viper	[3]
1955	-	1	P.74 helicopter	Research	2 x Napier Oryx	
1955	1960	28	EP.9 Prospector	Utility	1 x Lycoming O-480	[4]
1963	-	1	H.126	Research	1 x BS Orpheus	

Based upon *On the Wings of a Gull – Percival and Hunting Aircraft* by David W Gearing. Note: Gearing defines the Prince series as 'Percival' and the Pembroke series as 'Hunting'; to keep the twin family together, they have all been listed in this table. [1] Includes Mk.1 and 2 Sea Prince comms/crew trainer, RAF comms Pembroke and its civil equivalent, the President. [2] Prototypes and pre-production batch. [3] Includes export versions. See Chapter 13 for T.5 and Strikemaster. [4] Twenty-four built by Edgar Percival Aircraft at Stapleford, three transferred to Lancashire Aircraft Corp and completed Samlesbury. Four built by Lancashire Aircraft, one not flown.

Above: A pair of Jet Provost T.4s of the Manby-based College of Air Warfare's Macaws demonstration team at Colerne in July 1968. *Roy Bonser*

Right: Lancashire Prospector G-APWZ flying from Shoreham in mid-1983. *KEC*

Percival after Percival

When EPW left the company he founded in March 1940 he was not through with design. For the remainder of the war he was engaged in tasks for the British government on either side of the Atlantic – most likely to do with the Lend-Lease operation. Post-war he took US citizenship and is believed to have worked on guided weapons development. In the early 1950s he was in New Zealand acting as a consultant on aerial application systems for seed and fertiliser. During this time he came up with the P.9 – later designated EP.9 – a simple, rugged and versatile aircraft capable of crop-dusting and utility work.

In 1954 EPW established Edgar Percival Aircraft at Stapleford, Essex, to produce his EP.9. The prototype of this 'bushplane' first flew on 21 December 1955 and a batch of twenty was commenced. Rights to the design were acquired by Samlesbury Engineering Ltd, which revived the name Lancashire Aircraft Corporation (LAC) in October 1958. The EP.9 was remarketed as the Prospector but only another seven followed before LAC closed down in 1961. Edgar Wikner Percival, trilby wearer, creator of the lovely Gulls and the outstanding Mew Gulls, died on 21 January 1984, aged 87.

CHAPTER THIRTY-ONE

Government Issue

**Royal Aircraft Factory
1911 to 1918**

'…perhaps only a government organisation could perform the academic investigation necessary to determine of what use the new science of aviation might be to the military forces.' Paul Hare

WITH MORE THAN SIX DECADES separating them, British Aerospace and the Royal Aircraft Factory would seem to have little in common other than the manufacture of flying machines. Both were government owned, both arguably monopolies and both lasted less than a decade in that form. British Aerospace was the result of the nationalisation of the British Aircraft Corporation and Hawker Siddeley, among others, in 1977; eight years later the sale of its shares back into the private sector was completed. The Royal Aircraft Factory could trace its origins to the late Victorian era and it functioned as the aeronautical equivalent of bodies such as the Royal Arsenal, headquartered at Woolwich, or the Royal Dockyards, which originated at Portsmouth.

From 1911, what became the Royal Aircraft Factory determined that it needed to build aeroplanes and aero engines. This enraged the nascent aircraft manufacturers, who were struggling to gain a foothold in the only sizable marketplace available, the British military. Calls of 'unfair' became more organised and in 1918 the Royal Aircraft Factory gave up building aeroplanes to concentrate on research and development.

The Royal Air Force Museum's F.E.2b was the subject of a two-decade restoration project. It is based on an unfinished nacelle built by sub-contractor Richard Garrett and Sons of Leiston. *Dave Barrel*

Her Majesty's Balloon Factory arose out of the School of Ballooning at Aldershot on 1 April 1897 and seven years later began to relocate to Farnborough. To depict its changing role, it became His Majesty's Aircraft Factory, occasionally referred to as the Army Aircraft Factory, on 26 April 1911. The choice of the word 'aircraft' instead of the then more popular 'aeroplane' reflected dealings with balloons, airships and kites as well as the new-fangled fixed-wing machines. From April 1912 the prefix 'Royal' was granted. Inside and outside of Farnborough, the organisation was referred to as 'The Factory' and that is how this chapter will refer to the institution.

First to fly

From April 1904 American-born Samuel Franklin Cody was teaching the handling of man-lifting kites at Farnborough, as an extension of The Factory's role instructing in the art of operating gas-filled observation balloons. Army officer Lt John William Dunne, pioneer of swept wings, began experiments at Farnborough thanks to an arrangement with the War Office. Construction of an airship hangar began in 1904 and on 10 September 1907 *Nulli Secundus* – second to none – had its first flight from Farnborough.

In 1907 Cody decided to fit one of his kites with a 15hp French-made Buchet engine. This device was destined never to take a man aloft, but it did engage in *pilot-less* flights over Farnborough Common. The next step was the British Army Aircraft No. 1, which Cody piloted on 16 October 1908 to make the first powered, controlled and sustained flight in Britain. Despite this epoch-making achievement, in April 1909 the decision was made to stop all experimentation in wing-borne aviation at The Factory. Cody and Dunne were given their marching orders, although both were allowed to keep their aeroplanes, less engines, despite having been financed, at least in part, by the state. Dunne headed for Kent and the much more receptive Short brothers at Eastchurch. Cody persuaded the authorities to let him to stay at Farnborough, developing his flying machines in a ramshackle hangar on Laffan's Plain.

Mervyn Joseph Pius O'Gorman, superintendent of The Factory, 1909 to 1916. *Royal Aircraft Establishment*

Stealth manufacturer

The 'no aeroplanes' rubric was reversed within months and on 19 October 1909 the 38-year-old Mervyn Joseph Pius O'Gorman was appointed as the new superintendent of The Factory. With an engineering degree from Dublin, O'Gorman had worked in the electrical and motor vehicle industries. In his superb study, *The Royal Aircraft Factory*, Paul Hare sums up O'Gorman's objectives: '… to conduct experiments, research and tests; to prepare specifications; to analyse the results of tests upon trial designs, and to reply to scientific queries, proposals and theories which the civil and military authorities, or any official body, put to it.' The 'civil and military' bit was encouraging, but soon to be eclipsed by world events. Hare zooms in on the notion of 'trial designs', O'Gorman was convinced that the establishment needed to *build* aeroplanes and not just acquire them; otherwise it would only be a voyeur pontificating with theory but no real experience.

O'Gorman began to expand the workshop facilities at Farnborough and to find the right people to make his vision happen. He was aware that the authorities might well be wary of building experimental aircraft, let alone volume manufacture. Hare explains how the Irishman tackled this problem: 'anxious to conduct experiments with aeroplanes in different configurations, O'Gorman settled upon a subterfuge with which to bypass this tiresome restriction. To this end he requested permission to include, in the repair of the wrecked Blériot XII already at Farnborough, certain improvements and modifications so as to reconstruct the machine on more modern lines. Since the Master General of Ordnance was almost certainly ignorant of what was actually intended, and was influenced, no doubt, by O'Gorman's unaffected enthusiasm, such permission was eventually granted.' Part of his diversionary tactics was the creation of a series of classifications for Factory aeroplanes that *implied* an origin beyond the Farnborough fence – see the table.

Aircraft Factory/Royal Aircraft Factory type classifications

A.E.	Armed Experimental
B.E.	Blériot Experimental – tractor biplane, general purpose. After Louis Blériot, the trans-Channel exponent of the *monoplane!*
B.S.	Blériot Scout – tractor biplane, single seat
C.E.	Coastal Experimental
F.E.	Farman Experimental – pusher biplane. After the Farman brothers, Henri and Maurice
N.E.	Night-flying Experimental
R.E.	Reconnaissance Experimental – tractor biplane
S.E.	Santos Experimental – canard biplane. After Alberto Santos-Dumont. Later Scouting Experimental
T.E.	Tatin Experimental – monoplane with pusher propeller, behind tail. Frenchman Victor Tatin designed a monoplane of such format and it was exhibited in 1908; it is believed not to have flown. Despite this, the T.E.1 designed at Farnborough in 1917 was a conventional, two-seat, tractor biplane. Construction of the first of a batch of three was abandoned in mid-1917
H.R.E.	Hydro-Reconnaissance Experimental – floatplane

HM Aircraft Factory, Farnborough, including the airship sheds 1913. *Peter Green Collection*

The de Havilland era

O'Gorman turned to the motor industry for his first major appointment. In January 1910 he 'poached' Frederick 'Fred' Michael Green, working for the British arm of Daimler and appointed him as 'Engineer – Design'. A 'Designer – Pilot' was also needed. Within a year Green had met Geoffrey de Havilland and, after he had demonstrated his second biplane, The Factory had filled that vacancy. O'Gorman arranged for de Havilland's biplane to be bought by the War Office and he bestowed on it the first of his 'deception' designations: F.E.1 – Farman Experimental No. 1.

O'Gorman was determined to experiment with canard layouts – his Santos Experimental category – despite de Havilland's disastrous experience with his first biplane in 1909. So de Havilland's debut 'Factory' design was the S.E.1. As far as the War Office was concerned, this was a rebuild of an unfortunate Blériot XII that came to grief on Salisbury Plain around September 1910. The Blériot's flying characteristics were reflected in its nickname, *The Man-Killer*. de Havilland wrote in his autobiography *Sky Fever* that: 'The only vestige of the *Man-Killer* in the new canard, the S.E.1, was the engine [a 60hp ENV].'

The S.E.1 canard, Geoffrey de Havilland's first design for The Factory, 1911. *Royal Aircraft Establishment*

O'Gorman's assistant, Lt Theodore J Ridge, learned to fly on the F.E.1 and on 15 August 1911 he crash-landed it, very likely ending its flying days. Three days later Ridge was badgering de Havilland to let him have a go in the S.E.1 but was advised that it was not for a novice. *Sky Fever* provides the conclusion: 'He had only been in the air five minutes when he stalled and spun into the ground, dying within minutes. So the tradition of *Man-Killer* was sustained.'

de Havilland carried out the maiden flight of the F.E.2 – a much-improved version of his second biplane – on 16 August, the day *after* Ridge wrecked the F.E.1. Yet The Factory maintained that the F.E.2 was no more than a *rebuild* of the F.E.1! A two-seat pusher, the F.E.2 was a major step forward: it soon appeared in floatplane guise and later carried a Maxim gun in the nose. It was refined and enlarged in 1913 and the definitive F.E.2a family – really a brand new type – appeared in January 1915, becoming a practical bomber that was widely produced.

After the pusher F.Es and the S.E.1, de Havilland turned to the tractor format and began the steps that created the first practical military aircraft, the incredible B.E.2 family. Once again, the wool was pulled over the eyes of authority by declaring the B.E.1 as a 'rebuild' of The Duke of Westminster's wrecked Voisin, yet only its Wolseley engine was utilised. The B.E.1 was a tandem two-seater with docile flying characteristics, setting the biplane format for decades to come.

The more refined B.E.2 flew on 1 February 1912. That August military aircraft trials were held at Larkhill on Salisbury Plain and the B.E.2 looked every inch the winner. But The Factory could not enter it because it didn't make aeroplanes and O'Gorman was one of the judges. Cody's archaic-looking Military Biplane was the victor. To emphasize the B.E.2's qualities, de Havilland and Major Frederick Hugh Sykes climbed to 10,560ft in the early hours of 12 August to set an altitude record. The B.E.2 went on to be mass produced by a barrage of manufacturers. The B.E.3 and its follow-ons, the B.E.4, '5 and '6 general-purpose two-seaters, commenced testing in May 1912, all flown and created by de Havilland. The ultimate development of this incredible airframe was the B.E.12 of 1915, which brought the total of machines derived from the B.E.1 to just over 4,000.

In February 1913 de Havilland began testing B.S.1, the world's first single-seat scout, a type soon to be widely referred to as a 'fighter'. With assistance from Henry Folland and Sydney James Waters, de Havilland had produced a sleek biplane that could reach 91mph and climb at 900ft per minute on just 100hp. While testing the B.S.1 on 27 March 1913 de Havilland entered a flat spin and ended up in hospital with the aircraft wrecked. In typical 'Factory' procedure, the B.S.1 re-emerged almost totally rebuilt as the S.E.2 in October 1913. As Chapter 17 shows, de Havilland was sidelined into the Farnborough-based Aeronautical Inspection Directorate and began the hunt for another job. He became the Aircraft Manufacturing Company's designer in May 1914 in the next phase of his glittering career.

A B.E.2b of 1914; the pilot sat in the rear cockpit with the observer in front. *KEC*

Trials and triumphs

A look at the table reveals that in 1913 a string of prototypes appeared. With a 'private sector' firm that would probably have indicated impending financial collapse. Several of these machines gave rise to The Factory's 'Heath Robinson' image, but were no worse, or weird, than other prototypes generated in the wider industry. To use a modern phrase, Farnborough was supposed to 'push the boundaries' and it did that through O'Gorman's 'trial designs'. While it was advantageous to create a type that had a military application and went on to production in large numbers, that was not the principal aim.

The aero engine table shows that The Factory was also busy devising and building powerplants. Two engines emerged in 1916 that went no further with The Factory but had a major influence on the post-war industry. The 14-cylinder, 2-row radial R.A.F.8 was the launch pad for the Armstrong Siddeley (AS) Motors aircraft division, powering a wide range of types for a decade from the early 1920s. Napier's incredible 12-cylinder, 'W' format Lion was influenced by the R.A.F.10. Like AS, Napier was set up by the Lion, which first appeared in 1918 and was still in production in the early 1930s.

Royal Aircraft Factory aero engines

Name	Type/Format	From	Application*	Notes
R.A.F.1	V-8	1913	Airco DH.6	
R.A.F.2	9-cy radial	1913	R.A.F. B.E.8	
R.A.F.3a	V-12	1915	R.A.F. R.E.7	
R.A.F.4	V-12	1914	R.A.F. F.E.2b	[1]

Based upon *The Royal Aircraft Factory* by Paul R Hare. * Typical, or only, use. Engines that did not find an aircraft application are not listed. **[1]** R.A.F.5 pusher version of F.4.

As well as de Havilland, the other most prominent designer at The Factory was Henry 'Harry' Folland, who started at Farnborough in 1912 and went on to devise the exceptional S.E.5a. Along with the Sopwith Camel, the S.E.5a was the best British fighter fielded during the Great War. If Farnborough had done no more than sponsor this machine, the establishment's creation would have been worthwhile. Folland's highly streamlined S.E.4 of 1914 – by then the 'S.E.' standing for 'Scouting Experimental' – was the stepping stone to the S.E.5. The S.E.4 capitalised on de Havilland's B.S.1 and S.E.2 and among its innovations were 'I'-section interplane struts and a spinner with an integral cooling fan for the two-row Gnome rotary. Folland also came up with a clear-vision canopy but this was never taken aloft: *real* pilots sat in open cockpits! Typical of thinking at The Factory, Folland's next design – an entirely new machine – was designated S.E.4a and had its maiden flight on 23 June 1915. The S.E.5 was initially flown with a 150hp engine, but the availability of the 200hp Hispano-Suiza V-8 brought about the winning formula and in this form the prototype S.E.5a first flew in January 1917. Folland's subsequent career is charted in Chapter 20.

Having assisted de Havilland on the B.S.1 and the S.E.2, Folland and Waters collaborated on The Factory's only twin-engined design to fly, the F.E.4 of early 1916. Underpowered, it failed to meet both of the demanding requirements made of it: ground-attack with a Coventry Ordnance Works gun that fired 'one-pounder' shells or long-range bomber.

By 1906 Waters was a draughtsman for Napier, in those days most famous for motor car and boat engines. He had gravitated to Daimler – a fertile ground for Factory recruitment – by 1911 and worked as a designer-engineer at Farnborough from 1912 until 1917. Waters joined Hawker in 1923, graduating to assistant chief designer at Gloster in 1926 under his former Factory colleague, Folland. He departed Gloster in 1929, crossing the Atlantic to take the post of technical engineer with the newly founded de Havilland Canada.

O'Gorman's credo that experience was better than theory was applied by Edward 'Ted' Teshmaker Busk, Farnborough's assistant engineer–physicist. Busk argued that the best way he could put his ideas on stability to the test was in the air and so de Havilland taught him to fly. In mid-1913 the two-seat R.E.1 biplane designed with inputs from de Havilland, Folland and Busk started trials. Modifications to the rudder, the wing 'stagger' and the incorporation of ailerons instead of wing warping allowed Busk, on 25 November 1913, to fly for 7 miles without touching the ailerons, turning purely on the rudder. He had created the first inherently stable aircraft. This knowledge allowed the redesign of the B.E.2b and created the much-evolved B.E.2c. Tragically, on 5 November 1914 Busk was killed in a B.E.2; he was just 28 and had so much more to contribute to the study of aerodynamics.

After graduating in engineering at Durham, John Kenworthy started work in The Factory's drawing office in 1911. (This Kenworthy is not to be confused with Reginald Watson Kenworthy, Blackburn test pilot.) Kenworthy conceived the B.E.3 of 1912 and, via such experimentals as the B.E.7, B.E.8 and the R.E.5, arrived at the R.E.7 of 1915 and its definitive development, the R.E.8. The prototype R.E.8 first flew on 17 June 1916 and just over 4,000 were built. Rhyming slang based on its designation produced the nickname 'Harry Tate' after the stage name of Ronald Macdonald Hutchison, a well-known music hall entertainer of the time.

Left: Of the thirty-five S.E.5as handed on to the Royal Australian Air Force in 1921, A2-36 was converted into a two-seater trainer with the fuel storage moved to twin tanks on the upper wings. *Peter Green Collection*

Below: Siddeley Deasy-built R.E.8 E254 *Marple*, paid for by the residents of the Cheshire town of the same name. *KEC*

Among the R.E.8 team was John 'Jimmy' Lloyd, who carried out the stress calculations. Lloyd went on to design the incredible Armstrong Whitworth AW.52 jet flying wing of 1947. Another 'name' at Farnborough was Harold Bolas, later Parnall's chief designer. Kenworthy moved to the aviation division of Austin in 1918, creating the Greyhound fighter and the Kestrel and Whippet light aircraft. He was chief designer with ADC Aircraft from 1925 before conceiving the Redwing biplane tourer for Robinson Aircraft in 1930. John Kenworthy died in November 1940, aged 57.

The last three designs by Factory staff that were flown were all pushers. Farnborough's only flying boat, the C.E.1, adopted a format that would last into the 1930s, but the N.E.1 and its development, the A.E.3 Ram, were both throwbacks to the earliest days of the Great War. Ironically in 1918, The Factory, which throughout the conflict had supplied abundant work for the 'free enterprise' aircraft industry, reversed its position and became a sub-contractor. Pressures to build the potentially war-winning Handley Page O/400 and Vickers Vimy bombers absorbed the increasingly available production capacity at Farnborough.

The last Factory design to be completed, the anachronistic A.E.3 Ram pusher of 1918. It carried two Lewis machine guns in the nose. *Peter Green Collection*

Royal Aircraft Factory/Establishment sub-contracts

Type	Total	From	To
Handley Page O/400	24	1918	1919
Vickers Vimy	2	1918	

From all sides

In Volume One of *The War in the Air* by Sir Walter Alexander Raleigh (Oxford University Press, 1928) there is an eloquent explanation of the tensions between The Factory and the 'free market' manufacturers: 'There was a misunderstanding, which after a time became acute, between the factory and the private makers of aircraft. The factory, zealous for the public interest, believed that it could best serve their interest by encouraging, supervising, and co-ordinating the efforts of the makers. The makers, jealous of supervision and control, did not accept that view.

'A wise judgement will be slow to blame either. The officials of the factory were strong in the knowledge that their work was disinterested and aimed only at the public good. The makers, remembering that progress in aviation had come chiefly by way of private enterprise, feared the paralysing effect of official control, and the habitual tendency of officials to extend their ambitions and their powers. The makers, in short, dreaded a government monopoly. A difference of this kind, even when it is gently and considerately handled, always furnishes a happy hunting ground for the political agitator and the grievance-monger.'

If there was disquiet within the industry, there was thunder in parliament. During a speech in March 1916, the flamboyant Noel Pemberton Billing, the independent member for East Hertfordshire, a former Royal Naval Air Service (RNAS) pilot and the founder of manufacturer Supermarine, let rip that the airmen of the Royal Flying Corps (RFC) were 'Fokker fodder'. His implication was that the B.E.2c was an outmoded death trap and that The Factory was deficient in its continued production. In quick order two inquiries were launched: Sir Richard Burbidge to examine the Factory's role and function and Mr Justice Clement Meacher Bailhache to look into the RFC's administration, command and equipment. During 1916 The Factory flew the prototypes of two aircraft that addressed most of the inadequacies of the RFC, the R.E.8 and the S.E.5, both already in the pipeline and unbidden by parliamentary debate.

In July Burbidge's report was released and it outlined the tasks that The Factory should be doing, *including* the manufacture of aircraft. Burbidge wanted to introduce a board of management to put the running of the organisation on a more business-like footing. The Air Board was strongly against this as The Factory was first and foremost a military body and such a committee would be inappropriate. The prospect of a more efficiently run Farnborough would have been anathema to Billing and the wider industry.

While the judgements of m'lud Bailhache were awaited, O'Gorman was replaced on 21 September 1916 by Henry Fowler. The story was that the Irishman's contract was nearly up and that he was being retained as a consultant. O'Gorman had laid the foundations of a vital research and development institution and was paying the price for inadequacies in co-ordinating what the RFC and RNAS needed with the products of The Factory and the industry. O'Gorman slid over to work with the Aircraft Manufacturing Company in November 1917. Mervyn Joseph Pius O'Gorman CB died on 16 March 1958, aged 87.

Bailhache's deliberations were published in December 1916. He recommended that Farnborough stop making aircraft and the initiation of a better procedure to turn the needs of the air arms into functioning hardware. Other than priority programmes, including the S.E.5a and the already mentioned O/400s and Vimys, aircraft construction began to wind down at Farnborough. Production figures are very difficult to pin down, but from 1912 to early 1919 The Factory built about 550 aircraft while contracts for close on 10,000 units were released to the industry at large. The contraction of the Factory's activities led to key personnel leaving to find employment within the 'free market', where they were welcomed with open arms.

A Zephyr 7, development airframe for the Airbus Defence and Space Farnborough-based high-altitude pseudo satellite programme. *Copyright and courtesy Airbus Defence and Space*

Partially spurred on by Billing, Burbidge and Bailhache, and acknowledging the spectacular growth of aviation as a means of national defence, on 3 January 1918 Lord Rothermere took up his post as the first Secretary of State for Air. The Air Ministry would act as the go-between for industry, the military and – in due course – the airlines.

In 1918 the Royal Aircraft Factory changed its name to the Royal Aircraft Establishment (RAE) to better reflect its role fostering research and development. In doing so the word 'Farnborough' became world famous as *the* centre of excellence for aeronautical progress, immeasurably benefitting all of Britain's industry.

Pioneering the stratosphere

Today's Farnborough would be almost unrecognisable to a resuscitated O'Gorman. He would remember the former balloon school building, home of the Farnborough Air Sciences Trust museum and dedicated to telling the incredible story in which O'Gorman played such an important part. During October 1992 British Aerospace – now BAE Systems – established its operating headquarters at Farnborough, recognising the airfield's heritage.

Although beyond the remit of this book, the 98ft wingspan Zephyr 'pseudo satellite', which has the potential to have its endurance measured in *months*, deserves a mention as it has brought aircraft construction back to Farnborough. Initially conceived by the RAE's successor, QinetiQ, the programme is now in the hands of Airbus Defence and Space. As well as development airframes, several Zephyrs have been ordered by the UK Ministry of Defence and at least one overseas customer. Airbus describes Zephyr as 'the world's first solar-electric, stratospheric unmanned aerial vehicle'. Farnborough is still pioneering.

Royal Aircraft Factory types

From	To	Total	Designation	Type	Engine(s)	Notes
1911	-	1	F.E.1	1-seat pusher	1 x DH/Iris	[1]
1911	1913	2	F.E.2	Armed, 2-seat pusher	1 x Gnome	[2]
1911	-	1	S.E.1	1-seat pusher	1 x ENV	
1912	-	1	B.E.1	Military GP	1 x Wolseley	
1912	1917	c.3,400	B.E.2a to 'g	Military GP	1 x R.A.F.1a	[3]
1912	-	1	B.E.5	Military GP	1 x ENV	[4]
1912	1913	50+	B.E.8	Military GP	1 x Gnome	[5]
1913	-	5	B.E.3, B.E.4	Military GP	1 x Gnome	
1913	-	1	B.E.7	Military GP	1 x Gnome	[6]
1913	-	1	B.S.1/SE.2	Scout	1 x Gnome	[7]
1913	-	1	F.E.3/A.E.1	Gun carrier, pusher	1 x Chenu	[8]
1913	-	2	R.E.1	2-seat recce	1 x Renault	
1913	-	1	R.E.2/H.R.E.2	2-seat recce	1 x Renault	
1913	-	1	R.E.3	2-seat recce	1 x Austro-Daimler	
1914	-	1	F.E.6 pusher	Gun carrier	1 x Austro-Daimler	[8]
1914	-	1	S.E.4	Scout	1 x Gnome	[9]
1914	-	24	R.E.5	2-seat recce	1 x Beardmore	
1915	1916	450	B.E.12	Armed recce	1 x R.A.F.4a	[10]
1915	1917	1,418	F.E.2a	2-seat fighter/bomber	1 x RR Eagle	[11]
1915	1916	282	F.E.8	Scout	1 x Gnome	[12]
1915	1916	233	R.E.7	2-seat recce	1 x Beardmore	[13]
1915	-	4	S.E.4a	Scout	1 x Gnome	[9]
1916	-	2	F.E.4 pusher	Gun-carrier/bomber	2 x R.A.F.4a	[8]
1916	1918	4,077	R.E.8	Recce/GP	1 x R.A.F.4a	[14]
1916	1920	c.5,370	S.E.5, S.E.5a	Fighter	1 x Hispano-Suiza	[15]
1917	-	3	F.E.9	2-seat fighter recce	1 x Hispano-Suiza	
1917	-	6	N.E.1 pusher	Gun carrier	1 x Hispano-Suiza	[8]
1918	-	2	C.E.1 pusher	Flying boat, pusher	1 x R.A.F.3a	
1918	-	3	A.E.3 Ram I/II	2-seat ground-attack	1 x Sunbeam Arab	[16]

Based upon *The Royal Aircraft Factory* by Paul R Hare. Unless noted, all tractor biplanes. With respect to Paul, as warned in the Introduction, production figures should be regarded as a guide only. **[1]** Geoffrey de Havilland's first successful machine, sold to War Office January 1911. **[2]** Second example with a Renault in 1913, *possibly* a rebuild of the original. An entirely different design to F.E.2a. **[3]** Production version of B.E.1.; sub-variants B.E.2a to 'g. Also sub-contracted to: Armstrong Whitworth; Barclay Curle, Glasgow; Beardmore, Blackburn; Bristol; British Caudron, Cricklewood; Coventry Ordnance Works (COW); Daimler, Coventry; William Denny, Dumbarton; Eastbourne Aviation, Eastbourne; Grahame-White; Handley Page; Hewlett and Blondeau, Luton; Joucques Aviation, London; Martinsyde, Napier and Miller, Old Kilpatrick; Robey, Lincoln; Ruston Proctor, Lincoln; Vickers; Vulcan Motor and Engineering, Southport; G and J Weir, Glasgow; Whitehead Aircraft, Richmond; Wolseley Motors, Birmingham. B.E.2c converted to B.E.9 with gunner's position *ahead* of the propeller, 1915. **[4]** B.E.2 based. **[5]** BE.3 and B.E.4 based. Also sub-contracted to: Bristol; COW; Vickers. **[6]** B.E.3 and B.E.4 based. **[7]** B.S.1 rebuilt as essentially similar S.E.2, 1913. **[8]** 'Gun carrier', specifically the 37mm COW gun. **[9]** See narrative. **[10]** Improved B.E.2, sub-variants B.E.12a and 'b. Sub-contracted to: COW; Daimler; Standard Motor, Coventry. **[11]** No 'relation' to F.E.2 of 1911. Sub-variants F.E.2b to 'h. Also sub-contracted to: Barclay Curle; Boulton Paul; Garrett and Sons, Leiston; Ransomes Sims and Jefferies, Ipswich; Alexander Stephen and Sons, Glasgow; G and J Weir. **[12]** Also sub-contracted to: Darracq, Vickers. **[13]** R.E.5-based. Sub-contracted to: Austin Motor Co, Birmingham; COW; D Napier and Sons, London; Siddeley Deasy Motor Car Co (SD), Coventry. **[14]** Also sub-contracted to: Austin; COW; Daimler; SD; Standard. Two converted to R.E.9 status, 1917. **[15]** One S.E.5a converted to S.E.5b. Also sub-contracted to: Air Navigation Co (previously Blériot and Spad Ltd), Addlestone; Austin; Martinsyde; Vickers; Whitehead, Wolseley. Eberhart Steel Products Co, Buffalo, New York, USA assembled about 60 S.E.5as, mostly from British spares holdings, c.1919–20. US machines were designated S.E.5E – note capital 'E'. **[16]** Only factory type to receive a name; as in a male, horned sheep; not – as has been written – its intended method of attack!

CHAPTER THIRTY-TWO

Last of the Leviathans

Saunders, Saro and Spartan
1917 to 1959

'We rarely took off with all ten engines working. On one occasion we took off on nine and came back on seven.'
Princess flight test observer

SAMUEL 'SAM' EDWARD SAUNDERS crafted beautiful boats at his yard on the River Medina on the Isle of Wight. He was known as 'Slippery Sam', but this was not derogatory, it was recognition of the smooth hulls he created, giving owners of a Saunders-built vessel a competitive edge. The Saunders family had been in that business since the middle of the 19th century, with premises near Goring-on-Thames in Oxfordshire. Saunders's big breakthrough was Consuta – from the Latin *consutum*, stitched – a process that he patented in 1898. Layers of laminated ply were bonded together with copper wire stitching, which created the smoothest of hulls that were also very robust. At first the process was laboriously carried out by hand but once he had devised sewing machinery, Consuta revolutionised the construction of all sorts of vessels. In 1908 S E Saunders Ltd (SESL) was established at the Columbine yard, close to the mouth of the Medina at East Cowes.

Thomas Sopwith, a skilled yachtsman, was well aware of Consuta's qualities and in 1912 he approached Sam Saunders to make the hull for his Bat Boat biplane amphibian. Lt Cdr Charles Dennistoun Burney adopted the technique for his experimental Bristol X.3 'hydroped' monoplane of 1914. The aviation applications grew: a contract to build hulls for White and Thompson No. 3 flying boats in 1914 eventually led to SESL manufacturing entire NT.2Bs at Cowes towards the end of the Great War. As well as hull sub-contracts the company's boat designers turned their skills to refining the shape of floats, this generated commissions from Shorts to build Type 184 and 320 floatplanes at Cowes.

The prototype Princess running past cruise liners at Southampton, circa 1953. *Saro*

Despite all this maritime expertise, it is ironic that the initial wartime sub-contract was for Avro 504 *landplanes* that were test flown from Somerton, south of West Cowes. This led to the first SESL aircraft, the T.1 trainer of 1917 designed by Henry Thomas, who had started at the Bristol drawing office in 1914, before joining the Royal Aircraft Factory at Farnborough. The last thing the military needed as the war came to a close was a trainer – the final Avro 504Ks left RAF service in the early 1930s – and Thomas turned his thoughts to more appropriate flying boats. Aged just 32, Henry Haberfield Thomas fell victim to the so-called 'Spanish flu' global pandemic and died on 17 October 1918.

Norman Macmillan at the helm of the Saunders Kittiwake on its first flight, 19 September 1920. *Peter Green Collection*

Vickers took a half-share in SESL in 1918, awarding a contract for three Valentia flying boat hulls, and the Cowes firm assembled and flight tested the prototype. Vickers was looking for an existing company to take on flying boat production and development. It transpired that SESL was not the answer and Vickers sold its holding in 1921. It found what it was looking for in the acquisition of Supermarine in 1928.

Previously with White and Thompson, Frederick Percy Hyde Beadle took over the drawing board and came up with the Kittiwake flying boat. This odd-looking three-bay biplane had a passenger area above and behind the flight deck and employed copious amounts of Consuta. In *Saunders and Saro Aircraft since 1917* Peter London quotes a description of the Kittiwake as an: 'Isle of Wight ferry boat with wings'. First flown on 19 September 1920, trials of the Kittiwake were a nightmare; it went no further and Saunders was looking for its third designer.

Having conceived the Duiker parasol monoplane and the Woodcock biplane fighter for Hawker, Bertram 'Bertie' Thomson signed up as chief designer with SESL in late 1923. Arriving at the same time was Henry Knowler, latterly assistant to William Oke Manning on English Electric's Kingston and Ayr flying boats, having started his career at Vickers in 1914. Thomson tackled the Medina commercial flying boat while Knowler created the tri-motor Valkyrie patrol flying boat, both appearing in 1926. Neither got beyond the prototype stage: Thomson departed and Knowler remained. Knowler took the helm as chief designer, staying with the company all of the way through to the giant Princess flying boat of 1952. In that year Knowler handed over to Maurice Brennan and took the post of technical director until he retired in 1956.

Saunders-Roe

Knowler's appointment came as SESL realised that the days of Consuta were over and that all-metal construction was the future. Knowler came up with a strong but simple system of running well-spaced parallel 'corrugations' externally along the fuselage, providing for a relatively smooth surface. Changing over from wood to metal would be expensive in new tooling and retraining personnel, and was taking place at a time of 'fallow' in terms of orders. An all-new prototype was a huge gamble and a hybrid was the answer: Knowler designed a new fuselage and fitted it to the wings, powerplant and tail surfaces of a Supermarine Southampton. Trials were far from promising: the structure needed further strengthening and it was not until the advent of the London in 1934 that the method was validated on large structures. The company needed more than flying boats in its product line and Knowler found time to create a private-venture single-seat fighter, the so-called 'Multi Gun' biplane. The biplane lost out in a competition that was eventually awarded in 1933 to the Gloster SS.19, the excellent Gauntlet.

Meanwhile, the resources, and prospects, of SESL were sapping away. In 1928 Edwin Alliott Verdon Roe had concluded a deal with the Armstrong Siddeley Development Company, which acquired the business he had founded – Avro. This allowed the pioneer aviator to indulge his long-held liking of flying boats and the 51-year-old Roe set about looking for a suitable marine aviation manufacturer. In the autumn of 1928 Roe and his friend and colleague John Lord sold up their shares in Avro and acquired the controlling interest in SESL. In October 1928 it was renamed Saunders-Roe Ltd – Saro for short. Sam Saunders became the honorary president: the master boat builder died on 17 December 1933, aged 77.

Spartan interlude

A name like Roe was bound to attract others and his was not the only cash heading for the Isle of Wight. Formed in July 1929, the Aircraft Investment Corporation (AIC) aimed to stimulate civil aviation and it began to finance Blackburn and Saro. Acting as a consultant to AIC was the dynamic and charismatic Sir Henry Segrave, a former Great War pilot and the holder of speed records on both land and water. Segrave devised a high-speed, four-seat, twin-engined corporate conveyance or tourer and Saro manufactured the prototype, as the Segrave Meteor, which first flew on 28 May 1930. Sixteen days later Sir Henry was at the helm of his Saro-built speedboat, *Miss England II*, on Lake Windermere when it somersaulted, killing its 33-year-old captain. AIC vested production of an all-metal version of the Meteor with Blackburn – see Chapter 9. The link with Blackburn was maintained when Saro was contracted to assemble a batch of Bluebird IV biplane tourers in 1930, although up to twenty had to be returned to Brough when Saro's own fortunes began to improve.

As well as AIC, Whitehall Securities ploughed money into Saro and it snapped up Simmonds Aircraft in 1930. Simmonds had been building the Spartan two-seat biplane tourer in Southampton since 1928 and had followed this up with a more refined replacement, the Arrow and a three-seater version. Whitehall relocated Simmonds to the former John Samuel White aeroplane works at East Cowes and renamed the enterprise Spartan Aircraft. At this point another name enters the plot, Edgar Wikner Percival. He approached Saro with a proposal for a three-engined mailplane with the potential to become a small airliner. A joint venture was initiated and the resulting Mailplane was first flown from Somerton in early 1932. Wanting to concentrate on his Gull tourer, Percival sold the rights to the Mailplane and they were handed on to Spartan. The much modified, all-metal, Cruiser airliner entered limited production in 1932. Spartan's design office was absorbed by Saro in January 1933 and after the last Cruiser was handed over in the summer of 1935, the name Spartan Aircraft disappeared.

Simmonds and Spartan

From	To	Total	Name	Type	Engine(s)	Notes
1928	1930	49	Spartan	Tourer	1 x ADC Hermes	[1]
1930	1933	15	Arrow	Tourer	1 x ADC Cirrus	
1930	1933	26	Three-Seater	Tourer	1 x Cirrus Hermes	
1932	-	1	Clipper	Tourer	1 x Pobjoy R	
1932	1935	17	Cruiser	Light transport	3 x DH Gipsy Major	[2]

Based upon *Saunders and Saro Aircraft since 1917* by Peter London. Cruiser and Clipper monoplanes, all others biplanes. **[1]** Designed and built by Simmonds Aircraft at Weston, Southampton. Company became Spartan Aircraft in 1930, relocating to East Cowes, Feb 1931. **[2]** Redesigned Mailplane by Spartan Aircraft – see narrative. Includes one example under licence for Aeroput in Belgrade, Yugoslavia.

Spartan Cruiser III, G-ACYK, circa 1935. This machine crashed on the Hill of Stake, near Largs, Scotland, on 14 January 1938; without fatality. Its centre section was salvaged in 1973 and is displayed at the National Museum of Flight Scotland, at East Fortune. *KEC*

Turning the corner…into trouble

The first fruits of the Roe/Lord investment took the form of a family of amphibian or pure flying boat monoplanes with civil and military applications. In ascending size these were the Cutty Sark, the Windhover (an old-fashioned name for a kestrel) and the Cloud, seating four, eight and ten respectively. Knowler ingeniously mounted the tractor engines on pylons above the centre section on each type: this not only kept them well clear of spray but allowed for a wide range of powerplant choice. The RAF ordered sixteen Clouds, most serving as flying boat trainers and establishing Saro as a 'serious' RAF supplier.

Knowler's twin-engined London sesquiplane was a winner of Specification R.24/31 for a patrol flying boat – the Supermarine Stranraer also ultimately benefitting. The prototype London appeared in 1934 and was followed by orders for thirty that would keep Saro busy towards the end of the decade. Constructing 80ft span flying boats needed more space and in 1936 the huge Columbine hangar – using a Boulton and Paul supplied structure – was erected, along with a new apron and slipway. The need to increase factory capacity was met in 1937 when space was taken at Eastleigh, Southampton. The following year the company was restructured and the boat-building elements were placed under a new concern, Saunders Shipyard Ltd.

Other than its sesquiplane layout, the London was a very traditional biplane flying boat in an era that was increasingly dominated by monoplanes. Knowler's response to Specification R.2/33 for a long-range monoplane patrol flying boat was a radical departure. The A.33 was a four-engined parasol monoplane with fuselage-mounted sponsons to eradicate the need for wing-tip floats. Test pilot Frank Courtney captained the A.33's debut in October 1938. He found it reasonable in the air, but it had unacceptable porpoising tendencies in the water.

Moored on the Medina, Armstrong Siddeley Serval-engined Cloud G-ACGO, 1933. *Saro*

The one-off Severn, N240, at Felixstowe in 1930. As well as the sesquiplane layout, Knowler's 'corrugated' construction technique is apparent. *KEC*

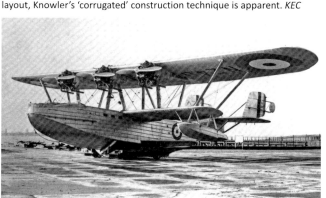

London I K5261 was initially issued to 201 Squadron at Calshot in the summer of 1936. *Saro*

The prototype Lerwick, L7248, at Felixstowe, spring 1939. *KEC*

On the 25th the A.33 hit the wake of a ferry boat and the 'bobbing' became more pronounced; the starboard side of the wing failed and twisted. The unfortunate aircraft was towed back and ultimately axed; the incredible Short Sunderland more than meeting the requirement.

Named after the administrative town of the Shetland Islands, the Lerwick twin-engined patrol flying boat was intended to replace the London and the Supermarine Stranraer biplane 'boats. The Air Ministry preferred Supermarine's response to Specification R.1/36 but fearing that an order would detract from the vital job of churning out Spitfires, Saro was awarded the contract. In the race to rearm, designs were less and less decided by a fly-off of prototypes; orders were placed 'off the drawing board'. The first Lerwick got airborne from the Medina in November 1938 and there were high hopes for substantial orders. Trials showed that the Lerwick was a handful to fly and its behaviour at speed in the water was also challenging. Only twenty-one were built and the type was pulled from operational flying in the spring of 1941.

The Lerwick's failure might have put paid to a small concern like Saro, but World War Two offered plenty of sub-contract work. In order to concentrate on Spitfires, manufacture of the Supermarine Walrus general duties amphibian was taken over at Cowes. This was followed by its Supermarine successor, the Sea Otter; the last of which was completed in July 1946. Saro devised an 'austerity' version of the Walrus, with a wooden fuselage, construction of which was carried out by glider manufacturer Elliotts of Newbury. Walrus IIs were assembled at a Saro-managed factory at Addlestone, Surrey. As well as whole airframe work, Saro built a large number of sub-assemblies, including a lot of Spitfire work.

Flying boat renaissance

A requirement for a very large, long-range patrol flying boat was shared by Shorts and Saro. The prototype of the massive Shetland took to the air in December 1944, with a purely civilian version following in September 1947. As shown in Chapter 34, the Shetland was a joint Short–Saro venture, with Cowes involved in design and building the wings. The Shetland turned out to be a cul-de-sac, but the brief Saro–Shorts liaison had a major effect on the future of the Isle of Wight business.

Disillusioned with the nationalisation of Shorts, its inspired chief designer Arthur Gouge (Sir Arthur from 1948), jumped ship and became Saro's vice-chairman in mid-1943. The combination of Gouge and Cowes' gifted designer Knowler made Saro the UK's centre of excellence of flying boat know-how. Both were convinced there was a promising future for flying boats, while the bulk of the industry regarded them as a diminishing, niche market. (Bound for retirement, Gouge left Saro in September 1959: his career is charted in Chapter 34.)

Gouge brought to Cowes his concept of a so-called 'guerrilla fighter', a jet-propelled, cannon-armed flying boat that could operate from calm waters with the minimum of support. There had been instances of *floatplane* fighters; probably the best-known was the Japanese Kawanishi N1K1 Kyofu of 1942. This *perhaps* influenced Gouge, that and the 'island-hopping' tactics needed to recapture the Pacific Islands from Japan. The idea appealed to the Ministry of Aircraft Production and under Specification E.6/44 three prototypes were ordered in April 1944, designated SR.A/1. The 'A' came from Anglesey, Saro having in 1940 relocated the design office to Beaumaris, where the company ran a flying boat modification and fitting out centre, specialising in Consolidated Catalinas.

By the time the first SR.A/1 got airborne on 16 July 1947 the Pacific War was long over. Nicknamed 'Squirt' at Cowes, the SR.A/1 performed impressively, but the whole programme had the look of something that should have been terminated long before. The other two examples took to the air in 1948 but were both written off the following year. The prototype was retired in the summer of 1951 and is today displayed at Solent Sky in Southampton.

Viscount lifeline

Sea Otter production ceased at Cowes in July 1946. Between then and 1948 only three Squirts were built. This was not going to keep the wolf from the door and the workforce active. Salvation came with more sub-contracts. Nearly 800 de Havilland (DH) Vampire wings were created and other work included sub-assemblies for DH Venoms and Supermarine Swifts. But *the* lifeline was provided by Vickers, which was getting ready to put its world-beating Viscount turboprop airliner into production. Saro was signed up to build the wings – 420 sets were made, the last in 1962. The relationship with Vickers was further cemented by the Valiant programme: Saro built the V-bomber's cockpits.

TG263, the first of three SR.A/1 fighter flying boats, 1948. *Saro*

Assembling airliner wings needed space that Saro did not have. The company already had premises at Eastleigh and in January 1951 Saro bought out neighbouring Cierva, which had collapsed. This purchase also provided a very welcome diversification into helicopters, of which more anon.

Saunders and Saunders-Roe sub-contracts

Type	Total	From	To	Notes
Avro 504A and 504J	200	1915	1916	
Short 184	70	1916	1918	
Short 320	10	1917	1917	
Felixstowe F.2A/F.5	150	1917	1919	
Norman Thompson NT.2B	24	1918	1919	
Vickers Valentia	1	1921	-	[1]
Isaaco Helicogyre	1	1929	-	[2]
Blackburn Bluebird IV	52	1930	1932	[3]
Supermarine Walrus I/II	461	1940	1945	[4]
Supermarine Sea Otter I/II	270	1943	1946	
Hiller XROE-1 Rotocycle	10	1959	1960	[2]

Complete airframe commissions only. [1] Three hulls built 1921–23, two Valentias assembled by Vickers at Barrow. Prototype Valentia assembled and tested at Cowes. [2] See narrative. [3] Built at West Cowes; up to 20 returned to Blackburn at Brough as unfinished airframes in 1931 for completion. [4] The Mk.II had Saro-designed wooden hulls, which were built by Elliotts of Newbury. The bulk of the 190 Mk.IIs were built at a Saro-managed factory at Addlestone, Surrey.

Double-decker

Gouge and Knowler were convinced that a very large commercial flying boat, using modern technologies, would find a good market in the post-war world. In 1945 they devised the SR.45, a pressurised, 330,000lb monster powered by *ten* turboprops. (See the table for a comparison of contemporary types.) Named Princess, the giant offered sumptuous accommodation for 100-plus passengers on two decks in one of the first applications of the 'double-bubble' fuselage layout.

The Ministry of Supply (MoS) was enthusiastic and ordered three to Specification C.10/46, believing that state-owned British Overseas Airways Corporation (BOAC) would be *bound* to buy some. MoS chipped in a cool £2.8 million and Saro started recruiting. Development contracts such as the Princess were on a cost-plus basis, or with a limit of liability. Payments from MoS could be withheld, or trickle-fed. If a keen minister moved on, the goodwill might dry up in an instant. Manufacturers could not survive on such stop-start arrangements, it was vital to secure regular, non-Ministry, work – hence the appeal of sub-contracts.

The first metal was cut in late 1947 but the Princess project evolved tortuously. Meanwhile, *five* different powerplants were pondered and rejected. Finally the Bristol Proteus turboprop was chosen, necessitating huge modifications to the already in-build wings. The ten propeller turbines were arranged as four coupled units driving contra-rotating propellers and two singles in the outboard positions.

On 3 November 1950 BOAC Short Solent 2 G-AHIO *Somerset* cast off from Berth 50 at the Southampton flying boat terminal. Finding clear space on Southampton Water, it took off, bound for South Africa. With that BOAC bade farewell to flying boat operations: the main 'target' of the Princess was standardising on landplanes. Three months later, worried about spiralling costs and the absence of customers, the MoS announced that the third Princess, would be scrapped to save £1 million. Construction of No. 3 was well advanced and the hulk was not dismantled; there were slim hopes that all might still be redeemed.

The first Princess was carefully extracted from the Columbine hangar during the autumn of 1951; the fuselage had to be 'see-sawed' in order to get the 55ft 9in tail out. Even then the maiden flight was a long way off. The outer wings needed to be fitted in the open air and although *some* of the engines had arrived, none had been fitted. The prototype was carefully floated on the Medina on 21 August 1952 and the following day Geoffrey Tyson and crew took the leviathan into the air. Like many British aircraft, the Princess proved to be a huge technical success and a monumental commercial failure.

Giants Compared

	Princess	Short Solent 2	Bristol Brabazon	Bristol Britannia 101
First flown	22 Aug 1952	11 Nov 1946	4 Sep 1949	16 Aug 1952
Powerplant	10 x Bristol Proteus 2,500hp	4 x Bristol Hercules 1,690hp	8 x Bristol Centaurus 2,500hp	4 x Bristol Proteus 2,800hp
Span	209ft 6in	112ft 9in	230ft 0in	142ft 3in
Max weight	330,000lb	78,000lb	290,000lb	155,000lb
Range	5,720 miles	1,800 miles	5,500 miles	4,580 miles
Passengers	105	30	100	90

The first Princess, G-ALUN (left), with the second example, G-ALUO, under assembly on the apron outside the Columbine hangar at East Cowes, 1952. In the foreground, providing scale is SR.A/1 TG263. *Saro*

Today, the Columbine hangar still dominates the River Medina at Cowes. *Ken Ellis*

Saunders and Saunders-Roe flying boats/amphibians

From	To	Total	Name/Designation	Type	Engine(s)	Notes
1920	-	1	Kittiwake	Light transport	2 x ABC Wasp	
1926	-	1	Medina	Airliner	2 x Bristol Jupiter	
1926	-	1	Valkyrie	Patrol/GP	3 x RR Condor	
1928	-	1	A.14 'Metal Hull'	Research	2 x Napier Lion	[1]
1929	1935	12	Cutty Sark	Light transport	2 x AS Genet Major	[2]
1930	-	1	Severn	Patrol/recce	3 x Bristol Jupiter	
1930	1935	22	Cloud	Light transport	2 x AS Serval	[3]
1930	1931	2	Windhover	Light transport	3 x DH Gipsy II	
1934	1938	31	London I/II	Patrol/GP	2 x Bristol Pegasus	
1938	-	1	A.33	Long-range patrol	4 x Bristol Perseus	[4]
1938	1940	21	Lerwick	Patrol	2 x Bristol Hercules	
1939	-	1	A.37 'Shrimp'	Research	4 x Pobjoy Niagara	[5]
1947	1948	3	SR.A/1 'Squirt'	Fighter	2 x Metro-Vick Beryl	
1952	1954	3	Princess	Long-range airliner	See note	[6]

Based upon *Saunders and Saro Aircraft since 1917* by Peter London. Kittiwake to A.14 and London all biplanes: all others monoplanes. Other than SR.A/1 – turbojet-powered – and Princess – turboprop – all tractor piston engine powered. [1] Newly designed 'corrugated' construction fuselage mated to Supermarine Southampton wings and tail. [2] Most produced as amphibians; two completed as flying boats. Several engine applications; all but one twins, one built with 1 x AS Lynx. [3] Amphibian. Several engine applications; all but one twins, one built with 3 x AS Lynx. [4] *Parasol* monoplane – see narrative. [5] Scale aerodynamic prototype for a large, long-range flying boat to Specification R.5/39, aiming to replace the Short Sunderland; later used for Short Shetland aerodynamic research. [6] Only prototype flew; two other examples substantially completed. Powered by ten Bristol Proteus turboprops: inboard and mid-position units coupled driving contra-rotating propellers; outer single unit driving single propeller.

MoS had no prowess in foreseeing civilian marketplaces. Despite being nationalised, BOAC recognised a dinosaur when it saw one … The plug was pulled on the Princess in June 1954. Perishing with it was the Duchess, a very sleek-looking six-jet commercial flying boat that had been schemed in 1950. The two other prototypes remained unfinished and were stored while desperate schemes were examined as ways of reviving the project. All to no avail: the three hulks were scrapped at Calshot Spit in 1967.

Rocket-power

With no future in flying boats, Saro had to find other ventures. It was already established in light helicopters – see below. In February 1952 MoS issued Specification F.124T for a ramp-launched, rocket-powered, supersonic interceptor. Saro's Maurice Brennan had been studying rocket-propelled concepts for some time; he became chief designer in October 1952, replacing Knowler. The company pitched for F.124T and won a contract for three prototypes, designated SR.53. These would be only the second landplane fighter built by Saro – the first was the solitary A.10 biplane of 1929.

The MoS requirement was full of impracticalities, so Saro retaliated by including such useful things as an undercarriage and dispensing with the whimsical ramp-launching. It also opted for a DH Spectre rocket *and* an Armstrong Siddeley Viper turbojet, the latter to bring the SR.53 back after the rocket fuel had expended. Despite this, the little delta could not take off on the Viper alone; it

needed to be blasted off the runway. The specification chopped and changed, and was rewritten as F.138D. In 1954, Saro commenced the design of a much more powerful and capable extrapolation of the SR.53, the SR.177. This was at the company's own risk but MoS support was forthcoming in 1955.

In March 1956 the Avro 720 mixed-power fighter, broadly similar to the SR.53 and well on its way to completion, was axed, as was the third SR.53. While aimed at different requirements, it was insanity to have two such projects running at once. In April 1957, the notorious Defence White Paper from Duncan Sandys cancelled all fighter programmes other than the English Electric P.1. There was some salvation for the SR.53, which was redefined as a research platform. The SR.177 struggled on with MoS encouragement until it was culled on Christmas Eve 1957. The P.1 became the superlative Lightning: more than up to the interceptor task.

Construction of the first SR.53 started in early 1954, but it was not until 16 May 1957 that it took to the air. On 15 June 1958 the second machine appeared to abort take-off at Boscombe Down and Sqn Ldr John Booth was killed when the delta exploded. Grounded at the time for repairs, the prototype never flew again and today is now displayed at the RAF Museum Cosford.

With the end of the SR.53, Brennan went to work briefly for Vickers before accepting the post of chief designer at Folland in 1959 – replacing 'Teddy' Petter. After graduating from Glasgow University, Brennan had joined Hawker in 1934 prior to crossing the Solent to Saro in 1936. After Folland he was appointed chief engineer at Hawker Siddeley, Woodford, in 1961. In retirement on the Isle of Wight, he lent his expertise to Sheriff Aerospace – Chapter 14 – during the early 1980s. Maurice Joseph Brennan died on 18 January 1986, aged 72.

Inherited assets

When Saro bought out Cierva in 1951, it was not the company's first experience with rotorcraft. In 1928 the Air Ministry awarded a contract to build an example of Italian designer Vittorio Isacco's Helicogyre. In the 1950s, this concept would have been known as a tip-driven, or compound, helicopter as typified by the Fairey Rotodyne. Isacco's first two Helicogyres had been tested with little success in France in 1927 and 1928 but the British ministry was determined to evaluate the concept. This machine was powered by *five* engines – a 105hp Armstrong Siddeley Genet driving a tractor

The first SR.53, XD145, at Boscombe Down. The Viper turbojet was housed above the Spectre rocket motor. *KEC*

Saunders and Saunders-Roe landplanes and helicopters

From	To	Total	Name/Designation	Type	Engine(s)	Notes
1917	-	1?	T.1	Trainer	1 x Sunbeam Nubian	[1]
1929	-	1	A.10 'Multi Gun'	Fighter	1 x RR F.XI	
1930	-	1	Segrave Meteor	Light transport	2 x DH Gipsy III	[2]
1932	-	1	Mailplane	Light transport	3 x DH Gipsy III	[3]
1951	1960	86	Skeeter	Light helicopter	1 x DH Gipsy Major	[4]
1957	-	2	SR.53	Fighter	See note	[5]
1958	1959	5	P.531, -0, -2 Sprite	Light helicopter	1 x Blackburn Nimbus	[6]

Based upon *Saunders and Saro Aircraft since 1917* by Peter London. T.1 and A.10 tractor biplanes; others monoplanes or helicopters. **[1]** A second example *may* have been completed. **[2]** Production transferred to Blackburn – details in Chapter 9. **[3]** Mailplane built under the aegis of Saro-Percival Aircraft – see narrative and Chapter 30. **[4]** Programme originated with Cierva as W.14, two prototypes built 1948–49 – see Chapter 15. **[5]** Mixed propulsion: 1 x DH Spectre rocket and 1 x AS Viper turbojet. **[6]** Programme taken over by Westland August 1959 as Scout and Wasp – see Chapter 38.

propeller and four 32hp Bristol Cherubs, one each mounted on the leading edge tip of the four-bladed rotor. The four Cherubs, with four-blade propellers, drove the rotor around. Unlike the two French examples, the Saro-built version had another, smaller diameter, four-unit 'rotor' mounted on an extension shaft above the main rotor hub, its 'blades' acting as 'flaps'.

Saro personnel found considerable problems in keeping all four Cherubs running during ground runs and were aware that if one of the tip-mounted engines flagged or failed completely, the Helicogyre would self-destruct. The device was delivered – by road – to the Royal Aircraft Establishment at Farnborough in January 1930. It never flew …

With the purchase of Cierva in 1951 Saro evaluated the assets it had acquired. The three-rotor Air Horse was dropped but the W.14 Skeeter two-seater, first flown in 1948, showed promise. It became the basis of Saro's Helicopter Division. Developing the Skeeter took a lot of time and effort and it was 1956 before the British Army took initial production versions. The final examples were delivered in 1960, with the German armed forces taking a batch of ten.

A growth version of the Skeeter, a turboshaft-powered four-seater with far greater military potential, was schemed in 1957 and the P.531 Sprite flew on 19 July 1958. A small batch was evaluated by the Army and the Fleet Air Arm. After Westland acquired Saro in August 1959 the P.531 series was turned into the Scout and Wasp money-spinners.

Saro's final flirtation with rotorcraft was a bizarre one-man mini-copter. French outfit Helicop-Air contracted Saro to assemble and test ten Hiller YROE-1 Rotorcycles. Some were for evaluation by the US Marines, others to act as sales demonstrators. Trials began at Eastleigh on 19 October 1959 and all had been completed by the following year.

As well as helicopters, Saro had taken the brave move to develop the brainchild of Christopher Cockerell, the hovercraft. The world's first practical example, the SR.N1, began 'flight' trials in June 1959; two months before the Westland take over.

With the rationalisation of the industry in the late 1950s and early '60s, Saro was a tempting acquisition for Westland as it restructured as Britain's specialist rotorcraft manufacturer. Eastleigh was wound down by 1962 and Cowes became Westland's Saro Division, making sub-assemblies for its helicopter projects and for other concerns, including Isle of Wight-based Britten-Norman. In 1966 Vickers and Westland combined to form the British Hovercraft Corporation, continuing hovercraft development and wide-ranging sub-contracting. Under GKN Aerospace, the Cowes factories thrive in the aerostructures business, building for Airbus and others.

Post-war, Saro manufactured three SR.A/1s, a trio of Princess – two flightless – and a pair of SR.53s. That was the sum total of the firm's indigenous fixed-wing designs that saw the light of day. Only via the helicopter division did it achieve series production and exports.

The nearly complete Isacco Helicogyre at Cowes, 1929. *Saro*

The first Skeeter 50 for West Germany, PC+117, under test at Eastleigh, 1958. In the background are Skeeter 6s XK773 and G-AMTZ. *Saro*

A Saro-assembled Hiller YROE-1 destined for the US Marines under test at Eastleigh. *Saro*

CHAPTER THIRTY-THREE

Prestwick's Pioneering

Scottish Aviation
1943 to 1978

'...we design aircraft for the small man and the smaller and more isolated communities of this world.' David McIntyre

WITH THE BACKING of the Marquis of Clydesdale, Scottish visionary David McIntyre established Prestwick Airport, near Ayr, in 1935. McIntyre was convinced that Prestwick was the ideal place to pioneer transatlantic services at a time when crossing that forbidding ocean by air was full of risk. The new airfield would be the gateway for aeroplanes arriving from Canada and the USA and the point of departure for traffic from Europe. Looking after the new airport was Scottish Aviation Ltd (SAL). Clydesdale and McIntyre were famed for their flight over Mount Everest in 1933 – see Chapter 38.

SAL's industrial ambitions kicked off 1940, as a sub-contractor making Hawker Hurricane rudders. During that year there was a proposal to move Lysander production from Westland to Prestwick, to allow the Yeovil plant to concentrate on Supermarine Spitfires and Seafires. This didn't transpire but it was ironic, given SAL's first 'home-grown' machine – the short take-off and landing (STOL) Pioneer, a Lysander for the 1950s. SAL built a batch of de Havilland (DH) Queen Bee target drones in Glasgow from 1943.

After the USA passed the Lend Lease Act in March 1941 McIntyre's prophesy for Prestwick came true; it was the preferred point of entry for eastbound flights. The Japanese attack on Pearl Harbor on 7 December 1941 brought about an enormous increase in traffic. Acting as the haven at the end of the transatlantic ferry route, it was logical that SAL worked on several US types, including the Consolidated B-24 Liberator. The Prestwick design office came up with an airliner project based upon the B-24's wing and tail. Called Concord, it got no further than a study.

The initial plans for Prestwick included an extensive, neighbouring, flying boat terminal and extensive hotel facilities for both sites. Having crossed the Atlantic, passengers would disembark, settle into sumptuous accommodation and, suitably refreshed, board an internal flight or a European service; or the other way around. These dreams were revived in 1945 and a scheme for a massive twin-hulled flying boat airliner also got no further than brochures.

Single and twin 'Pins'

Determined but inexperienced, in August 1945 SAL made a pitch for Specification A.4/45 seeking a light communications type for the RAF. Up against five other, more established manufacturers, the Prestwick company was rewarded with a contract for a prototype.

Three of the four Twin Pioneers ordered by Netherlands East Indies operator Kroonduif on a pre-delivery sortie in mid-1957. *SAL*

Cover of a 1950 Pioneer Mk.II brochure; illustrated is the prototype G-AKBF. *KEC*

Pioneer CC.1 XL703 was initially flown by 215 Squadron at Dishforth from May 1958. Today it is part of the RAF Museum's collection. *KEC*

The Pioneer, a three-seater powered by a DH Gipsy Queen, took to the air at Prestwick on 4 November 1947. It was not until 10 January 1949 that it was issued to the Aeroplane and Armament Experimental Establishment at Boscombe Down for evaluation. A long list of inadequacies resulted in the Pioneer being returned to Prestwick, where it was rethought.

A revised A.4/45 document was issued specifically to SAL, reflecting Downing Street's regional considerations; a Scottish manufacturing centre was long overdue. The RAF used the delay to refine its needs: it wanted greater capacity: pilot and four passengers or a stretcher and medic, and wing hardpoints for air-droppable containers or a variety of weaponry. On 5 May 1950 the Mk.II was flown with an enlarged cabin and an Alvis Leonides 502 radial. At 520hp the new engine had more than twice the power of the Gipsy Queen (240hp), making the Pioneer much more attractive for service in desert or jungle conditions. In this guise the Pioneer became a robust STOL workhorse for the RAF and it was also ordered by the air arms of Ceylon and Malaya. First deliveries were made to the RAF in September 1952 and production continued until 1961.

Perhaps the long, thin, fuselage of the Pioneer helped it gain the RAF nickname 'Pin'. It had exceptional STOL characteristics and although there were no further customers beyond the original trio, considerable interest in a twin-engined version with the same performance had been generated. Sticking to the reliable Leonides radial, the 'Twin Pin' employed its predecessor's wing for the outer sections, but otherwise was a from-new design. On 25 June 1955 the first Twin Pioneer flew from Prestwick. While on a demonstration tour, Twin Pioneer G-AOEO broke up over the Libyan desert on 7 December 1957 and the 57-year-old founder of SAL, David Fowler McIntyre, was among the three killed. The three Pioneer military purchasers placed orders, as did a variety of overseas civilian operators. The final Twin Pioneer was delivered on 30 June 1963. When the production line was closed, a dozen unfinished examples, including a new company demonstrator, were scrapped.

The design office had proposed further developments including the Turbo-Pioneer with rear loading ramp offered in 1956 and a tricycle undercarriage version, while the 'Single' was rethought as the nine-seat Pegasus in 1959. A series of light aircraft types also came off the drawing board. Each of these projects needed considerable investment and with orders dwindling, SAL's homespun product line ground to a halt.

With magnetometers housed in wing tip fairings, Twin Pioneer G-AOER displaying at the September 1959 Farnborough airshow. It had been handed over to Rio Tinto Explorations that month. Under the tail is the Saunders-Roe SR.N1 hovercraft. *Peter Green Collection*

Every cloud...

Had that been the end of the SAL story, its inclusion in this book would have been open to debate: a total production of 146 units of two types falls well below the criteria given in the Introduction. As Pioneer work was drying up, SAL increased its sub-contracting work. Lockheed placed a significant order on 2 December 1965 for C-130 Hercules fuselage panels. This was part of the offset deal for the RAF's purchase of the airlifter and the type remained 'bread and butter' for SAL until the last sections left Prestwick on 17 December 1982.

Hercules assemblies and other tasks kept the Prestwick factory floor busy and this gave SAL a commanding position when two other manufacturers went to the wall. As detailed in Chapter 7, Beagle collapsed in February 1970 with orders for seventy-one Bulldog trainers outstanding and a substantial purchase from the RAF pending. Beagle flew the prototype Bulldog, a military trainer version of the Pup tourer, at Shoreham on 19 May 1969. Tooling and jigs were ferried north and SAL lost no time in getting the Scottish version into the air on 14 February 1971. The RAF took on the type as a DH Canada Chipmunk replacement, and the first Bulldog T.1 flew on 30 January 1973.

While SAL had inherited the Bulldog, the programme was in its early days when Prestwick took it on. There was considerable development work still to be undertaken, particularly for the launch customer, the Royal Swedish Air Force. The turnaround from moribund project to export success was commendable. The last Bulldog was delivered in 1982 to Botswana. Attempting to expand the market, a four-seat, retractable undercarriage version, the Bullfinch, was flown on 20 August 1976 but it remained an expensive one-off.

Saving the Jetstream

An important element of SAL's sub-contracting had been making wings for the Handley Page Jetstream twin-turboprop since October 1967. The iconic 'HP' was wound up on 7 August 1969 and by March 1970 the Radlett factory was being stripped of assets. Several attempts to acquire the design rights to the Jetstream foundered but in the spring of 1970 W J 'Bill' Bright of Terravia Trading Services Ltd was successful. Bright's organisation had been responsible for delivering Jetstreams from Radlett and he was convinced that the

Instrument panel and controls of an RAF Bulldog T.1. *RAF Scampton*

Bulldog T.1 XX549, delivered to the RAF in March 1974, in service at Topcliffe with the Royal Navy Elementary Flying Training School, 1993. *KEC*

Instrument panel and controls of an RAF Bulldog T.1. *RAF Scampton* The one-off Bullfinch, G-BDOG, is currently flown by a Nottinghamshire-based owner. *Ken Ellis*

Jetstream T.1 XX492 of 6 Flying Training School, Finningley, circa 1978. Today it is on show at the Newark Air Museum. *BAe*

type had a good future. An arrangement was made with the College of Aeronautics at Cranfield to oversee the installation of Turboméca Astazou XVIs to create the new baseline Jetstream 200. Premises were secured at Sywell by September 1970 and three complete airframes were moved there, as well as ten or so unfinished fuselages.

Bright set up Jetstream Aircraft and an example originally delivered to the USA in 1969 was brought back to the UK to act as a demonstrator. While Jetstream Aircraft had saved the rights to the aircraft and plenty of hardware with which to recommence, it lacked the finances, design support expertise and the production facilities to go any further. Bright negotiated to sell the package on to SAL and the Prestwick company's chief engineer, Gordon Watson, joined the board of Jetstream Aircraft while the transition was completed. Jetstream Aircraft went on to complete five of the airframes it had acquired when HP collapsed: between the summer 1971 and January 1972 three were completed at Sywell and two more were finished at Leavesden in 1974.

By the beginning of 1972 the unfinished fuselages at Sywell had moved to Prestwick. On 24 February 1972 it was announced that the Jetstream had been chosen as the replacement for the RAF's Vickers Varsity crew trainers and that 'about twenty-five' would be ordered. In the same efficient manner as it had rescued the Bulldog – SAL wasted no time: the first Jetstream T.1, a reworked HP example, had its maiden flight on 13 April 1973. A year later SAL flew the first of fourteen airframes using Radlett-built fuselages and on 31 October 1975 the first of five 'all-Prestwick' Jetstreams had its debut.

Second generation

With the last Jetstream T.1 delivered to the RAF in 1977, the Bulldog and sub-contracts kept Prestwick going. That year was crucial to SAL, as on 17 March 1977 the Labour government announced the nationalisation of the bulk of Britain's aircraft industry. SAL fell below Lord Beswick's £10 million aerospace turnover limits for inclusion but strong union and regional pressure managed to get that figure lowered. SAL joined British Aerospace (BAe) on New Year's Day 1978. As shown in Chapter 12, BAe had plans for the twin turboprop. The much-improved Jetstream 31 was announced in December 1978 and a HP-built airframe was adapted as the prototype, first flying on 28 March 1980. The first pure-Scottish version followed two years later and an impressive 386 examples were made. A 'stretched' version, the Jetstream 41, had its debut on 26 September 1991. BAe announced in May 1997 that it was terminating its small turboprop interests, at which point 104 'J41s' had been made. On 29 July 1997 the last Jetstream 41 flew, bound eventually for Hong Kong – fifty years after the first Pioneer got airborne.

These days, the buzzword for sub-contracting is 'aerostructures' and in 2006 BAE sold its two plants doing such work – Prestwick and Samlesbury – to US-owned Spirit AeroSystems. Employing about 1,000 people, Spirit maintains stress and design offices at Prestwick and the airport is also home to the company's Advanced Technology Centre developing future techniques and processes. (In November 2019 Spirit acquired the Bombardier operation at Belfast, the former Shorts factory.) Always with transatlantic dreams, David McIntyre would be pleased to see that as well as major assemblies for Airbus, Boeing 767s and 777s have substantial Prestwick input.

Scottish Aviation sub-contracts

Type	Total	From	To	Notes
de Havilland Queen Bee	60	1943	1944	[1]

Whole airframe sub-contracting only: see narrative for examples of sub-assembly manufacture. **[1]** Built in Glasgow.

Scottish Aviation

From	To	Total	Name	Type	Engine(s)	Notes
1947	1961	59	Pioneer	Light transport	1 x Alvis Leonides	
1955	1963	87	Twin Pioneer	Light transport	2 x Alvis Leonides	
1971	1982	325	Bulldog	Trainer	1 x Lycoming O-360	[1]
1973	1976	26	Jetstream T.1	Crew trainer	2 x Turboméca Astazou	[2]
1976	-	1	Bullfinch	Tourer	1 x Lycoming O-360	

[1] Production taken over from Beagle – see narrative and Chapter 7. Prototype Bulldog first flown 1969. **[2]** Production taken over from Handley Page (HP) – see narrative and Chapter 24. Prototype Jetstream first flown 1967. Seven previously flown airframes completed as T.1s at Prestwick; 14 completed from HP-built fuselages; five built from new. Jetstream 31 programme began 1980 under British Aerospace aegis – see narrative and Chapter 12.

CHAPTER THIRTY-FOUR

World's First

Shorts
1908 to 1989

'...we must begin building aeroplanes at once, and we can't do that without Horace!'
Oswald to Eustace Short, 1908

'WHAT THE BLOODY HELL are you doing here?' Is how Horace Short is reputed to have greeted his younger brother, Eustace, in Mexico in 1894. Horace had left England four years earlier and his adventures in Asia, Australia and Latin America read like a novel featuring Indiana Jones. Eustace had tracked Horace down, finding him managing a silver mine in Mexico, where he had more than geological challenges; when organised crime was not threatening his business, corrupt government officials were muscling in. Eustace had travelled more than 8,000 miles to tell his brother that their father, Samuel, had died in 1891. The family was nearing destitution: his entrepreneurial skills were needed back at home.

The Short family hailed from Northumberland and had a background in coal mining. Samuel and Emma Short had three sons: Horace Leonard (born 1872), Albert Eustace (1875) and Hugh Oswald (1883), who chose to be called Horace, Eustace and Oswald, respectively. A head injury in his youth led to an attack of meningitis that left Horace with an enlarged forehead. This gave him a menacing look, useful when fending off ne'er-do-wells, and a learned appearance. Horace could be curt, but was genial enough with those close to him. 'Learned' did not even scratch the surface: the oldest Short brother was a man of exceptional intellect.

Horace needed time to sell off the silver mine before he followed Eustace back to Britain. The family settled in London in 1897 and Horace was soon engaged in several money-making pursuits, including

the invention of the Auxetophone, an early megaphone that led to the development of public address equipment. In London, Eustace was fascinated by gas balloons floating overhead and was convinced there was a living to be made from such devices. Horace disliked balloons, the idea of being blown where nature wanted instead of travelling with purpose was anathema to him. But he supported Eustace's ambitions; the Short family was embarked on a life in aviation.

The gathering of pioneers at Mussel Manor, Leysdown, 4 May 1909. Standing, left to right: T D F Andrews, Oswald, Horace and Eustace Short; Frank McClean; Griffith Brewer; Frank Hedges Butler, Dr William Lockyer, Warwick Wright. Seated, left to right: John Theodore Cuthbert Moore-Brabazon; Wilbur and Orville Wright; Charles Stewart Rolls. *KEC*

Before we go any further, when referring to the world's first aircraft manufacturer, is it Short, Short's or Shorts? In 1947 the marketing department announced that it was to be known as Shorts. This was explained as not being plural, or possessive, but as a contraction of Short Brothers. That said, it was a Short Belfast, not a Shorts Belfast, but, by the time of the commuterliners it was a Shorts 360! Throughout this book, the company is called Shorts.

Licensing the Wright stuff

A workshop in Battersea was turned into a balloon factory and in 1905 the War Office placed an order for a trio of gas balloons to take Army observers aloft. At this point, it is best to follow the lighter-than-air element of Shorts, led by Eustace and Oswald and scorned by Horace. In 1910 a contract to produce the gas bags for the Vickers-built Rigid Airship No. 1 was placed with Shorts. This contraption was given the nickname *Mayfly*, which proved optimistic: it was wrecked before trials began. The final 'static' gas balloon was made in 1914 and the following year Shorts created a non-rigid Submarine Scout airship – S.S.3 – but the pressures of fixed-wing manufacturing prevented further development.

Having made the world's first controlled, sustained flight of a powered, heavier-than-air aeroplane – albeit by blasting it off with a ballast-propelled catapult device – on 17 December 1903, Orville and Wilbur Wright were keen to capitalise on their achievement. Griffith Brewer had signed up as the Americans' patent agent for Britain and the Empire and was among those encouraging the Wrights to bring their Flyer to Europe for demonstrations. Arriving in France in August 1908, the Wrights began taking prospective partners aloft from Le Mans before spending the winter at Pau, near the Pyrenees. Brewer took a flight in October and returned to spread the word.

Even before he'd clapped eyes on the Flyer, Eustace knew that balloons were doomed, hence his exclamation at the chapter header. On receiving his brother's urgent call to arms, Horace extricated himself from an engineering contract in Newcastle and headed south. Eustace sent him to Pau with instructions to inspect and measure the Flyer.

Superb memorial to the Short brothers at Mussel Manor, Leysdown. Left to right: Horace, Oswald and Eustace. It carries a simple inscription: 'Magnificent makers of flying machines'. Ken Ellis

The pace quickened. In November 1908 Short Brothers Ltd was constituted as a business and later that month Eustace was taken for a flip in the Flyer by Wilbur. A deal was struck; Shorts could build six Flyers under licence. Eustace found customers for these with ease. Meanwhile, Brewer had been looking for a suitable venue for the Aero Club – the Royal Aero Club from 15 February 1910. He settled on Leysdown on the Isle of Sheppey and snapped up the adjacent Mussel Manor as a clubhouse. Shorts bought land at Leysdown and the world's first aeroplane factory was built. While the drawings of the Wright Flyer were being studied in February 1909, Shorts had *already* begun constructing a glider and Biplane No. 1, to the Wright format. On 4 May 1909 the famous 'summit' between the Shorts and the Wrights was held at Mussel Manor: the Americans were pleased with what they saw.

The table 'Short landplanes and floatplanes to 1914' shows the pace of early production and how quickly the Wright format was dropped. The much more practical and adaptable layout perfected by Frenchmen Roger Sommer and Henri Farman was the way forward. Leysdown was far from perfect and a better site, a short distance westward at Eastchurch, became the new Shorts factory and home of the Aero Club, in 1910. Among those taken on at Eastchurch was Charles Richard Fairey, who went on to form his own company in 1915 – see Chapter 19.

Having dropped the Wright format, the next turning point for Shorts was to abandon pushers. Horace devised a series of tractor biplanes, the first taking to the air from Eastchurch on 10 January 1912. These were refined and, fitted with floats, attracted the Admiralty's attention so much that an order for twenty-five was placed in 1913. This was the start of a successful relationship with naval aviation that lasted until 1918. Production of the Type 184 ran close to four figures, although the majority were manufactured by sub-contractors.

As Shorts increasingly turned to floatplanes, landlocked Eastchurch became redundant and premises on the east bank of the River Medway at Rochester were secured in 1913, soon to dramatically expand. Thirty-year-old Oswald, even at that stage referred to as 'The Kid' by Horace, became Rochester's first manager. Horace was the vital spark of the business in its first decade, the venture benefitting from his meticulous approach. Illness overcame Horace Leonard Short and he died on 6 April 1917, aged 44. In one brief lifetime he'd done more than most families could achieve in a couple of generations.

Commander Charles Samson and the First Lord of the Admiralty, Winston Churchill, in Short Admiralty Type 74 Tractor Biplane No. 76 at the Isle of Grain, June 1914. Shorts

Brush Electrical-built Type 184 N9089 at Loughborough, October 1918. *Brush*

Silver Streak

Shorts had forsaken gas balloons and 'blimps' by 1916, but Eustace was determined that the brothers should not ignore airships. Shorts began to manage the government-funded Cardington airship sheds and built the wooden-framed R31 and R32 in 1918. It commenced the huge R38, which capitalised on analysis of Zeppelin metal structures, and this eventually flew in 1921. Cardington was taken over by the state in April 1919, becoming the Royal Airship Works. Shorts was compensated and vacated the site, although the domestic area alongside the sheds was known for decades afterwards as Shortstown. In 1916, with a rosy future apparently ahead in airships, the process of registering the company as Short Brothers (Rochester and Bedford) Ltd had been begun. Ironically, the legal wheels took until 28 May 1919 to make the name official, just as part of it became irrelevant. Handing over the R38 was a complex and time-consuming task and several members of the Shorts airship drawing office, under Claude Lipscomb, stayed on until June 1921.

The airship era had been far from unproductive. Lipscomb, who had joined Shorts at Eastchurch in 1914, moving to Cardington in 1916, had gained a wealth of experience in Duralumin – an aluminium alloy containing a small amount of copper and other ingredients to supply greater strength. This know-how was going to transform the company's designs.

The ground-breaking Silver Streak, 1920. *Shorts*

Oswald was so taken with the new material that he decided to create an aircraft that, apart from steel tube spars, would be made entirely of Duralumin, including the covering of the wings and tail surfaces. In 1920 he proposed the Swallow, a general-purpose biplane, but the Air Ministry refused to fund such a radical proposal. Oswald continued as a private venture, dropping the name Swallow for the much more demonstrative Silver Streak: this machine seldom gets the accolades it deserves. In July 1920 the gleaming biplane with its monocoque fuselage dominated the Shorts stand at the London Olympia Aero Show and was the talk of the exhibition. It first flew on 20 August 1920 and an application to have it civil registered was rebuffed because not enough was known about the new material: such is the lot of innovators.

Try as it might, the Air Ministry could no longer ignore it and the Silver Streak was delivered to the Royal Aircraft Establishment (RAE) at Farnborough in February 1921, where it was well greeted by those invited to fly it. Its flying life was very brief; it was grounded in June 1921 and subjected to extensive fatigue and vibration testing. The Air Ministry relented; Duralumin had a future. Although the Silver Streak remained a one-off, it heralded the Springbok and Sturgeon series of 1923 to 1929. It was also resounding proof of the value of private ventures while provoking discussion and experimentation in design offices far and wide.

Short commissions and sub-contracts

Type	Total	From	To	Notes
Dunne-Huntington Triplane	1	1910	-	[1] [2]
Dunne D.5, D.6, D.7, D.8	4	1910	1912	[2] [3]
Airco DH.6	300	1917	1918	[3]
Avro 504J and 'K	500+	1917	1918	[3]
Handley Page V/1500	13	1918	1919	[3] [4]
Airco DH.9	100	1918	1919	[3]
Felixstowe F.3, F.5	73	1918	1924	[5]
Gnosspelius Gull	2	1923	-	[6]
Bristol Bombay	50	1939	1940	
Handley Page Hereford	150	1939	1940	
English Electric Canberra B.2, B.6	100	1952	1955	
English Electric Canberra PR.9	23	1958	1960	[7]
Bristol Britannia	35	1957	1960	[8]

Types built and flown by Shorts; not including sub-assemblies. Dunne types built at Eastchurch; Felixstowes at Rochester; Hereford to Britannia at Sydenham. **[1]** Bizarre triplane to initial layouts by John W Dunne, final design by A K Huntington; apparently flew well. **[2]** Swept wing, tail-less types to Dunne's design for the Blair Atholl Aeroplane Syndicate; assembled and tested by Dunne. **[3]** Built by Harland and Wolff at Belfast: included for completeness. **[4]** Eight flown from Aldergrove, five delivered as airframe sets to Handley Page; contract for 20 cut short. **[5]** Last F.5 delivered 1920, part of a batch of 12 for Japan. A special F.5 built 1924 with metal hull. **[6]** Single-seat ultralight for the Lympne trials, designed by Oscar Gnosspelius who worked for the Short experimental department – see narrative. **[7]** Shorts had design authority on this version – see Chapter 18. **[8]** Five Belfast-built airframes sets returned to Filton for completion.

Flying boat era

Contracts for Felixstowe F.3s and F.5s introduced Shorts to flying boats, which were to become the company's hallmark into the 1950s. The Felixstowes kept the Rochester factory busy in the early 1920s when other manufacturers were facing insolvency. Despite the big 'boats, Shorts still needed to diversify and from 1923 constructing bus and trolleybus bodies became a lifeline activity that continued into the 1930s.

Experience generated by the Felixstowes led in 1921 to the Cromarty – named after a Scottish port and a loch. Although this was the first 'all-Shorts' flying boat, it was not a great leap forward; that came with a tiny – 36ft span – single-seater of 1924. Australian aviation pioneer and adventurer Lebbaeus Hordern commissioned a sporting seaplane that he could use around Botany Bay for another of his passions – sea fishing. Oswald drew up a twin-engined, all-metal, monoplane flying boat with a monocoque fuselage. Initially called Stellite, the Air Ministry asked for this to be changed as it was a near clash with the Shorts entry for the 1924 light aeroplane trials at Lympne – the Satellite – and a blatant 'plug' for yet another aluminium 'blend'. So the Stellite became the Cockle: only one was built, but it pioneered all the attributes of the coming generation of big 'boats from Shorts.

In 1924 the Air Ministry commissioned an F.5 with a metal hull. This flew in January 1925 and was tested rigorously, earning much praise and the nickname 'Tin Five'. This led to an order for an all-metal flying boat, the first to carry the name Singapore, which had its maiden flight in August 1926. Although this Singapore remained a prototype, Imperial Airways ordered a larger, tri-motor, version – the Calcutta – and a bond between manufacturer and airline developed. The Rangoon of 1930 was a militarised Calcutta and with this Shorts entered series production; hulls were built on the west bank of the Medway and floated across the river to the assembly line for completion. The Rangoon also attracted a licence from Bréguet and an improved version, the KF.1, was made in Japan.

In 1930 an entirely new 'boat, the Singapore II, began trials. This featured four RR F.XIIs, the immediate predecessor of the Kestrel. Ordinarily these V-12s would have been placed side-by-side on either side of the fuselage. Designer Arthur Gouge came up with an innovation that made much better use of the F.XII's small frontal area, placing them in an innovative 'twin tandem' fashion. In a head-on view, the Singapore II gave the impression of a twin-engined flying boat: the engines were mounted port and starboard, back to back in a single nacelle, one pulling, one pushing. The Kestrel-powered Mk.III was ordered in quantity by the RAF, production running until 1937.

Suitably impressed with its Calcuttas, Imperial ordered a trio of four-engined Kents, which were delivered in 1931. Using a modified version of the Kent's box-like fuselage and all of its flying surfaces, two L.17 landplanes, *Scylla* and *Syrinx*, were assembled in the open at Rochester aerodrome, entering service with Imperial in 1934. The massive six-engined, one-off Sarafand – named after a settlement in Palestine – of 1932 marked the end of the Shorts biplane flying boats and paved the way for a golden era of monoplanes.

The first Calcutta, G-EBVG, taxiing on the Medway with its central Bristol Jupiter shut down, 1928. *Shorts*

Singapore III K8856 of the Pembroke Dock-based 210 Squadron in July 1937. Note the 'twin tandem' layout of the RR Kestrel engines. *KEC*

Derived from the Kent flying boat, the two L.17s G-ACJJ *Scylla* and G-ACJK *Syrinx*, at Croydon in 1935. *KEC*

Short landplanes and floatplanes to 1914

From	To	Total	Name/Designation	Type	Engine(s)	Notes
1909	1910	6	Wright Biplane	Pusher biplane	1 x ENV 'D'	[1]
1909	1910	3	No. 1, 2, 3	Pusher biplane	1 x Green	
1910	1916	60	Pusher	Trainer/GP	1 x Gnome	[2]
1911	-	1	Triple-Twin	Pusher biplane	1 x Gnome	[3]
1912	-	1	Monoplane	1-seater	1 x Gnome	[4]
1912	-	1	'Double-Dirty'	2-seat monoplane	2 x Gnome	[5]
1912	1914	37	Tractor Biplane	Trainer/Floatplane	1 x Gnome	
1912	-	1	Triple-Tractor	Trainer	2 x Gnome	[6]

Based upon *Shorts Aircraft since 1900* by C H Barnes. **[1]** Under licence from the Wright brothers, with degrees of modification. **[2]** Initially broadly to 1909 Farman-Sommer format, but increasingly developed with nacelles, floats, etc. Also sub-contracted to: Pemberton Billing; White and Thompson, Middleton-on-Sea. **[3]** Gnome rotary at front of nacelle, driving twin tractor propellers on inter-plane struts via belts; Gnome rotary at rear as pusher. **[4]** On Blériot lines; for Frank McClean. **[5]** Gnome tractor and pusher, tail surfaces on 'boom' framework. **[6]** Gnome rotary as conventional tractor, second Gnome behind driving twin tractor propellers on inter-plane struts via belts.

Men of 'boats

The man behind the flying boats and much more was Arthur Gouge: he conceived the hull of the 'Tin Five' and designed or oversaw everything through to the Shetland of 1944. Leaving school at 13, Gouge trained as a carpenter and joined Shorts at Eastchurch in 1915. His talents were soon recognised and by the early 1920s he was in charge of the small experimental department. Squeezing in studies at Chatham College, he graduated with an engineering degree and in 1926 was appointed chief designer.

Gouge's skills were not confined to the drawing board: he was at the forefront of the company's evolution from wood to metal and the role of general manager was added to his portfolio in 1930. Disenchanted with the nationalisation of Shorts in 1943, Gouge headed for the Isle of Wight. He became vice-chairman of Saunders-Roe and was to preside over the twilight days of big flying boats. Knighted in 1948, Sir Arthur Gouge, the man who created the wonderful Empire Boats and the Sunderland, died on 14 October 1962, aged 72.

Here is a good place to mention another member of the Shorts team, Oscar Gnosspelius, a pioneer of water-borne aviation. In 1910, aged 32, he built a floatplane of his own design that flew from Lake Windermere and he was a leading light in the Lakes Flying Company. During the Great War he was attached to the Admiralty's Air Department and later the Air Board. He was snapped up by Shorts in 1919 on a five-year contract, working in the experimental department. Gnosspelius continued to develop his own projects, including his elegant Gull ultralight of 1923, two of which he commissioned from Shorts. The early 1920s was a 'slow' period for the company and in 1924, with his contract expiring, Gnosspelius refused the eagerly offered renewal, declaring that he would stay on as an unpaid consultant. Oscar Theodor Gnosspelius died on 17 December 1953, aged 75.

In 1925, the Mussel, an all-metal, low-wing monoplane that could be fitted out as floatplane, appeared. Two were built and both were 'adopted' by Eustace Short. Test pilot, John Lankester Parker, taught him to fly on them; letting his boss go solo on 19 October 1927. Completing a flight in the Mussel II on 8 April 1932, Eustace was observed making a good landing on the Medway, only for the machine to run on. When the boat crew caught up, Eustace was found dead in the cockpit: a heart attack had taken the 57-year-old.

Sir Arthur Gouge, circa 1947. *Saunders-Roe*

Short biplane landplanes and floatplanes from 1914

From	To	Total	Name/Designation	Type	Engine(s)	Notes
1914	1916	163	Type 166, 827, 830	Patrol/Torpedo	1 x Gnome	[1]
1915	1919	928	Type 184	Patrol/Torpedo	1 x Sunbeam Maori	[2]
1915	1916	81	Bomber	Long-range bomber	1 x RR Eagle	[3]
1916	1917	109	Type 310	Patrol/Torpedo	1 x Sunbeam Cossack	
1917	1918	4	N.2A, N.2B	Patrol	1 x Sunbeam Maori	
1918	-	3	Shirl	Shipborne torpedo	1 x RR Eagle	
1919	1921	3	Sporting Seaplane	Light transport	1 x Beardmore	
1920	-	1	Silver Streak	Research	1 x Siddeley Puma	
1923	1925	5	Springbok I, II	Military GP	1 x Bristol Jupiter	[4]
1927	1929	4	Sturgeon/Gurnard	Fleet recce/fighter	1 x Bristol Jupiter	
1934	-	2	L.17 *Scylla/Syrinx*	Airliner	4 x Bristol Jupiter	[5]

Based upon *Shorts Aircraft since 1900* by C H Barnes. **[1]** Also sub-contracted to: Brush Electrical, Loughborough; Fairey; Parnall; Sunbeam Motor Co, Wolverhampton; Westland. **[2]** Also sub-contracted to: Brush; Mann, Egerton and Co, Norwich; Phoenix Dynamo, Bradford; Robey, Lincoln; Frederick Sage and Co, Peterborough; Saunders, Cowes; Supermarine; Westland; J S White, Cowes. **[3]** Also sub-contracted to: Mann, Egerton; Parnall; Phoenix Dynamo, Bradford; Sunbeam. **[4]** One Mk.II rebuilt as Chamois in 1927. **[5]** Landplane based on the Kent flying boat; see 'Flying boats and amphibians' table.

Landplane interlude

Of the few landplanes that Shorts produced prior to the Stirling, the Scions deserve greater attention. Appropriately, a scion is a younger family member and Oswald suggested in 1933 that a twin-engined, five-passenger light transport would be a good way to extend the product line. Part of his rationale was the arrival at Rochester aerodrome in 1933 of Douglas Rudolf Pobjoy's business building small radial engines. Pobjoy Airmotors had previously been located at Hooton Park on the Wirral, alongside major customer Comper Aircraft – see Chapter 16. Gouge's resulting Scion had its maiden flight on 18 August 1933 and began to attract orders. Adhering to his step-by-step approach, Gouge scaled up the Scion to create the Scion Senior with ten passenger seats. With its deep fuselage and four Niagaras – half the diameter of the Bristol Pegasus – the Scion Senior was in turn a half-scale aerodynamic prototype of the S.23 – the forthcoming Empire flying boat.

Pobjoy flew a prototype high-wing light aircraft in June 1935, the Niagara-powered Pirate, but it remained a one-off. Faced with an urgent need for investment in 1936, Pobjoy turned to Shorts for help. This provided Oswald with a solution to regain factory space needed for Empire production by licensing the Scion to Pobjoy and at the same time taking a sizeable share in Pobjoy Airmotors and Aircraft Ltd that was set up to cover the deal. Another six Scions followed before the Rochester aerodrome assembly line was closed; by that time Pobjoy was acting as a conveniently neighbourly sub-contractor to Shorts.

The last Pobjoy-built Scion, Series II G-AEZF, at Heston in April 1947 while serving with Air Couriers Ltd. Today, this machine is back at its birthplace, Rochester aerodrome, being restored to static condition by the craftsmen of the Medway Aircraft Preservation Society Ltd. *KEC*

Empire Boats and Sunderlands

The first big monoplane flying boat from Shorts was not bathed in glory: the R.24/31 was an advanced design, but suffered from its choice of engines. The Air Ministry was keen on the Rolls-Royce (RR) Goshawk V-12 that used evaporative, or 'steam', cooling, but it turned out to be a disaster. Nicknamed 'Knuckleduster' from the frontal aspect of its gull-wing format, the prototype R.24/31 had its maiden flight on 29 November 1933 and was soon forgotten.

The ever closer relationship between Shorts and Imperial Airways climaxed in 1934 with the most valuable order for a civil aircraft ever placed in Britain up to that time: twenty-eight flying boat airliners for a total of £1,750,000, straight off the drawing board. The four-engined, long-range, high-speed, high-capacity 'boats were to carry twenty-four passengers, their baggage and 1½ tons of mail on the so-called Empire routes to the Middle East, India and on to Australia. Orders would include the associated Qantas – Queensland and Northern Territories Aerial Services – and Tasman Empire Airways, and there was every chance of repeat business.

This heavenly commission allowed Gouge to approach the Air Ministry about the next round of flying boats for the RAF, which was formulated in November 1936 as Specification 22/36. The Sarafand, the 'Knuckleduster' and the Scion Senior all acted as stepping stones to this ambitious programme. A deep fuselage was required to get the Bristol Pegasus radial engines as far away from the spray as possible. In the airliner version this depth provided for spacious double accommodation decks, while in the military offshoot – soon to be named Sunderland – it allowed an ingenious 'bomb bay' within the centre section – the weapon racks slid out on rails under the inner wings for dropping.

The prototype Empire Boat, named *Canopus* as the first of Imperial's C-Class, lifted off from the Medway on 4 July 1936. Production continued until 1940, by which time the larger G-Class, *Golden Hind*, had also appeared from October 1937. The Empire Boats revolutionised the services operated by Imperial – British Overseas Airways Corporation (BOAC) from November 1939 – setting new standards of reliability and opulence.

The most spectacular Empire Boat was the Short-Mayo Composite, which attracted worldwide interest in 1938. Former Martlesham Heath test pilot Major Robert Mayo was in charge of technical development at Imperial Airways – he had formulated the Empire flying boat specification. With services to Africa, the Middle East, India and Australia well established, Mayo pondered links with North America and the West Indies. Initially he chose pioneer transatlantic operations with a mail-only service with his own proposal for a flying boat to take a smaller machine to height and launch it. Gouge and his team created an Empire boat, *Maia*, with a much greater

Above: The flight deck of C-Class Empire flying boat *Canopus*. *Shorts*

Right: The challenging process of lowering the upper component of the Short-Mayo Composite, *Mercury*, on to the 'mother-ship' *Maia*, 1938. *via Dean Wright*

wing area, modified rear fuselage and strengthened centre section. An entirely new four-engined floatplane, *Mercury*, capable of nearly 4,000 miles range and taking at least 1,000lb of mail, formed the upper component. The first flight as a combination took place on 20 January 1938 and on 6 February the inaugural separation was achieved.

The Short-Mayo Composite turned out to be a 'blip' in history, as did trials that commenced in 1939. Over Southampton Water on 24 May 1939 a Flight Refuelling Ltd Handley Page (HP) Harrow tanker successfully hooked up with a C-Class flying boat. This proved that Imperial's 'boats could be topped up en route without the need for mother-ships and the cumbersome infrastructure they required. By the time peace returned in 1945, the need for long-range flying boats was diminishing rapidly.

The prototype Sunderland flew on 16 October 1937, part of an initial batch of eleven and a production run that ran to an incredible 763 units. Sunderlands were built alongside Empire Boats until 1940 and a second production line began running at Sydenham in 1942: Sunderlands were also made at Dumbarton and Windermere. Support of the RAF fleet kept elements of the Belfast plant active into the late 1950s. Conversions of Sunderlands to civilian Hythe and later Sandringham status and new-build Solents satisfied civil operators through to 1949. BOAC Solent 2 *Southsea* was flown off the Medway on 8 April 1948, bringing a magnificent era to a close – it was the last flying boat made at Rochester.

On 14 December 1944 a four-engined flying boat with a 150ft 4in span – the Sunderland measured 112ft 9in – unstuck from the Medway to begin testing. This was the Shetland, built to Specification R.14/40, which was seeking a Sunderland replacement. Uniquely, the Shetland had been a combined programme from Shorts and Saro, with the Isle of Wight company designing and producing the wings. By the end of the war it was obvious that nothing would supplant the Sunderland: the role would be handed on to landplanes. The second prototype was completed in hopeful civil guise and it had its maiden flight on 17 September 1947. The giant was too big for a diminishing marketplace and was scrapped in 1951.

The prototype Sunderland, K4774, at the top of a slipway at Rochester, 1937. *Shorts*

Short flying boats and amphibians

From	To	Total	Name/Designation	Type	Engine(s)	Notes
1921	-	1	Cromarty	Patrol	2 x RR Condor	
1924	-	1	Cockle	1-seat sportsplane	2 x Blackburne Tomtit	[1]
1926	-	1	Singapore I	Patrol	2 x RR Condor	
1928	1933	16	Calcutta/Rangoon	Airliner/Patrol	3 x Bristol Jupiter	[2]
1930	1937	38	Singapore II, III	Patrol	4 x RR Kestrel	[3]
1930	1933	5	KF.1	Patrol	3 x RR Buzzard	[4]
1931	-	3	Kent	Airliner	4 x Bristol Jupiter	[5]
1932	-	1	Sarafand	Patrol	6 x RR Buzzard	[3]
1934	-	1	R.24/31	Patrol	2 x RR Goshawk	[6]
1936	1940	42	Empire C-Class	Airliner	4 x Bristol Pegasus	
1937	-	1	Mayo Composite	'Mother-ship'	4 x Napier Rapier	[7]
1937	1948	763	Sunderland I to V	Patrol/Anti-sub	4 x Bristol Pegasus	[8]
1939	1940	3	Empire G-Class	Airliner	4 x Bristol Hercules	
1944	1947	2	Shetland	Patrol/Anti-sub	4 x Bristol Centaurus	
1948	1953	25	Sealand	Light transport	2 x DH Gipsy Queen	[9]

Based upon *Shorts Aircraft since 1900* by C H Barnes. Cromarty to Sarafand biplanes, all others, monoplanes. All Rochester-built, except: Sunderlands built at Rochester from 1937 and at Belfast from 1942. Last 'Sunderland' type, a Solent, was completed at Rochester in April 1948. Sealands all built at Sydenham. **[1]** Originally named Stellite. **[2]** Licensed to Bréguet, Le Havre, France, four Calcuttas built 1932–33. Note: The Bréguet Bizerte and Saigon flying boats produced 1933 to 1940 were original designs, but employing patented Shorts construction techniques. **[3]** Tandem engines; two pulling, two pushing. **[4]** One built at Rochester; four licence-built by Kawanishi, Kobe, Japan, as H3K2. **[5]** See 'Biplane landplanes and floatplanes from 1914' table for the L.17 landplane version. **[6]** Nicknamed 'Knuckleduster'. **[7]** Lower component, *Maia* – see 'Short monoplanes from 1923' table and narrative. **[8]** Thirty-five Mk.IIIs built at Windermere, Cumberland, 1942–44. Mk.V with 4 x P&W Twin Wasp. Mk.IV with 4 x Bristol Hercules, renamed Seaford, eight built, 1945. Also sub-contracted to: Blackburn at Dumbarton, Mks II, III and V – total 240. Conversions: 24 to Hythe-class (Mk.III) 1946–47; Sandringham 1945–49 (30); Solent (from Seaford airframes) 1946–49 (19) and four new-build in 1949. **[9]** Amphibian, two completed as pure flying boats.

Edward Hulton's Sunderland 5 G-BJHS moored opposite the Tower of London on the Thames, August 1982. This machine is preserved at Polk City, Florida, USA. *KEC*

The elegant first prototype Shetland I, DX166, 1946. *Shorts*

First of the 'Heavies'

Although Gouge and Lipscomb had little experience of landplanes, by the time the demanding Specification B.12/36 appeared seeking a long-range heavy bomber they had a wealth of knowledge of large structures. The RAF requirement had its bizarre elements; the fuselage needed to accommodate a reserve crew, or twenty-four troops. As crisis after crisis rocked Europe, Shorts was given a straight off the drawing board order for 100 of what was destined to be the RAF's first operational 'heavy' – the Stirling.

As the Scion Senior had also served as a half-scale Empire flying boat helping to refine the latter's design phase, creating a half-scale Stirling also made sense. The choice of engines was easy, the locally made Pobjoy Niagaras. Designated S.31, the 'mini' Stirling first flew on 19 September 1938. Evaluation at Martlesham Heath was enthusiastic, but there were fears that the full-scale machine would need an excessive take-off or landing run: an extra 3 degrees of wing incidence was recommended as the 'fix'.

This was the second major redesign that the Stirling team had faced. In the initial response to B.12/36 Gouge had adopted the 112ft 9in wing structure of the Sunderland but the Air Ministry insisted on a span of less than 100ft, so that it could use existing hangars. The wing was rethought, with an increased broad chord profile that stunted the bomber's operating altitude. Production line commonality was abandoned; additional jigs were needed – just about acceptable at that stage.

Changing the wing incidence by 3 degrees would involve a massive redesign, incurring new tooling on the factory floor and unacceptable delays in getting the bomber to the squadrons. Gouge was well aware that expediency governed most decisions. The solution was to increase the Stirling's ground angle by 3 degrees, and that could be done by lengthening the undercarriage. The best means of doing that would have been a robust forged casting: too time-consuming. A lattice of multiple oleos was substituted: the Stirling was going to tower over everything else on an RAF airfield.

Short monoplanes from 1923

From	To	Total	Name/Designation	Type	Engine(s)	Notes
1924	-	1	Satellite	Ultralight	1 x Bristol Cherub	
1925	1929	2	Mussel I, II	Trainer	1 x ADC Cirrus	[1]
1927	-	1	Bristow Crusader	Racing floatplane	1 x Bristol Mercury	[2]
1930	-	1	Valetta	Transport	3 x Bristol Jupiter	
1933	1937	22	Scion I, II	Light transport	2 x Pobjoy Niagara	[3]
1935	1937	6	Scion Senior	Light transport	4 x Pobjoy Niagara	[4]
1937	-	1	Mayo Composite	Mailplane	4 x Napier Rapier	[5]
1938	-	1	S.31	Research	4 x Pobjoy Niagara	[6]
1939	1945	2,715	Stirling I to V	Bomber	4 x Bristol Hercules	[7]
1946	1952	27	Sturgeon	See note	2 x RR Merlin	[8]
1950	-	1	SB.3	AEW	2 x AS Mamba	[9]
1951	1952	2	Sperrin	Research	4 x RR Avon	
1952	-	1	SB.5	Research	1 x BS Orpheus	
1953	-	1	Sherpa	Research	2 x Turboméca Palas	[10]
1953	1957	29	Seamew AS.1/MR.2	Anti-sub/Patrol	1 x AS Mamba	[11]
1957	1958	2	SC.1	VTOL research	5 x RB.108	
1963	1986	153	Skyvan 1, 2, 3	Light transport	2 x Garrett TPE331	
1966	1967		Belfast C.1	Transport	4 x RR Tyne	
1974	1992	343	SD.330 and 360	Airliner	2 x P&W PT6A	[12]
1986	1993	160	Tucano	Trainer	1 x Garrett TPE331	[13]

Based upon *Shorts Aircraft since 1900* by C H Barnes. Gull to Sturgeon piston-engined; SB.3, Seamew, Skyvan, 330, 360 and Tucano turboprops; Sperrin, SB.5 and SC.1 jets. From production Sturgeons onwards, all built at Belfast. Stirlings built at Rochester from 1939 and at Belfast from 1940. [1] Both flown as landplane and floatplane. [2] Entrant for 1927 Schneider Trophy. Project overseen by Lt Col Whiston Alfred Bristow, designed by George Carter – see Chapter 22 – with considerable input from Shorts. Wrecked at Venice 11 Sep 1927. [3] Six built under licence by Pobjoy Airmotors and Aircraft, Rochester, 1936–37. [4] Last Scion Senior delivered early 1937. One airframe held back and converted into a test bed for the Sunderland III planing bottom. Flown in the form of a flying boat – central hull, outrigger floats – in October 1939. [5] Floatplane upper component, *Mercury* – see 'Short flying boats and amphibians' table and narrative. [6] Half-size Stirling aerodynamic test bed. [7] As well as Sydenham, Shorts assembled Stirlings at: Aldergrove, Long Kesh and Maghaberry. Also sub contracted to: Austin Motors, Longbridge (620). [8] First two built as torpedo/strike; remainder completed as TT.2 target tug. [9] Second example built, but not flown. [10] Re-engineered from SB.1 glider test bed of 1951. [11] Last two unflown when programme terminated. [12] Includes C-23 Sherpa for USAF. [13] Substantially re-engineered version of Embraer EMB-312 Tucano.

A war-weary Stirling of 149 Squadron. *Rolls-Royce*

Veteran Shorts test pilot John Lankester Parker took the prototype aloft at Rochester on 14 May 1939. The twenty-minute debut went well; the Stirling had good characteristics. As it touched down the big machine spun around, the undercarriage crumpled and collapsed. Nobody was hurt. A brake unit had seized; the prototype was a write-off. It was 3 December before Parker ventured skywards in the second example. That undercarriage was to plague many a pilot throughout the war.

The first Stirlings were issued to 7 Squadron at Leeming in August 1940: Gouge and his team had come up with the goods. However, with the introduction of the HP Halifax and Avro Lancaster, raid planners were faced with complications because the Stirling could not fly as high, requiring careful attention to target approaches. By mid-1943 Stirlings began to be phased out and the

type flew its last raid with Bomber Command in September 1944. That big fuselage, as originally requested by B.12/36, eventually paid dividends when Stirlings found new use as glider tugs and supply droppers on 'special duties' sorties. The Mk.IV was converted for exclusive transport duties and the final version, the Mk.V, was built from scratch as a turret-less transport.

Ulster transition and traumas

As part of the massive ramp up of warplanes in the late 1930s, the British government financed a huge factory at Queen's Island, Sydenham, alongside the Harland and Wolff shipyard at Belfast. This was operated 60:40 by Shorts and the builders of the *Titanic* by means of Short and Harland Ltd, which was incorporated on 2 June 1936. Strictly speaking, the Northern Ireland operation was a sub-contract for the Rochester parent. To ease the workforce in, Bristol Bombays and HP Herefords were sub-contracted – heralding an increasingly important element of the company's post-war activities. Stirling manufacture began in 1939 and the first Belfast-built Sunderland appeared in 1942.

By the end of 1942 Shorts was employing more than 20,000 people at sites across the province. There had been problems achieving industrial goals, but nothing that had not been experienced all over the rest of the UK. The Minister of Aircraft Production, Sir Richard Stafford Cripps, was irked that Sydenham was run from Rochester and was convinced this was the cause of the trouble. He came up with a dramatic solution: an action that was described by at least one pundit as a 'coup'. Citing defence regulations, Short and Harland Ltd was nationalised, without recompense, on 23 March 1943. In doing so, Cripps delivered a swingeing blow to the workforce, still bitterly regarded by veterans. Oswald Short was to step down as chairman, taking on the honorary role of life president. The youngest of the Short brothers, a trio of world innovators, Oswald died on 4 December 1969, aged 86.

Above: The Solent production line and Sunderland refurbishing tracks at Sydenham in 1948. In the foreground is Solent 2 G-AHIO *Somerset*, bound for BOAC. *Shorts*

Below: Sydenham, looking north-east, in the early 1980s. The main factory areas are to the left of the runway threshold and the triangular-shaped complex below that. *Shorts*

Oswald's loss was not the only fall-out from the Cripps axe. As already noted, Arthur Gouge headed for Saunders-Roe. Taking his place as chief technical officer was Claude Lipscomb. He had joined the payroll in 1914, aged 27, having previously worked at the Woolwich Arsenal. Under Gouge's tutelage, Lipscomb assumed greater responsibility within the drawing office and the Stirling was his creation. Lipscomb took the company through such types as the Sturgeon and on to the challenging Sperrin. In the late 1940s he was elevated to technical director, with David Keith-Lucas taking the mantle of chief designer. Claude Percival Thomas Lipscomb left Shorts in 1951; he died on 11 April 1974.

Even with the return of peace, the employment potential of aircraft manufacturing in Northern Ireland was considerable and in November 1947 a forced merger of the Short operation at Rochester and Sydenham resulted in the creation of Short Brothers and Harland Ltd and the demise of the Kent element. The iconic factory alongside the River Medway that had conceived the incredible Imperial Airways flying boats, the Sunderland and the Stirling closed its doors in July 1948.

The uniquely nationalised Shorts was touted by successive governments to the remainder of the British industry as a 'second force' sub-contractor of great potential. Supermarine was instructed that Swift jet fighters would also be built in Belfast, but with the collapse of that programme this did not come about. After a run of 100 Canberras, English Electric vested Shorts with the design authority of the significantly different PR.9 reconnaissance version, but only a disappointing twenty-three were eventually ordered. Two de Havilland (DH) Comet 2 jetliner fuselages were completed in 1956 before the variant was terminated. With high hopes for the success of the Britannia, Bristol invested in Shorts in July 1954 with a second assembly line for the turboprop. As Chapter 11 relates, at end of the unfortunate Britannia programme five airframe sets needed to be returned to Filton in 1960 to bolster Bristol's prospects. In 1965 a contract with Vickers building fuselage sections for the RAF's VC10 jet transports was commenced.

Return to naval aviation

Under Lipscomb, Rochester's design department created the Sturgeon twin-engined carrier-borne torpedo bomber and the prototype flew on 7 June 1946. This turned out to be the last landplane built and flown at the Kent factory. Events overtook the Merlin-powered Sturgeon and it was turned into a target tug for the Fleet Air Arm (FAA), with twenty-three TT.2s churned out up to early 1952. A radically re-engineered airborne early warning variant, the Mamba turboprop-powered SB.3, took to the air on 12 August 1950 but this potentially lucrative deal fell to Fairey with the exceptional Gannet AEW.3.

If large flying boats were no longer in vogue, there was a demand for smaller, more versatile, examples. To this end, the Sealand twin-engined amphibian was developed. This was not named after the airfield near Chester: 'Sealand' emphasized the type's amphibian nature. The prototype took to the air from Belfast Lough on 22 January 1948. Wartime surplus types such as the Grumman Goose and Widgeon and Consolidated Catalina were still easily snapped up and the market was not as buoyant as had been thought. In November 1953, the last of just twenty-three Sealands was despatched. With that, Shorts bade farewell to making flying boats.

Often referred to as the fourth V-bomber, two Sperrin four-jet bombers were ordered from Shorts in August 1948. Specification B.35/46, the requirement that gave rise to the HP Victor, the Avro Vulcan and, tangentially, the Vickers Valiant, was issued as a tender to the entire industry on 25 January 1947. Lipscomb and his team responded to this but on 26 September 1947 B.14/46 was drafted specifically for Shorts, effectively as a 'parallel' B.35/46. Working away at Rochester, Lipscomb presided over a relatively conventional layout except for the placing of its four RR Avon turbojets on top of

one another. This format was also chosen by English Electric (EE) for its Lightning interceptor, which had its debut, as the P.1A, in 1954.

Rochester was closing down and the new bomber was to be built at Sydenham; it was named Sperrin after a range of mountains in Northern Ireland. Three production standard jigs were created in 1948 at Sydenham, clearly in the hope of major orders. Relocating the design office from Kent to Belfast slowed things somewhat but in October 1950 everything changed. The Vickers proposal for B.35/46 had been rejected but was more appealing than the Sperrin and B.9/48 was written around the Brooklands product. The prototype Valiant took to the air on 18 May 1951 despite construction having started later. Such was the employment situation in Northern Ireland that the two Sperrins on order were to be completed as experimental test beds. The first Sperrin flew from the larger runway at Aldergrove (now Belfast Airport) on 10 August 1951, with the second following a year and two days later. (The reasoning behind the perceived need for three – or perhaps four – V-bombers is highlighted in Chapter 24.)

THE SHORT S.A.4

Long range, High level, 4 jet bomber now undergoing special trials for the development of some of Britain's latest secret equipment

Shorts THE FIRST MANUFACTURERS OF AIRCRAFT IN THE WORLD

Hollywood

Evocative 1952 advert for the SA.4 Sperrin featuring the artistry of William Hollywood. *KEC*

Three Short Sealands in late 1951. In the foreground are the two for Yugoslavia, with the company demonstrator, G-AKLV, in the background. *Shorts*

A Sturgeon TT.2 on HMS *Eagle*, with the wings folded back and the nose lowered to minimise deck space. Note the contra-rotating propellers. *KEC*

The prototype Seamew, XA209, flying along the shores of Belfast Lough, 1953. *Shorts*

During 1951 the Navy issued Specification M.123 for a simple, long-endurance patroller to supplement more complex sub-hunters. As well as the FAA, there was the likelihood that RAF Coastal Command would be interested. Shorts was awarded the contract for the Mamba turboprop-powered, fixed-gear, tail-dragger, Seamew. The first example flew on 23 August 1953 and an order for forty-one, mostly naval AS.1s and some RAF MR.2s, was placed. Production was embarked on immediately, but the requirement was cancelled by the RAF in 1956 and by the Navy the following year. Despite this, twenty-six flowed off the Sydenham line, many going from flight test almost directly into the hands of the scrapman.

Pushing boundaries

In 1948 Shorts engaged Professor Geoffrey Hill as a consultant, looking into new formats for a strategic bomber. As told in Chapter 38, pre-war Hill had been with Westland at Yeovil evolving the Pterodactyl series of tail-less aircraft. By the late 1940s, Hill had devised the aero-isoclinic wing, with pivoting elevons at the end of the wings doing away with horizontal tail surfaces. To test this out, Shorts came up with the SB.1 glider – its first aircraft wholly designed and built in Belfast – and this flew, fittingly behind a target tug Sturgeon, on 14 July 1951. The SB.1 was converted into the twin-jet powered Sherpa – the name is said to be derived from Short and Harland Experimental and Research Prototype Aircraft – which had its debut on 4 October 1953. This fascinating prototype is now under restoration at the Ulster Aviation Society's museum at Long Kesh.

The Sherpa in 1954, wearing 'B Condition' (or 'trade plate') markings G-14-1. The intake for its pair of Turboméca Palas turbojets was located behind the canopy. *Shorts*

Dramatic view of the SB.5 aerodynamic prototype for the EE Lightning in its final configuration with low-set tail. *Shorts*

Contracts for experimental types were offered by relevant ministries across the industry, often providing work for design departments that might otherwise be closed down. Such a lifeline arrived on the Sydenham drawing boards in the early 1950s; an urgent requirement for a low-speed jet to investigate highly swept swings and to trial conventional or 'T' format tailplanes. This was not academic curiosity: RAE thought that the low-set tail was unsuitable for what was to become the EE P.1A – the Lightning – but was proved wrong.

Powered by a single Derwent turbojet and with 50-degree sweep and a 'T-tail', the one-off SB.5 first flew at Boscombe Down on 2 December 1952 – just twenty-one months before the P.1A prototype. Soon, the sweep was increased to 60 degrees – this could only be done by reconfiguring in the workshop, this was not a 'swing-wing' design. In 1957 the SB.5 adopted its final format, 69 degrees of sweep, a low-set tail and a Bristol Orpheus powerplant.

The final Shorts experimental was a pioneer of vertical take-off and, of much greater long-term benefit, complex automatic stability systems. The SC.1 met Specification ER.143 for a single-seat, tail-less, fixed-undercarriage delta. Powered by *five* RR RB.108 turbojets, one mounted in the tail provided thrust; the others were mounted inside the portly fuselage to give lift.

The first of two SC.1s flew conventionally – with only the tail-mounted RB.108 installed – at Boscombe Down on 2 April 1957. The following year, the second machine made the inaugural free – untethered – hover on 25 October 1958. Seven months later, the Hawker P.1127 carried out its initial tethered hover at Dunsfold. The Hawker had just one engine providing lift and thrust – the precursor of the Harrier had taken its first steps. This did not negate the work of the SC.1; its contribution to flight control systems was immense.

SC.1 XG905 hovering clear of the special rig built at Sydenham on 2 June 1958. The massive structure was made from Bailey Bridge sections and known as the 'Goal Post'. *Shorts*

Large and small

By 1960, Sydenham had seen the last of the PR.9 reconnaissance Canberras and airlifter Bristol Britannia C.2s completed for the RAF. Future hopes rested with two transport projects, one regarded by some as whimsical, while the other would keep Shorts in the 'big league'. From the mid-1950s the RAF had been looking for a high-capacity, strategic airlifter and Shorts came up with several formats, all employing the Britannia's wing and called the 'Britannic' to reflect this. By the spring of 1959 the design was frozen: a high-wing, four RR Tyne turboprops and a capacious fuselage with a rear loading ramp. In 1960 an order for ten for the RAF, named Belfast C.1s, was placed and the prospect of up to twenty more for Transport Command was mooted.

Three Belfasts dominated the 1964 Farnborough airshow; the first and second, XR362 (left) and XR363, flew over each day while No. 3, XR364, towered over the static. *Shorts*

The first Belfast had its maiden flight on 5 January 1964. It was an exceptional design, with autoland technology and many refinements, but it was doomed to a tiny production run. Only the USAF had a need for anything this size and Lockheed was in the throes of building the mother of all transports, the C-5 Galaxy, which appeared in June 1968. The last of ten Belfasts was delivered to 53 Squadron at Brize Norton in June 1967. Only a decade later the fleet was axed as a cost-saving measure.

In the late 1950s Shorts had acquired the rights to a design concept developed by Miles and the French Hurel Dubois company for a light transport with a high aspect ratio wing – see Chapter 28. Considerably rethought at Sydenham, this emerged as the Skyvan and a year before the Belfast got airborne this private-venture, box-like, two-fin, twin piston-engined utility aircraft had its debut on 17 January 1963. In its first form it was underpowered and it was given French Turboméca Astazou turboprops, but this was another poor choice. In December 1967 chief engineer Tom Carroll selected the superb US Garrett AiResearch TPE331 turboprop, transforming its appeal.

If it were not for the Skyvan, as the last of the Belfasts were being created, Shorts would have been laying off staff and facing oblivion. The giant transport was built to keep a workforce going: Sydenham was being treated as though it were a shipyard – a strategic resource. But the political viewpoint was changing and the factory would need to stand up for itself.

The last Skyvan came off the track in 1986. Its box fuselage and wing structure was used in the Short 330 twin-turboprop, a thirty-seat 'commuterliner' that first flew on 22 August 1974. It was a huge export success, including freighters for the US military, and was built until August 1992. Stretched and given a single fin, the Short 360 version had its maiden flight on 1 June 1981, and the final example was rolled out in 1991.

Left: Skyvan 3 G-AXAG was leased to the Brazilian airline Sadia Salvador in 1969. *Shorts*

Below: Wearing the British registration G-BOEJ, Short 360-300 on test prior to delivery to Australian Hazelton Airlines in November 1988 as VH-MJU. *Shorts*

Lynn Irwin and Elizabeth Lacey, normally ensconced in the Shorts computer room, with an engineering mock-up of a Rolls-Royce RB.211 intake nacelle, 1969. *Shorts*

A new era

Shorts had been heavily engaged in the 1950s as a major sub-contractor. In the 1960s this venture was revived, not in the building and flying of complete aircraft, but in what in later years was to be called 'aerostructures' work. Wings for the Dutch Fokker F28 jetliner prototypes were made in Belfast in 1967 and Shorts went on to manufacture nearly 600 sets for the F28 and its second-generation Fokker 100 and 70 series. Boeing contracted Belfast to create sub-assemblies for its jetliner family. Nacelles for the RR RB.211 turbofan followed and led to a wide range of similar contracts. Production of nacelles remains a major operation, supplying RR, Airbus and General Electric.

In March 1985 the Brazilian-designed Embraer Tucano turboprop won the RAF's competition to replace the BAC Jet Provost T.5 trainer and these were built by Shorts. The Tucano required many modifications to meet the RAF's requirements and it emerged as a substantially re-engineered aircraft. Exports were made to Kenya and Kuwait; 160 units being completed in total. The first Tucano flew at Sydenham on 30 December 1986. When RAF Tucano T.1 ZF516 flew on 23 December 1992 it turned out to be the last Shorts maiden flight in a span of eighty-three years.

In 1977 the name reverted to Short Brothers Ltd and the company was privatised in 1984. With the Conservative Thatcher government writing off huge debts, Shorts was acquired by the Canadian Bombardier Group – which included the Canadair, de Havilland Canada and Learjet 'brands' – on 7 June 1989. Initially the new acquisition was known as Bombardier Aerospace Belfast, but it was not until the early 1990s that the historic title Shorts was finally phased out with the ending of 330/360 and Tucano production. The missile division kept the name going until 2001, when it became Thales Air Defence.

With four plants in Northern Ireland and a workforce of about 5,000, Bombardier became the largest manufacturer in Northern Ireland. Belfast became a major contributor to the Canadian parent's product line, building complete fuselages for Learjet 45, 70 and 75 executive jets, forward fuselages for Global 5000 and 6000 corporate jets, tail sections for the Global 7500, and major fuselage sections for Q400 turboprop airliners and CRJ twin-jet airliners, among others.

By 2010 the Belfast operation was known as Bombardier Aerostructures and Engineering Services. Bombardier flew the prototype CSeries regional jet on 16 September 2013 and its all-composite wings were Belfast-built. A series of major problems beset Bombardier and the CSeries and in October 2017 the entire programme was taken over by Airbus and rebranded as the A220. The prospects for the A220 changed dramatically, with the production line at Mirabel, Montreal, supplemented with one at Mobile, Alabama, USA, from August 2019. As part of a continued restructuring by Bombardier, the Canadian company announced in May 2019 that it was putting its Belfast and Moroccan aerostructures businesses up for sale. Six months later both elements were acquired by the US-based Spirit AeroSystems – already with a strong UK presence at Prestwick and Samlesbury – with assurances that aviation manufacturing would remain a major part of Northern Ireland's economy.

Tucano T.1 ZF139 had its maiden flight on 22 January 1988 and was delivered to the RAF six months later. *Shorts*

CHAPTER THIRTY-FIVE

Empire Builder

Sopwith
1912 to 1920

'Sir Thomas Sopwith, the genius who led from behind' Alan Bramson

Telegrams and letters, from the Royal family, President Ronald Reagan of the USA, captains of industry past and present, test pilots, yachtsmen and boat builders, racing drivers and motor manufacturers, previous employees and school children flooded in: too many to comprehend. Thomas 'Tommy' Octave Murdoch Sopwith, born in Kensington, London, on 18 January 1888, had reached his centenary and it was marked in fine style.

Sir Thomas, family and friends were at the home he acquired in 1945: Compton Manor set in 2,000 acres, near King's Somborne, west of Winchester, Hampshire. Among the many guests there was Lord Balfour of Inchrye; a decade younger than Sir Thomas. As an Under Secretary of State for Air in 1944, Lord Balfour had been instrumental in setting up Heathrow as the future London Airport, but that was not why he was on the invite list. On 6 March 1917 Lt Harold Harrington Balfour and his observer 2nd Lt A Roberts of 43 Squadron were flying in Vickers-built Sopwith 1½ Strutter A1097 over the Western Front. They engaged an Imperial German Halberstadt and sent it spinning away out of control. This was the first of Balfour's nine victories, all while he was piloting Sopwiths: two on 'Strutters' and seven on Camels, all with 43 Squadron. The

The RAF Museum's Dolphin recreation 'C3988' during a rare outing at Cosford in 2012. *RAF Museum*

presence of a Great War pilot reminded all those gathered of the era that most springs to mind when the name 'Sopwith' is mentioned. (Lord Balfour died on 21 September 1988, aged 90.)

Brooklands, about 40 miles to the north-east of Compton Manor, was the centre of a far larger party marking Sopwith's 100 years. It was at Brooklands that Sir Thomas had learned to fly in 1910 and from where many of the aircraft built by his companies had first taken to the skies. There was an aerial salute, beginning over the Sopwith family home, finishing at Brooklands. In turn the Shuttleworth Collection Pup, a Battle of Britain Flight Hurricane, a Hunter, a Harrier and a Hawk saluted Sir Thomas. As he had been totally blind for some time, he could not see them but he could hear them and appreciate the reactions of those around him. The Harrier and the Hawk, both in production at the time, paid vibrant tribute to Sir Thomas's greatest achievement – invigorating and consolidating the British aircraft industry.

The accepted figure for the number of Sopwith types manufactured from 1912 to the early 1920s is 18,106. That staggering figure is not reflected in the size of this chapter. That is partly because of the small time span of the company but also because the story is about the creation of highly successful aircraft and their tremendously efficient industrialisation. Writing about success takes far less words than those needed to explain failure. There are many books on Sopwith and Sir Thomas: two stand out and are well worth tracking down. *Sopwith Aircraft 1912–1920* by H F King is a pioneering journey though the complex genealogy of types; King has an engaging turn of phrase and yet is meticulous in his analysis. Alan Bramson's exceptional *Pure Luck – The Authorised Biography of Sir Thomas Sopwith* first appeared in 1990 and is a lyrical read, taking in every aspect of a crowded life.

Mention of Sir Thomas can be found all the way through this work. This chapter deals with his early life and adventures with the company that carries his name. Chapter 25 covers the Hawker years, Chapter 26 charts the Hawker Siddeley conglomerate and Chapter 12 explains his legacy to the present day. In this chapter the great man is referred to as 'Thomas' and his company as 'Sopwith'.

Breakthrough Tabloid

Thomas had too many interests and pursuits to cover within these pages and so we will stick to his aeronautical legacy. As the name 'Octave' implies, he was the eighth born – and the only son – of Thomas and Gertrude Sopwith. Thomas senior owned and managed a lead mine in Spain. While holidaying on the Isle of Lismore, near Fort William in western Scotland, the 10-year-old Thomas was boating with his father on 30 July 1898. A shotgun on the youngster's knee went off and his father was killed: a tragedy that scarred Thomas's long life. His father's estate was mostly divided between Gertrude and Thomas. This legacy did not leave the young man fabulously rich as some sources cite; Bramson quotes Sir Thomas as assessing his status as 'comfortably well off'.

His first flight was in a gas balloon owned by Charles Rolls – of Rolls-Royce fame – on 24 June 1906 and Thomas went and bought an example from the Short brothers; co-owning this with Phil Paddon, a business associate. His debut fixed-wing flight was with Gustav

Blondeau in a Farman from Brooklands, costing £5. Having acquired a Howard Wright Avis monoplane, Thomas taught himself to fly; his initial, tentative expedition on 22 October 1910 ending in a smash. He was awarded Aviators' Certificate No. 31 on 22 November 1910 on the Avis. Thomas took this aircraft to the USA for a successful tour.

By January 1912 Thomas had set up a flying school at Brooklands. With Fred Sigrist, previously engineer on his yachts, Thomas established the Sopwith Aviation Company in June 1912 and they were soon joined by Australian Harry Hawker. Fred set about modifying an American-built Wright by fitting a 40hp ABC and the trio began creating a series of biplanes of increasing sophistication. A former ice skating rink at Canbury Park Road, Kingston-upon-Thames, was turned into a factory. Like Alliott Verdon Roe, Frederick Handley Page and others, Thomas realised that his days flying and dreaming up new aeroplanes were over: he needed to evolve into a manager, decision-maker and planner, finding others to take on the 'productive' roles. He made the transition brilliantly, going on to create a world-class aviation empire.

The panel 'Sopwith types 1912 to 1915' charts the somewhat hit-and-miss early days of one-offs and the at times vague method of designation. Of the latter, a 'Sociable' was any aeroplane featuring side-by-side seating and a 'Tweenie' reflected the Kingston philosophy; an intermediate step from one type to another. First flown on 7 February 1913, the Three-Seater, or Tractor Biplane, was the first breakthrough, attracting orders from both the War Office and the Admiralty. By engaging Sam Saunders at Cowes on the Isle of Wight – Chapter 32 – Thomas combined his love of boats with aeroplanes in the form of Britain's first practical flying boat, the Bat Boat. Using his Consuta construction process, Saunders created a shapely two-seat hull that Sigrist mated to a biplane pusher in 1913.

Fred and Beatrice Sigrist during Sopwith's 1911 tour of the USA.
Peter Green Collection

Thomas Sopwith in his modified Wright biplane, at Brooklands, 1910.
Peter Green Collection

With Howard Pixton perched on the leading edge of the port lower wing, and a mechanic on the floats to help keep the tail at least partially out of the water, the Schneider-winning Tabloid under tow at Monaco, April 1914. *KEC*

The first Sopwith type to enter series production was the Tabloid, a 'Sociable' that Hawker tested on 27 November 1913. The name 'Tabloid' came from an era before it became universally associated with newspapers: in the early decades of the 20th century it was used to describe anything that was compact or smaller than usual, be it tablets or small cars.

Prospects for the Tabloid were good and Thomas felt that it had the potential to compete in the second Schneider Trophy contest for floatplanes that was to be staged at Monaco on 20 April 1914. A special, single-seat, version was built and Cecil Howard 'Picky' Pixton was to be both test pilot and competitor. The Schneider Tabloid's story exemplifies the determination and adaptability of the small Sopwith team. With a central float and balancing floats under each wing, Pixton tried out the Tabloid at Hamble in March but it promptly cartwheeled and sank. The float was positioned too far aft and it was clear that the layout was cumbersome.

Frenetic activity followed, with time ever-pressing. The Tabloid was roaded to Kingston and there Sigrist supervised a piece of adaptive genius: the float was cut down the middle and turned into a pair, and a new four-unit mounting was created and attached at the bulkhead and the centre section. There was no time to run the Tabloid back to Hamble; it was launched on to the Thames near Glover's Island, with Pixton carrying out the final test on 8 April. The Tabloid was packed and shipped to Monaco and flown again on the eve of the contest. Pixton was declared the winner at an average of 86mph. Not content with this, he flew for another two laps of the course to take the world air speed record for floatplanes of 92mph.

The Schneider version of the Tabloid also served the Royal Naval Air Service (RNAS) and was later developed into the more capable Baby. Thanks to the contest, the name Sopwith was becoming widely known and the floatplane scout was established as a practical warplane. Sopwith returned to the Schneider Trophy in 1919, held at Bournemouth, with the sophisticated Jupiter-powered Schneider. Piloted by Harry Hawker, the second-generation Schneider was retired during the first lap.

Sigrist's 'Bus'

Thomas's right hand throughout the formative days was Frederick Sigrist. Occasionally known as 'Uncle Fred', he started as a garage mechanic in Southampton, becoming the engineer on Sopwith's schooner *Neva* in 1911. Sigrist made the transition to the world of aviation with ease; he could scheme the layout of an aircraft almost

French-built 1½ Strutter F2211, complete with arrester wire 'grabs' on the mainwheel axle, during deck landing trials on HMS *Argus*, October 1918. *J M Bruce/G S Leslie Collection*

intuitively, relying on others to turn his thoughts into precise stress calculations and blueprints. In a retirement tribute to him in 1940 *Flight* magazine noted: 'In the early days Sigrist had an uncanny knack of producing the best results from primitive materials … He possessed great executive and organising ability and, like [Thomas] Sopwith, had the happy ability of picking the right men and getting the best out of them.'

Sigrist took the role of chief engineer; devising aircraft and managing the ever-expanding output. In late 1917 the government built a massive factory at Ham Common, between Kingston and Richmond, and this was leased to Sopwith. During 1918 this plant reached a peak of ninety aircraft a week. With the demise of Sopwith, the factory was sold to Leyland Motors. In 1948, under the Hawker Aircraft banner, Thomas had the satisfaction of buying it from Leyland and it became the centre of Hunter production.

By the end of the Great War, Sigrist was exhausted and he stepped into semi-retirement, returning with the advent of the Hawker company. Alongside Thomas, he faced the challenging days of forming the Hawker Siddeley Group and turning it into an industrial giant. By then both men were millionaires. Bramson quotes Sir Thomas regarding the origins of Sigrist's riches: 'When we got going at 'The Rink' [Canbury Park Road] in 1912 I said to him, "Fred, I'll give you fifty quid [£50] for every aeroplane we produce". We had an order for two, then we built four the next year; then the war happened and we built thousands of aircraft and I had to cough up.' Sigrist used some of his cash to invest in Sqn Ldr George Reid's aircraft instrument business in 1927; this became the very successful

Sopwith types 1912 to 1915

From	To	Total	Name/Designation	Type	Engine(s)	Notes
1912	-	2	Hybrid	Gen purpose	1 x Gnome	[1]
1913	-	c.12	Tractor Biplane	Gen purpose	1 x Gnome	[2]
1913	-	3	Anzani Tractor Seaplane	Military floatplane	1 x Anzani	
1913	-	1	Bat Boat I	Pusher flying boat	1 x Austro-Daimler	[3]
1913	-	2	Circuit Seaplane	Floatplane	1 x Green	[4]
1913	-	12	Folder Seaplane	GP floatplane	1 x Gnome	[5]
1913	-	1	Hydro Biplane Type S	Pusher floatplane	1 x Canton-Unné	[6]
1913	-	1	Gun-Carrier	Pusher floatplane	1 x Austro-Daimler	
1913	1914	c.38	Tabloid	Tourer/Scout	1 x Gnome	[7]
1914	-	1	Churchill	Trainer	1 x Gnome	[8]
1914	-	1	Gordon Bennett Racer	Sportsplane	1 x Gnome	
1914	-	c.3	Bat Boat II	Pusher flying boat	1 x Canton-Unné	[6] [9]
1914	-	7	Greek Seaplane	GP pusher floatplane	1 x Anzani	[10]
1914	1915	30	Gun Bus	Pusher 'gun carrier'	1 x Sunbeam	[11]
1914	-	3	Type C	Torpedo floatplane	1 x Canton-Unné	[6]
1914	-	1	Type 137	GP floatplane	1 x Austro-Daimler	[12]
1914	1915	18	Type 860	Torpedo floatplane	1 x Sunbeam	[13]
1914	-	24	Two-Seater Scout	Scout	1 x Gnome	
1914	1915	137	Schneider	Floatplane scout	1 x Gnome	[14]
1915	1916	c.386	Baby	Floatplane scout	1 x Clerget	[15]
1915	c.1923	5,466	1½ Strutter	Scout/Bomber	1 x Clerget	[16]
1915	-	1	SL.T.B.P	Scout	1 x Gnome	[17]

All piston-engined biplanes unless noted. [1] Also known as the 'Three-Seater Tractor', H F King (*Sopwith Aircraft 1912–1920*, Putnam, London, 1980) refers to it as the 'Hybrid', as it employed Wright-type wings, to avoid confusion with the later Three-Seater/Tractor Biplane. [2] King considers this to be the first true Sopwith type. It is also referred to as the Three-Seater Tractor Biplane. [3] First Bat Boat had a fuselage built by S E Saunders, Cowes, Isle of Wight – Chapter 32. [4] Built to compete in the *Daily Mail* 'Circuit of Britain' contest of August 1913. Broadly similar machine built for the cancelled 1914 event. [5] Also known as the 'Type 807', from the first serial number given to the batch. [6] Swiss-originating engine put into production, initially, by Salmson in France. [7] Thirty-six single-seaters, also known as Sopwith Scouts, plus unknown number of two-seaters. One of these became Pixton's Schneider winner – see narrative. [8] King's designation, also known as the 'Sociable' and 'Tweenie'. [9] Sharing the same *format* as the Bat Boat I, the Mk.II was very different in construction, larger and heavier. [10] Also known as the S.P.Gn – Sopwith, Pusher, Gun. [11] 17, plus another 13 knocked down as 'spares', built by Robey, Lincoln. [12] Designation taken from its Admiralty serial number. [13] First batch of nine carried serials 851 to 860; type designation adopted the latter. [14] Improved Tabloid, taking its name from Pixton's machine. Name reused for 1919 one-off. [15] Improved Schneider; includes an airframe supplied to the Marine Experimental Aircraft Depot completed with higher aspect wings and other modifications as the Port Victoria PV.1. Sub-contracted by Blackburn and by Ansaldo in Italy, the latter perhaps producing as many as 100. [16] Designated L.C.T – Land, Clerget, Tractor. Also used by the RNAS for shipborne fleet recce and known as 'Ship's Strutter'. Widely sub-contracted: Fairey, Vickers and Westland and by Hooper, London; Mann Egerton, Norwich; Morgan, Leighton Buzzard; Ruston Proctor, Lincoln; and Wells Aviation, London. Some 4,200 or thereabouts licence built in France from 1916, including 753 by Darracq; production apparently ended in the early 1920s. [17] Known as 'Harry's Runabout'; Pup precursor. There has been much conjecture about the meaning of SL.T.B.P, but the truth seems lost in the mists of time.

Reid and Sigrist Ltd. Ill health forced Sigrist to retire in 1940 and he moved to the Bahamas, seeking a kinder climate. Frederick Sigrist MBE died in Nassau on 10 December 1956, aged 72.

Although it doesn't get the same accolades as the Pup and the Camel, it was the 1½ Strutter that changed the fortunes of Sopwith, taking it into the realms of mass production. Its place in the company's development is similar to the leap that the 504 provided for Avro. Called in the factory 'Sigrist's Bus', the initial 'Strutter' was flown by Hawker to a new height record of 18,293ft on 6 June 1915. The name was derived from the additional support struts at the centre section; a classic practical adaptation. The definitive version appeared in December 1915 with orders from both the RNAS and RFC, and many were manufactured under licence in France. The type helped to develop what became known as the Sopwith-Kauper synchronizing gears, permitting reliable through-the-propeller-arc shooting vital to fighters of the period.

Pup and Camel

Some Sopwith designations have been lost in the mists of time: SL.T.B.P being much debated but not confirmed. This single-seater scout prototype of 1915 was a 'Tweenie', a clear step from the two-seat 'Strutter' to the elegant and practical Pup. Allegedly built straight from drawings chalked onto the ice rink floor by Hawker, the SL.T.B.P was nicknamed 'Hawker's Runabout'. Former school teacher Reginald J 'Pop' Ashfield was the draughtsman challenged with taking the

concepts of Hawker and Sigrist and turning them into a workable reality, the Pup among them. Ashfield joined Sopwith in October 1912 and by 1915 he had assumed the mantle of chief designer. He departed Kingston in 1916 or 1917, bound for the Gosport Aviation Company. He was back in Sopwith's empire – with Hawker Aircraft – in 1944, retiring in 1962, aged 71.

During August 1917 HMS *Furious* was engaged in trials intended to lead up to the world's first landing on a deck of an aircraft carrier while a vessel was under way. Flying Beardmore-built Pup N6452, Sqn Cdr Edwin Harris Dunning DSC made three attempts; his last one ended in disaster when the Pup stalled and crashed, killing Dunning. *Fleet Air Arm Museum*

Sopwith types 1916 to 1920

From	To	Total	Name/Designation	Type	Engine(s)	Notes
1916	1917	1,847	Pup	Fighter	1x Le Rhône	[1]
1916	1917	153	Triplane	Fighter triplane	1 x Le Rhône	[2]
1916	-	1	L.R.T.Tr Triplane	Zeppelin interceptor	1 x RR Mk.1	[3]
1916	1918	5,497	F.1 Camel	Fighter	1 x see notes	[4]
1917	-	250	2F.1 Camel	Shipborne fighter	1 x Bentley	[5]
1917	-	1	Bee	Experimental fighter	1 x Gnome	
1917	-	2	B.1	Bomber	1 x Hispano-Suiza	
1917	1918	233	T.1 Cuckoo	Torpedo bomber	1 x Sunbeam Arab	[6]
1917	1918	1,559	5F.1 Dolphin	Fighter	1 x Hispano-Suiza	[7]
1917	-	2	3F.2 Hippo	Fighter	1 x Clerget	
1917	1919	2,103	7F.1 Snipe	Fighter	1 x Bentley	[8]
1918	-	2	2B.2 Rhino	Bomber triplane	1 x BHP	[9]
1918	-	2	2FR.2 Bulldog	Fighter-recce	1 x Clerget	
1918	-	c.200	TF.2 Salamander	'Trench fighter'	1 x Bentley	[10]
1918	-	2	8F.1 Snail	Fighter	1 x ABC Wasp	
1918	-	2	Buffalo	Fighter	1 x Bentley	
1918		1+1	Scooter/Swallow	'Scout' monoplane	1 x Clerget	[11]
1918	1919	c.150	Dragon	Fighter	1 x ABC Dragonfly	[12]
1919	-	3	Snark	Fighter triplane	1 x ABC Dragonfly	
1919	-	3	Snapper	Fighter	1 x ABC Dragonfly	
1919	1920	2	Cobham	Bomber triplane	2 x SD Puma	[13]
1919		1	Atlantic	Long-range 'special'	1 x RR Eagle	[14]
1919	-	1	Wallaby	Light transport	1 x RR Eagle	[15]
1919	1920	c.12	Dove	Sportsplane	1 x Le Rhône	[16]
1919	1920	12	Gnu	Light transport	1 x Bentley	
1919	-	1	Schneider	Floatplane racer	1 x Cosmos Jupiter	[17]
1920	-	1	Rainbow	Sportsplane	1 x ABC Dragonfly	[18]
1920	-	1	Antelope	Transport	1 x Wols Viper	
1920	-	1	Grasshopper	Tourer	1 x Anzani	

All piston-engined, tractor biplanes unless noted. **[1]** Initially known as the Sopwith Scout; RNAS shipborne fighter versions were called 'Deck Pups'. Also sub-contracted by Beardmore (Chapter 8); and by Standard Motor, Coventry; and Whitehead Aircraft, Richmond. Considerably developed by Beardmore as the WB.III – not included in total, see Chapter 8. See also Dove. **[2]** Also sub-contracted, as follows: Clayton and Shuttleworth, Lincoln; Oakley, Ilford. **[3]** More of the Sopwith lexicon: Long-Reconnaissance, Tractor, Triplane. **[4]** Camels flew with Clergets, Le Rhônes and Bentley BR.1s. Extensively sub-contracted: Boulton and Paul, Nieuport and General; British Caudron, Cricklewood; Clayton and Shuttleworth, Lincoln; Hooper, London; Marsh Jones and Cribb, Leeds; Portholme Aerodrome, Huntingdon; Ruston Proctor, Lincoln. **[5]** Known as 'Ship's Camel' or 'Split Camel'. Sub-contracted to Beardmore and to Arrol-Johnston, Dumfries. **[6]** Sub-contracted to Blackburn (Chapter 9) and to Fairfield Shipbuilding and Engineering, Glasgow, and Pegler, Doncaster. **[7]** Also sub-contracted to Darracq, London, and Hooper, London. **[8]** Also sub-contracted to Boulton and Paul, Coventry Ordnance Works, Coventry; Kingsbury Aviation, Kingsbury; Marsh Jones and Cribb, Leeds; D Napier and Sons, London; Nieuport and General, Portholme Aerodrome, Huntingdon; and Ruston Proctor, Lincoln. **[9]** BHP – see Chapter 8. **[10]** Also sub-contracted to Glendower Aircraft, London. **[11]** Parasol monoplanes employing 'stock' F.1 Camel fuselages, in the case of the Swallow, Boulton and Paul-built B9276. **[12]** No operational service, majority issued straight to storage, or used as 'stock' to support Snipes. **[13]** The *second* Cobham, Mk.II, was first in the air, with a Puma; the *first* machine, Mk.I, did not fly until 1920 with the intended ABC Dragonfly. **[14]** See Chapter 25 for Hawker's exploits in the Atlantic. **[15]** Also referred to as the 'Atlantic Transport'. **[16]** Tandem-seat, smaller span version of the Pup. **[17]** Entered in the 1919 Schneider Trophy competition at Bournemouth. Piloted by Harry Hawker, it was retired during the first lap. Name previously used by 1914 floatplane scout. **[18]** Short-span, landplane version of the Schneider.

Working under Ashfield by the time the Pup first flew, February 1916, were Wilfred George Carter and Herbert Smith. Carter arrived in 1915 and within a year was appointed as chief draughtsman. With the collapse of Sopwith, Carter left and, as the designer of the Gloster Meteor, his story belongs to Chapter 22. Yorkshireman Smith worked with tool makers in Keighley and lift manufacturers in Northampton before joining Bristol, as a draughtsman for Frank Barnwell and Henri Coandă. Smith seems to have done all the 'leg work' on the Camel, but it was 1918 before he was acknowledged as chief designer: one of the strengths of the Sopwith style was that people 'manned the pumps' as and when necessary.

The Pup was a great success, but needed greater manoeuvrability. The result was the Triplane – a more powerful Pup with three wings. With the same span and slightly smaller wing area it had a superb rate of climb but it was not the winner that had been hoped for. Sigrist declared that the Triplane's extra set of wings – the most time-consuming sub-assembly – made it slower to build and less economic.

Hawker had devised a formula for a really good fighter: it would be a handful to fly, but offer incredible agility. The recipe was to group the pilot, guns, fuel and engine as close together as possible – bringing the centre of gravity well forward. Smith at times was at loggerheads with

the impetuous Hawker, but adopted this formula in the Camel. The new machine was essentially a Pup shortened by 12in, with higher aspect ratio wings, a smaller wing area and a pair of Vickers machine guns in a 'hump' in front of the pilot. The location of the guns is alleged to have determined the named 'Camel'. The evolution of Sopwith designs, taking the best from the preceding aircraft and adding refinements, resulted in the Camel prototype reportedly appearing six weeks after the drawings were finalised. Along with the Royal Aircraft Factory S.E.5a, the Camel – in the right hands – was the finest British fighter of the Great War and became the stuff of legend.

Smith's next success was the Dolphin, a fighter capable of ground attack. With up to 100lb of bombs on racks close to the centre section, a pair of forward-firing Vickers guns and two Lewis guns firing upwards and forwards, above the propeller arc, it was formidably armed. With a deep fuselage, a backward stagger on the wings and a generous cut-out of the upper wing centre section, the pilot had a commanding view upwards and around, if not forward. The excellent Snipe and heavily armed Salamander came off Smith's drawing board as a replacement for the Camel and Dolphin, respectively. The Snipe saw less than three months operational flying during the Great War, but became the RAF's main line of defence in the early 1920s.

Replica Triplane N5430, civil registration G-BHEW, at Duxford in May 1983 prior to it being sold to an American owner. *KEC*

Captain Arthur Cobby's Nieuport and General-built Camel C42 *The White Feather*, operated by 4 Squadron Australian Flying Corps. *KEC*

Painted in the colours of 1 Squadron, based at Hinaidi, Iraq, 1926, the RAF Museum's Snipe recreation 'E6655'. *Ken Ellis*

Turning off the tap

As the Great War approached its end, Sopwith continued to create designs in the hope of post-war contracts, then made the transition to types that might appeal to the burgeoning civil market place – such as it was. The table 'Sopwith types 1916 to 1920' charts a story of one-offs from 1919. Among the talent leaving Kingston in 1920 was Smith, who travelled around the world to Japan. From 1921 he was the chief designer for Mitsubishi at Nagoya. He was not finished with triplanes, the 1MT torpedo bomber of 1922 achieved a production run of more than twenty. Smith returned to Britain in 1924, apparently not taking up employment in aviation. Aged 88, Herbert Smith, the man who made the Sopwith Camel a reality, died in 1977 more or less unsung.

Thomas placed his company into voluntary liquidation on 11 September 1920. The demise is recorded in Chapter 25 as it is part and parcel of the birth of Hawker Aircraft. Bramson quotes Sir Thomas revealing just how swift the fall was: 'It wasn't a question of winding down. It was turning off the tap. We had scores of sub-contractors. I really can't remember how many – and suddenly, overnight, no one wanted any more aeroplanes.'

Sir Thomas retired from chairing the Hawker Siddeley Group in 1963 at the spritely age of 75: he enjoyed a long life beyond the boardroom. Sir Thomas Octave Murdoch Sopwith CBE, aviation pioneer, balloonist, aeronautical entrepreneur and industrialist, motorcycle competition rider, national ice hockey player, accomplished yachtsman and boat owner died on 27 January 1989, aged 101. His aviation endeavours had taken him from biplanes to vertical take-off jets.

The vast factory at Ham in December 1918: Salamanders in the foreground and row upon row of Snipes behind. *Peter Green Collection*

CHAPTER THIRTY-SIX

Masterpieces

**Supermarine
1914 to 1959**

'...not aeroplanes which float, but boats which fly...' Noel Pemberton Billing

Asking the telephone operator at the Southampton exchange for '38' in 1914 would result in a connection to the Billing yacht basin at Woolston, on the banks of the River Itchen. This was the premises of Pemberton Billing Ltd, makers of flying machines. This enterprise would ordinarily not show up on the 'radar' of this book, but for its telegram address – Supermarine – one of the most evocative names of the British aviation industry. Billing was fascinated by flying boats and he came up with the magic name 'Supermarine' to describe this form of aviation. He envisaged a 'flying lifeboat', that would seek out those in peril on the sea, land and jettison its wings and tail, allowing what had been the fuselage to became a cabin motor launch to effect a rescue. (Advertisements for Pemberton Billing Ltd from 1914 have the name hyphenated, and perhaps because of this some sources refer to the man as Pemberton-Billing.)

Prior to his founding the company that carried his name, Noel Pemberton Billing had already enjoyed a crowded life, including spells as an actor and soldier. Beyond Woolston he served in the Royal Naval Air Service (RNAS) and in September 1916 became an independent member of parliament – he pops up in Chapter 31 aiming his vitriol at the Royal Aircraft Factory and Royal Flying Corps. Noel Pemberton Billing died on 11 November 1948 aged 67, bringing to a close a tempestuous and controversial life – Barbara Stoney's *Twentieth Century Maverick* is well worth seeking out.

While looking for a base for his operations, Frederick Handley Page got to know Billing in 1908 when he visited the latter's 'Colony of British Aerocraft' at Fambridge, Essex: 'HP' was not impressed and settled for Barking Creek instead. In 1913 Billing and 'HP' had a lively argument about the stability of aircraft that left the usually

frugal Handley Page wagering £500 that it was not possible to get an Aviator's Certificate within twenty-four hours of sitting in a flying machine. Billing acquired a Farman and engaged Harold Barnwell, elder brother of the designer of the Bristol Blenheim, to teach him to fly at Brooklands. Starting at 5.45am on 17 September 1913, with a Royal Aero Club official on the spot, the tuition began. Billing described his first solo: 'Mr Barnwell jumped out of the machine, and I took her up at once, doing three successful eights [figure-of-eight 'circuits'] ...' After just over four hours, Billing ordered a hearty breakfast, clutching Aviator's Certificate No. 632.

In the run-up to the Dunkirk evacuation, on 24 May 1940, Spitfire I P9374 of 92 Squadron was shot down and force-landed on the beach near Calais. Salvaged in 1980, the remains were restored and, civil registered as G-MKIA, it flew again at Duxford on 30 August 2011. *Col Pope*

The Woolston works in 1940; Walrus on the slipway. *Vickers-Armstrongs*

The improbable PB.31E Night Hawk 'Zeppelin-killer' in its final form, wearing 'Supermarine Aviation Works' lettering. *KEC*

The following year, Billing turned Handley Page's cheque and his own, substantial, funds into Pemberton Billing Ltd, engaging Hubert Scott-Paine as works manager. The fruits of this venture can be found in two tables: it is fair to say that it was a much better sub-contractor than innovator. Billing handed control to Scott-Paine in 1916 and the Supermarine Aviation Works Ltd was born. That year a young man from Stoke-on-Trent arrived for an interview: his name was to become synonymous with Supermarine and a string of masterpieces.

Pemberton Billing (PB) and Supermarine sub-contracts

Type	Total	From	To	Notes
Short S.28 dual-control pusher	12	1915	-	PB
Farman Type III pusher	1	1915	-	PB
AD Flying boat	28	1916	1918	[1] [2]
AD Navyplane floatplane	1	1916	-	[1]
Norman Thomson NT.2B	3	1918	-	
Short 184	30	1918	1919	

Pemberton Billing Ltd became the Supermarine Aviation Works Ltd in March 1916. **[1]** AD – Air Department of the Admiralty had its own design office, but farmed out construction. Hulls built by May, Harden and May at Hythe. **[2]** Twenty-one acquired surplus and converted to Channel two/three-seaters 1919–21.

The third Sea Eagle, G-EBGS, in service with Imperial Airways in 1924 from Woolston on services to Cherbourg and the Channel Islands. *BOAC*

Transforming genius

One of the types schemed up by Pemberton Billing was the amazing Night Hawk. This twin-engined quadruplane was intended as a 'Zeppelin-killer', carrying a Davis non-recoil 1½-pounder gun and a searchlight. This ponderous machine must have shocked the young draughtsman asked to draw up a string of modifications: the blueprints carried the initials 'RJM'.

Born at Talke, near Stoke-on-Trent, Reginald Joseph Mitchell was apprenticed to a locomotive manufacturer. Close friends and colleagues were allowed to call Mitchell 'RJ'. Learning at the workbench and in the drawing office, he laid the foundations of his mastery of the theory and practice of engineering. Determined that aviation was his future, Mitchell travelled to Southampton in 1916 for an interview with Supermarine. He was taken on there and then as a draughtsman under Scott-Paine.

In 1919, chief designer F J Hargreaves, having conceived the Sea Lion flying boat for that year's Schneider Trophy, resigned his post. Mitchell was appointed in his place – this was a bold move as he was only 24, but it was obvious how talented and conscientious he was. In 1920, the company's faith in him was cemented when he became its chief engineer, and he was rewarded with a directorship in 1927. By the time the Spitfire flew, Mitchell had transformed Supermarine's prospects.

Delivered in 1925 as a Mk.I, Southampton S1043 was later updated to Mk.II status and served with 205 Squadron from Seletar, Singapore, in 1934. *KEC*

Military contracts were thin on the ground in the 1920s but civil aviation was showing prospects. An enlargement of the Commercial Amphibian of 1920 resulted in the six-passenger Sea Eagle of 1923. This experience led the Air Ministry to request a three-seat shipboard amphibian: the Seal II appeared in June 1921. A revised and more powerful military version, the Seagull, followed in 1922. The Seagull series ran to the Mk.IV, attracting orders from the RAF and the Royal Australian Air Force (RAAF) – taking the small company away from its previous hand-to-mouth existence.

In 1924 the first twin-engined type, the Swan commercial amphibian, appeared but it remained a one-off. Mitchell turned it into an armed, general reconnaissance flying boat. Called the Southampton, its maiden flight was on 10 May 1925 and a very successful series was born, ending with the all-metal, tri-motor, Mk.X of 1930.

Raising the game

It may not have seemed it at the time, but it was a marriage made in heaven. In November 1928 Vickers (Aviation) Ltd acquired Supermarine. At first glance, a diversified giant had swallowed an under-capitalised specialist: but both parties benefitted. Wisely, Vickers did not extinguish the Supermarine brand. Vickers brought capital, expertise in metal structures and access to wider markets; allowing the smaller company to raise its game. Vickers was planning massive expansion at Brooklands and during this period Supermarine provided valuable interim capacity: for example, the prototype Viastra transport was assembled at Woolston in 1930. The overall creative supremo was Vickers chief engineer Reginald Kirshaw 'Rex' Pierson: Mitchell viewed Pierson as 'old school' but he was a master of the practicalities of large-scale manufacturing.

Vickers' know-how was employed when it came to replacing the Southampton. In July 1932 chief test pilot Joseph 'Mutt' Summers was at the helm of what became known as the Scapa – named after the Orkney Islands naval base – twin-engined flying boat and a dozen were ordered. A larger version, the Stranraer, appeared in mid-1934 and the Vickers connection paid further dividends with a licence granted to Canadian Vickers: forty being built up to 1941. The early Southamptons were exceptionally elegant but the Stranraer had superb lines and was the pinnacle of Mitchell's 'grand' flying boats.

Three in a row

Supermarine and Mitchell had little experience of monoplanes. This was limited to the Sparrow ultralight biplane of 1924, which was converted into a parasol monoplane, and the three-engined Air Yacht commissioned by millionaire brewer Arthur Edward Guinness. All that changed with the 'S' series of racing floatplanes intended to seize the Schneider Trophy.

In 1919 the managing director, Scott-Paine, resolved that the newly revived speed contest for flying boats and floatplanes devised by armaments magnate Jacques Schneider was an ideal showcase for the company. Flying a Sopwith Tabloid, Howard Pixton had won the 1914 event and so Britain was host for the first post-war event.

Canadian Vickers-built Stranraer 914 of 5 (Bomber Reconnaissance) Squadron, Royal Canadian Air Force, operating from Nova Scotia, in 1939. *Public Archives Canada*

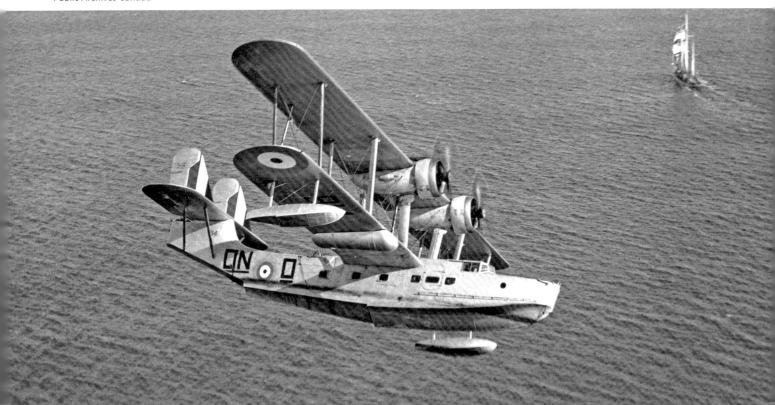

Assisted by Mitchell, F J Hargreaves created the Sea Lion I but it suffered a holed hull and retired on the first lap at Bournemouth.

The Italians triumphed in 1920 and 1921. Under the rules, any nation winning three times in a row would keep the Schneider Trophy in perpetuity and the tournament would cease. Scott-Paine was determined the Italians would not get the 'triple' in 1922 and Supermarine entered the fray. Mitchell devised the Sea Lion II and Henri Biard beat off three Italian Macchis to win at 145mph. So Britain hosted the 1923 competition at Cowes on the Isle of Wight. The 1922 winner was 'polished' into the Sea Lion III but was outclassed in 1923 by the American Curtiss CR-3 biplane floatplanes.

The stakes were rising every time and 'works' teams were being stretched to the limit. The British industry could not be expected to fund the next generation of racers on its own. Thankfully the Air Ministry stepped in, ordering a pair of Gloster III biplanes and a single S.4 monoplane from Supermarine for the 1925 tournament at Chesapeake Bay, Baltimore. The S.4 was the real mould-breaker, pioneering the way for its more sophisticated successors. In March 1925 the remarkable Southampton flying boat began testing from Woolston. It is hard to believe that it and the S.4 came from the same drawing board: such was the scope of Mitchell and his team.

Constructed largely of wood, the S.4 had a mid-set cantilever wing, a cockpit well aft, and tubular steel struts supporting all-metal floats. Ministry backing meant that Mitchell could tap the resources of the Royal Aircraft Establishment (RAE) to perfect the wing section. Biard took the S.4 for its maiden flight on 25 August 1925. Flying it nineteen days later, he clinched a world air speed record of 226mph. On 23 October the S.4 side-slipped violently and plummeted into the Chesapeake; Biard was rescued. James 'Jimmy' Doolittle took the trophy for the USA in a Curtiss R3C-2 biplane.

Right: The S.4 afloat at Woolston during flight trials, August 1925. *Peter Green Collection*

Below right: An advertisement declaring the role that the high-grade, ethyl-based fuel developed by Manchester-based fuel specialist Pratts played in the 1929 win. *KEC*

Below: Line-up on the ramp at Calshot in 1931 with the castle behind. Left to right: S.6B S1596, S.6 N248 and S.6B S1595. *Rolls-Royce*

Italian fascist dictator Benito Mussolini threw all his country's assets at the next contest, held at Hampton Roads, Virginia, in 1926. Britain did not enter; it was keeping its powder dry for the following year. The USA and Italy slogged it out, with the latter taking the laurels in a Macchi M.39. The chance to blunt Italian ambitions must have helped the British Air Minister, Sir Samuel Hoare, to decide not only to absorb the cost of the aircraft, but to turn to the RAF. In 1926 the High Speed Flight (HSF) was formed at Felixstowe and began training for an assault on the trophy. Three Supermarine S.5s, a trio of Gloster IV biplanes and a single Short-Bristow Crusader monoplane were ordered.

Dropping the mid-set wing of its predecessor for a wire-braced, low-wing format, the S.5 was proven in wind tunnels at the RAE and the National Physical Laboratory at Teddington, Middlesex. Of mixed construction, the S.5 had a semi-monocoque Duralumin fuselage. The wing surfaces included radiators and fuselage-mounted corrugated oil coolers to help tame the tightly cowled 12-cylinder Napier Lion VII. Flt Lt Oscar Worsley carried out the maiden flight of the first S.5 on 7 June 1927. The race was won by Flt Lt Sidney Webster in S.5 N220 at 281mph.

The RAF flying boat base at Calshot Spit was the venue for the next bout, which was delayed to 1929. Mitchell produced the slightly larger, all-metal S.6 that largely adhered to the S.5's winning format. Again, he made every inch of the airframe work hard for its living: the floats also acted as fuel tanks and housed engine coolant, the forward struts supported the engine as well as the floats and the fin was used as an oil tank and cooler.

The master stroke was to forsake the Napier Lion – which had run out of 'growth' – and adopt the untried Rolls-Royce 'R' (for 'Racing'). This was a geared development of the Buzzard V-12 that powered the Blackburn Perth and Short Singapore flying boats, among others. RR used high-duty alloys, a back-to-back supercharger for minimal frontal area, the latest in propeller technology and innovative fuel mixtures. Sqn Ldr Augustus Henry Orlebar first flew the S.6 on 10 August 1929, just twenty-eight days before the competition began. Newly elected Labour Prime Minister Ramsay MacDonald was in attendance at the contest. The Italians fielded Macchi M.52s and M.67s but Fg Off Henry Waghorn in an S.6 seized victory at 328mph.

Pleased with the 1929 win, the PM pledged that there would be a British team for the next Schneider, scheduled for 1931. But, when push came to shove, the funds were not made available and the HSF was stood down. Lady Lucy 'Poppy' Houston stepped forward: a former music hall dancer and suffragette, she was the widow of a shipping magnate and no lover of MacDonald's government. The sum of £100,000 was needed and Lady Houston was happy to oblige: the HSF was re-formed. Lady Houston's bank account got more exercise in 1933: she sponsored the Mount Everest Expedition, which involved climbing of the aeronautical sort in Westland PV.3 and PV.6 biplanes – see Chapter 38.

The 1931 Schneider was uncontested, but it could still be lost – HSF had to qualify. Mitchell had finessed the S.6 into the S.6B and on 13 September Flt Lt John Boothman averaged 340mph, winning the Schneider Trophy in perpetuity for the nation. To underline British domination, seventeen days later Flt Lt George Stainforth became the first man to travel at more than 400mph – setting a new world air speed record of 407mph.

Growing pains

Just as the Southampton was replaced by a new, all-metal type, so the single-engined Seagull line morphed into a sleeker, all-metal successor. Requested by the RAAF and designated Seagull V, the prototype flew on 21 June 1933. Summers asked Mitchell about the strength of the Seagull V's airframe and surprised everyone – including its designer – by *looping* the prototype at the Hendon airshow, *four* days after the maiden flight! In 1935, twelve were bought by the RAF under the name Walrus and increasingly large orders followed.

The Seagull V/Walrus was a pivotal programme for Supermarine; it was the first design to reach a three-figure production run. Up to that time, the factory had been building on a one-by-one basis, in a similar manner to the boatyards that lined the Itchen. The Southampton brought about batch construction, but as the eighty-plus ordered stretched over nearly a decade, this was not a great leap. The Walrus needed a lot of investment, in multiple jigs and tooling, factory space, existing workforce training and recruitment. While Vickers personnel were on hand to smooth out this process, it was clear that Woolston had a lot to learn about mass manufacturing. This was going to cause headaches when the Spitfire came along.

The last amphibian that Mitchell worked on was planned to succeed the Walrus. This was essentially an improved version, with a tractor engine, and originally to have been called Stingray. The prototype Sea Otter had its maiden flight on 23 September 1938 but it was not until 1943 that it entered limited production. With the Spitfire dominating all activities at Supermarine, the Walrus was handed on to Saunders-Roe (Saro) at Cowes in 1940. The Isle of Wight company developed an 'austerity' version of the Walrus, the Mk.II with a wooden fuselage. Saro also handled the entire run of Sea Otters.

Supermarine Schneider Racers

	Engine		Span	Empty	Event	Result /Notes
Sea Lion	Napier Lion 1A 450hp	35ft 0in	2,000lb	1919, Bournemouth	-	[1]
Sea Lion II	Napier Lion II 450hp	32ft 0in	2,115lb	1922, Naples	1st – 145.72mph	[2]
Sea Lion III	Napier Lion III 525hp	28ft 0in	2,400lb	1923, Cowes	3rd – 157.17mph	[2]
S.4	Napier Lion VII 680hp	30ft 7½in	2,600lb	1924, Baltimore	-	[3]
S.5	Napier Lion VIIA 900hp	26ft 9in	2,680lb	1927, Venice	1st – 281.65mph	[4]
S.6	Rolls-Royce 'R' 1,900hp	30ft 0in	4,471lb	1929, Calshot	1st – 328.63mph	[5]
S.6B	Rolls-Royce 'R' 2,300hp	30ft 0in	4,590lb	1931, Calshot	1st – 340.08mph	[6]

1919, 1922, 1923 Supermarine-funded entrants; 1924 Air Ministry-funded, Supermarine managed; 1927 onwards flown under the aegis of the RAF High Speed Flight. [1] Basil Hobbs had to retire on the first lap, the Sea Lion suffering a holed hull. [2] Pilot: Henri Biard. [3] Henri Biard crashed during pre-race tests. [4] First was Sidney Webster; Oscar Worsley was 2nd at 273.07mph. [5] First was Henry Waghorn; 3rd was David D'Arcy Greig at 282.11mph; Richard Atcherley averaged 325.54mph but was disqualified for cutting a turning point. [6] Contest uncontested, pilot John Boothman.

Air-sea rescue is the role for which the versatile Walrus is most remembered. *KEC*

Pemberton Billing

From	To	Total	Name/Designation	Type	Engine(s)	Notes
1908	1909	3?	Tail-less Monoplane	1-seat pusher	1 x NEC	[1]
1914	-	1	PB.1	1-seat flying boat	1 x Gnome	[2]
1914	-	1	PB.9	Scout	1 x Gnome	[3]
1915	-	21	PB.23E/PB.25	Pusher scout	1 x Le Rhône	[4]
1915	-	1	PB.29E	Anti-Zeppelin	2 x Austro-Daimler	[5]
1915	-	1	PB.31E Night Hawk	Anti-Zeppelin	2 x Anzani	[6]

Based upon *Supermarine Aircraft since 1914* by C F Andrews and E B Morgan. [1] Tricycle undercarriage; at least one iteration with foreplane/elevator. *Possibly* the same airframe rebuilt/altered over time. [2] Tractor biplane, also referred to as the PB.7: failed to fly. [3] Nicknamed the 'Seven-Day Bus'. [4] PB.23E prototype, nicknamed 'Push-Proj' and 'Sparklet'. PB.25 production version. [5] Two-seat pusher quadruplane. [6] Multi-crew tractor quadruplane.

Racing legacy

Part of Schneider mythology is that the S.6 led directly to Mitchell's masterpiece, the Spitfire. The floatplane paved the way for the disciplines and innovations needed to create a world-beating fighter, but it was not the next step. Between the S.6 and the Spitfire was a rare failure for Mitchell. His response to Specification F.7/30 for a single-seat day fighter, powered by a 600hp RR Goshawk II with evaporative cooling, was the gull-winged, faired, fixed undercarriage, open cockpit, Type 224. This first flew on 19 February 1934 and proved disappointing from the start. In Mitchell's defence, none of the bidders for F.7/30 were successful. The requirement was rewritten as F.14/35 and won by the Gloster Gladiator, destined to be the RAF's last biplane fighter.

The Type 224 was hamstrung by Air Ministry edicts, particularly its belief in the impotent Goshawk. The freedom that Mitchell had enjoyed with the 'S' series convinced the industry, and eventually the ministry, that unfettered Schneider-like radical new thinking was needed for the next generation of warplanes. Private ventures were the real legacy of the Schneider competition. Sydney Camm's Hawker Hurricane paved the way, followed by Mitchell's Spitfire and later de Havilland adopted the same mindset with the Mosquito.

All of those machines relied on the crowning glory of Britain's involvement in Jacques Schneider's tournament: the RR Merlin, another private venture. The experience of the 'R' was the springboard for the incredible Merlin and other areas of powerplant technology.

Birth of a legend

Millions of words have been expended on the story of the Spitfire. There is so much to cover: 20,351 Spitfires and 2,408 navalised Seafires of a bewildering number of variants were made, not to mention the post-war hopefuls, the Spiteful and the Seafang. The exploits of its pilots from the Battle of Britain onwards are the stuff of legend. More than thirty nations operated Spitfires or Seafires, including the Soviet Union and the USA. As noted in Chapter 35 dealing with Sopwith's vast output of fighters, the very success of the Spitfire means that it receives short shrift here. Once it was 'industrialised', it had so much growth and development potential – and was skillfully managed to maximise this – that it became a world-beater.

The Type 224 gave Mitchell the determination to plough his own furrow. When Specification F.37/34 came along demanding an advanced single-seat day fighter, the Type 300 was the accumulation of all that he and his design, structures, aerodynamics and engineering teams had learned. In 1933, at the age of 38, Mitchell was diagnosed with a cancer that medical knowledge was then ill-equipped to combat. He took this news with stoicism, all the while working his customary long hours.

Summers test flew the hand-built Type 300, K5054 – the prototype Spitfire – at Eastleigh on 5 March 1936, watched by the pale-looking Mitchell. After fifteen minutes airborne, Summers returned. Clearly well pleased, he is reported as telling the ground crew: 'Don't touch anything!' The Aeroplane and Armament Experimental Establishment at Martlesham Heath issued a glowing report in early June 1936: 'In general, the handling of this aeroplane is such that it can be flown without risk by the average fully trained fighter pilot.' This was exactly what the RAF was looking for – a super-plane that did not need to be piloted by supermen. The assessment was just as well: the pressure of world affairs was such that an order for 310 Mk.Is had already been placed.

In September 1936, Mitchell sent in the Supermarine response to Specification B.12/36 for a long-range strategic bomber featuring elliptical wings and a single spar, inherited from the Spitfire. As might be expected, it was a good-looking aeroplane. The prototype was destroyed in the devastating air raid on the Itchen Works on 26 September 1940.

K5054 was destined to be the only Spitfire that its designer saw in the air. Reginald Joseph Mitchell CBE died on 11 June 1937, aged 42. Up to the last he had been poring over layouts to put cannons in the Spitfire's wings. His loss was a devastating blow to the creative team at Supermarine. Mitchell had always praised those around him and his quiet, industrious manner engendered great loyalty. His deputy, Joseph 'Joe' Smith, stepped into the breach – from his fertile mind, and thorough adherence to the Mitchell design philosophy, all of the Spitfire variants sprang.

Informal gathering at Eastleigh, around R J Mitchell's Riley Nine, after the first flight of the Spitfire prototype, 5 March 1936. Left to right: Joseph 'Mutt' Summers, chief test pilot Vickers-Supermarine; Harold J 'Agony' Payn, Mitchell's technical assistant; R J Mitchell, Stuart Scott-Hall, the Air Ministry's resident technical officer; Jeffrey Quill, deputy chief test pilot. *KEC*

From Mk.I to Mk.24

Although Mitchell had bequeathed the prototype Spitfire to the nation, it was Smith that turned the fighter into a dynasty. Apprenticed at the Austin Motor Company, with the coming of the Great War Smith joined the Royal Navy at 17. Returning to Austin in 1919, he transferred to the aircraft division as a draughtsman, working on such types as the Whippet. Smith took the post of senior

Above: A line-up to celebrate the Seafire XVII entering service, September 1945. Fourth from the left is Joseph Smith; sixth from left is Jeffrey Quill, then: Admiral Sir Denys Boyd and Sir James Bird of Supermarine. *Vickers-Armstrongs*

Left: The 18th-century mansion at Hursley Park, home of the Supermarine design office and experimental shop, 1940 to 1957. *Alan Curry*

Mass production

Despite being part of the giant conglomerate Vickers-Armstrongs, Supermarine was a small concern, finding building Walrus amphibians challenging. Mass manufacturing a state-of-the-art fighter was a daunting prospect. Problems emerged at an alarming rate. A string of sub-contractors was engaged to help with the huge capacity expansion required. Co-ordinating ten different companies, all reliant on one another to keep the flow going, was a never-ending ordeal.

draughtsman with Vickers in 1921 and within five years was head of his department. By 1929 he had transferred to the Supermarine subsidiary as Mitchell's deputy.

Upon Mitchell's death in June 1937, Smith was curiously appointed as manager of the design department: it was 1941 before he was given the title of chief designer. Heading the Woolston design office was Harold J 'Agony' Payn, acting as the intermediary between Supermarine and Pierson at Brooklands. When Vickers bought Supermarine in 1928, Payn had been 'parachuted' in from Brooklands to oversee the transition, acting as Mitchell's technical assistant. A routine security clearance of Payn in 1939 revealed his second wife's German connections and 'Agony' was dismissed. In his exceptional *Spitfire – A Test Pilot's Story*, Jeffrey Quill notes that: 'Payn became unemployable in the industry and had a very hard time during the ensuing years.'

In late 1940 Smith's department was evacuated from Woolston to the delightful 18th-century mansion at Hursley Park, near Winchester. In 1948 Smith was made a director of Vickers-Armstrongs and he presided over Supermarine's jet age, taking particular pride in the Swift's world air speed record of 1953. His health deteriorated in the mid-1950s and Joseph 'Joe' Smith CBE, the man who took the Spitfire from Mk.I to Mk.24, died on 20 February 1956, aged 59. He was succeeded by his deputy, Alan Clifton.

That beautiful elliptical wing, and its square-tubes-within-square-tubes spar, was a nightmare to build and a specification change to the leading edge did not help the timetable. Production of fuselages was outpacing the wings and Supermarine was taking a lot of the flak from the Air Ministry. Alternatives needed to be considered: perhaps the Itchen and Woolston factories were better suited to other, less complex, types? The prospect of a switch to making the 'rival' Hurricane was real. The ministers held their nerve and a second contract, for 200 Mk.Is, was placed in March 1938. It was not until 14 May 1938 that the second Spitfire, Mk.I K9787, first took to the air. Thus, K5054 was an exceptionally precious airframe, for a worrying twenty-seven months it was the only development airframe.

Talks had begun with a giant of the manufacturing process, motor vehicle mogul William Morris – Lord Nuffield. The idea of 'shadow factories' – well-proven industries building aircraft to supplement the original constructor – had been commonplace in World War One. Construction of the vast Castle Bromwich Aircraft Factory, near Birmingham, began on 12 July 1938. The trickle of Spitfires soon became a flood.

In November 1944 the last major Merlin-powered Spitfire, the Mk.XVI, entered service. The secret of the type's longevity was its ability to evolve, stage by stage. Part of this transformation was a new

Above: Spitfire F.22s on the Castle Bromwich assembly line in late 1945. Many of these were completed and flight-tested at Keevil or South Marston. In the middle on the left is PK581, which was issued to the RAF in October 1945. *KEC*

Right: Westland-built Seafire III NN212 after a landing accident on HMS *Indefatigable* in January 1946. In August 1945, while flying this machine, Sqn Ldr G J Murphy downed two Japanese A6M 'Zero' fighters. *KEC*

engine developed from January 1939 – the RR Griffon. Based on Merlin thinking, although it was more powerful, it was kept compact. The Griffon turned left-handed, opposite to its forebear: this took some getting used to as pilots converted to the later Spitfires. The prototype Griffon version, the Mk.IV, had its maiden flight on 27 November 1941. To avoid confusion with the Mk.I-based photo-reconnaissance PR.IV, the Griffon Mk.IV was redesignated Mk.XX.

The first Griffon Spitfire to enter RAF service was the Mk.XII with 41 Squadron at Llanbedr in February 1943. Other fighter versions were the high-altitude Mk.XIV, from January 1944, and the Mk.XVIII of 1946. The pressurised, unarmed, long-range photo-recce PR.XIX had its debut with 542 Squadron at Benson in June 1944. The final three versions, Mks 21, 22 and 24, broke with the elliptical planform wing and adopted the laminar flow technology that was at the core of the North American Mustang's success. With very little fanfare, the final Spitfire, a Mk.24, was rolled out of the South Marston factory in February 1948.

Farewell to propellers

Supermarine responded to Specification S.24/37 of January 1938 for a shipboard torpedo dive-bomber to replace the Fairey Albacore. It was Fairey that carried off the prize, for its initially troublesome but ultimately effective Barracuda. Smith's proposal was intriguing, featuring a variable-incidence wing to lower approach speeds. Driven by an electric motor, the wing's angle relative to the fuselage could be altered in flight. Two prototypes were ordered, purely for research purposes, and it was stipulated that as much wood as possible be incorporated. With the Spitfire all-demanding, it was February 1943 before the first prototype, named 'Dumbo' because from the front the moving wing looked like flapping ears, flew. Smith returned to the concept of variable incidence for Supermarine's last flying boat, the second-generation Seagull.

All things must pass and with Specifications F.1/43 and N.5/45 the RAF and Fleet Air Arm (FAA) requested designs that would replace the Spitfire and Seafire respectively. Prominent in both requirements was greater speed, range and the laminar flow wing that had been adopted by the final Spitfire versions. With a new, two-spar wing that incorporated a wide-track, inward-retracting undercarriage, the time had come to drop the iconic name Spitfire. For the RAF the intended new fighter was the Spiteful, while the Navy settled on Seafang.

A Spitfire XIV was fitted with the new wing and it was test flown on 30 June 1944. The 'full' Spiteful prototype appeared on 8 January 1945. Four months later the initial production example was in the air. The first true Seafang F.32 had its maiden flight at Eastleigh on 18 June 1946. Overtaken by events and technologies, the Spiteful and Seafang never entered operational service.

Specification S.12/40 wanted a new fleet reconnaissance amphibian and Smith designed a sleek-looking monoplane that used a Consolidated Catalina-like pylon as the mounting for the wing. The Walrus and the Sea Otter were still in production and S.12/40 was not a priority. S.12/40 was rewritten as S.14/44 seeking an air-sea rescue amphibian, which appeared as the second-generation Seagull ASR.I. Smith returned to the

Spiteful XIV RB520, completed in 1945: behind is de Havilland Hornet F.I PX212. *Vickers-Armstrongs*

variable-incidence wing that had been pioneered by the 'Dumbo'. Two prototypes emerged from the experimental department at Hursley Park, flying in July 1948 and September 1949 respectively. No contracts followed: Supermarine's flying boat era had ended.

Jet transition

Vickers (Aviation) and Supermarine were taken back into the fold of the Vickers-Armstrongs conglomerate in October 1938 as Britain rearmed at an eye-watering rate. The conjoined companies emerged from World War Two as hugely successful, basking in the enormous success of the Wellington and the Spitfire respectively.

All of the development work on the Spiteful/Seafang laminar flow wing was not wasted. Smith and his team were aware that it was vital for both the RAF and the FAA to get a jet fighter of greater performance than the de Havilland Vampire and Gloster Meteor operational as soon as possible. The Spiteful wing and undercarriage was grafted onto a new, tail-dragging fuselage, fitted with a RR Nene turbojet. The prototype, initially known as the 'Jet Spiteful' was flown at Boscombe Down on 27 July 1946 – just a month before the full-specification Seafang had its maiden flight. A navalised, 'hooked' version with long-stroke undercarriage had its inaugural outing on 17 June 1947. The RAF did not opt for the new aircraft but, as the Attacker, it became the Navy's first front-line jet fighter, with 145 being received from August 1951.

The second prototype Seagull ASR.I, PA147, during deck-landing trials on HMS *Illustrious*, October 1949. *Vickers-Armstrongs*

Supermarine flying boats and amphibians*

From	To	Total	Name/Configuration	Type	Engine(s)	Notes
1918	-	1	N.1B Baby, pusher	1-seat patrol	1 x Hispano-Suiza	[1]
1919	1921	21	Channel, pusher	Light transport	1 x Napier Lion	[2]
1919	-	2	Sea King I, II*, III*	1-seat GP	1 X Hispano-Suiza	[3]
1920	-	1	Commercial*, pusher	Light transport	1 x RR Eagle	[4]
1922	1923	3	Sea Eagle*, pusher	Light transport	1 x RR Eagle	
1921	1926	33	Seagull I, II, III, IV*	Patrol	1 x Napier Lion	[5]
1924	-	12	Scarab*, pusher	Patrol	1 x RR Eagle	
1924	-	1	Swan	Transport	1 x Napier Lion	
1924	-	1	Scylla, monoplane	Patrol/recce	1 x RR Eagle	[6]
1925	1934	84	Southampton I–IV	Patrol	2 x Napier Lion	[7]
1927	-	1	Nanok/Solent	Torpedo/Transport	3 x AS Jaguar	[8]
1928	-	2	Seamew*	Patrol	2 x AS Lynx	
1930	-	1	Air Yacht, monoplane	VIP transport	3 x AS Jaguar	
1930	-	1	Southampton X	Patrol	3 x AS Jaguar	[9]
1932	1936	15	Scapa	Patrol	2 x RR Kestrel	
1933	1945	770	Seagull V/Walrus*	Patrol/Shipboard	1 x Bristol Pegasus	[10]
1934	1941	58	Stranraer	Patrol	2 x Bristol Pegasus	[11]
1938	1945	292	Sea Otter*	Air-sea rescue	1 x Bristol Mercury	[12]
1948	1949	2	Seagull ASR.I*, mono	Air-sea rescue	1 x RR Griffon	

Based upon *Supermarine Aircraft since 1914* by C F Andrews and E B Morgan. All tractor biplanes unless noted. [1] One converted in 1919 to Schneider race entrant Sea Lion I – see narrative. See also Chapters 9 and 38 for the Blackburn and Westland responses to the N.1B requirement. [2] Conversions of surplus AD flying boats – see sub-contracts table. [3] One converted in 1921 to Schneider race entrant Sea Lion II and in 1923 as Sea Lion III – see narrative. [4] Adapted from the unflown Seal I. [5] Prototype originally called Seal II. One-off Seal IV also known as Sheldrake. See also Walrus. [6] Taxied at Felixstowe March 1924, but not flown. [7] Mk.II onward with metal hulls; 24 metal hulls built to upgrade Mk.Is. See also Stranraer. [8] Nanok – torpedo carrier for Danish Navy, cancelled after flight trials. Reconfigured as civil 'air yacht' VIP transport. [9] Tri-motor version of Southampton with stainless steel hull and sesquiplane layout. [10] Twenty-four to Royal Australian Air Force as Seagull Vs; RAF, Fleet Air Arm and other exports all designated Walrus. Sub-contracted to Saunders-Roe (461), including 190 wooden-hulled Mk.IIs. [11] Originally designated Southampton V. Also 40 licensed by Canadian Vickers at Montreal, Manitoba, Canada. [12] Sub-contracted to Saunders-Roe (270).

Keeping to the step-by-step approach, on 29 December 1948 the Type 510 VV106, essentially an Attacker with 40-degree sweep flying surfaces, had its first flight. This became the first swept-wing jet to land on an aircraft carrier, HMS *Illustrious*, in November 1950. (Today it is preserved at the FAA Museum, Yeovilton.) By extending the 510's forward fuselage so that a nosewheel could be fitted and boosting the Rolls-Royce Nene with an afterburner, the resulting evolution was the Type 535 of 1950. From this came the Avon-engined Swift.

Much was expected of the first jet to enter operational RAF service from the hallowed Supermarine stable. Yet the Swift turned out to be part of the nightmare that brought about the hurried supply of stopgap Canadian-built North American Sabres to bolster RAF air defences. The prototype Swift had its maiden flight on 5 August 1951. By that time the Air Ministry had ordered 150 as 'insurance' in case the Hawker Hunter turned out to be a turkey. Mike Lithgow took the world airspeed record to 735.7mph over Libya on 26 September 1953 in Swift F.4 WK198.

Attacker F.1s of 800 and 803 Squadrons on HMS *Eagle* in Toulon harbour, France 1952. *KEC*

Supermarine landplane/floatplane* monoplanes

From	To	Total	Name/Designation	Type	Engine(s)	Notes
1924	-	1	Sparrow I, II	Ultralight	1 x Blackburne Thrush	[1]
1925	-	1	S.4*	Racer	1 x Napier Lion	[2]
1927	1928	3	S.5*	Racer	1 x Napier Lion	[2]
1929	1932	4	S.6/S.6A/S.6B*	Racer	1 x RR 'R'	[2]
1934	-	1	F.7/30	Fighter	1 x RR Goshawk	
1936	1948	22,759	Spitfire/Seafire	Fighter	1 x RR Merlin	[3]
1940	-	1	B.12/36	Heavy bomber	4 x RR Merlin	[4]
1943	-	2	S.24/37 'Dumbo'	Research	1 x RR Merlin	
1945	1947	29	Spiteful/Seafang	Fighter	1 x RR Griffon	
1946	1954	185	Attacker	Shipborne fighter	1 x RR Nene	
1948	1957	197	510/528/Swift	Fighter	1 x RR Avon	
1951	1954	2	Type 508, 529	Fighter	2 x RR Avon	
1956	-	1	Type 545	Fighter	1 x RR Avon	[5]
1956	1960	79	Scimitar	Shipborne strike	2 x RR Avon	

Based upon *Supermarine Aircraft since 1914* by C F Andrews and E B Morgan. **[1]** *Biplane*, 'parked' here for convenience; reconfigured as parasol *monoplane* 1926. **[2]** See narrative. **[3]** Includes Griffon-engined versions – see narrative. **[4]** Long-range heavy bomber, prototype destroyed in its jigs at Woolston in Luftwaffe raid 26 September 1940. **[5]** Prototype substantially complete when programme cancelled in 1956.

Above: Supermarine 510 VV106 during trials on HMS *Illustrious*, November 1950. *Vickers-Armstrongs*

Right: The world air speed record-breaking Swift F.4, WK198, in 1953. Today, its fuselage is preserved at the Brooklands Museum. *Vickers-Armstrongs*

Development problems bedeviled the Swift and orders were dramatically cut back. The RAF received its first Swift F.1s in early 1954 and a string of fatal accidents led to the permanent grounding of all F.1s and F.2s the following year. With a modified wing, incorporating a distinctive 'saw-tooth' leading edge, the FR.5 tactical photo-recce version first flew in May 1955. Operating at low and medium levels, the FR.5 became a potent asset with the Second Tactical Air Force in West Germany. The last of the breed, guided missile trials F.7s, were delivered to the RAF in December 1956.

Sophisticated weapon system

An experimental, twin-Avon, single-seat fighter, the Type 508, appeared in 1951 with a highly distinctive butterfly (V-shape) tail. By 1954 this had evolved into the swept-wing Type 525 with blown-flap technology and other sophistications; this became the Scimitar F.1. Taking over the helm from Smith in 1956 was Alan 'Cliffy' Clifton. An aero engineering graduate in 1922, Clifton served as a patent officer before enrolling with Supermarine in 1923. He began as Mitchell's technical assistant and was promoted the following year to lead the technical office. Under Clifton, the design department vacated the much-loved Hursley Park, moving to offices at South Marston.

In 1957 Conservative Minister of Defence Edwin Duncan Sandys had grasped the anomaly of too many manufacturers and too few contracts. His Defence White Paper of that year was intended as a 'carrot' to encourage mergers. But he lost all credibility with his 'Dan Dare' view that manned warplanes were in their final decades and that the future was missile-shaped. We are still waiting for this to ring true...

Scimitar forerunner, the second butterfly-tailed Type 508, VX136, 1952. *Vickers-Armstrongs*

Alan Clifton inside his office at Hursley Park, 1956 – note the model Scimitar. *Vickers-Armstrongs*

Entering service in August 1957, Scimitars provided the fleet with a low-level nuclear strike capability. Scimitars took over from the Swift on the South Marston production line, but only eighty-two emerged, the last one in 1960. The big, beefy naval strike fighter was the last type to carry the Supermarine name.

By the time that the British Aircraft Corporation was created in 1960, what had been Supermarine was set to fade away from aviation-related work as Vickers-Armstrongs (South Marston) Ltd. In 1959 Clifton's design office had been drafting responses to the famed Canberra replacement requirement, GOR.339. This task was subsumed under the Weybridge operation, and Clifton's lead man on the project, George S Henson and his team, relocated to Brooklands, where Vickers was fighting for its life.

The first production Scimitar F.1, XD212, prior to its appearance at the Paris Air Salon, June 1957. *Vickers-Armstrongs*

CHAPTER THIRTY-SEVEN

Heavyweights

Vickers
1911 to 1960

'Fancy having an interloper who did not know one end of an aeroplane from another coming in with equal status.'
Barnes Wallis

WITH A PORTFOLIO that included precision and electrical engineering, foundries, armaments, warships and commercial vessels, motor vehicles, locomotives and rolling stock, it was inevitable that Vickers Ltd, a massive industrial conglomerate, should want to enter the aviation business. There have been many subsidiaries and holding companies that have included the name 'Vickers' within their titles, but only the aviation-related entities need bother us here.

The first excursion into aeronautics ended in embarrassment. The Vickers, Sons and Maxim division, shipbuilders at Barrow-in-Furness, Cumberland, were engaged to construct His Majesty's Airship No. 1. Nicknamed *Mayfly*, but this contraption broke its back on the day it began trials, 24 September 1911. In that year Vickers entered the fixed-wing world with a licence to build the R.E.P steel tube monoplanes of Frenchman Robert Esnault Pelterie, and the Aviation Department was formally established on 20 January 1912. A factory at Erith on the south bank of the Thames, near Dartford, was the first venue for aircraft manufacture before larger premises not far away at Crayford were occupied in August 1914. The following year, Vickers moved to Brooklands and from 1916 the expanding division began to concentrate its operations there and at adjacent Weybridge.

In 1928 Vickers merged with another colossus, Armstrong Whitworth, to become Vickers-Armstrongs. The moguls decided that flying machines had no place in such an industrial combine and Vickers (Aviation) Ltd was let loose as a self-contained entity in

August. With ambitious expansion plans, the offspring went shopping and within three months had snapped up Supermarine. Vickers (Aviation) and Supermarine were taken back into the fold of the Vickers-Armstrongs conglomerate in October 1938 as Britain rearmed. When motor vehicle manufacturer William Morris – Lord Nuffield – pulled his organisation out from managing the vast Castle Bromwich Aircraft Factory – which opened in July 1938, building Spitfires – Vickers stepped in. The aviation division became a founder member of British Aircraft Corporation (BAC) in 1960. Ironically, armaments and shipbuilding elements of Vickers were taken on by the BAC successor, BAE Systems from 1999. Its portfolio includes: civil and military aerospace, defence electronics, munitions, naval vessels including nuclear submarines, and land warfare systems: BAE Systems is the modern-day Vickers.

The famed motor circuit club house, now the centrepiece of the Brooklands Museum. Barnes Wallis had his design office on the second floor. *Ken Ellis*

Gunbus breakthrough

Having obtained the R.E.P. licence, George Henry Challenger and Archibald R Low, both previously with Bristol, were hired to set up a design department. By 1914 Vickers had secured the services of Richard Leonard Howard Flanders and the Experimental Fighting Biplane – E.F.B. – series was initiated. Flanders had started off with Alliott Verdon Roe during his Lea Marshes Triplane phase in the summer of 1909. The following year Flanders started in his own name at Brooklands, building a successful range of monoplanes and biplanes that attracted small orders from the War Office. Optimistically named 'Destroyer', the E.F.B.1 of 1913, set the format of pusher biplane with a single- or twin-seat nacelle carrying a forward-firing gun. This led to the famous F.B.5 and F.B.9 Gunbus – although the 'Gunbus', as one word or two, was a generic name for any aircraft of this format. The first F.B.5s were issued to the Royal Flying Corps in 1914.

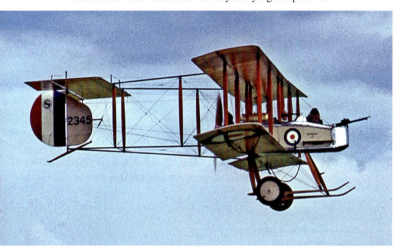

Replica FB.5 Gunbus '2345' (civil registered G-ATVP) built at Brooklands by the Vintage Aircraft and Flying Association in 1966. It was presented to the RAF Museum in June 1968. *Roy Bonser*

Vickers licences* and sub-contracts

Type	Total	From	To	Notes
R.E.P Monoplanes*	8	1911	1913	[1]
Royal Aircraft Factory B.E.2/a/c	134	1913	1916	
Royal Aircraft Factory B.E.8	35	1914	1915	
Royal Aircraft Factory F.E.8	50	1916	-	
Sopwith 1½ Strutter	150	1916	1917	
Royal Aircraft Factory S.E.5a	2,165	1917	1918	
Vickers-Wibault Scout	26	1926	-	[2]
Armstrong Whitworth Siskin IIIA	52	1929	1930	
Hawker Hart, Hart Trainer	211	1932	1936	
Avro Lancaster I	235	1944	1945	[3]

[1] Based on the designs of Frenchman Robert Esnault Pelterie, featuring a steel tube airframe. [2] Version of the Wibault 7.C1 parasol fighter. [3] Built at Hawarden, Chester.

In early 1915 Vickers test pilot Harold Barnwell flew a single-seat scout that he had designed and built himself, known as the Barnwell Bullet. Early on it suffered an accident but despite this, Vickers recognised its potential and requested drawing office apprentice Rex Pierson (of which much more anon) to redesign the little biplane. It is very likely Barnwell had given Pierson tuition at the Vickers School; Pierson got his flying 'ticket' – No. 660 – there in October 1913. The Bullet was reborn as the E.S.1 – Experimental Scout No. 1 and further improved as the E.S.1 Mk.II – some sources quote E.S.2. The type was used for trials with Vickers-developed interrupter gear for the forward-firing machine gun. Further developed, the type entered production as the F.B.19 in 1915. The F.B.14 of 1916, a two-seat armed reconnaissance biplane, was another success, more than eighty being made.

The Gunbus series and the F.B.14 and F.B.19 stood out from a string of prototype hopefuls. The company's greatest success during the Great War lay in efficient sub-contracting: including more than 2,000 Royal Aircraft Factory S.E.5as. This led to Wolseley Motors – suppliers of the fighter's Viper V-8 engine – being acquired and brought into the Vickers 'family'.

Bomber dynasty

Howard Flanders designed the first Vickers twin-engined type, the E.F.B.7 of 1915. Called a 'Gun carrier', it was intended to take a Vickers-developed one-pounder gun aloft and engage Zeppelins. A revised version, armed with lowly Lewis guns, was entrusted to 24-year-old Reginal Kirshaw 'Rex' Pierson, giving him experience that would blossom into the incredible Vimy of 1918. Norfolk-born Pierson was apprenticed at Erith in 1908 and his keenness for flying machines was rewarded in 1911 when he was transferred to the team building the R.E.P. monoplanes. As noted above, he qualified as a pilot in late 1913. Pierson was appointed chief designer in 1917 and remained at the helm of the drawing office through to his death in 1948.

As related in Chapter 36, when Supermarine was acquired in 1928, although Pierson was technically in command of both the Vickers and Woolston design offices, Reginald Joseph Mitchell was given free reign. Upon Mitchell's death in June 1937, Harold J 'Agony' Payn was appointed to act as an intermediary between Pierson and Mitchell's successor, Joseph Smith. Payn was removed in 1939 and Smith was also given virtual independence.

As well as Mitchell and Smith, Pierson also worked with another extraordinary talent, Barnes Wallis – as detailed later. Although Wallis insisted on parity with Pierson when he was appointed in January 1930, in truth it was Pierson that oversaw Wallis's output, monitoring his projects so that they could be turned into reality on the assembly floor.

Pierson was promoted to chief engineer in 1946, but the stresses of wartime pressures had taken their toll. He provided Vickers with a string of successes up to the Viking airliner, providing the company with a firm basis in commercial aviation that lasted into the 1960s. Reginald Kirshaw 'Rex' Pierson CBE died on 10 January 1948, aged 56: he was succeeded by George Edwards.

Along with the Handley Page O/400 and the de Havilland Amiens, Pierson's Vimy was designed as a bomber capable of striking at the cities of Imperial Germany. The prototype first flew at Brooklands on 30 November 1917 and several engine alternatives were tried before the Rolls-Royce (RR) Eagle was chosen for the definitive Mk.IV. Orders for 1,500 were placed, but events overtook the bomber. A single example was delivered to France in late October 1918, but it was not used in anger. With the Armistice, contracts were torn up and only about 200 Vimys were accepted for service. In 1919 Vickers was commissioned to make another thirty Mk.IVs and refurbish earlier models.

Alcock and Brown departing Lester's Field, Newfoundland, at the start of their epic transatlantic flight on 14 June 1919. *Rolls-Royce*

Above: A Virginia IX moments after being catapulted into the air at the Royal Aircraft Establishment, Farnborough, May 1931. *RAE*

Left: Interior of a Vimy Ambulance, showing the oval-shaped fuselage. *Vickers plc*

The Vimy became world famous when John Alcock and Arthur Whitten Brown flew a Vickers-owned, specially modified example non-stop across the Atlantic over 14/15 June 1919. The epic flight covered 1,890 miles in fifteen hours fifty-seven minutes at an average speed of 118.5mph from St John's, Newfoundland, to Clifden, Ireland. On 15 December 1919 the transatlantic Vimy was handed over to the Science Museum in London, where it still takes pride of place. From 1924, Vimys gave way to Vickers Virginias, which held the line well into the 1930s.

The Vimy provided the basis for the break into the burgeoning airline market. Pierson created an oval-section monocoque fuselage that was integrated into the Vimy's rear fuselage and tail surfaces and attached to the bomber's wings, powerplants and undercarriage to create the Vimy Commercial of 1919. This in turn gave rise to the Vimy Ambulance and the similar Vernon bomber-transport for the RAF. (The oval monocoque format was also used in the single-engined Vulcan biplane transport, but it failed to attract a large market.)

When 7 Squadron took delivery of its first Virginia III at Bircham Newton in June 1924, the Vimy's reign as the RAF's bomber of choice began to wane. Pierson had come up with a 'Super Vimy', although it represented only a slight improvement over its predecessor in terms of performance. In the 1920s, new types for the RAF were expected to serve for five or so years, a decade at most. The Virginia remained with front-line units until 1938, by which time the lumbering biplane was manifestly obsolete. The prototype first flew in November 1922. When the Mk.X appeared in 1928 all it had in common with the prototype was its format. Almost everything had changed: the wing shape, the length, the gun positions and the construction system. The Virginia started as wooden aeroplane; it ended with a metal airframe. Just as the Vimy was developed into the Vernon care of a large-capacity fuselage, the Virginia received similar treatment with the Victoria and the later Valencia transports.

Fighter ambitions

Although it built itself a 'name' as a manufacturer of heavyweights, Vickers did not give up on returning to the fighter market that it had penetrated with the Gunbus until the late 1940s. The most successful was a spin-off from a Pierson design to replace the Bristol F.2B Fighter and the Airco DH.9A – the two-seat Vixen of 1923. Frenchman Michel Wibault was taken on as a consultant in 1922; he had devised an easy-to-construct corrugated light alloy technique. Rather than reinvent the wheel, Vickers took up a licence for Wibault's 7.C1 single-seat parasol fighter in 1926 to fulfil a contract for Chile. In the mid-1950s Wibault came up with what he called the Gyropter, which was the springboard for the exceptional Bristol Siddeley Pegasus, the vectored-thrust turbofan that made the Harrier possible.

The single-seat Jockey of 1929 and the retractable-undercarriage Venom of 1936 were both relatively conventional prototypes aimed at specifications that, although hotly competed, went no further. When Vickers test pilot Joseph 'Mutt' Summers took the Venom aloft from Brooklands on 17 June 1936 for its first flight he must have known it was a redundant airframe. Sixty-three days earlier he had flown the Spitfire prototype: Woolston was the future of fighters, not Weybridge.

On 21 January 1931 Summers was at the controls of an aircraft that, other than its form of construction and some aerodynamic advances, would not have looked out of place in 1915 – it was the ultimate 'Gunbus'. This throwback was the COW Gun Fighter – designed around an upward-firing Coventry Ordnance Works (hence COW) 37mm gun that fired 1½lb shells. Specification F.29/27 was looking for a 'bomber destroyer', capable of flying under a bomber stream and decimating the enemy with well-aimed heavy firepower. Despite its looks, the COW Gun Fighter was full of engineering and aerodynamic innovations, but the entire concept was soon quietly dropped.

The incredible F.29/27 COW Gun Fighter of 1931; a throwback to the Gunbus. *Vickers plc*

The Type 432 under construction at the Foxwarren annexe, 1941. *via Tony Buttler*

On Christmas Eve 1942 the last Vickers fighter took to the air, from Farnborough. This was the first of two Type 432 high-altitude interceptors aimed at Specification F.7/41. Both 432s were built at the Foxwarren experimental annexe a couple of miles to the south of Brooklands. Although it was a very advanced, all-metal design it failed to rouse any interest; the requirement being met, at least in part, by the Westland Welkin. The second aircraft, although very nearly complete, was not flown.

Canadian venture

Vickers set up a shipbuilding and heavy engineering division in Canada from 1911. The pressing need for aircraft to link rural communities, or support fishing and mining outposts, was too good to miss and an aviation subsidiary began building Viking IV amphibians in 1923 at St Hubert, Montreal, Quebec. Pierson designed the Vedette, a simple pusher flying boat, for the Canadian market and the prototype had its maiden flight on 4 November

1924: it remained in production until 1930. To oversee the Vedette and to initiate indigenous production, Pierson appointed Wilfred Thomas Reid as chief designer for Canadian Vickers. As Chapter 11 explains, Reid had been chief designer for Bristol from the departure of Frank Barnwell – younger brother of Vickers test pilot Harold – in 1921. Barnwell was reinstated in 1924, putting Reid on the 'market'. Under Reid a variety of types appeared, but with limited success.

Reid left Canadian Vickers, but stayed in Montreal, forming Reid Aircraft in February 1928 to build his Rambler two-seat biplane. The American Curtiss company bought out Reid and Curtiss-Reid Aircraft was formed, constructing around forty Ramblers up to 1931. Post-Reid Canadian Vickers turned to licence manufacture of Bellanca Pacemakers and Northrop Deltas – see the table. During World War Two Canadian Vickers built Consolidated Catalinas at the government-owned plant at Cartierville, Montreal. By late 1944 Canadian Vickers had withdrawn from aircraft manufacturing.

Canadian Vickers indigenous production

Type	Total	From	To	Notes
Vedette flying boat	60	1924	1930	
Varuna flying boat	8	1925	1927	
Vista monoplane flying boat	1	1927	-	
Vanessa biplane floatplane	1	1927	-	
Velos sesquiplane floatplane	1	1928	-	
Vigil sesquiplane landplane	1	1928	-	
HS-3L Canadian Carrier	3	1928	1929	[1]
Vancouver flying boat	6	1929	1930	

Based upon *Canadian Aircraft since 1909* by K M Molton and H A Taylor.
[1] Biplane flying boat, based on Curtiss HS-2L. Additionally, two types built under arrangement with the British 'parent': Vickers Viking (6) 1923; Supermarine Stranraer (40) 1938–41. Licence production: Avro 504N (13) 1928; Bellanca Pacemaker (6) 1931; Consolidated PBY-5A/OA-10A Catalina (312) 1942–44; Fairchild FC-2 (11) 1928; Fokker Super Universal (15) 1929–30; Northrop Delta (20) 1936–40. Additionally: Handley Page Hampden fuselages for Canadian Associated Aircraft Ltd, Montreal, and up to 600 PBY Catalina hulls for Consolidated, San Diego, California, USA.

Airship rivalries

In 1908 Barnes Neville Wallis joined the shipwrights J Samuel White at East Cowes on the Isle of Wight. There, he met with H B Pratt, who had worked on the abortive *Mayfly* airship at Barrow up to 1911. Increasing rivalries with Imperial Germany meant that the military potential of Zeppelins could not be ignored and so Vickers re-established its airship works in 1913. Vickers wanted Pratt to head the new venture and he asked that Wallis join him at Barrow. The R.9 flew in 1916 and was followed by the very advanced R.80 in 1920. With no airship work coming to Barrow, Wallis took a degree in engineering in 1922 and dabbled with teaching for a while.

Convinced there was a future for commercial airships, Vickers formed a subsidiary, the Airship Guarantee Company (AGC) at Howden, west of Hull, to respond to a government requirement for a machine to fly to Canada and India. AGC received a fixed-price contract for the R.100 in October 1924. Meanwhile, the state-owned Royal Airship Works at Cardington, Bedford, was told to proceed with the R.101, without any such fiscal restrictions. Among those working with Wallis was Alfred Hessell Tiltman and his deputy, Nevil Shute Norway – the duo went on to found Airspeed – Chapter 3. Despite its bulk, R.100 was exceptionally sleek and said to have had the lowest possible aerodynamic resistance for its cross section. Weight-saving was the mantra, with much use of Duralumin and careful placing of load-carrying zones. Wire-mesh kept the fifteen gas bags in place and it is said that this criss-crossing, and the rigidity it brought for little weight, inspired the geodetics that became the hallmark of Wallis's fixed-wing creations.

Cardington's R.101 got airborne, on 14 October 1929 – it was underpowered, over-engineered and massively expensive. Sixty-four days later R.100 followed and showed immediate promise. It departed on a faultless flight to Canada in the summer of 1930. On 5 October 1930 R.101 crashed into a hillside near Beauvais in France; seven people miraculously survived, forty-seven perished. Britain's airship era was terminated; R.100 was dismantled in October 1931.

End of the biplane

Named after the African gnu, or vildebeeste in Afrikaans, the RAF opted for the simpler spelling of Vildebeest, without the final 'e'. The prototype of the big Vickers biplane had its maiden flight in April 1928 and 169 were built, in four different versions, replacing the Hawker Horsley. With minimal alteration, the Vildebeest was pitched at the RAF's need to replace the Fairey IIIF general-purpose biplane. The result was the Vincent, the first example – a conversion of a Vildebeest – first flew in 1934 and nearly 200 followed. The Vincent was named after the 18th-century Admiral John Jervis, the first Earl St Vincent. Between them the Virginia/Victoria/Valentia bomber/transport family and the Vildebeest and Vincent sustained Vickers from the early 1920s to the mid-1930s.

With the demise of the R.101, Barnes Wallis was jobless, but not for long. The chairman of Vickers and its Supermarine subsidiary, Sir Robert McLean, was determined to turn his talents to fixed-wing aircraft. He hoped that Wallis and his other 'young gun', Supermarine's Reginald Joseph Mitchell, would hit it off and provide new and vigorous approaches to Air Ministry specifications. The normally tolerant Mitchell, eight years Wallis's junior, took exception to Barnes and there was a famous moment when they took separate trains to head office to explain that they could not work together.

McClean offered Wallis the post of head of structures, under Pierson. Wallis took exception to this, so McClean upped the ante; Wallis was to work *alongside* Pierson at Brooklands. Hence the incredulity in the quote at the chapter heading: Wallis went on to describe Pierson as: 'the most generous man I have ever known'. So Wallis took the post of Chief Designer (Structures), although Pierson's remit encompassed far more; it was a clever piece of compromise to secure an incredible talent. Pierson must have seemed 'old school' to both Mitchell and Wallis, but he was a master of the practicalities of all-metal mass production. Pierson and Wallis took the aviation division of Vickers from promising sideline to industrial dynasty.

Vildebeest III K4163 of the Gosport-based Torpedo Development Unit's 'B' Flight, May 1937. *KEC*

Sir Barnes Wallis with a model of the Swallow aerodyne in his Brooklands office. *Vickers plc*

The first type Wallis worked on was the M.1/30 torpedo biplane, which adopted Duralumin for the spars, longerons and fuselage stringers. Vickers had a reputation for big, robust biplanes and while the M.1/30 looked the part, it was actually much more radical than it seemed. It first flew on 11 January 1933 but on 23 November it broke up in the air, while carrying an inert torpedo. Test pilot Summers and observer John Radcliffe successfully 'took to the silk'.

In mid-1931 the Air Ministry issued Specification G.4/31 for a general-purpose, light bomber or torpedo-carrier to replace Fairey Gordon and Westland Wapiti biplanes. In depression-ridden Britain, the winner of this contract was looking at long-term security. No fewer than nine companies built prototypes for a fly-off – see the table. Only three of these had the cushion of an Air Ministry order, the remainder were private ventures: expensive gambles with nowhere to go if rejected.

There was a great temptation to 'play safe' with G.4/31 and stick to Pierson's proven formula that had created the successful Vildebeest

and Vincent. McClean was inspired by Wallis and his new construction technique – the 'basket-weave' geodetics that made lighter, stronger aircraft. Tests at the Royal Aircraft Establishment found that the new structure exceeded all previous requirements by a significant margin. The geodetics formed a strong outer structure that could adopt complex curvatures – internal fittings, floors, etc, could be added as the airframe progressed down the assembly line.

Not only were geodetics light yet durable, the technique permitted ease of construction and repair. (Mitchell's Spitfire was also light and strong, but was a nightmare to mass produce.) By the time the Wellington was being finalised, Vickers stunned the Air Ministry by announcing in 1937 that, if ordered in hundreds, one bomber could be churned out every twenty-four hours. For G.4/31, a compromise was reached: classic Vickers biplane characteristics combined with geodetics for the fuselage 'shell' with conventional light alloy longerons.

Wallis also sketched monoplane layouts to meet G.4/31 and insisted that the time had come to drop biplanes. He got his way. A board meeting of 12 April 1932 decided to build *both* a biplane and a monoplane, at huge cost. The biplane first flew in August 1934. It was the victor of the hard-fought competition and the Air Ministry ordered 150 units. Hard on its heels was the monoplane, which took to the air in June 1935.

The two G.4/31s flew together at the Hendon Air Pageant in June 1935 and it was clear that the monoplane was a huge leap forward. The contract was reissued in October 1935 and eventually 176 were delivered. As well as this realisation, the mid-1930s showed that the 'G' for 'general purpose' was an anachronism. The big-span Vickers monoplane had the makings of an interim bomber and the other roles were forgotten. The new bomber was named in honour of Arthur Wellesley, who became the first Duke of Wellington after his dazzling defeat of Napoleon at the Battle of Waterloo in June 1815.

Often confused as external fuel tanks, the Wellesley carried a detachable pannier under each wing for up to 2,000lb of bombs.

The Vickers G.4/31 contenders, biplane and monoplane, displaying at Hendon in 1935. *Vickers-Armstrongs*

Competitors for Specification G.4/31

Maker, designation	Chapter	Basis*	Format	Engine	First flight
Armstrong Whitworth AW.19	4	PV	Biplane	AS Tiger	26 Feb 1934
Blackburn B-7	9	PV	Biplane	AS Tiger	28 Nov 1934
Bristol 120	11	PV	Biplane	Bristol Mercury	29 Jan 1932
Fairey G.4/31 Mk.II	19	PV	Biplane	AS Tiger	22 Jun 1934
Handley Page HP.47	24	Con	Monoplane	Bristol Pegasus	27 Nov 1933
Hawker PV.4	25	PV	Biplane	Bristol Pegasus	6 Dec 1934
Parnall G.4/31	29	Con	Biplane	Bristol Pegasus	1935
Vickers 253	37	Con	Biplane	Bristol Pegasus	16 Aug 1934
Vickers 246	37	PV	Monoplane	Bristol Pegasus	19 Jun 1935
Westland PV.7	38	PV	Monoplane	Bristol Pegasus	30 Oct 1933

* PV – private venture, designed and built at manufacturer's risk; Con – contract – built to Air Ministry order on cost-plus basis. Specification G.4/31 cancelled and rewritten as Specification 22/35 around the Vickers 246, as the Wellesley, with an initial order of 96.

These were needed because the 'egg shell' nature of the geodetic structure prevented large interruptions – such as bomb bays. (An egg is very tough, provided it keeps its shape.) By the time Wallis drew up the Wellington, he had realised that he could make large apertures in the airframe without compromising its integrity.

Decisive bomber

While the Wellesley was an important contract for Vickers, it had a greater purpose as a pathfinder for another Air Ministry requirement of massive potential and, ultimately, vital strategic importance. Specification B.9/32 was seeking a twin-engined medium bomber to transform the RAF's offensive capability. Ministry parameters changed as the design rolled on, but Pierson and Wallis were not just ready for these, they were ahead of them. Trevor Westbrook was given command of manufacturing the new bomber en masse and worked with Wallis to standardise the geodetic sections so that there were fewer variations, and made them lighter still. By thinking beyond the prototype, Vickers made sure the bomber would enter service smoothly and quickly. The 'one-a-day' claim mentioned earlier was far from an idle boast. As well as Brooklands, two satellite factories at Squires Gate, Blackpool, and at Hawarden, near Chester, also built Wellingtons.

On 16 June 1936 Summers took the Vickers Type 271 for its maiden flight at Brooklands. Also on board were Wallis and Westbrook: the consequences of a disaster during that first circuit do not bear thinking about. Two months later, 180 were ordered, long before the official RAF evaluation. At this point, the Type 271 was to be called Crécy, after Edward III's victory over Philip VI's forces of August 1346. That battle changed the face of warfare with longbows decimating the French. By September 1936 it was clear that the new bomber was very likely going to fight alongside France and it was renamed Wellington to avoid insulting an ally. One of Britain's greatest field marshals had managed to get his name – as Wellesley and Wellington – on two aircraft in quick succession!

The Wellington's contribution to Bomber Command was crucial; it took the brunt of the offensive until the four-engined 'heavies' gained momentum. At that point, its war was far from over, having already carved an important niche with the operational training units, as a bomber in the Middle East and with Coastal Command. On 13 October 1945 at Squires Gate the last-ever Wellington, a Mk.X, rolled off the production line. A grand total of 11,460 had been created, far more than any other British bomber. Wellingtons retired from RAF service, as crew trainers, in 1954, bringing to an end an astounding career.

Geodetic legacy

Hard on the heels of the Wellington specification, the Air Ministry issued B.1/35 for a bomber that could broadly be called the 'super' version. The prototype Warwick first flew on 13 August 1939 but was bedevilled with a slow gestation as its powerplant, role and abilities were altered. From January 1943 the Warwick was assigned to air-sea rescue and it became a very successful long-range saviour. Potentially a Wellington replacement, it was long outlived by its elder relative.

Pierson oversaw the Warwick and the follow-up, the Windsor. The last Vickers piston-engined bomber utilised the large proportions that geodetics permitted, with high aspect ratio, elliptical wings. Characterised by its four-unit main undercarriage – one in each engine nacelle – the first Windsor flew on 23 October 1943. It was a monster, carrying a 12,000lb bomb load, but Avro's Lancaster had become the weapon of choice for Bomber Command and only two more Windsors were built.

In September 1945, Pierson became chief engineer and George Edwards took over the design department – he is profiled in Chapter 13. The mother lode of the Wellington's legacy was not yet expended; Edwards knew that Vickers had to get into the civilian marketplace if it was to survive. On 22 June 1945 the Viking airliner, its wings showing its Wellington ancestry, had its maiden flight. From this stemmed the Valetta military transport and the Varsity crew trainer.

Wellington fuselages at Brooklands, at the start of the assembly process. *Vickers plc*

A Wellington I well on the way to completion, awaiting its outer wings. *Vickers plc*

Vickers to the Vimy 'family'

From	To	Total	Name/Designation	Type	Engine(s)	Notes
1912	-	1	Hydravion	4-seat pusher	1 x Gnome	[1]
1912	-	1	Tractor Biplane	2-seater	1 x Gnome	
1913	-	1	'Pumpkin'	2-seat pusher	1 x Vickers-Boucier	[2]
1913	-	1	E.F.B.1 'Destroyer'	2-seat pusher	1 x Wolseley	[3]
1913	-	7	E.F.B.2, '3 and FB.4	2-seat pusher	1 x Gnome	[3] [4]
1913	1915	321	F.B.5, F.B.9 'Gunbus'	2-seat scout	1 x Gnome	[5]
1914	-	1	Scout	2-seat	1 x Gnome	
1915	1916	c.80	E.S.1, '2, F.B.19	Scout	1 x Clerget	[6]
1915	-	2	E.F.B.7	Gun carrier	2 x Gnome	[3]
1915	-	1	E.F.B.8	2-seat scout	2 x Gnome	[3]
1916	-	1	F.B.12	Scout, pusher	1 x Le Rhône	
1916	-	1+	F.B.16 Hart Tractor	Scout	1 x Hispano-Suiza	[7]
1916	-	1	F.B.11	Zeppelin 'killer'	1 x RR Eagle	
1916	1919	80+	F.B.14	2-seat recce	1 x Beardmore	
1917	-	1	F.B.25	2-seat pusher	1 x Hispano-Suiza	
1917	-	3	FB.26 Vampire	Scout, pusher	1 x Hispano-Suiza	
1918	1919	c.6	F.B.24	2-seat fighter	1 x Hispano-Suiza	[8]
1918	1925	232	Vimy	Bomber	2 x RR Eagle	[9]
1919	-	35	VIM	Trainer	1 x RR Eagle	[10]
1919	1921	44	Vimy Commercial	Transport	2 x RR Eagle	
1921	1923	5	Vimy Ambulance	Transport	2 x Napier Lion	
1921	1925	55	Vernon	Bomber-transport	2 x Napier Lion	

Based upon *Vickers Aircraft since 1908* by C F Andrews and E B Morgan. All tractor biplanes unless noted. Majority manufactured at Crayford and, from 1916, Weybridge/Brooklands: fewer than a dozen at Bexleyheath. **[1]** Large, three-bay biplane; initially landplane, later floatplane. **[2]** Based on the Hewlett and Blondeau version of the Farman. **[3]** E.F.B. – Experimental Fighting Biplane. **[4]** Early 'Gunbus' types. **[5]** Includes one-off FB.6 sesquiplane version and licences to: Société Anonyme (SA) Darracq, Suresnes, France (99); unknown number completed as FB.9s: Nielson and Winthers, Copenhagen, Denmark (6 – perhaps 12). **[6]** Developed Barnwell 'Bullet'. E.S. – Experimental Scout, FB.19 production version. **[7]** Licensed to SA Darracq as F.B.16E – not known how many, if any, built. **[8]** At least one built by SA Darracq as F.B.24G. **[9]** Sub-contracted to: Morgan and Co, Leighton Buzzard; Royal Aircraft Factory (Establishment from 1918); Westland. **[10]** VIM – Vickers Instructional Machine; based on Royal Aircraft Factory F.E.2d.

Viking G-AGRW was delivered to British European Airways in August 1946. It last served with Autair from Luton 1963 to 1965. *Roy Bonser*

Dambuster

Wallis's visionary method of attacking Germany's dams – the 'bouncing bombs' of 617 Squadron – and the later series of huge, high-velocity weapons is beyond the remit of this book. His fertile brain had not abandoned aircraft; he made a return with typically revolutionary ideas. Travel at high-speed to Australia was his goal, but he was experienced enough to know that such a radical concept would be impossible without a military application to share the investment load.

To achieve aircraft capable of multiple-Mach figures, Wallis wanted to be rid of tail surfaces, to turn wings into the only control device and make 'fuselages' capable of a lift and/or control function. What he called the Swallow aerodyne was far more than a 'swing-wing' aircraft; it was capable of morphing its shape through all aspects of the flight profile, not just take-off and landing. What followed was one of Britain's longest research projects, from 1950 until it petered out in 1959. Given that most research ventures were aborted with great frequency in the 1950s this was all the more remarkable.

In many ways Wallis was what he had always been – way ahead of his time. High-Mach aircraft are still a rarity and only in the 21st century have aerodynamicists talked of morphing airframes. Knighted in 1968, Wallis retired from the successor of Vickers, the British Aircraft Corporation, three years later: he died on 30 October 1979, aged 92.

Turboprop contrasts

The 'low-tech' Viking lineage provided the bread and butter while Edwards and his team took massive risks and developed a world-beater: the Viscount. It originated with the machinations of the wartime Brabazon Committee tasked with scheming up commercial types that would be needed post-war. There was a major advantage of being part of the Brabazon 'club' – government orders for prototypes were up for grabs.

Pierson and then Edwards had to be tenacious to keep commercial reality to the fore. Vickers stuck to its guns: contrary to the Brabazon 'Type IIB' requirements, the new airliner would be pressurized, much larger than the projected twenty-four seats and be RR Dart turboprop powered. When Type 630 Viscount first flew on 16 July 1948 it was clearly an advanced machine with plenty of 'growth' built into it. By that time British European Airways (BEA) had become disenchanted with another Brabazon product, the Airspeed Ambassador. BEA warmed to a larger Viscount and took delivery of the first of many in January 1953. The last of 445, mostly for export, was handed over in April 1964.

Refusing to rest on the Viscount's laurels, as early as 1953 Edwards started to look at a replacement with Basil Stephenson, newly appointed as chief designer. The resultant Vanguard was much larger with substantial freight capacity within its 'double-bubble' fuselage. Powered by four RR Tynes, the prototype flew on 20 January 1959 but only another forty-three followed it, amid massive financial losses. BEA and Trans Canada Airlines, the only customers, were heavily involved in the specifications and Vickers had created a machine with little market appeal.

Vickers biplanes from 1919

From	To	Total	Name/Designation	Type	Engine(s)	Notes
1919	1925	34	Viking, Vulture, Vanellus	GP amphibian	1 x Napier Lion	[1]
1921	1923	3	Valentia	Patrol flying boat	2 x RR Condor	[2]
1922	1925	9	Vulcan	Transport	1 x RR Eagle	
1922	1932	126	Virginia I to X	Heavy bomber	2 x Napier Lion	[3]
1922	1936	125	Victoria/Valentia	Transport	2 x Bristol Pegasus	[4]
1923	-	1	Viget	Ultralight	1 x Douglas	
1923	1930	55	Vixen 'family'	Fighter/recce	1 x Napier Lion	[5]
1924	-	1	Vagabond	2-seat ultralight	1 Bristol Cherub	
1925	1933	16	Vespa	Army co-op	1 x AS Jaguar	
1926	1928	5	Vendace	Trainer	1 x Hispano-Suiza	
1926	1929	8	Hispano Scout	Fighter	1 x Hispano-Suiza	[6]
1928	1932	2	Vellore I and IV	Mailplane	1 x Bristol Jupiter	
1928	1937	209	Vildebeest	Torpedo bomber	1 x Bristol Pegasus	[7]
1929	-	1	Type 150/Vanox	Bomber	2 x RR F.XIV	[8]
1930	-	1	Vellore III	Mailplane	2 x Bristol Jupiter	
1931-	-	1	Type 161	Fighter	1 x Bristol Jupiter	
1931	-	1	Type 163	Transport	4 x RR F.XIV	
1933	-	1	M.1/30	Torpedo bomber	1 x RR Buzzard	
1934	-	1	Vellox	Mailplane	2 x Bristol Pegasus	
1934	1936	197	Vincent	Military GP	1 x Bristol Pegasus	
1934	-	1	G.4/31	Military GP	1 x Bristol Pegasus	[9]

Based upon *Vickers Aircraft since 1908* by C F Andrews and E B Morgan. Viking, Vulture, Vanellus and Type 161 pushers; Type 163 tandem format, 2-pushers, 2-tractors: all others tractors. **[1]** Vulture also known as Viking VI (2 built), Vanellus also known as Viking VI (1 built). Viking IV also built by Canadian Vickers (6). **[2]** Also known as Valencia; see below for second use of Valentia. All three had hulls built by S E Saunders at Cowes. First prototype built by S E Saunders at Cowes; other two assembled at Barrow. **[3]** See narrative. **[4]** Second use of name Valentia (see above): bomber-transport version of Victoria; Victorias also converted to Valentia status. **[5]** One Vixen rebuilt as the Vivid (or Vixen VII) 1927. Six Ventures for RAF trials, built 1924. Valpariso, export version of Vixen; licensed to Oficinas Gerais de Materiel Aeronáutical (OGMA) of Portugal – 13 built 1929–30. One Valiant, version of Vivid with Bristol Jupiter, 1927. **[6]** Bolivian Scout export version with Bristol Jupiter (6) plus Type 177 for Air Ministry evaluation. **[7]** Licensed to Construcciones Aeronauticas SA (CASA) at Cadiz, Spain (25) plus one from Vickers-built parts. **[8]** F.XIV became the Kestrel. Type 150 rebuilt/re-engined as Type 195, then Type 255 Vanox. **[9]** Parallel contender with the Wellesley – see 'Vickers Monoplanes from 1926'.

The first production Viscount 701, G-ALWE, was delivered to British European Airways in January 1953. *BEA*

British European Airways Vanguard G-APEK at Heathrow in April 1962; it first flew at Brooklands the previous August. *Roy Bonser*

Vickers post-war airliners and transports

Type	First Flown	Last delivery	Total built
Viking	22 Jun 1945	Apr 1949	163
Valetta	30 Jun 1947	Sep 1952	252
Varsity	17 Jul 1949	Feb 1954	163
Viscount	16 Jul 1948	Apr 1964	445
Vanguard	20 Jan 1959	Apr 1964	44
VC10	29 Jun 1962	Feb 1970	54

Bomber interlude

On 2 February 1949 Vickers was awarded an off-the-drawing-board contract for what became the Valiant – it was back in the bomber business. Vickers was to build the relatively low-risk type as the first of the trio of V-bombers – Avro and Handley Page opting for radical aerodynamics for the Vulcan and Victor, respectively. Chapter 24 takes a look at this lavish programme; the ordering of three types into production and allowing another – the delayed Short Sperrin – to reach prototype stage.

The first Valiant was flown from the grass at Wisley, near Brooklands, on 18 May 1951. (By 1953 Wisley had a concrete south-west–north-east runway.) The Valiant pioneered long-range jet operations for the RAF and lived up to Edwards's assessment of it as an 'unfunny' (ie. no frills) bomber.

There was a sub-plot to the Valiant. Inside the flight sheds at Wisley in 1955 a new prototype was coming together to meet a joint civil–military Ministry of Supply requirement. This was the V1000 jet transport, based on the wing of the Valiant and much of the know-how gleaned in the bomber's gestation. RAF Transport Command had ordered six; British Overseas Airways Corporation (BOAC) and even Pan American had expressed interest.

The RAF pulled out in November 1955 and the prototype V1000 was scrapped as no airlines could be tempted to commit. The RAF switched allegiances to the turboprop Bristol Britannia, but built by Shorts. The Belfast manufacturer was to have produced Swifts – from the Vickers sister company, Supermarine – and had suffered badly from the drastic cut back of that programme.

Hard lessons

The lessons of the Vanguard were not well heeded. The last Vickers type to be built was finalised in 1957 almost exclusively around BOAC's Far East and Africa services. The French Sud Caravelle, first flown in May 1955, pioneered putting jet engines on the rear fuselage to allow for a very 'clever' wing. The VC10 was breathtaking and set to be one of the most attractive of jetliners.

Convinced that the VC10 faced a long production run, Vickers erected a huge assembly hall, known as 'The Cathedral', specifically

A Valiant tucks up the gear on its first flight from Brooklands, with the motor circuit club house on the right. Its destination would have been the test airfield at Wisley, a couple of miles to the south-east. *Vickers*

Vickers monoplanes from 1928

From	To	Total	Name/Designation	Type	Engine(s)	Notes
1928	-	1	Vireo	Shipborne fighter	1 x AS Lynx	[1]
1929	-	1	Jockey	Fighter		
1930	1933	5	Viastra	Airliner	See note	[2]
1935	1938	177	Wellesley	Bomber	1 x Bristol Pegasus	[3]
1936	-	1	Venom	Fighter	1 x Bristol Aquila	
1936	1945	11,461	Wellington	Bomber	1 x Bristol Pegasus	[4]
1939	1945	845	Warwick I to V	Patrol/ASR	2 x Bristol Centaurus	
1942	-	2	Type 432	Fighter	2 x RR Merlin	[5]
1943	1946	3	Windsor	Bomber	4 x RR Merlin	[6]
1945	1949	163	Viking	Airliner	2 x Bristol Hercules	
1948	1951	252	Valetta	Transport	2 x Bristol Hercules	
1948	1964	445	Viscount	Airliner	4 x RR Dart	[7]
1949	1954	163	Varsity	Crew trainer	2 x Bristol Hercules	[8]
1951	1957	107	Valiant	Heavy bomber	4 x RR Avon	
1959	1964	44	Vanguard	Airliner	4 x RR Tyne	
1962	1970	54	VC10/Super VC10	Airliner	4 x RR Conway	

Based upon *Vickers Aircraft since 1908* by C F Andrews and E B Morgan. All piston engined, other than Viscount and Vanguard – turboprop; Valiant and VC10 jet. **[1]** Using Avions Michel Wibault construction technique. **[2]** First prototype assembled by Supermarine at Woolston. Built in 1-, 2- and 3-engined formats: Mk.I 3 x AS Lynx, Mk.II 2 x Bristol Jupiter; Mk.III 2 x AS Jaguar; Mk.VI 1 x Bristol Jupiter; Mk.VIII 3 x Bristol Jupiter; Mk.X 2 x Bristol Pegasus. **[3]** Prototype monoplane contender for G.4/31 – see also table 'Vickers biplanes from the Vulcan'. Production version named Wellesley. **[4]** Also produced at Hawarden and Squires Gate. **[5]** Second example nearly complete when programme cancelled May 1943. **[6]** Fourth example nearly complete when programme cancelled March 1946. **[7]** Total of 166 completed at Brooklands, remainder at Hurn. **[8]** Seventeen completed at Brooklands, remainder at Hurn.

for the new jetliner. The prototype thundered down the Brooklands runway on 29 June 1962. Even though the famed banking of the former motor racing circuit had been cut through to extend the runway, it was too tight for fully laden landings. (Airliner and Valiant first flights were 'commutes' to nearby Wisley or to Hurn at Bournemouth.)

BOAC chopped and changed its corporate mind and the type's prospects suffered accordingly. By the time the prototype had flown, top management at BOAC had their eyes firmly on Boeing at Seattle. When the airline discovered how high the VC10's customer appeal was, a U-turn was impossible. It came as a staggering blow to the Vickers boardroom and the workforce alike

that this radical, well-performing, type only beat the Vanguard's dire production run by ten. Other than BOAC, several airlines ordered in small numbers and the RAF took fourteen. (After the Falklands conflict, former airline VC10s were turned into long-serving tankers, greatly helping work-starved Filton.)

The illustrious name Vickers ground to a halt on 1 July 1960 when it became 40% of the new British Aircraft Corporation combine. Vickers had joined with English Electric and Bristol for the potentially glittering prize of GOR.339 – the TSR.2. Unlike the mutually beneficial union with Supermarine in 1928, this was a forced marriage and bound for a rocky ride.

VC10 G-ARVM, bound for British Overseas Airways Corporation, climbs away from the south-east runway at Brooklands on its maiden flight on 8 July 1964. Behind is 'The Cathedral' assembly hall. *Vickers plc*

CHAPTER THIRTY-EIGHT

Rotary Metamorphosis

Westland and Leonardo
1915 to date

'Designed, built and supported by Leonardo in the UK, our helicopters empower aircrews around the world...'
Leonardo website

WITH THE END of World War Two it was obvious that there would be far fewer military programmes and that they would be of ever increasing complexity. The airliner market was expected to expand rapidly, but new designs – especially those taking the leap into the jet age – would be phenomenally costly to launch and full of risk. What would become known as general aviation was at best a niche market and unlikely to sustain the bigger industry 'players' without dramatic downsizing. Too many companies were chasing a decreasing number of opportunities.

Among those realising this was the board of directors at Westland, who had wisely concluded that its Wyvern strike fighter was the company's last fixed-wing programme. The Yeovil-based enterprise had made a name for itself during the war as a very efficient Spitfire sub-contractor and Seafire specialist. Dating from 1936, its Lysander army co-operation type reached four figures in its production run, but its Whirlwind and Welkin fighters became also-rans. The prognosis for Westland was not good; perhaps it would be swallowed by one of the larger organisations.

Wildcat development airframe ZZ402 was first flown at Yeovil in November 2010 and was engaged in a series of deck landing trials until its retirement in 2016. *AgustaWestland*

That was not the case; Yeovil became a giant-killer, acquiring Saunders-Roe (Saro) in August 1959, Fairey Aviation Ltd in February 1960, finishing off the following month with elements of Bristol. (See the table 'Westland 'inheritance' programmes'.) What did these three 'victims' have in common? All three were in the rotary-wing business. Westland entered that sector in 1947 and thirteen years later it had transformed itself into Britain's *only* helicopter manufacturer of substance.

Matthew Uttley's *Westland and the British Helicopter Industry 1945 to 1960* is hardly edge-of-the-seat reading but it is a magnificent study of how a business should never be scared of opting for metamorphosis. Uttley explains that in the late 1940s and '50s the

Ministry of Supply (MoS) hoped that a functioning helicopter industry would emerge, but there was no obvious heir apparent. To help things along, the ministers fell back on the established tactics of scattering research and development contracts and what Uttley called a 'buy national' programme: Darwin's theory of evolution would do the rest.

Uttley describes Yeovil's rationale: '... to circumvent in-house research and development and focus instead on manufacturing proven US designs [to provide] the firm with a competitive edge and a route to British helicopter market dominance. ... Conversely, Bristol, Fairey and other UK firms bound by the MoS-sponsored 'all-British' programme were conducting development of unproven and experimental rotor technology, airframe layouts and components. These fundamental differences in activities, each involving radically different levels of technological risk, enabled Westland to enter [large] scale manufacture ahead of its UK competitors.'

Westland 'inheritance' programmes

Type	Last example	Chapter	Notes
Bristol Belvedere	1962	11	
Fairey Rotodyne	1957	19	[1]
Fairey Gannet AEW.3	1963	19	
Saro P.531 Sprite	1959	32	[2]

[1] Sole prototype first flew in 1957, development testing continued to February 1962, when the programme was terminated. [2] Programme evolved as the Scout and Wasp – see narrative.

A field near Yeovil

Petters Ltd began making ironmongery and agricultural machinery in Yeovil during the 1860s. Expansion was such that from 1913 the company settled on fields to the west of Yeovil, with plans to build a factory estate, and the name Westland was chosen. Twin brothers Percival Waddams Petter and Sir Ernest Willoughby Petter were at the helm as the Great War broke out. Determined to 'do their bit' for the nation, they embarked on a new venture, aircraft manufacture under sub-contract, from June 1915.

The Westland factory and airfield, looking west, in the early 1960s. *Westland*

Arthur Davenport, aged 24, was engaged as draughtsman to prepare drawings for the first commissions: Short 184 and 166 floatplanes. Davenport was previously engaged by Ruston Proctor and Company in Lincoln, another engineering firm that had turned its hand to aeroplane sub-contracts. The first Type 184 was completed in January 1916 and by then the decision had been taken to make aviation a stand-alone operation under the name Westland Aircraft Works. As can be seen from the table, Westland handled many types as a sub-contractor and its efficiency and quality were nationally recognised.

The relationship with the Aircraft Manufacturing Company (Airco) was particularly beneficial – for both parties. The DH.4 was followed by the DH.9 and, to take some of the load off Airco, Westland was chosen to redesign the DH.9 airframe to take the American 400hp Liberty engine: the prototype first flew on 19 April 1918. This type became a lifesaver for Yeovil beyond the Armistice: the standard DH.9A remained in production, rebuilding 'tired' DH.9A airframes was a steady task and the airframe became the basis of the Walrus shipborne reconnaissance type of 1920.

Civilian diversion

Davenport's first in-house project had been the N.1B scout floatplane of 1917, in which he assisted the works manager, Robert Bruce: it did not get beyond the prototype stage. Bruce and Davenport continued their collaboration with the Wagtail and Weasel fighters, but both failed to enter series production. Davenport was appointed chief designer in 1919 and, recognising the paucity of military work, turned to the civilian market. As the name implied, the Limousine biplane was aimed at the well-to-do, carrying three or five passengers in sumptuous accommodation: eight were built up to 1922.

Bruce was a biplane adherent, Davenport was a monoplane man. For the 1924 Lympne two-seater lightplane trials, the Woodpigeon biplane and the Widgeon parasol monoplane were entered. With considerable development, power going from the 35hp of the Mk.I to 120hp and the empty weight increasing from 475lb to the Mk.IIIA's 1,650lb, the Widgeon became a reasonable success. The duo agreed that their next civilian, a small airliner, should be a monoplane. Initially called Limousine IV, the new tri-motor later adopted the more prosaic name Westland IV. The prototype had its maiden flight on 21 February 1929 and four were ordered by Belgian airline Sabena. The sales department must have held sway; the improved version was renamed Wessex.

'Ninak' legacy

The legacy of the 'Ninak' – the DH.9A – loomed large at Yeovil. Specification 26/27 was looking to replace, among other types, the DH.9A in the 'general purpose' role: by the mid-1920s that encompassed day bombing, armed reconnaissance, army co-operation and communications. Davenport came up with a design that relied heavily on the DH.9A, including wings and tail surfaces. Although the requirement ideally wanted all-metal construction, the Wapiti was the clear winner of the contest. The prototype first flew on 7 March 1927. As time went by the Wapiti adopted metal-framed wings and rear fuselage: more than 500 were built, transforming Westland's prospects. With such a large production run a sub-contractor was needed and wing specialist Gloster was signed up. The mid- to late-1920s was a 'fallow' time for Gloster and this work was very welcome.

Davenport realised that there was still potential in the Wapiti and the board sanctioned a private-venture improvement, the PV.6, or Wapiti VII. This had mixed construction like its predecessor, a 2ft longer fuselage and the option of an enclosed cockpit. It had its maiden flight on 31 October 1931. The Air Ministry accepted the type as a day bomber for the home auxiliary squadrons and for general duties in the Near East and North West India. Westland had achieved a cost-effective way of continuing its assembly line well into the 1930s.

The new machine was called Wallace, which failed to conform to any of the naming protocols of the inter-war years: it should have been an animal, ideally four-legged. It *might* have been named after a small township in Ontario, Canada. It surely wasn't commemorating the 13th-century Scottish independence zealot Sir William Wallace, was it?

The first of twenty-eight Wapiti IAs for the Royal Australian Air Force at Yeovil, February 1929. *Westland*

Along with the private-venture, Wallace-derived, PV.3 torpedo bomber, the PV.6 was adapted for the Houston Mount Everest Flying Expedition of 1933. This had been sponsored by the saviour of the British entry in the 1931 Schneider Trophy, Lady 'Poppy' Houston – see Chapter 36. On 3 April 1933 Lt David McIntyre and Air Cdr Lord Clydesdale successfully flew the PV.3 and PV.6 over Everest. McIntyre and Clydesdale went on to found Scottish Aviation - see Chapter 33.

Westland licences* and sub-contracts

Type	Total	From	To	Notes
Short 184	12	1916	1916	
Short 166	20	1916	-	
Sopwith 1½ Strutter	125	1916	1917	
Airco DH.4	140	1917	1918	
Airco DH.9	c.260	1918	1918	
Airco DH.9A	355	1918	1927	
Vickers Vimy	25	1918	1919	
Cierva C.29*	1	1933	-	[1]
Hendy Heck	1	1934	-	[2]
Cierva-Lepère CL.20*	1	1935	-	[3]
Hawker Audax I	43	1937	-	[4]
Hawker Hector I	178	1937	-	[4]
Supermarine Spitfire I, V	685	1941	1943	
Fairey Barracuda I, II	18	1942	1943	
Supermarine Seafire II, III, XV, XVII	2,115	1943	1946	
Bell 47G-3B-4*	266	1964	1969	[5]
Sud SA.330 Puma*	48	1970	1981	[6]
Sud SA.341 Gazelle*	265	1972	1983	[6] [7]
McDonnell Douglas AH-64 Apache*	67	2000	2004	[8]

Note: See also the table 'Westland Sikorsky licences'. [1] Entered flight test, but failed to fly. [2] Prototype, series production by Parnall – Chapter 29. [3] Entered flight test, but failed to fly. Six production examples laid down, but not completed. [4] Contract originally placed with Avro. [5] Licensed from Augusta, Italy, from an original Bell, USA, licence. Sioux AH.1s for Army Air Corps/Royal Marines, HT.2s for RAF Central Flying School and 16 civilian examples for Bristow Helicopters. [6] Part of Anglo-French helicopter agreement – see narrative. Licensed from Sud Aviation, France; which became Aérospatiale in 1970. [7] Gazelle AH.1s for Army Air Corps/Royal Marines, HT.2s for Royal Navy, HT.3s for RAF and three examples for civil use. [8] Licensed from Boeing, Mesa, Arizona – having acquired McDonnell Douglas in 1997. Anglicized AH-64D Apache Longbow with RR/Turboméca RTM322 and other changes as WAH-64 Apache AH.1; assembled at Yeovil from US-built components.

PV.3 G-ACAZ photographed from PV.6 G-ACBR as they approach Mount Everest, 3 April 1933. *Westland*

Somerset exotica

Inspired by the thoughts of Russian designer M Voevodskii, the Royal Aircraft Establishment (RAE) and the Aeronautical Research Committee had tested some models in 1919. The Russian proposed a very deep aerofoil to create an all-metal cantilever monoplane wing that blended into the fuselage. In modern day parlance, the Dreadnought would be regarded as a pioneer of the blended wing body concept: it was well ahead of the investigations by George Miles – Chapter 28 – that took form as the 'X Minor aerodynamic test bed of 1942.

Issuing Specification 6/21 to Westland, the Air Ministry chose to call the required machine a 'Postal' with accommodation for eight passengers. (The 'Postal' ruse was used for commissions to Fairey, for the Long Range Monoplane, and to Boulton Paul, Bristol and Parnall – for 'mid-engined' types.) On 9 May 1924 test pilot Stuart Keep took the Dreadnought for its maiden flight, which ended quickly in disaster. Keep was rescued but both of his legs had to be amputated. The project was not resurrected.

Having flown Royal Aircraft Factory S.E.5s in the Great War with 29 Squadron, Captain Geoffrey Terence Roland Hill MC served as a test pilot with the RAE and, from late 1918, with Handley Page. Like Juan de la Cierva – Chapter 15 – Hill became fascinated by aircraft that could not stall. He came up with a tail-less configuration with rotating 'controllers' at the wing tips that acted as both elevators and ailerons. Small rudders mid-set underneath the wings provided additional directional control. Hill made a glider to prove his point and on the last day of 1924 he flew it at the wonderfully named Devil's Rest Bottom on the Sussex Downs. This got the RAE interested and eventually, the Air Ministry. Hill built a powered version, the Pterodactyl I, which he piloted at Farnborough on 2 November 1925. (This machine is displayed at the Science Museum in London.)

The Pterodactyl V two-seat fighter prototype, 1932. *Westland*

William Edward 'Teddy' Willoughby Petter in his office at Warton, with a model of the English Electric Canberra in the foreground. *British Aerospace*

With official interest increasing, Hill joined the staff of Westland in 1926, specifically to exploit his concept. In his superb *Westland Aircraft since 1915*, Derek James excels himself by describing the generic name that Hill adopted, Pterodactyl: 'It stemmed from the Greek meaning "winged finger", given to one of the feared tail-less pteranodons which flapped their way over the earth some 150 million years ago.' The Pterodactyl II and III remained on the drawing board but the Mk.IV two-seat pusher first flew in March 1931, leading to the tractor-configured Mk.V two-seat fighter in May 1934. Both were very advanced, but the Pterodactyls flapped no further.

Keeping it in the family

Many an offspring has joined the family firm to 'learn the ropes' and in June 1929 a 21-year-old started as an apprentice at Yeovil. He was William Edward 'Teddy' Willoughby Petter, son of Sir Ernest, who had studied aerodynamics at Caius (which, of course, is pronounced 'Keys') College, Cambridge, leaving with an impressive string of honours. Having worked his way around the departments, Petter settled in at the drawing office in June 1931: it was 1944 before he left it.

In January 1932 he became Bruce's assistant. Two years later, young Petter was given a seat on the board and the title of technical director. Horrified, Bruce – aged 65 – resigned and he was soon to be followed by Geoffrey Hill. From then on Davenport worked directly for Petter. During a reorganisation, the Westland Aircraft Works was renamed Westland Aircraft Ltd on 4 July 1935.

Petter's first design to fly became an exceptional warplane, in circumstances neither he nor the RAF could have foreseen. Meeting Specification A.29/34 to replace the Hawker Hector army co-operation biplane, the Lysander – named after the 4th-century BC Spartan warrior – first flew on 15 June 1936. A radical parasol monoplane, with a fully slotted wing and generous flaps, it could use very restricted fields. Ingeniously, each large spat that streamlined the mainwheels also contained a 0.303in machine gun and a stub wing carrying light bombs could be attached. More than 1,600 were built up to 1942, including licence manufacture in Canada. From 1941, the Mk.III (Special Duties) earned the type its fame, although it was some time before its role of 'delivering' and picking up Special Operations Executive agents – 'Joes' and 'Josephines' – in occupied Europe became public knowledge.

Concentrated firepower

Specification F.37/35 of February 1936 sought a long-range fighter with four 20mm cannon and an all-around view for its pilot. Petter created a beauty that solicited an order for 340 straight off the drawing board. The prototype Whirlwind had its maiden flight on 11 October 1938. The twin-engined layout allowed the four Hispano 20mm guns to be clustered in the nose, providing formidable concentrated firepower. Each cannon could spew 650 shells a minute at a muzzle velocity of 2,800ft per second and was fed by a drum holding sixty shells, so pilots had to be sparing with the trigger. Even so, a one-second burst from the four guns hurled forty shells, each weighing 9oz, in a devastating torrent of hot metal.

Westland biplanes

From	To	Total	Name/Designation	Type	Engine(s)	Notes
1917	-	2	N.1B	Scout floatplane	1 x Clerget	[1]
1918	1920	5	Wagtail	Fighter	1 x ABC Wasp	
1919	1920	4	Weasel	2-seat fighter	1 x ABC Dragonfly	
1919	1922	8	Limousine I–III	Light transport	1 x RR Falcon	
1920	1923	36	Walrus	Shipborne recce	1 x Napier Lion	
1924	-	2	Woodpigeon	Ultralight	1 x Bristol Cherub	
1924	1926	3	Yeovil	Day bomber	1 x RR Condor	
1926	1927	2	Westbury	Heavy fighter	2 x Bristol Jupiter	
1928	1932	558	Wapiti I–VIII	Military GP	1 x Bristol Jupiter	[2]
1931	-	1	PV.3	Torpedo bomber	1 x Bristol Jupiter	[3]
1931	1936	174	PV.6/Wallace	Military GP	1 x Bristol Pegasus	[4]
1934	-	1	F.7/30	Fighter	1 x RR Goshawk	

Based upon *Westland Aircraft since* 1915 by Derek N James. **[1]** See also Chapters 9, 36 and 39 for the Blackburn, Supermarine and Wight responses to the N.1B requirement. **[2]** Sole Mk.VII became PV.6 and prototype Wallace. **[3]** Himalaya expedition – see narrative. **[4]** PV.6, former Wapiti VII, became Wallace prototype: took part in Himalaya expedition – see narrative.

Above: Five of six Lysander IIs delivered to the Irish Air Corps at Baldonnel, near Dublin, July 1939. *KEC*

Left: Armourers at work on a Whirlwind; the nose section has been removed to show the battery of 20mm cannon. *KEC*

Development and manufacturing problems meant that the first deliveries did not take place until June 1940. Despite its potential, by then the Whirlwind was doomed. Pilots found it a delight to fly, but it was underpowered and its high landing speed excluded the twin from many airfields. For ground crews the Rolls-Royce (RR) Peregrine, the ultimate evolution of the Kestrel of Hawker Fury fame, proved to be very troublesome.

The Whirlwind was the only front-line type with the Peregrine, making the powerplant an 'orphan'. The Ministry of Aircraft Production deemed that it would be better if Westland built Supermarine Spitfires and Seafires, and that RR should concentrate on the Merlin. The plug was pulled and the last of 112 Whirlwinds rolled out at Yeovil in December 1941. By that time, Spitfire Vs were coming off the assembly line. A 'Seafire office' was set up to manage the carrier-borne version; the manual wing-fold system originating at Yeovil. Manufacture of Seafires by Cunliffe-Owen Aircraft at Southampton was managed from Yeovil.

Petter's final design for Westland was another shapely twin, the very large – 70ft 4in span – Welkin. Its origins lay with fears of high-flying Junkers bombers roaming free in British airspace. The prototype Welkin – Old English for 'tall sky' – first flew on 1 November 1942 and the type suffered considerable delays. The pressurised cockpit took a lot of time and effort to perfect, but it made

In his book *Adventure with Fate* (Airlife, 1984), Harald Penrose highlighted the yawning gap between practicality and adherence to aerodynamic purity: '… I had emphatically disagreed with Petter's perilous decision to run the exhaust pipes through the petrol tanks in the wing to avoid parasitic resistance. I stressed that this was a fighting machine and one bullet through the tank and exhaust would set the whole thing on fire. [Petter] coldly told me: "You pilots have to accept a few risks you know."'

Westland monoplanes

From	To	Total	Name/Designation	Type	Engine(s)	Notes
1924	-	1	Dreadnought	Research/'Postal'	1 x Napier Lion	[1]
1924	1930	26	Widgeon I, II, III	Tourer, parasol	1 x ADC Cirrus	
1927	-	1	Wizard	Fighter, parasol	1 x RR Falcon	
1928	-	1	Witch	Bomber, parasol	1 x Bristol Jupiter	
1928	-	1	Pterodactyl IA	Tail-less research	1 x AS Genet	[2]
1928	-	1	Interceptor	Fighter	1 x Bristol Mercury	
1928	1933	10	IV and Wessex	Light transport	3 x AS Genet	[3]
1930	-	1	COW Gun Fighter	Fighter	1 x Bristol Mercury	[4]
1931	-	1	Pterodactyl IV	Tail-less research	1 x DH Gipsy	[5]
1932	-	1	Pterodactyl V	Tail-less fighter	1 x RR Goshawk	[6]
1933	-	1	PV.7	Military GP	1 x Bristol Pegasus	
1936	1942	1,652	Lysander	Army co-op	1 x Bristol Mercury	[7]
1938	1941	116	Whirlwind	Fighter	2 x RR Peregrine	
1942	1945	77	Welkin	High-altitude fighter	2 x RR Merlin	[8]
1946	1956	124	Wyvern	Shipborne strike	1 x AS Python	[9]

Based upon *Westland Aircraft since 1915* by Derek N James. **[1]** Crashed on maiden flight, 9 May 1924. **[2]** G T R Hill design concept – pusher. **[3]** Two Westland IVs – later converted to Wessex status – and eight Wessex. **[4]** Upward-firing Coventry Ordnance Works (hence COW) 37mm gun firing a 1½lb shell. **[5]** G T R Hill design concept – pusher. **[6]** G T R Hill design concept – tractor. Wing failed during taxying trials 1932; successful maiden flight May 1934. **[7]** Around 17 constructed/assembled by Westland at Doncaster, 1940. Licensed to: National Steel Car Corporation, Malton, Ontario, Canada (225). **[8]** Twenty-six airframes completed 1945–46 but not flown. **[9]** Complex development history – see narrative.

The Welkin prototype, DG558, under test by the Aeroplane and Armament Experimental Establishment, Boscombe Down, early 1943.
Peter Green Collection

Westland Sikorsky helicopter licences

From	To	Total	Name/Designation	Type	Engine(s)	Notes
1949	1954	149	WS-51 Dragonfly	GP, military/civil	1 x Alvis Leonides	
1953	1966	292	WS-55 Whirlwind	Transport	1 x Alvis Leonides	[1]
1955	1959	12	WS-51 Srs 2 Widgeon	Gp. military/civil	1 x Alvis Leonides	[2]
1958	1971	382	WS-58 Wessex	Transport/Anti-Sub	1 x Napier Gazelle	
1959	1966	75	WS-55 Whirlwind Srs 3	Transport/ASR	1 x BS Gnome	[3]
1969	1995	344	WS-61 Sea King	Anti-sub/transport	2 x BS Gnome	[4]
1987	-	1	WS-70 Black Hawk	Transport	2 x GE T700	[5]

Based upon *Westland Aircraft since* 1915 by Derek N James. **[1]** Some conversions to turboshaft status, eg. Royal Navy HAR.9s, civil Series 3. **[2]** Plus three converted from Dragonflies. **[3]** Also conversions from piston-powered WS-55s. **[4]** Includes non-amphibious Commando transport, introduced 1973. Royal Navy variants included upgrades, eg. HAS.2 to HAS.6, and airborne early warning conversions. **[5]** Demonstrator assembled at Yeovil from Sikorsky-built components.

Yeovil an expert in such systems, so much so that a subsidiary, Normalair, was set up to pioneer industrial applications. Spitfires and Mosquitos that could climb ever higher coupled with the absence of the Luftwaffe at extreme altitude made the Welkin redundant: most were delivered direct to storage and scrapped.

By 1944 Petter was insisting that he be promoted to chief engineer, but he was rebuffed. He resigned in July and his story is taken up in Chapters 18 and 20 as the designer of the English Electric Canberra and the Folland Gnat, respectively.

Last of the line

Arthur Davenport took over from Petter as technical director in 1944. The role of chief designer was taken by John Wingfield Digby, who had trained as a RAF pilot in 1919 before studying aerodynamics at Cambridge. After graduating he moved to Yeovil's stress department, where one of his first tasks was the unfortunate Dreadnought of 1924. A decade later he was appointed assistant chief designer, under Davenport and Petter. From 1944 Digby and Davenport spent the next nine years getting the Wyvern naval fighter from the drawing board to squadron service.

Specification N.11/44 was overtaken by N.12/45; both looking for a turboprop-powered torpedo-strike fighter. Engine manufacturers were struggling to get a powerplant ready and on 12 December 1946 the prototype Wyvern was flown, fitted with a RR Eagle 22 piston engine. The first RR Eagle appeared in 1915 and was a 250hp V-12: the all-new second user of the name was a massive 24-cylinder H-format of 3,500hp that first ran in 1944. Fitting the Eagle 22 to the Wyvern was an interim solution allowing flight testing to commence while the turboprops were patiently awaited. The two competitors, the RR Clyde and the Armstrong Siddeley Python, were flown on development Wyverns on 18 January 1949 and 22 March 1949 respectively.

With a red wyvern painted on the nose, Wyvern S.4 VZ789 of 831 Squadron on the deck of HMS *Eagle*, February 1956. *Armstrong Siddeley*

By the time the definitive Python-powered Wyvern flew in May 1951 the torpedo requirement had been dropped and it was given the new 'S-for-strike' designation of S.4. Even then, the eight-blade, contra-rotating propeller gave angst. It was May 1953 before the Wyvern entered Fleet Air Arm (FAA) service. In 1956 the Wyvern went to war during the Suez crisis and acquitted itself well, but the following year it was withdrawn. Arthur Davenport left Westland, retiring in March 1952, aged 61. Some sources attest that he was 'pushed' after being blamed for the Wyvern's tortuously slow progress, most of which was out of his control.

Hands across the water

With the Wyvern turning into a costly and time-consuming programme, and before it flew with a turboprop, the Westland board had made the decision to get out of fixed-wing aircraft and build helicopters. For those who were around at the time, or who knew their company history, this was full of risk, especially as the firm's first attempts at rotary-winged flight were both fiascos. The Cierva C.29 of 1933 failed to get airborne. Great hopes were held for the CL.20 of 1935 and a production batch was laid down but the two-seater could not be persuaded to leave the ground.

Having decided that helicopters were the answer, the management was not going to build them from scratch – why run before you can walk? Two actions in early 1947 were pivotal to the future of Westland. Bell and Sikorsky in the USA were sounded out and it was the greater experience of the latter that clinched a licence agreement for the Sikorsky S-51 – as the Dragonfly – in January. Two months later, Westland took on O L Fitzwilliams, latterly overseeing the evaluation of rotorcraft at the Airborne Forces Experimental Establishment at Beaulieu. Between 'Fitz' and Sikorsky a dynasty was founded. Personnel from Yeovil had not been the only ones crossing the Atlantic in search of helicopter know-how. In *Westland Aircraft since 1915*, James notes: 'Ironically, Fairey Aviation had been offered a similar deal [with Sikorsky] but had turned it down.' Another early appointment was David Leonard Hollis Williams from Fairey and before that at General Aircraft – his 'CV' appears in Chapter 21.

By the time that the final Wyvern was delivered, in May 1956, Westland had produced three different helicopters (the Dragonfly, its Widgeon development and the Whirlwind) with the even more capable Wessex appearing in 1958. The programme culminated in the Sea King, which remained in production from 1969 to 1995. It must be stressed that this was not a case of bringing pattern airframes and boxes of blueprints over from Stratford, Connecticut, pressing a button and starting the assembly line. The task of 'Anglicizing' each type was daunting: they were re-engined, re-engineered and rethought to the extent that they eclipsed their Sikorsky origins. Even so, as explained at the beginning of this chapter, Westland was luxuriating in the notion that American taxpayers had footed the research and development bill for the Sikorsky types.

A 1948 advert for the Dragonfly: the strapline declaring Sikorsky helicopters having achieved 50,000 flying hours reflects the Westland rationale for adopting the American licence. *KEC*

Page from a late 1950s Westland brochure showing the Whirlwind production line, with a Dragonfly in the left foreground. *KEC*

Homespun helicopters

The first major revision was a modest step, the Widgeon that appeared in 1955. A Dragonfly with a stretched and reprofiled cockpit, the Widgeon could carry five passengers – one more than its predecessor – but that was the obvious change. The S-51 rotor blades were laminated wood and the gearbox left a lot to be desired; by substituting shortened metal rotors and the gearbox from the S-55-derived Whirlwind, the performance and handling was transformed. This thinking continued throughout the Westland–Sikorsky licences, with Yeovil creating a significantly changed and dramatically improved version each time. This

was particularly so with the almost total re-engineering of the WS-55 with a 1,050shp Bristol Siddeley Gnome turboshaft, which extended the helicopter's production life to 1966. The Gnome was another example of not reinventing the wheel; it was a licensed version of the American General Electric T58.

On 15 June 1958 the first of two Westminster heavy-lift helicopters was flown. Using Sikorsky dynamics, rotor, gearbox and tail rotor from the S-56 (CH-37 Mojave), it was Westland's first foray into original design. With no takers, the project was abandoned in 1960.

The Saro P.531 Sprite turboshaft light helicopter was part of the 'inheritance' of the buying spree of 1959 and 1960. Fitted with a

The prototype Westminster, G-APLE, along with Widgeon G-AKTW, 1958. *Westland*

Westland non-Sikorsky helicopters

From	To	Total	Name/Designation	Type	Engine(s)	Notes
1958	1959	2	Westminster	Transport/Crane	2 x Napier Eland	[1]
1960	1972	149	Scout AH.1	Army GP	1 x BS Nimbus	[2]
1962	1968	98	Wasp HAS.1	Shipborne anti-sub	1 x BS Nimbus	[3]
1971	2010	448	Lynx	Anti-sub/Army GP	2 x BS Gem	[4]
1979	1986	40	Westland 30	Transport	2 x RR Gem	
1987	date	164	EH.101 Merlin	Anti-sub/Transport	3 x GE CT7-2A	[5]
2009	date	70	AW159 Wildcat	Anti-sub/Army GP	2 x LHTEC CTS800	[6]
2015	2016	6	AW189	Coastguard	2 x GE CT7-2E1	[7]

Based upon *Westland Aircraft since 1915* by Derek N James. **[1]** Fitted with Sikorsky S-56 (CH-37 Mojave) rotor, gearbox and tail rotor. **[2]** Based on Saro P.531 programme, acquired 1959 - see Chapter 32. Includes eight P.531-2 development airframes built under Saro aegis 1960-1962. Scout production (141) at Hayes from 1961. **[3]** See notes for Scout - three P.531s used for Wasp development. **[4]** Part of Anglo-French helicopter agreement - see narrative. Includes 13 development batch WG.13s. **[5]** Joint programme with Agusta SpA, Italy, via joint organisation European Helicopter Industries, initiated 1980. Designated AW101 from mid-2000. Yeovil assembled aircraft, including 9 VH-71 Kestrels for US Marine Corps, delivered 2008-2009 but cancelled. Kawasaki Heavy Industries, Japan, licenced assembly of MCH-101 anti-mine version from 2007. **[6]** Major revision of Lynx; last example delivered May 2019. Production line 'held' in anticipation of more orders. **[7]** Batch for Bristow Helicopters assembled and fitted out at Yeovil.

Above: Scout AH.1 XR629 engaged in armament trials, mid-1970s. Note the anti-tank missile racks on the outriggers, sight above the cockpit and bulged rear compartment doors. *KEC*

Right: The first Wasp HAS.1 (Dutch designation AH-12), 235, for the Netherlands Navy, November 1966. *Kon Marine*

Gnome, the first pre-production Scout AH.1 flew on 4 August 1960. The Scout proved to be a reliable workhorse for the Army Air Corps (AAC), replacing the Skeeter. The same airframe was adapted for the Royal Navy, with castoring four-wheeled undercarriage and folding rotor blades as the Wasp HAS.1. From mid-1963 Wasps revolutionised naval anti-submarine warfare, the diminutive helicopters operating from the rear decks of frigates.

More, then fewer, licences

A major licence programme commenced in 1964, building Bell 47G light helicopters for the AAC and the RAF's Central Flying School as the Sioux AH.1 and HT.2, respectively, and a batch for Bristow Helicopters for contract training at Middle Wallop. This brought Westland into contact with Agusta of Italy. The agreement with Sikorsky precluded direct links with Bell in the USA and was instead finalised with the European licence holder, Agusta.

Britain and France signed an inter-government accord on 17 May 1965 that led to the Jaguar strike fighter and co-operation on three helicopters. On 22 February 1967 the helicopter element became contractual with Sud Aviation – Aérospatiale from 1970. Westland built the Sud Gazelle light helicopter for the British military and civilian applications, under a 'straight' licence arrangement. The other two elements were the Sud Puma medium transport helicopter

and the Westland Lynx battlefield support and shipborne helicopter, with both concerns making 30% of each other's design for the duration of the agreement.

On 1 October 1966 another corporate reorganisation came into effect with the inauguration of Westland Helicopters Ltd. On the same date, the British Hovercraft Corporation (BHC) was formed, 65% owned by Westland, 25% by Vickers and 10% by the National Research Development Corporation. Creating BHC 'tidied up' the Saro 'inheritance' but it was brought back into the fold in April 1983 as Westland Aerospace and today trades as GKN Aerospace, which is very active as an aerostructures manufacturer. Of the former Fairey assets, the assembly and flight test facility at White Waltham was disposed of in 1964 and the factory at Hayes was closed in 1972. The Bristol plant at Oldmixon, Weston-super-Mare, continued supporting Yeovil programmes until 2002.

In June 1989 Westland was granted rights to assemble the potent McDonnell Douglas (McDD) AH-64D Apache Longbow attack helicopter in anticipation of a major AAC order. A contract was eventually signed with Boeing – which had acquired McDD in 1997 – and a new assembly hall was completed at Yeovil in January 1999, with deliveries commencing the following year. The WAH-64 Apache was considerably 'Anglicized', including the fitment of RR/Turboméca RTM322 turboshafts and folding rotor blades.

A life-extension programme for the Puma in 2010 revealed a change of governmental attitude to its Yeovil helicopter specialist, by then named AgustaWestland. The substantial re-engineering contract for twenty-four airframes to HC.2 status with a 'glass cockpit' and Turboméca Makila turboshafts among other changes went to Eurocopter (Airbus Helicopters from 2014), with the work being carried out at Brasov, Romania, between 2012 and 2014. There was more writing on the wall in June 2016 when an order was placed direct with Boeing for up to fifty AH-64E Longbow Apaches – to be known as Guardians in British service – for delivery beginning in 2024. The Puma Mk.2 and AH-64E orders were the first major rotorcraft contracts placed without Westland involvement since the Dragonfly of 1949.

Lynx AH.9A ZG887 prior to delivery to the Army Air Corps, late 1991. *Westland*

World-beater

Westland's major contribution to the Anglo-French helicopter agreement was originally known as the WG.13. This evolved into the world-beating Lynx – Westland's first all-metric product. The summation of the vast experience gained through the Sikorsky alliance, the Lynx was a very advanced helicopter and the prototype first flew on 21 March 1971. Like the Scout and the Wasp before it, the Lynx was offered in two configurations, army battlefield support and shipborne anti-submarine. Westland continued to refine the Lynx and this was rewarded with a stream of export orders.

Having developed technologies including the British Experimental Rotor Programme (BERP) with composite construction and distinctive 'paddle' tips, Westland decided to fit the company demonstrator, G-LYNX, with 1,200shp RR Gem 60s turboshafts, a BERP III main rotor and other improvements to have a go at the helicopter absolute speed record. On 11 August 1986 G-LYNX achieved a speed of 249.1mph, which, at 400.87km/h, broke through the 'magic' 400km/h 'barrier'. (Today, G-LYNX takes pride of place at the Helicopter Museum, Weston-super-Mare.)

The Lynx's powertrain and dynamics were adapted to a new, high-capacity – seventeen passengers or twenty-plus troops – fuselage as the WG.30, which was marketed as the Westland 30. The prototype had its maiden flight on 10 April 1979 and the Westland board was confident enough to lay down twenty-five airframes, ahead of orders. Early sales success included commercial operators in the USA, all on lease and therefore still on Westland's 'books'. Problems with the tail rotor, allegations of poor product support and a non-fatal crash in November 1983 did nothing for the type's reputation; within five years the US examples were gathering dust.

A version with more powerful General Electric CT7 turboshafts flew in 1983 and two years later a fully militarised version with CT7s and a new five-blade BERP main rotor appeared. This huge investment saw no return. An order for twenty-one from an Indian offshore operator in 1986, largely funded by the British government,

German Navy Lynx Mk.88A 82+21 during search and rescue training, 1990. *Bundeswehr*

seemed to alleviate the Westland 30's woes. Three crashes during 1988 and 1989, two of which were fatal, put paid to the Indian venture and the programme was terminated.

In the late 1970s a consortium of Egypt, Qatar, Saudi Arabia and the United Arab Emirates set up the Arab British Helicopter Company with the intention to acquire twenty Yeovil-built Lynx followed by licence assembly and the full-blown manufacture of 200-plus. All of this was cancelled in 1979 and, despite a long-standing legal wrangle, Westland was denied contractual compensation and its losses were reported at £185 million. At the same time that the WG.30 was being re-engineered, Westland embarked on the Lynx 3, an updated version with a longer fuselage with revised tail section. This appeared in June 1984, but failed to attract sales. Costs were spiralling at Yeovil.

Despite the disastrous Westland 30 and the Arab debacle, the Lynx and continued demand for the Sea King kept Yeovil in business. By 2005 Westland was in a position to clinch an industrial 'Holy Grail': replacing the Lynx in AAC and FAA service. Featuring LHTEC CTS800 turboshafts, many aerodynamic improvements and enhanced systems, the prototype Lynx Wildcat – soon to be known as simply Wildcat – flew on 12 November 2009. By that date the first-generation Lynx had been in continuous production for thirty-eight years. As well as British forces orders, the Wildcat attracted exports from the Philippines and South Korea. In May 2019 the assembly line was put 'on hold' in the hope of further orders.

Anglo-Italian rapport

In November 1979 another European accord was reached, this time between Westland and Agusta of Italy to co-operate on a three-engined, anti-submarine and transport helicopter. European Helicopter Industries was initiated in June 1980, owned 50:50 by the two firms. The first EH.101 Merlin took to the skies over Yeovil on 9 October 1987 and deliveries began to the FAA in 1997. Export orders rolled in, the EH.101 replacing Agusta-, Sikorsky- and Westland-built Sea Kings, among other types.

Despite its export success, the EH.101 has had a rocky ride: a large order was cancelled in 1993 following considerable upheaval in the Canadian government; in conjunction with Bell and Lockheed Martin the so-called 'US-101' was chosen to replace US Marine Corps-operated Presidential Flight's long-serving Sikorsky VH-3As but the programme was terminated in June 2009; an order for VIP-configured EH.101s for India was placed in 2010 but was cancelled in January 2014 amid allegations of impropriety in the contract. Production of the EH.101 Merlin continues.

Cover of an AgustaWestland brochure for the maritime AW101, 2002. *KEC*

Problems, politics and mergers

Westland was not involved in the 1977 creation of the nationalised British Aerospace; an early indication that helicopters were not regarded in the same manner as fixed-wing programmes. The company had an ally in the Conservative Michael Heseltine, who had famously grabbed the mace on 27 May 1976 during a heated parliamentary debate on the Aircraft and Shipbuilding Industries Bill – see Chapter 12. Heseltine was to hit the headlines over Westland a decade later.

The decision to opt out of fixed-wing projects was rescinded in the early 1980s as the Somerset firm faced growing financial and technical troubles. In 1985 Westland proposed the Australian Aircraft Corporation A.20 Wamira turboprop trainer project for the RAF's AST.416 requirement to replace the BAC Jet Provost T.5. Hunting was similarly tempted, allying with NDN Aircraft – chapter 14 – with the Turbo-Firecracker, which at least had entered limited production. The award went to Shorts for a much re-engineered version of the Brazilian Tucano and Westland again shied away from fixed-wing ventures.

Despite both the Ministry of Defence and the Department of Trade and Industry declaring helicopters as a 'strategic resource', by the mid-1980s Westland was in dire straits and the vultures were circling. Already a shareholder, United Technologies, the owners of Sikorsky, and Italy's Fiat were vigorously campaigning to take a much larger slice of the company and the Treasury favoured this solution. As Defence Secretary, Heseltine wanted an entirely European consortium, including Italian rotorcraft maestro Agusta, already linked with Yeovil over the EH.101 project.

This erupted into the so-called 'Westland Affair', with Heseltine resigning on 9 January 1986 over what he believed to be a 'stitch up' by the Thatcher government that would leave the British military's purchasing options wholly reliant on the USA with an ever dwindling role for Yeovil. The Secretary of State for Industry, Leon Brittan, tendered his resignation fifteen days later over departmental leaks relating to the growing crisis. On 12 February 1986 the Westland board approved the Sikorsky–Fiat 'refinancing' package. An immediate result of this was the granting of a licence to produce the Sikorsky Black Hawk helicopter: a demonstrator was assembled from US-built components and first flew at Yeovil – perhaps appropriately – on April Fool's Day 1987. The British military did not take the bait and promised Middle East orders never materialised.

Fiat pulled its interests out in mid-1988 and the long-established, Midlands-based engineering titan GKN (from its days as 'nuts and bolts' manufacturer Guest, Keen and Nettlefold), already a Westland shareholder and with growing ambitions in the aerospace sector, took up the Italian concern's share, bringing its stake to 22%. By this time Westland was expanding its activities into aerostructures work and this remains a major venture to this day. Sikorsky baled out in 1994 and GKN took complete control on 18 April under the banner GKN Westland. Four years later GKN and Italian conglomerate Finmeccanica – the 'parent' of Agusta – announced a joint venture and on 26 July 2000 AgustaWestland came into being. Realigning to concentrate on aerostructures at the former Saro plant at East Cowes and, from 2008, at the one-time Bristol factory at Filton, GKN disposed of its 50% share in AgustaWestland to Finmeccanica on 26 May 2004. On New Year's Day 2017 Finmeccanica rebranded, taking the name Leonardo.

Westland, the one-time 'giant killer' of the British helicopter industry, swallowing Saunders-Roe, Bristol and Fairey during 1959–60, had in turn been consumed and is now a wholly owned division of an Italian colossus. Leonardo has expressed its desire to keep Yeovil as an airframe manufacturing site but with the Wildcat and Merlin both 'mature' programmes it remains to be seen if new types for the British military will continue to have maiden flights from a field west of Yeovil.

Bibliography and websites

Bibliography

A large number of books have been penned on the subject of Britain's aircraft industry. Most of these passed muster with distinction, some were found to be lacking in various ways. As beauty lies in the eyes of the beholder, I'm not going to delineate which I think should be in each category! To keep this listing within reasonable bounds, tomes devoted to individual types – many of which were referred to – are not included.

Air Ministry, *Maintenance – The Second World War 1939–1945*, AP.3397, Air Ministry, 1954

Amos, Peter, *Miles Aircraft – The Early Years*, Air-Britain, Tonbridge, 2009

Miles Aircraft – The Wartime Years, Air Britain, Tonbridge, 2012

Miles Aircraft – The Post-War Years, Air-Britain, Tonbridge, 2016

Andrews, C F and Morgan, E B, *Supermarine Aircraft since 1914*, Putnam, London, 1981

Vickers Aircraft since 1908, Putnam, London, 1988

Armstrong Whitworth Aircraft, *Pioneers of Progress – A Brief Illustrated History of Sir W G Armstrong Whitworth Aircraft Ltd, Coventry*, company brochure, 1982

Balfour, Christopher, *Spithead Express – The Pre-War Island Air Ferry and Post-War Plans*, Magna Press, Leatherhead, 1999

BAJ Coatings/Meggitt Aerospace, *Shadow to Shadow – A History of the Bristol Aeroplane Banwell Shadow Factory and Bristol Aerojet, 1941–1991*, Banwell, 1993

Barker, Ralph, *The Schneider Trophy Races*, Airlife, Shrewsbury, 2nd ed, 1981

Barnes, Christopher H, *Bristol Aircraft since 1910*, Putnam, London, 3rd Ed, 1988

Handley Page Aircraft since 1907, Putnam, London, 1976

Shorts Aircraft since 1900, Putnam, London, 1967

Blackburn Aircraft Co, *Blackburn Story 1909–1959*, Brough, 1960

Blackmore, L K, *Hawker – One of Aviation's Greatest Names*, David Bateman Ltd, Auckland, New Zealand, 1990

Blake, John and Hooks, Mike, *40 Years at Farnborough – SBAC's International Showcase*, Haynes, Sparkford, 1990

Bonser, Roy, *Aviation in Leicestershire and Rutland*, Midland, Hinckley, 2001

Boughton, Terence, *The Story of the British Light Aeroplane*, John Murray, London, 1963

Brett, Dallas, R, *History of British Aviation 1908–1914*, Air Research, Surbiton, 1987

Brew, Alec, *Boulton Paul Aircraft since 1915*, Putnam, London, 1993

Brooks, Peter W, *Cierva Autogiros – The Development of Rotary-Wing Flight*, Smithsonian, USA, 1988

Brown, Don L, *Miles Aircraft since 1925*, Putnam, London, 1970

Bruce, J M, *Aeroplanes of the Royal Flying Corps (Military Wing)*, Putnam, London, 1982

Carter, Graham, *ML Aviation Ltd – A Secret World*, Keyham Books, Chippenham, 2006

Chacksfield, J E, *Sir Sydney Camm – From Biplanes and Hurricanes to Harriers*, Oakwood, Usk, 2010

Costigan, F J, *Adventures of an Aircraft Designer*, Cortney, Luton, 1980

Cruddas, Colin, *In Cobham's Company*, Cobham plc, Wimborne, 1994

Davies, Glyn, *From Lysander to Lightning – Teddy Petter, Aircraft Designer*, History Press, Stroud, 2014

de Havilland, Sir Geoffrey, *Sky Fever*, Hamish Hamilton, London, 1961

Davis, Mick, *Airco – The Aircraft Manufacturing Company*, Crowood, Marlborough, 2001

Donne, Michael, *Pioneers of the Skies – A History of Short Brothers*, Nicholson and Bass, Belfast, 1987

Dudley, Roger and Johnson, Ted, *Weston-super-Mare and the Aeroplane 1910–2010*, Amberley, Stroud, 2010

Duval, G R, *British Flying boats and Amphibians 1909–1952*, Putnam, London, 1965

Ellis, Ken, *Testing to the Limits – British Test Pilots since 1910*, Vols 1 and 2, Crécy, Manchester, 2015 and 2016

Ellis, Ken, and Jones, Geoff, *Henri Mignet and his Flying Fleas*, Haynes, Sparkford, 1990

Ellison, Norman, *British Gliders and Sailplanes 1922–1970*, Adam and Charles Black, London, 1971

Eves, Edward, *The Schneider Trophy Story*, Airlife, Shrewsbury, 2001

Fostekew, Jean M, *Blossom – A Biography of F G Miles*, Cirrus Associates, Gillingham, 1998

Gardner, Charles, *British Aircraft Corporation – A History*, Book Club Associates, London, 1981

Gardner, Robert, *From Bouncing Bombs to Concorde – The Biography of Sir George Edwards*, Sutton, Stroud, 2006

Gearing, David W, *On the Wings of a Gull – Percival and Hunting Aircraft*, Air-Britain, Staplefield, 2012

Gibson, Michael L, *Aviation in Northamptonshire – An Illustrated History*, Northamptonshire Libraries, Northampton, 1982

Gunston, Bill, *World Encyclopaedia of Aircraft Manufacturers – From Pioneers to the Present Day*, Patrick Stephens, Sparkford, 1993

Hancock, Ian, *The Lives of Ken Wallis – Engineer and Aviator Extraordinaire*, self-published, Flixton, 2001

Handley Page, *Forty Years on ... 1909 to 1949*, Handley Page, London, 1949

Hare, Paul R, *Royal Aircraft Factory*, Putnam, 1990

Hayward, Keith, *British Aircraft Industry*, Manchester University Press, Manchester, 1989

Government and British Civil Aerospace – A Case Study in Post-War Technology Policy, Manchester University Press, Manchester, 1983

Hayes, Paul, and King, Bernard, *de Havilland Biplane Transports*, Gatwick Aviation Society, Coulsdon, 2003

Hitchman, Ambrose and Preston, Mike, *History of the Auster Aeroplane*, International Auster Club Heritage Group, Ratcliffe on the Wreake, 3rd Ed, 1989

Holmes, Harry, *Avro – The History of an Aircraft Company*, Airlife, Shrewsbury, 1994

Hyde, H Montgomery, *British Air Policy Between the Wars 1918–1939*, Heinemann, London, 1976

Jackson, A J, *Avro Aircraft since 1908*, Putnam, London, 2nd Ed, 1990

Blackburn Aircraft since 1909, Putnam, London, 2nd Ed, 1989

British Civil Aircraft since 1919, Putnam, London, Vol 1 and Vol 2nd Eds 1973, Vol 3 2nd Ed 1974

de Havilland Aircraft since 1909, Putnam, London, revised ed, 1978

Jackson, Robert, *V-Force – Britain's Airborne Nuclear Deterrent*, Ian Allan, Shepperton, 2000

James, Derek N, *Gloster Aircraft since 1917*, Putnam, London, 2nd Ed, 1987

Schneider Trophy Aircraft 1913–1931, Putnam, London, 1981

Spirit of Hamble – Folland Aircraft, Tempus, Stroud, 2000

Westland Aircraft since 1915, Putnam, London, 1991

Jenks, Alfred J, *Aviation in Warwickshire Between the Wars*, self-published, 2006

Kay, Derek R, *The Last Grand Adventure in British Aviation? A personal history of Britten-Norman*, Anthony Rowe Publishing, Croydon, 2008

Kershaw, Tim, *Jet Pioneers: Gloster and the Birth of the Jet Age*, Sutton, Stroud, 2004

King, H F, *Sopwith Aircraft 1912–1920*, Putnam, London, 1980

Kinsey, Gordon, *Boulton and Paul Aircraft – History of the Companies at Norwich and Wolverhampton*, Terrence Dalton, Lavenham, 1992

Lewis, Peter, *British Aircraft 1809–1914*, Putnam, London, 1962

British Racing and Record-Breaking Aircraft, Putnam, London, 1970

The British Bomber since 1914, Putnam, London, 1967

The British Fighter since 1912, Putnam, London, 1965

London, Peter, *Saunders and Saro Aircraft since 1917*, Putnam, London, 1988

Longworth, James, H, *Triplane to Typhoon – Aircraft Produced by Factories in Lancashire and the North West from 1910*, Lancashire County Developments, Preston, 2005

Lumsden, Alec S C, *British Piston Aero-Engines and Their Aircraft*, Airlife, Shrewsbury, 1994

Masefield, Sir Peter, with Gunston, Bill, *Flight Path*, Airlife, Shrewsbury, 2002

Mason, Francis K, *Hawker Aircraft since 1920*, Putnam, London, 1961

McIntyre, Dougal, *Prestwick's Pioneer – A Portrait of David F McIntyre*, Woodfield, Bognor Regis, 2004

McLelland, Tim with Tony Buttler, *TSR2 – Britain's Cold War Strike Aircraft*, Crécy, Manchester, 2017

Meekcoms, K J, and Morgan, E B, *The British Aircraft Specifications File 1920–1949*, Air-Britain, Tonbridge, 1994

Middleton, Donald H, *Airspeed – The Company and its Aeroplanes*, Terence Dalton, Lavenham, 1982

Molson, K M and Taylor, H A, *Canadian Aircraft since 1909*, Putnam, London, 1982

Negus, Geoffrey, and Staddon, Tommy, *Aviation in Birmingham*, Midland Counties Publications, Earl Shilton, 1984

Neil, William T, *Just One of the Pioneers – My Days With Scottish Aviation and de Havillands*, Cirrus, Gillingham, 2002

Ord-Hume, Arthur W J G, *British Light Aeroplanes – Their Evolution, Development and Perfection, 1920–1940*, GMS, Peterborough, 2000

Pasco, Dennis, *Tested – Marshall Test Pilots and Their Aircraft in War and Peace 1919–1999*, Grub Street, London, 1999

Penrose, Harald, *Architect of Wings – A Biography of Roy Chadwick*, Airlife, Shrewsbury, 1985

British Aviation – The Pioneer Years 1903–1914, Putnam, London, 1967

British Aviation – The Great War and Armistice 1915–1919, Putnam, London, 1969

British Aviation – The Adventuring Years 1920–1929, Putnam, London, 1973

British Aviation – Widening Horizons 1930–1934, HMSO, London, 1979

British Aviation – Ominous Skies 1935–1939, HMSO, London, 1980

Phipp, Mike, *The Brabazon Committee and British Airliners 1945–1960*, Tempus, Stroud, 2007

Pierson, Jean, *European Success in Global Competition*, Royal Aeronautical Society Toulouse Branch, Airbus Industrie, Toulouse, 1991

Preston, Mike, and Ames, Mick, *Austers – Nearly All You Wanted to Know*, International Auster Pilot Club, Ratcliffe on the Wreake, 2002

Pudney, John, *Bristol Fashion: Some Account of the Earlier Days of Bristol Aviation*, Putnam, London, 1960

Pugh, Peter, *Barnes Wallis – Dambuster*, Icon, Thriplow, 2005

Quill, Jeffrey, *Spitfire – A Test Pilot's Story*, Crécy Publishing, Manchester, 1996 edition, reprinted 2008

Ransom, Stephen and Fairclough, Robert, *English Electric Aircraft and their Predecessors*, Putnam, London, 1987

Reed, Arthur, *Britain's Aircraft Industry, What Went Right? What Went Wrong?*, Dent and Sons, London, 1973

Riding, Richard, *Ultralights – The Early British Classics*, Patrick Stephens, Wellingborough, 1987

Robertson, Alan, *Lion Rampant and Winged, A Commemorative History of Scottish Aviation Ltd*, self-published, Brarassie, 1986

Rogers, David, *Shadow Factories – Britain's Production Facilities during the Second World War*, Helion, Solihull, 2016

Roussel, Mike, *Spitfire's Forgotten Designer – The Career of Supermarine's Joe Smith*, History Press, Stroud, 2013

Russell, Sir Archibald, *A Span of Wings – An Autobiography*, Airlife, Shrewsbury, 1992

Russell, C R, *Spitfire Odyssey – My Life at Supermarines 1936–1957*, Kingfisher, Southampton, 1985

Scott, David and Simmons, Ian, *George Holt Thomas – The Man Who Created Airco*, self-published, High Wycombe, 2018

Scott, J D, *Vickers – A History*, Weidenfeld and Nicolson, London, 1962

Sharp, C Martin, *D.H. – A History of de Havilland*, Airlife, Shrewsbury, 1982

Shute, Nevil, *Slide Rule – The Autobiography of an Engineer*, Heinemann, London, 1956

Silvester, R John, *Percival and Hunting Aircraft*, self-published, Luton, 1987

Skinner, Stephen, *British Aircraft Corporation – A History*, Crowood, Marlborough, 2012

Hawker Siddeley Aviation and Dynamics 1960–1977, Crowood, Marlborough, 2014

Marshall of Cambridge, Tempus, Stroud, 2003

Smith, Adrian, *The Man Who Built the Swordfish – The Life of Sir Richard Fairey*, Tauris, London, 2018

Smith, Christopher, *Supermarine – An Illustrated History*, Amberley, Stroud, 2016

Smith, Ron, *British Built Aircraft – Greater London*, Tempus, Stroud, 2002

British Built Aircraft – South West and Central Southern England, Tempus, Stroud, 2003

British Built Aircraft – South East England, Tempus, Stroud, 2004

British Built Aircraft – Central and Eastern England, Tempus, Stroud, 2004

British Built Aircraft – Northern England, Scotland, Wales and Northern Ireland, Tempus, Stroud, 2005

Stoney, Barbara, *Twentieth Century Maverick – The Life of Noel Pemberton Billing*, Bank House, New Romney, 2004.

Tapper, Oliver, *Armstrong Whitworth Aircraft since 1913*, Putnam, London, 1988

Taylor, H A, *Airspeed Aircraft since 1931*, Putnam, London, 1970

Fairey Aircraft since 1915, Putnam, London, 1988

Temple, Julian C, *Wings over Woodley – The Story of Miles Aircraft and the Adwest Group*, Aston, Bourne End, Bucks, 1987

Thetford, Owen, *Aircraft of the Royal Air Force since 1918*, Putnam, London, 9th Ed, 1995

British Naval Aircraft since 1912, Putnam, London, 1971

Uttley, Matthew, *Westland and the British Helicopter Industry 1945–1960*, Frank Cass, London, 2001

Wallace, Graham, *Claude-Grahame-White – A Biography*, Putnam, London, 1960

Wallace Clarke, Ron, *British Aircraft Armament, Volume 1: RAF Gun turrets from 1914 to the Present Day* and *Volume 2: RAF Guns and Gunsights from 1914 to the Present Day*, Patrick Stephens, Sparkford, 1993 and 1994

Walls, John, and Parker, Charles, *Aircraft Made in Lincoln*, Society for Lincolnshire History and Archaeology, Lincoln, 2000

Wansbrough-White, Gordon, *Names with Wings – The Names and Naming Systems of Aircraft and Engines Flown by the British Forces, 1878–1994*, Airlife, Shrewsbury, 1995

Warner, Guy, *Shorts – The Foreman Years*, Ulster Aviation Society, Belfast, 2008

Warner, Guy, and Cromie, Ernie, *Aircraft and Aerospace Manufacturing in Northern Ireland*, Colourpoint Books, Newtownards, 2014

Wenham, Tom, *False Dawn – The Beagle Aircraft Story*, Air-Britain, Tonbridge, 2015

Wenham, Tom, Simpson, Rod and Fillmore, Malcolm, *Auster – The Company and the Aircraft*, Air-Britain, Tonbridge, 2018

Williams, David L, *Wings Over the Island – The Aviation Heritage of the Isle of Wight*, Coach House, 1999

Winkler, Eduard F, *Civilian Affair – A Brief History of the Civilian Aircraft Company of Hedon*, Flight Recorder Publications, Ottringham, 2003

Wixey, Kenneth E, *Parnall Aircraft since 1914*, Putnam, London, 1990

Wood, Derek, *Project Cancelled – The Disaster of Britain's Abandoned Aircraft Projects*, Jane's, London, 1986

Social, economic and political history

Many titles have been dipped into, but this is an aviation book, so here's some that are well worth reading: Stig Abell's work is particularly worthwhile.

A History of Modern Britain, Andrew Marr, Pan Macmillan, London, 2008

How Britain Really Works – Understanding the Ideas and Institutions of a Nation, Stig Abell, John Murray, London, 2019

Roller-Coaster – Europe 1950–2017, Ian Kershaw, Allen Lane, London, 2019

To Hell and Back – Europe 1914–1949, Ian Kershaw, Penguin, London, 2016

Websites

Bearing in mind that only a *fraction* of things beginning-with-www are helpful – let alone reliable, and that the rest ranges from the well-meaning but ill-informed, to fantasists shrouded in anonymity, to the outright malicious; the following occupy the 'real' world:

afleetingpeace.org – 'Golden Age Aviation' in the British Empire, Terry Mace's study of the inter-war years

airbus.com – Comprehensive site of a global triumph

airsciences.org – Superbly informative site from FAST, the Farnborough Air Sciences Trust

austerclub.org – Incredibly detailed site of the International Auster Club

austerhg.org – The Auster Heritage Group's informative site

baesystems.com – BAE Systems' vast site

britishaviation-ptp.com – Roger Moss's *British Aviation – Projects to Production* – labour of love

eurofighter.com – 'Home' of Europe's world-beater

flightglobal.com – *Every* page of every *Flight* and *Flight International*

leonardocompany.com/en/air/helicopters – Westland's current identity

Index

To keep the section on British manufacturers and their types within reasonable bounds, readers are reminded of the relevant chapter, eg Ch.2 for Airco. Only references to manufacturers and their types mentioned *outside* of the relevant chapter, or chapters, are individually indexed. Some personalities, eg Geoffrey de Havilland, and locations, eg Hatfield, receive similar treatment. Hopefully useful search notes appear in *italics*, including references to types carrying the same name, eg Avro, Fairey and Sopwith all had a Baby! Chapter 1, tables, illustrations and their captions are *not* indexed.

Airfields/Seaplane Bases – UK only

The knack of flying is learning how to throw yourself at the ground and miss! – Douglas Adams